Anonymous

The Granite monthly

A New Hampshire magazine

Anonymous

The Granite monthly
A New Hampshire magazine

ISBN/EAN: 9783337206048

Printed in Europe, USA, Canada, Australia, Japan

Cover: Foto ©Andreas Hilbeck / pixelio.de

More available books at **www.hansebooks.com**

THE

GRANITE MONTHLY,

A New Hampshire Magazine.

DEVOTED TO

Literature, History, and State Progress.

VOLUME TWO.

CONCORD, N. H.:
H. H. METCALF, PUBLISHER.
1879.

THE GRANITE MONTHLY.

A MAGAZINE OF LITERATURE, HISTORY AND STATE PROGRESS.

VOL. II. JULY, 1878. NO. 1.

THE SENATE AND ITS PRESIDENTS—HON. DAVID H. BUFFUM.

While the New Hampshire House of Representatives is the largest legislative body in the country, our State Senate is, with one or two exceptions, the smallest. The amendment to the Constitution recently adopted, which is to go into effect the coming autumn, however, makes a marked change in this regard, for, while reducing somewhat the number of Representatives, it doubles the number of Senators, placing our own upon at least an average footing with the Senates of other States throughout the Union.

Notwithstanding its comparative insignificance in point of numbers, the New Hampshire Senate has ever maintained an enviable reputation as an able, patriotic and eminently conservative legislative body. This is due largely, without doubt, to the fact that the office of State Senator has generally sought the man rather than the man the office. Demagogues and aspirants for popular favor, as well as active partisan leaders, have usually preferred seats in the House of Representatives, where as leaders of men and masters, or murderers, of rhetoric they have greater opportunity for achieving distinction or notoriety. It is true that it has been often alleged that the Senate of our State is a dangerous body, being easily corrupted or controlled, on account of the small number of members. This allegation, however, is an unjustifiable or inconsiderate one. When men's favorite measures are defeated, they are wont to cry out "corruption," or to allege other than patriotic motives as actuating those who caused their discomfiture, and it will generally be found that those who have charged the Senate with corrupt or improper action, have failed to secure at the hands of that body the passage or the defeat of some measure particularly affecting their own interests. The truth is, there is far more danger of bad legislation at the hands of a large and unwieldly body like our House of Representatives, than from a comparatively small body like the Senate. In the former a shrewd political leader or designing demagague, through his personal influence over numerous followers may readily secure the passage of an unwise act, which, in the latter, where such a thing as leadership is seldom known or attempted, and each individual member, as a general rule, acts and thinks for himself, could never have been carried through. The Senate, therefore, exercising its conservative power, through amendment or rejection, has protected the people from ill advised and even dangerous legislation, to a greater or less extent every year.

While the task of presiding over the deliberations of the Senate is far less difficult and laborious than that devolving upon the Speaker of the House, the position is, nevertheless, one of honor and distinction, and has been occupied by many illustrious citizens of the State. Sixty-two persons, in all, have holden the office of President of the Senate during the eighty-five years since the adoption of the Constitution of 1792. Following are their names, with their several places of residence and years of service:

Abiel Foster, Canterbury—1793; Oliver Peabody, Exeter—1794; Ebenezer Smith, Meredith—1795-6; Amos Shepard, Alstead—1794 to 1803, inclusive; Nicholas Gilman, Exeter—1804; Clement Storer, Portsmouth, 1805-6; Samuel Bell, Francestown—1807-8; Moses P. Payson, Bath—1809; Wm. Plumer, Epping—1810-11; Joshua Darling, Henniker—1812; Oliver Peabody, Exeter—1813; Moses P. Payson, 1814-15; William Badger, Gilmanton—1816; Jonathan Harvey, Sutton—1817 to 1822, inclusive; David L. Morrill, Goffstown—1823; Josiah Bartlett, Stratham—1824; Matthew Harvey, Hopkinton—1825-6-7; Nahum Parker, Fitzwilliam—1828; Abner Greenleaf, Portsmouth, and Samuel Cartland, Haverhill—1829; Joseph M. Harper, Canterbury—1830; Samuel Cartland, Haverhill, and Benning M. Bean, Moultonborough—1831; Benning M. Bean, 1832; Jared W. Williams, Lancaster—1833-4; Charles F. Gove, Goffstown—1835; James Clark, Franklin—1836; John Woodbury, Salem—1837; Samuel Jones, Bradford—1838; James M. Wilkins, Bedford—1839; James B. Creighton, Newmarket—1840; Josiah Quincy, Rumney—1841-2; Titus Brown, Francestown—1843; Timothy Hoskins, Westmoreland—1844; Asa P. Cate, Northfield—1845; James U. Parker, Manchester—1846; Harry Hibbard, Bath—1847-8; William P. Weeks, Canaan—1849; Richard Jenness, Portsmouth—1850; John S. Wells, Exeter—1851-2; James M. Rix, Lancaster—1853; Jonathan E. Sargent, Wentworth—1854; William Haile, Hinsdale—1855; Thomas J. Melvin, Chester—1856; Moody Currier, Manchester—1857; Austin F. Pike, Franklin—1858; Joseph A. Gilmore, Concord—1859; George S. Towle, Lebanon—1860; Herman Foster, Manchester—1861; W. H. Y. Hackett, Portsmouth—1862; Onslow Stearns, Concord—1863; Charles H. Bell, Exeter—1864; Ezekiel A. Straw, Manchester—1865; Daniel Barnard, Franklin—1866; Wm. T. Parker, Merrimack—1867; Ezra A. Stevens, Portsmouth—1868; John Y. Mugridge, Concord—1869; Nathaniel Gordon, Exeter—1870; G. W. M. Pitman, Bartlett—1871; Charles H. Campbell, Nashua—1872; David A. Warde, Concord—1873; Wm. H. Gove, Weare—1874; John W. Sanborn, Wakefield—1875; Charles Holman, Nashua—1876; Natt Head, Hooksett—1877; David H. Buffum, Somersworth—1878.

Of this list, eleven also held the office of Speaker of the House of Representatives, viz: William Plumer, Samuel Bell, Clement Storer, David L. Morrill, Matthew Harvey, John S. Wells, Harry Hibbard, Jonathan E. Sargent, Charles H. Bell, Austin F. Pike and William H. Gove. Of these eleven, three, only, are now living—Messrs. Sargent, Bell and Pike, and the two former are members of the present House. Twelve of the number held seats in the national House of Representatives, of whom Austin F. Pike is the only one now living; seven were members of the United States Senate, none of whom survive; and ten were Governors of New Hampshire, viz: William Plumer, Samuel Bell, David L. Morrill, Matthew Harvey, William Badger, Jared W. Williams, William Haile, Joseph A. Gilmore, Onslow Stearns and Ezekiel A. Straw, of whom the two last only are living at the present time. Of the entire sixty-two, twenty-two are now living, the oldest survivor being James B. Creighton of Newmarket, who was President of the Senate in 1840.

In considering the list with reference to localities, we find that of the several counties, or the towns composing them, Rockingham has furnished fifteen of the

HON. DAVID H. BUFFUM.

entire number, and Merrimack also fifteen; Hillsborough has furnished thirteen, Grafton seven, Cheshire four, Carroll three, and Belknap and Coos two each, while Sullivan has furnished none. Of the fifteen from Rockingham, five each were furnished by Portsmouth and Exeter. Concord has supplied four, Manchester four and Nashua two, but Dover has never had a President of the Senate, nor has District No. Five in which it is embraced, including the main portion of Strafford County, as now constituted, until the election of Hon. David H. Buffum of Somersworth, the present year. While a large proportion and perhaps a majority of those who have held the office of President of the Senate have been members of the legal profession, the Senate has usually contained among its members a large comparative representation of the business men of the State. A few clergymen, and physicians —Rev. Abiel Foster, a distinguished patriot and member of the Continental Congress, and Josiah Bartlett and Joseph M. Harper, both subsequently members of Congress, the former a clergyman and the two latter physicians, being among the number—have held seats in this body, but it has generally numbered more business men—merchants, manufacturers, etc., than representatives of the professions. To this fact, perhaps, may be attributed in large degree, the practical and conservative tendency of the Senatorial body in the work of legislation.

The present Senate contains one physician—Dr. Gallinger of Concord, (District No. Four,) three lawyers—Messrs. Cogswell of Gilmanton (No. 6,) White of Peterborough, (No. 8,) and Weeks of Canaan. (No. 11,) one farmer—Mr. Philbrick of Rye, (No. 1,) while the remaining seven are all business men, Messrs. Wheeler of Salem (No. 2.) Buffum of Somersworth (No. 5,) and Amidon of Hinsdale (No. 9,) being manufacturers, Mr. Slayton of Manchester (No. 3,) a merchant, Mr. Spalding of Nashua (No. 7,) a bank cashier, Mr. Shaw of Lebanon (No. 10,) a contractor, and Mr. Cummings of Lisbon (No. 12,) a merchant and manufacturer. The President,

HON. DAVID H. BUFFUM, President of the Senate, whose portrait accompanies this article, is a native of the State of Maine, which State, by the way, has contributed comparatively few to the list of the public men of New Hampshire, although on our part we have furnished Maine several of her ablest and most distinguished citizens, including Fessenden, Clifford, Cutting, Plaisted, and others of both State and National reputation. Mr. Buffum was born in North Berwick, November 10, 1820, being now fifty-seven years of age. He was the eldest child and only son of Timothy and Anna (Austin) Buffum. His father died when he was only six years of age, leaving his mother—a daughter of Nathaniel Austin of Dover Neck—with very little property and three small children, there being two daughters, younger than himself, both of whom are now living, one being the widow of the late John H. Burleigh of South Berwick, and the other the wife of Isaac P. Evans of Richmond, Ind. After his father's decease, he was taken into the family of an uncle, Benajah Buffum, with whom he remained until he was seventeen years of age, engaged for the larger portion of the time in a country store, of which his uncle was the proprietor, and where he laid the foundation for his subsequent eminently successful business career. His educational advantages up to this time, were only such as were afforded by the common school; but of these he had made the best possible use.

When he was seventeen years of age, his uncle sold out and went to Lynn, Mass., where he engaged in business. He accompanied his uncle, but remained with him but a few months, returning to his native place, where he made his home for a time with his step-father, Mr. Wm. Hussey—his mother having married a second time. He attended the fall term of South Berwick Academy the following autumn, and in the winter, being then eighteen years old, taught a district school in North Berwick. In the spring following he again attended the Academy. He had commenced teaching again the next autumn, but left his school to accept a position as clerk in the general store of William and Hiram Hanson in the village of Great Falls, Somersworth, which place has ever since been his home. He remained in the employ of the Hanson's about two years, when, being then twenty-one years of age, he bought the interest of William Hanson in the store and went into partnership with Hiram, under the firm name of Hanson & Buffum. Two years later the partnership was dissolved, and Mr. Buffum commenced the erection of the large brick block, known as Buffum's Block, upon the opposite side of High street from the old stand. This block contained three stores, one of which Mr. Buffum occupied himself, in the same business in which he had been engaged, until March, 1847, when he disposed of the business to attend to his duties as cashier of the Great Falls Bank, to which position he was chosen the previous year, and which he held for a term of seventeen years, until 1863, having also for six years been treasurer of the Somersworth Savings Bank. In 1863, Mr. Buffum resigned as cashier and treasurer of the banks, to take the management of the Great Falls Woolen Mill, a corporation which he had been chiefly instrumental in organizing, and whose manufactory had been commenced the previous year, under a joint stock arrangement. He held the position of agent, treasurer and general manager of the corporation for ten years, devoting himself untiringly to the business, which he conducted with great success. The capital stock of the corporation, which was originally $50,000, was subsequently increased, from the earnings, to $100,000. In 1873, having impaired his health by close and continued application to business, Mr. Buffum withdrew from the active management of the affairs of the corporation, and was succeeded by his brother-in-law, Mr. Stickney, the present agent. He spent several months in the autumn of that year in Colorado, and the spring of 1874 in California, and returned home with restored health.

Several years previous to the organization of the Great Falls Woolen Company Mr. Buffum had taken a large interest in a similar enterprise at South Berwick, known as the Newichawanick Company, of which his brother-in-law, the late Hon. John H. Burleigh, was the active manager, they two, with the well known "Friend" Hill being the principal stockholders, which enterprise, although a losing one at first, ultimately proved very successful. After the sudden and startling death of Mr. Burleigh, a few months since, Mr. Buffum was chosen treasurer of the Newichawanick Company. Aside from these important manufacturing enterprises, he has been for several years a partner with L. R. Hersom in the wool pulling and sheep-skin tanning establishment on Berwick side at Great Falls, and has, furthermore, extensive manufacturing interests at Milton Mills.

As would naturally be inferred from the foregoing, Mr. Buffum has not been largely engaged in public and political life. He has, however, had sufficient experience in that direction, taken in connection with his knowledge of practical business affairs, to qualify him for the efficient discharge of the duties now devolving upon him as a servant of the people, in the important office which he holds. He was chosen Town Clerk of Somersworth in March, 1842, it being the election at which he cast his first vote, and was re-elected the following year. In 1846 he was elected a member of the board of Selectmen, and was subsequently several times elected to the same position. In 1861 and 1862 he was one of the members of the House of Representatives from Somersworth, serving the first year as a member of the committee on Banks and the second year as chairman of the committee on the Reform School. In 1863, Mr. Buffum was the Republican candidate for Railroad Commissioner, running upon the ticket with Governor Gilmore. A third ticket placed in the field, defeated an election by the people, but the Republican candidates were chosen by the Legislature, and Mr. Buffum served as a member of the board of Railroad Commissioners for the full term of three years. In the spring of 1875, his name was brought forward, though against his wish, by some of his friends, in the Republican Senatorial Convention in District No. 5, and he received a very flattering vote. Last year he was again supported and received the nomination, by nearly a unanimous vote, his election following as a matter of course. He served with ability in the last Senate, as a member of the several committees on Judiciary, Finance, Banks and State Institutions, and although one of three members of the majority party, re-elected this year, he was accorded the Presidency by common consent. Among his associates in the Senate last year were three men who were fellow members in the House fifteen years ago, viz: Messrs. John F. Cloutman of Farmington, Natt Head of Hooksett, and James Burnap of Marlow. In the present Senate, there are also two members who were members of the House with Mr. Buffum—Messrs. Amidon of Hinsdale and Shaw of Lebanon.

Mr. Buffum was married, January 26, 1853, to Charlotte E. Stickney, daughter of Alexander H. Stickney of Great Falls, who deceased March 8, 1868, leaving him four children, three sons and a daughter, the latter also now deceased. The three sons, Edgar Stickney, Harry Austin, and David Hanson, are respectively twenty-two, twenty, and fifteen years of age. The oldest graduated at Yale College last year, and is now learning the manufacturing business in the woolen mill at Great Falls; the second is a member of the junior class at Yale, and the youngest remains at home.

Mr. Buffum's religious associations are with the Congregational church, where he attends public worship regularly and contributes liberally for its support, though not a member of the church organization. By strict integrity and courteous and gentlemanly bearing, he has secured the esteem of all classes of his fellow citizens who rejoice in his success both in private and public life.

NATURE'S CREED.

NATURE'S CREED.

BY FLINT CARMEL.

From the towering hills—over northward they rear—
   Whose mosses are fanned by the whispering breeze,
Happy homes, far below in the valley, appear
   To gaze upward in love thro' their tall shading trees.
Not a ripple disturbing the mirror beyond!
   With its beauty unbroken the scene becomes new,
Save where Purity rests in embraces so fond
   As the lily peeps into the sky's liquid blue.

On the deep fringed shore the sad willow droops low
   And is plaintively whispering "doomed to bemoan!"
But the wave as it rises will soothingly flow,
   Bringing kisses of sweetness for willows alone.
And the hills in their grandeur these things comprehend,
   Standing forth in protection above this retreat,
Seeming calmly to speak "we will last to the end,
   Keeping safe each warm heart till it ceases to beat!"

For a moment descend, ye time-fading old hills,
   To the homes that seem happy and peaceful below;
Pause and listen to discord of numberless ills,
   See how thankless thy mission their malice would show!
For the towering domes mounting upward toward thee
   As if thou to outreach in their heavenward flight,
Seem to speak of a faith which from sin pardons free
   In the place of a war that would sadden the sight.

Each tall spire, as upward it rises on high
   Looks in anger across at its neighboring foe,
And a battle goes on and opinions reply
   How we safest and surest may heavenward go.
As the eye of the pilgrim and sinner spells out
   All the guideboards to happiness, heaven and love,
On his ear harshly falling each deepening shout,
   He will heed not their warning—"They lead not above!"

From the discordant valley his sick soul he turns
   A deliv'rance to seek from the medley of creeds;
For his being is stirred, in a fever it burns,
   And cries out for a balm that will reach all its needs.
Up the brow of a hill with a soul-stricken mein,
   Till the summit is reached he waits not to rest—
Then he turns and is spellbound by rapture so keen—
   All beneath him, around him, in beauty is dressed!

The grand scene lies before him in quiet repose,
On the calm, sleeping lake, his glad vision returns,
Nature's harmony there his vague doubting o'erflows—
From the joy in his soul the true way he learns!
God is speaking in nature; once more by the breeze
Gently points to the spires—they something would say
As they lift up their heads from among the tall trees—
Chanted softly it comes—" we all point the same way."

MY FRIENDS AND I: MEMORIES.

BY L. W. DODGE.

> The day is done, and the darkness
> Falls from the wings of night,
> As a feather is wafted downward
> From an eagle in its flight.
> —Longfellow.

I have been standing with my face to the eastern window, watching the daylight fade away, and the night come down so gloriously, and the starry sentinels as one by one they take their stations in the deep-blue vault above. I was gazing dreamily, scarce knowing or caring why, when a meteor, a swift gliding star that seemed to have been resting in its allotted place near the zenith, left its throne of glory and went suddenly rushing down the farther sky, vanishing below the dim horizon, leaving behind a long train of fading splendor, as quickly to be gathered up, like stray sunbeams. Why may not our lives be thus, I mused, scattering blessings, as a train of brilliants, along our illuminated pathway?

But how incidents and happenings, trivial enough in themselves, sometimes will send our minds a wandering; and how one idea will follow another, until our thoughts run riot, like school-boys chasing butterflies in meadow pastures, running and leaping and singing with the mountain brook, hunting birds' nests in sunny glades, gathering nuts among the squirrel-haunted beech-woods.

These sudden flashes or passages of thought from one subject to another are sometimes quite startling, and yet there seems to be a sort of a gliding along, perhaps by association.

Just now, as that flying meteor went shedding its glories adown the east, it suggested—for it is the Christmas night—thoughts of that piloting orb which startled the shepherds, two thousand years ago, from their oriental slumbers upon the hills of Judea, and guided the Heaven-appointed seekers to the feet of the infant author of that simple faith which cheers the hearts of men wherever the story of the Christ-child is told among the sons and daughters of earth, to this day.

And perhaps that same gliding star that even now scattered its scintillations above this western world, may be looking down upon some weary watcher upon Bethlehem's plain, as he listens beneath a waving palm-tree for the muezzin's call to prayer at the first flush of expected morn.

Now comes a flood of overwhelming memories, and, seated by the firelight in my little library, I have been watching the cheerful glow of the bright-red coals, and dreaming away an hour in reveries whereof I must tell you, and if you listen you will know why that gleaming star, hastening beyond the east, suggested these musings; or, if I can put them to paper, and you follow my pen, you may see, although I shall fail to make them as interesting to you as I could wish.

We will not call it a story, but rather a history, for it is a narrative of events in the lives of two young hearts, even-while dwellers in a quiet New Hampshire village.

I had a friend once, and companion, in one of those years which we wish to remember and dream of. He was my junior by a year or two, but my superior in everything. How I loved his ardent nature, his great warm heart, void of all selfishness; how I admired his manly form, his brilliant intellect, and look, now, after this score and more of years, into his clear earnest eye, and worship the memory of his noble soul, of his better life!

It was during our later school-days that we first met; on one of those days between weeks, when, relieved from the weariness of conning our text-books, we sought that freedom which nature gives, and by shadowy, untrodden paths climbed a mountain slope, and upon its rock-crowned, topmost peak introduced ourselves to each other and to the world above us; not that there was any formal ceremony, for it was many days after that ere we exchanged names, or even thought of it. But we were acquainted, nevertheless.

You know it is always so in our every-day life; it is a certain principle of attraction and repulsion in our natures. What was it about that gentleman you called my attention to yesterday, as we were riding in the street car, that caused such a repulsiveness of feeling? It was nothing in outward appearance, for he was scrupulously and faultlessly dressed. Then why, I ask, that instantaneous, untaught repudiation independent of will or wisdom? And what was there in that sunny face and in those soul-stirring eyes that we passed upon the corner of the street to-day that caused us to stop and admire, and others to listen and smile, not guessing why? It was not that he was entertaining a little girlish sunbeam there, for the one in the car strove to awaken a child's love for novelty, but failed to interest, and the boy shrank away repelled. But I leave the why for philosophers to answer; we can know the facts.

But I was going to tell you; this was the first of many pilgrimages that we made together, my friend and I, and many pleasures unknown we sought in the forests and among the hills, wherever the wildness and the beauty of the scenery won us. I am not going to give you a narration of those experiences, lest they prove wearisome, but pass on to the incidents I intended to sketch.

My student life over, I entered into the more practical and busy affairs of life, leaving my friend to pursue his studies and strive for the fulfilment of his high ambition, which was a noble one. "I would be great," he said one day, as we stood upon an eminence, overlooking the little world of country around us, "I would go through the world like this wind, girded with power to freshen and purify, to sweep away old wrongs and prejudices, just as these leaves of autumn are scattered. I would stir the thoughts of men as these trees are stirred, and with words that would go echoing down the corridors of time. I would possess a knowledge of all lands and all nations; I would walk in the footsteps of the old masters, and muse above he ashes of departed greatness. I would wander among the time-hallowed ruins of Greece and Rome, and look upon those pyramidal monuments of ancient glory in the land of the Pharaohs; dream among those desolate ruins of antique palaces, the halls of Karnak and the temples of Luxor, century-laden relics of a mummied age. Or what more worth the living for than to see the sun rise above Olivet's sacred mount, or his glorious setting beyond the hills and forests of Lebanon? Think of bathing one's life-stained limbs in the waters of the Jordan, and baring his forehead to the dewy winds of Hermon! What more inspiring, think you, than to lie in the starlight of Bethlehem, gazing upon the misty outlines of the hills and valleys that had known the wanderings of the 'Son of Man;' or upon the hillside above the vale of Jehosaphat, watching the moonlight creeping over and around the walls of the 'City of David,' and across the hills of Judea, lighting up the shadows in Gethsemane's garden, and silvering the disturbed waters of far Galllee! Didst never think, oh, friend of mine, that that same calm moon and those changeless watchers in heaven's blue vault, which we so love to worship, looked down, in the ages that were, upon the scenes and incidents of 'Holy Land?' Didst never ask them, in your home in the up country, to tell you the story of that legendary eastern clime and the 'Boy of Nazareth?'"

I bade Wilbur Austin a reluctant good-bye that night, and saw him not again for many months; then our meeting was in this wise: In one of those far-off years of mine, full of rovings here and there, a soft, star-lit evening in early autumn found me at a quiet New Hampshire village. Many such are found at short intervals, scattered throughout the Connecticut valley, set like constellation gems along that watery way.

You may know the place; near where a spur of those grand old hills sets down his granite foot far across the valley, and the river goes fretting around it as though disturbed at the intended barrier. "Moosilauke," overlooking his humbler neighbors, lifts his shaggy summit into cloud-land toward the east.

There is a long avenue, the village street, stretching away beneath a shadow of wide-spreading elms, older than the century. A miniature park invites the wayfarer into its semi-solitude, and here the purple twilight falls early, for the sun sets before its time to the villagers atween the hills, and night comes down slowly.

Leisurely sauntering, almost unmindful, I lent a listening ear to the quaint song of a whippoorwill, sent from the gray cliffs a little back from the village street, and heard above the whisperings of winds and waters down below.

But now voices, less inspiring perhaps, but quite as familiar, aroused me from dreamy reveries, and, pausing, I became an involuntary though not an unwilling listener. I could not be mistaken; it was the voice of my old friend, though to-night somewhat tremulous and sad, and I knew the deep springs of his soul were stirred to their lowest depths and were welling up, up. I fancied I could hear other tones, too, of a crushed and fearful anguish, as of a heart bowed down.

"Yes, dear Ellen, it must be so; the cup is bitter, but it must be drained. I had anticipated no objection from your father to the realization of our fondest hopes. I know I am altogether unworthy your hand or your love, but somehow I had dared to hope, too fondly, alas, that our happiness was not to be disturbed in this way; but since the fiat has been spoken, I shut my eyes upon the bright picture of our future, tinted by 'love's young dream,' and shall open them on the morrow to the stern realities of the 'it must be so.' I love you too well to have you incur parental displeasure or sow the seeds for future unhappiness and sorrowful regrets. To-morrow I go to wander I know not whither, and we may never meet again, but I would not have you forget me soon, nor our brief dream of bliss, whether I tarry among the sunny scenes of life or go away beyond the hills of earth. On some quiet evening of midsummer, when there are no dampening shadows between the flowers and the stars we so love for companionship, and when the silvery moonlight creeps over the hilltop yonder and down into the valley, weaving around the soul its wizard spell, go out then upon the river's bank, and beneath the 'old oak' whose waving branches shelter the rock-hewn seat where we so oft have sat in the gloaming, listening to the wild songs of evening and watching the night come down with all the stars—sit there, I say, in the old familiar spot, and know for a verity, if the soul is superior to the clay, I will sit beside you, and we will talk of the past and its memories. And why not? Since sprits may commune with each other after this earthy form is abandoned, why may they not, too, while the blood is warm and the cheeks aglow and the eyes are bright?"

For many minutes there was no response, save in stifled sobs, and I could almost realize there was raging in the depths of some pure soul a tempest of intense love and emotion, and in his an indescribable and tumultuous agony. At length she spoke, and her voice was calm, save a lingering tremulousness: "And is this the end, dear Will? Must our love-laden bark here founder? Does my father think by driving you hence to turn my thoughts and affections into another and unnatural channel? It can never be. Wherever you may go, rest assured my heart goes with you. Time, you know, is the mother of change, and we may be happy yet. As the months go away, my father may relent, and see in a strong, noble soul, armed with true manhood, more of real worth than in the gold and glitter and lands of a cold-hearted man of the world. But, Will, it is hard to say goodbye—almost harder than I can bear. I must commence a new life, for all my present life and love will be gone, perhaps forever. But I will find companionship in our old haunts; I shall be alone on the bank of the river, where the shadows come and go, and there is wild melody of wind and waves; out upon the hillside at the foot of the cliff, where the night-bird sings the daylight away, and where we so love to worship the moon and the starlight as they come glinting into the evening sky; up in the glen, so full of sweet solitude, and where the laughing brook babbles among the rocks and the mosses. But, dear Will, should you never return to these scenes; should death come to you in a distant land—and now her voice became broken—I will name a tryst, and you shall treasure it in memory with this love of ours: If you go hence before me you shall be first to greet me upon the other shore; but if I tarry not long with these friends of earth, and your mission be not yet fulfilled, so I meet you not over there, my kiss shall awaken you upon that glorious morning. Shall it not be thus?"

"We will live and die in that memory, dear Ellen."

Just then a ray of moonlight stole in through the branches, and she blushed not to see two white arms wound around a manly neck, and a lovely form pressed lovingly to a breast where beat as noble a heart as ever warmed with human love; and I am very sure that compact was sacredly sealed with pure and ardent lips.

The intruder upon that sacred scene has long since been forgiven the innovation. It was my intention to steal away unnoticed with this unsought secret, and was moving with that purpose when a peculiar but well-remembered signal arrested my steps. I had heard it often in those days of which I mentioned—those later school days—and I obeyed its call with as much pleasure and alacrity as did my old friend a similar summons from me in one of our adventurous holiday excursions, whereof I may sometime tell you, but not now.

So novel a meeting would, under ordinary circumstances, have proved a very enjoyable one, for he was a glorious talker, and we would have walked and talked the night hours away and bridged over the almost three years of separation with the events of the lapsed period, whereof each formed a part, and of other days and their memories; but I knew the heart of my friend was o'er-filled with sad thoughts and dreary forebodings, and that of his fair companion, who clung so trustingly to his side as we strolled leisurely along toward her home among the maples, was brimming with meditations too sacred to commit to words; so I ventured not to turn the current of their moody reflections by idle, common-place utterances of my own. I shrank from entering the consecrated precincts where those agonized souls were worshipping at the shrine of true and holy love; so I awaited in silence, making companionship with the God-given glories of that summer evening, and turning at times with frank emotion to do homage to the world of beauty and true womanly loveliness that gleamed with heavenly radiance from the bright but sad young face of Ellen Burton.

Once, only once, was the silence broken by aught of the lips' expression:

"Better die then, since life has lost its joy; it were better to die that the aching heart may be at rest."

"No, dear Ellen, not so, for 'the darkest day wait till to-morrow will have passed away,' and these murky clouds may be hiding from us their sun-illumined face; after frost and the dreariness of winter come the flowers and the joys of spring."

The air had grown chilly and the evening far spent when we said "good-night" to Miss Ellen at the wayside gate leading to her father's house, where we left her in care of "Old Black Ben," the faithful house-dog, who came bounding down the walk to meet his young mistress. The moon smiled again as Will dropped a kiss upon those dewy lips, and entreating her to cheerful rest unmindful of to-morrow's adieus, he took my arm and we moved away in silence. Wrapping my cloak more closely about me to keep out the evening's damp, and lighting a cigar from Will's well-filled case, we wandered out into the starlight and adown the road by the river's bank. Had our hearts been free from this untimely sadness, and our spirits light as in those merry, happy days I wot of, we should have lain ourselves upon the grass, or upon some moss-upholstered rock beside the river, and, disturbed by no sound save those musical murmurs which we always loved, we would have talked the moon from out the sky, and the stars beyond the western hills; but now almost in painful silence the time sped along until the "High Rock" was passed, where the waters fretted so madly, and the cold gray walls of the "Haunted House" became dimly visible in the shadow of the "Hill of Pines." Here the wind sighed heavily, in sympathy, I suppose, with our saddest spirits. At the "Rustic Bridge" over the "Hemlock Brook," we turned to retrace our steps, and as villageward we wended our way, I learned what I was most wishing to hear from the lips of my old companion: the events of his life during the long months since that morning in a late autumn, when we, at a riverside depot, exchanged farewells, (and old hats, too, in memoriam, as I well remember), I, to step out into the world of busy life, he to return to the halls of learning. And most of all I wished to know of this late episode, this life of a lover, an interesting scene of which I had but now been an incidental witness. Gradually and strangely it unfolded, and I learned how, soon after I left him at school, the remittances from his agent or guardian grew smaller and less frequent, until one bright morning he awoke to learn that he was penniless. The small fortune that was left him by his father having been turned into cash by the miscreant in whose care it was placed, and he having fled with his ill-gotten gain to parts unknown.

Having fully satisfied himself of the fact, and deeming the recovery of it, or even the criminal himself, surrounded by an impenetrable shadow of doubts, he turned his attention to the realities of his new circumstances, and set about buckling on the armor of manhood to engage in the real battle of life. With extreme reluctance he severed his connection with the institution he had chosen as his Alma Mater, and gave up all idea of a complete college course. His little affairs, the necessary outgrowth of a student's life, were soon arranged, and he left in the care of a friend his nucleus of a library, and other accumulated effects, among which was a superb "Madonna" by some unknown author. This my friend greatly cherished, averring and always dreaming it the prototype of one yet to be found in all maidenly loveliness in some of the by-ways of the "yet to be." I shall never forget that artist's conception. I think one could sit for hours gazing into those dreamy eyes, and then the countenance! it seems impossible that so much loveliness could be put upon canvas, so life-like was it! such matchless lips! so rich, soft cheeks! and then there was a world of womanly loveliness and depth of soul beaming from out her gentle face.

You know there are few paintings representing the "Holy Mother" that are particularly striking, save as works of art, but this one of which I write, appealed to the heart; and one went out from it always with lingering dreams of those dove-like eyes beaming upon him from soul-full features.

Thus much have I said of this picture without intending it, but you will pardon me when I say, that although a score of years of life's experiences have left their impress here, yet the memory of that angelic face lingers as bright as a dream of Heaven.

But I was saying; these he left with a friend until time and circumstances should come for them, and then, sadly, but with hope and purpose strong, he stepped out to do and dare; a man among men, in and of the world.

CONCLUDED NEXT MONTH.

FORGETFULNESS OF SORROW.

BY MARY HELEN BOODEY.

Some precious moments of forgetfulness
I gain from out the web and woof of time,
Faint snatches from the future's perfect chime,
That fall upon the heart like a caress
Given by the soul that's steeped in tenderness:
  Peace wraps me like a mantle, faith is mine,
  And all my hopes in greater beauty shine,
Lit with a radiance that disarms distress,
Such hours do seem strange notes of harmony
  From heavenly choirs that reach me dwelling here
   Within the house of my mortality,
  Blinded, yet listening, albeit the soul's ear
Is dull and heavy, not what it will be
When the whole glorious strain, sweet, soft and clear,
Shall sound in ceaseless music through its sphere.

EARLY HISTORY OF THE METHODISTS IN NEW HAMPSHIRE.

BY JOSEPH FULLONTON.

There are different divisions of Methodists, but those most common in this section of the country, and the largest body of them, are called Episcopal Methodists. The denomination originated in England in 1739, mainly under the labors of Rev. John Wesley. A society was formed in London, and one in Bristol soon after. The corner-stone of the first Methodist meeting house was laid May 12, 1739. The annual conference of their ministers is peculiar to the denomination, and the first commenced in London, June 25, 1744, and consisted of six members.

The first Methodist Society in this country was organized in New York City in 1766. It was composed of immigrants from Ireland, who had been won to the faith by the preaching of Mr. Wesley. The first Methodist preacher in that city was Philip Embury. His first discourse was in his own hired house to five persons. As the congregation increased, a rigging loft was occupied in Williams Street; and, finally, a house of worship was erected. This was what has been since called the Old John Street Church. It was dedicated in 1768. The first annual conference was in 1773, when there were ten preachers appointed to six places, mostly cities, one of which was New York, another Philadel-

EARLY HISTORY OF THE METHODISTS IN NEW HAMPSHIRE. 13

phia, another Baltimore. There were six hundred in the membership. In 1784 there were 33 travelling preachers and 14,986 members. At Christmas, the same year, the first annual conference was held in Baltimore. In 1792, the first general conference was held in the same place.

It will be seen that these operations were south of New England, but it has been a characteristic of Methodism to make an aggressive war upon the empire of sin, and extend itself in all directions. New England was visited by several preachers, among them being Rev. Jason Lee, a pioneer often on the frontiers, travelling on horseback, and addressing, with great earnestness, zeal and fervor, multitudes that came to hear him. He was in Boston, where he preached once under the great elm on the common.

No sooner had a foothold been gained in Massachusetts than New Hampshire was considered a field to be cultivated. In 1794, the New England Conference appointed John Hill to labor in this State. What came of this is not known, as there is no record of his work. Possibly he did not come into the State. Yet, through the efforts of some one, a society was soon after formed in Chesterfield, which in 1797 had 92 members, and that year Smith Weeks was appointed to that place. The church there still exists, and is probably the oldest in the State. Two years later Elijah Batchelder was appointed there.

In the meantime other sections were visited. Jason Lee, above named, labored in the lower part of the State to some extent. Some opposition was encountered, but in general a good work is not hindered by opposition, but, on the contrary, is usually advanced. During the year 1800 a society was constituted in Landaff and one in Hawke, now Danville; in 1801, one in Hanover; in 1802, one in Bridgewater and one in Kingston; in 1803, one in Grantham; in 1804 one in Pembroke, one in Loudon and one in Tuftonborough; in 1805, one in Northfield and one in Centre Harbor; in 1806, one in Portsmouth; in 1807 one in Canaan and one in Rochester; in 1810, one in Greenland.

The several places to which a minister was appointed constituted a "circuit," receiving its name from the principal town; and this continued, especially in country regions, until within a very few years. A circuit embraced two, three or more towns. These the minister was to visit and hold evening or other meetings. When a circuit was very large, two ministers were assigned to it. On a circuit, a minister was much in the saddle, or travelling on foot in wilderness regions, finding his way by spotted trees.

During the times in which the above societies were established, and later, there were several distinguished ministers doing good service in the State, among whom should be named the following:

Rev. Elijah Hedding, who travelled over some of the rough portions of the State, preaching the gospel to many, but subsequently became a Bishop, and resided in Poughkeepsie, N. Y., where he died.

Rev. Wilbur Fisk, who was a Presiding Elder in New Hampshire, and afterwards became President of Wesleyan University, in Middletown, Conn., and was elected Bishop, but died before serving in that office.

Rev. John Broadhead, a native of Pennsylvania, who was for some time a Presiding Elder—a man of sterling ability and an effective preacher, who resided at what is now South Newmarket, was a Senator in the Legislature, and for four years Representative in Congress, and who died April 7, 1838.

Rev. Alfred Metcalf resided in Greenland as a local preacher, and labored successfully in the surrounding region. After a ministry of success for thirty years, he died June 4, 1837, aged fifty-nine years.

Rev. John Adams was born in Newington. He preached in Massachusetts, Maine, and, during the latter part of his life, as well as at times previously, in New Hampshire. He had some eccentricities, but many excellencies. He was apt, cutting in rebuke, fascinating and earnest, had great influence in his addresses, and was successful in bringing many into the churches. He was familiarly known as "Reformation John." He died in Newmarket, Sept. 30, 1850, aged fifty-nine years.

Rev. Joseph A. Merrill was for some time a Presiding Elder; also Rev. Benj. R. Hoyt. Rev. George Pickering did good service in helping to organize early societies. Rev. Martin Ruter, afterwards a Doctor of Divinity, labored for a time in this State. He died in Texas, where he went to preach to the destitute.

An academy was established by this denomination in Newmarket in 1813. This was near Newfields Village, in what is now South Newmarket. Its location was too far from the village for convenience, but it flourished for several years. In 1824 the funds were transferred to the institution in Wilbraham, Mass. Still the academy continued its operations for some years later, but in 1845 the State Conference opened a seminary at Sanbornton Bridge. After the buildings were burned, new ones were erected very near, in what is now Tilton.

Camp Meetings were not common till within the recollection of some now living. The first, a record of which is now at hand, was held in Sandwich in 1820. The first in Rockingham County was in Sandown, in 1823. Sprituous liquors were sold near by, which caused trouble. The following year another was held in that town. The celebrated Rev. John N. Maffit was present. The encampment was then a small affair, compared with those of more modern times. There were but about twenty tents in a circle, in which eight or ten hundred persons might be seated on rough seats.

MALAGA.

BY VIANNA A. CONNOR.

[The writer is a young lady of Concord, now visiting in Spain.—ED. MONTHLY.]

In one of the sunniest spots of "Sunny Spain" stands the quaint old city of Malaga, known to us in childhood by its delicious raisins, and, to our more advanced age, by its interesting history and the conspicuous part it has borne in the political struggles of the nation.

As we enter the harbor we are enchanted with the beautiful scene before us. The sea, calm and lovely in its glassy stillness, the mountains, rising on and on until their dim outlines are hardly perceptible in the distance, and the city with its domes and spires glistening in the rays of a tropical sun, form pictures of surpassing loveliness. As we approach, we obtain a fine view of the cathedral, the custom house, and the old Castle which has watched over its protegee for centuries.

Generation after generation has passed away, but this ancient fortress has been true to its trust, struggling nobly for the protection of its subjects, a bulwark of strength, and " a very present help in time of need." We drop anchor, and immediately our steamer is surrounded by small boats ready to carry us and our luggage to the shore. A medley of unintelligible sounds, accompanied by the high tones and frantic gesticulations of the boatmen, bewilders our unaccustomed ears, and we rejoice heartily when everything is satisfactorily arranged and we are on our way. Arriving on shore we proceed to find the Custom House officer, not without some anxiety, having heard various rumors of unreasonable duties extorted from foreigners; we, however, are more fortunate, and after a slight examination of our boxes, are allowed to depart in peace with the customary "Vaga Usted con Dios." Kind friends welcome us with loving words and our "Chateaux en Espagne" are more than realized in the happy hours which each day brings.

Who could be otherwise than happy in a climate of almost perpetual sunshine? To an inhabitant of northern climes it would appear incredible that weeks and even months pass without one cloudy day to obscure the brightness, and this without the penalty of a rainy season, which is not known in Malaga. In the months of November and December more rain falls than at any other portion of the year, but it is so interspersed with sunshine that there is little opportunity for dullness; even when the rain is falling the sun seems to be forcing its way through the clouds to remind us of its presence. The winter is charming beyond description; such a sky is not to be found even in Italy, and the air is uniformly mild and balmy We take our daily walks and drives as regularly as the Cathedral clock strikes the hours, planning excursions for days in advance without a fear of adverse weather. Invalids, especially those suffering from pulmonary complaints, are almost invariably benefitted by this climate. An equable temperature and strong sunlight are powerful remedial agents both for body and mind. In the year 1861 a phenomenon occurred in the form of a slight fall of snow which created quite a sensation among the Malagnenos. It disappeared as suddenly as it came and has never made a second visitation. The summer months are hot, but the heat is less enervating than in a climate where the temperature is constantly changing, and much less dangerous. There are no epidemics and we have never heard a case of sunstroke reported.

Malaga is very irregular in appearance; the ancient portion is quite a labyrinth of narrow streets laid out before the advent of carriages; those a little more modern are sufficiently wide to admit one carriage, while others made within the last half-century are broad and well paved. The favorite promenade is the "Alameda," so called from *alamos*, (elm), it being bordered on either side by those trees. It is adorned by occasional statues and fountains placed at each end. The largest of these was erected last year in honor of King Alfonso's visit to this city, its silvery spray rising to a great height, and reflecting the golden beams of the setting sun, producing a most brilliant effect. The other, less pretentious in size, is entitled to some consideration on account of having shared in the celebration of the marriage of ex-Queen Isabella, when it sent forth jets of red wine, to the admiration of all beholders.

On Sundays and days of *fiesta*, the Alameda presents an animated appearance, being filled with ladies and gentlemen promenading, or sitting in chairs arranged along the sides, which one may occupy a whole afternoon for the insignificant sum of half a real (two and a half cents), with the additional advantage of listening to gay music discoursed by a band of musicians furnished by the government. Here friends sit and chat over the current topics of the day; maidens and lovers cast furtive glances of unswerving fidelity, and little children, happiest of all, frisk about like young lambs, regardless of clean frocks and scolding nurses.

Running at right angles with the large Alameda is a smaller one, bearing the somewhat gloomy name of "Alameda de los Tristes," (of the sad). The name is an inappropriate one, as it is the gayest, most cheerful street in the city. The sun sheds upon it its life-giving rays "from early morn till dewey eve," while the merry birds fill the air with their joyous songs. Acacia trees afford a geateful shade for those who wish to pass the hours in "*dolce far niente*," a pastime much sought and enjoyed by inhabitants of southern climes. As the Alameda de los Tristes is the gayest street, so the Calle Peligro (Dangerous Street), is the safest; Calle Ancha (Broad Street), the narrowest; Calle Sucia (Dirty Street), the cleanest; and Calle dil Viento (Wind Street), the least airy. The Plaza de la Constitucion derives its name from having been the site of the City Hall at the time the Constitutional Law was first proclaimed, in the year

1812. It was an event of the greatest importance to the people, being a transition from absolute despotism to a Constitutional Monarchy. Hitherto they had been subject to the mandates of a capricious king, without a knowledge of their rights or power to assert them; but the new law extended its protecting hand and gave them a feeling of comparative security.

The Plaza de Riego a de la Merced (Mercy), as it is more commonly called, bears the name of Gen. Riego, a Liberalist who delivered an address in this square. He was afterwards executed in Madrid on charge of conspiring against the government. In the centre of the Plaza stands a monument on which are inscribed the names of forty-nine innocent men, executed here on the 11th of December, 1831. The principal one, a Spaniard by the name of Torrijos, who was known as a Liberalist, during a stay at Gibraltar, received a letter from the Governor of Malaga, informing him that great excitement prevailed among the citizens who were anxious for a change of government, and desired his immediate presence. Accordingly he embarked from Gibraltar in a small vessel containing forty-nine persons, who immediately upon their landing upon the coast west of Malaga, were seized and put to death without any opportunity of defending themselves. Upon two sides of the monument are the following couplets:

*" A vista de este ejemplo cindadanos
Antes morir que consentir tiranos."

†" El martir que transmite su memoria
No muere, sube al templo de la Gloria."

A blacker crime than this can scarcely be found recorded in the annals of Spanish history. Had it transpired in the less enlightened period of the middle ages, it would be regarded as the result of ignorance and barbarism, but the deliberate performance of a treacherous act in the very height of civilization is a stain upon the record of the nation which can never be effaced.

———

*" In view of this example, citizens, sooner die than consent to tyrants."

†" The martyr who transmits his memory never dies, but ascends to the temple of Glory."

TO MT. KEARSARGE.

BY WILL E. WALKER.

Lone mount, uplifting high thy storm-scarred crest,
  Oft veiled in clouds, amidst the circling hills,
Thy craggy sides and slopes in verdure dressed,
  The source of limpid springs and fruitful rills;
While many dwellers in the vale below,
  Who loved thee once have passed from earth away,
And we who love thee, too, like them shall go,—
  From age to age, dost thou, unmoved, stay,
And like the prophet who of old did cry,
  " Repent, repent, the Kingdom is at hand!"
So wouldst thou lift our worldly minds on high,
  To things eternal, to a Better Land.
Thy maker's glory thou dost well foretell;
  We greet thee, Hail! but soon must say Farewell!

CAPT. THOMAS BAKER AND MADAME CHRISTINE, HIS WIFE.*

BY REV. SILAS KETCHUM, WINDSOR, CONN.

On the 9th of February, 1704, a second great calamity and destruction by the Indians fell on Deerfield, Mass., the story of which has become familiar through the narrative of Rev. John Williams, minister of the town, who, with his wife and children, was carried captive to Canada. In this attack thirty-eight perished, and 100 were taken prisoners. Of this latter number nineteen were murdered and three starved before reaching Canada. Among the survivors was THOMAS BAKER, afterwards the celebrated Indian fighter.

He was born in Northampton, Mass., May 14th, 1682, a son of Timothy and Sarah (Atherton) Baker. Whether he was residing at Deerfield, or whether he was captured previously, in the raid of the Indians on surrounding towns, does not appear. He was then twenty-two years of age. How long he remained a captive in Canada is unknown, at least to the writer. What were his experiences, or manner of deliverance, how he was treated, or how employed, there is nothing to show. Two things, however, it seems safe to predicate of his captivity: That he acquired that knowledge of Indian modes and methods which contributed to his subsequent successes as an Indian scout, and that he made in Canada the acquaintance of a young woman who afterwards became as famous as he, and who, by becoming his wife, doubtless induced him to forsake his own and become a citizen of her native State.

---

* Since writing this article, my attention has been called to certain facts in relation to the subjects of it, communicated to the *N. E. Hist. and Genealog. Reg.*, in 1851, by Hon. John Wentworth of Chicago, and afterwards embodied in the *Wentworth Genealogy*, privately printed, in 2 vols., 1870, and soon to be published in an enlarged form, in 3 vols., by the same gentleman.

This lady was Madame Christine Le Beau, a daughter of Richard Otis of Dover, carried to Canada when an infant three months old.

A correspondent of *Farmer and Moore's Collections*, Vol. III., p. 100, says that "about the year 1720, Capt. Thomas Baker of Northampton, in the County of Hampshire, in Massachusetts, set out with a scouting party of thirty-four men, passed up the Connecticut river, and crossed the height of land to Pemigewasset river. He here discovered a party of Indians, whose sachem was called Walternummus, whom he attacked and destroyed."

That this date should probably be 1712, instead of 1720, is shown by Dr. Bouton in *N. H. Provincial Papers*, II., 635, where it is found in a transcript from the Legislative Journal of Massachusetts, in May of the former year, that £10 was voted to "Thomas Baker, commander of a company of marching forces in the late expedition against the Enemy at Coos, and from thence to the west branch of the Merrimack river, and so to Dunstable, in behalf of himself and Company for one enemy Indian besides that which they scalped, which seems so very probable to be slain." On the 11th of June following, the same assembly voted £20 "additional allowance" for still others of the enemy killed, on their own (i. e. the enemy's) showing. To both Gov. Dudley consented.

It was in this expedition that Capt. Baker came upon and surprised a camp of eight Indians at the confluence of a small stream with the Pemigewasset, between Plymouth and Campton, which has since, in remembrance of the exploit, borne the name of Baker's river. Penhallow says the number of the enemy was eight, and that all were slain without the loss of a man. [Coll. N. H. Hist.

Soc., I., 80]. This must have been early in May, 1712. The writer in *Farmer and Moore*, above quoted, says that Walternummus, the chief, and Capt. Baker levelled and discharged their pieces at each other at the same instant; that the ball from the Indian's gun grazed Capt. Baker's left eyebrow, doing no injury, while Baker shot the sachem through the breast, who leaped high in the air and fell instantly dead. They found a wigwam filled with beaver, of which they took as much as they could carry, and burned the rest. According to Penhallow, there were in Capt. Baker's company fifty men, instead of thirty-four. If so, the success of the exploit was not surprising.

At that time Capt. Baker lived in his native town of Northampton. In 1715, he married Madame Le Beau, and was still residing there. But in 1719 he represented Brookfield in the Massachusetts Legislature; and about 1721 he removed to Dover, which continued to be his home thenceforth until his death, probably in 1753. What the records of that town would disclose concerning his subsequent career, the writer would be glad to know. Of his history little enough is on record. Tradition has accorded him the character of a brave and successful scout. It is probable that this was not his first expedition, as an inexperienced man would not be likely to command such an one, and equally probable it was not his last.

His sword, with the initials, "T. B.," inlaid in the blade with gold, with the device of an eagle in a circle, and giving evidence of having seen hard service, is in the museum of the New Hampshire Antiquarian Society. We come now to the history of

MADAME CHRISTINE, CAPTAIN BAKER'S WIFE.

On the night of the 27th of June, 1689, the Indians fell on Dover, and wiped out their long-cherished sense of injury with a bloody hand. Belknap says there were five garrisoned houses in Dover at that time. One of these belonged to Capt. Richard Otis. He was an Englishman by birth, and was made an inhabitant of Boston, May 28, 1655, but was taxed at Dover the next year. For thirty-three years he had been one of the leading men of the town. He had been thrice married. His first wife was Rose, daughter of Antony Stoughton; his second, Shua, daughter of James Hurd; his third, probably a young woman, was Grizell, daughter of James and Margaret Warren. She had at the time of the attack a daughter, born in March previous, who had been named Margaret. Richard Otis was slain, his house rifled and burned, and his wife and child carried captives to Canada.

There Mrs. Otis embraced the Roman Catholic religion, being baptized May 9, 1693, by the name of Mary Madeline Warren, and was married on the 15th of October following to Philip Robitail,* a Frenchman, by whom she had several children, and died at a great age. The infant Margaret was taken in charge by the French, baptized by the name of Christine, educated in a Roman Catholic nunnery, but declined to take the veil. At the age of sixteen she was married to one Le Beau, a Frenchman, by whom she had certainly two, and possibly three, children.

She entertained a strong desire to visit her native land and be among her own people. How long she lived with Le Beau is not known. But in 1714 she was a widow, and, taking advantage of an exchange of prisoners, she returned to Dover. The Romanists would not allow her to take her children, the eldest of which could not have been more than eight years old, and a considerable estate which she possessed she had to abandon.

How much her remembrance of Capt. Thomas Baker had to do with her desire to return to New England we shall never know. When he was carried to Canada,

* This name is given as *Nobitail*, in Coll. N. H. Hist. Soc., VIII., 407, but is incorrect. I learn from Hon. John Wentworth that the name *Robitaile* is not unfrequent in Canada; that the Hon. Mr. Robitaile was, not long since, a member of the Canadian Parliament, and that a Dr. Robitaile recently graduated from the medical department of Harvard University.

CAPT. THOMAS BAKER AND MADAME CHRISTINE, HIS WIFE. 19

in 1704, she was barely fifteen years old, and unmarried. Whether she saw him before or after her marriage, which occurred within the first two years after his capture, or whether she saw him at all in Canada, is equally uncertain. It is assumed that she did, because certain it is that in the year 1715, being the next after her return, she is found at Northampton as Capt. Baker's wife. At that time he had led his scouting party into "the Cohos country," had received his bounty and established his fame.

At Northampton Madame Christine renounced the Romish faith and united with the Congregational church, then under the pastoral care of Rev. Solomon Stoddard, from which time she seems to have been called by the English name of Christina. It would appear that tidings of this renunciation did not reach Canada for many years.

At length, on the 27th of June, 1727, at which time Mrs. Baker had been six years a resident of Dover, M. Seguenot, who had been her own and her mother's confessor at Montreal, prepared and forwarded to her a letter of remonstrance and entreaty, exhorting her to abjure the faith to which she had apostatized and return to the church of Rome. The letter was written in French, and contained an elaborate presentment of the claims of "the Mother Church," and of the arguments commonly used against Protestant Christianity, chiefly composed of the calumnies and assumptions that had been used against Luther and Calvin. By this letter we learn that her mother, Madame Robitail, was then living, and that one of her own children, a daughter by Le Beau, had recently died. M. Seguenot advised her to show his letter to her ministers, thinking, doubtless, that as it contained profuse references to ancient and unusual authorities, they would be as little able as herself to answer him.

At that time the Rev. Jonathan Cushing was pastor of the church in Dover. He was, in 1727, thirty-seven years of age, and in the tenth year of a pastorate which lasted fifty-two years, the last two of which he had Jeremy Belknap for a colleague. He was a graduate of Harvard College, 1712, and a scholarly man in the learning of his time, but it is doubtful if he was acquainted with the French language, and altogether improbable that he possessed the historical volumes needful to make a conclusive reply to M. Seguenot's letter. The letter was placed in the hands of some competent person who translated it into English.

The following year William Burnett was transferred from the governorship of New York and New Jersey to that of Massachusetts and New Hampshire. He was the eldest son of the celebrated Gilbert Burnett, Bishop of Sarum, the historian of the Reformation in England and of his own time, the trusted minister and friend of William III., for whom his son was named by the king himself, who stood god-father at his baptism. Governor Burnett was an accomplished scholar, possessed a clear head, ready wit and a majestic presence. He came to his government in Boston on the 13th of July, 1728, but did not enter his Province of New Hampshire till, probably, April 19, 1729.* He died in Boston Sept. 7, following. From certain causes, New Hampshire was high in his favor, and Massachusetts under his displeasure.

Gov. Burnett never had any personal acquaintance with Mrs. Baker, By some means he was made acquainted with the character of M. Seguenot's letter, and the circumstances to which it related. Although a churchman, he was by education and disposition of mind favorably inclined to the Calvinists. He expressed a desire to see the letter, which was accordingly laid before him, and he prepared in French an equally elaborate reply, refuting the Romish priest's arguments, and exposing his falsifications of history. This was dated Jan. 2, 1729, and was addressed to Mrs. Baker, with leave to make such use of it as she deemed best, but concealing himself as the writer, and subscribing himself her "unknown but humble servant." This

---

*He made his speech to the Council and House of Representatives Tuesday, Apr. 22. Adams, *Annals of Ports.*, says he visited N. H. Sept. 7, 1729; but that was the day he died in Boston.

letter soon was, and the former was again, translated into English, and both were published, with a clumsy explanation by the bookseller, by "D. Henchman, at the corner shop over against the Brick Meeting-House in Cornhill: MDCCXXIX." This corner shop, by the way, was the same building now occupied by A. Williams & Co., opposite the Old South Church, and was built in 1712. Both were re-printed in the eighth volume of the N. H. Historical Society's Collections; and the original correspondence is in the Boston Athenæum.

On the 18th of Oct., 1734, Mrs. Baker petitioned the Governor and Council of New Hampshire for leave to keep a "house of public entertainment," which was granted on the 9th of May the next year. In 1737, she petitioned Gov. Belcher and the Honorable Council "to grant her a tract of land in this Province [N. H.], of such contents as you shall in your wisdom and goodness see meet," setting forth that she was captured in her infancy, lived many years among the French in Canada, and that she had purchased her liberty "with the loss of all her estate, which was not inconsiderable;" that since her return to New England she had met with many misfortunes and hardships, and had several children, which she might find burdensome to maintain, "especially considering that she was not in such comfortable circumstances as she had formerly lived in." The petition was, March 16, 1737, "ordered to lie for consideration till next session," and does not appear to have been again taken up.

The "several children" above referred to were six. One of these was Col. Otis Baker of Dover, who died in 1801. He represented Dover in the State Legislature in 1770, '72, '73 and '75, and under the revolutionary government; was Judge of the Court of Common Pleas, 1773-1785. State Senator two years, member of the Committee of Safety, 1776, '77, and Colonel of the 2d New Hampshire Regiment.

Lydia, daughter of Col. Otis Baker, married Col. Amos Cogswell of Dover, whose daughter, also Lydia, married Paul Wentworth, Esq., of Sandwich, and was the mother of Hon. John Wentworth of Chicago.

Mrs. Christina Baker died in Dover, Feb. 23, 1773, having nearly completed her 84th year.

MARY AND MARTHA.

BY LAURA GARLAND CARR.

"The sky is clear, the air is cool,
  The birds are full of glee,
The dew has dried from off the grass,
  The hills are fair to see;
Come, leave your sewing, Martha Gray,
  And roam the fields with me!"

"Ah, Mary, I would gladly go,
  But see this work to do!
These yards and yards to baste and stitch,
  And all this plaiting, too,
Before the dress I need so much
  Will bear the critic's view."

MARY AND MARTHA.

"But, Martha, while you're delving here
  These rare June days speed by,
Such days! when God seems reaching down,
  And heaven's own glories nigh!
Come, *live* this golden day with me
  And let the trimmings lie!"

"Nay, Mary, that will never do;
  I am not brave to dare
The whole gay world in quaker dress
  Like that you choose to wear;
So I must work away at home
  Though earth and skies are fair.

"Martha, you say that you believe
  When these frail forms decay
The thinking mind lives on and on
  In realms of endless day,
And all the good it gathers up
  It bears along its way.

"And yet, to deck this fading form
  You spend your time and care,
And let the living spirit starve,
  Shut off from all that's rare;
Bending its Godlike powers down
  To less than empty air."

"I know, friend Mary, what you say
  Is very good and true,
And yet, the folks that live your way
  You'll find are strangely few,
While thousands, wiser far than I,
  Live on just as I do.

"And so I join the crowd, although
  I like your way the best;
But 'tis so hard to face the world—
  Its ridicule and jest—
To know they write you down as 'odd,'
  'Strong-minded,' 'queerly-dressed.'"

So Martha turned to her machine,
  And straightened cloth and thread,
Then off, through weary lengths of seam
  The shining needle sped;
While Mary, out beneath the trees,
  Gleaned happy thoughts instead.

CHURCHES IN HOPKINTON.

BY C. C. LORD.

THE CONGREGATIONAL CHURCH.

One of the conditions upon which the original proprietors of the town of Hopkinton received their grant was an agreement "to build and furnish a convenient meeting house and settle a learned and orthodox minister." In the first plan of the division of lots, the land was parceled out upon opposite sides of four roads, diverging from a common centre towards the four cardinal points of the compass. By this arrangement, "the minister's" lot was the first "on the north range on the west side." The fifth lot in regular order on the same range and side was also a "ministerial lott."

The first settlers in Hopkinton came here probably as soon as 1739. At a public meeting held in the house of Timothy Knowlton, on the 24th of May, the same year, it was voted to build and furnish a meeting house by the last of the following October, said meeting house to be "thirty-five ft. in length, twenty-five ft. in breadth, and eight ft. between joints, with a basil roof." This house was not built. Troubles incident to frontier life came on, and twenty-seven years passed away before a church was erected. In the mean while the people worshipped in Putney's Fort, which stood near the angle of the roads diverging northwardly and easterly on the top of Putney's Hill, on land now occupied by Mrs. L. A. Stanwood, and where the first settled minister in town was ordained.

The first church was built in the year 1766. It was fifty feet long, thirty-eight broad, and the posts were twenty-two feet. Eight years more passed away before a pulpit and pews were added. Five hundred pounds, "old tenor," were originally appropriated for the erection of this house. A depreciated state of the currency made this appropriation equivalent to something over $1000. On the 5th of February, 1789, the church was burned. A local difference of feeling engendered a dispute which terminated in a crime. The first centre of the town was on Putney's Hill. Increase of population and incident circumstances gave a prominence and preference to the spot where the village now is. The first church was built on the site of the present Congregational house of worship. Some, of course, were dissatisfied. A certain young man testified to his dissent by burning the building. He was punished for a time by confinement in jail, and at labor. At a town meeting, May 8, 1789, it was voted to forgive him, his father binding him to labor for the town till satisfaction was rendered. The society of worshippers, thrown out of doors by the destruction of their meeting-house, accepted for a time the offer of Benjamin Wiggin, taverner, to open his barn for their accommodation. The house of Benjamin Wiggin is still standing, next building westerly to the Episcopal church. It was in front of Benjamin Wiggin's, under the trees now standing, that the Rev. Jacob Cram, third minister in town, was ordained, February 25, 1789.

In less than four months from the burning of the first house, a second one was erected. The old controversy was revived. It had only partially culminated on the day of the fire. A committee, consisting of Nathan Sargent, Samuel Farrington, John Jewett, John Moore, Isaac Chandler, James Buswell, Benjamin B. Darling, Enoch Eastman, and Joshua Morse, had reported on February 2, 1789, as follows;

"After we have considered the matter respecting the meeting-house, we have examined the rates and we find the east end of the town pays about 8 pounds in fifty in the minister tax more than the west end, and is eight parts in number more. Also the travel is thirty-six miles farther to the common lot on the Hill, so called, than where it now stands, according to our computation. As those two places are the only ones picked upon by the committee, therefore we think the meeting-house ought not to be moved."

Three days after, the meeting-house having been destroyed that morning, it was decided at a meeting held at the public house of Mr. Babson, and adjourned to his "barn-yard," to refer the settlement of the local dispute to the selectmen of Gilmanton, Linesborough and Washington. By this time several sites were proposed for the permanent location of a meeting-house. The disinterested committee of gentlemen from abroad reported *verbatim et literatim* as follows:

"*To the Town of Hopkinton, Gentlemen :*
"We, your Committee appointed to fix upon a Suitible Plac in your Town for you to build a meeting hous upon, do Report that we have Taken a View of the Principle part of your Town, and the Situation of Each Part of the Same, and have found it to be attended with difficulty Rightly to Settle the matter in such a way that Each part of the Town Should have theare Equality of Privileges. The Senter ot a Town in a general way is to be attended to in these Cases, but we are informed the Senter of the Land in your Town Cannot be Regarded for the above purpose; thearefore we have taken a View of the other Spots of ground Nominated by the Several Parts of the Town; (viz.) the Connor near Mr. Burbank's, the Hill, the Spot by the School Hous, and the old meeting Hous Spot, and Considered them thus: it appears to us that the Spot by Mr. Burbank's will accomedate the Southwest Part of the Town only; as to the Hill, it appears to us that it will accomedate the Northwesterly part of the Town only; as to the Place by the School Hous, the distance from the old Spot is so small it is not worth attending to. Thearefore, we, the Subscribers, are unanimus of the oppinion that near the Spot wheare the old meeting Hous Stood will be the most Convenient Place for you to build a Meeting Hous upon.

"Hopkinton, February 20, 1789.
PETER CLARK,   }
EZEKIEL HOIT,   } Committee."
JEREMIAH BACON.   }

The above report being accepted, the new meeting-house was erected promptly. It was 62x46 feet, and had a tower about twelve feet square at each end. It had seven entrances in all—two in each tower and three in front. It had the old-fashioned high pulpit, sounding-board, gallery, and square pews. A few of the front pews, according to custom, were of better finish. With the addition of a belfry and bell in 1811, the structure remained substantially intact till 1839, when it was remodeled into the form of the present church, which was dedicated on December 26th of the same year. A town clock was placed in the tower of the remodeled church.

The first church music was congregational. The hymns were often "deaconed" by some person whose superior musical attainments were popularly recognized. In time people began to desire something better. Musical societies, in different parts of New England were having their influence. The old "Central" society, organized at Concord, contained members from Hopkinton. At a town meeting September 8, 1783, it was voted that Thomas Bayley, Daniel Tenny, Jacob Spofford, Jonathan Quimby, Jr., Nathaniel Clement, and Isaac Bayley "should sit in the singing pew, to lead in singing and to take in such singers as they thought proper." With a proper social stimulus, progress in music advanced to a marked degree. The church choir sometimes included as many as fifty voices. Various instruments were used as accompaniments. In 1800, there were four bass viols, to say nothing of violins, clarinets, and other instruments, in the choir. There were notable singers, players and composers in the olden time. Among them were Isaiah Webber, Jeremiah Story, and Isaac Long. Orchestral music continued to be employed in the Congregational church till about 1850, when a seraphine was purchased and put in the gallery. In 1872, the seraphine was superseded by an elegant organ at a cost of $1800.

A Sunday-school was opened at Hopkinton in 1817, in the school house at Farrington's Corner. About 1821, another school was opened on Beech Hill. In 1822, a Sunday School was opened in the church. In 1848, a constitution was adopted and regular officers chosen. Stephen Sargent was the first superintendent under the new regulation.

In 1757, there were but ten members of the church. Now the church, society, and Sunday School are large and flourishing. The list of pastors ministering to this church since its organization is as follows:—James Scales, ordained November 23, 1757; dismissed July 4, 1770. Elijah Fletcher, Westford, Mass., ordained January 27, 1773; died April 8, 1786. Jacob Cram, Hampton Falls, ordained February 25, 1789; dismissed January 6, 1792. Eathan Smith, South Hadley, Mass., installed March 11, 1800; dismissed December 16, 1814. Roger C. Hatch, Middletown, Conn., ordained October 21, 1818; dismissed June 26, 1832. Moses Kimball, a native of this town, installed May 7, 1834; dismissed July 15, 1846. Edwin Jennison, Walpole, installed June 6, 1847; dismissed September 5, 1849. Christopher M. Cordly, Oxford, Eng., ordained September 5, 1849; dismissed February 4, 1852. Marshall B. Angier, Southborough, Mass., ordained June 8, 1853; dismissed March 22, 1860. Edwin W. Cook, Townsend, Mass., installed March 6, 1861; dismissed December 13, 1864. William H. Cutler, Lowell, Mass., ordained December 20, 1865; dismissed May 8, 1867. J. K. Young, D.D., of Laconia, supplied from June, 1867, till October, 1874. Clarendon A. Stone, Southborough, Mass., installed December 29, 1874.

The west part of the town was the location of a Congregational meeting house as early as 1803. This house was of the usual spacious, uncouth style of architecture prevailing at the time, and stood at Campbell's Corner. There does not appear to have been any separate organization of the church connected with it. It was taken down to be rebuilt into the present Calvinist Baptist church.

In 1834, Dea. Amos Bailey, of West Hopkinton, died, willing a large portion of his property to the Congregational church. One-half of this bequest was to be paid to any society maintaining preaching in the west part of the town. In the hope of securing the aid, a society was organized with its head-quarters at Contoocook. The Union meeting-house was used, and Rev. David Kimball, of Concord, employed to preach. However, it could not be made to appear upon trial that Contoocook was in that part of the town implied in the will of Deacon Bailey, and the bequest was lost. The Second Congregational Society, as it was called, kept up a nominal existence till the year 1851.

The old-fashioned, two-storied farmhouse standing near the old grave-yard on Putney's Hill, and occupied by the descendants of Moses Rowell, is said to have been the first parsonage in the town, the residence of the Rev. James Scales, the first minister. The land publicly held for the benefit of religion was at length disposed of by lease. On March 8, 1796, the town voted to lease it "as long as wood shall grow and water run." The income was divided among the different churches.

THE BAPTIST CHURCH.

Diversity of religious belief is natural among men. Although Hopkinton was settled by people nominally orthodox in faith, actual dissenters from the popular belief soon began to assert themselves. The first gathering of an organized Baptist church was effected through the missionary labors of Dr. Hezekiah Smith. At first this was a branch of the Baptist church in Haverhill, Mass., the subordinate organization occurring in 1769. On May 8, 1771, the church at Hopkinton became independent. In its earlier days, the influence of this church was widely extended. Branch churches were organized in Bow, Goffstown, and Londonderry. The organization included people of Bedford, Merrimack, Derryfield (now Manchester), and Nottingham West (now Hudson). Among the early laborers in the local Baptist field were Elders John Peake, Job Seamans, Thomas Paul, and John Hazen. Dr. Shepherd was also an advocate of Baptist doctrines.

The first years of this church were attended with trials. The war of the Revolution depressed it, but it rallied again in 1789. It received a new impulse from

CHURCHES IN HOPKINTON.

a great revival in 1793. The walls of a new church were enclosed in 1795, but the edifice was not completed till at least twenty years after. This house was very much like most of the country meeting-houses built at the time, being huge, square, high, and galleried. It stood on a spot of ground northerly opposite the house of Mr. Jonathan French, near the convergence of a number of roads, near the foot of the southern slope of Putney's Hill. The Baptist church suffered at length from internal doctrinal dissensions. At first, the members of this church were committed to no special Christian doctrine except such as are held in general by all Baptists. In time, they began to discuss the subtler themes clustering around Calvinism and Arminianism. A division of sentiments arose. The controversy reached its height about the year 1822, when the Rev. Michael Carlton, a pronounced Calvinist, became pastor of the church. In 1823, the scism between the Calvinists and Arminians resulted in a separation. Deacon Jonathan Fowler led off a large party which formed the nucleus of the present Free Baptist church. Since then, the two Baptist bodies have held on in their unmolested ways. In 1831, the Calvinists built a new church, of modern country style, in the westerly part of Hopkinton village, about a mile east of their old place of worship. Their new church was framed out of the timbers of the old West Congregational meeting-house. The old Baptist meeting-house was taken in bulk or in parts to Concord, where it formed a part of a new structure. The Baptist church in Hopkinton village was neatly repaired in 1854. A combined parsonage and vestry was erected nearly opposite the church in 1869.

The Calvinist Baptist church, in common with others, has felt the depressing effects of the later changes in the tide of population, though more and less than some. Its congregation has diminished. It has had important donations. The widow of the late Samuel Smith, about 1868, left a generous benefit to this church. Its cabinet organ was given in 1871 by Geo. H. Crowell, of Brattleboro, Vt. Its bell was a present by Mrs. Sarah Jones, of Hopkinton, in 1876. The list of pastors of this church is as follows:—Elder Elisha Andrews, settled in 1795; preached half the time for three years. For seventeen years after the church was supplied mostly by its deacons. Elder Abner Jones settled in 1815; resigned in 1821. Michael Carlton, ordained June 27, 1822; resigned September 14, 1832. Rev. A. J. Foss, installed March 27. 1833; remained 3 years. L. B. Cole, M. D., ordained and installed April 18, 1837; remained two years. Rev. Samuel Cooke, May 19, 1839; remained six years. King S. Hall, no date of ordination; resigned September 28, 1851. Rev. Samuel J. Carr, March 14, 1852; remained four years. Rev. J. E. Brown, April 2. 1857; resigned September 7, 1862. C. W. Burnham, ordained October 14, 1863; last Sunday in August, 1871. Rev. Abraham Snyder, January 1, 1872; resigned Dec. 27, 1874. William S. Tucker, Sept. 28, 1875.

THE EPISCOPAL CHURCH.

In 1800, Hopkinton had advanced to a position of wealth and influence. Social beliefs and forms were multiplying in proportion. In the village were many families of distinction. A large number of these were Episcopalians by faith or practice. There was also a quota of Episcopalians among the farming population. About this time, or later, also, a number of prominent families came over to the Episcopalians from the Calvinists. In 1803, an Episcopalian society, called Christ's Church, was organized, worshipping in the Court House. The Rev. Samuel Meade was the superintendent of this movement. Rev. William Montague, Rev. Robert Fowle, Rt. Rev. Alexander Griswold, and many others, officiated for Christ's Church for longer or shorter periods. In 1826, Rev. Moses B. Chase became the rector. During his leadership important changes took place. A new parish was formed. In 1827 it was incorporated under the name of St. Andrew's Church. The first wardens were John Harris and William Little. The first vestrymen were Matthew Harvey, Horace Chase, Nathaniel Curtis and J. M. Stanley. A new stone church was begun the same year. It was dedicated June 25, 1828. Rev. Mr. Chase continued rector till 1841. The church flourished during his ministry. In later years it declined with the business prosperity of the town. However, the church has been open most of the time. Important improvements have been made upon the interior of St. Andrew's church. During the ministry of Rev. Mr. Schouler the chancel was reconstructed. It was further improved, and the church frescoed and painted in 1875.

The first organ in town was set up in St. Andrew's church about 1846. It was purchased of the Rt. Rev. Carlton Chase; it had been his parlor organ. The instrument is still in its accustomed place in the unused gallery of the church. It did musical service for many years. In 1874 a new and handsome organ was set up at the left of the chancel, at a cost of about $2000. This church is much indebted to the energy and liberality of many of its friends at home and abroad. Its elegant font was obtained through the exertions of the late Elizabeth T. Lerned, about 1866. The present organ was secured by the energy of Miss C. C. P. Lerned. The altar and lectern cloths, together with the chandeliers and lamps, were the gift of Mrs. G. T. Roberts, of Philadelphia, Pa., about two years ago.

Since 1841 there have been clergymen of St. Andrew's :—Rev. Calvin Wolcott, one year from the second Sunday in May, 1842; Rev. Silas Blaisdell, 1845 to 1847; Rev. Henry Low; Rev. Edward F. Putnam; Rev. N. F. Ludlum; Rev. Francis Chase one year to November 3, 1862; Rev. William Schouler, July 1, 1865 to Jan. 29, 1868. Since Feb. 2, 1868, the church has been supplied by the Rev. H. A. Coit, D. D., of St. Paul's School, Concord. During the time Rev. Hall Harrison has been the almost, or quite, constant rector.

THE FREE WILL BAPTIST CHURCH.

We have already mentioned the defection in the original Baptist church which resulted in the separation of a party, led by Dea. Jonathan Fowler, who organized the Free Will Baptist church. This organization took definite form on the 17th of September of the year of separation, or 1823. The location of this church at Contoocook is suggestive in view of the valuable social results wrought by it. In the earlier times Contoocook had an unenviable reputation. The highest social laws were largely set at defiance. A minister on his way to preach at Contoocook was informed he was going to a bad place. Now all is changed. The influence of the Free Will Baptist church has been a prominent agent in promoting an improved state of society.

The original organization was known as the Union Baptist church. It consisted of twelve members. On the 28th of September, 1826, Jonathan Fowler and Thomas White were chosen deacons. The society was incorporated on the 30th of June, 1827. A meeting-house was constructed the same year; it was raised April 11, finished October 27 and dedicated October 29. Various improvements have from time to time been made on this house since its erection. In 1872 a bell was added.

Rev. David Harriman was pastor of this church from its foundation till May 10, 1828. Rev. Arthur Caverno succeeded till February 24, 1833. Rev. David Moody followed till February 27, 1837; Rev. Hiram Holmes supplied till November 30, 1839; Rev. John L. Sinclair continued a pastor till November 11, 1839 ? Rev. Abner Coombs was installed pastor July 16, 1840; dismissed May 15, 1842. Rev. D. Sidney Frost became pastor May 19, 1842; dismissed April 17, 1845. Rev. Barlow Dyer became pastor May 18, 1845; dismissed March 4, 1849. Rev. S. T. Catlin became pastor December 20, 1849; dismissed in 1851. Rev. Francis Reed became pastor May 20, 1851; dismissed in March, 1859. Rev. C. H. Witham became pastor the first of July, 1859; dismissed June 2, 1861. Rev. Thomas Keniston and others supplied from June, 1861, till May, 1863. Rev. Asa Raulett became pastor May 23, 1863; dismissed in October, 1865. Rev. John L. Sinclair became pastor a second time in January, 1867; dismissed in March, 1869. Rev. George W. Knapp became pastor in

March, 1869; dismissed in March, 1873 John C. Osgood became pastor in June, 1873; dismissed in March, 1878. Rev. C. W. Griffin became pastor May 13, 1878.

THE UNIVERSALIST CHURCH.

In the early part of the present century there was a great revival of Universalism in New Hampshire. Revs. Elhanan Winchester and Hosea Ballou preached the doctrine far and wide, gaining many hearers and making many converts. The church grew and multiplied in many places. Previously to 1840 there were many persons in Hopkinton who entertained some sort of preference for the Universalist form of religion. A church to be known as the Union meeting-house was projected as early as 1835. On the 5th of December of that year a meeting was held at the house of Clement Beck, at "Stumpfield," to take into consideration the erection of a church. Moses Hoyt, 2d, was chosen moderator, James Huse was clerk, and Moses Hoyt, Moses Copp and Nathaniel Colby were made a building committee. The enterprise was effected by the erection of shares, which were sold at $25 each. The whole number of shares sold was thirty-one. Representatives of different faiths in the vicinity took shares. The meeting-house was built in 1836, on a lot north of the road leading from Hopkinton village to Henniker, east of the house of Mr. Charles Barton, about three miles from the village.

There was never any settled minister in this society. Among those preaching here more or less, were Revs. A. A. Miner, J. P. Atkinson, N. R. Wright and J. F. Witherel. The meeting-house was seriously damaged by fire on the 5th of February, 1837, and was subsequently repaired. In 1865 the house was sold to Robert Wilson, and was moved to "Clement's Hill," where it was remodeled into a barn belonging to Alfred Hastings. The society had dwindled in common with many others in districts wholly rural.

A Second Universalist Society was organized shortly after the first. The new organization, had its headquarters at Contoocook. A church, called a Union house, was erected in 1837. It is now used by the New Church, or Swedenborgian Society. The Second Universalist Society for a time had considerable vigor. Rev. J. F. Witherel was a settled minister. A good deal of enterprise was shown in the efforts for propagating the faith. Mr. Witherel, in company with J. Sargent, of Sutton, published the "Universalist Family Visitor," a monthly periodical. The first number was published in April, 1841. The Visitor had twelve pages, was of common tract size, and set forth its favorite principles with talent and vigor. We have not been able to find any records of the Second Universalist Society, which kept up a nominal existence till quite late.

THE NEW JERUSALEM CHURCH.

The New Jerusalem Church, more commonly called the New Church, was founded through the missionary labors of Rev. Abiel Silver, a native of this town, who first preached a number of discourses in the Union church at Contoocook, in the summer of 1851. Mr. Silver was then a resident of Michigan, visiting his old home and family scenes. The appreciation of these discourses induced a contribution in money to the reverend gentleman, who returned the equivalent in theological works of Emanuel Swedenborg, or collateral publications of the New Church.

In a year or two after further interest in the New Church was awakened in Contoocook and vicinity. Mr. Silver returned and preached at length, and finally concluded to make the village his permanent place of residence. The Union church, which had stood for some years unoccupied by any regular society, became a place of weekly worship under Mr. Silver's ministrations. The interest grew till the meeting-house was filled to its utmost capacity. Hearers were found present from various parts of Hopkinton and surrounding towns. In 1857 a permanent organization was effected. On the 24th of May of that year the Rev. Thomas Worcester, of Boston, instituted the society. The following are the names of the original members of the church:—Abiel Silver, Edna N. Silver, Nathaniel L. Noyes, Sarah A. Noyes, Mary Nichols, Rhoda Cutler, Sullivan Hutchinson, Edna C. Silver, Charles Gould, Erastus E. Currier, Lucy H. Currier, Elizabeth C. Dean, Joseph Dow, Asa Kimball, John Converse, Urania N. Converse, Rhoda C. Putnam, Joanna L. Chase, Alonzo Currier, Emily Currier.

Rev. Abiel Silver continued to preach in Contoocook till April 4, 1858, building during his residence in Contoocook the house now occupied by John F. Jones, Esq. On the 15th of August, 1858, the Rev. George H. Marston, of Limington, Me., became the minister, continuing till the month of October, 1862. Since October, 1871, the Rev. Charles Hardon has been the regular minister of the church.

During the times when this church has been without a settled minister various persons have supplied the desk. The services have been frequently, and for months at a time, conducted by a reader. Mr. W. Scott Davis has officiated a great deal in the capacity of reader. This church has suffered a good deal by removals and deaths. A Sunday-school has been connected with the society since its earlier existence.

THE METHODIST CHURCH.

The Methodists quite early had a foothold in this town. In 1842 their allotted portion of the ministers tax was very small. Regular worship was held in the Academy at the lower village. Revs. Stephen Eastman, John English and Joseph Hayes were among the ministers supplying regularly. The Methodist Biblical Institute, at Concord, furnished preachers to a greater or less extent. We have not been able to find any record of this society, which abandoned regular services about 1850. Previously to the year 1871 there had been a number of Methodist families living for a longer or shorter time at Contoocook. Preaching had been sustaind also to some extent during a few previous years. On the 20th of March, 1871, at a meeting held at the house of George H. Ketchum, legal organization was effected as follows: Rev. L. Howard, President; George H. Ketchum, Secretary; W. A. Patterson, Treasurer; John F. Burnham, W. M. Kempton and Samuel Curtice, Financial Committee. The society purposing to build a church, on the 10th of the next month, at a meeting at Mr. Kempton's, D. N. Patterson, T. B. Hardy and Samuel Curtice were made a building committee.

The church was erected the same year at a cost of something over $2,000, on land purchased by the society of Samuel Curtice, and dedicated on the 16th of November. It it a neat and tasty edifice. The society, though small, is active. The following have been preachers:— Rev. L. Howard, from 1870 to 1873 inclusive; Prof. J. B. Robinson,1874; Rev. E. Adams, D. D., 1875; Rev. Joel A. Steele, 1876; Rev. L. Howard, 1877 and 1878.

AN OLD TIME TRIP IN NEW HAMPSHIRE.

BY HON. JOHN H. GOODALE.

That wide stretch of hilly country lying between the Merrimack and Connecticut rivers in this State was, a hundred and forty years ago, a densely-wooded wilderness. The few who would have ventured to occupy it well knew that so long as the French remained in possession of Canada this region was in continual danger from attacks by the Indians. In 1746 these attacks had become so frequent and successful that many of the settlements commenced in the central and southern parts of the State had been abandoned. There remained on the Merrimack small openings at Nashua, Litchfield, Concord, Boscawen and Canterbury, and one at

AN OLD TIME TRIP IN NEW HAMPSHIRE.

Hinsdale and another at Charlestown on the Connecticut; but the entire midland between these valleys was an unbroken, heavily-wooded country.

A TRAMP THROUGH THE WILDERNESS.

In the fall of 1747 two explorers from Dunstable, Nehemiah Lovewell and John Gilson, started from the present site of Nashua for the purpose of examining the slope of the Merrimack, and of crossing the height of land to Number Four, now Charlestown, which was known as the most northern settlement in the Connecticut valley. Knowing the difficulties in traversing hills and valleys mostly covered with underbrush and rough with fallen timber and huge bowlders, they carried as light an outfit as possible—a musket and camp-blanket each, with five days' provisions. Following the Souhegan to Milford and Wilton, they then turned northward, and crossing the height of land in the limits of the present town of Stoddard, had on the afternoon of the third day their first view of the broad valley westward, with a dim outline of the mountains beyond. The weather was clear and pleasant, the journey laborious but invigorating. On their fourth night they camped on the banks of the Connecticut, some ten miles below Charlestown. At noon of the next day they were welcomed at the rude fort, which had already won renown by the heroic valor of its little garrison.

A FRONTIER FORT.

At this time the fort at Number Four was commanded by Capt. Phineas Stevens, a man of great energy and bravery. Lovewell and Gilson were the first visitors from the valley of the Merrimack, and their arrival was a novelty. That night, as in later days they used to relate, they sat up till midnight, listening to the fierce struggles which the inmates of this rude fortress, far up in the woods, had encountered within the previous eight months. The preceding winter this fort had been abandoned, and the few settlers had been compelled to return to Massachusetts. But Governor Shirley felt that so important an outpost should be maintained. As soon as the melting of the deep snow in the woods would permit, Capt. Stevens, with thirty rangers, left Deerfield for Number Four, and reached it on the last day of March. The arrival was most fortunate. Hardly was the fort garrisoned and the entrances made secure when it was attacked by a large force of French and Indians. Led by Debeline, an experienced commander, they had come undiscovered and lay in ambush for a favorable moment to begin the attack. But the faithful dogs of the garrison gave notice of the concealed foe. Finding they were discovered the Indians opened a fire on all sides of the fort. The adjacent log houses and fences were set on fire. Flaming arrows fell incessantly upon the roof. The wind rose and the fort was surrounded by flames. Stevens dug trenches under the walls and through these the men crept and put out the fires that caught outside the walls.

REPULSE OF THE INDIANS.

For two days the firing had been kept up and hundreds of balls had been lodged in the fort and stockade. On the morning of the third day Debeline sent forward a flag of truce. A French officer and two Indians advanced and proposed terms of capitulation, which were that the garrison should lay down their arms and be conducted prisoners to Montreal. It was agreed that the two commanders should meet and Capt. Stevens's answer should be given. When they met, Debeline, without waiting for an answer, threatened to storm the fort and put every man to the sword if a surrender was not speedily made. Stevens replied that he should defend it to the last. "Go back," said the Frenchman, "and see if your men dare fight any longer." Stevens returned and put to the men the question, "Will you fight or surrender?" They answered, "We will fight." This answer was at once made known to the enemy, and both parties resumed arms. Severe fighting was kept up during the day. The Indians, in approaching the stockade were compelled to expose themselves. They had already lost over a dozen of their number, while not one had been killed in the fort and only two wounded.

The French commander, reluctantly giving up all hopes of carrying the fortification, returned toward Canada. The cool intrepidity of the rangers saved Number Four, and the news caused great rejoicing throughout the New England colonies. Sir Charles Knowles, then in command of the fleet at Boston, sent Capt. Stevens an elegant sword, and a letter of commendation to the intrepid soldiers. Subsequently, in compliment to the English Commodore, Number Four was called Charlestown. But while no further attacks were made upon the fort that year, the Indians continued to hover around this and the adjacent settlements of Brattleboro and Westmoreland. In August three men were killed and one captured in going from the fort down the river. Only a few weeks before the arrival of Lovewell and his companion several settlers were captured while harvesting and carried away to Canada.

A STORM AMONG THE HILLS.

Tarrying several days with the garrison, during which the weather continued clear and mild, the two explorers were ready to return homeward. In a direct line Dunstable was less than ninety miles distant. With the needed supply of salt pork and corn bread, Lovewell and Gilson left Number Four at sunrise on the 16th of November. The fallen leaves were crisp with frost as they entered the deep maple forests which skirted the hills lying east of the Connecticut intervales. The days being short it was necessary to lose no time between sunrise and sunset. The air was cool and stimulated them to vigorously hurry forward. Coming to a clear spring soon after midday, Gilson struck a fire, and resting for a half an hour, they sat down to a marvelously good feast of broiled salt pork and brown bread. One who has never eaten a dinner under like conditions can have no idea of its keen relish and appreciation.

It was now evident that a change of the weather was at hand. The air was growing colder and the sky was overcast with a thick haze. In returning it had been their purpose to cross the water-shed between the two valleys at a more northern point, so as to reach the Merrimack near the mouth of the Piscataquog. Their course was to be only a few degrees south of east. Before night the sleet began to fall, which was soon changed to a cold, cheerless rain. Darkness came on early and the two men hurried to secure the best shelter possible. With an ax this might have been made comfortable; at least fuel could have been procured for a comfortable fire. As it was, no retreat could be found from the chilling rain which now began to fall in torrents. It was with difficulty that a smouldering fire, more prolific of smoke than heat could be kindled. India rubber blankets, such as now keep the scout and the sentry dry in the fiercest storm, would have been a rich luxury to these solitary pioneers. The owls, attracted by the dim light, perched themselves overhead and hooted incessantly. Before midnight the fire was extinguished, and the two men could only keep from a thorough drenching by sitting upright with their backs against a large tree, and with their half-saturated blankets drawn closely around them.

LOSING THE WAY.

Daylight brought no relief, as the rain and cold rather increased, and the sleet and ice began to encrust the ground. After ineffectual attempts to build a fire they eat a cold lunch of bread. A dark mist succeeded the heavy rain and continued through the day. Both felt uncertain of the direction they were traveling, and every hour the uncertainty become more perplexing. All day long they hurried forward through the dripping underbrush which was wetting them to the skin. Night again set in, and although the rain and wind had somewhat abated, still it was impossible to build and keep a fire sufficient to dry their clothing, which was now saturated with water.

The third morning came with a dense fog still shrouding the hillsides and settling into valleys. Stiff with the effects of cold and fatigue, Lovewell and his companion felt that with their scanty supply of food, now mainly salt pork, they dared not await a change of weather. Yet there was a vague feeling that their journeying might be worse than useless. Deciding on what they believed a course due east they again hurried forward over a broken region—an alternation of sharp hills, ledges, low valleys and sometimes swamps, until a little past mid-day, when descending a hill they came upon the very brook where they had camped forty hours before! One fact was now established—they had been traversing in a circle. Thinking it useless to go further till the sun and sky should appear, they set to work to build a fire sufficient to dry their clothing and to cook their raw pork. By dark they had thrown up a light framework, and by a diligent use of their knives had procured a covering of birch bark. Piling the huge broken limbs in front they lay down and fell asleep.

Scouts in the olden time were proverbial for awakening on the slightest provocation. Lovewell was aroused by what he thought the rustling of a bear. Reaching for his gun he saw the outline of an animal climbing an oak just across the brook. The first shot was followed by a tumble from the tree. It proved a veritable raccoon, which, fattened on beechnuts, was " as heavy as a small sheep."

The fourth morning was not unlike that of the day previous. The fog was still dense, but it soon became evident that the storm was past, and that the sun would soon disperse the mists. Dressing the raccoon, whose meat was security against famine, they anxiously watched the clearing up of the atmosphere. Suddenly the mists dissolved and the sunlight touched the tops of the trees. The pioneers hastened up a long slope eastward, and toward noon gained the crest of a high ridge. The sky was now clear, and climbing to the top of a tree, Gilson announced that he could see some miles to the east, a high and naked summit which must mark the height of land they were so anxiously seeking.

A SYLVAN DINNER.

With this solution of their difficulties came the sense of hunger. Notwithstanding the hardships of the three past days they had eaten sparingly. The remnant of their bread had been accidentally lost the day previous, but this was far more than compensated by the rich, tender meat of the raccoon. Luckily a supply of fat spruce knots was near at hand. Gilson set himself to the work of furnishing fuel and water, while Lovewell attended to the culinary duties. The utensils of the modern hunter—frying pan, coffee pot, plate, spoon and fork—were wanting. The only implement in their outfit which could be of use was the jack-knife. The meat was cut into pieces two thirds of an inch thick and half the size of one's hand. Cutting several sticks two feet long, and sharpening them at each end, a piece of the salt pork and then a piece of the coon's meat were thrust upon the stick alternately in successive layers— so that in roasting, the fat of the latter, as it dropped down, basted and furnished an excellent gravy to the former. One end of each stick was thrust into the ground so as to lean over the glowing coals. With occasional turning the dinner was in half an hour ready to be served. Seating themselves on the bowlder by the side of which they had built the fire they fell to with sharp appetites. Rarely was a feast more heartily enjoyed.

NIGHT ON LOVEWELL'S MOUNTAIN.

It was past mid-day when the dinner was finished. Walking with renewed strength they reached the base of the mountain. The ground was wet and slippery and the climbing at times difficult, but while the sun was yet an hour above the horizon the two men emerged from the low thicket which lies above the heavy growth, and stood upon the bald summit. Like all New Hampshire peaks whose altitude approaches three thousand feet, the crest of the mountain was of solid granite. The air had now grown quiet and the clear sunlight illuminated the landscape. The two explorers had never looked upon so wide and magnificent a panorama. Westward was the far distant outline of a range now known as the Green Mountains. To the northwest were the bald crests of Ascutney and Cardigan. On the north Kearsarge was seen struggling to raise its head above the shoulders of an intervening range, and through the frosty atmosphere were revealed the sharp, snowwhite peaks of Franconia. Eastward the highlands of Chester and Nottingham bounded the vision—while nearer by reposed in quiet beauty the Uncanoonucks, at that time a well-known landmark to every explorer.

Warned by the freezing atmosphere they hastened down to a dense spruce growth on the northeast side of the mountain, and built their camp for the night. For some cause, perhaps because it was a sheltered nook, the tenants of the forest gathered around. The grove seemed alive with the squirrel, rabbit and partridge. But the hunters were weary, and as their sacks were still laden with coon's meat, these new visitors were left unharmed. The curiosity with which these wild tenants of the mountain lingered around led the two men to believe that they had never before approached a camp-fire or seen a human form.

Just before daybreak Lovewell awoke and telling his companion to prepare for breakfast, returned to the summit of the mountain. It was important to reach the Merrimack by the nearest route, and he could better judge by reviewing the landscape at early dawn. In after years he was wont to say that the stars never seemed so near as when he had gained the summit. The loneliness of the hour suggested to him what was probably the truth, that he and his companion were the first white men who had set foot on this mountain peak. It is situated in the eastern part of the present town of Washington, and its symmetrical, cone-like form is familiar to the eye of many a reader of the GRANITE MONTHLY. With the exception of Monadnock and Kearsarge it is the highest summit in Southern New Hampshire, and to-day it bears the well-known name of Lovewell's Mountain.

THE RETURN TO DUNSTABLE.

Before Lovewell left the summit, the adjacent woodlands became visible, and looking eastward down into the valley he saw only a few miles away a smoke curling up from the depths of the forest. It revealed the proximity either of a party of savages or a stray hunter. Returning to camp, breakfast was taken hurriedly, and descending into the valley they proceeded with the utmost caution. Reaching the vicinity of the smoke they heard voices and soon after the rustling of footsteps. Both dropped upon the ground, and fortunately were screened by a thick underbrush. A party of six Indians passed within a hundred yards. They were armed and evidently on their way to the Connecticut valley. As soon as they were beyond hearing the two men proceeded cautiously to the spot where the savages passed the night. They had breakfasted on parched acorns and the meat of some small animal, probably the rabbit.

Congratulating themselves on their lucky escape from a winter's captivity in Canada, Lovewell and his companion continued their route over the rolling lands now comprised in the towns of Hillsborough, Deering, Weare and Goffstown to the Merrimack. From thence, they readily reached their home in Dunstable. It may be well to add that Lovewell was a relative of the famous Capt. John Lovewell, whose name is so well known in colonial history.

THE GRANITE MONTHLY.

A MAGAZINE OF LITERATURE, HISTORY AND STATE PROGRESS.

VOL. II.   AUGUST, 1878.   NO. 2.

HON. JOSEPH D. WEEKS.

In the last number of the GRANITE MONTHLY there appeared a sketch and accompanying portrait of Hon. David H. Buffum, President of the State Senate. Appropriately following the same we take as our subject of illustration for this number Hon. Joseph D. Weeks of Canaan, Senator from District Number Eleven, and the Democratic candidate for President of the Senate.

Mr. Weeks is the eldest son of Hon. William Pickering Weeks of Canaan, a well-known and successful lawyer of Grafton County, and prominent member of the Democratic party, to whom some reference in this connection seems eminently proper. He was a native of the town of Greenland, born Feb. 22, 1803, a son of Brackett and Sarah (Pickering) Weeks. The families of Weeks and Pickering from which he sprang, were among the early and leading families of that town, and their descendants now constitute a very considerable proportion of its population. He fitted for college at Gilmanton Academy, among his schoolmates at which institution being Profs. Edwin D. and Dyer H. Sanborn and Dixi Crosby, and graduated at Dartmouth in the class of 1826, the late Chief Justice Salmon P. Chase being a member of the same class, and also his roommate. He studied law with Hayes & Cogswell of South Berwick, Me., and was admitted to the York County Bar at Alfred in 1829, but immediately removed to the town of Canaan and established himself in practice. By diligent application to business and careful attention to the interests of his clients, he soon secured a remunerative practice and won a high reputation as a safe and judicious counsellor. He continued in practice until 1861, a period of thirty-two years, when he retired, taking up his residence upon a large farm just below the village, where he lived until his death in 1870. He had devoted himself almost exclusively to the labors of his profession, but his firm adherence to the principles of the Democratic party, as well as his high character and ability occasioned a demand for his services in public life at the hands of his fellow townsmen of that political faith, by whom he was chosen a representative to the Legislature at several times between 1834 and 1851. He was elected to the State Senate in 1848 and 1849, and was chosen President of the Senate for the latter

HON. JOSEPH D. WEEKS.

year. He also represented the town of Canaan in the Constitutional Convention of 1850. Mr. Weeks' principal competitor in the legal profession was the late Judge Jonathan Kittredge, who went from Lyme to Canaan a few years after Mr. Weeks located there, and remained there in practice until his appointment as a Justice of the Court of Common Pleas, when he removed to Concord. Opponents in politics as well as rivals in the profession, the contests between the two were numerous and at times most exciting, enlisting the sympathies of their personal and political friends and adherents. Among those who were students-at-law in the office of Mr. Weeks may be mentioned Ex-Chief Justice Jonathan E. Sargent of Concord, as well as his present partner, William M. Chase, Esq., also, William T. Norris of Danbury, and Caleb and Isaac N. Blodgett, the former now a lawyer of Boston and the latter of Franklin. Judge Sargent commenced practice in Canaan as a partner of Mr. Weeks, remaining some three years, until 1847, when he removed to Wentworth. Isaac N. Blodgett also entered professional life as Mr. Weeks' partner, shortly before his retirement from practice.

Mr. Weeks married, in 1833, Mary Elizabeth Doe, only daughter and eldest child of Joseph Doe, Esq., of Somersworth, now Rollinsford, and a sister of Hon. Charles Doe, present Chief Justice of the Supreme Court of New Hampshire. Joseph Doe was a well-known merchant of Salmon Falls, but a native and former resident of Newmarket, who married Mary Elizabeth Ricker, daughter of Capt. Ebenezer Ricker of Somersworth, from whose family also came the wife of John P. Hale. By this union he had five children, three sons and two daughters, The eldest being Joseph Doe Weeks, the subject of this sketch, the second William B. Weeks, Esq., a lawyer of Lebanon, and the third Marshall H. Weeks, now residing at Fairbury, Neb., where he is extensively engaged in agriculture and the lumber trade. The daughters, Mary Elizabeth and Susan H. Weeks, the youngest of the children, accomplished young ladies, still remain at home in Canaan, though usually spending the winter abroad, either at the South or West.

JOSEPH DOE WEEKS was born October 23, 1837, being now in the forty-first year of his age. In early life he attended the district school and Canaan Academy. Subsequently he spent some time at the Academies at Meriden and South Berwick, Me., but returned home and completed his preparation for college at Canaan Academy, the principal at that time being Burrill Porter, Jr., of Langdon, an accomplished teacher, whose life has since been devoted to that occupation, and who is now principal of the High School at North Attleboro, Mass. Mr. Porter, by the way, graduated at Dartmouth in the class of 1856, Gov. B. F. Prescott, and Caleb Blodgett, beforementioned, being members of the same class. Mr. Blodgett, who was a Canaan boy, was a brilliant scholar and the leader of his class. In this connection it may properly be remarked that Canaan Academy, which was incorporated in 1839, was, for many years a popular institution of learning, with a large attendance of students from that and neighboring towns, and from abroad. Ex-Chief Justice Sargent was one of the early principals of this institution. Subsequently Hon. Levi W. Barton of Newport, then pursuing the study of law in the office of Judge Kittredge, became its principal. Mr. Barton was recently heard to remark, in speaking of this school, that while he was principal there were seven promising young men in attendance who afterward became members of the legal profession. These were Caleb and I. N. Blodgett, and William M. Chase, before mentioned, Joseph D. Weeks, the subject of this sketch, and his brother, William B., Delavan Kittredge, a son of Judge Kittredge, now a lawyer in New York city, and W. A. Flanders, now of Wentworth. In these days there were from 150 to 200 students in attendance at the Academy. Latterly the school has declined in numbers and prestige, and there are now but two terms a year—spring and autumn—with an average at-

HON. JOSEPH D. WEEKS.

tendance of about fifty scholars. Herbert F. Norris of Epping, Democratic candidate for Speaker of the House of Representatives at the late session of the Legislature, was principal of this Academy in 1873 and 1874.

Mr. Weeks entered Dartmouth College in 1857, graduating in 1861, his brother being a member of the same class, which also numbered among its members William J. Tucker, now an eminent Orthodox clergyman of New York city, formerly of Manchester, who was recently elected one of the Trustees of the College, George A. Marden and Edward T. Rowell, now joint editors and proprietors of the Lowell *Courier*, Henry M. Putney of the Manchester *Mirror*, and George A. Bruce, now Mayor of Somerville, Mass. Mr. Weeks was a diligent and faithful student, taking good rank in his class. Like a large share of the young men who have been students at Dartmouth, he passed his winters while n college in the occupation of teaching.

The first winter, that of 1857–8, he taught the school in his own district, at Canaan "Street," the next at East Lebanon, the third at Wellfleet, Mass., and the fourth in the " Littleworth" District, so called, in the city of Dover.

Immediately after graduating from college, in the summer of 1861, he commenced the study of law in the office of Samuel M. Wheeler and Joshua G. Hall, then partners in practice, in Dover, where he remained about two years. He then passed a year in attendance at the Harvard Law School in Cambridge, and completed his study preparatory to admission to the bar, in his father's office with Mr. Blodgett. He was admitted to Grafton County bar, at Haverhill, at the September Term in 1864. He soon after went west and located for a year at Janesville, Wis., but not fancying the western country as a place of residence, he returned home in the spring of 1866 and opened an office at East Canaan, where he engaged in the practice of his profession, having also an office at the "Street," where he remained a portion of the time, and making his home with his parents. His office and library at East Canaan were burned in the disastrous conflagration in that place, in 1872, since which time he has kept an office only at the "Street."

Mr. Weeks is an active and earnest Democrat, and has for several years been accorded the leadership of his party in the town. He was elected a member of the Legislature from Canaan in 1869 and again in 1870, serving the first year as a member of the Committee on Agricultural College, and the next on the Railroad Committee. The first year Mr. Weeks' Committee was an important one, as it was at that time that the friends of Dartmouth College made their strenuous and (as it resulted) successful effort to secure the location of the Agricultural College at Hanover, and several Dartmouth graduates, including Mr. Weeks, were made members of the Committee, unquestionably with a view to the promotion of that object, and for which they labored with due zeal. The Railroad Committee, of which he was a member during his second year's service, was busied with the consideration of important questions arising from the exciting controversy between the Concord and Northern Railroads. During his service in the House he established a reputation as an intelligent and industrious legislator, making no pretentions to display, but devoting himself faithfully to the promotion of the interests of his constituents and the State at large, as regarded from the stand-point of his own judgment.

In 1875 Mr. Weeks received the Democratic nomination for Senator in his District, then one of the so-called "close" districts of the State, and was elected. He served as a member of the Judiciary and Railroad Committees in that body, being chairman of the former. In 1876 he was again a candidate, but was defeated by James W. Johnson of Enfield, the Republican nominee, a man of great resources and tireless energy, who succeeded in carrying the district by a small majority. This year the Republicans again secured full control of the Legislature, and made such changes in the Senatorial Districts as to render a contest well nigh hopeless on the part of any Democratic candidate in Number Eleven, where Messrs. Johnson and Weeks were again the candidates of their respective parties the following year, and the former was re-elected, as a matter of course. In the last canvass, however, Mr. Johnson not being a candidate, the Democracy again insisted upon the renomination of Mr. Weeks, who after a vigorous campaign was elected over C. O. Barney, Esq., of the same town, the Republican nominee. At the opening of the late session of the Legislature he received the compliment of the Democratic nomination for President of the Senate, and served, during the session, upon the committees on the Judiciary and Education. In the Senate, as in the House, Mr. Weeks rendered efficient service as a practical legislator, and his judgment was seldom questioned on matters involving general public interests.

Mr. Weeks is unmarried, and his mother, sisters and himself have their home together. The large farm and extensive outlands of which his father died possessed, are still held, but in 1874 the family residence was changed to the Downing place, so called, a fine location on the "Street," which Mr. Weeks had purchased the previous year, and re-fitted and repaired in a thorough manner, building a first class stable, where he keeps about a half a dozen of the finest horses to be found in Grafton county. The love for good horses is, in fact, almost a passion with Mr. Weeks, and whoever of his friends and acquaintances is permitted to enjoy the hospitalities of his home is sure to be favored with a delightful drive behind some of his favorites, through that romantic region.

Canaan "Street," as the old village of Canaan has always been called, is one of the most charming localities, in summer, to be found in New Hampshire. The village is built upon the two sides of a single, broad street, extending a mile, north and south, in a straight line. The street is lined on either side with shade trees, the dwellings are neat and attractive, and the location, upon an elevated tableland, commands a fine view of the surrounding country, restricted only by the mountain ranges in the distance. Before the advent of the railway this was an important business point, being one of the old stage centres, but the passage of the railroad through the lower part of the town, and the building up of a village at the "Depot," or East Canaan, has carried the current of business in that direction. This renders the Street a quiet and pleasant resort for summer visitors, and of late, many people from the cities have been attracted thither, and taken up their abode during the summer months. The spacious mansion upon the Weeks farm, among other fine old residences in the place, is now occupied as a summer boarding house.

The care of the large estate left by his father in various investments, the oversight of his extensive farming operations, the attention to such legal business as naturally comes to his hands, and other business cares, including the management of a lumber mill, above Factory Village, so-called, which recently came into his possession, and which is adjacent to a large tract of heavy pine and spruce timber, of which he is the principal owner, together with the interest which he takes in general public affairs, educational, political and otherwise, keeps Mr. Weeks fully and actively employed, so that, although inheriting ample means, he has neither the opportunity nor disposition to follow a life of ease and leisure, which many in his situation would seek.

Mr. Weeks is an active member of the Mascoma Valley Agricultural Society, has been Superintending School Committee of the town, and in all movements involving the material, educational, and social welfare and progress of the community he always occupies a leading position. He was also one of the delegates from his town in the Constitutional Convention of 1876. He is a member of no religious denomination, but attends upon the services and contributes liberally to the support of the Methodist church in his village.

FINITIO.

Fast the minutes pass away,
Fades the day, and night is falling
O'er the earth. Beyond recalling,
Days like life will have their birth,
Life like days will pass away.
Slowly sinking from my sight
Pass dear faces, well-known places;
Death, you meet me, but I greet thee—
See! where yonder dawns the light,
The morn has come to life's dark night.
—*Will E. Walker.*

LOVE WINS LOVE.

BY HELEN M. RUSSELL.

"Good-bye, Josephine. You will not forget our pleasant companionship of the past few weeks, will you, little friend?" The summer sun was just going out of sight behind the tall hills which rose far above the little red farm-house covered with climbing roses and clematis, and its last rays lighted the tops of the tall trees in the distance, while the entire valley rested in the shade of the approaching evening. Afar off the call of the cow boy sounded, ringing out upon the stillness with a monotony that grated harshly upon the ear of the stylish young man who leaned so lazily against the fence that enclosed Farmer Granger's neat little home. His black eyes were fixed searchingly upon the sweet face of a young girl who stood just inside the gateway, one slender hand resting upon the gate, which stood open. At his words there had been an eager, upward glance of the brown eyes, which dropped beneath the piercing look of her companion. Slowly the color faded out of the perfect face, and a slight shiver passed over her slender form, but only for a moment—then she raised her head proudly and half defiantly as she replied;

"Indeed, Mr. Courtney, I cannot promise. Of course I shall not entirely forget, but time, you know, changes everything so completely that we cannot be sure of anything. In one month you will have forgotten that there is such a place as Glenville or Glen Cottage and its inmates. Is it not so?"

"Forget you, Josie? Never!" was the answer, a ring of falseness in the low tone as he replied.

"I prefer to be called Josephine, Mr. Courtney, and I do not wish you to make any rash promises." a laugh coming from the sweet lips as easily as if the little heart beating so rapidly was not filled with the keenest pain.

"How can you be so cruel to me, Josephine? Have I indeed been mistaken in thinking that you have enjoyed our companionship, even as I have? Oh, Josephine, you do not realize how your sweet face will haunt me as I go out from your presence into the world again."

There was a little truth in these words, and for the moment he really regretted the pastime which had been such cruel sport, and which had resulted in his winning the love of this sweet country lass, Josephine Granger. He knew she loved him, despite the coldness and light-heartedness she had assumed.

"Walk with me as far as the elm, will you not?" said he, turning slowly away at length.

"Certainly, Mr. Courtney, if you wish; although I might as well bid you goodbye here, I suppose," said Josephine, as she passed out through the gateway, bringing it shut behind her.

The road wound along beside a small river on the one side, while on the other rose the tall hills previously mentioned. There was a sad murmur in the music of the river this evening which Josephine had never noticed before. The twitter of the birds annoyed her; and the lowing of the cows, homeward bound, sounded, for the first time in her life, disagreeable. The sun had gone out of sight, leaving shadows in its place, just as the sunshine of her life was departing. She had been so happy here in her country home, content to perform her tasks without a wish for what lay beyond her humble sphere. Six weeks ago, Lee Courtney had presented himself at Glen Cottage and desired board for two weeks. The two had multiplied themselves into six, however, and now a summons from his father, in the form of a telegram, had caused him to pack up his effects without loss of time and take his departure. His stay at the little red farm-house, or "Glen Cottage," as he himself had christened it, had been most pleasant, and as he walked slowly along he thought of the girl who had met him so frankly upon his arrival at her home, filled his room with flowers, prepared his favorite dishes and picked the ripest berries for him, and involuntarily his eyes rested upon her now walking by his side. She seemed a different being. The former was a happy girl, without a trace of care in the lovely brown eyes; the latter seemed a woman. The erect, even haughty, figure walked steadily by his side, but there was a look of sorrow in the eyes which could not be concealed. The hand which carried a bunch of sweet clover trembled slightly as he took it gently in his own. They reached the "elm tree" at length, and, pausing, Josephine said with a smile:

"Well, Mr. Courtney, I wish you a pleasant journey home, and a pleasant one through life."

Her coolness vexed him, and he made a sudden resolve to compel her to own that she loved him. Where would be the harm, he reasoned. If harm there was, it had already been done, so turning quickly toward her, he clasped both her little toil-stained hands in his own, saying softly:

"Josephine, my darling, how can my life journey be pleasant unless you share it with me? My love, tell me that I may return to you, may win you and take you away from this country life to a home you are so much better adapted to adorn. My sweet girl, tell me that you love me."

Withdrawing her hands from his grasp, ne covered her blushing face with them, while the bunch of sweet clover feel unceded to the ground, but she made no reply.

"Tell me, Josephine, do you care for me?" said he, drawing her closely to his side and gently forcing the hands from her face. At length she raised her head mildly, the color coming and going in waves of crimson and white, as she murmured softly:

"Yes, Lee, I do love you with all my heart; but I—I—thought you were only amusing yourself at my expense."

There beneath the old elm they stood talking until the coming shadows of night warned Josephine that she must return home. The parting was bitter to the girl, and her evident sorrow touched even Lee Courtney's callous heart and caused him to exclaim to himself, when at length he found himself alone upon the road leading to the village of Glenville:

"I am a precious rascal, and no mistake! What possessed me to make the girl love me? Well, time will cure her of her folly, and I will stop this business. By George, I pitied her, but it cannot be helped now; so good-bye, my pretty wild flower, and now for home and Nora Weston's bright eyes and golden charms. I wish Josephine had Nora's wealth. I do believe I should like the former best if it were at all prudent to do so. I will write her a dozen letters or so and gradually let the affair die away. Confound it! I do believe I have got a conscience after all!"

Back again to the quiet home so lonely now, so desolate. One by one the stars came forth, and anon the moon shone down upon the quiet spot, lighting it with a tender radiance, and falling upon the sad face of the girl who leaned from her chamber window, her eyes misty with unshed tears, wandering toward the village whose tall church spires she could just distinguish in the distance—thinking of him who had made so great a change in her quiet life. She could never be the same again, free from care, content to perform her homely tasks, caring for naught but her home, her parents and the few humble friends of her girlhood. She must study—must fit herself for the home to which he had promised to take her. She would go away where she could learn all the graces he so much admired. Her parents would miss her, but they would learn to do without her, and when she had obtained the knowledge she so much desired, and she was Lee Courtney's wife, they should spend the declining years of life with her. At length she gave one last, lingering look to the village where he was stopping for the night, and then she sought her couch, but not to sleep. She heard the whistle of the departing train which bore him away in the early dawn, and she could but wonder at the dreary heart-ache, the utter desolation that came to her at the sound.

A lovely day—the sun shone, the birds warbled, the air was filled with the sweetest odors. Josephine Granger was seated in the shade of a tall maple which stood near her home. She held an open letter in her hand, and a sweet, glad light shone from her lovely eyes. Lee really loved her—he had not forgotten her as she had feared when day after day passed and there had come no word from him. The two weeks that had elapsed since he had left her seemed like so many months to the young girl, but now she held his first letter, brief and *not* just what she had fondly hoped it would be, but nevertheless a *letter*, and now the world had once more put on a look of beauty. There was not the faintest thought in her heart but that he loved her. She must tell her parents *now*, and they would let her go away where she would receive an education which would fit her to be Lee Courtney's wife. A step near by arrested her attention, and glancing quickly upward she saw a young man approaching her, tall and sun-burned, but nevertheless handsome and manly. A shade of annoyance passed over her face at being thus disturbed in her day-dreams, but it gave way to a look of pleasure as she made room for him at her side, at the same time saying:

"Well, Frank, you are back again. I am glad to see you. How do you like your new home?"

"Oh, little girl, it is just a jolly place. I really think there's not a handsomer farm this side the Connecticut than mine. Mother's a little lonesome, the folks being all strangers to her, you know," he replied, a little awed by the change he felt rather than saw in the girl by his side.

"Of course that was to have been expected, Frank. There are not many old ladies who would have so willingly given up the home which had been theirs for so many years, as did your mother! She is well, is she not?"

"Yes, oh, yes, she is well—but, I say, little girl, what's come over you? You don't seem at all like the Josephine I left at Glenville depot the day we went away. Are you sick?"

A flush dyed her face, but she laughingly replied:

"No, Frank, I am not sick—on the contrary, I am perfectly well and happy," a tender light coming into her eyes as she raised them to her companion's face. Why not tell him of the love which had come into her life? He had been her friend always, her companion to and from school, the one true and constant friend that takes the place of a brother. He had been the one to show her where the nicest berries grew, to gather pond-lilies for her—in short, she had loved him as if he had been her brother, and when he had sold the old rocky farm on the hill-side and bought a larger one upon the banks of the Connecticut, distant some twenty miles from her home, she had shed bitter tears. He had been absent but three months and it *was* pleasant to have him back again, and—yes, she would tell him; but first she would acquaint him with her intention of leaving home, so. looking up into his kindly face, she said suddenly:

"I am going away, Frank. I intend to go to some large school for young ladies, and I wish to be something more than an uneducated farmer's daughter." Then, not noting the pained look that came into his face, she said softly, hiding her blushing face from his eager gaze: "I—I wish to tell you something, brother Frank, but I don't know how to tell it."

There was no reply for a moment, then, looking up, Josephine saw that the browned face had grown quite pale.

"You don't need to tell me, little girl,"—his pet name for her always. "I heard something at the village, but I would not, could not believe it. I see now that it is true. Oh, Josephine, did you not guess that I loved you, that I was coming back for you? That city chap could not care for you a tenth part what I do and always have."

"I am so sorry, Frank. I never thought you cared for me in this way," murmured Josephine, bursting into tears of real sorrow.

"No, little girl; I see how foolish I was. I might have won your love had I told you of my own before Lee Courtney turned your head with his soft words that meant nothing to him, but which won your heart at once. Oh, Josephine! I can't realize it yet, you know—I can't believe I have lost you. I have loved you all my life, little girl."

There was an earnestness in the words and tone of Frank Clyde's voice that the girl had missed in the smooth, honied words of Lee Courtney, and it struck her more forcibly than ever before as she contrasted the two—the one rough and uncultured, but so good and noble, the other rich, handsome, well educated, but yet lacking something which she could not define, but it gave her the heart-ache nevertheless.

"Oh, Frank, don't talk to me any more about it, for it can never be, you know. You must always be my brother just the same, and we will try and forget you ever cared for me in any other way."

"Forget you, little girl? I shall as soon forget the sun that shines as to forget the love I have given to you. I shall go away, but I shall always love you just the same. Good-bye, little girl." His voice grew husky as he spoke, and rising from his seat by her side, he threw both arms around her, held her one moment to his heart, pressed a long, lingering kiss upon the flushed forehead, and turning quickly he hurried away, not pausing or looking back. It was years ere they met again.

It was a lovely day in autumn when at last Josephine stood in the door-way of her humble home, ready equipped for her departure. Her mother stood near by, wiping the fast falling tears upon the corner of her calico apron, her heart filled with grief at this parting. There had been expostulations and entreaties when her daughter had made known her determination to leave home, but they had been of no avail, so at last the worthy farmer and his wife had set about preparing for their daughter's departure with sorrow-filled hearts. The day long dreaded had arrived, and now the hour of parting had come. Her father carried her to the village, where she was to take the afternoon train for her destination, a large flourishing town in New York. Old ties were broken now, and a new life, new associations, were to be formed. Her heart beat high with hope, notwithstanding the real grief she felt at leaving home. I would gladly follow her through the weeks that came, but space will not permit. I will simply say that her school life proved all that she had anticipated. She learned easily and rapidly. Letters came from home every week, and from Lee Courtney *occasionally*. She stifled any fear she may have felt at his coolness, and time passed quickly away.

It was in the early spring-time when she knew at last that the one hope of her life had crumbled, as it were, into ashes. Several weeks had elapsed since she had received a letter from Lee, and her companions had noticed that the sweet face had grown paler and her happy laughter no longer rang out in unison with their own. One evening the mail-bag had been carried into the long dining-hall to be opened and the contents to be distributed among the many pupils assembled there. There was no sign from Josephine, when at length it was emptied and carried away, that she had expected a letter, yet she had felt *so* sure that she should hear from him that night. Her head ached and throbbed terribly, so, arising, she asked to be excused and left the room and sought her own, where she knelt down by the window—an old habit which clung to her in her new life—and gazed wearily out upon the grounds surrounding the seminary. A long time she knelt there, but at length her room mate, Ellen Weston, entered the room with a song upon her lips. She carried a paper in her hand.

"I declare, Josephine, what *has* come

over you? You are sober as an owl," she said.

"You have received good news. I conclude, Ellen," said her friend, wearily arising from the window.

"Yes, and you have none. That accounts for your long face. You recollect hearing me speak of my cousin Nora, do you not?"

"Yes, and you promised to show me her picture," replied Josephine, with an attempt at animation.

"Yes, I will do so, and also that of her husband. They were married last Wednesday, and this paper contains an account of the wedding. After you have looked at their pictured faces I will read you what this paper states in regard to them," returned Ellen.

A moment later she had procured two photographs, and after a hasty glance at them, threw them on the table beside which her friend was seated. Josephine took up the pictures, and her gaze fell upon the face of Lee Courtney.

"How came *you* by Lee Courtney's picture?" she asked, turning her white face toward her friend.

"Why, he is cousin Nora's husband, Josephine; but where did you ever see him, in the name of wonder?" replied Ellen in surprise.

She did not faint; even the bliss of unconsciousness was denied her. Afterward she remembered that she had given some common-place answer, and then, making some remark about her aching head, had sought her bed, and through the long hours of the night had fought with the pain at her crushed heart. She saw it all now—saw how blind she had been from the first. Two weeks later there came a letter to the anxious parents at the farm-house, saying:

"Father — mother — you will have learned ere you receive this how basely I have been deceived. I cannot talk of it yet—the pain is too severe; neither can I remain here at school or return to you. So by the time you receive this I shall be far away. A lady—a friend of my room mate—wishes a companion on a journey to Europe, and has kindly consented to allow me to fill that place. If I live I shall return to you in time. Good-bye, dear kind parents.

Your unhappy daughter,
JOSEPHINE."

Through all the years that followed there came no sign that she yet lived, until ten long years had passed—then to the care-worn parents there came at last a letter, telling them that she was yet alive and would be with them almost as soon as her letter reached them. Josephine Granger left home a young girl full of hope. She returned a woman, beautiful and wealthy, and no more to be compared with what she had once been than is the choicest garden flower to the simple field daisy. The lady in whose company she had travelled had learned to love the sad, pale-faced girl, and when at last death overtook her, Josephine learned to her surprise that her kind friend had bequeathed a large portion of her vast wealth to herself.

Home again, at last! There was infinite rest in the knowledge, and she would remain there until she could decide what to do in the future.

"Mother," said she, the day after her arrival home, "I have never heard one word concerning Frank Clyde since I left home. Is he yet living?"

"Yes, my child; and if you will go to church with us to-morrow you will see him," said her mother.

On the morrow she once more entered the little white church at Glenville, but the faces raised to her own were nearly all strange to her. Involuntarily her eyes sought the pew where, years ago, she had been wont to see the kindly face of her friend, Frank Clyde. Mrs. Clyde sat there alone.

"Frank is late, doubtless," she thought, settling herself back into her seat, and raising her eyes to the old-fashioned pulpit. The minister arose, and in a clear, impassioned voice began the services of the day. Surely somewhere she had heard that voice. Could it be her old friend, Frank Clyde? An hour later she stood before him and felt the warm clasp of his hand and heard him welcome her home in the same old voice, cultivated now, to be sure, but still the same. Her true friend always, she realized at that moment what she had thrown away—the pure gold for the glistening tinsel. Afterward she learned how his disappointed hopes had caused him to sell the farm he had bought thinking *she* would share his home with him, and go away; and how his mother came to live with the lonely parents she had deserted, during his absence from his native place. Two years before Josephine's return he had addressed the people of Glenville from the little pulpit in the little old church.

One year after her return the wedding bells rang out a joyful peal as arm in arm Frank Clyde and Josephine Granger walked into that same little church to be made one for the remainder of their lives; and when later on that same day she entered her own home, there stole into her heart once more perfect rest and peace.

POLITICS IN HOPKINTON.

BY C. C. LORD.

Internal politics have but a little chance for agitation when a new country is harassed by external foes. The first inhabitants of this town, besides being loyal subjects to the colonial authority of the Crown of England, were too actively engaged in the pursuit of a material existence to indulge to any great extent in local political discussion.

The Bow controversy, as it is sometimes called, was early a cause of litigation to the inhabitants of this town. In 1727, Jonathan Wiggin and others obtained a grant of the township of Bow from the authorities of New Hampshire. This act ultimately led to contention with other parties holding grants of townships from the authorities of Massachusetts. Concord, Pembroke and Hopkinton were all involved in this controversy. Bow was at length obliged to yield over two-thirds of its territory * to these three towns, the final boundary lines being settled at different times from 1759 to 1765. In this controversy the town of Hopkinton was represented by Dea. Henry Mellen, Adj. Thomas Mellen, and Timothy Clement.

During the pending of the Bow claim, the town of Hopkinton became involved in the Mason controversy. John Tufton Mason, presumed heir of John Mason, in consequence of an alleged defect in the sale of lands to Samuel Allen, in 1691, conveyed his interests in New Hampshire to twelve leading men of Portsmouth, for fifteen hundred pounds. This was in 1746. The new proprietors, however, were liberal, granting new townships for the simple conditions of a guaranty for improvements by the occupants and the reservation of fifteen rights for themselves. Under the date of November 30, 1750, we find a record of conditions obtaining in the case of the grant of this town. Henry Mellen, yeoman; Thomas Walker, cooper; Thomas Mellen, cordwainer, and their associates, were grantees. One-fifth of the land was to be set apart on the west, to be exempt from all taxes till improved. One share was to be set apart for a minister, one share for a school, and a reservation for a mill privilege. There were to be thirty families in three years and sixty in seven years. There was to be a meeting-house in three years, and a minister in seven years. The suitable white pine was to be reserved for His Majesty. In case of an Indian war the times expressed in this agreement were to be extended. In case Bow took any territory the equivalent was to be made up from ungranted lands. The absence of local records during nu-

*Bow claimed a notch of a few square miles in the south-east corner of Hopkinton.

merous years about the time of this transaction prevents a confident statement in regard to all the conditions that may have been implied in the Mason grant of this township. The absence of any reference to the "fifteen rights" of the Mason proprietors, leads to the conjecture it may be that those rights were bought by the grantees.

The distribution of the rights of the proprietors of the township under the new grant was as follows: Thomas Mellen, 4;* Dea. Henry Mellen, 3; John Jones, Esq., John Chadwick, Jonathan Straw, Sampson Colby, Peter How, Jr., and Enoch Eastman, 2 each; Daniel and John Annis, 2; Joseph Haven, Esq., Rev. Samuel Haven, John Haven, Thomas Bixbee, Peter How, Joseph Haven, Timothy Townsend, Elder Joseph Haven, Simpson Jones, Esq., Isaac Pratt, Jedediah Haven, Mark Whitney, Nathaniel Gibbs, Isaac Gibbs, John Jones, Jr., Benjamin Goddard, Eleazer Howard, Daniel Mellen, James Lock, David Woodwell, Nathaniel Chandler (heirs of), James Chadwick (heirs of), Samuel Osgood, Aaron Kimball, Thomas Eastman, Timothy Clement, John Rust (heirs of), William Peters, Ebenezer Eastman, Jacob Straw, Samuel Putney, Joseph Putney, Thomas Merrill, Joseph Eastman, Jacob Potter, Matthew Stanley, Abraham Colby, Isaac Chandler, Jr., Abner Kimball (heirs of), John Burbank, Caleb Burbank, Samuel Eastman, Stephen Hoyt, Isaac Whitney, Thomas Walker, Isaac Chandler, and Joseph Eastman, Jr., 1 each; John and James Nutt, 1; Enoch and Ezra Hoyt, 1.

Soon after the first occupation of the territory by the proprietors, this township began to be called New Hopkinton, though known at first as No. 5. The present name of Hopkinton became the legal appellation under the act of incorporation. Our readers will be interested in our notice of

THE INCORPORATING CHARTER.

Anno Regni Regis Georgii Tertii, Magnæ Brittanicæ, Franciæ, et Hiberniæ, etc., Quinto.

[S. S.] An Act to incorporate a Place

*This is a doubtful figure in the original record.

called New Hopkinton, not within a Place heretofore incorporated, together with that Part of the Township of Bow which covers a Part of the said New Hopkinton, into a Town, invested with the Powers and Privileges of a Town. WHEREAS the Inhabitants of New Hopkinton (so called) together with the Inhabitants of that part of the Township of Bow which covers a part of said New Hopkinton have petitioned the General Assembly, representing the Difficulties which they are under for want of the Powers and Privileges of a Town, and therefore prayed that they might be joined, united and incorporated together into a Town and be invested with the Powers and Privileges which other Towns in the Province enjoy,

THEREFORE

BE IT ENACTED by the Gouvernour, Council and Assembly, That that part of the Township of Bow which covers a Part of New Hopkinton be, and hereby is, separated from the rest of the said Township of Bow, and is joined to and united with the said New Hopkinton, to all Intents and Purposes: and that all the Land contained within the Bounds and Limits hereafter mentioned, and all the Persons who do or shall inhabit the same, their Polls and Estates, be and hereby are incorporated together into a Town, including all that part of the township of Bow which covers a part of New Hopkinton, with the Polls and Estates; and are hereby invested and enfranchised with all the Powers and Privileges of any other Town in the Province; and shall be called Hopkinton.

A description of the boundaries of Hopkinton, together with certain general laws and regulations, conclude the act of incorporation, done in the House of Representatives for the Province of New Hampshire, on 10th of January, 1765, and signed by H. Sherburne, Speaker; recorded in the Council the next day as passed, and signed by T. Atkinson, Secretary; consented to by B. Wentworth, Governor; and copies attested by the Secretary of the Council, and Enoch Eastman, Town Clerk.

The act of incorporation provided that

annual town meetings should be held on the first Monday of March. Acting under this provision the first board of selectmen were chosen the same year. They were Capt. Matthew Stanly, Jonathan Straw and Serg. Isaac Chandler. The incorporation of the town gave a new impulse to internal affairs, and improvements progressed rapidly.

The struggle for colonial independence occasioned the entertainment of provisions for the maintenance of independent civil government. The people of this town recognized this necessity of civil government as well as others. At a town meeting held on July 18, 1774, Capt. Jonathan Straw was chosen delegate to the convention held at Exeter on the 21st of the same month to succeed the previous assembly dispersed by Governor John Wentworth. This convention chose Nathaniel Folsom and John Sullivan delegates to the Provincial Congress at Philadelphia. On the 9th of January, 1775, Joshua Bayley was chosen delegate from Hopkinton to a second convention at Exeter, to appoint delegates to a second Congress to be held on the 10th of May. John Sullivan and John Langdon were appointed to the approaching Congress. On the day that Joshua Bayley was chosen delegate to Exeter the town of Hopkinton voted " to accept what the grand Congress has resolved." On the 11th of December, 1775, Capt. Stephen Harriman was chosen representative to Exeter for one year.

The success of the struggle for independence secured to the inhabitants of this town and all others the possession of their lands in fee simple, and the consciousness of an existence of free governmental privileges. However, it opened the door to an earnestness and intensity of political controversy that many had not expected to experience. The task of establishing a permanent civil government awakened a discussion between the doctrines of the concentration and distribution of governmental agencies which have plagued legislators throughout a long historic past, and probably will continue to plague them for a long time to come. On the 13th of January, 1778, the town voted to accept of the articles of confederation, but on the 22d of the July following the people, as states the town clerk, " Tryed a Vote for Receiving the Plan of Government—none for, But 106 against it." On the 30th day of May, 1781, Joshua Bayley was chosen a committee to attend an assembly* at Concord for the purpose of forming a plan of State government; yet on the 21st of January, and again on the 11th of November, of the following year, the town voted not to accept the plan of government as it then stood. On the 4th of March of this year, Capt. (Jonathan) Straw, Benjamin Wiggin and Isaac Bayley were chosen a committee to petition the General Court for a repeal of the oath of fidelity. On the 23d of December it was voted to accept the plan of government " with the amendment made by the committee, there being 100 votes." The substance of this matter related to the powers and privileges of the Governor of the State; a compromise was effected by the recommendation of the convention that the Governor be elected by the people, which plan was adopted.

Under the new condition of affairs, Meshech Weare, of Hampton Falls, was elected President† of the State of New Hampshire. The vote of the town of Hopkinton that year stood fifty-six for Josiah Bartlett, of Kingston, and two for Timothy Walker, of Concord, and none for Weare. On the following year John Langdon of Portsmouth received eighty-nine votes and Timothy Walker one.

The unanimous character of the votes cast in Hopkinton for chief executive of the State for many years subsequently to the independence of the American colonies attests the little progress that had been made in national politics. When at length the people became conscious of the great struggle between Federalism and Republicanism, the sympathies of this town gravitated steadily toward the

---
*This assembly, or convention, held nine sessions and was in existence two years.

---
†The chief executive of the State was not called governor vntil 1792, when a new constitution came in force.

Republican side. The growing state of the population, and the consequent increasing multiple character of the inhabitants, soon prevented that degree of political unanimity at first prevailing. In 1812 the contest between Federalism and Republicanism was at its height. The progress of the existing war was bitterly opposed by the Federalists; the Republicans were as intensely ardent in its support. In 1812 William Plummer, of Epping, a Republican, was elected governor of New Hampshire. He had been a prominent Federalist but had seen fit to change his political position to the Republican side. His opponent was John Taylor Gilman, a life-long Federalist and popular citizen and official. Yet Hopkinton, zealous of the principles and measures of the Republican party, gave 192 votes to Plummer against 108 for Gilman. In 1813, the town cast a much larger vote than on the previous year. The popular excitement occasioned by the war impelled the increased attendance at the polls. The candidates for the office for governor of the State were the same as the previous. The great personal popularity of the man gave Gilman the election. Yet Hopkinton attested her devotion to Republicanism by giving Plummer 220 votes against 152 for the successful candidate.

Among the changeable things in this world are the names of political parties. In the progress of popular events, the body of voters representing the essential principles of government held by the Federalists, came to be known as Whigs, and later as Republicans; the upholders of the original Republican doctrines came to be known as Democrats. The later Republican party in this town has absorbed the most of the representatives of the once Free-soil party (which at one time attained to a respectable representation here), as well as also the voters of the American or "Know-nothing" party. The former Republicans and later Democrats held the advance on party votes in this town till 1865. In 1846, when Anthony Colby, of New London, a Whig, was chosen governor of New Hampshire, the vote of Hopkinton stood 245 for Jared W. Williams of Lancaster; 134 for Nathaniel S. Berry of Hebron; 78 for Anthony Colby of New London, and two scattering. Williams was a Democrat and Berry a Free-soiler. In 1855 there was a close contest in this town between the Democrats, Americans, and the remnants of the Whig and Free-soil parties. The Democrats maintained a plurality on the governor's ticket. The vote stood 248 for Nathaniel B. Baker of Concord; 219 for Ralph Metcalf of Newport; 29 for James Bell of Meredith, and seven for Asa Fowler of Concord. Baker was a Democrat, Metcalf an American, Bell a Whig and Fowler a Free-soiler.

The Democrats lost this town on the State ticket for the first time in 1865; the vote stood 240 for Walter Harriman of Warner, Republican, against 229 for John G. Sinclair of Bethlehem, Democrat. The Democrats rallied again in 1872, gaining a plurality. James A. Weston of Manchester, Democrat, had 243 votes; Ezekiel A. Straw of Manchester, Republican, 241; there were two votes for Lemuel P. Cooper of Croydon, Labor Reform candidate. In 1875, the town went back to the Republicans, giving Person C. Cheney of Manchester, 256 votes, against 241 for Hiram R. Roberts of Rollinsford, Democrat. The next year the Democrats carried the State ticket, giving Daniel Marcy of Portsmouth, 256 votes, against 252 for Person C. Cheney, and two scattering. In 1877 the Republicans took the ascendency, giving Benjamin F. Prescott of Epping, 261 votes, against 215 for Daniel Marcy. The Republicans still maintain the balance of power.

POEM.

BY REV. SILVANNUS HAYWARD.

[Delivered at the Quarter-Century Meeting of the Class of '53, Dartmouth College, June 26, 1878.]

Stay, Clotho, stay thy fervid wheel,
    Let Lachesis cease twining;—
The quarter skein upon her reel
    Our threads of life combining.

Threads tinged by Life's "dissolving views"
    In shades of countless number;—
Some decked with Joy's celestial dews,
    Some smirched with sorrow's umber.

We come from out the dusty maze
    Where weapoued warriors glisten,
Into each other's eyes to gaze,
    Each other's accents listen.

Nor absent those whom duties hold
    To-day from our collection,
Nor those whose dust 'neath grassy mold
    Awaits the resurrection.

We feel the presence of our dead;
    There are no vacant places;
Though Atropos has cut their thread
    We see their vanished faces.

For bonds which classmates here assume
    Nor Time nor Death can sever;
The shuttle flies in Friendship's loom
    Forever and forever.

On Time's tempestuous, trackless sea
    A momentary meeting,
Then gliding to the far To Be,
    "Hail and Farewell," our greeting.

Heavenly Pilot, do Thou guide
    To that fair port of entry
Beyond this billowy, treacherous tide,
    Guarded by angel sentry.

Who next of our departing band,
    The crown immortal winning,
Shall pass within that vailed land?—
    Clotho, resume thy spinning.

CONGRESSIONAL PAPERS. NO. II—THE SENATE.

BY G. H. JENNESS.

The Senate differs from the House in numbers, in membership, and in the character and methods of its legislation. Comparatively small when measured with the House, it is free from the turbulence and disorder so frequent at the other end of the Capitol. In the House the Speaker pounds the desk with his mallet until he seems exhausted with his efforts to preserve even the semblance of order. In the Senate a slight tap of the Vice President's gavel is sufficient to repress any undue excitement among the honorable Senators. As a whole, good order and parliamentary courtesy reign supreme in the Senate chamber. Sometimes in an animated partisan debate an ill-timed remark may evoke a personal rejoinder and lead to hot and hasty words; but a night's sleep, and a friendly reminder of the "dignity" of an American Senator, sets everything right again, after the usual "personal explanations."

In all of its visible surroundings the Senate resembles the House. The presiding officers, the clerks, the Sergeant-At-Arms, the official stenographers, each occupy the same relative positions, and perform nearly similar duties. The Chamber is simply the Hall of the House made smaller. There is the same gorgeous gilding, the heavy cornices, the beautifully-designed, richly-painted glass panels overhead, the mellow light from above, the paintings, the frescoes, the uncomfortable desks, the lounges, the ante-rooms, the galleries, the diplomatic gallery conspicuously empty amid surrounding crowds, the newspaper reporters' perch in the rear above the Vice President's chair, these, and other points of similarity are held in common by the two rooms of our American Parliament. Of the manner of election and duration of the term of service of Senators it is not my purpose to speak, that being a subject upon which all intelligent citizens are presumably well informed. It is to the differences in the character and methods of legislation of the Senate, to which attention is particularly invited, and to which the bulk of this article will be devoted. Briefly, then, the action of the Senate is revisory in matters of business, and practically paramount in matters of law. The House originates all appropriation bills. The Senate revises, suggests and amends. The Senate takes care of international affairs, negotiates foreign treaties, gives or withholds its approval to the men selected by the President to represent our government abroad, and exercises a fatherly and supervisory care over the Revised Statutes. Either House may be obstinate, and can, if it chooses, put the other to much inconvenience and delay; but the constitution and common consent prescribes the course that, under ordinary circumstances, each will pursue. Under our system of government, which has been aptly termed a system of "checks and balances," neither the President, the Senate, or the House can change a law or appropriate a dollar, without the other's consent. With these existing conditions, certain legislative amenities *must* be regarded—else all the machinery of government would stop. No party *dare* take the responsibility of allowing the eleven regular appropriation bills to fail in either or both houses of Congress. The result would be, simply, that at the close of the fiscal year there would be no money that could be legally used to run any branch of the government. As long as our country comprises its present vast extent of territory, its commercial intercourse, and its multiplied and varied industries, it must have the services of at least 80,000 to 100,000 persons to perform the work required to administer the government with any reasonable degree of efficiency. It must have, also, under the most favorable circumstances, not less than $150,000,000 annually, for the same purpose. To indicate how this vast sum shall be wisely and economically expended is the principal problem that confronts the legislator, in either branch of Congress, and one to which he must give earnest and careful attention if he would avoid political shipwreck. A nation of money-worshippers may forget a vote given upon matters purely political, one unworthily bestowed, or one against which many objections can be urged; but a false step in the vicinity of the "almighty dollar," may often prove fatal. Hence the sensitiveness of the House in regard to everything involving an expenditure of money. The House *knowing* that a hundred dollars is needed for a certain purpose, appropriates ninety-nine, and sends the bill to the Senate. The Senate adds the needed dollar. The House disagrees. The Senate "insists." They have a "conference." The House "recedes from its disagreement"—as it intended to all the while. Then the House calls the country to witness that it is finally compelled to submit to adding the extra dollar, and denounces the Senate for its extravagance.

This is, in brief, a history of all legislative "conferences" between the two houses, upon money appropriations. It is safe to say that for the last twenty years the Senate has carried, in "conference," three of every four amendments previously "insisted" upon in open Senate. As a whole, the Senate is composed of much abler men than the lower branch of Congress. Generally, they are men who have had many years experience in the House. They must, of necessity, know more concerning the needs of the government. They are elected for an official term of six years. They are less under the necessity of trimming and hedging to secure a re-election. They can afford to wait longer than a member of the House for the "vindication" of their motives which it is said time will

surely bring. They can better afford to consider every public measure upon its merits, rather than its immediate consequences upon their personal ambitions. These, and many other reasons equally potent, make it possible for a Senator to exercise a more careful judgment, and a more intelligent comprehension of measures that must receive his consideration. The ever changing character of the House, its great number of new members, and the time required to become at all familiar with the complicated machinery of legislation, consumes its time, and limits its usefulness as a legislative body. The Senate with one fourth the membership, and three times the term of service, can give to all important matters much more attention than it is possible for them to receive in the House. Hence of the thousands of bills rushed through the latter, generally less than half secure the approval of the Senate. The balance remain in the Senatorial pigeon-holes, wherein slumber many thousands of schemes originally designed to extract "very hard cash" from the coffers of our beloved Uncle Samuel.

In the matter of giving or withholding its approval of measures referred to it, the Senate has to bear more than its just share of the burden, for the House will frequently pass bills that it *knows* the Senate will kill—and which the House really desires it *should* kill. It only wishes to shift the responsibility of the execution to the other end of the Capitol. The lobbyist says "I can get your little bill through the House well enough, but, gentlemen, there's the Senate." This is particularly true of bills involving small money appropriations, and bills of a private nature. The big railroad schemes and steamship subsidies are as vigorously advocated and opposed, and as thoroughly discussed in the House as in the Senate; but of the smaller matters, many a member votes against his better judgment for a bill to please some influential constituent, knowing all the time that it can never pass the Senate. In the House, very important measures are sometimes passed under a suspension of the Rules—a two-thirds vote being required for that purpose. In the Senate this is rarely done. The usual course is to refer every bill to the appropriate committee and await the Committee's action as reported by their chairman. If not reported in the usual manner the bill may be regarded as dead, unless the committee are directed to consider the subject by special vote of the Senate. When once reported favorably, without amendment, and placed upon the "calendar" its passage is a foregone conclusion. It is only a question of time, regulated, generally, by its numerical order upon the calendar. By common consent, whenever *any* bill or resolution, has been favorably reported from committee, the report adopted, and the bill or resolution placed upon the calendar, its final passage is conceded, and the yeas and nays are never called except upon important bills, or upon such measures as it is desired to make a "record." A knowledge of this simple fact will explain to the amazed spectator who for the first time visits the Senate galleries, the apparent indifference of three or four score Senators to what is passing before them. The presiding officer will put through, perhaps, thirty or forty bills of greater or less importance, in as many minutes, calling for the ayes and noes, verbally, in the usual way, declare the bills passed, one after another, and all the while not a Senator responds for or against. This method of passing bills is called "by unanimous consent," which presupposes every vote *in favor* of a bill, and is so recorded unless open objection is made. It does not indicate, as would seem to the casual observer, a sublime indifference of Senators to important legislation, but is only an expeditious method of passing measures that have been carefully considered and agreed upon. The adoption of this method, practically unknown in the House, except during the closing hours of a session, enables the Senate to gain time, both in the consideration and final passage of bills. It also enables the enrolling clerks of the House to "anticipate" some of their work, and to enroll a large number of bills in advance. A given number of bills having passed the House, and having been reported favorably to the Senate and placed upon the calendar without amendment, their final passage in exactly the same form as reported, is only a question of time. Consequently, the House enrolling clerks can enroll the bills, leaving the date of the passage blank, and thus do much work that would otherwise fail for want of time. No bill—even if passed without opposition by both houses of Congress—can become a law, unless it is enrolled upon parchment and presented to and signed by the President of the United States before the hour fixed for final adjournment. The Senate and House might pass a thousand bills in good faith and every one of them fail to become laws if sufficient time was not given to enroll them. Owing to the indecent haste with which all kinds of bills are crowded through Congress during the closing hours of the session, many bills fail for this reason, and the number would be largely increased were it not for the "probabilities" indicated by the Senate Calendar which enables the enrolling clerks to "take time by the forelock."

The Senate has numerous other advantages over the House which enables it to transact business more rapidly, or rather to give more time to the consideration of important matters. It has less members. Much less time is consumed in calling the yeas and nays. The immense amount of work required to prepare the great appropriation bills, is all done by the House. The Senate has only to revise and amend. If the House Committee on Appropriations does its work well,—the Senate has but little to do comparatively.

Ordinarily, the Post-Office, Pension and Indian appropriation bills pass the Senate with few amendments. The Military Academy, Navy, the consular and diplomatic, the River and Harbor, and the fortification bills, will be considerably amended. The Deficiency bills pass substantially as reported, while the "tug of war" comes on the Legislative, the Sundry Civil, and the Army. The Sundry Civil, is known as the "Omnibus" bill, as, like the vehicle from which it derives its name, there is always "room for one more"—appropriation. On the "Omnibus" bill, if anywhere, the watchful lobbyist, is able to get his little amendment tacked on, and trusts to the chances of the hurry and confusion of final adjournment to put it through. Failing in this, all his hopes are blighted.

In the House there is never a session to which the public is not admitted. Even during a "call of the House" when the doors are locked and members can get in only under the escort of the Sergeant-at-Arms, or his deputies, the public are admitted as usual to all the galleries. In the Senate, the "Executive Session" bars out everybody but Senators and a few officials sworn to secrecy. Here, at least, no prying reporter can penetrate, and only by skillful cross-questioning of Senators, or in some instances by downright bribery of susceptible officials, can the proceedings in "executive session" be ascertained. Nevertheless State secrets *do* leak out in spite of all precautions, and generally the statements elicited are so distorted, that it may fairly be questioned whether it might not be advantageous to entirely remove the ban of secrecy in the highest legislative body of a Republic.

The writer is not among that numerous class of people who believes that the Senate of the present decade has been an essentially weak body of men, and that all senatorial capacity, intelligence, and dignity was confined to the times of the famous triumvirate, Clay, Webster and Calhoun. Washington "society" abounds in "seedy" croakers of the ancient *regime* who sigh—between drinks—for the "good old times," and lament the present "degeneracy" of Congress in general, and the Senate in particular. Such men never realize the fact that they are merely the sunken rocks whose only use is to measure the depth of the wave of progress that has rolled over them. The Clays, Websters, Calhouns, Napoleons and Bismarcks, are the kind of men who flourish once in a century. They impress their characteristics upon the statesmanship of a century. In all the common practical details of every-day legislation, many men of less pretensions, unknown to fame, are infinitely their superiors. Fancy Daniel Webster in "conference" on the Legislative bill, wrangling over a coal-heaver's salary, or a doorkeeper's wages! or Henry Clay fixing up a post-route bill providing for a tri-weekly mail from Pumpkinville Post Office to Grasshopper Gulch! And yet all such legislation is just as necessary as Webster's reply to Hayne, or his letter to the Austrian Minister. Indeed, it is absolutely indispensable. As the country grows larger, as it extends its vast network of railroads, canals, and telegraphs; as it increases its capacity for production, and consequently its need for a better market; as its foreign and domestic commerce expands or contracts in accordance with the laws of trade, all these problems of tariff, revenue, internal improvements, transportation and navigation, must of necessity claim the legislator's most careful attention. On their successful solution depends the wealth and material prosperity of the country. To solve them needs clear-headed, intelligent, practical, common-sense men, and of such I believe the American Senate to be mainly composed.

MY FRIENDS AND I: MEMORIES.

BY L. W. DODGE.

> Like warp and woof our destinies
> Are woven fast,
> Linked in sympathy like the keys
> Of an organ vast.
> —Whittier.

A June morning unfolded its glories to the susceptible nature of Will Austin at a bright New England village on the banks of the lordly Connecticut. The lonely beauty and the wild, romantic surroundings of the locality at once won his poetic heart; and having no spot particularly endeared to him by the fond ties which cluster around the place we call home, he resolved to tarry here until fully persuaded in mind what course in life to pursue; or where, and in what manner, to begin his life work.

Being of a joyous disposition, and social withal, my friend had soon made many acquaintances among the first families of the village, and found himself a welcome guest, wherever chance or fancy found him, at the homes of the villagers.

Among his new-found friends, one of the first was the merchant of the place, a jovial, whole-souled sort of a man generally, and who prided himself mostly upon being *the* wealthy man of the town; and in fact it was so; which fact, too, he seemed not too modest to magnify. His home was a picture enjoyment; beautiful in its choice surroundings, showing no lack of taste and judgment in its arrangements, being really what it was often termed, a "paradise of beauty and comfort."

Within the well-ordered store of the merchant Will often found himself in pleasant chat with the good-natured proprietor, upon subjects of mutual interest; and as the days passed away and the busy season of trade was ushered in, his aid was invoked, sometimes at the desk, at others behind the counter at the service of customers, and ere long his services became apparently indispensible; accordingly he was duly installed merchant's assistant, and became, likewise, a member of the merchant's family, consisting heretofore of the storekeeper, his amiable wife and lovely daughter Ellen, an only child, just stepping beyond eighteen, and rich in all the charms of young and innocent womanhood. Shall I tell you of her as I afterwards knew her?

She was indeed a winsome girl, the impersonation of loveliness, and with a heart as light as her footstep. Her life had never known a cloud, and her dark and radiant eyes shone with the light of pure and hopeful girlhood. Her soul, which gleamed from out those blue depths, was an ocean of purity and love. She had grown to these years with all the beautiful and attractive adornments of a good, true woman's heart; not frozen to ice by worldliness, or by contrast with the coldness of so-called fashionable society and its false motives. Her personal charms I cannot well describe, but her face was an attraction, fair and fresh, and joyous as a June morning; her voice was a musical echo; she loved the bright flowers, those wild children of Eden, growing in sunny nooks; she loved the mountains and the forest, and the wind among the trees; the babbling of the brooks and wild dashings of the river; she loved the silent stars and the golden glow of sunset; and she adored Will Austin, too, with all the fervor of a true woman's love.

And do you wonder that he worshipped her in return? You might search the country through and you would never find one so universally beloved. She was the village pet, and we all know what that means. Gray hairs and children, middle age and youth, all were happy from her words of cheer, and joyous in the smiles of her ruby lips; for such smiles! they were like the blessings of angels. But I am dwelling too long upon her loveliness, and you sneer—at what? The picture I have given you of her love or her beauty? Well, doubt it if you will. You did not know her. There is such love in the world, and such excellence, and such beauty, too. You may not have seen it.

A twelvemonth came and went, as all years have, and will, and naught seemed to occur to disturb the quiet river of the lives of the young lovers. But now a change came over the spirit of their "love's young dream," the nature of which we already know; and it appeared in this wise.

An undeserving scion of a gold-bearing stock, a stern, cold-hearted man of the orld, who knew no love but the love of wealth, and possessed in his soul no music but the click of gold, a business friend of the merchant Burton, was introduced to the family and cast a shadow into the quiet home; and that shadow grew.

He was wealthy, as the world counts riches, in stocks and lands, and the gold that glitters; but of the wealth that enriches the heart, builds up the divine manhood, and makes the world brighter and better, he was sadly barren. There was in his nature no sunny spot where could grow and blossom bright flowers to scatter in bouquets of love and charity along the pathway of life. But I will not describe him. We all know such, and meet them in our daily walks and feel the icy chill of their presence.

Did you ask me if he was welcomed at the Burton mansion? By the father he was; and Ellen, who loved her parents with all the love of a fond and dutiful heart, accorded to him that respect and attention due her father's guest. But it was not until a recurrence of his visits again and yet again, that his true intentions were manifest to the mind of the innocent girl; and when next he came, for come he did, ostentatiously apparelled and outfitted, Ellen was not at home, and diligent inquiry failed to find her. A messenger was sent throughout the village, but no one had seen her, and when hour after hour had passed and she returned not, the wooer reluctantly relinquished the purpose of his coming; and the early-rising moon of that evening saw the aristocratic carriage of the heir of the house of Ross, disappearing southward along the valley.

A week later saw its return, and this time unannounced; but the bird had flown again, and no one knew whither. Shall I tell you a secret? I will, since it is difficult to keep, and I am not sure but it has been told, for this was years ago; more, indeed, than I care to remember, so fast do they come and go.

The winds knew of her hasty flight; the birds welcomed her to their shadowy retreats; and the wild mountain stream that went laughing adown the glen and among the rocks, bearing no impress where those dainty feet had trod, told not the secret of her flight and hiding-place. I think Will knew, however, although he never told me so; but he did tell me how, very soon after the disappointed visitant had bidden his perplexed host " good night," and said adieu to the genial hostess, a light glimmered suddenly out, like a guiding star, from the west window of the old garret, facing toward the mountain and the glen, and half an hour afterwards came "Black Ben" from up the ravine, followed by a rustling among the shadows, as of the evening wind among the bushes. And I think, too, the moon was in the secret, for as Will and " the rustling" met at the pasture gate, she came smilingly from behind the hill, beaming with joy at the meeting; but then, she always laughs at those glad scenes.

But I am wearying you with details. I must hasten to tell you how the next day brought around an interview between the father and daughter, at which he told her his wishes, that she should encourage the attentions of "Walter Ross" with a view of becoming his wife. He looked upon it as a very desirable match, as, in addition to his actual possessions, which were ample, he was the prospective heir to a large estate of tenanted lards, and much well-paying bank stock. He was a man of fine personal appearance, fairly intellectual, and quite moral, as the world goes. To be sure he was somewhat wild and given to excess, but all this he would outwear with years of experience and the counter charms of wedded life; and then he was of a very aristocratic progeniture, being in direct line of descent from Geo. Ross, a signer of the Declaration of Independence, and a distinguished member of the Continental Congress.

Now we must not judge from this that the father of Ellen Burton was altogether a mean and selfish man; there were in his nature many warm and sunny spots, and, as I have said, he loved his only child with all the fondness of a devoted parent, and in urging the suit of this petitioner for the hand of his daughter, he was not at all unmindful of her future happiness; but he, like many another that you know, fancied that the amount or degree of earthly bliss depended upon the extent of earthly possessions, and standing in what the world is pleased to term society. He was wealthy, and consequently, he thought, happy; hence his conclusions; so we need not wonder that when Ellen declined to accept his views or comply with his wishes, telling him she could not give her hand where her heart could never go, he was overcome with a mingling of grief and offended authority; and when later she ventured to tell him of her deep love for Will Austin, and that she preferred the wealth of his heart and noble manhood to the boasted opulence and sumptuous surroundings of this stranger, he waxed ireful, the cloud of his anger gathering fury, until an hour later, it burst woefully upon the head of the innocent lover.

You know already with what effect. We heard it as we stood in the starlight of that evening, as the shadows gathered in the park; and we heard it again from the lips of my friend as we sauntered along that valley road until the night grew old and the stars disappeared in the flush of the morning's dawn.

I left him that morning, his soul oppressed with sad thoughts at the prospect of parting with her he loved with a pure and holy affection, and who he believed worshipped him as divinely.

"She will be true to me. I know," he said, in one of his moments of rapture. "The heart of the father, too, will yet relent, and I will come back in time, and then:——"

Here his voice was checked with emotion, and pressing my hand passionately, we parted.

He left, next day, for Europe, and I heard from him casually as he flitted here and there. First a greeting from Switzerland; then a line from that "City in the Sea," throned on her hundred isles: "I stood in Venice on the Bridge of Sighs; a palace and a prison on either hand." A few weeks later another, in Will's peculiar hand and style; "At the 'Arch of Titus,' gray with centuries, and away through the deep blue skies of Rome I waft a message to thee." Then again, after a time: " Dreaming of home in this Sabbath evening twilight, from Thebes of a hundred gates — travel-stained with dust that throbbed with life four thousand years ago; wandering above the ruins of ancient temples, while the night sweeps down loaded with glory; gazing upon the stony face of 'Memnon,' gloomy with ages forgotten, while the shadows steal across the plain and over the time-hallowed graves and city of Pharaohs. In the misty silence of the halls of Karnak, among whose gloomy ruins the dun fox and the wild hyena call, and owls and flitting bats startle the echoes and fill the imagination with visions of uncanny spirits and ghosts of long-mummied Egyptians."

A month later and he was at Jerusalem, the holy city, realizing thus the cherished dreams of his boyhood: "Lying in the starlight of Olivet, gazing with tear-dimmed eyes above the hills of Judea; breathing inspirations of glory from above the 'Mount of Ascension,' made sacred in the eyes and faith of millions by the footsteps of the 'Son of Mary'; following in imagination the career of those strange but brave men, those zealous followers of the humble Nazarene, who came from afar to lay down their lives, and thereby expiate their sins in endeavoring to wrest the sepulcher from unholy hands; from the possession of the "Camel driver of Mecca."

But I am getting along slowly with my memories. I must hasten to tell you. This was the last I heard from the wanderer, and when weeks lengthened into months and no tidings came of him, I could but conclude he had, in some of his lonely ramblings, fallen a victim to Bedouin rapacity, and thought his pilgrimage ended in that sunny land.

I saw Ellen Burton but twice during all this time, and once was to convey a message from her noble lover. It was indeed painful to mark the change these months had wrought. She was no longer the happy, light-hearted girl of former times. The bloom of health had faded from those rosy cheeks, and brightness from her eye. Her step was no longer elastic, but lingering, and her friends saw her less frequently among them; and it began to be whispered that she was going by the dark road. Few knew wherefore she pined and faded, but she was dying, the doctor said, and he should know, for he was their old family physician, and was skilled and wise. The father knew whereof she was dying, and he sighed as the great waves of his agony rolled over his soul. Also he would give all of his possessions to be able to turn back the events of past months, or stem the consequences of that tide of circumstances; but he knew he could not, and that is why the iron frame shook with suppressed grief.

It was in October; a golden day near its close; one of those brightest of Indian Summer days, when the whole world is as radiant as a gleam of Heaven. I had been all day revelling amid the scenes of summer-garnered sunshine glories; riding over the hills toward the valley whereof you know.

A message came for me, and I knew instantly whence it came, and whereof, and I went immediately to the home of the Burtons, for I knew I was called to the bedside of the dying girl. I hardly waited to be announced, and waving ceremony, passed quietly, following the servant, to the sick room.

Many eyes were red with weeping; the members of the family were standing around the bed, and the old doctor scattering his words of comfort. There were circles of sad-eyed friends about the room, watching that young spirit pluming itself for heavenly flight. I was motioned to the bedside, and taking gently in mine the withered hand of the pale form, I stooped to catch in broken whispers:—

"Tell Will, if you ever meet him, I will remember our tryst."

This was all; and closing again those dimmed eyes she seemed quietly sleeping.

A window was opened toward the river, and once, when the breeze came in, bearing with it a murmur of waters and a sighing of the wind among the old pines near the house, a smile lighted up her calm face, and the lips moved, and we knew the listening soul was charmed into lingering by the familiar melody; but again the eyelids drooped and the sunny eye was closed, but the lips still smiled sweetly as if pressed by the kisses of angels; and the angels were glad, for they were again welcoming to their number a loved one so long a wanderer from her native heaven.

I was standing near the door opening into the broad hall, and gazing listlessly out upon the hillside, now tinged with the last rays of the setting sun. The shadows up the glen were growing deeper and more gloomy; the brooklet laughed not, but tinkled sorrowfully; the winds up among the pines and the old rocks whispered mournfully, for they were lisping to each other the sad story.

The servant announced a stranger, and at the instant, unceremoniously but quietly, a dark form glided past, and I looked to see, kneeling at the couch of the silent sleeper, one whom I did not at first recognize. The nerveless hand was held caressingly in his, and the pale lips erewhile so lifeless, were pressed with the warm kisses of love. There were no words around that wondering group, but many tears and loud beating hearts. I stepped forward as the lips parted, and "dear Will," was whispered almost inaudibly; nothing more.

I deemed it best to retire and leave the frail flower to those who loved her best, and to whom she was dearest, and only pressing the hand of my friend, travel-worn and almost overcome with this sudden grief, (he had been told of Ellen's death before reaching the village) I went out and over to my room at the hotel.

The dim-lighted windows, and shadows moving silently about in the mansion across the river, disturbed my sleep until long after the noon of night had studded the sky with starry watchers.

I only heard next day that the weary soul still tarried among friends on this side; and receiving a promise from Will that he would inform me when the change came, I left the place and friends, hoping against feeble hope.

A telegram reached me a week later, only saying: "She is still with us, and doctor says she is better."

But why need I trouble you longer with details? The sequel is soon told in an extract received from my friend some months after I left them as above, in which he says:

"You must be sure and come; the circle will be incomplete without you. We shall have a quiet wedding, but it will be a happy one. E. says, as you have been a sharer in our sorrows, so should you witness our highest joy. We are to have the old homestead on the river, and it is a sunny home since the light of it has returned to us. Poor, dear girl, how she must have suffered during those long months of loneliness. But it is all past, and the sun shines brightly where erst but cloud shadows spread. Be sure and come, and we will have a 'Merry Christmas,' indeed."

And I was there.

RICHARD POTTER.

BY REV. SILAS KETCHUM, WINDSOR, CONN.

Read before the Annual Meeting of the New Hampshire Antiquarian Society, July 16, 1878.

"In Memory of RICHARD POTTER, the Celebrated Ventriloquist, who died Sept. 20, 1835, aged 52 years."

Such is the legend on the stone that marks the resting-place of a very remarkable man. To the generation now passing and nearly passed away, no man in New England was better known, probably, than he. From Quebec to New Orleans there was scarcely a man, woman or child that had not beheld with vacant wonder his marvelous tricks, or laughed themselves weak at his endless ventriloquial imitations and inimitable drollery.

How he would compare for skill with men of his own craft in our day it would be impossible to determine. Professors of his art were by no means so common in the days of our fathers as now. The chemistry of the atmosphere, of liquids and heat was less generally understood. The principles of electricity and magnetism were scarcely understood at all. Tricks with these, which would have been incredible except on demonstration, are now familiar to every school-boy. In Potter's day the notion of magic and the possession of occult powers, was by no means eradicated from the popular mind. Whether he was greater or less than Signor Blitz. the Fakir of Ava, Jonathan Harrington and "the Great Hermann," it would be only a matter of speculation to enquire. Probably the latter; as all arts tend to elimination of the crude and the perfection of their methods.

But, if all that has been reported of Potter is true, he must have possessed powers not only marvelous, but supernatural. He could handle and swallow melted lead. He could go into a heated oven, with a joint of raw meat, and remain in the oven till the meat was cooked. He could dance on eggs and not break them. He could cause a turkey-cock to draw a mill-log across the platform. He could cause any lady in the audience to find a peeping chicken in her pocket; or gentleman a "bumblebee" imprisoned in the handkerchief in the top of his hat, without himself leaving the stage or their leaving their seats. All these and other feats equally impossible, the writer has heard related of Potter, by persons who declared they had seen him do them.

Of the nationality of Richard Potter various statements have been made, widely circulated and believed, and nothing certain is known. Of any part of his early history no more than probabilities can be reached, by piecing together parts of various stories, of which he appears to have been the author.

He was commonly called "Black Potter," and had the appearance of a mulatto. The story was currently reported, in the vicinity of his own home in Andover, that he was the son of a negro woman in Boston, and that Benjamin Franklin was his father. That the mother was a servant in a Boston family, and that, after the birth of the child, Franklin furnished her a home in a back street behind the State House, where Potter lived till he was ten years of age. Stephen Fellows of Grafton, who was Potter's assistant during the last years of his travels, and, with Potter's son, succeeded to the business, and who now possesses all of the great magician's kit there is in existence, assured the writer that Potter told him this story in confidence. It is entirely probable; and that Potter told it in one of his fits of humor, to parry enquiries as to his early life, concerning which he appears to have been always reticent. Nevertheless, the story became current, and was confidently believed by many who ought to have known better.

The folly of the assertion is seen in the fact that Franklin was not in America after November or December 1776, till 1785; and was not probably in Boston after his departure to England, in 1764, until after the latter date; while Richard Potter, if the date and age on his tomb-stone are correct, was born in 1783, at which time Franklin was 77 years old.

Potter told Fellows that he was at ten years of age, picked up by a ship-captain, and carried as a cabin boy to London. Being there turned adrift upon the city, he fell in with a travelling circus, with which, in the capacity of a servant boy, he remained four or five years, visiting all the large towns and cities of England; that the circus then came to America, and was the first that ever exhibited in the United States; then he returned to America with the company, being then past fifteen years of age, and continued in that service two or three years, during which time he acquired from his employers and associates the knowledge and practice of the art he afterwards pursued; and that, when about eighteen years old, he left the circus and set up business for himself as a magician and ventriloquist.

There was, however, an opinion widely prevalent, within the territory of his most frequent exhibitions, that Potter was a native of the East Indies. It was confidently affirmed, by many persons who professed to be acquainted with him, that he had himself so reported. And that he *had* so stated is rendered probable, by the currency of this story among those who had witnessed his performances, and held desultory conversation with him before tavern fires, in places widely remote from each other. The writer has heard it repeated, with variations, but with a general agreement of points, in Maine, New Hampshire, Vermont, Massachusetts and New York.

Among his townsmen in Andover, the general understanding seems to have been that he was a native of one of the West India islands. But his complexion and physiognomy it was said, by those whose acquaintance with both races enabled them to judge, indicated the presence of Asiatic rather than of African blood. And among many, who had never heard of the Franklin story, though living in sections far apart, it was firmly believed that he was the son of an Englishman by a Hindu mother. This was the version which, in northern Vermont, the writer as a boy always heard and never questioned. But it was, undoubtedly, false.

Nevertheless, in both versions of the origin and early life of "the celebrated ventriloquist," there are some points of agreement, that not only point toward a common authorship, but give rise to the suspicion that, with whatever of romance there may be in either, there may be also some grains of truth. And this supposition receives some encouragement from certain corroborative circumstances, known to be historic.

Whether Potter ever told the Franklin story to any one beside Stephen Fellows, does not appear. But even if he did not, it is no matter of surprise that it should obtain a considerable circulation. For Fellows, as his assistant, supposed to be conversant with his affairs, would be the party most easy of access, and most likely to be questioned, in all places where they exhibited, concerning his employer's origin and history. And that Potter had given him a true history, Fellows seems never for a moment to have doubted.

But in both the Franklin and the Hindu version are certain points of identity. In both he is the son of a white father and of a colored mother. By the believers in each it was understood that he was not born in wedlock. By both it was said he was picked up by a ship-captain—the one said in the streets of Boston, the other in the streets of Calcutta—and carrried to London. Both agreed that he there drifted about, without care or guardianship, until he came to America under twenty years of age. Both understood that he first landed in this country in Boston. Both had heard that he learned his tricks of hand and voice in boyhood, and in foreign parts. And, by those who believed in his Hindu origin, the assumption was natural that, being quick and bright, he had acquired them in his native country from the Hindu jugglers.

In 1872, Moses B. Goodwin, Esq., formerly a correspondent of the *National Intelligencer* at Washington, was editor of the *Merrimack* (N. H.) *Journal*. In issue of Nov. 8, of that year, he gave an account of an interview, which took place in 1848, between Joseph T. Buckingham, editor of the Boston *Evening Courier*, and the Hon. Geo. W. Nesmith of Franklin. At that time the Northern (N. H.) Railroad had just opened to travel. The two gentlemen above named were journeying together from Franklin toward the northern terminus of the road, engaged in conversation. When the train reached the Potter Place, and the name of the station was announced by the conductor, Mr. Buckingham enquired for whom the station was named, and on being informed that it was formerly the abode of the great magician, he proceeded to state the circumstances of his first acquaintance, and subsequent business and friendly relations, with that gentleman.

Mr. Buckingham said that when he had finished his apprenticeship in the office of the *Greenfield* (Mass.) *Gazette*, he went to Boston and set up business as a job printer. That he boarded at an old and well-known tavern called *The Bite*, kept by one Bradley, near Market Square. That one day a small-sized, sharp-eyed, dark-complexioned young man sat down with him to dinner. That after the meal was finished, this young man enquired of Bradley for a suitable man to do some printing. That Bradley thereupon introduced him to Mr. Buckingham. The small-sized, sharp-eyed, dark-complexioned man was Richard Potter.

Between the two there soon sprung up relations of confidence, respect and friendship; and Mr. Buckingham believed that, when exhibiting in this country, and within such distance of Boston as to render it possible for him to do so, Potter from that day forth to the end of his life, gave him all his patronage in printing. He stated that Potter had paid him thousands of dollars; that he always paid promptly and dealt honorably; and that, in his long career as a printer, only two other men had ever given him more encouragement or pecuniary aid.

Mr. Buckingham spoke with much feeling of the "Genial Showman," and with a "tender respect for his memory;" dwelt at length on the details of his long and intimate acquaintance with him; and declared him to be one of the noblest and most generous men he had ever known.

Now Buckingham left the office of the *Greenfield Gazette* and went to Boston in 1800. He had but recently established himself there when he was introduced to Potter. The fact that Potter enquired of Bradley for a printer, coupled with the generally-understood fact that the renowned magician commenced his career in Boston, would indicate that he was just starting in business for himself, and had had no printing done before. This might have been in 1800, and was not probably later than 1801. In 1800, Potter was seventeen years old.

In the story told to Fellows he said that he left the employ of the circus and started business when about eighteen years of age, which would exactly coincide with the time at which he was having his first printing done in Boston. This would tend to enhance the probability that the story was not all fiction, and that he learned his art from some company of mountebanks with which he was associated when a boy.

From that time forward there is no trace nor tradition of Richard Potter, connected with any fixed date or location, that I have been able to discover, for the next twenty years. An examination of files of newspapers, published in Boston, and various other towns and cities of the Eastern and Middle States, would doubtless throw some light on his history during that period. But such examination I have not been able to make.

His headquarters, and whatever "home" he had, are supposed to have been in Boston. It is certain, however, that he travelled widely, and had become known and famous, previous to 1820. It is certain that he had, within that time visited Europe, for he was for a time with Napoleon; though not as a soldier. It is certain that he had married and that his two children were born before the latter date. It is certain that his wife travelled and performed with him, until she became unfitted to do so, from habits of intemperance.

But with what particular successes or adventures he met; how extensively he circulated, what countries he visited; when, where and whom he married, or where his children were born, the writer knoweth not.

In the winter of 1875, at my suggestion and request, and in order to procure for me the information I desired, Moses B. Goodwin, Esq., above named, visited Andover (N. H.), where Potter spent the last fifteen years of his life, and made minute enquiries of the old residents of the place, who had been acquainted with him and his family.

From a near neighbor to Potter, during his residence in Andover, whose son was, at one time, Potter's travelling assistant and partner in the business; from Hon. Geo. W. Nesmith of Franklin, who was acquainted with Potter's affairs; and from Mrs. Isabella West, an aged and intelligent lady of Franklin, whose husband in Potter's day, kept a tavern in Boscawen, at which Potter and his wife were frequent guests, Mr. Goodwin obtained much reliable intelligence concerning the great magician. From his subsequent letters, and from his article in the *Merrimack Journal* above referred to, a large part of the facts of this history were obtained; for which the writer hereby expresses his grateful acknowledgements.

About 1820 Potter purchased a farm of about 175 acres in that part of Andover which now bears his name. On this he erected a residence 22x38 feet, fronting on the turnpike, the whole second story of which was one room; the lower story being divided by a hall running through the house. This he finished and furnished with elegant display, regardless of the cost; and, it was said, with taste and judgment. He was generous to a fault, kept open house, and dispensed a liberal hospitality. In another house, entirely separate from the mansion, was done all the cooking and housework.

located all the servants' offices, after the manner of the South, and there, also, were all the sleeping-rooms.

Mr. Potter carried on extensive farming operations, raised excellent crops, and cultivated choice breeds of cattle, horses and swine; raising great numbers of the latter. The grounds about his house were tastefully laid out, well kept, and ornamented with a great variety and profusion of shrubs and flowers, of which both he and his wife were passionately fond.

Both of them affected considerable display in dress, selecting rare and costly materials of foreign make, distinguished for rich and brilliant colors. In this each followed the characteristics of the people from which they sprung.

Stephen Fellows assured me that Potter told him that Mrs. Potter was a full-blooded Penobscot-Indian squaw. If he did it was but one of his freaks of humor. No one, acquainted with the characteristics of the native American women, would probably ever have mistaken her for one of them. According to Mr. Goodwin, she was, when in her prime, a finely-formed, beautiful and graceful woman, who had an easy carriage, bright and expressive eyes, danced charmingly, and knew how to dress. She was intelligent, refined, well informed, engaging in her manners and conversation, and proud as a princess. She had a rich voice, and was a sweet singer. All the authorities above quoted agree without hesitation in declaring her a native of India. It seems to have been always so understood by those who knew her best, and they had their information from her and her husband. *Where*, nobody knows, but somewhere in his travels, most likely while in Europe, Potter came across this brilliant and fascinating daughter of the East, and married her. He was fond and proud of her and cherished her with loyal affection, even after she had contracted habits which disgraced both herself and him.

They had an only son and an only daughter. The former was a spendthrift and a drunkard; the latter a half-idiot, given to uncontrollable lewdness. It is said that the perpetual and untold shame and anguish of the proud and sensitive mother, because of the conduct and condition of her children, drove her to seek "some nepenthe to her soul" in the oblivion of constant inebriation. Certain it is that she became disqualified for all duties, either in public or at home; caused her husband immeasurable trouble; indulged in scandalous extravagance, compelling him to seek remedy at law to prevent her from running him ruinously in debt; that her charming beauty and quick intelligence were utterly wrecked; and that she died the victim of her own indulgence.

With unqualified confidence the same authorities all assert that Richard Potter was a native of one of the French West India Islands, the Franklin and Hindu stories to the contrary notwithstanding. His hair was soft and handsome, but it testified to his African extraction. He was once turned out of a hotel in Mobile, while Thompson of Andover traveled with him, by a landlord who would not entertain a "nigger." Potter did not deny the charge, removed to another hotel, performed twelve nights in the town, and carried off $4,800 in silver, in a nail cask, as the net result. Learning that there was danger of being waylaid, he gave out that he was going to a certain place on a certain day, and departed the night previous in the opposite direction. He was often called a mulatto, and never contradicted the aspersion. His characteristics raise a strong suspicion of Creole origin.

He was proud, high spirited, courteous in deportment, independent, the soul of honor, generous and brave. As a citizen of Andover, to which town he came to remove his wife and children from the influences of city life, he was public spirited, honorable in business, prompt to pay, a kind neighbor and trusted friend. He was kind and liberal to the poor, and an early mover in the cause of temperance. He was a man of rare executive ability, of endless native resources, and possessed a mind enriched by experience, and well stored with information. His wit was fertile, quick as thought and sharp as steel.

The more I have learned of the history and character of the "Celebrated Ventriloquist," the more I have been compelled to pay him honor. When I remember the race to which he belonged; the probable deteriorating influences under which he passed his early life; the absence of all family and social ties and restraints; the incentives and allurements to recklessness and ruin; the lack of all the ordinary processes and opportunities for education and discipline; the profession which he chose and followed; the disgrace of his wife and infamy of his children; and that, under all these, he lived honorably and died respected; I seem to see a man whom nature has royally endowed, struggling against vast odds which finally threw but never vanquished him. "He was as good a citizen as ever lived in Andover; and one of the truest and best men that ever lived!" This was the testimony of his nearest neighbor for forty years after Potter died.

The lewdness of the half-idiot daughter occasioned litigation, after Potter's death, in which Judge Nesmith and the late Samuel Butterfield were counsel, out of which grew a curious decision in law in relation to adultery, that obtained considerable notoriety in New Hampshire.

Potter was buried in his own front yard. When the Northern railroad was built his remains had to be moved back some yards, the limits of the road covering his first resting-place. The wife did not long survive her husband, and a simple marble slab "In Memory of Sally H., wife of Richard Potter," who died Oct. 24, 1836, aged 49 years," preserves her name from oblivion. The two graves have been pointed out by the conductors on the Northern road, to numberless travellers within the last thirty years.

The daughter died and, it is said, was buried beside her parents. But no trace of a grave is discoverable.

The son's name was Richard Cromwell. He was sometimes called "Dick" and sometimes "Crom." He was dissolute and unprincipled. The property which his father left he soon squandered. He sold the farm to a Mr. Colby of Bow, who sold it to Aaron Colby of Andover, who sold it to Wm. Howe, Esq., who sold it to John E. Morrison, the present owner.

Taking his father's apparatus he traveled, in company with Stephen Fellows, for a time, giving exhibitions, but was not successful. He finally mortgaged the kit, and when it was taken from him under the mortgage, he broke into the premises where it was kept and stole it; in consequence of which he became a fugitive, as he had long before been a vagabond, and was last heard of at Lansingburg, N. Y. Thus is the family of the "great Magician" become extinct; but his name and his fame appear to have become historic.

ILLEGIBLE MANUSCRIPT IN PRINTING-OFFICES.

BY ASA MC FARLAND.

In every well-regulated printing-office inflexible rules are observed regarding manuscript that is to be put in type. The necessity for such rules is obvious; for authors, in general, have no standard themselves, and their manuscripts differ as much as the peculiarities of those who prepare them. Many thoroughly-educated men write a hand of which they ought to be ashamed; others, with meagre educational advantages, make lines so fair that the youngest apprentices at the printing-business have no difficulty in putting their "copy" into type. The late Rufus Choate, so eminent as a lawyer and so eloquent as an advocate, wrote a hand so obscure as to confound printers and all others who undertook to decipher his letters and other papers. He also made sentences two of which have been known to fill an octavo page, and put no punctuation marks into his work. Some writers, and those, too, of ambitious pretensions to scholarship, seem to have no proper idea of punctuation, and distribute capital letters with the utmost freedom, and in defiance of all rules laid down in the books. Others, again, employ no other punctuation than a dash (—) which, with them, takes the place of the comma, colon and semicolon. Another class of writers underscore about one word in every three—the purpose being to impart emphasis to the underscored words, since such are, according to the rule, put in *italic* type. But they can carry the practice to such an extreme that they not only fail in their object, because of the multitude of their italic words, but mar the printed page. A book that is well printed should contain as few italic words as possible, and those be employed only where, according to well-established practice, they are required. Hon. Henry Hubbard, Governor of New Hampshire in 1842 and 1843, wrote annual messages of great length, plentifully supplied with italic words, to the discomfort of printers in the office of the New Hampshire Patriot, and those in all other newspaper offices in the State which published the messages of that chief magistrate.

If all manuscript sent to newspaper and book printing-offices was printed as written—and it is very common for authors to direct the printer to "follow copy"—many aspiring public men would cut a sorry figure after their productions appeared in print. Men have been known to place a capital letter at the commencement of every line, as if engaged in making verses; others, as before remarked, employ the (—) with "perfect impunity and great boldness," and others punctuate hap-hazard. Sensible men, however, submit their compositions to the printer with directions to capitalize and punctuate as to him seems proper; well aware that if he is master of his business he will make straight whatever is crooked, and present the author to the public in better plight than he could himself.

In most cases the proof sheets of manuscript sent to the offices of daily and weekly journals are not sent to the authors. It is otherwise in book and job printing establishments, and it is common for authors to make the final correction. This is a procedure that affords mutual satisfaction; for, when the writer has revised his work, no other responsibility rests upon the printer than to see that the types are not disarranged and that the press-work is properly done. And right here is a point where many printers have had experience of a trying character, namely, in material changes from the copy, and sometimes to such an extent as to greatly enhance to the author the cost of his work. In a well-remembered instance in the experience of the writer of this article, an address before a literary society in Dartmouth College, printed in pamphlet form in the office of the New Hampshire Statesman, was so changed by the author's corrections as to more than double the cost of the work. The additional expense was of course borne by him; but even if the printer be reimbursed for his time, labor and perplexity, the work itself is marred by a multitude of typographical changes, and the satisfaction of producing a good specimen of printing greatly lessened. The prolific power of some writers seems greatly quickened by the sight of their proof sheets.

The difference between fair and illegible manuscript is like that between a day in June and one in mid-winter. One causes smiles, the other frowns. If the hand-writing of a writer is illegible, he should employ a copyist, and every one who writes for the press should cover only one side of the sheets. Many newspaper offices reject all manuscript written on both surfaces of the paper, however eminent the author or important and seasonable the topic he discusses. In a business experience of many years we found it greatly to the advantage of the office to examine and prepare for composition most manuscript that came to us. Unless this course was pursued with the larger portion of it, the inevitable consequence was increased labor and vexation in correcting the proofs. The manuscript of some writers can never be forgotten for its illegible and slovenly character, and that of others will be long remembered for its excellence. JOHN FARMER, Esq., one of the founders and many years the right arm of the New Hampshire Historical Society, wrote a hand that a child could read, and his pen, too, moved with much rapidity. Much of his manuscript is deposited in the rooms of that institution at Concord. His patient researches were mainly of genealogical and historical character, and appeared in the Historical Collections of the Society, and caused him to be well known throughout New England, although he was most of life an invalid, and rarely went abroad. Several manuscript volumes treating of graduates of Harvard College, deposited in the rooms of the Historical Society, bear testimony to his careful toil in a department of literature that has few attractions to most people of literary taste. The manuscript of Hon. JOHN J. GILCHRIST, a Justice, and subsequently Chief Justice of the Supreme Court of this State, was absolutely perfect. In a long experience we have never had to do with better "copy."

He prepared a Digest of all the Reports of Cases decided up to the time he was Chief Justice, and it was printed by McFarland & Jenks for Gardner P. Lyon, bookseller. It is a volume of more than six hundred octavo pages, and rarely or never has an equal amount of work moved along more pleasantly. Other Justices and Chief Justices of that Court made excellent manuscript, but that of Judge Gilchrist was perfection itself.

Every author desirous of ascertaining how much space his manuscript will fill in page and type of prescribed size, and would count the cost before he commences to build, should write upon paper of uniform size and place the same number of lines upon a page. The printer can then determine the number of printed pages the manuscript will fill and the cost of the work. This is, of course, upon the presumption that the author makes no additions while the work is in press, and no material alterations from the copy. We printed a small work many years ago which the writer thought would fill about twenty-four pages, but he made such copious additions that it exceeded seventy-five.

PROCEEDINGS OF THE NEW HAMPSHIRE ANTIQUARIAN SOCIETY.
CONTOOCOOK, JULY 17, 1878.

The day was auspicious, and the attendance larger than on any former occasion. The Society's rooms were found too small to accommodate those present, and to transact business with comfort.

The meeting was called to order at 10 A. M., the President, Rev. Silas Ketchum of Windsor, Conn., in the chair. After the reading of the minutes of the last Quarterly Meeting, the President read his annual address, setting forth the condition of the Society's affairs, a general review of its transactions for the past year, and making several recommendations, *to wit:* The weeding out of the duplicates and undesirable articles in the museum and library; the donation and exchange of articles to and with certain societies; the careful husbanding of the Society's resources; the vigorous prosecution of the work of the Historical Committee, particularly in the collection of the perishing materials for history, and in gathering lists of sepulchral inscriptions from the various towns.

George H. Ketchum, Curator, reported the donation of about 3000 articles to the library and museum during the year, making the whole number to the present time a little over 33,000. Among the recent additions was a collection of about 150 manuscripts formerly belonging to

Gen. Amos Shepard, consisting of documents relating to the early settlement and settlers of Alstead; also valuable mineral specimens from the Yellowstone Park by Hon. Chas. H. Bennett of Iowa, and from Arizona by G. S. Davis of California.

H. A. Fellows, Chairman of the Historical Committee, presented the folds of the fifth volume of the Society's Ms. Collections. In it are copied the papers of the late Gen. Aquila Davis of Warner, and a memorandum book kept by his father, Capt. Francis, first settler of the town. Also interesting papers relating to the early settlement of Boscawen and Dixville, formerly belonging to Col. Henry Gerrish, Col. Timothy Dix and Daniel Webster. The Committee was given more time to arrange, index and bind the volume.

Charles Gould reported that he had nearly completed the copying of the sepulchral inscriptions of Hopkinton. The Society has already extensive lists, some of them complete, of inscriptions in Bristol, Hill, Ashland, Alexandria, Franklin, Concord, Henniker, Dunbarton, Exeter, Hanover and other towns. Most of these are already recorded and indexed.

William H. Stinson, Esq., of Dunbarton read an interesting paper, prepared hastily, but with great good taste and judgment, on the sepulchral records of Dunbarton. A copy was requested for the Hist. Colls. of the Society.

Wm. A. Wallace, Esq., gave some account of his endeavors towards a history of Canaan, a considerable part of the early history being already in manuscript. Mr. W. was appointed to read a paper on the subject at the next annual meeting. Col. L. W. Cogswell was appointed to present a paper at the same time on the sepulchral records of Henniker, and Robert Ford to collect the entire list of inscriptions in Danbury. Also to copy the records of the first church in Danbury, now extinct. Mr. Wallace presented valuable donations to the museum and library of matters relating to the history of Canaan.

The President read a paper on the life and character of Richard Potter, published in this number of the GRANITE MONTHLY.

Col. Cogswell presented appropriate resolutions on the death of Dr. Bouton, an honorary member, which were adopted.

The Society elected Rev. Silas Ketchum, President; Capt. G. A. Curtice and S. L. Fletcher, Esq., Vice Presidents; John F. Jones, Esq., Treasurer; Charles Gould, Esq., Recording Secretary; Walter Scott Davis, Esq., Corresponding Secretary; Geo. H. Ketchum, Curator; D. C. Blanchard, Rev. Silas Ketchum, Col. L. W. Cogswell, Wm. A. Wallace, Esq., Wm. H. Stinson, Esq., S. L. Fletcher, Esq., Wm. M. Chase, Esq., Historical Committee.

The Society acknowledges the receipt of valuable additions during the year, besides those above referred to, from Col. Albert H. Hoyt of Cincinnati, O., Gen. Wm. S. Striker of New Jersey, Dr. Samuel A. Green of Boston, Hon. Clark Jillson of Worcester, Elijah Bingham, Esq., of Cleveland, O., the Mass. Hist. Soc., N. E. Historic Gen. Soc., Worcester Society of Antiquity, the Essex Institute, Gov. Prescott and others.

The Society has published during the year A Diary of the Invasion of Canada, edited with notes by Rev. Silas Ketchum, and A List of the Centenarians of New Hampshire who have deceased since 1705, by D. F. Secomb.

THE GRANITE MONTHLY.

A MAGAZINE OF LITERATURE, HISTORY AND STATE PROGRESS.

VOL. II.   OCTOBER, 1878.   .   NO. 3.

WILLIAM J. COPELAND.

In previous numbers of the GRANITE MONTHLY there have been presented sketches of representative men of New Hampshire, in business, and public and professionanal life, with accompanying portraits. Herewith we give a short biographical notice, with portrait, of a well known lawyer, who, although not an actual resident of the State, is a member of the Strafford County bar, and extensively engaged in practice in this and other counties of eastern New Hampshire, as well as in the State of Maine.

WILLIAM J. COPELAND is a son of Rev. William H. Copeland, a Baptist clergyman, yet living and a resident of Lebanon, Me. He was born in Albion, Kennebec County, Me., Jan. 24, 1841, being now in his thirty-eighth year. The Copeland family trace their ancestry to Sir John Copeland, who fought at the battle of Neville's Cross, under Edward III., October 17, 1346, and with his own hand captured King David of Scotland, whom he bore from the field with a company of attendants, and, proceeding to Calais, delivered him into the hands of his royal master, then in France. For this service he was created a banneret by the king, and given a pension of five hundred pounds per annum. He was also made Warden of Berwick, Sheriff of Northumberland and Keeper of Roxburgh Castle. Lawrence Copeland, a lineal descendant of Sir John, from whom sprang all the Copelands in America, came to this country and settled at Mount Holliston, Mass., where he died December 30, 1699, aged 110 years. Moses Copeland, a great-grandson of Lawrence, and from whom William J., the subject of our sketch, is a direct descendant in the fifth generation, went with his brother Joseph from Milton, Mass., to Warren, Me., in 1763, being among the early settlers of that place. He was a man of great activity, shrewd and calculating, and gained wealth and distinction, taking a prominent part in the enterprises of the town. In early life he had served in the army, entering at seventeen, under Capt. Boice; was at Ticonderoga in 1758, and at the taking of Quebec the following year. Soon after his settlement in Warren he was appointed sheriff, and held the office eleven years. He also held the office of crier of the court several years. From constant con-

WILLIAM J. COPELAND.

WILLIAM J. COPELAND.

tact with lawyers and observation of legal proceedings he gained a good knowlege of the law, and finally became the principal lawyer of the place, for, although not educated to the profession, his practical information and ready knowledge of human nature rendered his advice and assistance in legal controversies the most valuable that could be obtained in that region. This Moses Copeland was a cousin of President John Adams, and a grandson of John Alden upen the maternal side.

William J. Copeland attended the common schools in Shapleigh and Berwick, where his father was then preaching. In 1855 he attended the academy at South Berwick, and afterwards, for a time, the West Lebanon and Limerick Academies, earning the money to defray the necessary expenses by teaching in the winter and farm labor in the summer, teaching his first school, at Shapleigh, before he was sixteen years of age. Having a strong inclination toward the legal profession, he entered the office of Hon. Increase S. Kimball of Sanford, Me., at an early age, where he pursued the study of the law until he was admitted to the bar, which was before he was twenty-one years of age. He then located in Presque Isle, Aroostook County, where he entered upon the practice of his profession, remaining there until April, 1868, when he removed to Berwick, opposite Great Falls, where he has since resided, having established his office at the latter place.

During the past ten years in which he has been in practice at Great Falls, it is safe to say Mr. Copeland has attained a degree of success in his profession seldom equalled and never surpassed by any practitioner in the country outside the great cities. This is attributable, it may fairly be presumed, to his indomitable energy, intense application and thorough devotion to his professional work. With powers of physical endurance far greater than those with which most men are endowed, with a keen insight into human nature, and a strong love for the contests of the legal arena, he has the ability to command success in cases where others would see only failure from the start. Without any of the graces of oratory, he exercises, nevertheless, a wonderful power over the jury, through his ready perception of their individual characteristics, enabling him to appeal directly to their understanding and judgment, and the earnestness with which he enters into the case, carrying us it does the appearance of a settled conviction of the justice of his cause.

In a description of Mr. Copeland's phrenological character, recently written out by Prof. O. S. Fowler, that distinguished phrenologist says: "*Power* is your predominant characteristic, and much greater than I often find it. It appertains to your constitution, intellect, will and whole character, so that you have brought and will bring more to pass than any one man in thousands who started evenly with you. This comes from the predominance of your muscular system, which renders your mental operations remarkably virile and effective, to which you superadd great memory, especially of facts, faces and places. Are pre-eminently adapted to the study and practice of law. Can be a public man and leader. Are remarkable for looking right into and through things at a glance, and particularly sagacious in spelling out men."

As has been stated, Mr. Copeland has a large practice at the Strafford County bar, being engaged, upon one side or the other, in a great proportion of all the cases coming to trial in the county. In Carroll County, also, he has been extensively engaged, having been retained in most of the important cases tried there for several years past, prominent among which was the famous Buzzell murder case, wherein he secured the acquital of the respondent upon his first trial, in May, 1875, though he was subsequently tried and convicted of the statutory crime of "hiring and procuring" the murder. In the management of this case, especially at the first trial, Mr. Copeland displayed his remarkable powers to the best possible advantage, manifesting a force of character, command of resources and influence over men seldom shown. His services have also been called into requisition at the Rockingham and Belknap County courts, while his practice in Maine even exceeds that in this State. As few men are able to accomplish as much professional labor as Mr. Copeland, there are few who receive so large an income therefrom—certainly not more than one or two in this State—and should he continue to devote himself exclusively to his profession for the next ten years, he will have gained not only a remarkable reputation for professional success, but material wealth fully commensurate therewith.

Mr. Copeland married, in March, 1862, Miss Ellen L. Wade, youngest daughter of Loring and Sarah (Foster) Wade, formerly of Machias, Maine, and a granddaughter of Col. Benjamin Foster, Jr., of Machias, prominent in the early history of that town. By this union he has had three children, all daughters, two of whom are living—Mabelle, born April 10, 1864, and Kate, January 13, 1867. His home is one of the finest and most elegant residences in that section, the abode of comfort and domestic enjoyment, and his few leisure hours, here passed, are not without their happy influence upon his busy and earnest life.

In politics he has always been a Republican, but has never held office, or engaged in political life beyond the manifestation of decided opposition to what is generally known as the "machine" in party management, until during the recent campaign in Maine, when he espoused the cause of the new National Greenback party, and made several effective speeches upon the stump.

A DAY AT OLD KITTERY.

BY FRED MYRON COLBY.

Two distinct and breathing worlds lie open for the sojourner in this fleeting life; the world of the present and the world of the past. Those who love the present derive most enjoyment in visiting great cities and centres of fashion, picture galleries, and splendid libraries. They are enraptured by the pageantry and grandeur of imperial palaces, the glitter and show of courtly ceremonies, and all the gay dissipations of fashionable life. The devotees of the past prefer rather to dream away the hours on the spot where great men fought for a worthy cause, or linger among the ruined halls of greatness. The eloquent voices of another age, though only in imagination, speak greater truths to them than the loudest utterances of the present.

To those who possess this secret, Kittery Point, in Maine, possesses many points of deep interest. Whittier, in his sweet verse, has often mentioned some of them, yet the traveller has to carefully seek for them, for like Hamlet, they dread to be "too much i' the sun." Once found, however, and they reward the explorer with suggestive and noble pictures of the past. In an article like this, too little space is granted for more than a brief mention of its chief attractions.

Kittery lies opposite to Portsmouth, the Piscataqua river flowing between, and the visitor to the latter place usually visits the former. You cross by a long bridge set upon piles, where the water is more than thirty feet deep. On either hand lies the loveliest scenery in New Hampshire. Blue as the interior of a hare-bell the broad, romantic river, sanctified by John Smith's wanderings and Whittier's lays, flows southward to the sea, which you can discern in the distance through the soft violet haze. Behind you lies Portsmouth, its spires rising in the air; old Fort Constitution towers at your right, seaward are White Island, Boar Island, Great Island, and Whale's Back, the whole coast clothed with villages as far as the eye can reach. Fronting you is the famous navy yard, with its arsenals and its shop-houses. A long undulating highway runs in a sinuous line before the eye, hedged in by green orchards and clustering farm-houses, reminding the English traveller of those emerald lanes that lead down into Kent and Sussex. Three miles on you view a little hamlet, the spire of a small church rising above the roofs, and nearer you behold mouldering old docks upon which boys sit with their feet over the water, fishing. Groups of sail boats and fishing schooners ride in the harbor, their broad white sails flapping listlessly in the breeze. This is the outline of the scene that is spread before you.

There is a suggestion of the antique, and of quiet decay in the general aspect of the town. The stranger is reminded by a hundred evidences that he is looking upon the seat of past prosperity and vanished splendor. Distinct and widely separated indeed is the present with its quiet, half mournful life, and that famous past when Kittery was a commercial and social centre, when the activity of trade made it a new world Tyre, and ships sailed from its decks to India and the Southern seas—ships that circumnavigated the globe.

On the whole Atlantic coast there is no better harbor than that afforded by the widening of the Piscataqua below Portsmouth and Kittery, and in the colonial period it was a great channel of commerce. At Kittery and Portsmouth were mercantile centres which vied with Salem and Boston, Newport and New York. Some of their merchants had a hundred vessels at their command, engaged in commerce and fisheries, and large trad ing parties were ever coming in on land from the lands of the Abenequis, the Coos, and the St. Francis. Gay and romantic must have been those expeditions into the summer forest; the encounters with Indians, half-breeds and squaws; the wild adventures, and the return to the populous towns. Those were the golden days of Portsmouth and Kittery.

It is delightful to lounge about the old worm-eaten wharves on the sunny afternoons. There is a fascinating air of dreams and idleness about the place which is very soothing. Very little business is transacted here now-a-days. Three or four barges laden with coal, and a few schooners bearing the valuable produce of the Maine forests, with here and there a fishing smack, constitutes about the whole of its commercial prosperity. In the great navy yard there is comparative quiet. Only now and then is there a vessel launched from the stocks. It is only by a great effort that you can imagine all the past glory of the old maritime town—its merchants as rich as princes and almost as powerful, its large, noisy ship-yards, its huge warehouses stocked with merchandise from all parts of the world, its numerous fleets going and coming to and from China, the Indies, and the Mediterranean.

Before leaving the river side we must say a few more words about the navy yard. It contains an area of nearly sixty-five acres. Permanent gray walls of dimension split granite enclose it on all sides. There is every convenience and facility for constructing the largest class of government ships. The water at the wharves is of sufficient depth to float the largest man-of-war at the lowest tide. Three large ship-houses, seven large timber sheds, a mast house, and a rigging house, machine shops, and wood shops on the most extensive and improved plans pertain to the yard. There is a floating dry-dock for the repair of ships, which cost nearly a million of dollars. It is three hundred and fifty feet in length, one hundred and fifteen in width, and thirty-eight feet in height. The quarters for officers and men are not excelled by those of any naval station in the country. Some over five hundred hands are usually employed in the yard.

As we pass up-town, through the historically famous streets, we have time to more leisurely notice the architecture of the buildings. Most of the houses are modern, but among them are now and then seen a more ancient type of dwelling—relics of the revolutionary epoch. Their quaint, small paned windows, ample door porches, glittering brass knockers, and enormous chimneys are at once old fashioned and suggestive. One could, gazing at these antique houses, almost fancy that from them would issue gentlemen of colonial days, dressed in knee breeches, silken stockings, plum colored coats, cocked hats, and silver buckles. Every one of these houses has its treasere of tradition, and if allowed to speak could tell rare tales of auld lang syne. There is one great mansion which we cannot summarily dismiss with a passing notice, for though curtailed somewhat of its fair proportions, it is still the object of frequent pilgrimages to Kittery Point. We refer to the old Pepperell House, built one hundred and ninety years ago, which has seen more of splendor and sheltered more famous individuals than any other private residence en this side of the sea.

The house was built by the first William Pepperell, the great merchant and ship-builder of his time. He accumulated vast wealth by trade, and his mansion reflected the boundlessness of his means. Grand as any old English castle, it stood looking out to sea, girt by a great park where droves of deer sported. His son, the famous Sir William Pepperell, enlarged and adorned it at the time of his marriage in 1734. This Lord Pepperell, the only American baronet after Sir William Phipps, was a remarkable man. He was the richest merchant in the colonies, and had at times two hundred ship at sea. His success at Louisburg proved him a skillful general, and his political influence was second to that of no man's in the colonies. The style he lived in recalled the Feudal magnificence of the great barons. The walls of his great mansion were adorned with rich carvings, splendid mirrors, and costly paintings. In his side-board glittered heavy silver plate and rare old China. Wine a hundred years old from the delicate, spicy brands of Rhineland to the fiery Tuscan, was in his cellars. He kept a coach with six white horses. A retinue of slaves and hired menials looked to him as their lord, and he had a barge upon the river, in which he was rowed by a crew of Africans in gaudy uniforms. The only man in all the colonies worth two hundred thousand pounds sterling, reigning grandly over grand estates, for, like an English peer, he might have travelled all day long upon his own lands, sovereign lord, in fact, if not in name, of more than five hundred thousand acres—timber, plain and valley, in New Hampshire and Maine—Sir William Pepperell could do this and yet not live beyond his means.

The memory of all this baronial magnificence fills the mind as you stand before the old mansion where he lived, or at the Knight's tomb in the orchard across the road, a few hundred yards from the goodly residence that he built. Faded is the escutcheon on the marble tombstone. Curtailed of its fair proportions, and sadly decayed is the grand old mansion, but they recall visions of splendor still. The house looks down from its three story grandeur with scorn upon its humble and more modern neighbors, and well it may. Its experiences have been unique. British Admirals, belted Earls, grave statesmen, and the noblest chivalry of the old and the new world have abode under its roof. Its master was one of the most brilliant personages of his generation; and although the famous men who came after him, Langdon, Washington, Adams, Franklin and Livingston, with many others—figured in greater ovents, still the name and memory of Sir William Pepperell are well nigh as famous as those of the *Dii majous* of our history.

Half a mile to the West is another famous old mansion, the Sparhawk House, built by Lord Pepperell in 1741, for his daughter, who married Col. Sparhawk. This structure is in better repair than the other, and is one of the stateliest houses of that age in America. Its great parlor is thirty by twenty feet, and very high posted. The other rooms are smaller but stately. The orginal paper remains on the walls of the wide hall, as do the deer antlers above the doors. The observatory upon the roof affords a fine view of the surrounding country. A noble avenue of elms, a quarter of a mile in length, formerly led from the street to the door. The trees were about one rod apart. The perspective effect of this grand avenue must have been peculiarly graceful and impressive. Some vandal cut down the trees twenty-five years ago. But no one can destroy the beauty of the noble site on which the mansion stands. James T. Fields has lately endeavored, among others, to purchase it for a summer residence.

We pass from the atmosphere of these ancient structures once more into the light and life of the sea-port town. A change has taken place during our absence among the memories of the past. For the first time, we are reminded of the fact that Kittery has claims as a popular summer resort. Yes, the old town has Rip Van Winkled into life again, acquiring fresh fame in its new dignity. It is now four o'clock in the afternoon, and the quaint streets have become a sort of Hyde Park. Equestrians and carriages dash thither and hither, making a pleasant and brilliant promenade. The friends who breakfasted together a few hours before, have now the satisfaction to bow to each other from barouches or from the saddle. The lovely ladies who wore bowling costumes this morning, wear driving costumes this afternoon, and tonight they will flaunt gaudy ball-room attire. How they smile and bow! How the ribbons flutter and the gloves glitter! The air is soft and mild. The music from a brass band chimes pleasantly on the ear. Over all shines the warm sun, from a spotless sky.

But all this bustle and gaiety and splendor is far apart from the life of the town. It preserves its indomitable repose despite the fury of the brief summer episode of excitement around it with a smile of scorn as it were. For one short month the saturnalia of fashion reels along its wide beach, and holds high festival in the very heart of its quaintness, but during the rest of the year the old town dozes silently upon the water and dreams of its great days departed.

The last spot we visited was the ancient grave-yard,—a fitting finale of this brief sojourn. As the grave closes the mortal career of man, so we chose that this cemetery should be the end of this day's scene of active, varied, picturesque transitions. Verily a good place to forget the vanities of this life. The old grave-yard itself is dead. Pomp, pride, ambition, and even grief itself are all at an end. Black slate headstones and the costlier marble monument, stand in a ruinous state side by side. Noble dust slumbers beneath the sod, and once in a while we can decipher an ancient crest or the name of some colonial magnate.

"History numbers here
Some names and scenes to long remembrance dear,
And summer verdure clothes the lonely breast,
Of the small hillock where our fathers rest.

Theirs was the dauntless heart, the hand, the voice,
That bade the desert blossom and rejoice."

We wish we could have lingered longer within its sacred precincts. It is good for man sometimes to forget the things of this life, and to realize the common fate of all mankind. And these old cemeteries have charms yf their own. Both the ethical and the historical faculties are aroused as well as the spiritual in the contemplation of such burying-grounds. Among all our old cities places of similar historic interest are found. Translate these localities north of the White Mountains and how many annual pilgrimages they would receive. So long as they remain within a pleasant foot ramble they are rarely visited, but if the circumstanc transpired that we suggested, those localities would be designated by some enduring monument, and a pebble from the soil would be treasured as a mantel curiosity.

TRAVELING ACCOMMODATIONS IN HOPKINTON.

BY C. C. LORD.

HIGHWAYS.

Roads are generally constructed in fulfilment of the immediate wants of the existing community. The first roads in Hopkinton were laid out to suit the then present condition of things. One of the earliest acts of the proprietors was to take measures for establishing needed roads. On the 14th of February, 1737, a vote was passed appropriating twenty pounds for clearing a road from Rumford (now Concord) to the centre of the new township, and to be used in constructing roads north and south to the extent the appropriation would allow. On the 13th of May it was enacted that the money appropriated for clearing roads be collected by the first of July. On the 20th of December a sum of forty-four pounds, accumulated in the treasury, was appropriated for the clearing of the road to Rumford. Dea. Henry Mellen, Daniel Claflin, John Jones and John Brewer were made a committee to confer with the selectmen of Rumford in reference to the proposed road. On March 29, 1738, it was voted that the money granted to clear the road should be assessed in the following May, showing that a previous vote to collect had not as yet been fulfilled. One the 30th of September of the same year, it was voted that a road be constructed from Rumford line to the meeting-house spot or place; also from Meeting-House Hill west to Contoocook river; also a road on the east side, to accommodate lots; also from the meeting-house place to the Great Meadow, so called; and from the meeting-house to the township north.

The first roads were merely paths traced through the native wilderness. As population and occupation increased, fences and walls became in demand.

Roads and attendant accommodations were multiplied with the growth of the local settlement. On May 12, 1766, it was voted to build a boat in the Contoocook river, said boat to be as large as Deacon Merrill's boat in Concord, for the accommodation of people passing between Hopkinton and New Amesbury (now Warner). On March 2, 1772, a vote was passed appropriating thirty pounds in labor for the construction of a bridge across the Contoocook.

The increasing need of facile intercommunication between more distant localities at length led to the establishment of better public thoroughfares. In 1805 the present communication between the two villages was established, by building the road from Putney's Hill to the meeting-house, relieving people of the necessity of climbing the southern brow of the hill or taking the easterly route leaving the lower village just north of the blacksmith shop of Horace Edmunds, and thence running to a point just west of the house of S. B. Gage, where it connected with the present highway at this spot. In 1815 the road known as the "turnpike" was constructed. It was a main line to Concord, avoiding the toilsome Dimond Hill road on the east. In 1827 the so-called "new road" from Hopkinton village to Dunbarton was built. This was to accommodate a public stage route between Boston and Hanover, which, south of Hopkinton took a westerly direction. The well known Basset Mill road was constructed in 1836. The so-called "new road" to Concord was built about 1841. This was also in accommodation of a stage route between Hopkinton and Concord and more distant points.

HOTELS.

Among the first taverners in Hopkinton were Benjamin Wiggin and Theophilis Stanley. Several persons quite early were engaged in hotel keeping on the site of the old Perkins House. The most notable of these earliest landlords was Mr. Wiggin, who was justice, postmaster and trader also. He came to this town from Stratham, N. H., and became established as a landlord as early as 1774, which date was inscribed upon his old-fashioned swinging sign-board, one-half in each upper corner. On the bottom of this sign-board was the significant announcement, "Entertainment by B. W." This sign-board also bore a painted representation of a man on horseback followed by two dogs. Never were worse proportions delineated. The man's waist was shrunk up to comparative nothingness, while his lower extremities enlarged into feet of enormous proportions. Benjamin Wiggin's hotel is still standing, being the house next westerly to the Episcopal Church. In front of this situation the Rev. Mr. Cram, the third minister in town, was ordained out of doors in the month of February. A reception was given to General Lafayette in the same place, on his visit to this country in 1824. Mr. Wiggin died in 1822. He was a man of much public spirit and social generosity. After his death the tavern stand was sold to Benjamin Greenleaf of Salisbury, N. H. Subsequently it has passed through various hands.

Capt. Birnsley Perkins' tavern was for many years a hotel *par excellence*. It was the grand hotel of all this region. It stood on the site of the late remodeled "Perkins House." In the days of its highest prosperity there were three lines of stages passing through the town. Hopkinton was then one of the shire towns of old Hillsborough county, and for a time the capital of the State. Here came the old legislators—John Langdon, John Sullivan, Daniel and Ezekiel Webster, and a host of others. Great times were seen here on public days. The best fare was always to be had. Although Capt. Perkins was the most noted ruler of this house, he was not its first landlord. Public house was kept here by several persons previous to him. It is not definitely known to us when the tavern was erected, but once a piece of plaster fell from a wall, revealing the date 1786 on the lathing. When the old meeting house was burned in 1789, it was kept by a Mr. Babson. Subsequent to the burning a town meeting was called at this tavern, and the gathering being large, it was adjourned "to Mr. Babson's barn yard," where important business was transacted. Being the principal public house in this part of the town, and the natural resort of most all traveling characters and enterprises, its patronage was of an incongruous nature, including statesmen, lawyers, transient travelers, teamsters. show-men, etc. Captain Perkins opened this house in 1811, was landlord about forty years, and died on the premises in 1856.

For many years this ancient house was closed to the public. The innovation of railroads turned the course of travel and shut off patronage. But times revived a few years ago, when the "Perkins House" passed under the management of Mr. D. B. Story, who kept it open until its destruction by fire in October 1872. During Mr. Story's conduct of the establishment, it underwent important repairs and was largely patronized by summer boarders. It was also a resort for winter sleighing and dancing parties from Concord. Its loss was a great misfortune, both on account of its historic memories and business advantages.

Elder Joseph Putney's tavern stood on the highest point of road between the two villages in town, on the site now occupied by the house of Mr. Charles Putnam. It was part of a large farming establishment and was patronized by the more lowly among travelers. To obtain a clearer idea of life in a public accommodation like Elder Putney's we must understand a feature of ancient travel which was more or less exhibited in or round all country inns. In the olden time all freight was of course carried through the country on wheels and runners and in many instances by the owners themselves. Teamsters were often inclined to indulge only the most economical fare. When teams large and small put up for the night, the drivers often brought their own provisions, thereby saving all expenditures except for lodgings, grog and hay. It was a picturesque sight when a large company of travelers gathered around the open fire, and refreshed themselves each from his own box of edibles. Elder Putney was particularly hospitable to his guests, always furnishing them with plenty of cider for nothing. His supply of winter apples was just as free. The average patronage of a house like Elder Putney's would surprise the modern enquirer. The number of horses and men required to transport freights was large, and the accumulation of small teams swelled the road travel immensely. Mr. Putney was a man of remarkable generosity and integrity. His temperament was strongly religious, impelling him to officiate publicly in the school house close to his home. From this fact it is probable he received the universal title of "Elder." Upon the death of his wife he abandoned public hospitalities. He died Sept. 20, 1846, aged 93. He was a soldier of the Revolution.

The first public house in Contoocook stood on the site of Curtis & Stevens's present store, which is a part of the original structure, since remodeled. At first there was a plain, one-storied, ungainly building opened to the public by Daniel Page. When the later Central House was first projected the idea of the necessity of competition first entered into the mind of the proprietor of the old hotel, and an extra story was added. Not far from this time Mr. Page sold out the stand to his sister Susan, afterwards the wife of Simeon Tyler, who lived in the district known as Tyler's Bridge. Miss Page was sadly unfortunate in the ultimate of her proprietorship. She sold the house for railroad stock and lost it all. The stand ceased to be open to the public about the year 1834.

The second hotel built in this village was erected in the autumn of the year 1831, by Messrs. Sleeper & Wheeler. Both landlords were young men. The enterprise did not flourish in their hands, and in about a year the property went into the hands of Mr. Herrrick Putnam, who kept the doors open for about a dozen years. Mr. Putnam was followed by Mr. Rufus Fuller, of Bradford, who conducted the establishment till about twelve years later, when he died. For years the place was kept by Henry Fuller, son of Rufus, and afterwards by Mr. Walcot Blodget, son-in law of the older Mr. Fuller. It changed hands frequently till 1872 when it fell into the possession of Col. E. C. Bailey, who kept it open till 1878, when he tore it down and erected just east of it the present hotel.

The Putney House in Hopkinton village was built to supply the place of the Perkins House, burnt in 1872. In the summer of that year Mr. Geo. G. Bailey determined to make Hopkinton village a place of residence, bought the old Isaac Long place and fitted it up for the convenience of his family during the hot months. A year or two after, he purchased the old Dr. Wells house, adjoining the Long place, moved it back, established connection between the two, and made the present Putney House, a nice and convenient hotel in a pleasant shady spot. The structure includes two stories with a Mansard roof. The complete establishment has a front extension of 125 feet and a rear one of 190. Since the erection of this house an elegant hall, a bowling alley and other additions have been constructed.

The old Parker Pearson stand at "Stumpfield" and French's Tavern, now burned, on the Basset Mill road, at "Sugar Hill," were instances of smaller country establishments for the accommodation of the traveling public.

THE RAILROAD.

A little over a quarter of a century ago a stranger came to Contoocook, and lectured in the small hall in the rear projection of the Contoocook House, in the attempt to illustrate the feasibility of steam locomotion. He had a small engine, for which he laid a narrow track across the hall, and actually conveyed himself back and forth to the observation of the interested audience. Heads were shaken when he predicted that in twenty years freight would be brought to this village by steam power plying the rails. Yet in less time the prophecy became true. The Concord & Claremont Railroad was projected; the line passed through Contoocook, from which there was also a branch line to Hillsborough Bridge. In the early fall of the year 1850 the cars began to run regularly to this village. A day of great festivity was held. The railroad officials extended the favor of a free ride to and from the city of Concord. The proffered courtesy was accepted by a large company, filling a long train.

The people of Contoocook determined to be liberal in furnishing the festivities. A subscription was raised, a public dinner provided, music and artillery secured. About one thousand persons sat down to eat. The food was set upon a row of tables at the station, a shed having been erected for their accommodation. About fifteen members of the Warner artillery came with a gun and music to do the military honors. The gun was posted on the intervale on the north side of the river just below the railroad bridge, towards which spot a signal was given when to fire. Speeches were made, the band played, the cannon thundered. It was indeed a gala occasion. The pecuniary expense of the dinner eaten on this occasion amounted to $200.

Many citizens of Contoocook, as well as others of the town, paid dearly for their enthusiasm and enjoyment. Assessments on primitive stock did the work. To get rid of the personal liabilities many threw up their whole interests, in some instances amounting to thousands of dollars. Yet the public benefits afforded by railroad facilities have been entirely incalculable.

"MIRON."

BY MISS CARRIE A. SPALDING.

[This poem, written for the occasion, was read at the recent silver wedding of "Miron," (Myron J. Hazeltine), well known in the world of chess, at his beautiful home known as "The Larches," in the town of Thornton. It was published in a New York paper, but is worthy of republication in the GRANITE MONTHLY. The author, Miss Spalding of Haverhill, is a young lady of fine literary talent, whose productions have been much admired.]

In other realms, where kings and queens bear sway,
Their subjects have no will but to obey:
To every mandate, howsoe'er unjust,
They bow in silence—since, forsooth, they must!
But lo! a change in our progressive land—
We see a man who can all kings command;
Queens move submissive at his sovereign will,
Or, as his word directs, in turn stand still.

The moss-grown castles far beyond the sea
For ages yet to come unmoved may be;
The ivy clambers o'er the turrets high,
The arches echo as in years gone by;
But this enchanter of the modern times
Brings back the wonders of Arabian climes,
Takes up the Castles as "a little thing,"
And moves them without aid from lamp or ring.
The knights of old, mounted on prancing steed,
Who fearless sought each brave and daring deed,
Bowed only to the will of lady fair—
No other ruler would they deign to bear;
Behold the change! these craven, soulless men
Retreat, advance, and then retreat again;
The lightest touch, the softest, swiftest word,
Holds them in check as soon as it is heard.

Bishops, who in the sacred chancel stand,
Arrayed in flowing surplice, gown and band,
While at their feet a kneeling, prayerful crowd,
In true devotion, to the earth is bowed,
Aside their litany and prayer-book lay—
One "not in orders" they at last obey;
Across the checkered path they move with speed,
And neither ritual nor canon heed.

Not often do the gods such power bestow
On common mortals in the world below;
To hold at will, through all its changing scenes
Pawns, Knights and Castles, Bishops, Kings and Queens.
But, lest this privilege should foster pride,
To share the honors and the spoils divide,
They also sent a "help-meet," skilled no less
In realms of poesy and fields of Chess.

And now, upon this merry, festal day,
The silver milestone of the earthward way,
I, too, would add my wishes most sincere,
For richer blessings in each coming year;
And when the "game of life" at last is done.
Each foeman vanquished and each victory won,
May these dear friends, resigning earthly things,
Be crowned with glory by the "King of Kings."

FOREST VEGETATION IN NEW HAMPSHIRE.

[From the Report upon Forrestry, Department of Agriculture, for 1877.]

The whole State was originally covered with a dense forest growth, the principal kinds of timber being pines, spruces, oaks, and hickories, beech, chestnut, white, red and sugar maples, butternut, birches, elm, white and black ashes, basswood, and poplars. A striking contrast is shown in the aspect of the northern and southern portions of the State, caused by differences of temperature due to altitude, the transition being gradual, some species becoming scarce, and finally disappearing, while others first appearing in small numbers increase as we go north or south until they may become the prevailing kinds. A few species occur throughout the entire State. A line drawn from North Conway to Lake Winnipiseogee, and from thence to Hanover, would somewhat distinctly divide the northern from the southern types. This transition area would be at an elevation of about 600 feet above tide, corresponding with the annual mean of 45°, or of 20° in winter and 65° in the summer months.

Among the species characteristic of the more southern type, which here find their northern limit may be mentioned the chestnut, white oak, spoon-wood or mountain laurel, and frost-grape. The range of pines and walnuts, of white or river maple, red oak and hemlock, is also mainly southern. The more characteristic trees of the northern class are the sugar-maple, beech, balsam-fir, black and white spruce, and arbor-vitæ, and of smaller trees the mountain ash and striped maple. Of these the white spruce and arbor-vitæ have the most limited range. The former is abundant about Connecticut Lake, but occurs rarely, if at all, South of Colebrook. The latter (*Thuja Occidentalis*), is also common in this section, extending south to the vicinity of the White Mountains, and is also occasionally found in highland swamps farther south.

The pine family forms the most important feature of the landscape, and has been an important source of wealth to the State. The white pine originally filled all the river valleys with a heavy growth, extending along that of the Connecticut to the northern boundary. This growth has now nearly disappeared before the lumberman's ax, but the great abundance of saplings in the southern part of the State shows that this species is still the principal conifer of that section. Passing northward into Coos County, we find the white pine much restricted in area, occurring mostly at the headwaters of the streams, and mainly confined to the first-growth specimens, saplings being of rare occurrence, even where the land is allowed to return to forest after clearing.

The pitch and red pines are of more limited range, the former (*P. rigida*) occurring most along the sandy plains and drift knolls of the river valleys, scarcely growing on hills that attain much elevation above the sea level. It is found most abundantly in the southeastern part of the State, and in the Merrimack

Valley and around Lakes Winnipiseogee and Ossipee, extending northward as far as North Conway. In the Connecticut Valley it appears less abundantly. The red pine (*P. resinosa*), often called "Norway pine," "is the most social of the pine genus," occurring in groups of from a few individuals to groves containing several acres. Although much less common, its range is about the same as that of the pitch-pine, probably attaining a higher elevation above the sea level. This species is of handsome and rapid growth, and is well worthy of being planted for ornament.

In the White Mountain region the balsam-fir and black spruce, growing together in about equal numbers, give to the scenery one of its peculiar features. They are the last of the arborescent vegetation to yield to the increased cold and fierce winds of the higher summits. North of these mountains, the arborvitæ forms the predominant evergreen, mingled with the white spruce about Connecticut Lake. In the southern part they are mostly confined to the highlands between the Merrimack and Connecticut Rivers, the black spruce being most abundant.

The hemlock is common in the southern part of the State, ranging most abundantly around the base of the Rocky Mountains, southward along the highlands, becoming less near the coast. Its northern limit is in the vicinity of Colebrook and Umbagog Lake, reaching an elevation of 1,200 feet above tide.

The tamarack does not enter largely into the flora of New Hampshire, being chiefly confined to swamps of small extent, and ranges along the highlands from Massachusetts to north of the White Mountains. The red cedar is chiefly limited to the sea-shore. The juniper is sometimes troublesome by overspreading hilly pastures. The American yew is often present in cold-land swamps.

The maples are best represented among deciduous trees. The river maple is most limited in range, being confined to intervales of the principal streams, and rarely far away from them. The red maple is common in all parts of the State, and the sugar-maple is abundant, filling an important part in the economy of the State, supplying both timber and sugar. It is common in most parts, but less towards the sea-coast. This with the beech makes up the greater part of the hard woods of Coos County. Southward the beech is common on high lands only, often growing with spruce and hemlock.

Four species of birch are common, of which the black, yellow and canoe birches have about the same range as the red maple. The canoe or paper birch grows high up the sides of mountains. The fourth and smallest, the white birch, is most abundant in the southeast part of the State, affording the "gray-birch hoop-poles" used in the manufacture of fish-barrels.

Five or six species of oaks are found, of which the hardiest is the red oak. Although the only species found along the water-shed between the Merrimack and Connecticut, it does not extend much beyond the White Mountains, having its upper limit at about 1000 feet above the sea. The white and yellow oaks usually appear together, on the plains and hillsides along the rivers. The former extends northward in the Connecticut Valley nearly to the mouth of the Passumpsic, in the Merrimack Valley to Plymouth, and in the eastern part of the State to the vicinity of Ossipee Lake. Its limit in altitude is about 500 feet above the sea, which is also very nearly that of the frost-grape. The barren or shrub oak is abundant on the pine plains of the Lower Merrimack Valley, thence extending eastward to the coast, and to the sandy plains of Madison and Conway. The chestnut oak seems to be local in this State; at Amherst and West Ossipee it can be found abundantly.

The chestnut is found in the same situations as the white oak, but the chestnut is the first to reach its limit of altitude, which is about 400 feet above the sea. It occurs in a few localities about Lake Winnipiseogee· at a somewhat greater height, the neighborhood of the lake producing less severity of temperature than the river valleys at the same altitude.

The American elm attains probably the largest size of any deciduous trees. It grows best in alluvial soil, and is the most extensively planted for shade and ornament of all trees, unless, perhaps, the sugar-maple.

Butternuts also prefer the borders of streams, and in the valley of the Pemigewasset extend northward to the base of the mountains. Hickories are most common in the Lower Merrimack Valley, the shell-bark extending northward to the vicinity of Lake Winnipiseogee. Basswood is found mostly on the highlands, but is not very common. The black cherry is found throughout the State, usually most common near streams. Two species of poplar are common; the first a small tree, very common in light soil, and often springing in great abundance where woodland has been cleared away. The other, the black poplar, may be a large tree.

The Hon. Levi Bartlett of New Hampshire has given in the result of his experience, an interesting illustration of the profits that might be realized from tree-planting in this State, covering a period of about fifty years. A tract had been cleared and thoroughly burned over in a very dry season, about the year 1800. It immediately seeded itself with white and Norway pines, and about twenty-five years after came into his possession. He at once thinned out the growth on about two acres, taking over half of the smallest trees, the fuel much more than paying the expense of clearing off. From that time nothing was done with the lot for the next twenty-five years—having sold it, however, during that time. Upon examining it he found that, by a careful estimate, the lot which had been thinned was worth at least a third more per acre than the rest which had been left. It was worth at that time at least $100 an acre. He thought that had the land been judiciously thinned yearly, enough would have been obtained to have paid the taxes and interest on the purchase, above the cost of cutting and drawing out, besides bringing the whole tract up to the value of the two acres which had been thinned out. At the time when this part was thinned (twenty-five years from the seed) he took a few of the tallest, about eight inches on the stump, and forty to fifty feet high, and hewed on one side for rafters for a shed. At the next twenty-five years (fifty from the seed) he and the owner estimated that the trees left on the two acres would average six or eight feet apart. They were mostly Norway pine, ten to twenty inches in diameter, and eighty to a hundred feet high. He was greatly surprised, seven or eight years after, to see the increase of growth, especially the two acres thinned thirty years before. The owner had done nothing, except occasionally cutting a few dead trees. It was now the opinion of both that the portion thinned out was worth twice as much as the other; not, however, that there was twice the amount of wood on the thinned portion, but from the extra size and length of the trees, and their enhanced value for boards, logs and timber. There were hundreds of Norway and white pines that could be hewed or sawed into square timber, from forty to fifty feet in length, suitable for the frames of large houses, barns and other buildings. There were some dead trees on the two acres thinned at an early day, but they were only small trees shaded out by the large ones. On the part left to nature's thinning there was a vastly greater number of dead trees—many of them fallen and nearly worthless. Of the dead trees standing, cords might be cut, well dried, and excellent for fuel. Estimates were made that this woodland would yield 350 cords of wood, or 150,000 feet of lumber per acre. Allowing that these were too large, the real amount must have brought a very large profit on the investment.

A RHAPSODY ON OLD CLOTHES.

BY LUCIA MOSES.

In these days of æsthetic raving over everything old it surprises me that old clothes receive so little attention. I do not mean worn-out garments, fit only for the second-hand clothing shop, the rag-bag or the beggar at your door, but the partially disused adornments and habits that you wear on rainy days, when you know that no callers can venture forth, or that you pack in your cedar chest as being capable of further use by some future "making over." These superannuated servitors of a deposed queen of fashion are irresistibly fascinating to me by reason of their garrulity.

I am by nature a quiet body, and by stress of worldly circumstances an untraveled one, but I have my failings as well as the best, and indulge them when I can. My especial weakness is a pardonable fondness for that sort of gossip known as reminiscences, and happily for me I learned long ago that by bringing my imagination into active play I could gratify my small whim without mental labor or pecuniary outlay.

There is a cedar-lined closet and chest I know of, the contents of which have enabled me to travel from the Golden Gate to "far Cathay," and revel in opera, balls, college life, and "love's young dream." I have crossed the Atlantic by simply sitting quietly before an old rough serge dress. It is rugged and tired-looking, for it has made four sea voyages. As I open the door of the closet where it hangs, a strong, fresh, salt air seems to blow in my face; I hear the wash of the waves; I feel the breeze on my cheek. Shining sand from the bay of Naples shakes from the ruffles fringed by long tramps over Scotch hills. A dark stain on the front is a rivulet of beer spilled by a clumsy waiter in a German concert garden. By the trailing, dejected braid hangs a tale of a dark, foggy night on her Britannic Majesty's Channel steamer; a surging sea, a dizzy head, an impertinent nail, and "'Ere we are at Dover, mem, at last."

In the dimmest corner of this same closet hangs a battered, faded dressing-gown. The elbows and quilted scarlet silk cuffs of this once luxurious, gay garment are sadly dilapidated, as if the wearer had spent his college days leaning out his window on folded arms. In one of the deep pockets is a smoking-cap embroidered in a fanciful pattern with tarnished gold braid. In another there is a dainty, scented billet-doux, a bit of blue ribbon, a meerschaum case, a sonnet in halting Latin, and a pair of small primrose-colored gloves. The hands that wore the gloves and wrought the cap to cover a lover's brown curls are folded in that sleep that knows no waking, and the college boy, who, years ago, held the little gloves to his lips, sits by a lonely fireside in a far-off land.

But my chief delight is in a cedar chest. There I hear again and again a love story that will never grow uninteresting. 'Tis simply a pearl-gray velvet hat with sweeping plume and pale blush roses that babbles to me so deliciously. The bud of a girl who wore this saucy hat is now a blooming matron, but how beautiful she looked as she came down the stairs with it on twenty years ago. The young man impatiently awaiting her said involuntarily, "Fresh-blown roses washed with dew." Indeed, she must have been a vision of rare loveliness—the pure young face, the soft brown hair, the dreaming eyes. "So sweet, so daintily sweet and dear," he thought. I fear neither of them heard the opera that evening. They heard instead love's beguiling overture and the music of each other's unspoken words. Poor old hat! You were tossed carelessly aside soon after that to give place to bridal flowers, but your roses are still faintly blushing in memory of the kiss they guarded that night—what kiss so perfect as a kiss *sub rosa?*

In a corner, almost hidden from my prying eyes, is a pair of tiny red shoes. The restless feet that once pattered about in them are lightly keeping time, in high-heeled French absurdities, to the witching strains of a Strauss waltz. Helen and her brother Tom wonder why their ancient aunt will romance over their cast-off habiliments, and scoff good-naturedly, and ask me to give my opinion of a new bit of Limoges with no earthly association in which I have an interest. Now Tom's "Knickerbockers" amuse me vastly more than a Satsuma or Nankin cup. They have patched knees, and bits of string, chipped marbles, crumbling chalk, and all the *olla podrida* a boy usually carries, are still in the much-abused pockets. Tom half blushes as I shake out these childish garments, and says, "It's deuced queer that you should keep such baby things;" but he adds compassionately, "women are such romantic geese."

Yes, he is a mighty senior now; he carries a cane, smokes many and strong Havanas, whistles "Fair Harvard," and considers himself altogether too manly and practical to see a story in his old "small clothes," but in his heart of hearts I know he wishes he were, if only for a day, a Knickerbockered boy again, climbing trees, playing for "keeps," and going nightly to confess all his naughty acts to his mother. He has outgrown these things, but however much he scoffs, I know the sturdy little knee breeches have stirred sweet and bitter memories in his heart even more deeply than in that of the "goose."

Ah! hush! Here, folded tenderly in fine linen, is an epic bound in blue and gold. It is a lieutenant's coat. The gilt braid is dull; the eagles on the few remaining buttons are barely discernible. I read with filling eyes this sad, grand poem. The poor faded coat lies before me, a mute, blind Homer. I close my eyes, and I hear the roar and din of cannon, the whistling of bullets, the tramping and snorting of horses, the groans of the dying. The hero who proudly wore this is dead, shot through the heart. Here on the breast is a dark stain where his life blood flowed away. Ah! how it moans out the solemn, terrible tragedy of those awful years of carnage!

And now, O, scoffer, can you speak lightly of old clothes? Why, here is a white silk whose slim waist has been encircled by the arm of the fair-haired Duke—no, no, I'll forbear, and will not be as eloquent as I can, lest your unaccustomed mind lose itself in the mazes of my fancy.

But let me give you a word of advice. Be not too eager to put aside old garments. There is a certain air of respectability and refinement about an old but well preserved dress that gives the wearer an enviable individuality and importance. A dress that has traveled and seen the world—how much to be preferred to a garment ostentatiously new, that has, perhaps, a vulgar, shop odor. New clothes are so pretentious, so pushing, so grasping. But my prophetic eyes see coming the golden age for old clothes, for I know a maiden who has dared wear the same hat two winters, and I take heart of hope and smile defiantly on the man who jovially offers to take all your old clothes and give you a very small red Bohemian (?) glass rose. I say to him, "My good Othello, your occupation will soon be gone, for we are growing wise in our day and generation."

THE WAY TO GRANDPA'S.

BY LAURA GARLAND CARR.

A well-worn path across the field—
Round barley-lot and through the corn—
Here showing clearly, there concealed
 By drooping grass, at dewy morn!
  The older people walked straight through,
  But many curves our young feet knew!

Out through the barn for just one glance
 At swallows flitting to and fro—
At queer black heads, with look askance,
 From out mud nests, at us below—
  For just one tumble on the hay,
  Then off, through back-doors, on our way!

Down by the stone-heap, framed around
 By raspb'ry bushes young and old.
Just there, beneath a rock, we found
 A whole ant city in the mould!
  'Twas but a step outside the way—
  We'd not been there for one whole day!

Then over yonder, by the ledge,
 The blueb'ry bush that stood alone
Seemed wooing us with offered pledge
 Of berries ripe and fully grown;
  And close beside, in grassy rest,
  We found a tiny chip-bird's nest.

We reached the style—a pleasant place
 Beneath a spreading maple tree—
And there we tarried long to trace
 The wayward flight of bird and bee,
  Or watched the chipmunk rise and fall,
  Darting adown the pasture wall.

The pasture bars—too wide and high
 For little fingers to undo—
But many crevices were nigh
 Where little forms could " sidle " through!
  Beyond, the orchard, darkly green,
  While " cat-tail " flags grew rank between!

The garden gate—the garden gate!
  O, we could never pass it by!
There holly hocks rose tall and straight,
And sweet red roses charmed the eye;
  There currant bushes, all aglow
  With ripening fruit, were in a row.

And just beyond the low stone wall—
  No sweeter music e'er was known—
We heard a brooklet's tinkling fall
Along each moss-enveloped stone.
  We followed on, for well we knew
  Where fragrant beds of pep'mint grew!

The house was reached! Agleam with red
  The cherry trees stood round the door;
And scolding robins, overhead,
Fluttered and reveled in the store!
  While noisy thumps of grandma's loom
  Came sounding from the " open room."

'Twas long ago—O, long ago—
  That we went bounding o'er the way;
We have grown sober-faced and know
Of many changes since that day;
  But Mem'ry picture's all so plain
  We seem to live it o'er again.

MEN AND THEIR PROFESSIONS.

BY WILLIAM O. CLOUGH.

THE PROFESSIONAL TEACHER.

We boldly assert, while in the belief that it will provoke discussion, that the most important person in every community, to the community, is the professional teacher. That a good many women, as well as men, succeed as teachers in public schools, seminaries, academies and colleges, who would be useless to the world in any other calling is true, and that the ideal teacher, whom we conceive, is in a large degree a myth, is also true. Moreover we desire it understood in the outset that what little we have to say concerning this necessary public servant does not include that ever present individual who has no heart in the work, who teaches between the day of graduation and the day of marriage; who groans, whines and complains; who hesitatingly accepts a school to oblige the committee; who is an aristocratic snob, with not even the pride of family wealth behind; who drags a weary body through the drudgery of the day because of the dollars and cents it puts in an empty purse; who has no higher motive than the belief that it is an eminently respectable way of earning broadcloth, silk and ribbons, with which to dazzle the ignorant and cause the thoughtful to suggest that there must have been a good deal of pinching to accomplish such a show; who snaps, snarls and vexes the pupils, and shows a decided partiality to those of their neighborhood or church; who—but the outs are too numerous to mention. We have nothing to do with this teacher in considering the genuine, the ideal teacher.

The teacher we have in mind loves the occupation, has fitted expressly for it, is appointed of God, is ambitious to succeed and devotes energy and all attainable knowledge to the work, is not troubled with day and night dreams of fortunes that are to be won in mercantile marts; is not disturbed by ignorant public sentiment; has no jealousies to avenge; no fancied wrongs to set right, and no "axes to grind" or bosom friends to favor at the expense of some worthier persons inalienable privileges. The ideal teacher has the best balanced mind in the community; never spends valuable time in discussing pet ideas and isms; never cripples usefulness by too great a familiarity with the affairs of town, city or parish; does not dabble or mix in politics; is not a bigot in creed or a self-appointed theologian whose business it is to impress upon the youthful minds the certainty of future punishment as a cure for insignificant shortcomings. The ideal teacher has a religious faith as simple as childhood, as sweet as the rose, as fragrant as the incense from the holy Catholic altar, as pure as the ritual of the Episcopalian, as fixed as orthodoxy, that is infinitely beyond the comprehension of narrow sectarianism, that sees and recognizes God and goodness in everything, that patterns life after bright examples, and realizes that the impressions of the schoolroom are more enduring upon the mind of the youth than all else, and have far greater weight in molding future destiny.

Of what shall be taught from books, and of the precise method of teaching we have nothing to say. There has been a revolution in such matters since our time, and we are not therefore familiar with the routine of studies, or competent to express an opinion that the public is bound to respect. We have a conception, however, of what the ideal teacher should be. The ideal teacher recognizes the great responsibility of the calling, and is ever on guard against uneven deportment, peevishness, impoliteness by word, look or gesture, selfishness, fashion-plate conceit, lawlessness, deception, theft of time for private purposes, and a thousand and one little irregularities of conduct that young people observe and magnify to the destruction of a symmetrical character. The ideal teacher is never in violent temper; can inflict greater punishment by kind words fitly spoken than with a hickory switch, can command the respect of pupils in school and out of school alike, and is the friend above all friends to whom application is made for counsel when the troubles of childhood are tormenting the mind. In short, the ideal teacher—'My teacher!' as the pupil who is satisfied says with enthusiasm—conducts the youthful aspirant for the honors and emoluments of life to the great door of the world and says, practically, "I leave you here, having done the best for you that it is possible to do. You understand the beauty of piety, the necessity of honesty, the grandeur of purity, and the obstacles between you and complete success. Let all the ends you aim at be honorable. You know what is expected of you. Act well your part, there all the honor lies. You have my blessing. Go and be useful in the world."

Let us admit that although there are but few ideal teachers, there are some who are all the fancy pictures, and we honor them. The calling of the teacher is the most important, and to our mind, the most honorable—to the individual who enters it in the right spirit and with the right motives—that is known among men. It towers above all others, it guarantees greater peace of mind, is of more real dignity—the dignity that fathers and mothers respect—and grants greater satisfaction than any other profession. The affairs of the world,—except in momentous epochs,—its hurry, worry and confusion, its 'ups and downs,' its price currents, sensations, and the failures that bankrupt men in purse and reputation, need not enter his philosophy or vex his mind. He may live on a plain high above all worldly bickerings and strife; he may be comparatively free from sin, and, if he will, eminently respectable, hopeful of the life that is and is to come, without making any considerable effort as compared with those mortals, who, by force of circumstances over which they have no control, are compelled to dicker, trade and associate with the rabble.

THE PREACHER.

The preacher of to-day is decidedly unlike the preacher of the past. To many this is undoubtedly a matter of regret and lamentation. It is nevertheless a fixed reality, the sequel of which is obviously in the fact that the sources of education have increased and the masses thereby advanced to the point where the utterances of the most profound thinker are subjected to the rigid examination of a multitude of men of equal intelligence and argumentative ability. Time and institutions of learning have wrought wonderful changes, and instead of the simple, unquestioning faith of the fathers there is a spirit of determined inquiry— not to say doubt; a disposition to investigate, to ignore acceptance simply because the Rev. Mr. So-and-so says so. This being in a large degree the animus of the public mind, the minister who sermonizes the year round on themes that provoke discussion, loses his hold on his hearers; while the minister who is anxious mainly to impress the beauty of the Christian religion—whose concern is that men shall live better, think holier, study the amelioration of humanity, and feel more of love to God and man, and take more interest in deeds of charity and mercy than in discussing Adam's fall— comes nearer the wants of the people and the mission which the masses of this generation are content to hear and espouse. Those who accept the latter as the ideal find two classes of ministers.

1. The first is cold and formal. He comes to you like an apparition from a refrigerator. His 'good morning' and 'good evening' freezes the blood of the individual to whom it is addressed, and the mind quickly suggests that he should walk in the sunlight an hour at morning and evening before coming into the presence of men. He addresses his acquaintance emphatically as 'Mister,' and never condescends to smile or be cheerful. The average sinner is ill at ease in his company and gets the impression that there is no happiness here; that all of joy and good fellowship is 'way over there somewhere,' and it is a wicked sin to be sociable, comfortable and companionable, till he get there. Men who are in trouble do not seek this sort of a clergyman. They shun him and scold about him.

2. The second is warm and fraternal. There is no formality in his greeting, no ice in his hand with which to chill the blood, no suggestion that it is a sin to be happy, no indication that he would like to give somebody a theological nut to crack, no mannerism that asserts 'I'm holier than thou.' He has evidently left his creed—which doesn't amount to much anyhow—in his study, put aside his sermon paper, and started out with a view of dispensing and receiving just as much of good fellowship as can be conveniently crowded into an hour. He enters into conversation on the things that concern the daily life, and, feeling that he is accorded privileges that men will not grant the multitude, drops a word in one place and a remark in another, that lightens burdens and leaves those whom he has met more contented with their surroundings. In short this much is observable. 'The minister who mingles with the people and participates in their joys and sorrows, discovers their need, and is enabled to preach directly at them, while the minister who stands aloof preaches over their heads and leaves only the impression that religion is a gloomy article that belongs to sick people and those who have no further pleasure in the world.'

The first mistrusts a thorn in every bush, and the wicked one as manager of all public amusements. He is a sort of parish monitor; a censor whose behest everybody is bound to obey. He vents his spleen on things that are none of his concern, orders straight jackets for persons who are abundantly able to govern themselves, and never omits an opportunity to exhibit his spite against the Masonic body and Odd Fellowship. The second sees roses where the other discovered thorns; does not live in fear of being spirited away by the evil genius; is satisfied that on general principles the world is not so bad as some would like to make it appear, and that by the exercise of a little judgment and discrimination it is possible to be pretty cheerful for the most part of the journey from the cradle to the grave. When the first speaks on the questions at issue in this paragraph, he offends and shows that his vision is exceedingly narrow; his estimate of the wants of the multitude and what it will have, whether or no, considered from the wrong standpoint, and his knowledge of the secret institutions painfully out of keeping with the facts. The votaries of the former deny him the poverty of thanks, while the patrons of the latter close their lips and way down in their hearts pity his weakness. When the second speaks he shows that he has rubbed against the people of the world, knows what they want and what they cannot be prevented from obtaining, and is determined to so educate and refine the masses that good taste shall prevail and the very things which the first condemned become a power for good. He is a warm-hearted brother with the men who meet in secret conclaves, and, like Father Taylor of blessed memory, and many another eminent minister to guilty men, he counts it no sin and no shame to kneel with them and beseech God to bless and continue them in fraternal fellowship and in the faithful service that men are likely to need at their hands. The first avoids the crowd as he would the plague, and the latter is always seeking admittance to places where men congregate, and he will tell you that he is always welcome; that men grasp him warmly by the hand; that the class who have something mean to do and therefore repel the minister, is small, very small, so small indeed, that he never blundered into their company.

WHAT CONSTITUTES A MINISTER?

But why do we speak of the profession of the minister as second to that of the teachers in public schools and other institutions of learning? Let us be understood as saying, 'we do not place this exalted office second because of any preconceived purpose to underate it, but simply on the ground that its opportunity, in our judgment, is second—the competent and conscientious teacher being first to impress the mind with those principles and examples which mould the character and are most lasting. But we had purposed to conclude this theme with a summary of some of the observations we would make to young men concerning the ministry:—

They, the candidates, must have special training in addition to that of the college and theological school; they must possess traits of character unlike the multitude, and it will not profit this generation if they are deep in books and nothing in 'common with everyday life.' They must understand human nature and have the proper methods of approaching widely different minds, else all their efforts will miscarry, and they will be the constant recipient of rebuffs that will rob them of their peace of mind and make their life short and of little service to their fellow men. They must be a connoisseur in the art of knowing just what to say and how and when to say it, for—although they may think otherwise—this is one of the great secrets, in fact the only secret, of the successful man in all professions. They must have a good constitution—for it is a well known fact that a sickly minister preaches sickly sermons, and sickly sermons are not what a healthy people will naturally be satisfied with. Sentiment may satisfy those of a congregation who are at that interesting period of human affairs when cupid is the controlling medium, but it will never do for the old folks who pay the bills. They will cry out that it is veal, and become hungry for something that is largely made up of practical common sense. They must make up their minds to be diligent workers; to submit to privations; to be subjected to occasional persecutions; to be a servant rather than a master; to endure all sorts of trials of their own and for others; to be cheerful when overworked, and of even deportment when afflicted with the ills that flesh is heir to. They must expect to meet with obstinacies in men who profess better things; to be unfavorably criticised by those who should overlook their shortcomings; to be, in short, a public man who has no time to devote to his own whims and fancies. Should a young man enter this profession he will discover strange things regarding human nature, and will often have his faith in men and women put to the severest test.

The young thinkers of this generation will learn, as they develop and discover the ways and manners of this wicked world, that 'all is not gold that glitters;' that if a minister is bold of speech and progressive—if he speak right to the point on the sins and shortcomings that are nearest the doors of his parishioners —he is in danger of empty pews and a hint from a certain clique that his usefulness is greatly impaired. They will also learn that if these things are not mentioned, another offensive clique will circulate the idea that he is a coward, and tries to suit everybody; if he unhesitatingly presents his views on political questions which concern the public weal —and concerning which every right-minded citizen should be gratified for information such as only an observing student can impart—he is in danger of being derisively mentioned as the 'political parson'—'a weak-minded minister turned ignorant statesman;' if he fails to speak, to sound the alarm, to endeavor to persuade men what is right and what God would have them do in the premises, he is berated as a man who halts between two opinions or sympathizes on the wrong side of the question at issue. If he fail to warn his people against the evil—a decreasing evil I am rejoiced to say—of intemperance, he is accused of being the bosom friend of the rumseller, of having rumsellers in his congregation, of taking their ill-gotten gains for the advancement of the cause of religion. If, on the other hand, he earnestly and consistently advocates the cause of temperance and all moral and legal means to crush the demon that seeks the ruin of mankind, he is said to be lacking in good judgment and detracting from the peace and amiability of the community, and, sometimes, is invited to 'step down and out.' If he confines himself closely to the tenets of the gospel, he is an old fogy, and the people cry out for a modern preacher; if he fail to draw a full congregation, he is in trouble with the trustees of his society; if he visits Deacon Brown's family once oftener than he does Deacon Smith's, he is partial; if he is a little reserved and the madams of the parish cannot have their own way, he is made a target for town talk; if he is not all things to all men, and all women, he is not social; if he is all things to all men and women, he is double faced.

They will learn that the times have changed, and this profession is not, as we hinted in the beginning, what it was in the eighteenth century. Free thinkers; free speakers and advanced ideas, together with thoughtlessness and frivolity, the elements of doubt and uncertainty, and the desire to be the most fashionable church in town or city—regardless of pointing to the cross and salvation, and being humble examples of the better way of living—have demoralized the occupants of the pews and thereby inflicted erroneous impressions on the non-churchman's mind. They will understand, therefore, that the clergyman's life has come to be one of trial and long suffering; that patience, forbearance and brotherly love will not prevail except through the well directed efforts of a well balanced mind, and the exercises of a discretionary diplomacy such as few men possess. We would not, however, attempt to persuade any man, who feels that he has a mission to perform, to enter another field. Brave and conscientious men are wanted, and we bid all candidates God's speed and a just reward. Our only caution is 'be sure you enter with the right motive and with a right understanding.' Do not enter with the idea that it is an easy way of earning your living, because of a desire for wealth, or in the belief that it is to be to you a life free from annoyances. It has its hardships and its trials; its triumphs and its rewards. It has its perplexities such as few men can satisfactorily master; its burdensome crosses, and its dark gloomy, and desponding hours, which nothing but a consecrated life can withstand. We are therefore persuaded that he who enters here should pause and consider his way.

THE PHYSICIAN AND SURGEON.

The third useful profession—and we are not sure that it is not the first and most important to the human family—is that of the physician and surgeon. The more we contemplate this profession the more we honor it, and the longer we live the greater is our respect for ninety-nine in every hundred of the men that are in it. We have observed, and it cannot be that we are alone in our observation, that there is no class of men in this community that go about their business with the quiet demeanor that marks the true physician. He meddles little in public matters, and he seldom pauses to tell long stories. He is generally a model man, and there is an honor about him that no other profession possesses. He never remarks unkindly of a rival, nor does he by word or conduct inform the mind of the rabble with explanation or insinuation of the delicate cases of disease or surgery which he has been called to treat. His lips are sealed; his tongue is silent, and we sometimes wonder whether or no he has been conducted into the deep recesses of some gloomy dungeon, and amidst suggestive surroundings and oppressive silence, taken upon himself a more solemn obligation to secrecy and circumspection than any society on earth can boast.

The graduated physician and surgeon is a good and true man. To his skill, to his knowledge, to his honor, men and women implicitly commit themselves. Are we disposed to complain of his charges, a moment's reflection convinces us that an awful responsibility is his. Are we inclined to doubt his coming at our call, the second thought reveals the fact that in his faithfulness—we speak now of ninety-and-nine in a hundred—he outranks the world; for, be it recorded to his praise, he responds to the wail of distress whether it be in the heat of a high-twelve summer sun or the low-twelve of the cold, gloom and darkness of winter, and that, too, in innumerable cases where he knows there is to be no compensation. In him we confide when the days are dark, the nights long, the pain almost unendurable; when hope is but a faint ray, when dear ones are in danger, when distress is upon us. Let him who can cry out 'unfaithful!' The physician has little time of his own, and little time for speculations in which other men indulge. His average comfort—as other men see comfort—is in the main a myth. He is everybody's servant. He is in the mansion at one hour and the cottage the next, and his profession knows no distinction—his teaching and practice no favoritism. Both obtain the best service he can render, and it often occurs that the cottage obtains a discount in his charges.

We have observed that the world would be in a terribly bad way were it otherwise, and hence we take occasion to say that we have no sympathy with that mistaken zeal—as it appears to our understanding—which in any way tends to weaken the esteem in which all right-minded men and women must of necessity hold them. We have no desire, however, to discuss public measures in this article, and so we pause and pass to the consideration of other professions.

THE LAWYER.

The man who 'puts out his sign' in this profession must be an individual who has a well-balanced head, and is 'thick skinned' in the matter of public abuse. There are a good many people, and they are usually those who are two-thirds of the time in a scrape, who cannot command adjectives sufficiently expressive to speak his condemnation. He may be as honest, as conscientious and as pious as any man in the community, and yet there are those who consider and proclaim him a pirate. That he lives and thrives largely by other men's misfortunes and misunderstandings; that his fees for services rendered are generally five times what they ought to be, is true; but that he is worse than the average of his fellow men is not true. We have observed, however, that men who are never so happy as when they are 'head over heels' in a law suit—and there are a good many such

—are not entitled to a great amount of sympathy, and we opine that they should not complain bitterly about lawyers. Those people who have no scrapes, who do not trespass on their neighbors, who, if their neighbors trespass upon them are not angered to revenge, or 'mad,' past becoming pleased, and in a condition of mind that forgives all the world at evening prayer, should not complain, except perhaps, when they aspire to office of honor, trust or profit, and find an attorney and counsellor at law ready to fill the bill to their exclusion. But we are not kindly disposed, enthusiastically speaking, towards lawyers, and therefore cannot be expected to give them the character we award to a professional teacher or clergyman. There is a good deal about the profession that we do not like. Lawyers are clanish. They 'tickle' and 'feed' each other, and are 'deaf, dumb and blind' to the pockets of other professions. To use a slang phrase, 'they know too much' for men who are not burdened so heavily with knowledge as by cheek; but, inasmuch as we have no purpose or desire to offend, we will not particularize. Suffice it to be said that it is our observation and experience that a barrister can serve God and Mammon more successfully than the multitude. His is not, however, as bad as the average mind pictures him, and even among our friends and acquaintance there are worthy and honorable exceptions from the rule that marks the profession as one to be dodged by that man who hopes to live a life acceptable to himself and the community.

THE JOURNALIST.

In this profession there is less money and more trouble and torment to the mind and body than all others combined. The journalist serves a wicked and perverse generation, and sees more of the shams and meanness of men than any of his compeers. He is bounded on all sides by critics, and is every day making the acquaintance of idiots, who, with more cheek than brains, flatter themselves that they—who have spent their lives in some other calling—are more competent in the matter of editing a newspaper than he who has devoted a quarter of a century to the profession. He is annoyed by ignorance that assumes intelligence, and if he avoids a discussion on some issue that in his judgment is in the interest of an individual rather than the public, it is hinted that he has been bought; if he denounces evil and unfairness he is meddlesome and malicious; if a free puff is denied he is mean; if a free puff is given, the person who receives it thinks he has only obtained what he is entitled to because of his great merit, and sometimes he comes around to find fault because it was not stated a good deal stronger; if he pursues a course in politics that he believes most advantageous for patriotic and party ends, the men who should give support turn their noses in condemnation. A journalist is expected to denounce, politically, his best friend, and to compliment a party man, politically again, and that, too, when the 'denouncing and complimenting' is of no more consequence to him as an individual than a copy of a last year's almanac. He is expected to praise everything—be it good, bad or indifferent, professional or amateur—and he is certain that the man of whom he is compelled, in order to maintain his equilibrium before the public, to speak censorious, will curse him, even though the same individual has been favorably mentioned in his newspaper writings ninety-nine times, for which the person thus complimented has never bestowed the poverty of his thanks. And then, if he is a live journalist, he is always writing and publishing something that some pious soul does not like, and is receiving calls from good people who want their neighbor shown up, and a promise that he will not mention the source of his information. He is bothered by typographical errors, assailed by his political opponent, hated by those who have cases in the criminal court, annoyed by those who are not reported every time they open their mouths, and in danger of a club or law suit from some one whose merit is not appreciated. In short, the journalist is a victim of men's spleen, and he must be a man of temper like a dove, and a constitution like an ox,

MEN AND THEIR PROFESSIONS.

or make his arrangements to be with the angels at forty.

POLITICIANS AND SPORTING-MEN.

Both are professions—we guess—and both are to be given the 'cut direct' by all men who have made up their minds that salvation, at the end of life, is desirable. Not that all will be 'lost,' but that the 'chances' are nine out of ten in favor of it. The 'professor of politics' needs no special notice in New Hampshire. He is an ever present individual, and what he don't know—unless he is mightily mistaken, and he never will admit as much—no magazine writer can tell. The professor of the art of gambling—for that is what constitutes a sporting man's career—may be briefly mentioned.' His ways are devious, dark and damning. He is the jackal of society that does more mischief than the church can counteract. He seeks the ruin of the body, the peace of mind and the soul of his victim, and, alas, too often accomplishes his purpose. He prospers for a time, but the end is invariably terrible to contemplate. He is the abhorrence of all men—even those who are not particular in morals—the culprit who gives the police the greatest uneasiness, the despised of the community, the forsaken of God, the hated and ignored of virtuous women. And more than all, this bleareyed loafer, this would-be important gentleman, knows that he is under the ban of society, knows that he is a reprobate, a fugitive from justice, a worthless being who preys upon men and morals. Rum and its *et cœtera* ruins his health, and eventually—if he escapes prison, where he rightfully belongs—he dies, to be unmourned and speedily forgotten, save by the victims who live to curse his memory. This is a profession that no young man can contemplate with any degree of satisfaction, or seek to enter unless he has 'made up hi mind' to be useless, and have it said, 'it were better had he never been born.'

THE MERCHANT.

If there is any man in the States that is, and has been for several years past, deserving of sympathy, that man is the merchant, who has had his all—his necessity of the present and his hope of old age—invested in 'stock in trade.' The fall in prices on staple articles, rents, which are at 'war figures,' taxes, which have increased rather than diminished, and customers who do not pay their bills promptly, if at all, have made his life full of trouble and anxiety. In fact, in ninety cases in every hundred, his is a daily anxiety of which the professional man—who enjoys a long summer vacation—knows absolutely nothing by experience. The merchant's nerves are at tension the greater part of the time, and the multiplicity of cares with which he is surrounded robs him of that enjoyment which, in the course of human events, all men who labor are entitled to receive. With notes becoming due, current expenses to meet—be the times never so dull—he often finds himself in fine meshes, and enduring hardships of which the laboring man is entirely ignorant. There is, however, no necessity of minutely depicting the trials of the merchant, for the certainty that he is the man who, in these days of financial embarrassment and uncertainty, 'carries the heavy end of the plank,' is obvious to those to the 'manor born.' Moreover, those who entertain the belief that the merchant is the man who is in the majority at fashionable summer resorts, who spends his money the most freely, will, upon investigation, find themselves deceived. We speak for the average merchants, for we know that while the public school teacher, the clergymen, lawyers and others, have opportunities of 'rest and refreshments' to body and mind, while they may sun themselves at morn and eve and bask in cool seclusion at midday, the merchant and those other 'watchmen on the towers'—the physician and journalist—are mired in business. Those, therefore, who envy the merchant, who imagine that he is the man who has the 'easiest time of it,' who see only the millionaire picture, are mistaken in their estimate.' They should keep their eyes open to obituaries like the following, which we clip from a current number of a well-known newspaper: 'He was for many years the senior partner of the firm and was a prosperous merchant. But adversity and ill health gathered over his way. Afflicted with mental disease, his last years were clouded, and he passed away the victim of care and disappointment, and the object of sympathy.'

THE MERCHANT'S CLERK.

It is due that I should mention the merchant's clerk. The popular belief that his is a life free from the trials, temptations and perplexities of the man who has a trade or tills the soil is an erroneous one. There is no man who is compelled to labor for his daily bread—and all men ought to be compelled to do diligence or go hungry—that has a more disagreeable task. Through summer's heat and winter's cold he is ' cooped up ' behind a counter and is face to face all the day long with customers. Some of these customers know what belongs to good manners, but the greater number behave only a vague idea of ' shopping etiquette,' and are nice, polite and aristocratic in their imagination only. This latter class—and we know enough of human nature to feel confident that there is not a woman in America who will make a personal application of what is here truthfully said—are an unmitigated annoyance, a libel on good breeding, and are liberally hated and emphatically despised by clerks who have no alternative but to shirk them upon their fellows. There is not a merchant's clerk of our acquaintance—we have no fear of contradiction—but can give the names of a hundred persons who are dreaded as the plague and dodged as a timid man would a dog with the hydrophobia. There are other trying ordeals to which clerks are subjected; such as dull days when there is nothing to do but stand around, first on one foot and then on the other, and wait for a storm to clear up and customers to put in an appearance; such as irritable and unreasonable masters; such as insufficient salary to meet their expenses; such as the impossibility to accumulate the wherewith to clothe their family—if they happen to be blessed with one—or pay their tired and need-of-rest wife's expenses to her country home; such as an inability to save a few dollars to pilot them through sickness and support them in their old age. All these things should be considered by country boys who have got the merchant clerk maggot in their crazy heads, and the truth should be stated in all candor that not one in a hundred of those who go behind the counter become ' merchant princes.' It has been our observation that when a business man wants a partner, or is compelled to promote some one, the person who has the preference is a son, brother or individual who is backed by money not his own and who comes to the establishment without experience and with monstrous, overbearing and presuming airs, while the faithful clerk, who has spent his strength to build up the business, is snubbed, and, if the times be a little dull, so that he can not readily find employment elsewhere, is cut down in the matter of salary because the expense of the concern has become greater than the income. These are facts that admit of no cavil, and therefore we say to every young man who is about to become a participant in the struggle for place, consider well the situation. Do not despise the lessons of the experienced or imagine that you are so much smarter than others that you will escape their grievances, for it is not so much in the possibility of success now as it has been in the past.

THE MECHANIC.

Concerning the mechanic, whether he be first, second or third class, much may be said. Were we to speak at length it would be with great respect and sympathy, for we realize that he is indispensable to the world, that much of the prosperity of the people depends upon him, that by his inventions he has conferred blessings that cannot well be estimated, and that just now he is, in consequence of the general depression of business, a victim of low wages and in most cases has a hard chance in the matter of obtaining employment and supporting his family. To discourage young men from learning a trade is a responsibility—even with a full knowledge of the times and the belief that low wages are to continue—that but few men would care to take, and hence we must dodge the subject with the commonplace remark that 'we hope the times will be better, that they will soon be enabled to earn the honest dollar of their daddies and be relieved from the annoyances and embarrassments which now surround them.'

THE FARMER.

Those who have read this article to this caption will not expect 'sound advice;' from us in this paragraph, and although we should chance to 'hit the exact truth,' would be slow to acknowledge it. We will therefore be brief. That farming is hard work is an indisputable fact. That farmers have cares and anxieties we will admit. But farming has, to a large degree, been reduced to a science, and the man who uses the intelligence which is easily obtained succeeds better than those in professions and numerous other callings, and although he may not have so much ready money, he has that which answers the same great purpose and which is about all the multitude can hope for at any time, viz.: 'the creature comforts.' He is also, as a rule, free from embarrassments; is subject to no man's caprice; is in no fear of a sheriff; can have a holiday now and then without losing his pay; and if he is a willing man in the 'seasons,' may place his family beyond the pinching and worryment that come to those who are dependent upon 'quick' or 'glutted' markets. All these possibilities, with many other advantages—such as distance from the temptations of the grog-shop, the society of dead-beats and loafers, the familiarities of vice, and animosities and jealousies—are less, and why, in view of all that has been said and written, there is such an unsolved problem as 'How shall we keep our young people upon the farms?' is beyond our comprehension. We note, however, that multitudes of mechanics, traders and others have become disgusted with the treadmill of their chosen callings and compelled to acknowledge from the 'book of experience' that the most reliable feeder of the family is the soil, and the farmer who 'means business' quite as honorable and more profitable than the average. Therefore, young men, consider well your situation and your opportunity. Let your 'air castles' in which wealth abounds be but the dream in the dark. Let your judgment master the situation. Consider that there are more applicants than places, more blanks than prizes, and if you have a gloomy outlook, stick, make it bright, and by your grit and industry make it pay.

DYER HOOK SANBORN, A. M.

BY REV. SILAS KETCHUM, WINDSOR, CT.

The writer of this sketch was, in 1853 and 1854, a mechanic, working in Hopkinton. In his frequent visits to the stores and post-office he was accustomed to meet the students of old Hopkinton Academy, with Greek and Latin books, an algebra or geometry in their hands, which they were supposed to be studying. Subsequent developments have shown that, in some cases, there was no fact in the supposition. But at that time they seemed to the writer to be of another order of beings. Some of them have since become such—eminently. And the supposed ecstacy of their employment, and profundity of their learning, excited ambitions and aspirations which he then had no means of gratifying or promoting.

The teacher at that time was Prof. Dyer H. Sanborn. To get him from Tubbs Union at Washington was thought by the trustees and townsmen a considerable acquisition. His fame had preceded him, and was probably at that time at its climax, and extensive. An unusual advent of students from abroad was anticipated and realized. So many pupils, it was said, (the writer does not speak from data or personal knowledge) had not attended that institution at one time for many years, as did attend it during Prof. Sanborn's preceptorate; and it is doubtful if so many ever did in any one term afterward.

As the writer was walking home one evening he was accosted by the Professor, to whom he had never before spoken. The popular teacher made enquiry in an easy and kindly way as to the opportunities, position and antecedents of the boy mechanic, and learning that the mechanic was not altogether content to remain as he was, gave him some encouraging words, advised him about his reading, and was the first man who ever showed to him the possibility of pursuing those studies toward which he had looked with longing eyes afar off.

The acquaintance thus begun by the condescension of the Professor was by him encouraged and improved, and eventually ripened into a closer and more intimate friendship than often exists between two of such disparity of years. In the days of his activity many men doubtless enjoyed his confidence, and thoroughly knew him in the various relations which he sustained to society. But during the years of his retirement at Hopkinton, the writer believes there were few men to whom the Professor spoke, of himself, of his history, his affairs and designs, more unreservedly than to himself.

While therefore he feels conscious that he thoroughly understood the man, and appreciated him for not more nor less than he actually was; and esteemed him more highly as he knew him more intimately than the generality of his townsmen; he confesses himself disqualified, by the very circumstances, from attempting an impartial analysis of his character and acquirements.

But Professor Sanborn's life was busy and fruitful, his talents versatile and variously employed. He sustained at different times relations to interests widely diverse and unrelated. His influence with the young of both sexes was marked and unusual. For full fifty years he was an instructor of youth, and at the time he laid down the ferule had had perhaps a greater number under his tuition than any other man in the State. For a generation at least his name was familiar to the people, and the positions he filled, if not eminent, were at least not inconspicuous in public affairs. His personal acquaintance was vast beyond any enumeration. And yet, so far as the writer is aware, no connected history of the laborious services rendered by this man, or the changes that marked his useful career, has ever been put on record.

Of the facts herein brought together some were obtained from an obituary in a Seminary paper printed at Tilton, some from his brother, Prof. E. D. Sanborn of of Dartmouth College, some from an examination of catalogues, registers, masonic proceedings, school reports and other documents, and many were communicated by the gentleman himself in the latter years of his life. He has served his generation and his record is on high. These scanty and partial memoranda may also serve to preserve some knowledge and remembrance of it to the posterity of those who were in early years his pupils, and in after life his friends.

Dyer Hook Sanborn was named for his maternal grandfather, Capt. Dyer Hook of Chichester, formerly (1760) of Kingston, and one of the original proprietors of Wentworth, whose daughter, Hannah, married David E. Sanborn of Gilmanton, and became the mother of three sons who rose to distinction. Of the father, David E., and of the Hon. John S., his youngest son, a slight account is given in the sketch of Prof. Edwin D., GRANITE MONTHLY, I, 289.

Dyer H. was born in Gilmanton, 29 July, 1799; and died in Hopkinton, 14 January, 1871. Brought up on his father's farm, which was a mile square, he was early engaged in the rural pursuits common to the life of a farmer's boy at that period. But having an active and enquiring mind, and being of a feeble constitution, he turned his attention to study and prepared for college at Gilmanton Academy, but for some reason gave up the intention of going to college and never entered.

At the age of seventeen he commenced teaching and taught winter schools for about ten years, in Pittsfield, Deerfield, Gilmanton, Wiscasset, Me., and Amesbury, Mass., working on a farm summers. He had in the mean time married and had bought a place in Gilmanton which he carried on, and served some time as a captain of militia. He then removed to Lynn, Mass., and engaged in teaching as a profession. While there he commenced and pursued a course of medical studies, and it is believed he received the degree of M. D.; but he never practiced medicine.

In 1828 he removed to Marblehead, where he taught for several years. Returning to New Hampshire he became principal of the Academy at Sanbornton Square, and prepared for the press an "Analytical Grammar of the English Language." In its construction he used many of the definitions which had been employed in the Grammar of John L. Parkhurst, published in 1820, for which purpose he purchased and held the copyright of Parkhurst's Grammar; but gave that gentleman credit for all he used, with scrupulous care. His Analytical Grammar was first printed at Concord, in 1836. The sale of the first edition was rapid, and in 1839 it was revised and stereotyped. In 1846 it had gone through eight editions.

In 1833 he received from Waterville College, and in 1841 from Dartmouth College, the honorary degree of Master of Arts.

He also taught at Sanbornton Bridge, now Tilton, and became Professor of Mathematics and of the Natural and Intellectual Sciences in the New Hampshire Conference Seminary, which was then located on the Northfield side of the river. While in this position he formed classes for normal instruction, and published an abridgment of his larger work under the form and title of "Sanborn's Normal School Grammar," Concord, 1846, which passed through eight editions in five years, being extensively used in certain sections of New Hampshire, and probably in other states, till superceded by Weld's. In this appeared the well-known grammatical rhyme, commencing,

A noun's the name of any thing,
As ball, or garden, hoop or swing,

of which he claimed to be the original author.

At what time the writer is not aware, but thinks it was while connected with this institution, Professor Sanborn received ordination and became a local preacher in the Methodist Episcopal Church. He never took an appointment, or belonged to conference, but he often supplied vacant pulpits, in his own and other denominations, and married a great number of people, particularly among his former pupils.

In 1848 he left Sanbornton and was principal of Andover Academy one year, when he became principal of Tubbs Union Academy, Washington, and was appointed School Commissioner of Sullivan County in 1850, serving two years. He also represented Washington in the Constitutional Convention in 1851.

With the fall term of 1853 he entered upon his duties as principal of the Hopkinton Academy. Of his popularity at that time, and of the success of the school under his administration, mention has already been made. He purchased a small place in Hopkinton village which was henceforth his residence during his life. This he took a great delight in adorning and improving, and paid particular attention to the cultivation of the best varieties of grapes, pears and apples.

Having long been a personal friend and political associate of Franklin Pierce, he was offered and accepted a clerkship in the Treasury Department at Washington, under that gentleman's administration, and entered upon his duties in 1855. In 1857 and 1858 he taught a select school in Pittsfield; but receiving the appointment of postmaster of Hopkinton in 1859, in place of Joseph Stanwood, deceased, he never taught any except private pupils afterward. He continued in the office until his death, and was for many years also superintendent of the town schools.

After retiring from the active duties of his profession his former pupils gave him a complimentary reception and benefit, with an elaborate dinner, and literary exercises adapted to the occasion, and as a testimonial of their good faith they presented him a purse of several hundred dollars.

In Freemasonry he was a Knight Templar, and was a chaplain of the Grand Lodge of New Hampshire from 1849 to 1856. He held for many years a commission of Justice of the Peace and Quorum throughout the State, and did considerable justice business. Before the war of the Rebellion he affiliated with the Democratic party; but during and after that war with the Republican.

Professor Sanborn published, besides the books above named, "A Geographical Manual," 1856, and "School Mottoes," 1858. He was a frequent contributor to the *N. H. Journal of Education*, while published, and for various periodicals in and out of the state. He collected with great labor materials for a history of the Sanborn Family, a portion of which he edited and prepared for the press, but did not live to complete the work.

About two years before his decease he experienced a partial paralysis, severely effecting one side, from which he never fully recovered; and although his exit was not unexpected, his final illness was very brief. His second wife survives him, but by neither wife left he any issue.

A HYMN.

BY MARY HELEN BOODEY.

I can but trust in God
  And rest within His arms,
Whether I lie beneath the sod
  Or face life's wild alarms.

In Him is all my joy;
  In Him is all my peace;
I work in His employ.
  And at His bidding cease.

He doeth all things well,
  He loveth every soul;
All things His goodness tell
  And His supreme control.

Father of life and light!
  Being all-wise and kind!
Oh, give me clearer sight
  Who am so weak and blind.

Let me not faint and fail
  Before the close of day,
Oh, let not doubts assail
  The heart that owns Thy sway.

And when my work is done,
  And I am gathered home,
How bright will be the sun!
  How sweet a voice say—Come!

THE TWO LAST SAGAMORES OF NEWICHAWANNOCK

BY W. F. LORD.

[This sketch, from the pen of the historian of Berwick and Somersworth, will be, we believe of sufficient interest to our readers dwelling in the eastern section of the state, as well as to all interested in Indian history, to warrant its republication in the GRANITE MONTHLY.]

Rowles, a noted Sagamore of Newichawannock, during its early settlement by the English, had his domicil on the easterly side of the river near Quampheagen falls. All the Indians from the upper waters of the Newichawannock to the sea were his subjects, though he was under the great Passaconway. His subjects had been greatly diminished by the fearful plague that had flapped its malarious wings along the New England coast, a few years before permanent settlement had been made in Newichawannock.

He possessed the gift of prophesy and predicted to the early settlers the impending bloody conflicts between the Indian and white man. He said "at first the Indian will kill many and prevail but after a few years they will be great sufferers and finally be rooted out and destroyed."

The dwelling place of Rowles upon the banks of the Newichawannock was well chosen for sustenance and picturesque beauty. It was at the head of tide water; the upper waters were not then as now yarded up to be daily parceled out and harnessed to a ponderous mechanism and ladened with the filth of factories and street sewers, but it flowed freely from the crystal lakes, dancing and laughing through the high mossy gorges to the tide water. In their season, countless salmon and migratory fish sported in its crystal waters on their passage to its upper sources; an hour in his light canoe upon a receding tide would take him to the broad Piscataqua which the early explorers found so crowded with delicious fish that they named it Piscataqua (fish water).

Near the soft green meadows on the sligo shore was his small and rudely cultivated cornfield; around him was a dense forest filled with game; near his dwelling were several small moulded hills irrigated by pure, gushing springs, upon whose summit there clustered luscious grapes and sweet and nourishing nuts. At his fireside could be heard the gurgling waters of Assabumbadoc as they fell through the craggy chasm into the fathomless pool.

If he turned to the rising sun he saw old Agamenticus sitting upon the rim of the ocean, the pulpit of the Great Spirit, where their traditions taught them He came down concealed in the great storm cloud to watch the angry moods of the ocean. If he turned to the setting sun he saw towering above the forest, draped in hazy veils, the long chain of mountains that brace up the valley of the Merrimack, the home of Passaconaway, his great lord and master,

"Who could change the seared and yellow leaf
To bright and living green."

Ferdinando Gorges had by royal favor obtained a charter of all the land in the western part of Maine, where he hoped to build up an empire for his prosperity. He founded the Agamenticus plantation in 1623; within its limits was Newichawannock. He sent over scores and hundreds of tenants and servants. Some having no taste for agriculture were early attracted by the excellent timber that grew upon the banks of the Newichawannock and its wonderful facilities for the manufacture and transportation of lumber.

In 1643 Humphrey Chadbourne, for a pittance, purchased the homestead of Rowles, the land on which the village of

South Berwick now stands. Seven years later Gov. Godfrey and council granted to Richard Leaders, Assabumbadoc falls and adjacent lands. Dams and mills were erected there, and at Quampheagen and Salmon Falls. The forests melted away, the game disappeared and migratory fish could no longer ascend the river. Every means on which Rowles and his people had relied for support had been swept away.

In 1670, five years before the commencement of the Indian wars. Rowles being bedridden with age and sickness, complained of the great neglect with which he had been treated by the English. At length he sent a messenger to some of the principal men of Newichawannock to make him a visit. He told them "he was loaded with years and that he expected a visit in his infirmities from those who were now tenants on the land of his fathers. Though all of these plantations are of right my children's, I am forced in this age of evil, humbly to request a few hundred acres of land to be marked out and recorded for them upon the town books as a public act, so that when I am gone they will not be perishing beggars in the pleasant places of their birth."

This modest request of the dying Rowles was deemed of sufficient importance to be attested to by Major Waldron and others, but it was never granted. Rowles passed away beyond the setting sun, leaving no inheritance for his children in the places of their birth.

His son and successor, Blind Will—who received that name from having lost one eye—regarding the premonitory counsel of his father with sacred respect, at the commencement of the King Philip war, about 1675, he entered the English service where he remained two years, or until his death. Although sometimes distrusted by his comrades because he had a red skin he always proved himself loyal to the English and is spoken of by the early historians as a Sagamore of note and ability. He became the trusted friend of Maj. Waldron, accompanied him on various expeditions against the Indians and acted as pilot in the expedition to Ossipee lakes.

After the English made an alliance with the "Mohawks" against the Eastern tribes, strange Indians were reported to be in the vicinity of Cochecho. Maj. Waldron sent Blind Will with a company to ascertain who they were. The "Mohawks" mistaking them for enemies rushed upon them and only three escaped. Blind Will was dragged away by his hair and perished in the woods at the confluence of the Isinglass and Chochecho rivers in the south-west part of Rochester. a short distance above the line between Rochester and Dover. This location still bears the name of "Blind Will's Neck," and the old inhabitants in that locality will point out the spot where he was buried, and some of them insist that they have heard his "war-whoop" as they pass it with their teams in the midnight hour. Few of the subjects of Rowles remained long in the valley of the Newichawannock after his death. A century ago one had his home on the banks of Worster's river, near the Newichawannock, by the name of Sunset, a suggestive name. He was buried in an unmarked grave in the old Worster burying ground and not a ray of twilight from the departed race lingers in the pleasant places of their birth.

THE GRANITE MONTHLY.

A MAGAZINE OF LITERATURE, HISTORY AND STATE PROGRESS.

VOL. II. NOVEMBER, 1878. NO. 4.

GEN. NATT HEAD.

Passing up the romantic valley of the Merrimack, that queen of New England rivers, the nursing mother of our greatest industries as well as the brightest adornment of our most beautiful landscapes, the traveler observes, when nearly midway between Hooksett and Suncook, upon the table-land, commanding an extensive view of the valley in either direction, an elegant and spacious brick mansion which seldom fails to attract more than mere passing notice. It is indeed one of the finest country residences in New England, the elegance as well as the substantial comfort and convenience of its interior appointments fully bearing out the promise of its exterior. This mansion is the residence of one of New Hampshire's self-made men —men who through the avocations of manual labor and the stirring discipline of business life have won their way to competence and honor—commanding the confidence of their fellow citizens as manifested in their elevation through the suffrages of the people to positions of trust and responsibility.

Here lives Gen. Natt Head, whom the people of New Hampshire at the recent election—the first holden under the amended constitution—selected for their chief magistrate for the term of two years from June next.

Gen. Head is a descendant of Nathaniel Head, who, with his brother John, came from Wales to America and settled in Bradford, Mass., but subsequently removed to Pembroke in this State. He had three sons, Nathaniel, James and Richard. The former was the grandfather of the subject of our sketch. In the history of Chester, by Benjamin Chase, it is related of him that in his youth he paid his addresses to a young lady of Scotch-Irish descent named Knox, a daughter of one of the leading families of the town. Between these families there was a feeling of hostility. While driving the cattle in the field for his father one day the old gentleman asked young Nathaniel if he intended to marry that Irish girl. "Yes, father," was the reply. "Then understand," said he, "you can never share in my property." "Very well," said the youth, "I will take care of myself," and dropping his goad-stick in the furrow, he left the field and his home, and went out to make his own way in the world. He served for a time in the Revolutionary army and attained the rank of Captain. Having married the young lady of his choice, Anna Knox, he established his home in a log cabin in that part of the old town of Chester now embraced in Hooksett, upon the very site now occupied by the residence of his grandson. He prospered in life and accumulated a handsome property. He was a man of great energy and independence of character, as well as sound practical judgment, and, holding the position of Justice of the Peace, as well as the confidence of the people throughout the community, he became practically the lawyer for all the surrounding region, and was largely engaged in the settlement of disputes and the transaction of legal business for his neighbors and townsmen. He had nine children, five sons and four daughter. Of these, Samuel, the eldest, was the proprietor of the celebrated "Head Tavern" in Hooksett. John, the youngest of the five sons, and the father of the subject of our sketch, remained upon the homestead. He married, in 1791, Anna Brown, a daughter of William Brown, a retired sea captain, and sister of Hon. Hiram Brown, the first mayor of Manchester, now a resident of Virginia, and father of the wife of Hon. Isaac W. Smith of the Supreme Court. He became an influential citizen of the town, was a successful farmer, and engaged in the manufacture and sale of lumber. He was prominent in the militia, and attained the rank of Colonel. He died in middle life, August, 1836, leaving five children to the care of his widow, a woman of rare mental powers, and executive ability surpassing most men, who proved herself fully equal to the task of administering the large estate, and managing and even enlarging the extensive business in which her husband had been engaged, as well as rearing her children to become true and earnest men and women, and valuable members of society.

NATT HEAD was the eldest son, and third child, two sisters being older and two brothers younger than himself. The eldest of the sisters married the late Col. Josiah Stevens, formerly of Concord, who died in Manchester a few years since; while the younger, now deceased, was the wife of Hall B. Emery of Pembroke. The eldest of his two brothers, John A. Head, has resided many years at the West, and is now Auditor of Broome County, Iowa. He was for some time engaged as a contractor in the construction of the Northwestern railroad, and subsequently several years Superintendent of the Iowa division of that road. The youngest brother, William F., still resides in Hooksett, living in a substantial residence not far from that of Natt; the two having all along been in partnership in the various operations in which they have been engaged, farming, lumbering, brick-making, contracting, etc., or rather they have done business in common, never dividing a dollar, but each using what he needed or pleased, the interest of the other brother and sisters having been purchased by Natt when he became of age. His father died when Natt was but eight years old, and the advantages afforded by the district school, supplemented by a few terms attendance at Pembroke Academy, furnished all the education he secured, aside from that obtained through discipline of active life, in the various departments of labor and of business in which he has been engaged. Few men in the State are more extensively engaged in agricultural operations, and certainly no one has done more to promote the interests of the cause of agriculture. The Head farm contains some two hundred acres of cultivated land, upon which is cut, annually, from two hundred to two hundred and fifty tons of hay. Altogether, the brothers own some fifteen hundred acres of land, which includes several valuable tracts of timber land in other towns, one of 600 acres lying in the town of Groton.

The lumber business in which their father was engaged has been continued, from 500,000 to 1,000,000 feet of lumber being manufactured annually at their mills. As manufacturers of brick, however, they have attained their greatest celebrity, their business in this line being the most extensive in the State, and the quality of their brick unsurpassed. This business was commenced by their mother after her husband's decease, soon after the beginning of mill building at Manchester, which opened a ready market for vast quantities of this valuable building material, for the manufacture of which the extensive beds of superior clay along the river at this point afford superior facilities. They manufacture from three to six millions of brick per annum, selling the same in all parts of New England. Ten millions were furnished by them for the construction of the new Massachusetts State Prison at Concord, and several millions for the Lawrence Water Works. In their extensive operations of farming, lumbering and brick-making, altogether, the brothers Head give constant employment to nearly two hundred men, with thirty horses and several yokes of oxen, all of which are kept on the farm, upon which there are also more than a dozen dwellings, occupied by the families of those of their workmen who have been long in their employ.

Aside from, or supplementary to, the extensive business already mentioned, Gen. Head has been largely engaged upon contracts for the construction of railroads and of buildings. A large portion of the work on the Suncook Valley railroad was done by him, as well as much upon other roads. The firm of Head & Dowst, contractors and builders, of Manchester, well known as among the most extensive building firms of the city, embraces the General and his brother, whose enterprise, energy, and ample resources have contributed largely to the success of the firm.

Gen. Head inherited from his ancestors a strong taste for military affairs, which, with musical talents of high order, early led him into prominence as a military musician. He became leader of the Hooksett Brass Band at sixteen years of age. This, by the way, was the first band that ever played in the city of Manchester, its first visit being on the occasion of a grand Fourth of July celebration at Amoskeag in 1844, the first year of his leadership. He was subsequently, for a number of years, a member of the Manchester Cornet Band. In 1847 he became fife major in the Eleventh Regiment of the State Militia, and served four years in that capacity. He was also chief bugler in the celebrated organization known as the Governor's Horse Guards. He has been many years an active member of the Amoskeag Veterans, and commanded that famous battalion four years, from 1869 to 1872, inclusive. He is also a member of the Ancient and Honorable Artillery of Boston, and an honorary member of the Boston Lancers.

In the position of Adjutant General of the State, to which he was appointed by Gov. Gilmore in 1864, and which he held until 1870, Gen. Head may truly be said to have won his greatest reputation, as well as the lasting regard of a large portion of our people, especially the soldier element. He came into the administration of this office at a time when its duties were manifold and great, and to their proper fulfilment constant and varied effort and executive ability of high order were absolutely essential. It is but just to say that he gave his best energies to the work of the office, and although finding its affairs in a most unsatisfactory and perplexing condition, by constant and persevering effort he placed the same in systematic order. In Waite's "New Hampshire in the Rebellion," it is said of Gen. Head, referring to his administration of this office, "that on assuming its duties he found the department very incomplete, but little matter having been collected relating to the outfit of the troops and their achievements in the field, although New Hampshire had, up to that time, sent to the war twenty-six thousand soldiers. In fact, not a complete set of muster-in rolls of any regiment could be found in the office. In the face of these obstacles and discouragements, and with no appropriation to draw from, Gen. Head at once entered upon the duties of his position, employing upon his own responsibility three clerks, and procuring the necessary outfit of the office, trusting in the Legislature to reimburse him, which it not only promptly and cheerfully did, but made all additional appropriations for the department that were asked for. During the remainder of the war no State in the Union had a more faithful, efficient and popular Adjutant General than New Hampshire. The clerical duties of the office were performed in an admirable manner, and the method by which the records of our soldiers were persistently hunted up and placed on file, and the order and system exhibited in carrying on and preserving the extensive and valuable correspondence of the department were worthy of the highest praise." The reports of the department during Gen. Head's administration of the office are voluminous and complete, embracing the record of every officer and soldier who entered the service of the State during the war, with a sketch of the history and operations of each of the several regiments, and also embodying a complete military history of New Hampshire from the first settlement of the province to the outbreak of the Rebellion. The preservation and arrangement of the battle-flags of the New Hampshire regiments, in the rotunda of the State House, is one of the numerous evidences of Gen. Head's thoughtful care in the administration of this office.

Aside from his experience in the Adjutant General's office, Gen. Head has been considerably engaged in public affairs. He has served his town most efficiently in various official capacities, and was a representative therefrom in the Legislature for the years 1861 and 1862. He was a candidate for the State Senate in old District No. Two, in 1875, when the famous controversy over the spelling of his name upon the ballots occurred, and was elected to the Senate from that District the following year, and re-elected in 1877, when he was chosen President of the Senate, and discharged the duties of the office acceptably and efficiently.

For several years past the friends of Gen. Head in the Republican party have advocated his nomination as a candidate for Governor, and at the Convention in January, 1877, when Gov. Prescott was nominated, he received a very flattering vote, leading all candidates except Prescott. This fact, along with his universal popularity, gave his name such prestige before the Convention in September last, that, although the friends of Hon. Charles H. Bell made a vigorous effort, aided by a large proportion of the party press throughout the State, to secure the nomination of that gentleman, Gen. Head was nominated by a decided majority upon the first ballot, and, although on account of the third party, or so-called Greenback movement, it was scarcely expected by his most sanguine friends that he would be chosen by the popular vote, he received a majority of four hundred and eighty-eight votes over all, and will succeed Gov. Prescott in the gubernatorial chair, if he lives until June next. It is safe to remark in this connection that no man, not even excepting Gov. Prescott himself, has ever entered upon the duties of the executive office in New Hampshire with a more extensive acquaintance with the people, or a more intimate knowledge of their practical wants and requirements than Gen. Head enjoys.

He is one of the Directors of the Suncook Valley Railroad, in which enterprise he was one of the active movers. He is also a Director of the New Hampshire Fire Insurance Company, and President of the China Savings Bank at Suncook. He has been a member of the N. H. Historical Society for ten or twelve years past, and has taken a strong interest in its work and progress. He is also an active member of the Manchester Art Association. In Free Masonry he is both active and prominent, being a member of Washington Lodge, Mt. Horeb Royal Arch Chapter, Adoniram Council and Trinity Commandery of Manchester. He is also a member of the Supreme Council, having received all the degrees of the Ancient and Accepted Scottish Rite, and all in the Rite of Memphis to the 94th. He was recently made an honorary member of the "Mass Consistory S∴ P∴ R∴ S∴ 32° Boston." He is also a member of the Independent Order of Odd Fellows, belonging to Friendship Lodge of Hooksett and Hildreth Encampment of Suncook. Aside from these connections, he is a member of Oriental Lodge, Knights of Pythias, and Alpha Lodge, Knights of Honor, of Manchester, and Excelsior Temple, of Concord; is a member of Pinnacle Lodge of Good Templars at Hooksett, and Master of Hooksett Grange of the the Patrons of

Husbandry, which organization he was one of the pioneers in forming.

As Director and President of the State Agricultural Society, which latter position he has held constantly since 1868, Gen. Head has labored zealously to promote the welfare of the farming interest in the State, and the success which has attended the annual exhibitions of the Society proves conclusively that his efforts have not been in vain. He originated the movement looking to the holding of Farmers' Conventions in New Hampshire, the first holden in the State, and we believe the first in the country, having been gotten up at Manchester in 1868, mainly through his efforts and under his direction. At this meeting prominent friends of agriculture throughout New England and New York were present and made addresses, and much was done to give fresh impetus to agricultural progress in the State. In 1869 he was appointed by the Governor and Council one of the Trustees of the State Agricultural College.

Gen. Head was united in marriage, Nov. 18, 1863, with Miss Abbie M. Sanford of Lowell, Mass., by whom he has had three children, two of whom, both daughters—Annie twelve and Alice eight years of age—are living. He is now just fifty years of age, having been born May 20, 1828, and is in the full prime of his physical and mental powers. That he may live long, not only to enjoy the comforts and honors which he has won by his constant and varied labors and faithful discharge of duty, but also to render the State and his fellow-men many more years of valuable service, is the hope of his thousands of friends in all parts of the Granite State, and beyond her borders.

BIRTHPLACE OF GEN. STARK.

[The following article was recently published as a communication in the Boston Journal. Since its publication the correctness of the writer's assertion has been questioned by the Manchester Mirror, which paper states that a great-granddaughter of Gen. Stark—Mrs. N. E. Morrill—is now living in that city, and that she knows it to have been generally understood in her childhood, that her illustrious ancestor, whom she well remembers, was born upon the Atlantic Ocean during his mother's passage to this country. That his early childhood was passed in the territory now known as Derry, is unquestionably true, and probably upon the spot described by the writer.]

Seven cities of Greece contended for the honor of Homer's birthplace. More than half this number of towns are emulous of the honor of having given to the world New Hampshire's greatest hero. Londonderry, Derryfield, Derry, the mythical Nutfield and substantial Manchester, are by various authorities assigned as the place where John Stark first saw the light of day. Edward Everett, in his biography of Stark, solemnly gives Nutfield as his birthplace, the truth being that there never was any Nutfield for anybody to be born in. That was as unreal a name as "Molly Stark," though both were properly used on occasion.

Now a familiarity with Everett's biography of Gen. Stark is as much a part of a New Hampshire boy's education as the Ten Commandments and Lord's Prayer. It ought to be just as familiar to every boy in the whole country; but Everett, in that case, needs to be as correct as Scripture itself. As now printed he certainly is not. A brief recital of the history of the naming of these different towns will set this matter right and clear up the confusion now existing as to the birthplace of Gen. Stark. There was an indefinite and extensive tract of land in the region of what is now Manchester, and to the southeast of it, called before it was settled by the whites, Nutfield, on account of the abundance of walnuts, chestnuts and butternuts which it produced. The original settlers of Londonderry, arriving on this tract in 1719, called their settlement after this familiar name; but when Stark was born, in 1728, a town had been incorporated, which they named Londonderry from their old home of that name in Ireland, they having come from Scotland through Ireland to America. The settlers, previous to their incorporation as a town in 1722, had organized for mutual government and protection, and this organization was called Nutfield, but it was never a town for any purpose of taxation or for holding town meetings.

Londonderry as incorporated in 1722 was a very much larger tract of land than is now covered by its territory. In 1751 Derryfield was chartered, being formed from parts of Londonderry and Chester and the whole of Hurrytown. In 1810 the name Derryfield was changed to Manchester, and in 1846 Manchester became a city, parts of other towns being added to it afterward. In 1742 the parish of Windham was incorporated by the Provincial Assembly from the territory of Londonderry, a part of which was afterward annexed to Salem, and the rest became the present town of Windham. A part of Hudson once belonged to Londonderry, though it is not intended here to narrate in full the partition of Londonderry. It is enough to add that in 1827 Derry was set off and became a town by itself, and that it was in what is now Derry that Stark was born. Not unfairly, though, can all the places named, and possibly more, claim something of the prestige which properly attaches to the birthplace of so distinguished a character as General Stark proved to be. Mr. Everett needs not to be corrected when he says of the services of General Stark that they were of the highest character and of an importance not easily surpassed, those of Washington excepted, "by any achievements of any other leader in the army of the Revolution."

A visit to Derry was recently made by the writer, a resident of Bennington, Vermont, and, of course, interested in everything connected with the hero of the battle of Bennington, a short account of which may interest the readers of The Journal. Through the kindness of the corresponding secretary of the old Londonderry Historical and Antiquarian Society—one of those modest and useful societies which are doing so much to preserve our early history—he found himself on one of these bright autumnal mornings, in company with a descendant of Stark, residing in Manchester, at the Windham station of the Manchester and Lawrence railroad, ready to take conveyance to the southwestern part of Derry near that section of the town known as "Derry Dock." The historic spot of Stark's birthplace is on the farm of Mr. John H. Low, and is about two miles from the Windham depot on a road running east of and parallel, or nearly so, with the Londonderry turnpike. It is a short distance, say one quarter of a mile, north of the crossing of the Nashua & Rochester Railroad, on the left side of the road, in a wooded nook, a secluded and romantic spot, facing extensive meadows—probably the very meadows where a marauding party from Massachusetts were put to route by the early settlers, headed by their minister, a true McGregor, who did no discredit on this occasion to the fighting qualities of the noted Highland chieftain of whose country he was and whose name he bore.

As these meadows were a part of the "one thousand acre wildernesse farme" which Massachusetts granted to her Gov. Leverett, inhabitants of Massachusetts claimed and exercised the right to mow them. Hence the dispute, which with the Scotch-Irish refugees in possession, could result in but one way.

A ravine runs up from the road on each side of the place where the house stood. The site itself is plainly marked by the cellar walls, which are almost intact. A pine tree a foot and a half in diameter grows up out of the cellar; a large elm spreads its graceful branches just behind, and the remnants of an apple orchard are scattered about among the frequent chestnut, walnut and other trees which more than half cover the place. The house evidently faced not to the road but to the south. In what was its front is a large rock on which, after a survey of the spot and its surroundings, we partook of a lunch provided for us by our host. With a wise forethought our antiquarian caterer had appropriately brought with him a cork-screw of an antique manufacture, found on the battle-field of Bennington, and doubtless once the property of an officer captured or killed in the battle. With this he drew the cork from a bottle of rare old cider, the contents of which were even more appropriately offered us in a wine glass which once was "Molly Stark's." We had read of the nectar drank at the banquetting tables of the gods, but what was that to a glass of foaming New England cider—the cup that cheers but not inebriates—quaffed at the birthplace of John Stark, from a glass that once his own hand had filled; filled, too, from his own decanter, and perhaps a decanter of that old Tobago rum which John Langdon gave to raise funds for the Bennington campaign; or perhaps of that which Stark himself ordered from Charlestown, Number Four, as a part of his ammunition with which he fought and won the Bennington victory. It will be remembered in explanation, that Stark, at Charlestown, on the Connecticut river, discovered that rum—so necessary in those days to any great undertaking—was scarce where he was going, and ordered a supply to be forwarded. It was forwarded and used.

The attention of the artist should be called to this spot, full of such historic interest. As there is no house upon it now, and as aside from its associations it possesses a beauty of its own, the continuance of which in this world of change cannot be assured, no time should be lost in obtaining a sketch. Its authenticity as the birthplace of Stark is believed to be beyond question. As time goes on, and the past recedes further and further from our view, the value of all such places identified with our early times is proportionately enhanced, and it is therefore important that their exact locality be securely fixed, and their appearance transferred to canvas and preserved.

We lingered about the place for a short time enjoying in addition to what of the past the occasion had brought us, the fine Indian summer day which nature had given us for our visit. Then, turning away, we journeyed on through Derry, the upper village of which gave us a magnificent view of an extended prospect, Wachusett, Monadnock and Kearsarge, with the wide expanse of country between being all embraced in the range of vision at the same time. A charming day, and one long to be remembered, was ended, after parting with our kind host, by a short ride to Manchester, and by one of us, at least—to bring him back to the nineteenth century—a political meeting in the evening.   C. M. B.

CONTOOCOOK RIVER.

BY EDNA DEAN PROCTOR.

[This poem is from "Light at Eventide," a paper made up of contributions from New Hampshire authors and writers of note, and published in aid of the "Home for the Aged," a charitable institution projected at Concord.]

Of all the streams that seek the sea
By mountain pass, or sunny lea,
Now where is one that dares to vie
With clear Contoocook, swift and shy?
Monadnock's child, of snow drifts born,
The snows of many a winter morn,
And many a midnight dark and still,
Heaped higher, whiter, day by day,
To melt, at last, with suns of May,
And steal, in tiny fall and rill,
Down the long slopes of granite gray;
Or, filter slow through seam and cleft

When frost and storm the rock have reft,
To bubble cool in sheltered springs
Where the lone red-bird dips his wings,
And the tired fox that gains its brink
Stoops, safe from hound and horn, to drink.
And rills and springs, grown broad and deep,
Unite through gorge and glen to sweep
In roaring brooks that turn and take
The over-floods of pool and lake,
Till, to the fields, the hills deliver
Contoocook's bright and brimming river!

O have you seen, from Hillsboro town
How fast its tide goes hurrying down,
With rapids now, and now a leap
Past giant boulders, black and steep,
Plunged in mid water, fain to keep
Its current from the meadows green?
But, flecked with foam, it speeds along;
And not the birch trees silvery sheen,
Nor the soft lull of whispering pines,
Nor hermit thrushes, fluting low,
Nor ferns, nor cardinal flowers that glow
Where clematis, the fairy, twines,
Can stay its course, or still its song;
Ceaseless it flows till, round its bed,
The vales of Henniker are spread,
Their banks all set with golden grain,
Or stately trees whose vistas gleam—
A double forest in the stream;
And, winding 'neath the pine-crowned hill
That overhangs the village plain,
By sunny reaches, broad and still,
It nears the bridge that spans its tide—
The bridge whose arches low and wide
It ripples through—and should you lean
A moment there, no lovelier scene
On England's Wye, or Scotland's Tay,
Would charm your gaze, a summer's day.

And on it glides, by grove and glen,
Dark woodlands, and the homes of men,
With now a ferry, now a mill;
Till, deep and calm, its waters fill
The channels round that gem of isles
Sacred to captives' woes and wiles,
And, gleeful half, half eddying back,
Blend with the lordly Merrimack;
And Merrimack whose tide is strong
Rolls gently, with its waves along,
Monadnock's stream that, coy and fair,
Has come, its larger life to share,
And, to the sea, doth safe deliver
Contoocook's bright and brimming river!

Brooklyn, N. Y.

THE WIDOW'S MISTAKE.

BY HELEN M. RUSSELL.

The widow Montgomery's snug little house was looking its best. The "Fall cleaning" was all completed, and from the kitchen to the attic everything was as neat as two energetic hands could make it—while the widow herself, dressed in a neat home suit of brown alpaca, stood watching, from the sitting-room window, the dead leaves which were blown about by the chill November wind. She was a happy looking little woman, with jet black hair and eyes, and an unmistakable air of gentility about her. The time had been when she was the petted daughter of wealthy parents, but the wealth had "taken wings,"—the fond parents had died, and she had married Alvin Montgomery, a plain carpenter, for the sake of a home, and because she knew he loved her. In short, she "married in haste to repent at leisure." The young husband had built the cottage and taken his bride home soon after their marriage, and Hattie Montgomery had tried hard to be content; but she found this life very different from what had once been hers, and when death stepped into the home circle and took from thence her husband, she could not mourn with any deep and lasting grief. It is true she missed him, and really mourned for him, because she thought it her duty so to do, and because he had always been kind to her, but when she laid aside her robes at the end of a year, people said she laid aside her regrets likewise. Whether she did or not is nothing to me—I have only to tell her story in the fewest words possible. Just across the way from the widow's cottage stood a large white house, with long piazzas and deep bay windows, which quite threw into the shade the little cottage in question, but Mrs. Montgomery cared little for this. To be sure, she worked hard, and the sewing machine was seldom allowed to remain idle long at a time, but she somehow managed to find time to read her favorite books and practice her favorite selections upon the piano, which was the only memento she possessed of olden days. She also found time to build castles in the air, which, like all castles of a similar nature, tumbled to pieces as soon as they were built.

There was one thing which Mrs. Montgomery particularly disliked, and that was matchmaking. "In ten cases out of a hundred such marriages proved unhappy," she often declared, and as her own marriage was reckoned in with the hundred, she evidently knew whereof she spoke. It *is* a pity that people cannot find pleasure of a less questionable character. There are unhappy marriages enough which people enter into of their own free will, without those which are, in one sense of the word, directly brought about by interested parties, who, when they discover the evil they have wrought, lift their hands in surprise and exclaim: "Well, I am sure I am not to blame. I told him [or her] to consider everything, and then do as he [or she] thought best, and if they really decided to marry, never to blame *me* if the marriage proved otherwise than happy." Of course they are not to blame—no one would think of blaming them; and they can go on their way with a clear conscience, and perhaps do the same thing over again, and, quite as likely as not, with the same result. In spite of her horror of matchmaking, however, Mrs. Montgomery had a scheme in her little head that she thought a very wise one. In the great house across the way, previously mentioned, lived Lester Pierce. He was a bachelor somewhere in the forties, wealthy, handsome and honorable, a noble specimen of what a man should be. For over ten years he had lived there alone, with the exception of his housekeeper and her husband, and although he bore his years lightly, the silver was beginning to creep into the brown hair and long silken beard. "Time he had a wife," the little widow had said many times to herself, and if he was not disposed to help himself to one, why, she would try and select one for him, only it must be brought about very quietly.

In the city of L——. lived her only brother. He had once been quite wealthy, but the hard times and sudden failures had swept away his property, and now, with a sick wife and family of seven children, he found life to be a round of toil and trouble. His eldest child, a daughter, was very beautiful—so at least thought the widow when she received a letter containing an account of her brother's misfortunes, together with a photograph of her niece, Ida Hartwell, and there at once sprang up in her wise little head a scheme whereby she could secure a home for Ida—and a wife for Lester Pierce. Not for worlds would she have had either party think she was matchmaking, however, so she decided to write and invite Ida to pass the winter with her. The letter had been written, dispatched and answered, the invitation accepted, and she was now awaiting the arrival of the train upon which she expected her neice to come.

"It is time I was on my way to the depot," soliloquized Mrs. Montgomery at length, turning away from the window, and placing upon her head a brown velvet hat, and throwing over her shoulders a warm shawl. "I hope I shall like Ida, and I hope Lester Pierce will like her, too. It will be so nice to have a relative live so near me. Oh, how cold it is!" she exclaimed, as she left the house, locking the front door securely behind her.

A brisk walk of a quarter of a mile brought her to the depot just as the cars steamed slowly up to the platform. Hurrying forward, she eagerly scanned every face as the passengers alighted one by one. At length she saw the sweet face of her niece, and in a moment more she had taken the small hands in her own and welcomed her in the most cordial manner.

"Are you my Aunt Hattie?" questioned the softest, sweetest voice Mrs. Montgomery had ever heard.

"Yes, Ida, and I am so glad to see you. Come this way and we will find your trunk. Have you a check?"

"Yes, here it is, Auntie," replied the girl, as she hastened to assist her aunt in securing her baggage.

Fifteen minutes later and Mrs. Montgomery, Ida and the baggage were snugly ensconced in the little cottage, having been transferred there by the "hotel team," and the widow silently contemplated her niece as she helped to remove the girl's wrappings. She was very lovely, with an innocent, doll-like expression in the pure young face. Rings of sunny hair rippled away from the somewhat low forehead, and hung down over her slender shoulders. Her eyes were dark blue, with a merry, roguish light in their depths. Her face was quite pale—too colorless for perfect health, thought the widow, as she bustled about to prepare refreshments for her guest.

"I am so glad you sent for me, Aunt Hattie. I mean to be as happy as the day is long here with you. You must let me assist you, so that I shall not feel myself a burden to you, and then I can stay as long as I like, can I not?"

"Indeed, what can you do to assist me, my dear? Your company will more than repay me if I like you as well as I think I will," returned her aunt, as she led the way to the cosy dining room, where a delicious supper awaited them.

"Oh, Aunt Hattie, how nice and pleasant it is here!" said Ida, when the window shades were at length drawn, the lamp lighted, and they had seated themselves beside the round table which stood in the center of the room. "Do you know I fancied you were old and gray, and lived in a horrid, old-fashioned village with rickety, tumble-down houses, your own the most of all? I must write to papa to-morrow and tell him how surprised and happy I am."

"Your ideas of country life were undoubtedly as unpleasant as the picture your imagination drew of me and my surroundings," said her aunt with a smile. "But did not your father enlighten you in regard to my being old and gray?" she inquired.

"No, he only laughed when I told him that I knew you were old and cross, and said I must come and see for myself," returned Ida.

Then followed questions and answers concerning family affairs, and it was quite late when they at length retired for the night. As days passed on, the young girl's delight by no means diminished. The brisk walks which her aunt urged her to take every day, together with her happy spirits, soon brought roses to take the place of lilies in the sweet face. How to bring about a meeting between Lester Pierce and Ida now became a matter of concern to Mrs. Montgomery, for, as she was but little acquainted with that gentleman and seldom met him, there were not so many opportunities for so doing as one would suppose; but fate at length took the matter in hand. It happened on this wise.

One day Ida entered the sitting-room, where her aunt sat at work, and hastily throwing her hat and sacque upon the nearest chair, she waltzed around the room once or twice, finally stopping and throwing her arms around Mrs. Montgomery's neck, and giving her a kiss on either cheek.

"What has happened to you, Ida?" said the widow, disengaging herself from the girl's grasp, and turning around in surprise.

"Oh, Aunt Hattie, I am so surprised and delighted! I was returning from the post office, and was just at the street crossing this side of Johnson & Hall's, when I heard my name called. I turned around and saw a gentleman and lady coming rapidly towards me. At first I did not recognize the lady, but as they drew nearer I saw to my delight that it was my old schoolmate and dearest friend, Susie Pierce. I have not met her before for two years. She was with her uncle, Lester Pierce, and talks of stopping with him through the winter. I invited them to call, and Mr. Pierce said, turning to Susie, 'My dear, I am under great obligations to you if by your coming I can form the acquaintance of Mrs. Montgomery and her niece,' and then, not waiting for her to reply, he thanked me very politely and said they would call this evening, if agreeable. Of course you don't care if they do come," concluded the girl, as she raised her hat and sacque from the floor, where they had fallen during her pirouette around the room.

"Certainly not, Ida; I would be very glad to know your friend, and to become better acquainted with her uncle," replied Mrs. Montgomery with a smile.

Never in her own girlish days had she taken half the pride in herself that she did that evening in her niece. Certainly the girl had never looked more lovely, and when the expected guests arrived it was no wonder that Lester Pierce's eyes rested in admiration upon her.

"You will lay aside your wrappings, Susie, and pass the evening with us," insisted Ida, after introducing the young lady to her aunt. "This must not be a formal call, for I have so much to say to you."

"I promised uncle that I would attend the lecture with him," replied Susie, turning toward her uncle with a smile.

"I will excuse you, if such be your wish, my dear, and will call for you as I return home," replied Mr. Pierce.

"Thank you, uncle, I will stop, I think, as I really have no desire to attend the lecture," said Susie, as she threw aside her hat and shawl and seated herself in the easy chair Ida had placed at her disposal.

Susie Pierce was as plain as Ida Hartwell was beautiful, yet one seemed to forget the lack of beauty in the dark face when they came to know her intimately. She was a brunette, and the only beauty her face afforded was her large, lustrous black eyes. There was so much soul in them (if I may use the expression) that instinctively one felt the beauty of the soul which looked out from their inmost depths. She was dressed in a black cashmere, relieved only by snowy lace at the neck and wrists.

Mr. Pierce attended the lecture. The

evening passed very pleasantly to the young ladies in recalling their school-days, while Mrs. Montgomery busied herself with her work.

It was ten o'clock when Mr. Pierce called for Susie, and Mrs. Montgomery managed to make his call so pleasant that it was nearly eleven when they at length rose to take their leave. Mr. Pierce invited the ladies to a party at his house on the following Tuesday eve.

"The old house needs warming up with young faces and happy hearts. I have lived alone so long that the very walls have become like myself—desolate and lonely. I thank the good angel that put the thought in Susie's heart to visit me."

"Then she came unexpectedly," said Mrs. Montgomery.

"Yes, I knew nothing of it until she came into my reading room yesterday afternoon," returned the gentleman.

"His reading room, as he calls it, is a perfect bachelor's den," said Susie, with a smile.

"Don't slander me to my good neighbors, Susie," said he, a smile lighting up his somewhat sad face; then turning to Ida, he said: "Don't be ceremonious, Miss Hartwell, but call upon us whenever you wish—the oftener the better. I expect Susie will get homesick and leave me at the end of a fortnight."

Susie immediately declared her intention of remaining until her uncle should send her away. Then, after a cordial good-night, the door closed upon their retreating forms.

"I can see that he is charmed with Ida already," said Mrs. Montgomery to herself as she retired to rest that night. "I really believe that in less than six months she will be his wife."

Some may think that the widow was strangely disinterested as regarded herself, and perhaps she was so. Certainly she had never had a thought that there was any chance for her. She had somehow missed her chance in life for true happiness—if there had really ever existed one—and she fancied herself done with that sort of thing forever. She was not sure, even, that she had a heart like other women, and consequently was satisfied to let matters remain as they were.

The night of the party came and passed. Nothing quite so grand had ever before taken place in the village of A——. From the night of the party there was a continual round of gayety—parties and (when the snow came) sleigh-rides, festivals, skating parties, etc. Lester Pierce seemed to enjoy them all with all the zest of a younger man. The widow laughingly shook her head at all entreaties and remained at home, while Ida and Susie remained inseparable friends and depended always upon Lester Pierce as their escort. Scarcely a day passed that he did not call at the cottage, and it had come to be an acknowledged fact that he found great attraction there—people being divided in their opinions as to which should prove the favored one. Thus the winter passed quickly away.

One evening in the early spring-time Ida and Susie were invited to attend a select party of young ladies to see about arranging matters for a festival. Mrs. Montgomery sits alone in her sitting-room. Her work has fallen in a heap on the floor, and her head rests against the back of her easy chair in a weary, listless way, quite the reverse from her usual energetic manner. In fact, she has somehow changed since we first saw her. Her round, happy face has lost its roundness, and there is a look in the black eyes that tells of a mind not quite at ease. Suddenly she hears a step without, and then the bell rings a quick, peculiar peal, the sound of which brings the color to her face in a scarlet wave.

"He has come to ask my consent to pay his addresses to Ida. I ought to be glad, but I am afraid I am not," she murmured, as she hastened to open the door. As she had supposed, Lester Pierce stood before her, and she welcomed him with a smile and cordial good evening. At her invitation he entered the house, and, after removing his hat, he seated himself with the air of one very much at home. A half hour passed in general conversation, when he suddenly drew his chair nearer that of Mrs. Montgomery, and said in a low voice, his eyes resting upon her face with an eagerness unusual to him:

"Mrs. Montgomery, you and I have been very good friends for the past three months, and I have long been wishing to tell you that I wish much to become something more than a friend. You have certainly noticed my frequent visits here, and have doubtless guessed the state of my feelings. I am not much given to love-making," a smile passing over his face, "but I wish much to know if my suit is to meet with success."

He paused, waiting for her to speak, but as she did not, he continued:

"Susie goes away very soon now, and then I shall be more lonely than ever before, and,—well, some say I have lost the best years of my life, wasted them living alone, and perhaps I have. I am not a man to love lightly, and once having given my love away, it must be for all time. Will you tell me if that love is in vain?"

"Indeed, Mr. Pierce, I cannot tell you, for although I have long known the state of your feelings, I can form no sort of an idea as regards Ida's. At times I have thought she cared for you; at others I have thought she didn't," replied Mrs. Montgomery quietly, raising her eyes to her companion's face. He was looking at her in surprise, and for a moment made no reply; then he said slowly:

"Is it possible that my visits here have been misinterpreted? My friend, it is your dear face that has been the attraction, and you are the one I love and have loved since long before Ida came here, although I was but little acquainted with you. As for Ida, she is as dear to me as my own niece, which is saying much, but if I do not call Hattie Montgomery wife, I shall never call any one by that title. Can you give me any hope, Hattie?"

At his words the color had receded from her face, and her head had fallen upon her clasped hands. The surprise was so complete, the reaction so great—for she had discovered during the past few weeks that she had a heart—that several moments passed ere she could utter a word, and then I expect she did a very foolish deed for a woman of her years, for she laid her head upon Lester's shoulder and actually burst into tears. They were soon wiped away, however, and when the young ladies returned home they found a very happy couple awaiting them.

It was not until years had come and gone, and she was a happy wife and mother, that Hattie Pierce told of her first and last attempt at matchmaking, but I think she never owned, even to herself, how glad she was that the attempt had so signally failed.

CONGRESSIONAL PAPERS. NO. III—THE "THIRD HOUSE."

BY G. H. JENNESS.

In the popular mind nearly all congressional legislation is supposed to be more or less unduly influenced by the organization known as "the lobby." Exactly what it is, who supports it, who constitutes it, where it is located, and how it operates, are points upon which the popular mind aforesaid is less clear than in a general belief in the lobby's existence. That eminent statesman from the backwoods of Tennessee, Mr. Crutchfield, who held a seat in the Forty-third Congress, gave *his* opinion of the lobby in language, which, if not elegant, is at least terse and vigorous. In reply to an inquiry as to whether there was a "lobby" working for the extension of a certain sewing-machine patent, Mr. Cutchfield, who was a member of the House Committee on Patents, said: "Lobby? that's the spook that is always arter me. I hain't been in Congress only one term, and I don't want to no more. I'll be dogged if I can stand it. I am just pulled and hauled until I don't know where I am. * * * * This is my last year in Congress. I am goin' to get shet out of it at once. I can't stand it. Young man, when this yer Congress is busted and I ken in honor tell ye all I know, I will give ye still more than enough to fill a book of the blamedest stuff ye ever dreamed about. I'm goin' to have my experiences published if I have to write 'em out myself. Lobby, did ye say, backin' of 'em sewing-machines? I should say so! Lobby? If ye were a member ye'd find that out. When I came here I learned a few things. Does a member love good feedin'? Then it rains invitations to the biggest kind of feeds. Does he love drinkin'? Whiskey runs in rivers for him upon every hand. Is it women he wants to persuade him? Then women it is of every kind, big, little, old, young, and nary one of 'em with any morals to bother 'em. Last, if all these fail to fetch him, money can be had in bales rather than to loose him. I am a pore man, but I want to stay an honest one. I have stood it out two years in this yer place, and I ain't goin' to resk myself here any longer."

At the close of his term Mr. Crutchfield renounced the pomps of Congressional life, returned to the purer atmosphere of his mountain home, where it is reasonable to suppose he is engaged in preparing his great work "showing up" the "lobby" at Washington. His vivid description is that of a steady-going old farmer, ignorant of the world, suddenly brought into contact with the most disreputable phase of Congressional legislation. Unlike many others, Mr. Crutchfield evidently does not believe the "lobby" to be a mere creature of imagination. To him it was a stern reality, or to use his more expressive language, "the spook that was always arter him," and which finally induced him to leave Congress rather than to risk the chance of having his integrity questioned. Other members have had similar experiences, and have withstood all the blandishments the "lobby" could offer; while still others, possessed of less Spartan integrity and firmness, stand all over the land, thrifty monuments of the mysterious power that sits enthroned at the Capital.

The "lobby" is no myth; neither is it so offensively conspicuous as many imagine. Whoever expects to see somebody rushing around whispering in Congressmen's ears "I'll give you ten thousand dollars to vote for the Pacific Railroad bill," and "five thousand dollars to vote for the Brazilian 'subsidy' bill," will be disappointed. Nothing of the kind occurs. In fact, the experienced lobbyist is careful that his scheme of operations shall "take any shape but that." A person might haunt the corridors of the Capitol for years without ever hearing a proposition of this kind openly made. There are better methods of exerting "influence"—as witness the relations of the Credit Mobilier and other gigantic schemes. An invitation to "take stock" in what promises to be a "safe investment," a suggestion that a certain project will prove to be "a good thing," or a mild hint that a European tour is needed to perfect a congressman's health, are among the thousand and one little insinuations thrown out by the professional lobbyist. The details may be left to such times and circumstances as are mutually satisfactory to the contracting parties. That the great majority of Representatives and Senators are corrupt, is not, for a moment, to be believed; but that *some* of them have shamelessly betrayed their trusts, and enriched themselves at the public expense, is too plainly evident to admit of denial. The "lobby" has an existence, and is a fixed fact as much as the existence of Congress itself. Its influence is far-reaching, powerful, and sometimes potential. It takes advantage of everything, and scruples at nothing. It leaves no methods untried, however base, to accomplish its purpose. It embraces in its membership the least reputable of both sexes. It has talent, wealth, and beauty at its command. It can and does to all outward appearances, make and unmake those who should have avoided its fatal clutches. *Apparently*, it has no tangible existence. You cannot find its headquarters, or its private office. You cannot interview its president, secretary, or executive committee. You don't know where to look for it, or where to find it: but *somehow* or *somewhere* there is a mysterious, unaccountable, and powerful influence emanating that facilitates or retards the progress of legislation involving great monied interests of a public or private nature. There are always before Congress numerous and cunningly devised schemes to plunder the Treasury. Many of them are of vast magnitude, and some of them are made to appear to be a national necessity. They are introduced to public notice and pushed forward by able, persistent, and unscrupulous men. They easily find their way into Congress through the manipulation of some friendly or interested member. Once introduced they are subjected to the ordinary chances of legislation, and must pass through the customary *routine* of Congressional pulling and hauling. To push all such schemes through both houses of Congress, and to favorably "influence" the President, is the principal object of the lobby. It must not be presumed that all schemes in which the lobby is interested are dishonest. Far from it. All is fish that comes to its net. If it is an honest claim there is less need of secrecy, and the work can be done openly and aboveboard. It is only necessary for the claimant to change his figures. He must add a sum sufficient to cover the expenses of the lobby. Then if he gets his bill through, and escapes the clutches of the rapacious sharks that lay in wait for him, he is fortunate indeed. The great railway and subsidy rings "lobby" upon a grand scale. Champagne suppers, railway and steamboat excursions, junketing parties of all descriptions, fashionable dissipation, superb dinners at "swell" restaurants, board at the best hotels, costly wines, cigars, and stylish turnouts, are among the many numerous appliances that a powerful lobby always has at its command. The condition and circumstances of every member of Congress is inquired into and known. If a member is poor and in need of money, advantage will be taken of that fact to capture him if possible. If he takes the bait, all right. If he refuses he is quite likely to be held up to public scorn in some form or other. To its shame be it said the press has frequently been an active and unscrupulous ally of the lobby. Cheap newspapers and cheaper writers have sometimes prepared the way for the favorable consideration of disreputable schemes for public plunder, and abused those who resisted them. Indeed the great metropolitan journals of the country have not been found entirely guiltless, as has been proven by past investigations. The lobby will leave no stone unturned to secure the aid of every newspaper of influence, no matter what its name or politics. As an illustration of this there is a scheme involving millions which failed at the late session of Congress. The fight was a hot one and the lobby was beaten. One of the interested parties is chief owner in a great newspaper. To increase the chances of success, howver, efor his favorite measure, he furnished a large sum of money to maintain another brilliant newspaper of exactly opposite political faith. Whether final success awaits this enterprising gentleman remains to be seen; but it is reasonably safe to predict that at least one newspaper funeral would speedily follow the passage of a certain bill.

The lobby will always maintain an existence at Washington so long as the private claims upon the government aggregate hundreds of millions of dollars. There always has been, is now and always will be hundreds and thousands of such claims of varying amounts and infinite variety. Selfish interests will always prompt interested parties to take every advantage and use every appliance to hasten legislation upon such of these claims as may directly concern them. The lobby is a pliant tool to be used for all such purposes, and will be found conveniently near whenever needed.

OLIVER CROMWELL.

BY PROF. E. D. SANBORN.

It is not probable that an impartial history was ever yet written. No writer can, with greater justice, lay claim to impartiality than the learned Athenian who wrote "for eternity." Next to Thucydides stands the philosophic Tacitus, the uncompromising enemy of oppression, and the fearless defender of the oppressed. In modern historians and biographers it is in vain to look for strict impartiality. The writers of histories are partisans. They have a creed to defend or a system of government to support. They are wily advocates, making use of the facts of history to prove their own dogmas; or they are the pensioned hirelings of an oppressive aristocracy, perverting the truth for a reward. A partisan or a pensioned dependant can not write history well. They neither write as they ought nor as they know how to write. They judge of men by the creed or politics of their party, hence they fail to do justice to individuals. No man expects justice from an opponent. A statesman's biography cannot be written with fidelity, while the principles he advocated remain unpopular. The advocate of necessary reform will always be abused by the majority. Tyrants never relish discourses upon liberty, nor wily bigots endure homilies upon toleration. "As a man thinketh in his heart, so is he." Let him once be convinced of the divine right of Kings and Priests and his hostility to democrats and independents will know no bounds. If such a man's opinions are adopted and perpetuated by others, neither time nor distance will abate the virulence of their advocates. The Catholic of to-day hates Luther as cordially as did his Catholic contemporaries. The cavaliers and churchmen of Victoria's reign assail the character of Cromwell with as much bitterness as did those of the time of Charles the First.

The injustice of contemporaries is proverbial. The injustice of a partisan posterity is equally notorious. The parties which the living patriot encountered dispute over his tomb, nay, they continue to dispute after his very dust has mingled with its parent earth, and the place where his bones repose is forgotten. Socrates, who is said by one of the wisest of the Romans to have brought philosophy from heaven to earth, was held up to the contempt of an Athenian populace by a distinguished comedian as an impudent charlatan and a reviler of the gods of the people; and after the lapse of 2000 years there are not wanting men who defend the shameless satirist. It is never safe to repeat or admit the charges even of an enemy who is reputed honest, without careful examination. Some men seem to be born partisans. Their peculiar mental constitution inclines them to adopt particular opinions, and to imbibe particular sentiments. They adopt what they feel to be right; not what reason commends. They reject what their feelings oppose, not what virtue condemns. Hence the integrity of a partisan witness cannot secure him against errors of judgment. The more honestly he entertains his own views, the more injurious will he be to his opponent.

These remarks apply, with peculiar significancy, to those men, who, from their austere lives and devoted piety, were called Puritans. Their history has been written by their enemies. Their errors, their foibles, and their innocent peculiarities, have been exaggerated into the most odious crimes. The good deeds they performed have been studiously discolored or concealed; the virtues they practiced have been blackened by the grossest slanders, and the inconsiderable weaknesses which they, being men of like passions with others, shared, have been diligently set forth in the garb of the most repulsive cant and hypocrisy. Among these men thus willfully traduced by malicious enemies, stands pre-eminent the leader of the great rebellion, Oliver Cromwell. At the mention of his name, the mind is at once beset with images of violence, of oppression, tyranny, falsehood and hypocrisy. Why should the name of Cromwell be associated with all that is vile in men or odious in demons? Did he walk the earth an incarnate fiend? Was he, as his foes maintained, in league with the Prince of darkness? Why has his name become, in history, synonymous with usurper, tyrant, and hypocrite? 'Tis true he won a kingdom by his valor. So did David, the man after God's own heart. 'Tis true he consented to the death of an imbecile, perjured tyrant. If David did not as much, he was as undoubtedly reconciled, eventually, to the removal of Saul, and wore his royal honors without reluctance. 'Tis true that Cromwell punished those who conspired to overthrow his government and refused to obey his laws. So did the Hebrew monarch. 'Tis true that Cromwell believed in a special Providence, and ever acknowledged the reign of Jehovah. 'Tis no less true that he prayed earnestly and devoutly to the God of Heaven for divine counsel and guidance; and he believed, too, in his inmost soul, that his prayers were heard and answered. All this did the sweet Psalmist of Israel. It does not, therefore follow, because Cromwell consented to the death of Charles, that he was a regicide, nor because he wore the regal honors that he was a usurper, nor because he prayed and sung psalms that he was a hypocrite. Had he been as reckless as Macedonia's "Madman or the Swede," had be been as profligate as Cæsar and as bloodthirsty as Napoleon, had he combined and in his own character, all the vices of military chieftains from the days of Nimrod to Andrew Jackson, and at the same time been as undevout as Paine or Voltaire, he might have stood in peerless grandeur among earth's mightiest heroes, without a stain of meanness upon his character. Men have been so long accustomed to reverence power, and to admire the conqueror's nodding plume and glittering helmet, when surrounded with all the "pomp and circumstance of glorious war," that they have learned not only to tolerate but to laud the vices of their heroes. They expect a great man to be a wicked man. Public character and private virtue are dissociated. The trappings of royalty, the diadem, the purple robe, and the studded baldrick, conceal the moral diseases of the monarch; and when, like Herod of old, arrayed in royal apparel and seated upon a throne he makes an oration, the people shout; "it is the voice of a god and not of a man," though he may already be smitten with a moral plague by the angel of the bottomless pit! Had Cromwell been as immoral and profligate as other conquerors whom the world delights to honor, his very wickedness would have abated one half of the slanders with which the press has teemed against him. But he was a religious man, a man of prayer. In this he was so unlike other conquerors that the multitude, at once, pronounced him a hypocrite. The like was never known in the biographies of a thousand heroes. Great men never pray—never make God's word the standard of their conduct. For a pretence he makes long prayers. He is a deceiver—a mean, canting hypocrite, say they. The reputation of the Protector has suffered from this one cause more than from all others. It was not so strange a thing in the world's history, or in England's history even, that a king should be deposed or murdered, that the trial and condemnation of his most sacred majesty, Charles I. should have so filled the hearts of men with horror and loaded the memory of his judges and executioners with ignominy. Had the king been removed by secret assassination, his murderer might have filled his throne with no reproach of meanness. Men would have called him wicked, no doubt, but the very daring of the villany would have cloaked its enormity. Men look upon Richard III. with more complacency than upon Cromwell; and why? Because they, erroneously, suppose that the one was an open and fearless usurper, the other a disguised and hypocritical one. Cromwell and his compeers acted under a deep sense of religious responsibility, and with a strong and unwavering conviction that their cause was the cause of God. Their victories were all ascribed to God's mercy. His guiding hand was everywhere acknowledged, and everywhere proclaimed. Believing that they were, in a sense, engaged in a holy war, they sought out good men to do battle for the Lord.

In one of the Protector's speeches to a large committee of his second Parliament, he briefly alludes to his early efforts in the revolution, in connection with his friend and relative, John Hampden: "At my first going into this engagement, [meaning the civil war] I saw our men were beaten on every hand. I did indeed; and desired him [John Hampden] that he would make some additions to my Lord Essex's army, of some new regiments; and I told him I would be servicable to him in bringing such men in as I thought had a spirit that would do something in the work. This is very true that I tell you; God knows I lie not. Your troops, said I, are most of them old decayed serving men, tapsters, and such kind of fellows; and, said I, *their* troops are gentlemen's sons, and persons of quality. Do you think that the spirits of such base and mean fellows will ever be able to encounter gentlemen that have honor and courage and resolution in them? Truly I did represent to him in this manner, conscientiously and truly I did tell him: 'You must get men of spirit, and take it not ill what I say. I know you will not—of a spirit that is likely to go on as far as gentlemen will go;—or else you will be beaten still.' I told him so; I did truly. He was a wise and worthy person, and he did think that I talked a good notion but an impracticable one. Truly I told him I could do somewhat in it. I did so, and truly I must needs say this to you, the result was —impute it to what you please—I raised such men as had the fear of God before them, as made some conscience of what they did, and from that day forward, I must say to you, they were never beaten, and whenever they were engaged against the enemy they beat continually. And truly this is matter of praise to God, and it hath some instruction in it to our men who are religious and godly."

In another speech, he uses the following language: "If I were to choose any servant, the meanest officer for the army or the Commonwealth, I would choose a godly man that hath principles, especially where a trust is to be committed. Because I know where to *have* a man that hath principles." Truly he did know both where to have men of principle, and how to choose them. He selected the best and wisest for places of trust and responsibility. Even his enemies admit it. Such were his uniform declarations, and his practice corresponded to them. Does any one call this cant, hypocrisy and meanness? To such a one I would say in the words of Carlyle: "The man is without a soul that looks into this Great Soul of a man, radiant with the splendors of very Heaven, and sees nothing there but the shadow of his own mean darkness. Ape of the dead sea, peering asquint into the Holy of Holies, let us have done with thy commentaries. Thou canst not fathom it." No great man, much less a good man, ever lived, of whom all men spoke well. Not even he "who went about doing good" received testimony from men. "Some said he is a good man, others said nay, but he deceiveth the people." Because bigots and the tools of tyrants have represented the Puritans as ignorant, besotted fanatics, are we bound to believe them? There are not wanting men in our own land who still take pleasure in abusing the Pilgrims, denouncing them as mere political adventurers, unscrupulous partisans, knavish, time-serving hypocrites. And who are the men who at this late period, attempt to set aside the verdict of many generations, and to pour contempt upon our honored ancestry, of whom the world was not worthy? These are they who light wax candles in the day time, who venerate Holy Mother Church, who make genuflexions before a crucifix, and consign men better than themselves over to the uncovenanted mercies of God. These are they that venerate the faithless Charles as a martyr of blessed memory, and devoutly lisp the praises of the sainted Laud! It is right to judge of men by their works. Revelation pronounces those blessed who die in the Lord: the reason, too, is annexed: "That they may rest from their labors; and their works do follow them." This goodly land in which we dwell is eloquent of the works of the Puritans; if we should altogether hold our peace concerning them, the very stones would cry aloud in their behalf. "English history," says Bancroft, "must judge of Cromwell by his influence on the institutions of England."

If the Protector were now alive, he would assent with his whole heart to this standard. While he lived, he said fearlessly to his Parliament: "this government [is] a thing I shall say little unto. The thing is open and visible, to be seen and read of all men; and therefore let it speak for itself." And what does this government say for his Highness? Before answering this question, let us look at Cromwell's previous history. Little is certainly known of his early life. Indeed we know little of him till he was forty years of age. The gay butterflies that swarmed about the Court of Charles II. sought for themselves an ephemeral celebrity by inventing scandalous reports, not only of Cromwell's reign, but of his early life. Most of the anecdotes that have come down to us are derived from a little book called "Flagellum, or the Life and Death of Oliver Cromwell, the late Usurper," by James Heath. From this polluted source has flowed a continuous torrent of filthy slime and mud to bury, in ever accumulating infamy, the memory of departed greatness. When royal spite and priestly vengeance were digging the earth from mouldering corpses; "when St. Margaret's churchyard was polluted with the decayed bodies of a hundred patriots, torn from their last resting place to glut the malice of His Most Christian Majesty, together with his retinue of harlots and ghostly advisers;" and among them the remains of Admiral Blake, who contributed as much as any other man that ever lived to make England mistress of the seas; "when the gallows was graced with the rattling bones and mouldering clay of the high-souled Oliver and his coadjutors;" when such fantastic tricks were enacted in the face of high Heaven; what could we expect from the mean, cowardly, sycophantic Heath, who, like his prototype in the desert, sees not when good cometh, who comes like Falstaff to battle upon the slain, and flesh his maiden sword in the body of the dead hero? Of this man and his work, Carlyle says: "Heath's poor, little, brown, lying Flagellum is described, by one of the moderns, as 'Flagitium,' and Heath himself is called 'carion Heath,' as being an unfortunate, blasphemous dullard, and scandal to humanity;—blasphemous; who when the image of God is shining through a man, reckons it, in his sordid soul to be the Image of the Devil, and acts accordingly;" who in fact has no soul except what saves him the expense of salt: who intrinsically is carrion and not humanity; which seems hard to measure to poor James Heath."

Considering the origin of these tales of his boyish irregularities and dissipation, we may safely set them down to the credit of his slanderers, and at once pronounce them false. The stories of his profligacy while a student at law, have not the least foundation in fact; for he never was in the Inns of Court, as his veracious biographers pretend. The books of all the Inns have been diligently searched, and the name of Oliver Cromwell no where appears. The strongest proofs of his early impiety are the penitential confessions of Oliver himself in a private letter to a friend. Here his language is vague and general. He does indeed admit that he had been the chief of sinners, and so did Paul; but we may not wrest this confession to the injury of either. Cromwell early became a truly religious man, and from the time of his making a public profession of religion till he became the most prominent man in the realm, by the confession of his enemies, he led a consistent life. If he afterwards became all things to all men, to gratify boundless ambition, which was his easily besetting sin, we can only say, that like most good men, he sometimes acted inconsistently with his principles and profession. While he lived as a retired and quiet farmer in Huntingdon, and afterwards at St. Ives, no man hath found aught to censure in his character or conduct.

At the age of twenty-nine he was a member of the 3d parliament of Charles, to represent his native Huntingdon. Is it probable that his fellow citizens, who knew his whole history, would have selected such a scape-grace as he is represented to have been, to fill the place which his honored and honorable uncle, Sir Oliver Cromwell, had so long and so creditably occupied? While he lived in retirement, his enemies being unable to impeach his morals, would fain undervalue his capacity for business. He is represented as having squandered his mother's and his wife's estate so that he was reduced almost to beggary. After inheriting a considerable estate from his uncle, Sir Robert Stewart, one of the turkey-buzzards of that age says: "Shortly after having again run out of all, he resolved to go to New England." The testimony of Milton will set this forever at rest. He says: "Being now arrived to a mature and ripe age, which he spent as a private person, noted for nothing more than the cultivation of pure religion, and integrity of life, he was grown rich at home." The fact that he was able to subscribe £1000 for raising soldiers at the first out-breaking of the civil war, shows that he was no beggar. In parliament, he does not seem to have acted a prominent part. Whenever he does appear, it is always in defense of liberty and religion. The civil war stirred his mighty mind to its depths. He entered into it as a true patriot should have done, with spirit, energy and decision, and he never deserted the true interests of his country; nor did he desert the parliament, even, till that parliament became a quarrelsome faction and deserted him. In the commencement of his career, his future destiny had never dawned upon him. Hampden first discovered his superior talents, and he is said to have remarked, "should this contest end in a war, yonder sloven, (pointing to his cousin), will be the first man in England." Cromwell followed fortune, or, in his own language, the "leadings of divine Providence." He made the most of his position on every step of the ladder by which he rose to supreme power. He was not conscious even of his own strength. He acted under strong convictions of the 'necessity' of the course he adopted. To a spectator, therefore, he seemed almost like one inspired. He moved forward with a directness of purpose, an earnestness and a certainty of success unparalleled in the world's history; and yet it was a favorite remark of his: "No man often advances higher than he who knows not whither he is going." As he rose, in rank and power, he filled each successive office with the dignity and grace of a hereditary prince. His mind expanded as his sphere of influence enlarged. An English Essayist observes: "Cromwell, by the confession even of his enemies, exhibited in his demeanor the simple and natural nobleness of a man neither ashamed of his origin nor vain of his elevation; of a man who had found his proper place in society, and who felt secure that he was competent to fill it. Easy even to familiarity, where his own dignity was concerned, he was punctilious only for his country."

His private letters to his family show the kind father, the affectionate husband, and the true economist. His public dispatches, while in the army, breathe the purest patriotism with the most fervent piety. He ever acknowledges the good hand of God in every victory; and it is said Cromwell never lost a battle. No one can reasonably impute this habitual recognition of God's power and providence to sheer hypocrisy. We can see no possible motive for such deception. It was uncalled for, and could answer no important purpose. It is far more charitable to believe and to maintain that his prayers, his repeated appeals to the inspired word, and his fervent thanksgivings to Almighty God for his success, were the spontaneous outpourings of a devout and grateful heart. His numerous speeches to his several parliaments are all characterized by the same zeal for religion; the same earnest and apparently sincere desires for the highest good of the people. 'Tis true he spoke with great caution, because every word was treasured up, and would be made, if possible, a weapon for his own destruction. His sentences, are, therefore, sometimes involved, intricate, and obscure, encumbered with repetitions, and frequently unfinished. We can find other motives for this hesitancy and circumlocution besides fraud and intrigue. The critical position in which he was placed sufficiently explains them all. But, says one, palliate his conduct as you will, he was still a usurper and a tyrant. Let us hold up this charge to the light of truth. We admit that he held power which the people had never delegated to him, and which he had not gained by hereditary descent. If no circumstances will justify such an assumption of authority, then Cromwell must rest under the stigma of exercising unjust power. Let us look at the state of society and the condition of the government. As Cromwell was situated, it was a question of life and death with him, whether he should put himself at the head of the State. Had he doubted, or hesitated, or shown fear he would have been crushed, and anarchy dark, fearful and bloody, would have followed. The Commonwealth was rent with factions. No party had sufficient influence to lead the others. All were seeking for the supremacy. Royalists and Republicans, levelers and fifth monarchy men, Episcopalians and Presbyterians, Independents and Quakers. The nation was one mighty seething pot of isms, political and religious. No man could control these hostile and turbulent factions but Cromwell. He saw it and acted accordingly. I do not mean to assert that while he acted from an evident necessity, that he did not act in accordance with a fully developed and inexcusable ambition; but as Guizot asserts, "if he had abdicated his power one day he would have been obliged to resume it the next." "Puritans or royalists, republicans or officers, there was no one but Cromwell who was in a state at this time, to govern with anything like order and justice." That fragment of a constitutional assembly denominated by way of derision the "rump parliament," were as ambitions of power as the Protector. They wished to make the power which the people delegated to them for a season, perpetual and perhaps hereditary. They were about to curse the nation with a permanent oligarchy. Cromwell saw it and resisted their usurpation. The violent dissolution of this parliament was not generally ungrateful to the people. Cromwell says himself: "So far as I could discern, when they were dissolved, there was not so much as the barking of a dog, or any general and visible repining at it." When he assumed the reins of government, though he acted arbitrarily, he did not assume unlimited power. "For himself," says Macaulay. "he demanded indeed the first place in the Commonwealth; but with powers scarcely as great as those of a Dutch Stadtholder or an American President. He gave the Parliament a voice in the appointment of ministers, and left to it the whole legislative authority—not even reserving to himself a veto on its enactments. And he did not require that the Chief Magistracy should be hereditary in his family. * * * Had his moderation been met by corresponding moderation, there is no reason to think he would have overstepped the line which he had traced for himself." When the Parliament which he summoned began to question his authority to rule, the same authority, too, by which they were called, and under which they acted, he became more arbitrary and dismissed them; and who would not have pursued the same course? The necessity under which the Protector lay of assuming despotic power, does not prove him guiltless in this matter, but it certainly palliates the crime. if crime it may be called. But, says an objector, why pull down one tyrant to set up another? The domination of Cromwell was as odious and oppressive as that of Charles; what, then, had the people gained by ten years of suffering, toil and bloodshed? I answer, much, every way. The two administrations, though both were despotic, were as unlike as light and darkness. I do not assert this without authority.

Of Charles, Macaulay, than whom no man is better versed in English history, says: "All the promises of the king were violated without scruple or shame. The Petition of Right to which he had in consideration of money's duly numbered, given a solemn assent, was set at naught. Taxes were raised by the royal authority. Patents and monopoly were granted. The old usages of feudal times were made pretexts for harrassing the people with exactions unknown during many years. The Puritans were persecuted with cruelty worthy of the Holy Office. They were forced to fly from their country. They were imprisoned. They were whipped. Their ears were cut off. Their noses were slit. Their cheeks were branded with red-hot iron." Another able critic observes: "The sovereign was, in fact, a Rob Roy on a large scale; the Richard Turpin of the nation; and his representatives were licensed highwaymen and freebooters, levying an abominable blackmail from their fellow subjects." Such, in brief, was the reign of the faithless tyrant, Charles I. England was bleeding at every pore. The rights of her citizens were all abrogated. The land, the property, the lives of the people, according to the prevailing politics and religion, belonged to the king by divine right. Nothing but resistance to oppression could arrest the encroachments of the government. Resistance was made. The tyrant was defeated. The abuses of many years were reformed; and even under the usurper Cromwell England was essentially free. Listen to some brief testimony on this point. Bancroft says: " Cromwell was one of those rare men whom even his enemies cannot name without acknowledging his greatness. The farmer of Huntingdon, accustomed only to rural occupations, unnoticed till he was more than forty years of age, engaged in no higher plots than how to improve the returns of his farm, and fill his orchard with choice fruit, of a sudden became the best officer in the British army, and the greatest statesman of his time; subverted the English constitution, which had been the work of centuries, held in his own grasp the liberties which the English people had fixed in their affections, and cast the kingdoms into a new mould. Religious peace, such as England, till now, has never again seen, flourished under his calmer mediation; justice found its way even among the remotest Highlands of Scotland; commerce filled the English marts with prosperous activity under his powerful protection; his fleets rode triumphant in the West Indies; Nova Scotia submitted to his orders without a struggle; the Dutch begged of him for peace as for a boon; Louis XIV. was humiliated; the pride of Spain was humbled; the Protestants of Piedmont breathed their prayers in security; the glory of the English name was spread throughout the world."

Such, too, is the concurrent testimony of all historians, both friends and foes. Even Clarendon admits his ability as a statesman and his successful administration. He applies to him what was said of Cinna, "Ausum eum quæ nemo auderet bonus, perfecisse quæ a nullo nisi fortissimo perfici possent." The same prejudiced historian adds: "He reduced three nations to obedience at home, and it is hard to say which feared him most, France, Spain or the Low Countries;" and while he thinks that he will be looked upon by posterity as "a brave, wicked man," he admits that "he had some good qualities which have caused the memory of some men, in all ages, to be celebrated." The best men and the wisest men in the kingdom admitted the equity of Cromwell's administration. Such men as Milton, Locke, and Cudworth eulogized, and we trust, sincerely too, the virtues of the Protector. Never had England been so prosperous. Never had her subjects before enjoyed such freedom of worship. Cromwell was far, very far in advance of the religious men of his own times in toleration. He always maintained that men had a right to think and act for themselves in matters of religion, and that, as long as they behaved peaceably they were free to dissent from the magistrate and the priest. To his parliament in 1654, who had failed to regulate matters in religion as he wished, he said: "Those who were sound in the faith, how proper was it for them to labor for liberty, for a just liberty, that men should not be trampled upon for their consciences? Had not they labored but lately under the weight of persecutions, and was it fit for them to sit heavily upon others? Is it ingenuous to ask liberty and not give it? What greater hypocrisy than for those who were oppressed by the bishops to become the greatest oppressors themselves as soon as the yoke was removed? " Cromwell ever acted in accordance with these sentiments. Though some religious impostors were punished during his Protectorate by the Parliament, it was not done by his approbation or consent. He was liberal in opinion and practice. He was a sincere and honest Independent, both as a citizen and a monarch. His views of Apostolic succession would be not a little unpalatable at Oxford at the present time. Of this he says: "I speak not, I thank God it is far from my heart—for a ministry deriving itself from the Papacy, and pretending to that which is so much insisted on—Succession. The true succession is through the Spirit given in its measure. The Spirit is given for that use. To make proper speakers forth of God's eternal truth, and that's right Succession." With all the theological light of the 19th century who can define Succession better? Who at this day entertains juster views of religious freedom and of the true end of a church organization than did Oliver Cromwell? Here is no scourging, no boring of tongues, no cutting off of ears and slitting of noses for dissent, as in the days of the sainted martyr, Charles. No, if Cromwell had not been thwarted by his Parliament, plotted against by the royalists, insulted and abused by sectaries he would have made the English nation the freest, the happiest people on earth. The true difference between him and Charles was this: Charles ruled for his own advantage; Cromwell for the advantage of the people. Charles sought to aggrandize himself. Cromwell, the nation. Charles wished to compel a uniformity of belief; Cromwell aimed at a unity of spirit and action. Charles impoverished the nation; Cromwell enriched it. Charles fled before his enemies; Cromwell subdued them. Charles failed to command the respect of his own subjects; Cromwell gained the respect of the whole world. Charles contended for prerogative; Cromwell for principles. The Court of Charles was the resort of intriguing politicians, fawning sycophants and shameless harlots; the Court of Cromwell was little more than a well regulated christian family, characterised by simplicity, purity and decorum. Such was Oliver the Protector. England has never known his equal. The conqueror of Napoleon, the "iron duke" had not a tithe of his liberality and far-reaching sagacity. The character of Cromwell will never be appreciated till the principles he advocated have become popular in England. That time hastens on apace. During the last half century whole mountains of mean slanders have been rolled from the clay of the insulted hero. Another half century will reveal to an admiring world the man Oliver as he was, such as Milton saw him when he penned the following lines:

"Cromwell, our chief of men who through a cloud,
Not of war only but of detractions rude,
Guided by faith and matchless fortitude,
To peace and truth thy glorious way hast plow'd,
And on the neck of crowned fortune proud
Hast reared God's trophies, and his work pursued,
While Darwent's stream with blood of Scots imbrued,
And Dunbar field resounds thy praises loud;
And Worcester's laureate wreath yet much remains
To conquer still: peace hath her victories
No less renowned than war; new foes arise
Threat'ning to bind our souls with secular chains.
Help us to save free conscience from the paw
Of hireling wolves whose gospel is their maw."

SORROW.

BY MARY HELEN BOODEY.

Sorrow sits and softly sings
    While she flings
    O'er the strings
Of her lute her fingers white,
With tear-diamonds bedight.

Diamonds deck her, head and foot,
    Well they suit
    On her lute,
Glitter, glitter, like the rain,
Sparkle, sparkle, without stain.

Every diamond is a tear;
    Jewels dear;
    Without fear
Sorrow wears them and doth shine
As she were a diamond-mine.

Sorrow gathers hour by hour
    Such a dower,
    Such a shower
Of the bright, translucent gems
Which she wears in diadems.

When her holy work is done
    Every one
    In the sun
Glows and flashes living light
That would dazzle mortal sight.

Now she comes and sits by me,
    Moments flee
    Dreamily;
As I weep she closer clings,
Working, ever, as she sings.

Sorrow! Sorrow! go thy way,
    Do not stay
    Here to-day,
I've shed tears enough for thee,
Haste away! I will be free!

But my guest doth still remain
    And again
    Falls the rain
Of my tears, which she doth take
Singing low, "For faith's sweet sake!"

INDUSTRIES IN HOPKINTON.

BY C. C. LORD.

AGRICULTURE.

An early occupation of civilization is tilling the soil. In a new country farming is often the main support of the population. The first settlers in Hopkinton were mostly farmers. The condition of agriculture was, of necessity, crude. Its profits were uncertain in a corresponding degree. Besides the natural uncertainty of the seasons, the lack of intercommunication between localities, and the attendant imperfect means of transportation, made the consequences of local failure more disastrous. The soil, however, was new and fertile. When it brought forth it did so abundantly. It was only when it failed through drought, flood or cold that population suffered—mostly through the difficulty of communicating with immediate and abundant supplies.

As population and social facilities increased, the farms were not only self-supportive, but on fertile years corn and grain were stored in the granaries of the industrious. Consequently, in the earlier times, the farmers of Hopkinton sold corn and wheat, instead of buying them as they do now. In the case of infertile seasons, the stores of accumulated products became available in the suppression of famine. In 1816, there occurred a prominent illustration in kind. The year was very unfruitful through an intensity of cold. On inauguration day in June, there was snow to the depth of four inches on a level. An early frost in autumn killed all the corn. The farmers cut it up and shocked it, but, being in the milk, it heated and spoiled. As a consequence of the induced scarcity, corn sold in Hopkinton as high as $3.50 a bushel.

Corn and grain have been sold in this town and taken to Vermont for consumption. People then could not anticipate the times that were coming. One of our townsmen tells us he very well remembers the first time his father bought a barrel of flour. The price paid was only four dollars, but the act of purchase was deemed so extravagant as to be almost culpable. It could not then be popularly forseen that the time was at hand when it would be almost as rare for a farmer in Hopkinton to raise his own flour as it was then rare for him to purchase it.

In the earlier times, the production and maintenance of farm animals was also much larger. In districts where it is now comparatively rare to find a yoke of oxen, the supply of this kind of stock was multitudinous. Nothing was more common than to own several yokes of large oxen, to say nothing of the usually attendant array of steers. Not more than fifty years ago, Mr. R. E. French, our present townsman, seeking cattle for the down-country markets, bought over seventy head in one day. They were all purchased in one district in this town, and the transaction required less time than half of the day. At the present time it is nothing uncommon for a man to travel over parts of several towns to buy a single yoke of oxen.

Besides the usual complement of horned stock and general farm animals, there was at one time quite a specialty in sheep. Stephen Sibley and Joseph Barnard were prominent growers of this kind of stock. Their flocks were counted by hundreds. Considerable effort was made to secure improved animals. Stock was imported from Vermont, New York, and perhaps other states, and the quality of the local flocks materially advanced. The prosperity of this branch of farming industry soon met with an ignominious defeat. The revenue laws of 1832 and 1833, reducing the duties on imports and discouraging local manufactures, so reduced the price of wool as to materially depress the interests of sheep growers. The flocks declined. A little impulse was given to this branch of industry during the war of 1861, owing to the demands for wool created by the army, but it was only temporary.

The soil of this town was adapted to growing all the staple crops of New England, but its subjection to the uses of the husbandman was a work of prodigious effort. The dense, heavy forests so extensively prevailing, were subdued by labor without direct profit. Wood and timber, so much in excess of the demand, were comparatively worthless. Even many years after the complete occupation of the township, a large pine tree, several feet in diameter and full of clear stuff, was sold on the stump for the insignificant sum of twenty-five cents. The freedom with which the best of timber was employed in the humblest uses of building attests the low marketable estimate placed upon it. Acres upon acres of primitive forest were cut down, the logs rolled in heaps, and the fallen debris—trunks, branches and boughs—burned to ashes. Following this exceedingly laborious toil, came not only the difficult task of plowing and planting, but the almost endless labor of removing the rocks and stones that thickly cumbered the surface of the ground. Stones were utilized in the division of lots by walls, which were often thick, or double. On an ancient location on Putney's Hill, can be seen stone walls that are six or eight feet in thickness. Heaps of stone thrown up in waste places are significant monuments of the severe toil through which the early inhabitants of this town reclaimed the wilderness.

With experience and increased social facilities, came improvements in the quality of the products of the soil. The introduction of improved varieties of fruit was a more notable event on account of the facilities for improvement afforded by the process of grafting. About seventy years ago the Baldwin apple was introduced into this town by Stephen Gage. Since then it has become the standard winter apple in every household in the community. We need not speak of the many varieties of roots, seeds and scions that have come and gone, or come and remained, since the earlier times. The history of our town, in this respect, is substantially uniform with that of many others in its vicinity.

Upon the ancient farm of Mrs. Eliza Putney, upon Putney's Hill, lies an ancient broken grindstone, a symbolic relic of a past rude husbandry. It is of common granite rock, and for a long time was the only grindstone in the immediate vicinity. People came long distances to grind their scythes upon it. Before its use, people from this town used to go to Concord to grind their scythes. A general scythe-grinding took place only occasionally. The scythes were kept sharp with whetstones as long as practicable, and then a party gathered up the dull scythes in the neighborhood and took them away for grinding. Snaths at that time were made by hand. The axe-handles were straight. The plows were at first of wood, faced with iron. Implements of all kinds were rude and imperfect, besides being mostly the products of the skill of the local blacksmith and carpenter. The introduction of modern implements has been a gradual but comparatively thorough work. The ancient richness of the soil having been in a great measure exhausted, the introduction of fertilizers from outside has become a permanent traffic. The utilization of the newer and richer fields of the West has brought to our doors an abundance of corn and grain, and the accidental forms of cereal products. In the accidental improvements of farming—draining, building, etc.,—our town has made creditable progress. The proximity of Hopkinton to Concord and Fisherville, populous places, has latterly given an impulse to the department of the dairy. Improved dairy stock has been introduced to a considerable extent. Among our most enterprising farmers may be mentioned Joseph Barnard, James M. Connor, Woodbury Hardy, John W. Page, S. S. Page, Horace Edmunds, H. H. Crowell, and others.

MANUFACTURES.

In 1738, Henry Mellen received a promise of a gratuity of twenty-five pounds from the incipient township, on condition that by the first of October of the same year he should erect a mill " on the reservation" and keep it in repair for three years next following, with the implied privilege of each proprietor to obtain sawing at a stipulated price. The list of proprietors' and other lots given on the plan of occupation originally drawn gives no specific location of the " reservation." Wherever this reservation was, if there was ever a mill built upon it, the structure was probably not located on any very considerable stream. The circumstances of the new township would hardly admit of an immediate important manufactory of lumber. In very early times there was a mill on the brook now utilized by Dea. Timothy Colby, but farther up than the present lumber works, at the head of the present pond. The foundations of the ancient structure can be seen to this day. We have heard it said that this spot was the site of the first mill in town. It may have been, but we cannot prove it.* From the few facts in our possession we conclude that, after the permanent settlement of the town mills increased with considerable rapidity. In 1791 the following persons were taxed for mills:—Nathaniel Clement, Moses Titcomb, Jeremiah Story, Amos Bailey, Levi Bailey, Joseph Barnard, John Currier, Eliphilet Poor, Abraham Rowell and Simeon Dow, Jr. The principal business done at these mills was probably sawing lumber, grinding corn and grain, or fulling and dressing cloth. Nathaniel Clement and Jeremiah Story were in partnership, continuing so, probably, till 1798, when both ceased to be taxed for property in mills. Their first mill, possibly in activity before 1791, was on or near the site of the old Phillip Brown mill, just east of the village, below what is now known as Mill's Pond. Moses Titcomb's mill was afterwards known as Webber's; the site is no the well-known Sibley farm, now owned by Dr. C. P. Gage, of Concord. Joseph Barnard's mill was also on Dolloph's brook, so-called, near its outlet into the Contoocook river. John Currier's mill was in " Stumpfield," on the well-known brook coursing through that district. Abraham Rowell's mill was on the Contoocook river, at West Hopkinton, near Rowell's bridge, on the present mill site. Simeon Dow's mill was at Contoocook, as was the mill of Eliphilet Poor, the first in this location. We cannot give the location of the others.

In the earlier times, manufactures were very much scattered. In fact every household was a manufacturing establishment in a small way. Once small mills and shops, manufactories of lumber, leather, and various domestic articles in whole or in part, were scattered through the town, occupying nearly or quite every available water privilege, while some, like the tanneries, were often on highland locations. Since the earlier times, many men have been engaged in manufactures in this town. We can only mention some of the more important establishments and owners.

The principal water-power being on the Contoocook river, at the village of the same name, which has grown up in a large measure in consequence of the local, natural privileges offered by the stream, there have been a number of the more important works in this locality. Mills of greater or less importance were located early at this point, among the operators being Benjamin. Hills, who was taxed for mill property in this town as early as 1795*, and whose family name gave the euphonious title of " Hill's

---

*Since writing the above we have received information which leads us to believe that the first mill in town was located on the site of the old Philip Brown mill described in this article.

---

*In 1797-99, Moses Hills was taxed for Mill property in this town.

INDUSTRIES IN HOPKINTON.

Bridge" to the present village of Contoocook. As the place increased in size and importance more notable works were established. As soon as 1825, Abram Brown was a mill operator or owner. In company with John Burnham, he carried on a notable business in the lumber and grain line for about thirty years. The grist mill operated by these two men was conducted by the sons of John Burnham till the fire of 1873, which consumed it. In 1826, or thereabouts, Joab Patterson established himself here in the business of a clothier. Subsequently he took into partnership his brother, David N., and till about 1860 the two carried on business, but subsequently to 1844 following the manufacture of woolen cloths, which they sold largely to people in the vicinity in exchange for wool or cash. For a short time another brother was connected with them. On the north side of the river, a mill, on the site of the present saw mill operated by the Burnham brothers, was built by Hamilton E. Perkins about 1835. It was subsequently burned and rebuilt. The present grist mill, owned by Col. E. C. Bailey, occupies a building erected for miscellaneous purposes by H. E. Perkins a short time after his first. Messrs. Kempton & Allen began the manufacture of mackerel kits about 1850, first in the present Burnham saw mill; afterwards one or both occupied the old Patterson factory, where business was kept up till the fire of 1873. For a few years subsequently to 1864, Messrs. Jonathan M. & George W. Morrill carried on woolen manufacturing in the present grist mill building, which was then the property of Capt. Paul R. George, or his heirs. In 1874 the brothers Morrill & Kempton, kit manufacturers, erected their present steam mill about a half mile north of the village. Grinding was also done at their mill during the first years of its existence. A year or two subsequently to the erection of this mill, Colonel Bailey put in the machinery of his present grist mill. He is at present the exclusive owner of the site of the water power at Contoocook.

About 1815, Thomas Kast began the manufacture of leather on the spot now occupied by Horace J. Chase, employing the present water power. He kept up the business for about thirty years, and then sold out to Jonathan Osgood. In 1852 the works passed into the hands of Mr. Chase, who has made numerous important additions and improvements to them. This establishment has been twice burned out—once during its occupancy by Mr. Kast and once since owned by Mr. Chase. About 1830, Benjamin F. Clough established a mill at what is now known as "Cloughville." Several sons of Mr. Clough have since been engaged in different kinds of wooden manufactures here, and several mills have at times been in operation. As soon as 1835, John Smiley became engaged as a miller at West Hopkinton, on the site of the old Rowell mill. For about thirty years "Smiley's Mills" was a popular grinding station for the vicinity. Grinding is no longer done at this station. The traveler who now takes his way in the valley between Putney and Beech Hills, crossing the tortuous Dolloph's Brook where it runs easterly across the road, at the site of what was formerly Richard Kimball's mill, will hardly conceive that here, where is now nothing but trees and bushes, was once a mill three stories in height, where, in addition to sawing lumber, the managers ground and bolted as good meal and flour as perhaps can be made at any place. Yet it was so. Several parties were at different times interested in this mill. Nathaniel Clement and Jeremiah Story once did business in partnership at this location. The Clement family was prominently connected with this mill in later times. The mill site was in the possession of the Story family till 1877.

About forty-five years ago, much enthusiasm was aroused over the manufacture of silk. Silk worms and mulberry trees were procured from older New England States and work begun in earnest. Silk thread and cloth were manufactured, but the enterprise died about as suddenly as it was born. The products of this business cost more than the income. Our people could not successfully compete with the cheaper labor of Europe. In some instances remnants of the old mulberry orchards can be to this day seen.

The following parties are taxed for mill property the present year:—Eli A. Boutwell, Charles F. Clough, Benjamin C. Clough, Timothy Colby, Henry H. Crowell, Carr & Wheeler, Wadsworth Davis, Amos Frye, Jr., Kempton & Morrill, Nathaniel V. Stevens, Samuel Spofford, Nahum M. Whittier.

TRADE.

Trade is essential to civilization. An incipient community has its quota of tradesmen. Soon after the first occupation of the township of Hopkinton, stores, or domestic trading posts, for the accommodation of the public, began to spring up. Reliable data of the earliest conditions of trade in this town are very meagre. In 1791, the following persons were taxed for stock in trade and money at interest:—Capt. Joshua Bailey, Capt. Chase, Daniel Herrick, Samuel Harris, Capt. Stephen Harriman, Theophilis Stanley and Benjamin Wiggin. It is reasonable to believe that only a part of these were engaged in actual traffic in merchandise. Some may have been small manufacturers. Theophilis Stanley and Benjamin Wiggin were taverners, though Wiggin also kept a store, while Stanley worked a tannery.

There was a combination of circumstances tending, in the earlier times, to make Hopkinton a comparatively thriving trading post. Besides the natural wants of the local population, an incentive was afforded in the fact that for many years Hopkinton was a shire town of old Hillsborough County; the town also occupied a prominent position on the northern frontier of New Hampshire settlements. In consequence of these circumstances, the local business interests advanced rapidly for a number of years. In 1800 the following persons were taxed for stock in trade:—Joshua Bailey, Esq., Samuel Darling, Reuben French, Ebenezer Lerned, Isaac Long, Nathaniel Procter, Theophilis Stanley, Silas Thayer, Samuel G. Town, Town & Ballard, and David Young. Of these Isaac Long was a book-binder and seller; David Young a cabinet-maker. There were others whose business we cannot describe, unless they were common traders. In 1810 there were Abram Brown, Thomas W. Colby, Reuben French, Ebenezer Lerned, Isaac Proctor, Theophilis Stanley, Stephen Sibley, Joseph Town, and Thomas Williams; in 1820, Buswell & Way, Calvin Campbell, Thomas W. Colby, Timothy Darling, George Dean, Thomas Kast, Isaac Long, Jr., Ira Morrison, Stephen Sibley, Joseph B. Town, and Thomas Williams.

For a time it was thought that Hopkinton might become the permanent capital of the State. The year 1805 decided in favor of Concord. It may be said that here was the beginning of a tide of events that ultimately took away the business ascendancy of this town, which rapidly declined in thrift in the latter part of the first half of the present century. In the days of greatest prosperity Hopkinton village was the center of a large wholesale trade. Town & Ballard were wholesale and retail merchants, occupying the building now used by Kimball & Co. The whole lower floor of this building was in use by this firm, and numerous clerks found busy employment, while strong teams from the upper country resorted here for the products of trade and barter. During this period the stores of Thomas W. Colby, Lerned & Sibley, and Thomas Williams were notable places of business. Colby's store occupied the corner now used by Gage & Knowlton; Lerned & Sibley, the building now occupied by Miss Lydia Story; Thomas Williams, a building standing between John S. Kimball's and the Congregational meeting house. At this time, besides other stores, were the usual attendant establishments representing the multiple business wants of a complex community.

In the earlier times trade was not so closely confined to the villages as now. One of the outposts of business was on the Concord road, near the present residence of Mr. William Long. Nathaniel Proctor was a trader at this point, as may have been others. Different parties have also traded in a store that stood near the present residence of Mr. Perley Beck, at the four corners at "Stumpfield." Among those trading in Hopkinton village in later times Joseph Stanwood, Stephen B. Sargent, James Fellows and Nathaniel Evans are prominent. Among the earlier traders in Contoocook was Solomon Phelps. Ebenezer Wyman came to Contoocook over forty years ago, and till lately has traded most of the time since, doing a miscellaneous business. Herrick Putnam and Isaac D. Merrill were also well known merchants in this locality.

The following parties are at present engaged in trade in this town:—Gage & Knowlton, Kimball & Co., Curtice & Stevens, W. H. Hardy, Rufus P. Flanders, G. H. Ketchum (stoves, tin and hardware), Miss Julia M. Johnson (ladies' goods). The first two firms mentioned are in the lower village; the other parties in Contoocook.

THE BRITISH ACT OF PARLAIMENT, KNOWN AS THE BOSTON PORT BILL, OF 1774, AND THE LIBERALITY OF NEW HAMPSHIRE, AND OTHER PLACES, FOR THE RELIEF OF THE SUFFERERS IN BOSTON.

BY HON. G. W. NESMITH.

This act of Parliament went into effect on the 14th day of June, 1774. The harbor of Boston was blocked up by four large ships of war, with orders to interdict all trade by sea. Five regiments of troops were stationed in different parts of the town to prevent trade with the country. The intent of the statute was to punish the rebellious citizens of that town, who had not only refused to pay duties on British goods, but had dared to throw overboard cargoes of imported teas, in vindication of the claim that taxation and representation should go together, or, in other words, that the colonies should be heard before taxes on imports should be imposed. Again, Boston had complained of the *quartering of troops* within the limits of their city in a time of peace, and as a consequence of this tyrannical act the massacre of March, 1770, had ensued and a hostile spirit between the citizens and troops had been engendered. The tendency of the Port Bill was to produce immediate want and suffering. The ordinary commerce and trade of the town being prohibited, the industries of the citizens destroyed, their sources of living dried up, their only resource left was either to abandon their homes entirely, or to appeal to the charity and liberality of their friends elsewhere for a supply of the necessaries of life. The appeal was made. The friends of liberty yielded a ready response. The conduct of Britain was everywhere regarded as oppressive, and a deep sympathy was felt in behalf of the sufferers. The newspapers of the day inform us that the bells in the town of Falmouth (now Portland) and in the city of Philadelphia were tolled all day, and all business suspended on the aforesaid 14th day of June, in consequence of this grievous act of Parliament being enforced upon the inhabitants of Boston. Large meetings of the citizens of Philadelphia, Baltimore, New York, Portsmouth, and various other cities and towns assembled, and passed resolutions recommending the people to purchase no more British goods, and to consume no more tea, strongly sympathizing with the oppression of Boston, and exhorting her people to stand firm at this trying crisis.

The Provincial Congress of Massachusetts and New Hampshire, representing the people of each State, among their spirited resolves, requested their fellow citizens to contribute liberally to alleviate the burdens of those persons who are the more immediate objects of ministerial resentment, and who are suffering in the common cause of their country. Donations soon began to flow into the town of Boston from all quarters. On the 20th day of June, 1774, Newburyport contributed two hundred pounds. June 30th, Charleston, South Carolina, sent two hundred and five casks of rice. The editor of the South Carolina Gazette severely critisized the character of the Port Bill, stigmatizing it as being not a production of Lord North, but of *h—l*. On the 15th of July, Wethersfield, Conn., and vicinity, sent one thousand bushels of grain for the *Boston poor*. On the same day the editor of the Boston Chronicle remarked "that this town was visited by Col. Putnam, of Pomfret, Conn., a hero renowned, and well known throughout North America. His generosity led him to Boston to succor his oppressed brethren. A fine drove of sheep was one article of *comfort* he was commissioned to present to us." Putnam saw enough at this visit to induce him, when first hearing of the battle of Lexington, some months after, to leave his plow in the furrow, and fly to the rescue of his friends.

Soon a quantity of provisions was received from the friends of liberty in Quebec, and one hundred pounds sterling from Montreal, and one thousand pounds worth of West India rum from the Island of Barbadoes. A constituent of Edmund Burke, resident in Bristol, England, wrote to his friend and correspondent here to pay on his account fifty pounds, and five hundred pounds, if, in his judgment, the good cause demanded it. We cannot stop to recount the liberal donations from the State of Massachusetts and other States. Some of the donations from our State are not defined. The account is quite general in this language:— This day was received from Londonderry, Amherst, Hampton, New Ipswich, etc., provisions, money, etc., for the relief of Boston. In other cases we have the following items: Portsmouth contributed three hundred pounds, Exeter two hundred pounds, Rye twenty pounds, South Hampton fifteen pounds, Temple ten pounds, Poplin (Fremont) her pair of oxen, delivered to Mr. Foster by Zacheus Clough, Esq. Mr. Foster was chairman of the donation committee for the town of [Charlestown, which was embraced in the common calamity with Boston. John Sullivan, Esq., afterwards Gen. Sullivan, of Durham, and the minister of the parish, Rev. John Adams, constituted a committee who collected some funds in Durham, and the vicinity, and forwarded the same by a messenger no less distinguished than Alexander Scammell, who was then a student at law in Sullivan's office, accompanied by the following letter, which we give for purpose of showing the spirit of the hour. The letter was addressed to the donation committee of Boston, of which Samuel Adams was chairman:—

"DURHAM, Nov. 21, 1774.

Gentlemen—We take pleasure in transmitting to you by Mr. Scammell, a few cattle, with a small sum of money, which a number of persons in this place, tenderly sympathising with our suffering brethren in Boston, have contributed toward their support. With this, or soon after, you will receive the donation of a number in Lee, a parish lately set off from this town, and in a few days the contribution of Dover, Newmarket, and other adjacent towns. What you herewith receive comes mostly from the industrious yeomanry of this parish. We have but few persons of affluent means, but these have most cheerfully contributed to the relief of the distressed in your metropolis. This is considered by us not as a gift, or an act of charity, but a debt of justice. It is a small part of what we are in duty bound to communicate to those truly noble and patriotic advocates of American freedom who are bravely standing in the gap between us and slavery, defending the common interest of a whole continent, now gloriously struggling in the cause of common liberty. *Upon you* the eyes of all America are now fixed. Upon your invincible patience, fortitude and resolution, depends all that is dear to us and our posterity.

May that superintending Gracious Being, whose ears are ever open to the cries of the oppressed, in answer to the incessant prayers of his people, defend our just cause, turn the counsels of our enemies into foolishness and deliver us from the hands of our oppressors, and make those very measures by which they are endeavoring to compass our destruction the means of fixing our invaluable rights and privileges upon a more firm and lasting basis. It seems to us that it may prove to the ultimate advantage of this good cause in America, that the attacks of our enemies are made to that quarter where the virtue and firmness of the inhabitants could brave the shafts of the military tyrants and set at defiance the threats of an exasperated and despotic minister.

We are pleased to find that the methods sought to divide, have happily united us, and by every new act of oppression our union has been more and more strengthened; and we can with truth assure you, gentlemen, that in this quarter we are engaged to a man in your defence, and of the common cause.

We are ready to communicate of our substance largely, as your necessities shall require, and with our estates to give also our lives, and mingle our blood with yours in the common sacrifice to liberty. We renewedly assure you we will not submit to wear the chains of slavery which a profligate and arbitrary *ministry* are preparing for all of us. That Heaven may support you under your distressing circumstances, and send you a speedy and happy deliverance from your present troubles, is the earnest prayer of your cordial friends, and very humble servants.

(Signed)
JOHN ADAMS,
JOHN SULLIVAN. } Committee.

This letter was published in the Boston Chronicle at the time. Its determined zeal and fervor naturally tended to influence the public mind, and to prepare the friends of liberty to strike for the common cause.

The patriots of Boston, amid all their severe trials, were encouraged by salutary advice and substantial aid to persevere to the end by the lovers of freedom everywhere. They were doomed to encounter the perils and privations of two sieges. The first, commencing with the 14th of June, 1774, continued about one year, until open hostilities commenced, and was prosecuted to gratify the vengeance of a spiteful British Ministry. During this year the town lost nearly one-third of her population, who felt compelled to remove in order to obtain the means of living. Many of those who remained, who had been in comfortable circumstances, were reduced to abject poverty. All classes of people were made poorer; none were enriched. After the engagement at Bunker Hill, the *besiegers* found themselves *besieged* by land, and for the next nine months the American army held the avenues to the town, and the hopes of the patriots were revived and their condition somewhat improved by a friendly intercourse with the troops without. During these nine months the British troops were obliged to depend upon their shipping for provisions. The patriots within the town derived much consolation from the fact that the British troops were involved with them in a common suffering for a supply of necessary food and fuel. In March, 1776, Washington was prepared to bombard the town.

This resort was expected by the patriots, and the owners of property feared the results. Gen. Howe threatened to fire the town if Washington persisted in his purpose. Finally Howe proposed to evacuate the town if no attack were made. This arrangement was concurred in, and on the 18th of March Howe withdrew his army, giving relief and great joy to the inhabitants of the town.

In the afternoon of the next Sunday after the evacuation, in presence of the American army, Rev. Mr. Bridge, Chaplain in his brother's regiment, preached an appropriate discourse from II. Kings, 7th chap., 7th verse—"Wherefore, they arose and fled in the twilight, and left their tents, and their horses, and their *asses*, even the camp as it was, and fled for their life." The application of the text was as follows: "The text describes the flight of our enemies, as they left their tents, and their horses, and quite a number of *Tories* for *asses*."

THE GRANITE MONTHLY.

A MAGAZINE OF LITERATURE, HISTORY AND STATE PROGRESS.

VOL. II.   DECEMBER, 1878.   NO. 5.

HON. MOODY CURRIER.

[The following sketch is from the history of Boscawen, by C. C. Coffin, recently published.]

The subject of this sketch was born in the town of Boscawen, April 22, 1806. At an early age, his parents removed to Dunbarton, and thence to Bow, where his early years were passed on a farm, attending the district school about six weeks during the winter. He had an insatiable desire for information, and devoured all the books he could lay his hands on, reading through the long winter evenings by the light of a pitch pine knot, or a tallow candle.

He fitted for college at Hopkinton Academy, and graduated at Dartmouth in 1834, Hon. Daniel Clark of Manchester, of the U. S. District Court for this District, being one of his classmates.

Soon after leaving college he taught school in Concord, and, in company with Hon. Asa Fowler, edited the New Hampshire Literary Gazette. He was afterwards principal of the Hopkinton Academy for one year, and in 1836 became principal of the High School at Lowell, Mass. He held that position for five years, and in 1841 removed to Manchester, where he has since continued to reside. During his residence at Hopkinton and Lowell he studied law, and on going to Manchester was admitted to the Bar, and became a law partner with Hon. George W. Morrison. In 1842 he purchased an interest in a weekly newspaper, the Manchester Democrat, and devoted a part of his time to editorial labors for about a year. His partnership with Mr. Morrison was dissolved in 1843, but he continued in the practice of his profession independently until 1848. In that year the Amoskeag Bank was organized, and he became its cashier and has continued in the banking business since that time.

Upon the organization of the Amoskeag Savings Bank, in 1852, he became its Treasurer, and still holds the office. When the Amoskeag National Bank was organized to succeed the old Amoskeag Bank, in 1864, he became its President. He has been a Director in the People's Bank at Manchester since it was organized in 1874; a Director in the Blodgett Edge Tool Company during the existence of the corporation; President and Treasurer of the Amoskeag Axe Company since its organization in 1862; a Director in the Manchester Gas Light Company since 1862; a Director in the Manchester Mills since the organization of the corporation in 1874; Treasurer of the Concord & Portsmouth Railroad Company since 1856; Treasurer of the Concord Railway Company in 1871-'72; and is now Treasurer of the New England Loan Company, and President of the Eastern Railroad Company in New Hampshire.

He was Clerk of the New Hampshire Senate in 1843-'44, and was elected a member of that body from the 3d District in 1856-'57, and was President of the Senate in the latter year. He was elected Councillor in 1860-'61, and was Chairman of the War Committee of the Council during the first fifteen months of the War of the Rebellion. In that position he exhibited great ability and energy, and rendered efficient service to the state and the nation. He entered with his whole soul into the business of raising and equipping troops, and won great praise from all parties for his efforts in this direction. The first eight regiments of infantry, the First New Hampshire Battery, together with four companies of cavalry and three companies of sharp-shooters, were organized, equipped and sent to the front with the utmost dispatch, while Mr. Currier was at the head of the War Committee. In compliment to him, the rendezvous of the Eighth Regiment at Manchester was named "Camp Currier."

Mr. Currier has been three times married. His first wife was Miss Lucretia Dustin to whom he was married, Dec. 8, 1836. His second wife, to whom he was married September 5, 1847, was Miss Mary W. Kidder. He was married to Miss Hannah A. Slade, his present wife, November 16, 1869.

He has had three children, one of whom, Charles M. Currier, survives, and is the Teller of the Amoskeag National Bank.

Mr. Currier has an ardent temperament and versatile talent. His practical judgment is shown in the success of the banking institutions which he has managed for many years, and also in the success of the various other enterprises with which he has been connected in an official capacity. He is methodical and cautious in his habits, and has always sustained the reputation of being honorable and upright in all his business relations.

He maintains a high rank as a scholar and, unlike many other men who have enjoyed the advantages of a liberal education, he has throughout his whole life taken a strong interest in the study of literature, science and philosophy. He retains a taste for the ancient classics and is quite familiar with the French, German, and several other modern languages; he has written many pieces of poetry, at intervals of leisure, which are very creditable in taste and composition. He is an independent thinker upon all subjects, and though he is decided in his convictions and frank in the avowal of his opinions, cherishes a tolerant spirit, and entertains the highest respect for those with whom he is obliged to differ.

By industry and prudence he has acquired a handsome fortune, and his residence is a model of taste. He is liberal of his gifts to worthy objects and especially to those which relate to intellectual culture. In 1876 he presented to the Manchester City Library upwards of 700 volumes of valuable books,—standard, classical, illustrated, ecclesiastical, and scientific. These books were numbered and classed in the catalogue of the library as the "Currier Donation." In acknowledgment of this generous gift, resolutions of thanks to Mr. Currier were passed in both branches of the City Government, and by the Board of Trustees of the City Library.

He has been for many years a member of the Unitarian Society of Manchester, and one of its most liberal benefactors.

NEW HAMPSHIRE HILLS.

[Among the prominent men of the last generation, few are better known or more widely honored than Governor Colby. Living in the quiet town of New London, he originated and carried on a variety of business operations, much in advance of his times. He was as active and successful in politics as in business. He held many important offices in town and state, and, in 1846, was chosen Governor of New Hampshire. His only daughter was educated at New London Academy, and became for some years, one of the most thorough and successful teachers our State has ever produced. She was afterwards married to James Colgate, Esq., one of the most distinguished bankers of New York City. Mr. and Mrs. Colgate are widely known for their munificent gifts to public institutions and private charities. Mrs. Colgate loves her native state. The following poetic tribute to the New Hampshire Hills, is from her pen:]

New Hampshire hills! New Hampshire hills!
Ye homes of rocks and purling rills,
Of fir trees, huge and high,
Rugged and rough against the sky
With joy I greet your forms, once more
My native hills, beloved of yore.

Engraved upon my youthful heart
With keener point than diamond's art,
I see you when the world's asleep
And memory wakes, with fancies deep,
Visions of scenes, though old, still new,
Then lost in dreams, I gaze on you.

New Hampshire hills! New Hampshire hills!
The electric sound my spirit thrills,
With thoughts of childish ecstacies,
And dreams of glorious symphonies,
While now as then, I see you stand,
Erect to guard our granite land.

I've watched you, at the early dawn,
Before the shades of night had gone,
Arrayed in robes of soft gray mist
Before the sun your brow had kissed,
Then laying this pure vest aside,
Stand, nobly dressed in royal pride.

I've seen you in the moon's full light,
When every dell was brought to light;
When rock and leaf and crag lay bare,
Suffused with gleaming, glint and glare,
Then blent with tints that knew no name,
Thy hues and dies seemed all the same.

I've watched you when departing day
Shed o'er your forms a softer ray,
Empurpling all your verdure o'er
With richer hues than e'er before;
Then touching quick your peaks with gold,
Too glorious, made you to behold.

I've loved you when the moon's mild beams
Shed lights and shades on hills and streams,
Too strange, mysterious, dark and bright,
For realms designed for human sight;
In silence then, I've stood amazed,
And lost to all but you have gazed.

New Hampshire hills! New Hampshire hills!
The sight of you my spirit fills
With raptures such as minstrels feel,
When at the shrine of love they kneel,
And all aglow with poet's fire,
Strike with delight the living lyre.

New Hampshire hills! New Hampshire hills!
Sweet peace and health your air distills,
As fresh as when the earth was new,
And all the world was good and true;
Emblems. ye are of royal state;
Majestic hills, bold, grand and great.

New Hampshire hills! New Hampshire hills!
Your presence every passion stills,
And hushed to peace I long to pass
Far up your heights of lovliness,
And stand, the world beneath my feet,
There earth and heaven enraptured meet.

LAWYERS AND POLITICIANS.

BY HENRY ROBINSON.

A writer upon "Men and their Professions," in the GRANITE MONTHLY for October last, assumes to slur lawyers. Defence is unnecessary, yet we venture a few suggestions in their behalf. Had his ungenerous insinuations been couched in more respectful language, they might have been worthy of more considerate notice. With an air of authority, he summarily denounces lawyers in general as "Men who are not burdened so heavily with knowledge as *by Cheek*." Imagine the modest writer before the seven able and erudite judges, who constitute the august tribunal of the highest court of our own State, or before the Supreme Bench of the United States, giving vent to such a sentiment! We would call his attention to the history of his country, wherein he may learn that from the ranks of the legal profession have come our leading statesmen, our most gifted orators, our best writers and finest scholars in various branches. The presidents, with very few exceptions, have been lawyers, and a large majority of the cabinet officers, senators and congressmen were students and practisers of the law, and whoever states that these men succeeded through "cheek," rather than by knowledge and ability, insults the intelligence of the American people. "Check" is a low word, and has a low meaning, but *pluck* is an essential element of legal and other success. Lawyers as a class, are as well educated and as well cultured men, as can be found in the community, and any well informed, unprejudiced teacher, clergyman, doctor, or even school-boy, will tell you so. They are preferred for public stations,—for members of the Board of Education, for offices of trust and responsibility in various organizations, and for important positions in society, church and state. Undoubtedly, there are dishonorable lawyers as well as dishonorable barbers and butchers, bakers and candlestick-makers, but the statistics of criminality show lawyers to be better behaved than journalists and doctors, and even the ministers, who generally conduct themselves pretty tolerably well. Undoubtedly, there are ignorant and "cheeky" lawyers, as well as ignorant and "cheeky" scribblers for the magazines; but the writer speaks of them as a class, when he writes down the profession " as one to be dodged by that man who hopes to live a life acceptable to himself and the community."

"No rogue e'er felt the halter draw,
With good opinion of the law."

Has the writer recently received a curt collection letter, or has he been righteously whipped in a law-suit? Ah! here may be a clue to his biliousness. He says, people should not complain, "except, perhaps, when they aspire to office of honor, trust or profit, and find an attorney and counsellor at law ready to fill the bill to their exclusion." We are sorry that the writer has met with disappointments in his aspirations, but he is unreasonable in blaming lawyers as a class for his personal misfortunes. He says, " lawyers are clannish;" but he is in error in his statement, for they are almost invariably arrayed one against another. He would lead us to believe that lawyers are a mean set of people, for even amongst *his* friends and acquaintances "are worthy and honorable *exceptions*." We do not happen to know what the writer's associations are, but do know that your average lawyer is a good, whole-hearted citizen. He is a practical man, —he can harness a horse and drive it; he can make a speech, write an article for the newspaper, and saw a cord of wood. The sun does not go down upon his passion,—he will oppose you to-day; but go a-fishing with you to-morrow. He investigates many subjects; sees many things; he thinks much, travels much, reads much, writes much, talks much; he is a broad and deep student of human nature, the grandest of studies; he can give and take hard blows. He has a deep respect for members of his own and other professions and trades, and has warm friendships and many acquaintances amongst them. He is a genial companion, a good family man, well-informed and handy as a friend. He is public-spirited; does not sit in judgment on other men and their vocation and cases, but does his best for his clients. He has an immense sense of the ridiculous; but a deep reverence for things holy, and is charged with a fund of interesting anecdote. His is a grand and deep science. It may not be grander and deeper than theology or medicine, but a life-time of application to it would fall far short of its accomplishment. To be a good lawyer, he must love his work. Law is that order which pervades and constrains all existence, and in these days of civilization, enlightenment, invention, improvement, progress,—in these days of a million competitions and complications of trades, governments, laws, transactions, no one can afford to sneer at an upright lawyer. Wherever are law and order and peace, there are lawyers. Where all is chaos and confusion, there is no mission or opportunity for lawyers.

The writer referred to has gone on to discuss the members of other professions and has drawn some very invidious discriminations. The truth is that we are all dependent one upon another; each is important in his place, and each puts his own profession, his own trade, craft or calling at the head, and such pride is laudable, for every man's vocation, be it legitimate, should be the highest in his own estimation. The writer is no very keen observer, else he would have learned that there are no totally depraved callings. Human nature runs about the same throughout all kinds of business. There are good and bad men in every decent department of life, and—thank God! —the good are in the majority, and our friend ought to know it. It may seem otherwise at times; the day is not always bright, but the sunshine is much more plentiful than the thunder clouds; men may lie, but truth is far more frequent than falsehood. We have not the time, the inclination or the space to point out all the erroneous impressions conveyed in the writer's article, but it seems a duty to call attention to one more, at least, now that we have given the matter any attention.

He classes all politicians with blear-eyed, drunken loafers and culprits, who escape prison, where they rightfully belong, who give the police the greatest uneasiness,—"the despised of the community, the forsaken of God, the hated and ignored of virtuous women." But what does he mean? A saintly teacher of ours, now beyond the river of time, taught us that *Political Ethics*, the Science of Government, was one of the grandest, broadest and deepest studies, and in later days, with the utmost deference, we have revered the names of the noble statesmen, as we have been wont to call the politicians who have comprehended the mighty fabric of our organic laws, and have marshalled the people into a peaceful union, under a republican Government and a Glorious Old Flag! Alas! these men were professional politicians, and, the gentleman declares, should be given the "cut direct." Yet Washington and Webster, Lincoln and Sumner, and hundreds and thousands of other great men were politicians. What would we be without politicians? Are there any politicians in Kamtschatka or Fegee Islands? Every great leader is a politician. Every loyal, intelligent citizen and voter takes an interest in politics, and is in some measure a politician. Our presidents, our senators, our congressmen, are politicians, and the better politicians they are, the better qualified they are to serve their constituency to the best advantage. The wide scope of learning has divided men into specialties; the ministers preach to sinners; the doctors visit the sick; the editors prepare their sheets; the blacksmiths fashion and weld iron; but when the affairs of State and general government get entangled, and we are threatened with revolution and ruin, we look, for a helmsman, to somebody who has made politics a study and a business. Are these somebodies, "blear-eyed, drunken loafers," or are they the first men of the nation, essential to our welfare and prosperity? Ah, sir, do not denounce all lawyers, because you are so unfortunate as to have a tilt with a resolute collector; nor all politicians, because you happen to meet at the ballot box, some petty ward-fugler, who never had the slightest conception of the science of politics. To good and true politicians we must look for purification, for harmony, for peace, for prosperity, for good government, and when we give the profession of politics the "cut direct," down goes our hope of union, of progress, of civilization, of Christianity and all honorable advancement. Young men, if your tastes, inclinations, opportunities and circumstances will admit, become upright and able politicians, scholars, statesmen, leaders in the land.

BAKER'S RIVER.

BY HON. J. E. SARGENT.

Baker's River is located in Grafton County, mainly in the towns of Plymouth, Rumney, Wentworth and Warren, and has a history, like all the other rivers and mountains in the State, and particularly in the northern part of it, many of which histories, if they could be written and read and understood, would prove rich in stirring incident and fraught with instruction.

This river is made up of two principal branches, known as the North and the South branches, and of many smaller streams or brooks that flow into them and into the main river after those branches are united. The North or principal branch of the river rises in Moosehillock mountain in the town of Benton, formerly Coventry. Its source is north east of the northerly or highest peak of the mountain. There is a cascade a little way down the slope of the mountain, and about north east from the Summit House, which is visited by many travellers, the waters of which descend to a level piece of bog or swampy land at the foot of the mountain, which is some half a mile in diameter and out of which flows a small stream which is the origin of the North branch of Baker's River. After descending a mile or two, a branch from the west unites with it, which comes down in the ravine between the two spurs, which extend easterly from the two principal peaks of the mountain. At Warren Village, there is another stream entering it from the west, affording valuable water power and mill sites, and a half a mile below, near the old Clough house is another stream, entering it from the east, in the bed of which, up toward the mountains, were discovered the first grains of gold, that were found in the neighborhood of Warren.

At Wentworth Village, a branch, sometimes called the South Western branch, but more commonly Pond Brook, which is the outlet of Baker's Pond, so called, in Orford, unites with Baker's River from the west. This stream was so swollen by the great freshet in August, 1856, that it swept away mills, shops, dwelling houses, barns and out-buildings, and utterly destroyed all of Wentworth Village that was located upon the street that extended up by the side of this stream towards Orford, carrying away all the foundations even, and the soil upon which they stood down to the solid ledge, which remains to this day in nearly the same condition. This river has a general direction nearly south down through Warren and perhaps half through Wentworth, then it turns south easterly and then easterly, passing out of Wentworth through Rumney and Plymouth, and empties into the Pemigewassett, just north of Plymouth Village.

Just before it passes from Wentworth into Rumney, the stream known as the South Branch flows into it from the south west. This branch is said to have its rise in the town of Orange, takes a circuitous route through the easterly and north easterly parts of Dorchester, thence through the south easterly part of Wentworth to its union with the North Branch, which is known as Baker's River. Just below Rumney meetinghouse, another branch called Stinson's Brook, which is the outlet to Stinson's Pond, so called, unites with Baker's River from the north. The whole length of the river from its source in Moosehillock to its mouth is something over thirty miles. The length of the South Branch is something less than that of the North Branch, though not very materially less, on account of its very circuitous course.

BAKER'S RIVER.

The Indian name of Baker's River was "Asquamchumauke," which means "the place of the mountain waters." This name was given to it by the natives, because of the place where it rises, and also perhaps, because all the streams that flow into it, have their source in the mountains that lie on either side as it descends to the Pemigewassett.

Moosehillock, the name of the mountain on which Baker's River rises as it was formerly spelled and pronounced, would seem at first to be a compound English word, made up of moose (an animal) and *hillock*, meaning a little hill. But if this were the origin of the name, then it must have been most inappropriately applied. There is little reason in calling this noble mountain, which is 4800 feet high, and the largest and highest in all the northern part of New Hampshire or Vermont west of the White Mountains, a *hillock*, or *little hill*. If the word moose had any connection with the origin of this name, it surely should have been *Moose Mountain* instead of *Moose Hillock*. To have called it Moose Hill would have been entirely out of place, but *Moose Hillock* is still worse. But we understand that the name of this mountain is derived from the Indian words *Mo-ose*, meaning *Bald*, and *auke*, meaning *place*, the letter *l* being thrown in for the sake of euphony, making Moose lauke, the "Bald place" or the "Bald Mountain," a much more appropriate and significant appellation than to apply the word hillock to a mountain of that size and consequence. There are points from which this mountain may be viewed, where the resemblance to a bald head is most striking, and where every beholder would at once be struck with the appropriateness of the Indian appellative. The name has now come to be spelled in accordance with this theory.

The original dwellers on Baker's River were a tribe of American Indians known as the *Coos auks* or Coosucks, as they were more frequently called. This is also an Indian name, made up of two words, *Coos*, meaning *a pine tree* and *auke*, meaning *place*, "the place of the pine tree," and the Coosauks were the dwellers in the place of the pine. The word *auke* in their language, meaning the same as place in English, was applied to everything that had locality, like our word place. Rivers, mountains, countries, lakes were all *places*. Coos was the name given by the whites originally to all that portion of New Hampshire, which was located north of Concord on the Merrimack River, and of Charlestown, formerly known as Charlestown, No 4, on the Connecticut river; these being for a considerable period of time, the most northerly towns that were settled in the State by whites. All north of this was called the Coos Country or the country of the pine tree, from the large quantities of pine that grew originally, in the valleys of the Merrimack and Connecticut rivers and their tributaries.

Portions of the counties of Sullivan, and Merrimack and all of Grafton, have been made of what was once the Coos Country, and after taking all these, we have remaining the present country of Coos, still as large in extent of territory as any other in the State. The Coosauks thus named from the country they inhabited, wandered over the valley of the Connecticut to the country of the St. Francis tribe in Canada on the north, to the Green Mountains on the west, and to the White Mountain range and to Squam Lake on the east, including the valleys of the Pemigewassett and Baker's River. The Squam Indians occupied the region east of Squam Lake and so north on the east side of the White Mountains and extended to the territory of the Penobscots in Maine.

On the south were the Penacooks, the largest, most warlike and most powerful tribe in the State, who used the territory now occupied by Concord, then called Penacook, for their hunting and fishing grounds and also for agricultural purposes, to raise their corn and beans. The Coosauks and also the Squam Indians were subject to the Penacooks; received their laws, if laws they might be called, from them, and paid them tribute in furs and beads and ornaments, which in fact, constituted not only the currency, but all the personal property of the Indian, except his canoe and his hunting, fishing and cooking apparatus, all of which were of the roughest and most simple character.

Up to the year 1700 and later, these hardy Coosauks traversed freely the places where thriving villages now stand and the intervales along the banks of their own Asquamchumauke. This river from its mouth to just below Wentworth Village was a great resort for the Indians. As they passed back and forth between the Pemigewassett and the Connecticut, on hunting and fishing excursions, or for the purpose of traffic with the Squams or Pemacooks, on the one side, or with the Canada tribes on the other, they followed up this river to just below Wentworth Village, sometimes in their canoes and sometimes by land. Here they left the river and followed up the valley of Pond Brook to the ponds in Orford and Piermont, over what was termed a carrying ground or place, and from thence one route led directly across to the Connecticut River in Piermont and another turned north from the upper pond and extended up to the place where long afterwards and now long ago, was Tarleton's Tavern, thence to the valley of the Oliverian Brook, so called, and thence to their encampments on the "Ox Bow." A line of spotted trees indicated these routes, known as carrying grounds.

Some of the early exploring parties of the whites followed this route from Plymouth to Wentworth, thence up Pond brook to the upper pond in Piermont and then turning northward sought the valley of the Oliverian Brook or River, and thence west to Haverhill. Other parties followed. Baker's River up as far as Warren Village and thence by one route or another crossed over to the Haverhill Valley. Above the present site of Wentworth Village, the Indians did not use the river much as a thoroughfare, but they pitched their tents along upon its borders, dwelling there in summer, and following their usual avocations of hunting and fishing. The location of some of these camping grounds have been discovered, by the arrows and hatchets of stone, which have been found in these places.

The Indians had undoubtedly explored this river to its source, and were well acquainted with its origin, as the name they gave it would imply. They had an encampment, or a place of favorite resort at the mouth of the river upon the north side of it upon the intervale near where it unites with the Pemigewassett. Here they built their wigwams; here they deposited their furs and game; here they had their sports; here they sang their songs; danced their war' dances, and smoked the pipe of peace. Here, Indian graves and bones have been found, also stone mortars, pestles, hatchets, arrows and other Indian utensils.

As they passed up and down the river by land, they soon found and marked paths from point to point, cutting off the bends in the river and thus shortening the distance and making the route more direct, and hence many of the first roads laid out by the whites in the several towns upon the river were laid out and built upon these lines of spotted trees, which originally marked the wandering Indians path from hill to hill, and along the valleys.

But a question naturally arises here, why was this river, the Indian "Asquamchumauke," called in English, "Baker's River?" We find that it was so called, when the first settlers came on; it is so called in the journal of Capt. Powers in 1754, of whose travels we shall hereafter speak.

It seems that early in the year 1709, one Thomas Baker was taken captive from Deerfield, Mass., by the Indians and carried up Connecticut River to Lake Memphremagog and thence to Canada. The next year he was ransomed and returned by the same route to his home in Northampton, Mass., thus having gained a knowledge of the route and of some of the haunts of the Indians. In 1712, he raised a company of 34 men, including one friendly Indian, as a guide. His object was to ferret out and destroy, if possible, the Indians having their encampment somewhere upon the waters of the Pemigewassett River. He then held the title of Lieutenant, and went directly by the old carrying place with which he was familiar to the Coos or Cowass intervales in Haverhill and Newbury. There he halted and following the lead of the Indian guide up the Oliverian Brook to the height of land south of and in plain sight of Moosilauke and then followed a small brook down to the Indian Asquamchumauke in Warren and thence through Wentworth, Rumney and Plymouth to the mouth of the river.

When Baker and his men, who had kept on the west and south side of the river, came near its mouth, the guide signified that it was now time for every man to be on the lookout, and so every one moved with the utmost circumspection, and when near the junction of this river with the Pemigewassett, they discovered the Indians on the north bank of the Asquamchumauke, sporting among their wigwams in great numbers, secure as they supposed from the muskets and the gaze of all "pale-faces." This was in fact, their principal village or settlement, where they deposited their booty and stored their furs.

Baker and his men chose their positions and opened a tremendous fire upon the Indians, which was as sudden to them as an earthquake. Many of the sons of the forest fell in death in the midst of their sports; but the living disappeared in an instant and ran to call in their hunters. Baker and his men lost no time in crossing the river in search of booty. They found a rich store of furs, deposited in holes, dug in the bank of the river horizontally—in the same manner that bank swallows dig their holes.

Having destroyed their wigwams and captured their furs, Baker ordered a retreat, fearing that they would soon return in too large numbers to be resisted by his single company. And it seems that the Indians were fully up to his expectations or apprehensions, for notwithstanding, Baker retreated with all expedition, the Indians collected and were up with them, when they had reached a poplar plain in Bridgewater; a little south of where Walter Webster formerly kept tavern, here a severe skirmish ensued, but the Indians were repulsed and many of them killed—several skulls have been since found on this plain by the early settlers, some of which had been perforated by bullets, which were supposed to have belonged to those who fell in this engagement.

The leader of the Indians in these engagements was Walternumus, a distinguished sachem and warrior, and in one of these engagements and possibly in this one at Bridgewater, he was slain. It is said that he and Baker fired at each other the same instant; the ball of the Indian grazing Baker's left eyebrow, while his passing through the Indian's heart, he leaped in the air and fell dead. The Indian warrior was royally attired, and Baker hastily seizing his blanket, which was richly ornamented with silver, his powder horn and other ornaments, hastened on with his men.

But notwithstanding the Indians had been repulsed, the friendly Indian advised Baker and his men to use all possible diligence in their retreat, for he assured them that the number of the Indians would increase every hour and that they would surely return to the attack. Accordingly Baker pushed on the retreat with all possible dispatch, and did not wait for any refreshment after the battle. But when they had reached *New Chester* now *Hill*, having crossed a stream his men were exhausted, through abstinence, forced marches and hard fighting and they concluded to stop and refresh themselves at whatever risk, concluding that they might as well perish by the tomahawk as by famine.

But here again was a call for Indian strategem. The friendly Indian told every man to build as many fires as he could in a given time; as the pursuing Indians would judge of their numbers by the number of their fires. He told them also that each man should make him four or five forks of crotched sticks, and use them all in roasting a single piece of pork, then leave an equal number of forks round each fire, and the Indians would infer, if they came up, that there were as many of the English as there were forks and this might turn them back.

The Indian's counsel was followed to the letter, and the company moved on with fresh speed. But before they were out of hearing and while the fires they had left were still burning, the pursuing Indians with additional reinforcements, came up and counting the fires and the forks, the warriors whooped a retreat, for they were alarmed at the numbers of the English. Baker and his men were no longer annoyed by these troublesome attendents but were allowed peacefully to return to their homes, owing their preservation, no doubt, to the counsel of the friendly Indian who acted as their guide. Baker's River is supposed to have been so named to perpetuate the remembrance of this brilliant affair of Lieut. Baker at its mouth.

This is the first party of whites that we have any authentic account of having passed along the course of this winding river, which was from that time forth to take the name of their illustrious leader. The date of this expedition of Baker is stated by Whiton in his history of New Hampshire to have been 1724, but this is evidently an error, as the journal of the Massachusetts Legislature shows that Lieutenant Thomas Baker, as commander of a company in a late expedition to Coos and over to Merrimack River and so to Dunstable, brought in his claim, for Indian scalps, which was allowed and paid, in May, 1712 and an additional allowance made for the same, June 11, 1712, which would seem to fix the time beyond question. In addition to other pay, Baker was promoted to the rank of Captain, by which title he is generally known.

The next time that Baker's River was explored above Plymouth by the whites, that I find any account of, was just forty years after Baker's expedition, viz: in the spring of 1752. That spring, John Stark, afterwards General Stark of New Hampshire, the hero of Bunker Hill and Bennington, in company with his brother, William Stark, Amos Eastman, then of Rumford (now Concord), but afterwards of Hollis, N. H., and David Stinson of Londonderry were upon a hunting expedition upon the Pemigewassett and so passed up Baker's River into Rumney. Here just below Rumney meeting house near the mouth of the brook that flows in to Baker's River from the north, this party was surprised by a party of ten Indians under the command of Francis Titigaw, who is supposed to have belonged to the St. Francis tribe in Canada. John Stark and Eastman were taken prisoners; Stinson and Wm. Stark attempting to escape were fired upon by the Indians and Stinson was shot, killed, scalped and stripped of his wearing apparel. Wm. Stark escaped. This event and the death of Stinson, as connected with it, will long be perpetuated by the mountain, pond and brook in Rumney, which bear his name and at the union of which brook with Baker's River, he was slain. This event is said to have taken place April 28, 1752.

From the mouth of Stinson's Brook, John Stark and Eastman were led as captives, up Baker's River through Wentworth, and so through the *Meadows* at Haverhill, (then so much talked of in Massachusetts and New Hampshire) to the headquarters of the St. Francis tribe in Canada. These men being ransomed, returned from their captivity in the autumn of the same year, by the way of Lake Champlain and Charlestown, No. 4.

At that time, the Indians were masters, —the whites were captives. Then the forests were unbroken and silence and solitude reigned, where now the peaceful farm house is seen, dotting the cleared and cultivated soil, and where the din of business and machinery is now constantly heard. How little could the gallant Stark, then foresee or conjecture the changes that a hundred years and more would produce in the face of the country; the relative position and power of the races; of the march of civilization and of improvement in the arts of peace and of war. The idea of railroads, cars and telegraphic lines was not then conceived.

And who can predict that the changes produced in the next century, shall be less astonishing than those that have occurred since John Stark first wandered a captive, along the banks of the red man's

Asquamchumauke and pursued his winding and sorrowful way up through the valleys, now so pleasant and peaceful, and by the site of the present villages, now so busy, bustling and active.

The second exploring party on this river was a company sent out by the General Court of New Hampshire, in the spring of 1753, to explore the "Coos Country", with directions to pursue the track of the Indians as they came from the great valley to Baker's River and the Pemigewassett and returned again with their prisoners. This company was led by Col. Lovewell, Major Tolford and Capt. Page, with John Stark for their guide. They left Concord March 10, 1753, and in fifteen days reached the Connecticut River at Piermont. They spent but one night in the valley and returned by way of Baker's River. This expedition having proved a failure, the Government sent another company under Capt. Peter Powers of Hollis, N. H., Lieut. James Stevens and Ensign Ephraim Hall, both of Townsend, Mass., to effect if possible, what had hitherto been attempted in vain.

This company started from Concord, then Rumford, June 15, 1754. They passed up the Pemigewassett and Baker's River to Pond Brook; thence up to Baker's Pond; thence northerly, through the east of Piermont and Haverhill, till they struck the Oliverian Brook; thence west to Connecticut River and thence up as far as Lancaster and then returned by the same course.

We have been furnished with the journal of Capt. Powers on this excursion by the Rev. Grant Powers, formerly of Haverhill, who was a descendant of the Captain. We will give a few extracts relating to their journey up Baker's River, introducing such comments as seem appropriate, and will commence with the entry in the journal for Thursday, June 20, 1754, which is as follows: "We steered our course one turn with another, which were great turns, west, north west, about two miles and a half to the crotch or parting of the Pemigewassett River at Baker's River mouth; thence from the mouth of Baker's River up said river north west by west, six miles. This river is extraordinary crooked and has good intervales; thence up the river about two miles north-west and there we shot a moose, the sun about half an hour high and then encamped."

(This was about 8 miles from the mouth of the river and must have been near where Rumney village now stands, and near where Stinson had been shot, something over two years before.) "Friday, June 21, we steered up the said Baker's River with our canoes about five miles as the river ran, which was extraordinary crooked. In the after-part of this day there was a great shower of haile and raine, which prevented our proceeding any farther, and here we camped and here left our canoes, for the water in the river was so shoal that we could not go with them any farther. (This was probably somewhere in the vicinity of Smart's Mills in Wentworth.)

"Saturday, June 22. This morning was dark and cloudy weather; but after ten of the clock, it cleared off hot, and we marched up the river near the Indian carrying place from Baker's River to Connecticut River and then camped and could not go any further, by reason of a great shower of raine, which held almost all this afternoon.

"Sunday, June 23. This morning dark and cloudy weather and we marched up the river about one mile and came to the Indian carrying place, and by reason of the dark weather, we were obliged to follow the marked way, that was marked by Major Lovewell and Captain Tolford and others, from Baker's River to Connecticut River, and this day's march was but about six miles, and we camped between the two first Baker's Ponds, and it came on a great storm of rain, which prevented our marching any farther, and on this day's march we saw a considerable quantity of white pine timber and found it was something large, fit for thirty inch masts as we judged. But before this day's march we saw no white pine timber that was very large on this Baker's River, but a great quantity of small white pine, fit for boards and small masts. And on this river there is a great quantity of excellent material, from the beginning of it, to the place where we left this river, and it layeth of a pretty equal proportion from one end to the other, and back of this there is a considerable quantity of large mountains."

"Monday, June 24. This morning it rained hard and all the night past and it held raining all this day, and we kept our camp, and here we staid the night ensuing and it rained almost all night."

"Tuesday, June 25. This morning fair weather and we swung our packs, the sun about half an hour high, and we marched along the carrying place or road, marked about two miles and then steered our course north, twelve degrees west, about twelve miles and came to that part of the Coos intervale, that is called Moose Meadows and then steered our course up the river by the side of the intervale about north-east and came to a large stream that came into the intervale, which is here about a mile wide. This stream came out of the east and we camped here this night."

This last mentioned stream was the Oliverian and the next day's journal gives an account of their following this stream to the Connecticut River to the great intervale there, now known as the Ox Bow. This party proceeded on up as far as Lancaster and some of the party took an excursion as far north as the present town of Northumberland, while the rest of the party as the journal says, tarried to mend their shoes and to make preparations to return homeward. We have an account of their journey back as far as Haverhill Corner or thereabouts, and then the journal ceases and we have no account of their progress or encampments. It would seem that they camped on the night of Saturday, June 22, 1754, near where Col. Joseph Savage of Wentworth now lives. As the record shows that their encampment was about a mile below the Indian carrying place, which started at the fording place a little below Wentworth Village, and that they passed Sunday, June 23, mostly in the town of Wentworth, in pursuing their journey up to near the place where the village now stands, then after fording the river in passing up Pond Brook to their encampment between the two Baker's Ponds. This encampment was of course that night in the edge of Orford, probably near the former dwelling and tavern of Mr. Nathan Davis.

After this party of exploration, we have occasional accounts of parties passing up Baker's River. It seems that one Capt. Hazen in 1762, with a party of men among whom was Col. Joshua Howard, settled in the present town of Haverhill, N. H., and went about erecting a saw mill and grist mill there, the first that had been undertaken in the Coos Country, north of Charlestown and Concord. Col. Howard used to relate that he and two others of the Haverhill party were the first among the settlers that came from Salisbury in the straight course to Haverhill. They came on in April, 1762. Jesse Harriman and Simeon Stevens, were Col. Howard's companions and they employed an old hunter at Concord to pilot them through. They came up west of New-found Pond in Hebron, and so up to Rumney or West Plymouth, thence up Baker's River through Wentworth and a part of Warren, to where the brook comes down from the summit and unites with Baker's River. They then followed that brook up to the summit, and thence followed the Oliverian to Haverhill. They performed the journey from Concord to Haverhill in four days, which was for *that time* considered, far ahead of the present rail road speed.

We also learn that the crank for the first saw mill at Newbury, was drawn on a hand sled from Concord to Haverhill on the ice and snow, in the winter probably of 1762 and '63. The party that went after it and drew it up were Judge Woodward and John Page and some three or four others. They made their sled and took their provisions and started. They accomplished the down journey with ease, but on the return, their load proved rather heavy; the snow was very deep; the weather very severe and the whole party came near perishing with cold, fatigue and hunger. They came by New Found Pond to Baker's River, thence up the Indian carrying place through Orford and Piermont to Haverhill Corner, but at last they arrived in safety, at their rude homes and happy firesides.

The first settlements of the towns on Baker's River by the descendants of the English, were as follows: Plymouth was granted July 15, 1763, to Joseph Blanchard, Esq. and others. The first settlement was made in August, 1764 by Zachariah Parker and James Hobart, who before the next winter were joined by Jotham Cummings, Josiah Brown, Stephen Webster, Ephraim Weston, David Webster and James Blodgett, all of whom except Weston were from Hollis.

Rumney was first granted to Samuel Olmstead, afterwards on the 18th of March, 1767, to Daniel Brainard and others. The first settlement was made in October, 1765, by Capt. Jotham Cummings, who was joined in 1766 by Moses Smart, Daniel Brainard, James Heath and others. Wentworth was granted November 1, 1766, to John Page, Esq., and others. It received its name from Gov. Benning Wentworth. The first settlements were said to be made in 1765, probably before the date of the charter, by a Mr. Davis, probably Abel Davis, who I find was an inhabitant of the town at the earliest date I can find on the records of the proprietors. Warren was granted July 14, 1763, being prior to the Wentworth charter, but this charter ran out and was afterwards extended. The first settlement in Warren was in the year 1767. The first settler was a Mr. Joseph Patch.

For many years after the first settlements in these towns, many of their articles of subsistence, flour, potatoes and seed for the propagation of vegetables, were transported thither from Concord and the towns in that region upon pack horses, hand sleds and in knapsacks. There were no roads or even cart paths for a time.

The first time an ox team ever came through from Haverhill to Plymouth down Baker's River, it was effected by a company of men, who went out expressly for the purpose, with Jonathan McConnel of Haverhill as the leader. It was an expedition that excited much interest with the inhabitants at home, and the progress of the adventurers was inquired for from day to day and when they were returning and approached Haverhill Corner, the men went out to meet them and congratulated them upon their safe return.

Thus we see some of the hardships and privations that the first settlers in the neighborhood of Baker's River were subjected to. After the early settlers had got the wilderness so far subdued as to raise their own bread stuff, they were compelled to go from this quarter to Concord and Salisbury to mill, before they could get their flour and that when there was no road or hardly a path through the wilderness.

But soon the numbers of the settlers increased. Mills were erected, roads were constructed; the forests were felled, farms were cleared and improved; more capacious and convenient dwellings were built; schools were established; churches erected and so civilization and the arts have advanced, and knowledge has increased. The people have become better and better educated, more and more intelligent, until we find at this time, after a lapse of a century and a half and more from the time when the Indian's "Asquamchumauke" was first explored by the white man, that there is as enlightened, as intelligent, as enterprising, as active and as prosperous a people, scattered along on the banks of Baker's River, as any other tract of territory in our State or country can boast.

During all these changes Baker's River has continued to flow with the same ceaseless, constant, quiet current, regarding not whether her banks are peopled by the red or white men; whether encampments of Indians' huts and wigwams skirt her borders; or, whether the more stately habitations of the independent husbandman, rise upon her banks; or, thickly settled villages are built on either side. It matters not to her whether she be called Asquamchumauke or Baker's River. Under whatever name, she still remains what the rude native Indian called her, "The place of the mountain waters." But among all the changes that this river has witnessed upon her borders, perhaps none are greater than the changes produced within a century in the facilities and means afforded for transportation and for travel.

Then, the Indian with his birch canoe paddled up its waters, or carried his game and furs on foot upon its banks. And in this way the whites were obliged for a long time to travel and transported their necessaries. Then rough paths were made, so that pack horses and men with hand sleds passed up and down the river laden with such necessaries as the early settlers were able to procure; then the roads were widened and the logs removed and the stumps cut down so low, that an ox team with a cart could pass; then the more opulent could travel in their gig wagons; and at length, after great improvements in the roads, and carriages, a new idea was started, which was the idea of a turnpike, a *stage coach*, and a four or a six horse team.

And for a time there was as much excitement in regard to turnpikes and stages as there has since been in relation to railroads. For many years did the old stage coach groan under its load of passengers, as it passed up and down daily upon the banks of Baker's River, until at length, the amount of business seemed to exceed the facilities for transportation. Then, new plans are laid; projects more vast and important are discussed, and for a time, the great idea of a rail road engrossed the public mind, in the valley of our favorite river. When at length, she saw upon her banks, a road graded to a level; hills cut through; valleys filled up; and upon this level grade those iron bands were placed, which are fast encircling the earth, and binding states and nations together by ties of interest as strong as human love of gain.

And soon the iron horse was heard and seen; the cars sped their way upon the iron track; and the age of steam had come and was duly inaugurated on Baker's River. And following in the train of these improvements came the telegraph. Men could not long wait for steam to convey their thoughts, but the electric fluid is made obedient to the will of man and does his bidding and conveys his thought with lightning speed; overcoming all distance, annihilating space, and enabling men, thousands of miles distant to converse with each other as it face to face. Along the course of Baker's River does the magnetic wire convey to all the dwellers upon its borders, the events transpiring in the distant portions of our country.

What changes our quiet river shall witness in another century, none can predict; no eye can see; no thought can conceive what changes the next century, or even the next fifty years, will produce and witness. Shall we in that time be enabled to navigate the air? Shall electricity and magnetism be still further applied so as to not only afford us light and heat, but also to furnish us with a motive power, so as to do away with the use of steam and water power altogether? or will some new agent be discovered, or some new application of the agencies already understood, be made, so as to revolutionize all our present ideas of speed, all our modes of business and all our habits of thought? But whatever these changes in the future may be, Baker's River will still move on as it has done in all the changes of the past, in its winding course; fulfilling silently but constantly, every moment as well as every year and every century, its great mission of conveying our mountain waters, downward and onward, to the bosom of the mighty deep, and at the same time, of watering, fertilizing, refreshing and beautifying the whole region of country through which it flows, thus teaching a lesson which all would do well to learn and to practice.

THE DEAD OF 1878.

During the year just past the "grim messenger" has summoned fully the usual number of the world's good and great—useful and honorable men in the various walks of life—from the scenes of earthly labor to higher spheres in the world beyond. And while princes and potentates, statesmen, scholars, heroes, poets and divines—men of world-wide distinction and honor have been called away in other lands and states, New Hampshire has lost no inconsiderable number of her distinguished citizens, representative men in the different professions and callings.

From the ranks of the legal profession in the State, a number of well known men have been taken during the year. Among them may be mentioned William H. Y. Hackett of Portsmouth, long prominent in public and official life as well as at the bar; William B. Small of Newmarket, late member of Congress, and George William Burleigh of Somersworth, all men of ability and distinction.

In the record of names of New Hampshire clergymen, who departed this life during the year, we find those of Rev. Nathaniel Bouton of Concord, eminent as a historian as well as a leading divine of the Congregational denomination; Rev. Hosea Quinby, D. D., of Milton, a prominent Free Will Baptist; Rev. Lemuel Willis of Warner, one of the oldest and most efficient members of the Universalist clergy in the State, and Rev. Michael Lucy of Exeter, a Catholic priest of high character and reputation.

The medical profession has lost a goodly number of its members; the most distinguished of whom was Dr. Albert Smith of Peterborough, long a member of the faculty of the Dartmouth Medical School and one of the most learned and experienced physicians in the country. Others in the list worthy of note are Drs. John Morrison of Alton and John McNab of Woodsville, the latter dying at the advanced age of ninety-five years and retaining his intellectual and physical activity in a wonderal degree almost to the day of his death.

Among our well known educators deceased in 1878, were Lorenzo D. Barrows, D. D., President of the N. H. Conference Seminary at Tilton, who was also a prominent clergyman of the Methodist denomination, and Ephraim Knight for many years, Professor of Mathematics at the New London Institution. The more prominent representatives of the press, who departed this life during the year were the venerable John T. Gibbs of Dover, who published the Dover Gazette nearly forty years, and William H. Gilmore of Henniker, formerly of the Manchester Democrat and Journal of Agriculture, and subsequently, for many years, agricultural editor of the People at Concord.

Of the railway managers of the State, the two ablest, most notable and successful, whose enterprise, energy and sagacity had contributed more than that of any score of other men to the extension of our railway lines and the consequent development of our material resources—ex-Governor Onslow Stearns of Concord, President of the Northern and Concord roads, and John E. Lyon of the Boston, Concord and Montreal, (who although a resident of Boston was to all practical intents and purposes a New Hampshire man), both made their exit from earthly life during the year.

Among prominent manufacturers dying in 1878 were Alexander H. Tilton of Tilton and Nicholas V. Whitehouse of Rochester; among the representative farmers of the State deceased, may be named Col. Ezra J. Glidden of Unity and Arthur Clough of Canterbury.

THE DEACON'S PRAYER.

BY WILL E. WALKER.

'Tis Christmas day. The cloudless morn
Recalls to earth the Light once born
Beneath that glorious, kindly star
Which led the wise men from afar—
That Light whose glory ne'er shall cease,
The fount of life, and love, and peace.

New England hills are cloaked with snow,
And snow-white are the vales below,
Save where, 'mid leafless trees, is seen,
The foliage of the evergreen.
The widespread forests rule the land.
Though scarred by man's relentless hand.

Within a quiet valley, where
The colonists, with toil and care,
Have built their dwellings, without fear
The people come from far and near
To hear what Elder Gray would say
Unto his flock this Christmas day.
The new-built church is small and plain;
What matters that, if souls but gain
The blessing of the Lord, which waits
Within the humblest temple's gates?

Peace dwells within this vale; afar
The devastating tide of war
Rolls on, as 'gainst imperious might
The men oppressed fight for the right.
Brave men have left this quiet spot,
And in the struggle cast their lot
For indpendence, leaving all
The joys of home at Freedom's call.
Brave women bade their loved ones go,
And, anxious, wait their weal or woe.

The little church is now well filled;
The buzz of whispering voices stilled.
The hymn is sung, the prayer is said,
A Scripture lesson has been read
Which warns the people of their sins;
Then thus the Elder's text begins:
" Peace on the earth, good-will to men!"
He told the story old, again,
Of Bethlehem's glory, of the Child,
All holy, harmless, undefiled;

THE DEACON'S PRAYER.

The Son of Man, who, separate
From mankind's sins, to high estate
Had lifted those who humbly gave
Their hearts to Him—who came to save
From sin and woe, whose love divine
Would last when suns no more should shine.

But sin still lived, and still gave birth
To woes that long would trouble earth.
" E'en now, within your very doors,
Fell war its desolation pours
Upon your households, nor departs
Till it has stricken many hearts,
Laid many a loved one 'neath the sod.
Whence comes our help except from God?
It seems in vain to seek redress
From man for wrongs which selfishness,
Oppression, tyranny and pride
Hath righteous deemed, and justified.
Nor wrongs shall cease, nor woes be stayed
Till God the righteous cause shall aid.
We all are sinful, and we need
The spirit of our Lord in deed
And truth; so let us humbly pray
That soon may come that blessed day
When tyranny and strife shall cease,
And foemen say, ' Good-will and peace?'
Surely in this our hearts will share;
Will Deacon Adams lead in prayer?"

Thus closed the Elder's sermon. Near
The preacher, with attentive ear,
The Deacon listened. He had dared
War's dangers, and but ill had fared,
When Braddock, at a heavy cost,
Indulged his pride, his army lost;
For, maimed in body, from the field
By comrades borne—who slowly yield—
This soldier brave can join no more
The ranks in which he fought before,
But, crippled, he is patriot still,
And to his country nobly will,
Through sacrifice, in word and deed,
Prove true in this her hour of need.
Three sons he to the war has sent,
And two have fallen; he is content,
Since they fought well, and bravely gave
Their lives their country's life to save.

But yesternight had brought the news
That Washington must surely lose
His army; 'twas in full retreat,
His men with shoeless, bleeding feet,
Half-clothed, and lacking arms and food,
By twice their number fast pursued.

THE DEACON'S PRAYER.

All night before the Deacon's eyes
The weary patriot army flies.
He seems to hear the panting breath
Of those to whom repose is death
Or capture; those on whom depends
His country's welfare; son and friends
Are struggling there for right, not wrong;
They ask but justice. "Lord, how long
Wilt Thou withhold Thy mighty arm?
Wilt Thou not save the weak from harm?"

These anxious, troubled thoughts will find
A place within the Deacon's mind
As he attends to the discourse
Of Elder Gray; and still will force
Itself upon him, that worn band
Of patriots; while with upraised hand
Seems Freedom standing at their side,
A suppliant. What will betide
Ere God the righteous cause shall seal,
And peace the wounded land shall heal?
By these and kindred thoughts possessed,
He hears good Elder Gray's request.

The Deacon paused, then slowly knelt,
And prayed. The trouble which he felt
Found utterance, and sore he plead
That He who oppressed Israel led
From bondage would this people free,
And bless their land with liberty;
Make right prevail, e'en though its price
In pain, and woe, and sacrifice,
Were great. And less for peace he prayed
Than justice, and that God would aid
The patriots in this their hour
Of doubt, distress and waning power.

Like Moses, when he humbly dared
To pray that Israel might be spared—
Although the judgment of their God
Had risen with its avenging rod
To smite them—so this patriot stood
Between his Lord and nation; would
Not let the wrestling angel go
Until he would his grace bestow.

The congregation sat in awe,
With faces pale or tearful, for
The presence of the Lord seemed there
In answer to the fervent prayer.
And not one heart but many thrilled,
As tremulous with feeling, filled
Anon with deep entreaty, then
With argument, and yet again

THE DEACON'S PRAYER.

With hope, that earnest voice is heard
Pleading fulfilment of God's word.

The Deacon ceased; and silence fell
Upon the people, till the spell
Was broken by the blessing given,
" Good-will and peace to thee, from Heaven!"

A week has passed, and from the South
Comes, flying on from mouth to mouth,
The news of that successful feat
At Trenton. Pausing in retreat,
The patriot leader backward turned.
And, at their cost, the Hessians learned
The daring zeal of Washington.
'Mid drifting ice and tempest, on
Blest Christmas night, his brave men crossed
The Delaware, and only lost
Four comrades in the raid, but took
A thousand prisoners; well might look
The people to this chief to save
Their country with his soldiers brave.
Now changed the people's fear to joy,
Fresh hopes their hearts and hands employ.
Old troops, their time of service o'er,
Agree to stay, and try once more;
While with their service just begun,
From town and country, one by one,
Come new recruits, with ardor fired,
By Freedom's victory inspired.

Unto our quiet, snow-bound vale
This strangely-moving, wondrous tale
Has reached at last; and tears and smiles
Greet news which over many miles
Had passed. spreading such joy around
As now within this vale is found.
And many heartfelt thanks ascend
To Him who will the right defend,
And oft one to another saith.
" Not vainly shall we ask in faith
For help and comfort from the Lord;
The Deacon's prayer had its reward."

LIBRARY QUESTIONS.

BY C. W. SCOTT.

When the first congress assembled at Philadelphia, that library which then opened its doors to the delegates, was one of the thirty possessed by the colonies, and had upon its shelves a tenth of the 45,000 volumes in similar collections north and south. A hundred years more, and when in the same city the congress of the world assembled to commemorate the success of that national venture, the government laid before it a twelve hundred page volume to give but a brief account of our 3,700 libraries, with their 12,000,000 of volumes. The hundred years represent the growth from such libraries as was that of Brown University, to such as is that of the city of Boston. The first described by "250 volumes, and they such as our friends could best spare;" the latter perhaps the best public library which the world has ever seen.

The libraries in their growth have been an exponent of general information and of public education. We have ceased to be sensitive over such subjects as whether cultivated people read American books, and are considering how part of the American people can best get the material for reading, and how the rest can be made to read. But while there has been so large a growth in the number and size of libraries, there has not been a corresponding advance towards uniform methods in their administration. Here and there have been devised and carried on at great expense, systems apparently perfect in their plan and successful in their operation; but towards a library science and its acknowledgment by the public, comparatively little has been done, and most of that little has been accomplished within a few years. It is a question whether the last ten years have not done more than the preceding ninety towards the recognition of such a science. The responsibility for having made no more progress must be decided between libraries and the public. Or perhaps to state it better, it results from the officials and the mode in which they have worked. There has been no special training for the majority of men who have taken charge of collections of books, and in many cases there has been no attempt to make up the deficiency, or to do better than second-class work. With that comfortable feeling of capacity which inclines the average American to believe that he can do everything, newspaper editing and office-holding included, nine men out of ten who have received more than a common school education, or have a taste for reading, think, if they are out of employment, that they are fully equal to library administration. Hence a library has come to be considered as a kind of panacea for those ills which come to superannuated and unsuccessful men in all the professions. This view is frequently seen in practice; in fact one can hardly meet with an article on library organization, where it is not mentioned. Many an applicant for the position of librarian speaks of his qualifications much as did the Maine man, who upon presenting himself at a shipping station, said "he was not exactly a green hand, for he had tended saw mill."

Generally speaking, the man who draws a book thinks there is but little labor required to get it from and return it to the case, and he understands nothing of the real labor which lies back of this; hence he sees nothing very intellectual in arrangement and management. With such the librarian will get little credit if he does his work well. At best he must do much which is difficult, is not comprehended by the public, and is ignored by perhaps the majority. Many have regarded his work as purely mechanical, classed him far below the professions, estimated his services by those of the laborer, and been satisfied with the work of a shoddy contractor. This is illustrated by the case of a fine town library containing several thousand volumes and kept to public satisfaction. In its catalogue one finds new chemistry and manual of chemistry in different places, an and the treated as leading words, and no assistance in topical research. When people look through a large library and then remark: "how long it must take you to read all of these books," we are not surprised if they think that in some way every book can take care of itself. But there are those who are familiar with the results of the best work and do not begin to appreciate the high grade of experience and education which enters into it. As Mr. Winslow remarks, doubtless having certain Boston officials in mind, "they say we have nothing to do and are fully equal to it."

Not long since one of the most flourishing New England cities, almost persecuted a cataloguer who spent over two years on ten thousand volumes instead of disposing of them in six months as was expected. Take the matter of catalogue, or as it has been called "the eye of the library," and we have a work which is never completed. It alone requires more labor than is publicly supposed to be necessary for the entire administration of a library. "The catalogue of the Boston Athenæum library will cost $100,000; and the cataloguing of Harvard College library has employed eighteen persons for sixteen years, and the work is not more than half completed." But cataloguing, although the heaviest, is only one of the eighteen routine duties mentioned by Rhees in his library manual. Again, routine work is not sufficient; there is a demand for as high a grade of education and as much training as enters into any of the professions. More, there is a claim that library administration does belong to a profession rather than an employment. Not that librarians, in imitation of quacks and sleight of hand performers, will bestow upon themselves the title of professors of bibliography. Nor will colleges soon be likely to follow the suggestion made by Mr. Perkins, and appoint professors of books and reading, although it would be both practical and useful.

But at least librarians may claim the same distinctions as are made elsewhere; as are made between the man who pumps the organ and he who fingers the keys; as are made between the teacher of a primary school and the ripe culture which fills the chairs of a college. They have a right to claim that the man who comes to the business with the training of years, or has by experience fitted himself for the work, shall no more be classed with the man who can do nothing about a library, except to dust books and charge them in a ledger, than the inventor shall be classed with the hod-carrier or the lawyer with his copyist. Not to say much of the qualifications of a librarian — whether business ability shall be first, or whether the book-worm is alone competent, or again whether the man is best whose mind is a cyclopædia, inert in itself but useful to any one that cares to turn the leaves. Leaving out these questions, it is evident that a good general education is necessary, and that it must be only the basis for his training. It is this special training which will develop library science, give it a rank with the public, and allow the public in turn to be helped by it. In Germany a plea for this science has been made by Dr. Rullman* of the University of Freiburg. He argues the advantages of a uniform system, and says in regard to special training, "Both theoretically and practically the opinion is gaining ground that only a man specially trained for it can successfully fill the place of librarian. Such training belongs very properly to the university course." The plan

---

*See government report on libraries. The statistics used are mostly from the same source.

mapped out covers three years of lectures, and contains among others, these subjects: general history; encyclopedia of science, with special regard to the best way of defining the limits of each science; history of literary productions, printing, and the book trade; some knowledge of the fine arts; and instruction in library economy. In this country even, with the tact of doing without it, special training is fast becoming a necessity. A college education is only a starting point, and a subordinate place in a library has a tendency to give only a knowledge of part of the routine duties, and to produce skilled, rather than educated labor. The student who has passed through his three years' course and graduated from a school of theology, law or medicine, has probably done less work than would be required to make him reasonably proficient in library management. While so many technical and professional schools like civil engineering are maintained throughout the country, it seems reasonable to suppose that there could be supported one school for making teachers for book uses. The course of such a school might extend through two years, part of the time being given to lectures and recitation, and each person attending being required to be a student for the rest of the year in some library. Such a plan would reduce the expense, aid libraries in much of their work, and give a class of men educated and practical, who would be familiar, not with a particular library, but with libraries. And this introduces a second reason why there has been no more progress in library science —it is because every man has worked for himself, and has made little use of the improvements introduced by others. So in the beginning there is the loss of time in working out plans which are no advance on existing ones, instead of adopting settled ones as a starting place for improvements. Systems of classification illustrate this. Further on there is a loss when in every library is being done that which might be multiplied at a small cost by printing. And in the end there is the greatest loss in those things most essential for the use of readers, but, from their expense, out of the reach of most libraries. Many of these difficulties may be met by co-operation. Reference has already been made to cataloguing; this is costing, without printing, from fifteen to fifty cents a volume, and may cost even more. As has been proposed this work might be done at some central library, and the cards printed and furnished at a small cost; or, as again suggested, the publisher might print slips with each book. Most libraries—particularly college libraries where most of the reading is done towards an object or around a subject—cannot use more than half their value without an index catalogue; a co-operative system of cataloguing will give it at the expense of a make-shift. Again a large part of the thought most useful to scholars and many others, has been expressed through the reviews. It is hopelessly locked up without an index; but there is none covering the last twenty-five years, and no library alone can hope to fill the blank. This work, which is a revision of Poole's index, is in a fair way to be completed, either by American co-operation or by the English index society. Then there would be a gain to users as well as to managers, if there existed a uniform system for libraries. There should be hardly more difference in the manner of managing these than in the modes of teaching, and a book user should be almost as much at home in one library as in another, meeting new books as new faces, but feeling the general atmosphere unchanged. Some have gone so far as to hope for a universal system of classification, which would give to every book at the time of its publication, an unchanging number, designating its place in every library. For the greatest utility this would need to be accompanied by general catalogues, or bibliographies, so that those books in a given library could be designated by marks, and users would know what books to look for elsewhere.

The plan of a fixed number is partially met by the "Amherst system," which makes use of a decimal classification in such a way that all books on a given subject have a common number. If this was in general use shelf catalogues would become classified lists, and any person could locate a book as easily as a letter in a word, or having given the number of a book, know the subject treated by it.

To settle such, and many other questions, to forfeit by the results of experience, to secure uniformity and economy in administration, and to give the profession a better and more useful position with the public, is the aim of the recently formed library association. As far back as 1853 there was a meeting looking toward such a result. Since then there have been from time to time volumes of library sketches or statistics, discussions by the Social Science Association, articles in the reviews, and notes by the press on improvements made or needed. But the interest for several years increasing, found expression during the centennial year. There was first the government report on libraries, which contained the results of the best work and thought in the country, and took the place of a cyclopædia. Then was formed the Library Association which held its first annual meeting at Philadelphia in October. During the summer appeared the first number of the American Library Journal. The first volume of this monthly comprises 450 quarto pages, in its appearance has few equals, and contains probably the best index ever printed with an American periodical. It numbers among its contributors representatives of nearly all the large libraries, treats of no literary subjects and working with committees, discusses all questions relating to libraries from capital letters to catalogues. Of course some recommendations are not binding, but as they come from a comparison of the best methods, and there is a strong desire to get at uniformity, they are pretty sure to recommend themselves and come into general use. The work done has awakened much biblic interest and there have been frequent comments and discussions in the daily press. Among longer articles the most noticable is one on a librarian's work in the Atlantic for November, 1876. There was also a conference at London, during October of the last year, and it seems that such meetings will become common. At this meeting seven countries were represented, and the American delegation took a leading part in all the discussions.

If a librarian seeks for discoveries and wants his Africa, he will find it in bibliography. No one man can ever fully explore the subject, and hence he must always feel that he has not perfectly mastered his profession. Not only that, he may expect to be approached from every department of learning and must not be surprised if specialists deem him ignorant. More than this, there is a field which stretches from the present back into the past as far as pen and ink have left a record. It is filled with titles, authors, printers, prices, histories of editions, and literary notes. It has its scholars and writers, going back from Allibone through Lowndes and Brunet, and among these are the specialists. There are the men who, as have some of the French, consider the bibliography as the science of all sciences, dividing it into material and intellectual, and introducing a special science for manuscripts. Some of these have written volumes which are marvels of usefulness, and have made of books, divisions and subdivisions so learned and minute that it is less labor to do without than to master them. Others have made classifications purely fanciful, like that of Denis who had a division into seven classes, based upon the words of Solomon: "Wisdom hath builded a house, she hath hewn out her seven pillars;" or like that of another writer who proposed to group all books under morals, sciences, and devotion. Then there are the men who are misers of books, whose happiness is bound up in large paper copies and rare editions— Aldines and Elzivers. They are the collectors divided by Burton in his Book Hunter into "private prowlers" and "auction haunters." "Book madmen," they are called by Dibdin, who was the much honored historian and admirer of the disease. Its symptoms we have in his "Bibliomania," as well as many notes on men who have spent their lives in the collection of books "cheaply bought with thrice their weight in gold." In his imagination an auction was a skillfully manœuvered battle, and the sale of a "Boccacio" "a Waterloo among books."

But pleasant as this field may be to a man of leisure, and profitable as it is to librarians, few are those who can indulge the taste, or become book-hunters. An American librarian, with indexing, circulation and the books of the day crowding every department, must, in a majority of cases, consign bibliography as well as antiquarian and many other kinds of research, to specialists. He must first be practical, and administer for the majority, yet if he would be in the highest sense successful, he must not only live in the atmosphere of the catalogue, but also consider bibliography, with its more than twenty thousand volumes, as a continually to be drawn upon and inexhaustible storehouse.

A perfect library system is one of those things which are many years in the future. We can tell some of the conditions which must enter into it and quite definitely many things which must be excluded. The old world has priceless treasures in manuscripts and untold wealth in volumes, but from the very bulk of the collections as found in the large libraries, a change of system becomes impossible. The past has bequeathed them methods cumbersome and unsuited to the present and to a reading people. The improvements in methods of administration are not to be found in the old collections, with their flavor of scholarship and antiquity, but in the libraries which have grown up in the manufacturing places like Manchester and Leeds. The model library is not to be arranged by gilt edges as was said of one old collection. It is not to be an inaccessible buried assemblage of books and manuscripts like that of the Vatican. And it must not be without an index, and hence open to the charge of being pathless, as is said of the British Museum. It may not, like the library of Paris, count its books by millions; but every volume must be like a sentinel on duty, and the arrangement must be such that it can be determined at once what belongs to any department or subject. The old world has beyond comparison more resources for the scholar in its libraries; but in rapidity of circulation, inflexibility of management, in ability to reach the people, and in much that goes to constitute the true public library, Europe must yield to America. In fact it is claimed that the popular library, taking that of Philadelphia as the representative, is older here than in England. The public library of the future is to be like the school, within the reach of every one. It is to have the benefit of special laws and possibly special taxes, to be paid the most cheerfully of all. Small assessments accomplish large results in furnishing reading, and there is the constantly increasing assistance of endowments. The commissioner of education notes that of thirty seven towns and cities where libraries have been established, thirty-two voted unanimously for them, and in the remaining five cities the vote was three to one in their favor. Eight states already have library statutes and eleven states have public libraries. It is noticable that of the libraries mentioned Massachusetts possesses two-thirds, and the same ratio of the 1,300,000 volumes. But while this small part of our really public libraries has only a fifth more volumes than the British Museum, it represents a wide influence in a circulation of nearly five millions, and probably twice that number of readers. As the use of all classes of libraries increases, so must the scientific knowledge of how to use them. And it is probable that in the future library manuals will become text books rather than catalogues, and that their principles will be deemed as essential to readers as book-keeping to business men.

In colleges there is no sufficient reason why a limited time should not be given to the study of bibliography or something allied to it; and any student would be doubly paid for the time given by the ease with which he would get at any desired subject. Judging from their tendencies, libraries will grow into a common form; classifications will be used which will save time and convey information; co-operative systems of cataloguing will reduce the drudgery of the librarian; divisions into special and professional libraries will enable him to know books better than by their titles; and indexes will make available all articles of the day in periodicals.

There is no slight question as to what books shall be characteristic of the library of the future. Shall we attempt to create a higher standard of taste? or shall we feed the mind in its crude form? Shall we draw the line between the false and the true at fiction? or shall we make that the nucleus supplying it to the full demand and believing with Mr. Poole that people read books better than themselves? Shall we agree with George Ticknor that a second-class book that will command one reader is better than a first-class one which will remain upon the shelf? Shall we attempt to save every printed scrap? or shall we with the founder of the Rush library leave out all newspapers, calling them "teachers of disjointed thinking?" Settle these and many other questions as we may, the library of the future is to go hand in hand with the school and to that alone will its educational influence be secondary. The librarian must in the best sense of the word, be a teacher as well as a guide-board and a cyclopædia in quotation marks. He is to furnish facts for the business man and artisan, help the scholar to the best thoughts, have at his command that which will give to every mind amusement and sympathy, and be the means of making many a never to be dissolved friendship between the living men of the dead past and the living men of the living present. Holmes has spoken of libraries as chemical laboratories where all the best thoughts of men have been crystalized. But the large library of which we are speaking, will be a university on the most liberal plan, where the doors will never be closed and the sessions never end; where every man will elect for himself and the course cover the entire domain of knowledge.

MILITARY AFFAIRS IN HOPKINTON.

BY C. C. LORD.

The early settlers in Hopkinton soon experienced the effects of war. It was in consequence of the French War that the Indians broke into Woodwell's garrison, surprised six persons in their beds and hurried them away into captivity, on the 22d of April, 1746. From the same cause Abraham Kimball and Samuel Putney were captured by the Indians on the 13th of April, 1753. From the second volume of the report of the Adjutant General of New Hampshire for 1866, we take the following item:

"On the 27th* of April [1746] an attack

*The reader will notice a slight discrepency between the statements of this quotation and our foregoing account; it is a result of a difference between authorites.

was made at Hopkinton, by the Indians, and eight persons taken captive. Capt. John Goffe was ordered to pursue the enemy, and in six days he was at Penacook (now Concord), with a company of fifty men in pursuit of them. While at Penacook, news came of an attack upon Contoocook (now Boscawen). Capt. Goffe immediately went in pursuit of the enemy, but without success. This scout ended about the 20th of May. Only a few of the men composing it are known, as the roll is lost, and those only from the fact that Capt. Goffe persuaded them to re-enlist for another scout of ten days."

These re-enlisted men were John Goffe, Nathaniel Smith, William Walker, Philip Kimball, James Stickney, Stephen Flood, Jonathan Stevens. Josiah Heath, Solomon Goodwin, Herbert Morrison, James Vants, William MacAdams, William MacKeen, Joseph Simons, Zachariah Eastman, Caleb Dalton.

In all new countries the administration of government is largely dependent upon military force. The first provincial militia law affecting the people of New Hampshire was passed in 1718, and required that all persons from sixteen to sixty years of age, excepting negroes and Indians, should be liable to military duty. When national independence came to be agitated and a new government anticipated, new laws were demanded. In 1776, a law was passed instituting two military bands, known as the Training Band and the Alarm Band. The first band included all the able bodied men from sixteen to fifty years of age, excepting public officers, negroes, mulattoes and Indians; the second, all persons from sixteen to sixty-five, not included in the first.

The active interest in the war for independence taken by the citizens of Hopkinton is attested by the following scrap of an account:

Hopkinton Account.

Capt. Jonathan Straw, pay Roll to Cambridge, 1775, £60, 17 s., 9 d.
Capt. Joshua Bayley, pay Roll, Alarm at Coos, 1780, £12, 8 s., 7 d.

The local population in Hopkinton was profoundly stirred by the passing events of the Revolution. On March 4, 1776, Maj. (Isaac) Chandler, Joshua Bayley and Moses Hill were made a committee of safety. On January 14, 1777, an act was passed procuring shovels, spades, one hundred pounds of gun powder, with lead and flints*. On March 31, the town voted to raise sufficient money to procure twenty-six men for the army; and on April 14, that service already done should be considered equal to service to come; and again, on June 9, that the militia should have the same pay as soldiers. On the 15th of January, 1778, a vote was passed making the selectmen a committee to provide for the families of non-commissioned officers and soldiers. In 1779, March 1, the town passed a significant vote, affecting the pecuniary compensation of its "continental soldiers," who, it decreed, should "be made good as to the depreciation of money." The fact that a man was then demanding fifteen dollars a day for labor attests the importance of this act. In 1780, Nov. 20, the soldiers' rates were made payable in coin as well as in money; and on the 5th of February of the following year, Maj. Chandler and the commissioned officers were authorized to employ soldiers and hire money for the purpose.*

Hopkinton men fought on many battle-fields of the Revolution, side by side with others of the different New England provinces. The records of the distinctive part performed by Hopkinton men are very meagre. While the soldiers were fighting abroad, public vigilance was alert at home. On March 4, 1776, the town passed an act deposing certain resident parties suspected of disloyalty from the privileges of public trust, and making official recognition of such a deed of public hostility. The list of soldiers representing this town in the Revolution is long and honorable. In fact its length prevents its introduction into the present article.

The success of the war for independence and the formation of a permanent plan of government determined new military laws. In the year 1786 the Legislature of New Hampshire passed a law instituting a training band, of men from sixteen to forty years of age, and an "alarm list," of men from forty to sixty. Each town of thirty-two privates and

---

*At that time an old law required each town to keep on hand for emergencies, one barrel of gunpowder, two hundred pounds of lead and three hundred flints.

*In elucidation of the price paid to Revolutionary soldiers from this town, we offer the following from the records of a town meeting held on the 15th of May, 1777:

"Voted to accept the raits that is already made for the warefare.

"Voted to allow to those Persons which hired men for three year before thear was any Committee Chose in Town for to hire men for three year Equal month with those which the Committee hired at Ninty Dolars the three year."

the proper number of officers, should be entitled to form a company; a town of ninety-two should have two companies.

In the year 1792, a law was passed making companies in Boscawen, Salisbury, Andover, New London and Kearsarge Gore constitute a first battalion, and the companies in Hopkinton, Warner, Sutton, Fishersfield and Bradford a second battalion, which should together constitute a 21st regiment. In 1819, the companies in Boscawen, Hopkinton, Salisbury and Andover were made to constitute a 21st regiment. In 1842, the companies in Hopkinton, Henniker and Warner were made to constitute a 40th regiment. In 1851, the New Hampshire militia, excepting what existed upon paper, was practically abolished.

The militia law of 1792, with some modifications and amendments, was the essential law until the abolition of ancient military customs. Under this law the militia of this town were called out for inspection and exercised in drill at least twice a year, in spring and fall, dressed in their common garb of citizenship. The officers of companies were attired in a swallow-tailed coat, with bell-buttons, and wore a bell-crowned cap and plume. Independent companies, however, were thoroughly uniformed. A body of cavalry known as "The Troop," belonging to the old 21st regiment, and subsequently mustering with the new 40th regiment, contained members from Hopkinton, who were dressed in a red coat trimmed with yellow facings, white pants, a bell-crowned cap, and a white plume with a red tip. Connected with the 21st regiment, and continuing until 1851, was a company of Hopkinton riflemen, who for many years wore a blue suit—spencer and pants—a bell-crowned cap and black plume; afterwards they adopted a gray suit, with a modern cap surmounted with three black feathers. There was also a company of light infantry dressed in a blue coat and white pants, ornamented on the lower leg with two rows of black buttons, and wearing a bell-crowned cap with a white plume tipped with red. The light infantry was subsequently superseded by the "Cold Water Phalanx," a company of men dressed in a black velvet coat, trimmed with red, and white pants bearing a red stripe, and also wearing a modern cap with three white feathers.

There are still living in Hopkinton many of the old officers of militia. Among them are Col. William Colby Capt. Benjamin Lovering, Capt. William Palmer, Capt. Moses Hoyt, Capt. Isaac Story and Capt. E. E. Currier.

In the earlier times a tract of land was set apart by the town for a "training field." The spot selected was on Putney's Hill, on the present Rowell farm, south of the house, on the west side of the principal road. In the year 1796, the town voted to lease the field for 999 years, and it passed into the possession of Nathaniel Rowell, and subsequently into the hands of Moses Rowell, whose descendants own it to this day. In later times rents were paid for the use of grounds for military parade.

The war of 1812 found the people of Hopkinton ready to do their part in maintaining the integrity of the country. On July 6, 1812, the town voted to allow a compensation of seven dollars a month to all soldiers detached from their regiments as a relay corps by order of the general government. Ten dollars of each man's wages was to be paid in advance, and two dollars upon "signing his name." In 1814, October 5, twelve dollars a month was voted to all soldiers put under special governmental requisition, with two dollars upon entering actual service. The last clause of this vote, however, was afterward rescinded.

During the progress of hostilities, two recruiting officers, Gibson and Peck, were stationed for a longer or shorter time at Capt. Brimsley Perkins' tavern, where they enlisted men for the army. Many men enlisted for this war have lost their identity in the regiment to which they belonged. The first volunteers from this town were mostly or wholly included in the 1st regiment of New Hampshire troops, enlisting for one year and rendezvousing at Concord.

The field and staff officers of this regiment were as follows:—Aquila Davis, Colonel; John Carter, Lieutenant-Colonel; William Bradford, Major; James Minot, 1st Lieutenant and Adjutant; Joseph Low, 2d Lieutenant and Quartermaster; Henry Lyman, Acting Surgeon's Mate; John Trevitt, Acting Surgeon's Mate; Timothy D. Abbott, Sergeant Major; Nicholas G. Beane. Quartermaster Sergeant; Thomas Bailey, Drum Major; Nehemiah Osgood, Fife Major.

This regiment went into camp on the first of February, 1813, and left for Burlington early in the spring. On the first day of its march it passed through Hopkinton, halting at the village for rations. This halt gave many people an opportunity to reflect upon the trials of soldiers. Although the troops had marched only seven miles, some were already jagged and footsore.

The 1st Regiment of New Hampshire Volunteers was soon disbanded. On the 29th of January, 1813, Congress repealed the "Volunteer Act," and the soldiers enlisting under this act were re-enlisted into the regular United States Army, or reformed into new regiments, to serve till the time of their volunteer service expired. The soldiers of the 1st New Hampshire Regiment of Volunteers who were not re-enlisted, were consolidated with Col. McCobb's regiment from Maine, becoming known as the 45th regiment, with field and staff officers as follows:—Denny McCobb, Colonel; Aquila Davis, Lieutenant-Colonel; H. B. Brecvort, 1st Major; Daniel Baker, 2d Major; Joseph Low, Paymaster; Daniel G. Kelley, Sergeant Major. This regiment, at the expiration of the term of enlistment, was recruited by Paymaster Low, and was at Burlington for service in the early spring of 1814.

The well-remembered alarm at Portsmouth aroused afresh the military spirit of New Hampshire in 1814. During the winter of 1813 and 1814, British vessels of war were cruising along the New England coast, while maintaining a rendezvous at Bermuda Islands, as well as one at Gardiner's Bay, at the east end of Long Island, their naval depot being at Halifax, in Nova Scotia. On the 8th of April, 1814, a British force ascended the Connecticut River and destroyed about twenty American vessels collected there for safety. On the 23d of the same month, Admiral Cockburne, rendezvousing at the Bahamas, issued a proclamation declaring the whole Atlantic coast of the United States in a State of blockade. Soon after about thirty or forty American coasting vessels were destroyed in Massachusetts Bay. These circumstances spread great alarm, not only throughout New England in general, but throughout New Hampshire, particularly on account of the insecurity of the harbor and town of Portsmouth and the adjacent navy yard at Kittery, Me. A detachment of eight companies of militia, under the command of Maj. Edward J. Long, were ordered to the defense of Portsmouth.

Very soon an event occurred arousing the ardor of the people of New Hampshire to a high pitch. We copy an account of the occurrence from the "Annals of Portsmouth," by Nathaniel Adams:

"Tuesday, June 21st, between the hours of ten and eleven o'clock in the evening, the town was alarmed by a report that the British were landing at Rye Beach. Alarm bells were rung and signal guns fired. All the military companies turned out with alacrity and prepared for the attack. A martial spirit pervaded all ranks, and they glowed with ardor to be led to the place of danger. Expresses were dispatched to ascertain the situation of the enemy, and the report proved to be without foundation. It was occasioned by some boats of a suspicious character that were observed off Rye Harbor by the the guard stationed. The inhabitants again retired stationed ther the sweets of repose."

Although the above affair was only a "scare," there is no doubt the British intended an attack on the defenses of Portsmouth and destruction of the adjacent navy yard. Report tells us that, after the close of the war, a British officer confessed to an American colonel that, during the Investment of the New England coast, he ascended the Piscataqua river, in the disguise of a fisherman. and inspected the defenses of Portsmouth, reporting to his commanding officer on his return that the place was abundantly defended and swarmed with soldiers. This information doubtless had its influence in diverting the British from the proposed attack.

The popular excitement created by this alarm at length induced the Governor, on the 7th of September, to order out detachments from twenty-three regiments of militia for the stronger defense of Portsmouth. Two days after he issued general orders putting all the militia of the State in readiness for marching at a moment's notice; the detachments from the twenty-three regiments were to march to Portsmouth immediately. Arrived at their place of destination, the detached infantry was organized into a brigade of five regiments and one battallion, under the command of Brigadier General John Montgomery, assisted by James I. Swan, Brigade-Major, and George H. Montgomery, Aid-de-Camp.

The following soldiers from Hopkinton were in the First Regiment, Lieut. Col. Nat. Fisk, in Capt. Jonathan Bean's company:—Thomas Towne, 1st Lieutenant, acting Quartermaster from September 18; Moses Gould, Sergeant; Robert A. Bradley, Samuel Burbank, Barrach Cass, David C. Currier, Amos Eastman, John J. Emerson, Ebenezer Morrill, John Morey, Isaac Pearce, Hazen Putney, Jacob Straw, William Wheeler, privates. These men were all enlisted for a service of ninety days from September 11, 1814. The following were in the Second Regiment, Lieut. Col. John Steele, in Capt. Silas Call's Company:— Nathaniel Morgan, Sergeant; Jacob Chase, Amos Frye, John Johnson. John Hastings, Alvin Hastings, Francis Stanley (died in service). James Eastman, Amos Sawyer, Jonathan Gove, William M. Crillis, John Burnham; privates. These men were all enlisted on the 2d of October, 1814, to dates running from November 8 to November 19.

The citizens of this town took but little active interest in the Mexican War. Capt. Paul R. George was a Quartermaster in that war, taking with him Elbridge Burbank and David Calton. We do not know that there were other residents of this town in that service. All three of the parties returned.

The civil war of 1861 found the citizens of this town in a state of mind common to a large part of our country's population. So long a time had passed since the people of our town had taken any active interest in war, the experience had come to be looked upon as a comparative impossibility, or the threatened contest would be an event of the shortest possible duration. However, when, on the 13th of April, the bombardment of Fort Sumpter made the presence of war inevitable, the ardor of our populace became deeply aroused. Bells were rung, flags suspended, processions formed and speeches made. The call of the President on the 15th of the month, for an army of 75,000 men, confirmed the patriotism of our young men, and they soon began to enlist into the ranks. The first man enlisted in the town was James B. Silver; he was enlisted in Dea. Nathaniel Evans' store, where Kimball & Co. now trade, by J. N. Paterson, of Contoocook, who had just taken out enlistment papers. Other parties from this town had already enlisted in Concord. Patterson enlisted a number of men, who rendezvoused at Contoocook until they were ordered to join the Second Regiment of New Hampshire Volunteers at Portsmouth. On their departure they were escorted through the main street to the depot by the Hopkinton Cornet Band, which also accompanied them to Portsmouth. A large number of people witnessed their departure with evident manifestations of grief at the occasion and the loss.

During the progress of the war the town of Hopkinton did her part in maintaining the cause of the Union. One of her first public acts, after the beginning of hostilities, was to adopt the State law, passed June session, 1861, authorizing the towns to provide assistance for

MILITARY AFFAIRS IN HOPKINTON.

the families of volunteers; this was done on the 29th of October.

The summer of 1862 witnessed a new impetus to military affairs. On the 4th of August of that year the President of the United States issued a call for 300,000 men for a service of nine months. Under two calls, both issued in July, 1861, the government had already made demands for 600,000 men for three years. Impelled by these calls, at a public meeting held on the 26th of August, 1862, the town voted to pay $150 each to all soldiers who had enlisted for the war since the last call for troops; to all who had or would enlist after the first of August to fill up old regiments, $200 each; to all who would enlist for nine months, $75 each; and to all who would from that date enlist for three years, and during the war, $200 each. The same day a vote was passed to assist the families of soldiers to an extent not exceeding twelve dollars a week,—or four dollars for a wife and the same amount for each child not exceeding two. Soon after, Patrick H. Stark and Daniel E. Howard were made enlisting officers. On the 2d of October the same year, another vote was passed, giving $150 to men enlisting for nine months, or $200 each if the quota was filled.

The year 1864 was one of great activity in the United States. The resolution to maintain the integrity of the Union became as determined as the urgency of the situation was great. On February 1st of that year, a call was issued for 500,000 men for three years, a part of whom were to be credited to the darft, under a call for 300,000 men, on the 17th of October, 1863, the enforcement of which draft was not completed, owing to a defect in the law under which it was made. The call of February 1, therefore, formed a total of all calls after 1862. On the 14th of March, 1864, an additional call for 200,000 was issued; this was succeeded by a call for 500,000 on the 18th of July, and another and a last one for 300,000 on the 19th of December of the same year.

The urgency of the national situation during the memorable year of 1864 gave a spirited activity to the people of New Hampshire. Such words as were uttered by Gov. Gilmore in his proclamation of the 16th of July fully awakened the people of the different towns to a practical comprehension of the situation. "Our quota," said the Governor, "is to be filled by volunteering if we can, by drafting if we must." In view of the reigning crisis of that year, the town of Hopkinton took formal action on the 4th of June, voting to raise $40,000 for the encouragement of voluntary enlistments, and also to pay $300 each to drafted men or their substitutes. On the 8th of November, the town voted to authorize the selectmen to enlist or otherwise procure soldiers in anticipation of any call.

Enough has been written to illustrate the general promptness and liberality with which the town of Hopkinton assumed her share of the pecuniary burdens of the war. The responses to her appeals for volunteers were fully as ready and prompt as could be expected in a town of her population and character. Only a few of her population were drafted into the army of the United States. We think, also, that none of our people were compelled by the draft to take a position in the ranks of war. Of those entering the army, many returned, but also many died. Some of the bodies of the dead were brought home and interred, but others sleep in distant or unknown grounds; their memory is cherished in the hearts of a grateful people.

The Report of the Adjutant General of New Hampshire. Vol. II. 1865, thus states the summary of our war record: Enrollment, April 30, 1865, 180; total of quota under all calls from July, 1863, 86; total credits by enlistments or drafts, 115; surplus, 29.

The amount of money authorized to be appropriated for war uses, exclusive of sums paid to soldiers' families, was something over $100,000.

The length of this article precludes mention of the names of our soldiers engaged in the war of 1861.

DECEMBER 2, 1878.

A dull, brown earth, o'erarched by dull gray sky;
   Cold, sobbing raindrops dripping over all;
   Stark trees with arms that wildly rise and fall,
Made frantic as the dirge-like winds sweep by.
Like tattered rags the vines hang from the rack;
   No spot of color shows, the eye to cheer;
   The wet, black walks, like mirrors picture back
The dismal scene, and make it doubly drear.
One lonely face looks from a window nigh;
   One lonely passer plods the sloppy street.
The world is dead; and nature's wailing cry
   Thrills human hearts with its own anguish deep.
O, spread the snowy pall and hide from sight
This wreck of what was once so fair and bright.
                     —*Laura Garland Carr.*

FROM THE GERMAN OF HEINE.

Art thou truly, wholly changed?
   Have I truly, wholly lost thee?
To all the world will I complain
   That thou hast hardly used me.

O, say ye most unthankful lips,
   How can ye speak in scornful ways
Of the man who oft and fondly
   Kissed you in the happy days?
                     —*Ellen M. Mason.*

THE GRANITE MONTHLY.

A MAGAZINE OF LITERATURE, HISTORY, AND STATE PROGRESS.

VOL. II. MARCH, 1879. NO. 6.

HERBERT F. NORRIS.

Among the young men of New Hampshire whose names have been prominent in our state politics during the past few years, Herbert F. Norris of Epping, is one of the most active and well known.

The Norrises of Epping, and most of those bearing the name in this section of the country, are the descendants of seven brothers who were among the first settlers of that town, then a portion of Exeter, who located upon farms in the same vicinity, all lying along the road from Epping village to West Epping. The name was prominent in the early history of the town, several of its representatives taking a prominent part in public and military affairs. We find, in fact, that precisely one hundred years previous to the election of the subject of our sketch as a member of the legislature from Epping, in 1877, the town was represented in that body by one Josiah Norris.

Herbert F. Norris was born in Epping, July 28, 1849. He is the eldest of five children (two sons and three daughters) of Israel F. Norris, a farmer, of that town. His early years were spent in labor upon his father's farm, and in attending the district school. Subsequently he attended the high school in the neighboring town of Raymond about a year, and was afterwards engaged in teaching several terms in his own town. In December, 1870, he entered the N. H. Conference Seminary at Tilton, and graduated in the college preparatory course in the summer of 1872, taking high rank in his class, which was one of the largest ever graduated from that institution. While in the Seminary he developed a decided talent for debate, and was an acknowledged leader in society matters. He had contemplated a college course at Dartmouth, but was prevented from entering with the class that year, by a severe illness, and finally relinquished the idea. Upon his recovery he engaged in teaching, being successively engaged at West Epping, Fremont, and South Newmarket, and going immediately from the latter place to take charge of the Academy at Canaan, for the spring term of 1873. Subsequently he taught another term of school at Epping, returning to Canaan as principal again in the fall, and also teaching the next spring term of that academy. Meantime, in December, 1873, he entered as a student at law in the office of Eastman, Page & Albin at Concord, and upon the close of the spring term of 1874 at Canaan, he established himself in the office for the completion of his legal course. While pursuing his studies here, he was engaged to some extent in newspaper work, and became the regular New Hampshire correspondent of the Boston Post. He also served for two years as clerk of the Concord police court, and taught for two terms in the Concord schools. He was admitted to the bar at the October term for 1876, at Concord, and immediately commenced practice in the office where he had pursued his studies, as a partner of W. T. Norris, Esq., of Danbury, who had previously become a member of the firm, in place of Mr. Albin, the firm of Page & Norris then being dissolved. The firm of W. T. and H. F. Norris continues, and enjoys a liberal share of patronage, especially in criminal practice. The firm were engaged in the defence of the notorious La Page, and also of Johnson, the Bristol wife murderer.

Mr. Norris comes of Democratic stock, and has from boyhood been strongly attached to the principles of the Democratic party, for whose success he has earnestly labored. He has been a delegate to the Democratic state convention from his native town, where he has always maintained his voting residence, nearly every year since attaining his majority, and has taken an active part in the deliberations of that body. He was also for two years previous to October last, secretary of the Democratic state committee, and did efficient work in the conduct of political campaigns.

In 1877, Mr. Norris was chosen a member of the legislature from Epping, and during the session of that year took an active and prominent part not only in the debates upon the floor, but in the work of the Judiciary Committee, of which he was a member. Re-elected to the house in 1878, he was honored by the Democratic members with a unanimous nomination for the speakership, a position which he was eminently qualified to fill had the strength of his party been adequate to his election. During the protracted session of last summer, which tested severely the capacity of various members on each side of the house for leadership, debate and general legislative work, he won a high reputation in all these capacities. With large mental resources and perfect self-control, never taken by surprise by any device of his opponents, he proved himself equal to all emergencies, gaining in the various contests which occurred, the fullest confidence of his own party as an able and fearless leader, and of the opposition as an honorable though uncompromising foe.

He was the youngest member of the Judiciary Committee in the house, and the youngest man who has served upon that committee for many years. As a ready debater he had few equals, and no superiors in the house. His manner as a speaker is easy and pleasing. He states his positions plainly and forcibly, and draws his conclusions in a clear and logical manner.

The Manchester Mirror, in reviewing the history and personnel of the last legislature, alluded to Mr. Norris in the following terms: "No Democrat in the house has grown so much in popular estimation this session as he, and he is altogether the worst customer the majority have to deal with. He has improved much as a parliamentarian and a speaker, and there are not many men on either side who can match him in either capacity. His strongest point is his ability to use all his powers at a moment's notice, and to adapt himself to the demands of the occasion."

The Independent Statesman also paid him the following handsome compliment: "Herbert F. Norris, 'the Young War Eagle from Epping,' and the parliamentary leader of the minority did full justice to the confidence reposed in him by his party associates. Alert and ready, he gave the majority a good deal of trouble and the Speaker no end of perplexity. * * * Cool of manner, moderate of speech and persistent in purpose, he could not be easily disconcerted or put down."

Mr. Norris is the youngest man who has received a nomination for congress from either party in this state, since the time of Franklin Pierce, being now under thirty years of age. He was united in marriage in May last, with Miss Belle E. Mower, daughter of L. L. Mower, Esq., clerk of the common council of the city of Concord.

As a member of the Rockingham county delegation the past two years, Mr. Norris has actively participated in the consideration of county affairs, and was appointed one of the county Auditors each year by the delegation.

At the Democratic Congressional Convention for the First Congressional District, at Rochester, on the first of October last, Mr. Norris was nominated with remarkable unanimity upon the first formal ballot, as the candidate of his party for Representative in Congress, receiving 194 votes, against 28 for Lafayette Chesley, 17 for Thomas J. Smith, and 8 for Thomas J. Whipple, and this without any effort upon his part to secure the nomination. He accepted the candidacy, and immediately entered upon an active canvass, addressing the people upon the issues of the day in various sections of the district, and making a gallant contest, although little hope of the success of his party in the district was entertained from the start.

VARIATIONS.

LAURA GARLAND CARR.

We turn dame Nature's plans about
  To suit our wayward fancies.
When driving storms and winds are out,
  And frost views meet our glances;
The fruits and berries that grew bright
  In pleasant sun and showers,
Bring summer flavors to delight
  The dreary winter hours.

By a few tricks of light and heat
  The floral seasons vary,
And wax-like May buds open sweet
  In snow-bound January.
The cold grows fierce. In many a farm
  The icy evils gather;—
In vine-decked rooms, by firesides warm,
  We laugh at winter weather.

O, happy they who can defy
  Years as we do the season!
Who keep youth's buoyant spirits by
  To blend with age's reason.
Though hair grows white, and face and form
  Show Time's defacing finger,
He cannot chill the heart-beats warm,
  Where youthful fancies linger.

EARLY HISTORY OF THE CONCORD PRESS.

BY ASA McFARLAND.

The first weekly newspaper published in Concord, made its appearance January 6, 1790. It was issued by Mr. George Hough, a native of Bozrah, Conn, who came to Concord from Windsor, Vt., where he had published the Vermont Journal. The four pages of the Herald were each nine by fourteen inches, and bore the marks of care and correct taste. Within a year or two the paper was enlarged and appeared as the "Courier of New Hampshire."

I have derived great satisfaction in examining such files of "Hough's Concord Herald" and his "Courier of New Hampshire" as came in my way; and am of opinion that if those files were now submitted to a discriminating committee of printers, they who composed it would be surprised, that with his scanty materials and the rude hand press of those days, Mr. Hough contrived to bring out a sheet, which, for typographical correctness, methodical arrangement, and general good taste, would come off victor in a competitive examination with many journals of the present day.

I knew George Hough in my boyhood days—he being a frequent and ever-welcome guest in my father's house, and a favorite whithersoever he went. He permitted his "moderation to be known of all men," and I can never forget the care with which he always prepared and the deliberation with which he ate an apple, when that was the fruit passed around, or how systematically he punctuated his path, as he walked from his dwelling, now the abode of Dr. Russell, to his office. I was several months in his office, supplying the place of Moses G. Atwood, Esq., who died some years ago in Alton, Ill., and, in common with all who were ever in his service, bear testimony to his uniform kindness. As was apt to be the case with printers of papers at that time, he had not much aptitude with his pen, except to write a very round, legible and faultless hand. He had passed through no training that prepared him to perform literary labor, even for the columns of a village journal. He wrote, however, with grammatical accuracy, but had very little mental vigor, and it may be doubted if he could have written a pungent paragraph, however favorable the opportunity, or whatever his provocation. But his correct mechanical taste and natural good sense were auxiliaries which enabled him to produce a weekly paper that was by no means so far behind those of Boston as Concord was less than the commercial metropolis of New England. He had such appreciation of the necessities of readers that he was careful to select, from the meagre supplies at his command, an amount of foreign and domestic occurrences fully equal to the capacity of his columns, and to issue his supplies with as much promptitude and completeness as was practicable at a period in our history when the transportation of mails was irregular, the arrival of ships still more so, and village journals were diminutive sheets. I have many times taken notice, in files of Hough's "Courier of New Hampshire," of its foreign news feature, and been entertained by perusal of its columns long after the events there recorded ceased to disturb and interest mankind. The celebrated speech of Maximilian Robespierre, delivered in the national convention of France, July 26, 1794, three days only before its author ascended the scaffold, is to be found in the Courier,—a proof that Mr. Hough was desirous of doing all in his power to supply readers with the momentous transactions of that period.

Mr. Hough was not without a competitor, even in this circumscribed newspaper field. "The Mirror," by Elijah Russell, was issued several years at the north end of Main street. It never, I think, equaled Hough's Herald, or his Courier of New Hampshire. Such numbers as I have seen lacked evidence of the good sense and correct taste perceptible in sheets of which Mr. Hough had the supervision.

Many of the inland journals of that period partook of scrap-book character. Riddles, acrostics, *bon mots*, anecdotes, bad verses, weak communications, and wretched "hits" at one another by rival local politicians, constituted the average bill of fare of "The Mirror" and its north-end successor "The Star." Neither in the Mirror, the Star, nor the Courier was such a production ever found as what has been known as "a leader;" an article occupying a conspicuous position, and treating some topic of timely popular concern with vigor and ability, and at sufficient length to set it forth in a proper manner. If articles of that character, since so common in the journals of New Hampshire, had appeared in those published in the closing years of the last century, or early ones of this, the people would have believed that indeed "a Daniel had come to judgment." The town would certainly have been stirred, and the author, if discovered, been regarded as a miracle of literary power. The "leaders" of journals here spoken of were apt to be the record of a marriage, the weight of an overgrown beet or calf, or such a paragraph as this, in Hough's Herald, December 7, 1790: "No Boston post arrived; all news, we believe, is frozen up by the cold weather. We have not even a report with which we can serve up a paragraph for our hungry customers."

I am not in possession of the means by which to trace the rise, progress and fall of the several papers which bore the Concord imprint from 1790 to 1809, but it is certain that the life of each was a constant but unavailing struggle against circumstances, the discouraging nature of which can, even at this distant day, be readily appreciated. The people had not become accustomed to the expenditure of money for the gratification of literary taste; indeed, many mechanics, traders and farmers were often at their wit's end to obtain money with which to pay their taxes and provide for more imperatively necessary articles than books and papers. Inter-communication, also, was slow and uncertain. Partisan politics had not become permeated by enduring heat, and only few men, not the mass as now, had formed the habit of diligently following up current political events. Within my recollection all the papers received in a week in Concord from abroad could be placed in the crown of a stove-pipe hat of the present day, and the garment worn without much discomfort, while town subscribers of the local press did not probably number an hundred and fifty.

But the papers of that period were equal to the encouragement they received. Greater expenditure in their behalf would not have materially augmented their income, and I have no hesitation in saying that Hough's "Courier of New Hampshire" was as fully up to those times, and as completely answered the requirements of the people, as journals of the present day.

In 1806, William Hoit and Jesse C. Tuttle commenced a paper bearing the title "Concord Gazette," of which more will be found in a succeeding portion of this essay. How long the firm of Hoit & Tuttle existed, I cannot say, but in October, 1808, the senior member was encouraged to embark in a second enterprise, and commenced the publication of "The American Patriot." Its projectors were influential men, then bearing the partisan name of Republicans, afterward assuming that of Democratic Republicans, and, later still, Democrats. I knew Mr. Hoit well, for he here labored in his profession, I think, nearly fifty years, and I obtained some particulars regarding the establishment of the "American Patriot," which, but for him, would have passed into oblivion. The Patriot was commenced in a small one-story building, standing where is now the dwelling of the family of the late J. Stephens Abbott, Esq. Mr. Hoit had within him a humorous vein, and his narrative of circumstances attending the birth of the Patriot was of an amusing character. The plan, he informed me, was that the literary labor upon the Patriot should be performed by an "Association of Gentlemen." Several of this class assembled in the office the night preceding the appearance of the first number, and remained until morning, to the discomfort of Hoit and his workmen. Of the number was Phillip Carrigan, author of the map of New Hampshire, which bears his name. The occasion became of very hilarious character, and would undoubtedly have been more so had the "Association of Gentlemen" been capable of penetrating the future, and discerning the long period which the paper then about to appear would endure. But, according to the narrative to us, some members of the association became so full of good drink that they fell asleep, and so remained through the night.

The commencement of the "American Patriot" was attended by circumstances of no more favorable character than accompanied preceding attempts, except that Concord had been chosen in which to permanently hold the sessions of the legislature. In all probability the Patriot, after brief existence, would have gone into the same grave as its predecessors, but for the fortunate circumstance that it came into the custody of a gentleman of the ability, industry and tact necessary not merely to rescue it from the fate of other village journals here, but to make it a power in New Hampshire. This person was the late Hon. Isaac Hill, who in his day acquired a reputation as a political writer and journalist second to that of no other newspaper conductor. He came to Concord soon after the expiration of his apprenticeship with Joseph Cushing, proprietor and publisher of the "Amherst Cabinet." The "American Patriot" had been six months in existence. The first number printed by Mr. Hill is dated April 18, 1809, and thenceforward the people of New Hampshire came within an influence they had only imperfectly realized—the power of the press to mold and guide popular opinion. Mr. Hill was a man of decided convictions and untiring industry, wrote with great facility and vigor, and possessed that electric force by which a writer upon political affairs imparts to others the convictions and zeal possessed by himself. Under his guiding hand the success of the Patriot was certain. It soon became a successful journal, attaining a wide and constantly increasing circulation; greater than that of any preceding or contemporary journal in New Hampshire. A circumstance which accelerated its growth was that difficulty with England which culminated in what is known as the war of 1812-15. That the Patriot, in the hands of Mr. Hill, would have become permanent, even in years of profound calm, there is no reason to doubt: but it is equally certain that its growth would have been less rapid, because of the natural sluggishness of mankind until moved by exciting causes; the disinclination of the people, during the first twenty years of the period here in review, to expend money for the gratification of literary taste, and the limited amount of money in circulation.

The only competitor of the "New Hampshire Patriot," from its commencement until the year 1823, was the "Concord Gazette" of which mention has just been made ; Hoit & Tuttle proprietors and publishers. The scanty materials employed in printing the Gazette were purchased of Dudley Leavitt, the celebrated almanac author, and were brought hither from Gilmanton Corner in a two-horse wagon. They had been used for printing one number of the almanac, and a village paper. The circumstance that only two horses were required to transport two men and the materials with which a weekly paper was equipped, sixty-five years ago, is of sufficiently suggestive character, without any elaboration, to prove the slender resources and the equally moderate requirements of the people of that generation upon the craft.

The "Concord Gazette" was commenced with the advice and under promise of material aid from gentlemen of the Federal party in Concord and vicinity. Its various publishers were Hoit & Tuttle, Tuttle alone, and Joseph and William Spear. Excepting a brief period when the paper was in charge of the late Hon. John Kelley of Exeter, it really had no reliable hand at the helm. But through the force of external circumstances the Gazette had a good circulation during several years; but when the war was over, and the political excitement it caused had subsided, the Gazette languished, and languishing expired, in 1818—in the twelfth year of its age. I remember the paper well as it appeared through those years of its life that succeeded 1812. It had, for a vignette, a wretched imitation of the eagle, a "counterfeit presentment" of the emblem bird, so badly engraven that its groundwork was black as ink. This caused the Patriot to adopt the practice of speaking of the Gazette as the "crow paper." But the party whose views it espoused had no other journal in central and northern New Hampshire, and they were subjected to "Hobson's choice"—the Gazette or nothing. William Hoit and Jesse C. Tuttle were the only publishers of the Gazette whom I knew, and only them because they ended their days in Concord, within the recollection of some men now in our midst: each living many years after the Gazette ceased to be. Mr. Hoit was a native of Concord, but when a lad went hence with his father's family to Wentworth. He served five years as an apprentice to the printing business in Peacham, Vt., which town he left on becoming of age, and entered into the service of Mr. Hough, in Concord. His was almost wholly a printing-office education, but he became a good scholar in the English language, and was the most correct compositor whose proofs I ever read. He rarely omitted or duplicated a word: but his surprise one day amounted to consternation—a day, too, in the evening of which the Statesman went to press—when the discovery was made that he had left an "out" of somewhat colossal proportions: being all the toasts or sentiments at a celebration of American Independence in Plymouth, written in the close chirography of the late N. P. Rogers, Esq. His general information was far above that of his associate, Mr. Tuttle, and the anecdote is not fictitious that a dispute arose between Hoit and Tuttle in regard to capitalizing a certain word found in the foreign news then being put in type. The sentence was as follows: "The army of Bonaparte is in jeopardy." Mr. Tuttle maintained that *jeopardy* was a place in Europe, and therefore should commence with a capital letter, while his associate took the negative of the question. Hon. Thomas W. Thompson being in the office, or passing in the street, was chosen arbiter, and of course decided for Mr. Hoit. Mr. Tuttle was a native of Goffstown, and became an apprentice to Mr. Hough. He was a worthy man, but without aptitude for the successful pursuit of his chosen calling. He did not remain long in the printing business after the discontinuance of the Gazette, in 1818, but became otherwise employed; finally becoming the lessee of a grist mill, now known as Brown's, in Bow.

During the interval between the disappearance of the "Concord Gazette" and the commencement of the "New Hampshire Statesman"—1818 to 1823—a sectarian paper, known as the "New Hampshire Observer," made its appearance. Its establishment was encouraged by Congregational clergymen and laymen. George Hough was printer and publisher; but, as seems often to have been the case in newspaper undertakings of that and a preceding period, no arrangement of reliable nature was made for regular literary assistance. The scheme for an "Association of Gentlemen" was as much the plan as there was one at the start. Samuel Fletcher, then a young Concord lawyer, was to furnish "leaders," Mr. Hough to make selections, and various clergymen were to furnish articles upon such topics as came to mind. My father, being the only Congregational clergyman within six miles of the Observer establishment, was of course expected to perform regular and gratuitous service in its behalf. But Mr. Fletcher undoubtedly soon found that he could not prosper with two irons in the fire, as my father did, that he had parish work enough to occupy his time, while the out-of-town clergymen gradually ceased to make contributions. The result was that good Mr. Hough was not long in ascertaining—as others had before him—that an "Association of Gentlemen" is not a newspaper support of reliable character. The "Observer" was commenced January, 1819, and Mr. Hough contrived to sustain it until the autumn of 1822, when it was sold to Mr. John W. Shepard, a gentleman several years in trade at Gilmanton, his native place. He commenced with an office of his own, in a chamber over the old corner store, where the Masonic Temple now stands. Thence the office was transferred to a building which stood opposite the State House yard, now placed back of the bakery of Mr. Bradbury, and occupied by Mr. Daniel A. Hill, for the repair of household furniture. Mr. Shepard made a change which was no improvement, as many did before and have since. He dropped the word "Observer" and thenceforth the paper was known as the "New Hampshire Repository." It had a life of trial and vicissitude, the stages of which it is unnecessary to trace. It is sufficient to say that in the course of its existence it took a journey to Portsmouth, and was published for a time by Messrs. Miller & Brewster, and even another to Portland, but eventually returned to the place of its birth. It was known through many of its last years as the "Congregational Journal," which title it bore at the time its subscription list was purchased of B. W. Sanborn, Esq., by the proprietors of "The Congregationalist." The life of the paper embraced a period of forty-four years, and during its last years there was no lack of ability in its columns; Rev. Henry Wood and Rev. Benjamin P. Stone having, separately, had charge of it. It was published seventeen years by Mr. Sanborn; but it having ceased to be self-sustaining, that gentleman sold the subscription list, as stated above.

There were jealousies between North-End Democrats and their down-town political brethren so long ago as fifty years. They at the North-End regarded those beneath the shadow of of the State House as desirous of giving law to the Democratic party. The last-named men were spoken of as "Parliament-corner politicians;" a term which included Isaac Hill, William Low, Joseph Low, Richard Bartlett, Jacob B. Moore, and a few other active and influential men south of the present City Hall. Those North-End gentlemen of the same party who were becoming, if not alienated from, at least jealous of their down-town brethren, and who immediately or more remotely partook of this feeling, were John George, Robert Davis, Samuel Coffin, Abiel Walker, Francis N. Fiske, Charles Walker, Samuel Sparhawk, and other less conspicuous men. There were also Democrats in other portions of New Hampshire who had become jealous of the "Parliament corner" leaders, and this at first slight misunderstanding, or disaffection, culminated in the commencement of the journal known as the "New Hampshire Statesman," January 6, 1823; a paper that is one of the very few which, growing out of a mere feud among local politicians, became a permanent establishment. Luther Roby, then in business at Amherst, moved to Concord, and became printer and publisher of the Statesman, and Amos A. Parker, then in the practice of law at Epping, was engaged to conduct it.

To revert to the preceding year: In June, 1822, Hon. Samuel Dinsmoor, senior, of Keene, was nominated for governor by the Democrats (or Republicans as they were then styled), in the legislature of that year; candidates for governor and for congress being then nominated in June by members of the lesislature. In the following winter Hon. Levi Woodbury of Portsmouth, then one of the Justices of the Superior court, was nominated for governor by an irregularly constituted assemblage of people in attendance upon a term of court in session at Portsmouth. The Patriot sustained the nomination of the legislative convention, and came out in strong rebuke of this procedure at Portsmouth, which really was an open revolt, by so many Democrats as participated in the nomination of Judge Woodbury, against the regular nomination of the party the preceding June. But the Portsmouth transaction was countenanced, if not shaped, by the Plumers of Epping, Judge Butler of Deerfield, the North-End Democrats in Concord, and other equally conspicuous and influential politicians in various parts of the state. Although the Federal party had been disbanded, yet thousands who were members of it naturally sympathized with any procedure in conflict with the Patriot, and, with nearly one accord, went into the support of Judge Woodbury, who was chosen over Gen. Dinsmoor by 4026 majority.

The Statesman of course advocated the election of Judge Woodbury; indeed, I have supposed that when it was commenced it was understood that a rebellion was on foot against the nominee of the June convention. But the triumph of the North-End gentlemen was transitory, for one of the first important appointments by Governor Woodbury was that of Hon. Richard H. Ayer of Hooksett, to be sheriff of the newly formed county of Merrimack. This was a suitable selection—fitness being the standard—but one which created disappointment; indeed, displeasure throughout the ranks of those by whose votes Judge Woodbury was made governor. Mr. Ayer was brother-in-law of Mr. Hill, and exerted all his power to thwart the election of Gov. Woodbury, who, in fact, by this and other procedures, turned his back upon his supporters, and distinctly indicated to them that he should henceforth seek promotion in another quarter. He was governor only one year.

The generous promise of material aid to Mr. Roby, if he would commence the Statesman, having failed of fulfillment, and the chief motive for setting it on foot having been thwarted, at least for the time, and the zeal of its godfathers having become indifferent to its fate, the paper commenced to languish, and would have ceased to be, but for an arrangement of which I proceed to make mention, finding it necessary to retrace my steps, and speak of another journal, which came into existence a year and four months after the birth of the Statesman.

In May, 1824, the good George Hough being still alive, though far advanced in years, and without much worldly substance, was induced by his fast friends to commence a paper, which bore the name of "Concord Register." The promises to Mr. Hough were made good at the start, and he was furnished with such means that he brought out a paper surpassed in typographical appearance by no other in the state. It was of large dimensions for those times, printed with new materials, and arranged with the good taste and care for which Mr. Hough was distinguished. The Register was, in truth, a very comely publication, filled with useful and entertaining matter, and in its editorial columns there was no lack of ability. These columns were nominally filled by George Kimball, Esq., who had read law, but was for a time teacher in the public schools here. He was a native of New Hampshire, but had been a resident of the island of Bermuda, where he married a lady who was said to be the owner of several slaves. As the Patriot disposed of the Concord Gazette by styling it "the crow paper," so it put Mr. Kimball, of the Concord Register, in a disadvantageous position by uniformly alluding to him as "the Bermuda man." Mr. Kimball was a gentleman of intelligence; a pleasant companion, of amiable disposition, good at telling a story or relating an anecdote, and a writer of fair ability. But he had, like other men, his infirmities. He was exceedingly indolent, a great snuff taker, and fond of exhilarating and intoxicating liquors ; and it often came to pass that when publication day was at hand there was a lack of supplies for the editorial columns. Then he was wont to resort to George Kent, Esq., whose pen had been all along the chief instrument by which the Register was making its way in popular regard.

But without dwelling farther upon this portion of the topic, I proceed to say that in September, 1826, the "New Hampshire Statesman" and the "Concord Register" were united, the full title of each being retained. The Statesman abandoned its North-End quarters, in a building that was the abode of the late Dr. Ezra Carter, and came down to the office of Mr. Hough, situated upon ground now occupied by Phenix Block. The united paper was, however, not long printed by Mr. Hough, who had passed his seventy-fifth year ; for about the time of the consolidation here spoken of, Mr. Thomas G. Wells, who had been publishing a paper entitled the "Amherst Herald," the subscription list of which, with the printing materials, were brought to Concord,—Mr. Wells having purchased an interest in the Statesman and Register. But being desirous of trying his fortune in a new and distant field, Mr. Wells sold his interest in the paper to Moses G. Atwood and Asa McFarland, February, 1826, and within a few months sailed for Valparaiso.

It here comes in order to speak of the rise of another paper. In 1826, John Quincy Adams being president of the United States by a congressional, not popular, election, and a strictly minority president, it was very obvious that his re-election would be sharply contested, and that Gen. Andrew Jackson—his most formidable competitor in the election of 1824—would be brought forward again in 1828. It was also apparent, as early as 1826, that although Mr. Adams was the choice of New England, and a favorite of a large portion of the Democratic Republicans of New Hampshire, the Patriot, nevertheless, which had in 1824 sustained Wm. H. Crawford of Georgia, would support Gen. Jackson in 1828. Among the Democratic supporters of Mr. Adams was a host of influential men, found in every portion of New Hampshire. To name a few of those in Concord is to indicate the character and position of Mr. Adams' supporters in this state. Jacob B. Moore was one of these. He was associated with Mr. Hill in the Patriot up to the year 1822. Richard Bartlett, secretary of state ; Joseph Low, adjutant and inspector general ; Samuel Sparhawk, cashier of the "Upper Bank," so called, in distinction from the Lower Bank ; Gen. Robert Davis ; and others, less prominent, but equally active politicians. The Statesman and Register was sustaining Mr. Adams, but that journal being regarded by the Adams Democrats as the representative of what remained of the Federal party, and in the interests of such men as William A. Kent, Stephen Ambrose, Abel Hutchins, Wm. Kent, Richard Bradley, Robert Ambrose, Benjamin Gale, Charles and George Hutchins, and other well-known men of Concord and elsewhere in New Hampshire, a new paper was, by the Democratic wing of the Adams party, regarded as necesssary. This desire came to maturity, and in September, 1826, Jacob B. Moore, then carrying on the business of bookseller and printer, commenced "The New Hampshire Journal." The first number contained an account of the frightful and melancholy occurrence in the Notch of the White Hills, August 26, known as the destruction of the Willey family. This narrative was from the pen of Mr. Moore, who, with Richard Bartlett, were upon an excursion to the mountains at the time of the awful deluge which fell upon those hills and valleys, and themselves narrowly escaped being swept into a swollen and raging torrent.

Mr. Moore was a gentleman of untiring industry, much ability as a writer, good executive capacity, well read in political history and general literature, and an enterprising man of business; pushing with all his might such undertakings as he projected. Through the force of his own pen and that of others whom he enlisted in his service, and a thorough canvass of the state for subscribers, the Journal, early in 1828, had more than four thousand subscribers; a great circulation for that period, when every inland paper was printed upon a hand-press. Having just before—February, 1828—embarked in the Statesman, and being young and timid, I was fearful that our establishment would be wrecked and my investment of five hundred dollars go to the bottom. But when the presidential election of 1828 had become a receding incident in public affairs, and the heat of the fiery campaign was succeeded by comparatively calm weather, the Journal rapidly lessened in circulation. Mr. Moore, becoming weary of journalism, transferred the establishment to Richard Bartlett, who, as secretary of state, had been superseded by Col. D. S. Palmer, his deputy in the office. Mr. Bartlett was pronounced one of that description of men who can do better writing for others than themselves. He had performed yeoman service while the Journal was in possession of Mr. Moore, but, when in his own custody, ruined his articles by putting too fine a point upon them. The paper continued to decline—which it probably would into whose possession soever it had fallen; and my fear, in 1827, that the Statesman would be irreparably damaged by its vigorous competitor, then sweeping all before it, not only proved groundless, but entirely the reverse, for in May, 1830, the Journal was united with the Statesman, and the consolidated paper took the title, " New Hampshire Statesman and State Journal." Except for this arrangement,—perfected by leading men to save the feelings and property of Mr. Bartlett, —The Journal must have been discontinued for want of support.

THE AFFECTIONS.

BY MARY HELEN BOODEY.

My friend, it does not seem that there should be
    Comparisons 'twixt bond and bond ;—I think
Each plummet in the heart doth deeply sink,
    Each tie holy in its own degree.
    And truth, like air, is full as it is free.
Why need we fear, as, leaning o'er the brink
Of our own being, we yet long to drink
    In larger draughts of God's equality.
    Of kindly care for all; we can but see
That He hath planned so infinitely well
    For every human heart, for you and me,
That in the rapturous gladness that will swell
    The sweet, sweet future's music there will be
Not one tone missing from the perfect spell.

DECISIONS OF CHIEF JUSTICE SMITH.

[SMITH'S DECISIONS. Reports of the cases decided in the superior and supreme judicial courts of New Hampshire from 1802 to 1816, with opinions in the circuit and district courts of New Hampshire, with extracts from the treatise on probate law, &c., by Chief Justice Smith. Selected, edited and annotated by his son, Ex-Judge Jeremiah Smith. Boston: Published by Little, Brown & Co. From the press of John Wilson & Son, 1879.]

This volume is a mirror of the law of "the olden time," in its best estate. Chief Justice Smith was the pioneer in the field of jurisprudence in New England as Kent was in New York.

Kent at thirty-four, in February, 1798, became *puisne* Judge of the supreme court of New York, and at forty-two, in July, 1806, its chief justice.

Parsons at fifty-six, in July, 1806, was made chief justice of the supreme judicial court of Massachusetts.

Smith, after serving four terms in congress, and as judge of probate in the county of Rockingham, was at forty-one, on Feb. 20, 1801, made Judge of the circuit court of the United States for the district of New Hampshire; and on May 17, 1802, chief justice of the highest court in this state. He held this position until 1809, when he was over-persuaded by certain of his political friends, among whom was Daniel Webster, to abandon it for that of governor, because the supposed interests of the federal party required the nomination of its most available candidate.

On July 12, 1813, he again became chief justice, and held that place until June 29, 1816, when he was swept from it by the political revolution of that year.

Prior to the appointment of Judge Smith in 1802, the law in this state as a science had no existence. For this there are two principal reasons:

1. Under the proprietary government of Mason, we had no law of our own, either statute or common. As late as 1660, Mason claimed that New Hampshire and Maine were governed by the law of the mother country. Portsmouth, Dover, Exeter and Hampton were little principalities, and did substantially as they pleased. The province as such had no existence before the union with Massachusetts, in 1641, nor until after the forced separation in 1679.

The first code of laws enacted in this province in 1679-1680 was in substance a re-enactment of the Mosaic code, was sent to the mother country for royal sanction, and was disallowed by the Privy Council as many others afterwards were.

During the reign of James II. the laws were silent. A trinity of pro-consuls ruled and robbed the people. In 1692, seventy years after the settlement, we were entirely destitute of what is called *written* law. Many statutes were enacted after this time which never received the sanction of the king and council.

No laws were published until 1716, when an edition of sixty pages folio was published in Boston. In 1718, seventy-two pages were added, and in 1719, twenty-four pages more. After this, and before 1728, sixteen pages more were added, making in all a volume of one hundred and seventy-two pages. There was no printing press in this province till 1756. An edition of the statutes was published here in 1760, but discarded as not authentic, and a new and carefully printed edition was published in 1771. After the revolution, the statutes were printed in folio till 1789, when an octavo edition, containing the public and some of the private laws, was published by order of the legislature. The dissatisfaction of the public compelled the publication of a new and revised edition in 1792, which was followed by the edition of

1797, and afterwards by the more copious one of 1805.

The statute law when Judge Smith came to the bench was in a crude, chaotic, and unsatisfactory condition, and the common law far worse.

2. With notable exceptions, like the Livermores, which prove the rule, the bench was filled with broken-down ministers, lumbermen, bankrupt traders and cheap lawyers. From two to four of these judges as the quorum varied, attended each trial term, if they did not, as sometimes happened, forget the time ; and not unfrequently they all charged the jury in the same cause, differing oftentimes as much as the opposing counsel. Chancellor Kent told the rest in describing the condition of things when he came to the bench in New York. "When I came to the bench," says the Chancellor, "there were no reports or state precedents. The opinions from the bench were delivered *ore tenus*. We had no law of our own, and nobody knew what it was. I first introduced a thorough examination of cases and written opinions."

Smith was a strong man. It needed some iron hand to purge the Augean stable and he came. He was one of the best representatives of that industrious, tough, enduring, Scotch-Irish stock, who regarded it as recreation to work or fight from dawn till set of sun, and then to spend half the night in jest, and song, and story. At forty, Smith was a profound lawyer. He had absorbed the history of New England, and especially of this province and state, as a sponge does water. At this time he was the greatest master of probate law in New England. No one since has equalled him ; and no one in this state has approached him except the late Charles H. Atherton. He prepared two large manuscript volumes on the subject. It cost a vast amount of time and labor and was an able work of great value. It was the reservoir from which Webster, Chief Justice Richardson, and others hardly less eminent, continually drew. Notwithstanding he was a busy man of affairs, he was top-heavy with law learning when he came to the bench, and when he retired at the age of fifty-six, he had accomplished more than ought to be expected of those at seventy-five, who now stand in the fore-front of the profession with the aid of all the modern appliances. How he did it, heaven only knows !

Upon coming to the bench Judge Smith promptly introduced the practice of allowing a single judge to direct the course of trials, at the trial terms of reserving cases and questions for the consideration of the whole court, and of preparing written opinions.

This brought order out of chaos, but the labor was immense. Besides that expended on the great work of his life, the treatise on probate law, he presided at the trial terms, examined the cases, and prepared the written opinions in all cases heard *in banc* numbering from sixty to seventy yearly, and making fourteen manuscript volumes with a manuscript digest.

Partisan madness prevented the publication of these opinions when that publication was demanded by every rational consideration of the public interest. Had they been published when they ought, thousands and tens of thousands of the money of individuals and the public would have been saved, for a very large proportion of the questions heard before Judge Smith have since been litigated at great expense.

The volume before us is mainly a selection from the cases and the treatise referred to. We fear that the editor from an excess of caution, and from considerations which would naturally influence a son, has given us less than he ought.

The cases reported are in the main, valuable. *First*, because they involve important questions of constitutional and municipal law, taxation, the construction of statutes relating to deeds and other instruments, the rights, powers and duties of judges of probate, sheriffs and receiptors. They contain a very able discussion of the great questions of religious toleration, the right to tax clergymen, and the history of proprietaries and town corporations not to be found elsewhere in so compact a form. *Secondly*, the principles underlying these decisions have been frequently considered in a variety of forms by many of the American courts as well as our own. *Thirdly*, the compiler himself, late one of the ablest and clearest headed members of our supreme court, has, by the notes which he has appended to these cases, given the profession in a compact form a concordance of the decisions here and elsewhere, wherever the same or similar questions have been considered. These notes show great care and are exceedingly valuable.

We note the following as cases of interest : Muzzy *v*. the Assessors of Amherst, N. H., 1-38.

This was the pioneer decision here in favor of religious toleration. A majority of the court, Wingate, J., dissenting, held that Presbyterians and Congregationalists were not the same religious sect, &c., within the meaning of the constitution. Before Smith was appointed, the court had decided that Universalists were of the same "persuasion, sect, or denomination," as Congregationalists, and could be taxed for the support of settled ministers of the Orthodox church. This decision was affirmed in Henderson *v*. Erskine, Cheshire, Oct. term, 1802, by Judges Farrar and Livermore. Smith took no part in this decision, though he seemingly acquiesced in it as the settled law of the state. But though a Unitarian himself, when it came to the question whether the Presbyterians must pay tribute in this way to the Congregationalists he stood up stoutly for the independence of the church of Scotland, to which his kith and kin belonged.

In Kidder *v*. the Assessors of Dunstable, 155, Cheshire, April term, 1807, the case of Kelly *v*. the Selectmen of Warner is cited, but without any attempt to summarize the history of that once famous case, nor does the chief justice seem to have understood what the facts really were.

The Rev. William Kelly was born at Newbury, Massachusetts, October 30, 1744, graduated at Harvard, in 1767, and was ordained at what is now Warner, N. H., February 5, 1772, where he resided till his death, May 18, 1813. Warner, at the time of the ordination, was so thinly inhabited, that after the council had convened it was rumored among the people that there were not enough professors of religion in town to form a church, and therefore the ordination must fall through. In this emergency an old Dutch hunter, who had lately moved into town from New York, anxious to help the council out of their supposed dilemma, sent them word that rather than not have them proceed he would join the church himself, but if they could get along without him he would rather not. The council went on without his assistance. Kelly received, by way of settlement, $100, with an annual salary of £40, to be increased till it should equal £60 per annum, and twenty cords of wood. About 1792, Kelly found such inroads made upon his society as to render his support burdensome to his friends, and thereupon gave up his contract, and afterwards was repeatedly refused a dismission. Soon after this an unfriendly board of selectmen taxed his property, and collected the tax by distress. Kelly brought suit against the selectmen which the town defended, and at the May term, 1798, the court decided that the property of a settled minister of the gospel, under his own management, was exempt from taxation. On March 11, 1801, after he had won this cause, Kelly was dismissed by a council called at his own request.

Fisher *v*. Steward, 60, is a Claremont case. The court held that one who finds a swarm of bees in a tree on another's land, marks the tree, and notifies the land-owner, has no right to the honey. This case shows the strength of traditional law. Many people believe to this day that the contrary is true because the tradition has come down to them on the stream of generations as an heir-loom.

In Melven *v*. Darling, 74, it was held that an unsatisfied judgment against a trustee in foreign attachment for the amount of a debt secured by a mortgage, is a bar to a suit afterwards brought by the principal defendant upon the mortgage against the trustee. The *dicta* in this state upon this point have been very conflicting and it must be a wise man who knows what the law is.

Morey *v.* Orford Bridge, 91, contains a valuable discussion of the constitutional question as to whether a grant of a ferry and the like is a contract which the constitution of the United States prohibits the states from impairing. This decision was made six years before the opinion was given by Chief Justice Marshall, in Fletcher *v.* Peck. Judge Smith held that the grant of a ferry is against common right and must therefore be construed strictly. This doctrine was affirmed in the supreme court of the United States in the Charles River Bridge case, contrary to the opinions of Marshall and Story. Judge Smith also held that a ferry and a bridge, though they serve the same end, are things totally distinct in their nature; that a grant of a ferry does not prohibit persons from crossing or enabling others to cross in any other way; and that the grant of a ferry would not infringe the grant of a bridge.

In Frost *v.* Brown, 113, it was held that where a minor had contracted for his own services, and his employer had agreed to pay him therefor, his earnings could not be attached on trustee process by a creditor of his father. Ignorant of its existence, the legislature many years afterwards, re-enacted this decision.

In the case of St. John's Church at Portsmouth, 178, it was held that the exercise of corporate privileges for upwards of a century, recognition in ancient records and papers, and in acts of the legislature, were evidence of due incorporation.

In Currier *v.* Basset, 191, it was held that towns may settle disputed lines so far as respects jurisdiction.

In the case of Flanders *v.* Herbert, 205, it was held that a writ of attachment, without a declaration, is not a writ, and that no officer could justify under it.

In Doe *v.* Morrell, 255, it was held unlawful for one tenant in common of a house, to make partition with a saw. We had before heard of an eccentric lawyer in Vermont, who summarily dissolved the firm of which he was a member, by sawing his partner's name off their common shingle.

In Cornish *v.* Kenrick, 270, the history of the origin of proprietary and town governments is summarized. An examination of the reports of the supreme court of the United States and of the states, shows that nobody outside of New England, and comparatively few within it, ever understood either.

The opinion in Boynton *v.* Emerson, 298, was the foundation of the magnificent argument of Parker Noyes which carried the court with him in the noted case of Weld *v.* Hadley, 1 N. H., 295, in which it was held that a tender of specific articles, unaccepted, vested the property in the chattels in the person making the tender.

In Hodgdon *v.* Robinson, 320, it was held that where an execution is extended upon two tracts of land, it is not necessary that the same persons should be appraisers on both tracts.

Thompson *v.* Bennet, 327, contains a masterly opinion by the chief justice that a deed attested by only one witness is inoperative. This decision was afterwards disregarded by the majority of the superior court, and from that time to this confusion has reigned. The decision in French *v.* French, 2 N. H., 234, was as bold an act of judicial usurpation as that in Taltarum's case.

The editor makes an ingenious effort to reconcile the decisions in Hastings *v.* Cutler, 24 N. H., 481, and in Barker *v.* Bean, 25 N. H., 412, and we presume would reckon Gooding *v.* Riley, 50 N. H., 400, as in harmony with Barker *v.* Bean. It would seem impossible to any one who knew the real facts to reconcile these two cases. The truth is that when Hasting *v.* Cutler and Barker *v.* Bean were decided, one judge as a rule knew little about the opinions of any other judge. The cases were divided among the judges.

Each one wrote the opinions in the cases assigned to him, and to use the pointed language of Judge Perley, "took the responsibility of it." The judges who in form decided these two cases, never looked far enough to see that they had made two antagonistic and irreconcilable decisions; and Gooding v. Riley has a history of its own.

In Chesterfield v. Hart, 350, it was held that an infant of sufficient property, was liable under the pauper statutes for the support of her grandmother.

In Porter v. Tarlton, 372, it was held that a sheriff who delivered attached goods to a receiptor, did so at his own risk, unless the taking of the receipt was directed or ratified by the creditor. This was undoubtedly the ancient law in this state. It has also been so held in other jurisdictions. The modern doctrine in this state that a sheriff was bound to accept a receiptor was the result of judicial legislation. Whether it was rational or not, is one thing; whether it was the law or not, another. It is obvious that a receipt is a contract. Like other contracts it should receive a rational interpretation. To meet the supposed equities of particular cases, the courts have warped such contracts, and adopted abortive views of them, and in order to support refinements without reason, and distinctions without sense, they have been compelled to invent a history which they ought to have known never existed. Not a few of these contradictory decisions, owe their existence to the fact that the judges were not aware of the decisions which had been previously made upon the same point. As illustrations, Phelps v. Gilchrist, 28 N. H., 266; and Sanborn v. Buswell, 51 N. H., 573, are in point as respects Remick v. Atkinson, 11 N. H., 256. In their attempts to reach justice, our court, in the matter of receipts, and the supreme court of the United States, in the bond and tax cases, have created an anomalous class of contracts and made a deformity of the law so that it now depends upon arbitrary precedents instead of legal principles.

In Bryant v. Ela, 396, the court held in effect, that where no personal service is had upon the defendant, the court had no jurisdiction over him for any other purpose than as affects the property attached; that such suits were proceedings *in rem*; that they were restricted in their scope to the property attached; and that the attachment was the necessary foundation for any further proceedings. This decision receives strong support from a recent decision of the supreme court of the United States, that in those states where a sale is allowed instead of an attachment, no jurisdiction can be acquired without personal service.

GOOD LUCK.

FROM THE GERMAN OF GEIBEL.

Good luck is only a flighty thing,
And has been from the beginning;
You may hunt for her all the world round
And yet the creature may not be found.

Throw yourself on the dewy grass,
And sing your songs to the fickle lass;
Quickly, perhaps, from out the blue skies,
She may descend to sooth your sighs.

Then you must seize and hold her close,
But do not make your complaints verbose;
Though she so long has kept you waiting,
Mayhap a new flight she is meditating.

—*Lucia Moses.*

CONGRESSIONAL PAPERS, No. 4.—ILLUSIONS DISPELLED.

BY G. H. JENNESS.

Many erroneous ideas prevail concerning congress, among those not familiar with its interior workings. The newspaper, that omnipresent vehicle of modern intelligence, fails to delineate all the peculiar phases of our American parliament. Even the Congressional Record itself, which is supposed to be an exact official record of proceedings, is also made to convey a harmless deception by its burden of long-winded speeches that were never delivered. Take a case in point. The "Record" of the forty-fifth congress, second session, contains many very able speeches upon American finance, purporting to be the extemporaneous eloquence of approval, disapproval, or indignation generated by the president's veto of the silver bill. The actual delivery of those speeches would have occupied one or more of the entire daily sessions of the house. As it was, the bill was passed in both branches of congress, and became a law in spite of the president's veto in less than four hours after it left the White House, all debate being cut off in the house by Mr. Alexander H. Stephens' demand for the previous question. "Leave to print" is the mysterious process by which this feat of parliamentary legerdemain is accomplished. The advantages of the plan are obvious. It affords time for preparation, relieves the listeners and avoids the pangs of delivery. It also conveys to the honorable member's constituents the pleasing delusion, that, in times of great public emergency, the honorable member aforesaid is at his post, flinging his eloquence into the congressional arena, and fiercely gesticulating to the admiring crowds who listen with breathless attention to his impassioned oratory. The local newspaper takes up the theme, and with the Congressional Record for a breastwork, marks out a campaign, throws up the lines of defense, and challenges the political enemy to prove that the failure to re-elect the author of so much extemporaneous (?) eloquence would not be a national calamity, and perhaps imperil the very existence of the government itself.

Another safety valve for the escape of congressional eloquence when it reaches the danger line, is the Saturday session, and an occasional evening session "for debate only." At these momentous gatherings the audience upon the floor of the house numbers from three to twenty-five, the latter, in congressional parlance, being considered "a good house." The best speakers on either side never resort to this method of firing the hearts of their constituents, for it is considered a great waste of the raw material. Banks, Butler, Garfield Hale, Frye, Kelley, Cox, Blackburn, Tucker, Gibson, Clymer, and McMahon, are never found talking to empty benches and galleries, but carefully husband their resources for the "field days" that seldom come unannounced. A judicious expenditure of printer's ink generally conveys to an anxious and expectant public the intelligence that "something is up" in the house at the proper time before that "something" occurs. There are exceptions to this, as, for instance, when some unguarded "hit" brings on a running debate, in which the heavy artillery are compelled to take the field, even if not rewarded by the smiles and plaudits of "fair women and brave men" in the gallery. The few men who command the attention of the house, or the country, are alternately praised and abused by the press, and their names perpetually paraded before the people. The "evening session" member drops into obscurity after the customary "notice" of his effort by the local newspaper, and his popularity with such of his constituents as judge congressmen by their speeches only, is measured by the number of printed copies sent into his district.

Those who estimate the work of congress by the speech-making, or the proceedings in open session, fail to do that honorable body common justice. The real work in both branches is done in the committee-rooms. Here is where the multitude of petitions are sent, papers referred, arguments offered, witnesses examined, and all the details of legislation perfected. The "sacred right of petition" is being indulged in to an extent never before known in the history of American legislation, and it adds heavily to the burdens of committees who are obliged to take cognizance of their contents. During the first five months of the forty-fifth congress, the number of petitions referred, daily, to the appropriate committees varied from one hundred to three hundred, the bulk of which went to the committee of ways and means, commerce, and invalid pensions. The humblest citizen in the obscurest hamlet in the land may petition congress for a redress of greivances, payment for services rendered, or for damages inflicted upon his barnyard fence during our "late unpleasantness," and rest assured that his petition will be as carefully introduced, referred, indexed, filed, and considered as if it were a matter of the gravest national importance. During the five months previously referred to, over five thousand bills were introduced in the house alone, nearly all of which were read and referred to committees. A few pass, under a suspension of the rules, but by far the larger portion are carefully considered in committee before being reported to the house. The house meets at noon, daily, and usually adjourns before five o'clock; but the committee-man's work, like a woman's, is *never* done. The ablest men on all the leading committees work more hours, and tax their physical endurance and mental powers to a greater degree than they would if at home in their counting-rooms or offices. The ability of the practical legislator is tested more in the committee room than upon the floor of the house, for it has been found upon many noted occasions that fine oratory and practical hard work are not closely related. Both are essential, and neither can well be dispensed with, particularly the hard work. There are many men in congress who seldom make a speech, whose names are scacely ever seen in the papers outside of their own states, who are comparative strangers to the readers of the *Record*, whose good judgment and practical sound sense has great influence in shaping legislation and enacting good laws. The daily sessions then, instead of being a true exponent of the work being done by our law-makers, are merely for the purpose of comparing notes, supplying omissions, perfecting details, or smoothing up work roughed out by the different committees. The "field days" are elaborately reported and highly colored by correspondents whose fertile imaginations are equal to any emergency; but the *business* days and weeks when no "oratory" is heard or expected, are but little noticed either in Washington or the country at large. These are the days and weeks when the clear-headed and far-seeing practical men of business lay aside all nonsense and political buncombe, and use their best judgment in devising ways and means whereby our good uncle, whose surname is Samuel, is enabled to provide for the support of his large and growing family, and to pay his honest debts. The appropriation bills are drawn with very great care and require many weeks of the severest mental labor to perfect them. To provide for the support of every branch of the government in all its details is the task allotted to the committee on appropriations. The army and navy, the consular and diplomatic, the river and harbor, the pension, the post-office, the Indian, the legislative, the deficiency, and the sundry civil are the principal appropriation bills that emanate from this committee. Four or five of the eleven will contain from fifty to one hundred and ten printed pages each, document size, which fact is sufficient to convey the idea that a position on the appropriation committee, at least, is no sinecure. Indeed the amount of work performed by the average congressman is much greater than is popularly supposed. The work in committee, the daily attendance at the regular sessions, the calls at the departments on official business, the immense private correspondence from clamorous constituents who want a book, or a speech, or an office, all add to the cares and responsibilities of the honorable M. C. Then if his family, if he has one, is desirous of cutting a dash in "Washington society," the poor man is "toted" around to all the balls, pound-parties, lunches and "receptions" given by the notables from Lord A down to Esquire Z, and filled up with frozen cream, boiling coffee, terrapin soup, and iced champagne. He must call on all the officials, high and low, stand the "crush" at the president's reception, and furnish the female interviewer the full particulars concerning the style and cost of his wife's wardrobe.

The preparation of speeches, if he be given to speech-making, requires much care and time on the part of the congressman who aspires to renown in that direction. On all possible subjects connected with legislation the field has been thoroughly gleaned many times over. International and constitutional law, diplomacy, the tariff, internal improvements, and every conceivable subject upon which any considerable number of citizens are supposed to take the slightest interest, has been a matter of public discussion in the two houses of congress ever since their existence. It is not expected, therefore, that, upon general topics, the average member will be able to say anything remarkably new, or strikingly original. He will be fortunate indeed if somebody does not hop up and point him to the volume, page, column, and paragraph in the *Record* or *Globe*, of ten, twenty, or forty years ago, where almost his exact language may be found. This strange condition of affairs may be accounted for by the fact that upon certain specific questions of a public nature, the reference to standard works in the congressional libraries are the only reliable data upon which to build the superstructure of a speech. It is not to be wondered at, then, that hundreds of men, searching for the same facts upon the same subject, in the same books, should frequently stumble upon the same paragraph in elucidating their views. Then, again, they must rely on the knowledge and judgment of the librarian, who hunts up the "references" on a given subject. Without the librarian and his assistants, *any* man would be as helpless as a ship at sea without a rudder. The various libraries in the capitol contain a half-a-million volumes, which is a pile of books the size of which no one would form any adequate idea, who has not seen them. Amid the miles of shelving, and the hundreds of alcoves, one might hunt a year for a certain book and not be able to find it. The librarian, however, with his wonderful system of indexing, and his vast practical knowledge, gained only by years and years of experience, will soon find whatever is needed. Let a member make known his desire to find the decision of a county, state or supreme court upon any case, the opinion of any noted jurist upon any question of law, the cost of keeping a soldier in 1840, the price of army blankets in 1850, the revenue derived from the importation of quinine in 1860, the number of tons of pig-iron produced in Pennsylvania; in short, if he wants any particular information upon any given subject, the old "book worms" in the libraries can produce it for him in an incredibly short space of time. There is a man in the house library who knows it so well that he is regarded as a permanent fixture. He has been discharged once or twice on account of political changes, but soon reinstated. *They can't do without him.* He has probably contributed indirectly, more pages to the *Congressional Record*, during the last dozen years, than any man living. He is not an M. C. and is not much seen upon the floor, but there would be some fearful gaps in a good many congressional speeches if his work were blotted out. He is one of the "book worms" of the house library, belongs to the noble family of Smiths, and, horrible to think of (to some), is an American citizen of African descent.

Under the circumstances herein alluded to, the charge of plagiarism, to which the honorable member may have laid himself liable, should be lightly treated and generously overlooked. It is well nigh impossible to get up an "original" speech in congress upon the standard legislative subjects, and the few attempts to do so are not well calculated to stimulate enterprise in that direction.

The purpose of this article is not to tear away too much of the veil that surrounds our lawgivers, but just enough to dispel some of the harmless illusions that exist in the public mind.

SUNSHINE AFTER CLOUDS.

BY HELEN M. RUSSELL.

CHAPTER I.

"You are very tired tonight, are you not, Margie? Your work has been harder than usual today, I know by your flushed cheek and heavy eyes. Oh my child! how I wish I might take a portion of your heavy burden upon myself." Mrs. Benson raised herself from the lounge where she had been reclining and gently drew her daughter to her side. It was a poor room, but neat as wax. The uncovered floor was white and clean. The few chairs and small table, and well-worn lounge were neatly dusted. The window curtain which shaded the one small window was snowy white; but over all the signs of extreme poverty cast a shadow that told of toilsome days and weary nights. Mrs. Benson was a confirmed invalid. The thin cheeks, with their hectic flush, told that death was very near her. Her large brown eyes were filled with unshed tears as she tenderly drew her daughter to her side. Margie Benson laid her head for a moment upon her mother's shoulder, with a low sigh, then she lifted it, and the dark brown eyes rested lovingly upon the face so dear to her, as she replied: "No, mother, my work has not been more tiresome than usual; but our wages have been lowered. Mr. Brown says he cannot afford to pay as much as he has been paying, and I don't know how we shall live. If I could find something else to do I would leave the mill, but that I cannot do, I suppose. If father would not drink!" This last, with a bitter sob, as the brown head sank down again to its resting place. "If father would not drink!" How many hundreds, aye thousands of poor girls have uttered that self-same cry, wrung from their inmost hearts. The shame and misery, the anxious days and fearful nights of a drunkard's family, are known only to themselves. For a moment Mrs. Benson made no reply. It was not often that Margie gave way to her feelings like this, but tonight she was so heart-sick and discouraged that she gave up to the sorrow that cast a blight upon her young life. Compelled oftimes to furnish her father with means to procure his potations, her very soul shrank from the injustice of her unnatural parent. Gently Mrs. Benson stroked the curling hair away from her daughter's flushed face ere she replied. Then she said softly: "Margie, where has your courage gone? If you lose that, what will become of us?" "Oh, my mother, forgive me. I do wrong to worry you like this." She paused for a moment, and then said: "I shall not give him any more money. I do not think he will beat me and I do not mind his harsh words—much. After all, it is not so bad as it might be, mother," said she, trying to speak cheerfully, as she arose from her seat and bustled about to prepare her frugal supper. Twenty minutes later she assisted her mother to a seat at the table, and altho' she pressed the invalid to partake of the toast she had prepared for her, she ate but little herself. Her heart beat rapidly at every footstep near the door, for she well knew that if her father returned at all that night, he would return intoxicated, as she had herself seen him reeling into a drinking saloon when on her way home from the factory. She felt the disgrace keenly, this young girl whose thoughts and aspirations were so much above the sphere in which circumstances placed her. Her only sister, Clara, had married, two years before, a well-to-do farmer, residing in Vermont, and she had been very kind to the mother and sister in their bitter sorrows, often sending them money and cheering words, which came like rays of sunlight into the drunkard's home. Margie sat thinking sadly of their poverty, her mother's ill-health and her father's intemperance, until Mrs. Benson slowly arose from the table, then she hastily sprang forward and assisted her to a seat near the fire, and bustling about, soon had the room restored to its usual order. "Mother, had you not better retire? It is getting quite cool here and the coal is nearly gone. You will be more comfortable in bed. I will throw my shawl over my shoulders and wait up for father. I fear he will be late tonight." Mrs. Benson raised her eyes to her daughter's face and said sadly: "Yes, Margie, I will do as you wish. I cannot see him in his degredation tonight, I am not equal to it. Rest here on the lounge until he comes. If you refuse him money he will pawn this miserable furniture, and we shall have nothing. Oh, Margie, what a curse rum is. It has changed your father from a noble man to a miserable wretch, as it has done many others. What will become of you, my poor child, when I am gone?" Slowly and feebly she arose, and, leaning on her daughter, she sought her own room. "Mother seems more feeble tonight than ever before," said Margie to herself, as at length she stood alone in the little kitchen. "She will soon be out of this grief and trouble, while I must live on, doubly wretched without her dear presence. Oh, surely my lot is very hard," she moaned, as extinguishing the lamp, she drew aside the window curtain and knelt beside the window, thus beginning her long watch. Night after night she had knelt there, watching for her father, that she might be ready to open the door for him and keep him quiet if possible. Usually he was stupid and sullen and easily led, but if he was thirsting for liquor, and had no money to obtain it, he would curse and swear at his poor wife and wretched daughter until he got what little money they had, then he would leave them, and spend the money thus obtained at some of the many filthy dens which infested the city. The fire died entirely out in the little stove, and at length Margie arose shivering from the window, and wrapping a shawl around her, threw herself upon the lounge, dropping into a light slumber which lasted until the little clock on the mantel struck two. "He will not come home tonight. Doubtless he has got into the station house again. I am sorry I didn't try to induce him to come home with me, but how could I enter that vile, filthy place? And, beside, mother has strictly forbidden it, too. Oh, the shame of being a drunkard's daughter," said Margie, as she arose, and shivering with cold, stole noiselessly into her mother's room, and without disrobing lay down beside the invalid, whose regular breathing told Margie that her mother, at least, was resting peacefully, forgetting in sleep her many sorrows. Margie was up long before day, and had prepared the scanty breakfast for her mother and herself. It was snowing rapidly, the flakes falling thicker and faster as the morning deepened. At half-past six Margie stood ready to depart for her day's labor, everything that her mother would need being placed close at hand, she at length bade her goodbye, and hastened away. After her daughter's departure, Mrs. Benson sat for a long time before the fire. Anon it began to grow light, and then she amused herself by watching the flakes of snow as they fell faster and faster upon the window ledge. The days were very long to the poor woman, especially those which found her unable to busy herself with some light needle work with which she essayed to earn a little money, much against Margie's wishes. Her thoughts this morning had somehow gone back into the past—a past that seemed like heaven when compared to the misery of the present. Could it be that she was the daughter of wealthy parents, carefully guarded from every want, idolized as only daughters often are? Ah, well! that was ended. She had chosen her own lot in life and the consequences, let them be what they would, must be borne. She knew that all trouble would soon end for her, but the thought of the dear ones she must leave behind, especially Margie, filled her already aching heart with keenest anguish. Suddenly there came a knock upon the outer door, and in answer to her low "come in," the door was thrown open, and a gentleman, well wrapped up in a heavy coat and muffler, his fur cap drawn down over his face, entered the room.

Throwing off his wet outer garments, and tossing them into one corner of the room, he turned toward Mrs. Benson, who sat watching him in surprise. "Don't you know me, Margaret?" The rich mellow tones of the gentleman's voice fell upon Mrs. Benson's ear like strains of half forgotten music, while one glance into the dark brown eyes, which looked sadly into her own, and were so strangely like her own, told her that her only brother stood before her. With a low cry of intense joy she half rose to her feet, sinking back again and holding out both hands, while the single word, "brother!" fell from her pale lips. "My sister, my poor, wronged sister!" said the gentleman, as he clasped the fragile form close to his bosom, and mingled his tears with her own. "William, my brother! Oh! it must be a dream. It cannot be true that we meet again, meet when I most need your strong arm to lean upon," she murmured, drawing away from him and gazing eagerly into the handsome face of the gentleman, who was regarding her with joy and sorrow both depicted on his noble countenance. "Thank God! I have found you at last," said he, reverently. "We will never part again until death parts us. Poor sister, that I should find you thus. What a change, Margaret! I can hardly believe my own eyes," and burying his face in his hands, he groaned aloud. Then he started up and glanced around the miserable room, strode to the little bedroom where the wretched pallet, which served as a bed for his poor sister, met his eye; then he burst forth angrily, fiercely. "And so this is what that rascal of a Tom Benson has brought you to. He was never half good enough for you in his best days. Alas! poor, stern, unyielding father was right, when he said you had better been laid away in your grave than to have become the wife of such a man. It proved to be the hovel instead of the palace, Margaret." Over the pale, thin face of the invalid the blood rushed in a crimson wave, and receding, left her paler than before, while her thoughts flew back to a scene far different from this. The large, magnificent drawing-room and all the insignia of wealth surrounding them—herself and this selfsame brother, standing side by side—and in answer to the words, "Margaret, he is not good enough for you, even if he were your equal in other respects, what will you do, reared as you have been, as the wife of a man comparatively poor?" She had made answer: "I love him, William, and could be happier with him in a hovel than with any one else in a palace." Young and impulsive, she believed for the time being that she spoke the truth; experience, however, had taught her a bitter lesson. Experience is a hard teacher, but a most thorough one. I wonder if anyone in the world ever did, or ever will live just such a life as he or she fondly hoped and expected to live. For example, one sees upon a rosebush, a fair, perfect rose, and essays to pluck it, when lo! at a touch the leaves fall out and lay upon the ground beneath, or if perchance allowed to gather it in its beauty, there are thorns hidden from sight that were little thought of. Just so with many—I had nearly said most lives. The future seems "bright with promise," but often, too often, we find that "distance lends enchantment to the view." But to return to my story. "Not much better than a hovel, William," she said, the tears coming afresh to her eyes. "But, indeed, I never regretted my marriage until he took to drink." Forgive me, sister, I was wrong to speak as I did, but the surprise and sorrow of finding you like this must be my excuse. How many children have you?" "Two, living. My Willie died when only two years of age. I thought it hard to part with him then, but I am so glad now that he was spared this misery and his father's wretched example. Clara, my eldest daughter, is married. Margie is at work in the factory, and it is to her that I look for what few comforts I have. Ah, brother! my life is *not* much like the one I knew when I was Margaret Roden. When father disinherited me, I thought my heart would break, at first, for I missed you all so much; but you were kind to me, and my home, tho' humble, was neat and comfortable, and I had all the real necessaries of life. That was twenty years ago, brother, and for ten years, all went well. We had two lovely daughters, and when our little Willie was born, we thought our cup of happiness nearly full, especially as Tom was succeeding very well in business. When only two years old, our lovely boy was taken from us, and soon after we lost about five thousand dollars at one time, and two thousand more at another, nearly all we had. I never blamed Tom for that, but with all the trouble, he got discouraged, took to drinking, and so things have gone from bad to worse. I have lost my health, and the end for me is not far distant. And now, after all these years, why are you here?" She paused, exhausted, and leaned her head upon her clasped hands. "Let me help you to the lounge, that you may rest there while I tell you my story," said her brother, and he tenderly assisted her to the miserable apology for a lounge, and adjusted the cushion as handily as Margie could have done. Lastly he threw a comforter over the invalid, then after waiting until the violent coughing spell, which racked her poor frame, was over, he said sadly:

"Father died six months ago, and since that time mother and I have sought for you, advertised in dailies, far and near, with no success whatever. Mother was discouraged, but I would not give up. I had secretly been on the search for many long years, sister. Do not think you have been forgotten. I arrived here day before yesterday and began a search with little or no hope of success. Last night I saw a young lady enter a small grocery store, and her likeness to yourself startled me. I followed her, intending to question her, but I saw that the proprietor knew and trusted her, so I waited until after she had left the store, and then made inquiries. At first he would tell me nothing, but when I told him my reasons for inquiring, he gladly told me all I wished to now, with one exception, he did not know where you lived. He promised to ascertain as soon as possible and let me know. This morning he came to my hotel with the desired information, and I hastened hither at once." "Did my father ever forgive me?" asked Mrs. Benson, huskily. "Yes, Margaret, and wished so much to see you before he died, that he might ask your forgiveness. His death was very sudden. He had no time to alter his will, but he trusted me to give you one half of his property, and I gladly promised to do so, if I could find you. Thank God, I have succeeded." "And mother is well," asked Mrs. Benson. "Yes, Margaret."

"Have you no family, William?"

"No, sister, I have never married and probably never shall. I entered the store as clerk soon after your marriage, and for ten years have been junior partner, succeeding to the whole business at father's death. And now, Margaret, this miserable life must end. You have killed yourself for Tom Benson. I can see that, but at least you can die in peace and plenty. I shall take rooms for you where you can be quiet, and telegraph for mother at once. As soon as practicable you must be moved out of this den, Margie bids adieu to factory life at once. As for Tom, he can take care of himself. I'll have nothing to do with him," he concluded, bitterly. "William, I cannot leave him like this, indeed I cannot. After all he is my husband." murmured Mrs. Benson sadly. "Well, well, sister, when Margie comes we will see what can be done. Just be as quiet as you can while I go out for an hour or so." Tenderly William Roden bent over his sister, loved so dearly in other days, and pressing a kiss upon her wasted cheek, he turned away with tears in his eyes, and hastily replacing his coat and muffler, he hurriedly left the house. Left to herself, Mrs. Benson burst into tears of mingled joy and sorrow. For twenty long years her parents and only brother had been the same as dead to her. After her marriage, she had written letter after letter to her father, praying for forgiveness, but when she found they were of no avail, she resolutely tried to forget them all. Her mother and brother, she well knew, still loved her, but Mr. Roden, stern and unyielding, had forbidden them to see her, even going so far as to threaten to disinherit his son if his commands were not obeyed. About two years after their marriage, Mr. and Mrs. Benson removed to the city of M———, leaving behind them no trace of their whereabouts. Through all the long years that followed, Mrs. Benson had never heard one word concerning her relatives, and therefore her surprise was great indeed, when her brother so unexpectedly entered her home.

CHAPTER II.

"I tell you it is of no use! Go away and let me alone, William Roden!"

Tom Benson sat in his miserable home near the close of a bitter cold day, about a week after the events narrated in the preceding chapter. There was no fire in the stove, and dreary and cheerless enough seemed the drunkard's home, as Mr. Roden entered it, having been searching for the miserable man for several days. True to his promise, he had conveyed his sister to a pleasant suite of rooms in a quiet locality, and then telegraphed for his mother, who had soon arrived. Margie had seen her father and told him of the change in their lives, and begged him to see her uncle William. This he had utterly refused to do, and had managed to keep out of the gentleman's sight until the afternoon in question. But at length he had been compelled to drag his miserable body to his old home, the tenement where his wife and daughter had passed so many weary hours. Here Mr. Roden had found him, and had sought to awaken within his heart, hope that he might yet reform. It is true he had shrank from the task his sister had aloted him, for he despised the besotted wretch, and had no pity for him, until he saw him so worn out and despairing, seated before the fireless stove, his face buried in his trembling hands. He remembered him as he had seen him in other days, tall, erect and handsome, and for his sister's sake resolved to do everything in his power to help him overcome the passion for strong drink that had been his ruin.

"Tom, your wife loves you yet, and only this morning, begged me to find you and bring you to her side. She is very comfortable in her new home, and the physicians bid us hope that she may be much better, with good care and nourishment, such as she is now receiving. Now, Tom, let me hear you say you will try and you shall have every facility in my power to bestow, to help you on your way. Only say you will try." During his words, William Roden had kept his eyes fixed upon the poor wretch before him, and he saw that he was visibly affected, but he made no reply. Mr. Roden resumued after a few moments silence. "I will go out and get some coal for a fire, and something for you to eat, and then after you are warmed and have had a good dinner, you will feel more like talking with me. Will you promise to remain here while I am away?" At that moment the outer door opened and Margie entered the room. One week had made a great change in her appearance. The beautiful brown eyes had in a measure lost their look of sorrow, though a cloud darkened their brightness as they rested on the bowed form of her father. The sweet face, however, wore a happier look, and just the faintest of pink flushes rested in the delicate cheeks. She was dressed neatly and warmly, and her step light and elastic with new life, told how much a little comfort can do for one who has suffered the pangs of poverty and despair. Mr. Roden's eyes rested longingly upon her as she stepped forward, and pausing by her father's side, she laid one slender gloved hand upon his worn, threadbare coat and said:

"Father, have you no word for your daughter Margie? Mother wishes to see you at once, she is much better or would be if you would but go to her. Say, father, will you go?"

"I am ashamed to go, Margie, I have abused you so much that I—Oh, Margie, my child, my child!" Down upon her knees sank the young girl, and throwing her arms around her father's neck, she drew his head down until it rested upon her shoulder. Then she tenderly drew off the old battered hat, and brushed back from his forehead the matted hair, sobbing all the while. "Oh, my dear, dear father, we will forget that dreadful time, and you will be my loving father once more. Say you will go with me."

"If you think you can save me, I will go with you, but William—Margie —I am not worth the trouble," he replied, raising his head from his daughter's shoulder and brushing away the tears that had rolled down his cheeks. "Will you go at once?" said Margie, eagerly. "I cannot go to her looking like this, Margie," said her father as he looked down upon his ragged clothes and worn shoes. Mr. Roden then spoke : " I think, my dear, that he had better have a fire here, and something to eat, and then we will make a few calls before going to your mother. He wants to leave behind him every possible trace of the life he has led, and he is right. Yes, uncle William, I will soon have a fire and some nourishment for him." She left the room as she spoke, but soon returned bearing kindlings and coal, and very soon had a warm fire burning in the little stove. Then she hurried out upon the street, returning soon with oysters, crackers and tea, which she quickly prepared and placed upon the little table. Her father ate but little, but arose from the table evidently refreshed.

It was growing quite dark when the two men left the house. Margie waited only long enough to tidy up the little kitchen for the last time. When all was arranged to her satisfaction, she, too, left the house, locking the door behind her. Meeting their landlord soon after, she gave him the key, telling him he was welcome to the furniture, or anything else the rooms contained. Then she hurried on her way, feeling that she had really done with her old life and its surroundings forever. An hour later as she sat beside her mother telling her over and over again the joyful news, the door opened and Mrs. Roden entered the room. She was a lovely lady, with silver gray hair, and a sweet, sad look in the gentle blue eyes that rested so lovingly upon her daughter, as she came slowly forward. "Margaret, your husband has come and is waiting to see you. Shall I bid him come in?" "Yes, dear mother, I would see him at once." Even Margie could hardly believe that the man who soon entered the room and knelt so penitently before her mother, could be her father. His long, unkempt hair and beard had been closely trimmed, and a neat suit of black had taken the place of the rags he had so lately worn. It was no easy task for him to conquer his appetite for strong drink. Those who witnessed the struggle never forgot it. They pitied and helped him, and Mrs. Benson lived to see her husband entirely cured. For a time they fondly hoped and believed her better, but toward spring she grew worse. It was her great desire to return to her old home, where she had passed her happy girlhood days, and the first of May they departed from M——. She bore up wonderfully and when they reached home, declared herself better than when she started, but as soon as the excitement and pleasure of reaching her loved home was over, in a measure, she began to sink, and there came a day, at last, when her weeping friends gathered around her bedside to receive her last, kind, loving words. Clara had been summoned home, and with all her friends surrounding her, Mrs. Benson breathed her last.

Margie had already become the light of her grandmother's home, and as soon as her grief at her mother's death had in a measure subsided, she began to look eagerly forward to an education, and succeeded in becoming an accomplished woman. Mr. Benson entered the large establishment of Roden & Co., as clerk, and came to be much respected by all who associated with him. Most especially was he noted for his kindness to those who were treading the downward path, he had once trod, and more than one owed their entire reform to him.

MANNERS AND CUSTOMS IN HOPKINTON.—No. 1.

BY C. C. LORD.

DOMESTIC.

In the early days of this township, the domestic customs were copied from the olden districts of Massachusetts, and were largely in common with those of all rural New England, so far as the conditions of this primative wilderness would allow. The dwellings were at first small and incommodious, as well as built of logs. Such habitations were often if not always floorless, with seldom if ever more than one room, though they might have afforded a loft for the depositing of articles, or for other purposes. An open fire place and a chimney, and sometimes an oven, were necessary appendages of a local domestic establishment. Subsequently to the log hut followed the framed house. Framed houses were largely built upon a substantially uniform plan. A huge chimney stack, a brick oven and fire places proportioned in number to the represented competency of the owner, occupied a central position in every dwelling. The back part of the house was mostly taken up by the kitchen, which was often flanked on one side by three small apartments—a buttery, an entry and a cellar-way. The last was generally surmounted by a stair-way leading to the chamber or attic, by a door leading from the entry. A front room and an entry, the latter in front of the chimney stack, and often large enough to contain a bed, completed the accommodations of the lower floor. The chamber was generally an open space covered by the naked roof. This description, however, applies to the house of the poorer resident. Sometimes an additional joint, affording two extra rooms, a front and a back, was built to the structure; sometimes, also, the original plan allowed two, square front rooms, a front entry, and a kitchen in the rear, flanked by such accommodations as the taste of the builder directed, but very often on one side by the buttery, entry and stairways, and on the other by a bedroom.

As the material prosperity of the early inhabitants increased, there was evinced a decided inclination to build houses with two stories. Many of the two-storied houses erected were only duplicates of the apartments of the prevailing lower edifice. The matter of size was apparently entertained as an element of importance in the construction of two-storied houses. Pride may have borne its part in this matter, since some of these large buildings were never finished completely. On the other hand, the early attractions of the newer western country left many of the provided prospective domestic accommodations unneeded.

The early framed houses in this vicinity were very strongly built. Near the top of Putney's hill stands the first parsonage in the town, said to be also the first framed house, built for the Rev. James Scales, the first minister. The ancient edifice is 36 feet and 4 inches in length, and 28 feet and 4 inches in width. Its posts are 15 feet high, and the slope of the roof is 10 feet. The corner and side posts are of solid oak, 8 inches square, with expansions at the top for the accommodation of upper timbers. The plates, of clear, solid hard pine, are 10 1-2 by 7 inches; the attic beams, of similar stuff, are 9 by 8 inches; the rafters, of oak, are 6 by 5 inches, the end ones also being braced; the oak ribs are 6 by 3 inches. The fact that $400 has been spent upon this house since its occupation by the Rev. James Scales, and it is even now unfinished, suggests some idea of the rudeness of the home of that pious gentleman. This house, like many others of its time, was located with its front to the south, thus enabling it to serve as a sun-dial. This custom of locating houses was often followed without regard to the position occupied with respect to the highway.

The ancient kitchen fireplace was the largest of all and yearly devoured immense quantities of fuel, selected and arranged as fore-stick, back-stick and superimposed material. Resting on fire-dogs or andirons, the fuel burned, while pots and kettles suspended on the crane by pot-hooks and trammels, contained the resolving culinary preparations of divers kinds. Baking was done by the assistance of the reflecting surfaces of the tin baker, or by the cruder method of burying the material to be cooked in the ashes. The brick oven was also periodically brought into requisition in the preparation of food.

The introduction of stoves* gradually brought about a revolution in domestic affairs. The work of change began about sixty or seventy years ago. The innovation was at first attended with ridicule and scorn. Necessity, however, wrought its own modified results in spite of captious opposition. Among the patterns of stoves first introduced were the James, the Morse, and the Moore. Neither of these would compare favorably with the present styles of kitchen stoves, either in economy of fuel or ease of culinary results. However, the adoption of the first stoves was an important step in the path of domestic prudence. With a continued complement of ancient fireplaces in every dwelling-house, the native supply of fuel would before this time have been practically exhausted.

In the earliest days of this settlement, the fire of the domestic hearth was renewed by the use of a flint, a steel and a supply of tinder. The introduction of the lucifer match put an end to the less convenient practice of kindling. The introduction of the ancient clock, with open works and visible pendant weights, relieved society of the necessity of locating dwelling-houses directly with respect to the cardinal points of the compass. The tall, encased clock†, now frequently seen, fol-

---

*Daniel Chase is said to have been the owner of the first stove ever used in this town. It was of very thick iron castings, and much heavier than an average stove of the present day.

†Many ancient clocks were made by Abel and Levi Hutchins of Concord. Sometimes the uncased works were purchased ot the manufacturers and afterwards enclosed. David Young is said to have been the maker of the first clock-case constructed here. In the rooms of the New Hampshire Antiquarian Society, at Contoocook, may be seen the first complete tall clock ever brought into this town. It was made in 1733, by JONATHAN BLASDEL, and was brought to this town in 1776, by Benjamin B. Darling.

lowed, to be in its turn superseded by timepieces of still more modern construction. The kitchen ware, sometimes of wood, or of porcelain, or of pewter, exhibited features of less distinctive importance, though of different relative value when china was as rare as now is silver, and pewter as rare as china. The general furniture of a household, of which there are so many lingering representations, needs no special description.

Out of doors, improved utensils were adopted as time advanced. We have already given some account of these in our article on local industries. Joshua Morse owned the first wheelbarrow used in the town. The wheel was a simple, solid truck, wrought from a piece of plank. This implement was in use many years ago. The first waggon had wooden axles, and the body had no braces or springs. The seat was suspended on a pair of wooden strips running longitudinally and acting in some degree as springs. The first sleigh was double, being capable of conveying at least six persons. The first single sleigh was owned by Jonathan Chase, father of Daniel. The first wagon seat, like the first sleigh seat, contained a cavity or "box" for the convenient transportation of different articles.

We have already, in a previous article, spoken of each household of the olden time as a local manufactory. Men, women and children wore largely only cloths of domestic manufacture. Wool was carded, spun, and wove by hand, fulled at the mill, and at home made into garments for both sexes. Flax was treated in a similar manner. The implements employed in the manipulation of wool and flax can now be found scattered here and there in different places. Cotton was frequently purchased in the form of yarn and woven in textile combination with wool. The laborious and slow production of fabrics necessitated a stinted economy in dress. Ladies' gowns had fewer breadths and both sexes had fewer changes of raiment. The provision of comfortable supplies of domestic conveniences required diligent labor of the whole available household throughout the year.

In the olden time, as now, improvements were at first within the privileges of the wealthier class. Consequently, they were more properly included in the department of domestic luxuries. As the local tendencies of population became more defined, the village became the natural centre of refined domestic attractions. Here luxuries early became more generally known than in the more rural districts and their glare and fascination proportionally influenced the imagination of the less favorably endowed. To cite a case, John Harris, Esq., owned the first floor carpet ever seen in Hopkinton. The introduction of this luxury excited unmeasured popular comment.

SOCIAL.

The privilege of socially commingling is always highly esteemed in every local community. Very soon after the settlement of this town, the universal taste for sociability began to exhibit itself. People met in lesser circles with their private friends or joined the general company on occasions of greater social festivity. In every locality more stated occasions of popular gatherings are selected or set apart. In the earlier days of this township, a "raising" naturally became the incentive to a popular demonstration of sociability. The erection of the frame of an important edifice brought out the majority of the entire settlement — men, women and children. It was often followed by a grand demonstration of hilarity. When, about one hundred years ago, Jeremiah Story raised the frame of his two-storied dwelling house, the younger people in the neighborhood supplemented the event by a grand party in the temporary house of their host, where some of them "danced all night till broad daylight." The autumnal husking was another occasion of joviality. Both sexes collected at huskings, shucked the corn-ears, paid forfeits of red ones, consumed a hearty supper, of which baked beans, pumpkin pies, and attendant gratuities of the farmer's kitchen, formed an important part, and frequently crowned the festivity with a social dance to the music of the violin. When instrumental music was wanting, dancing was kept up to the jingling melody of the best singers in the company.

Hopkinton being several times the seat of the State Government, and always close to the permanent Capitol, inauguration day, or "'lection," naturally afforded the people of this town a regularly-recurring opportunity to exercise their taste for social amusement. The fascination of official dignity, the display of military, and accidental array of attractive and diverting sights and sounds,—all conspired to present an entertainment not likely to be overlooked by the masses of any society. Training and muster days also implied attractions appealing to the same social passion. The muster day, particularly, was a time of greater local interest and excitement. The mimic war, attended by the thousand and one features that always cluster around an out-door public exhibition set the hearts of the whole community agog. Nor would our references be complete unless we mentioned further those opportunities of social festivity arising from the general inter-dependence of society in the prosecution of personal enterprises. The raising and the husking are only preliminary in a list including the quilting, the apple-paring, and similar events of a more social character.

In the past history of this town was developed a social feature for which we cannot to-day show an adequate compliment. When Hopkinton was a centre of commercial and political influence, there was a corresponding representation of those who tread only the higher paths of social popularity and privilege. There were gentlemen and ladies of the old school, who not only enjoyed the better surroundings afforded by their position and power, but also trained their households in a rigid etiquette that placed a social value on the words and acts of the individual unentertained in the ranks of the great commonalty. Inevitable later changes have left but comparatively little of that higher sociability once so prominent.

MORAL.

In general, throughout the history of this town, its people have exemplified the traits of character proverbially ascribed to New England. Great crimes have been few, the population being mostly of that industrious class finding no place for overt acts against the laws of good society. However, a person familiar with only the present state of our social life can have but little conception of the peculiar features of human character always largely obtaining in a pioneer state of civilization. They are only individuals of resolute will and overwhelming personal force that can subdue a wild region, full of wild beasts and wild men. Such as subdue such a wilderness are both positive and stern both in their morals and immorals. In an intense illustration of a vigorous ideal, the first settlers in a new country strike heavily right and left, dealing energetic and telling blows, whether battling for the right or wrong. In time the increase of social and refining facilities tends more to soften than to obliterate the essential outlines of character pertaining to an incipient community, struggling for existence in a new country.* Hence, in contemplating the mental character of a people like ours, assuming the essentials to have been the same since the beginning of local history, it becomes our imaginations to intensify their conceptions the further back they extend into the past.

There was one feature of the earlier moral life of this town that requires a more special explanation. All frontier life is liable to be involved with the experiences of criminal adventures. When Hopkinton occupied a prominent position on the northern New

---

*In perusing the earlier records of this township, one sees an illustration of this theory in the progressive conduct of local legislation frequently required to accomplish various ends. Acts were at first passed and rescinded in multitudinous instances. The incorporation of the township, in 1765, in a large measure appears to have softened many asperities and essentially established the unity and prosperity of the community.

Hampshire frontier, it became the facile resort of thieves, smugglers, counterfeiters, and other outlaws, seeking the awards of their nefarious traffic. The obscure haunts of wood and dell afforded many an opportunity of conducting outlawry, which has left too few reliable data to encourage an exact narration. Horse-thieving, smuggling and counterfeiting were conducted by gangs of accomplices that operated on a line extending from Canada to Massachusetts. Secret meetings were held in out-of-the-way places, like the dark glen on the Sibley brook, as it approaches the meadow on Dolloph's brook, where, on a dark, rainy night, a party is said to have discovered a whole convention of men, supposed to be consulting for mutual criminal advantage. Smuggling was carried on in goods surreptitiously conveyed across the Canada border and thence southwardly to places of profitable destination. Goods were conveyed in parcels, united in lots, and distributed again in packages, to suit the convenience of the operators. The partially settled state of the country facilitated these operations so far that, with all the wariness of public officials, very little progress was made in arresting the crime. The counterfeiters dealt both in spurious notes and coin; the former were largely purchased in Canada, and the latter to some extent, possibly, manufactured here. In the chimney of an old house on the Sibley farm, taken down in 1878, by Dr. C. P. Gage of Concord, was a vault or cavity, unlike anything customarily found in old chimneys, and supposed to have been designed in furtherance of counterfeiting. The fact that a former proprietor was confined in the State Prison in Charlestown, Mass., for dealing in spurious money, added force to the suspicion. Different places in this town have been pointed out as possible or probable scenes of former criminalities in the line described, and which now belong to a shadowy historic past.

The present subject would be incomplete without a reference to the use of intoxicating liquors. At the time of the settlement of Hopkinton, the practice of alcoholic stimulation was essentially universal. Rum, or some other intoxicant, was considered an indispensable household article. Alcoholic liquors were drank at home and abroad. All social courtesies were confirmed in drinking. The neighbor who congratulated at the event of birth, the friend at the fireside, the laborer in the field, the customer at the counter, the guest at the wedding, the clergyman on his parochial rounds, and the mourner at the funeral, were all treated to liquor. On gala days and occasions fabulous quantities of intoxicants were consumed. When the first Baptist church in the town was raised, the brethren provided a barrel of rum, and a complimentary supply of sugar, for the refreshment of the company. During one town-meeting in the older time, over sixty dollars worth of liquor was sold in small quantities* in one store alone. During the continuance of the general traffic in liquor, Ira A. Putney, a teamster, conveyed from the lower country into one store in this town, thirty-six hogsheads of rum in six weeks. Possibly a considerable part of this quantity was consumed in other places, being distributed to traders more distant from the southern centres of wholesale traffic.

Previously to the great temperance reformation, which begun in this town about fifty years ago, the popular traffic in and consumption of alcoholic liquors was carried on without special moral consideration, though to some extent under legal cognition.† The redemp-

---

*In 1783, Rev. Elijah Fletcher settled a bill at the store of Abel Kimball. There were thirty-eight charges in the bill, and they were all for small quantities of liquor, ranging from a dram to a "point," including glasses and "mugs of flip." The evidence of mutual settlement at the bottom of the account is as follows:

Jan. 29, 1783. Reckoned and Settled all accounts from the Beginning of the World to this Day, and nothing Due on either Side.
ELIJAH FLETCHER.
ABEL KIMBALL.

†The following extract from the records of this town illustrates:
STATE OF NEW HAMPSHIRE.
MERRIMACK ss.
To the Honorable Samuel Morrill, Judge of the Probate for said County.
We, your Petitioners, humbly sheweth that—— —— of Hopkinton, in said county, is in a habit of being almost continually intoxicated, which un-

tion of local society from this extended sway of alcohol was however mostly effected by moral suasion. Rev. Roger C. Hatch of the Congregational church, Rev. Michael Carlton of the Calvinist Baptist church, Rev. Arthur Caverno, of the Freewill Baptist church, Dr. James Gregg, and perhaps others, were prominent local apostles of temperance. Through the influence of men of high moral stamina, who presented economic, moral and spiritual motives, a great work of popular reform was instituted. However, a strict regard for historic truth requires us to suggest that, in reviewing this great revolution, allowance must be made for the fact that among those abandoning the use of intoxicants at that time there were many who had adhered to the use of liquor, not from any passion for it, but simply in fulfillment of a popular custom. The knowledge of this fact incurs a charitable consideration for the moderate success of the modern temperance reformer, who has almost wholly to combat causes that lie in the deeper recesses of the human mental or moral constitution; since men who are accustomed to commit acts in the face of popular sentiment are more difficult of effective moral approach through any avenue.

Since later times, permanent societies have been formed here in the name of temperance. In 1874, an organization of Good Templars was formed in the village of Contoocook; in 1878, one in Hopkinton village.

fits him for any kind of business, and is spending his property, and when under the influence of ardent spirits is very violent and abusive to his family, and there is some property still left under very peculiar circumstances. We therefore pray your Honour to appoint Guardian over said ―― agreeably to the laws of said State in such cases made and provided, as in duty bound will pray.
July 6th, 1826.

B. DWELL EMERSON, } Selectmen
STEPHEN DARLING, } of
STEPHEN SIBLEY, } Hopkinton.

A REVIEWER REVIEWED.

BY WILLIAM O. CLOUGH.

The author of the flattering tribute to "injured innocense"—a studied eulogy of the wonderful learning, eminent talent, honest purpose, respectability, disinterested and distinguished public and private services, ability to "harness a horse," drive a duck to water, and the beautiful christian virtues of the men who "see many things," who "think much, travel much, read much, write much, talk much," smoke much and pray without ceasing—vide the GRANITE MONTHLY for December, 1878—is undoubtedly a lawyer of the class complained of as thriving on the misunderstandings and misfortunes of their fellowmen in the humbler walks of life. A lawyer forsooth! To attribute a review of this character to any other professional man would be to do an injustice, violence if you please, to the public estimate of the cloth. The ear-marks, and the arraignment, the avoidance of context in the matter he would criticise, and the begging of the question at every point all bear too true a resemblance to the style of composition of the average lawyer to be mistaken by even a billious magazine scribbler. Yes, my would be smart critic must be a cheeky lawyer. No other professional man who is in his right mind, certainly no mortal of common clay, who respects himself and venerates the truth, would be guilty of such unfairness as is manifest throughout "Lawyers and Politicians." But why do I complain?

1. This reviewer, this "Daniel come to judgment" lawyer, like the world over, argues but one side of the cause. He introduces testimony not warranted by the facts, and draws upon his imagination for conclusions in a manner

that makes him ridiculous even to those favorable to vices. An honest reviewer makes mention of the article in which he finds sentiments that conflict with his own as a whole. He throws no mud at its author, and seeks no quarrel. He does not guess at grievances or hypothicate motives. He is exceedingly careful to understand the author's creation that he would desert, to commend whatever is commendable as well as to condem whatever seems to him wrong in theory and spirit. Not so with this new school reviewer. He brushes aside all these considerations and proceeds with the "cut direct." We complain, therefore, of ungenerous treatment, and insist that we have been placed in a wrong light. And why? For the simple reason that what we said about lawyers was very meager, and, on the whole, quite complimentary. Taken in connection with other matter in the article, its spirit need not be misunderstood—the whole being a review of the lesser side of professional men rather than the larger; of the things to be avoided by those starting out in life, rather than a measure of the measurer of success or failure those far advanced in life have attained. The very text was balanced with exceptions, so that the application was in every readers possibility. The argument, if argument there was, accommodated itself to a "class" within a profession, and with those who understand the mystery of a mouse-trap there is no occasion for misunderstanding. Those, therefore, who are above the pettifogger and the cheap demagogue, are not disturbed by what is unquestionably true of men in the law business, and, unlike vain and silly women, are content that others should sound their praise or speak their condemnation.

2. No other professional man, aside from the "class" of lawyers mentioned, would attempt to magnify the virtues of a mere politician, on the hypothesis that the article he is grieved about assails them, when in truth and in fact every word he quotes (as he must know) is set down against another class—the gambler and sporting man. In this particular his review ceases and bitter irony possesses him. He is terribly out of joint with the times, and withal severe on the author. "The 'professor of politics' needs no special notice in New Hampshire. He is an ever present individual, and what he don't know —unless he is mightily mistaken, and he never will admit as much—no magazine writer can tell." Only this and nothing more is said about politicians, and hence my learned and discourteous reviewer, who quoted me as saying all manner of evil against them, must stand convicted of perverting the facts to make out a case—not an uncommon occurrence with cheap lawyers. My conclusion is that he should summons for the spirit of his "saintly teacher," and request to be taught that the first, last, and only qualification of a reviewer is honesty. After he has learned this lesson he should be told by some "billous magazine scribbler, who has been righteously whipped in a law-suit," that his argument—it is not a review—reputes itself; that no better evidence of the statement that lawyers are "not burdened so heavily with knowledge as by cheek" is needed among ordinary people than the exhibition he makes of himself as a would-be reviewer.

THE GRANITE MONTHLY.

A MAGAZINE OF LITERATURE, HISTORY, AND STATE PROGRESS.

VOL. II.   APRIL, 1879.   NO. 7.

COL. JOHN HATCH GEORGE.

When a biographer encounters the duty of describing, in the abstract, a character which demands greater elaboration in order to do it reasonable justice, he must be excused for the roughness of the outlines, which, with the proper shadings thrown in, would give his descriptive picture more satisfactory approximation to its required fidelity. In the present instance limitation of space, and partial opportunity to glean matters of fact and incident suitable for biographical record, justify the claim on the reader for such excuse. In so far as details are given, however, they will be found correct.

JOHN HATCH GEORGE, son of John George, Esq., and Mary Hatch, his wife by a second marriage, was born in the house in Concord, N. H., now the Colonel's residence in that city, on the twentieth day of November, 1824, and is now, therefore, in his fifty-fifth year. The native place of his father was Hopkinton, but from his early manhood until the period of his death he was a resident in Concord, where he held the common respect of the citizens as a man of great energy and of unalloyed integrity. He died in 1843. Mary Hatch, mother of the subject of this sketch, survived her husband four years. She was a daughter of Samuel Hatch, Esq., of Greenland. Of the same family were the father of Hon. Albert R. Hatch of Portsmouth, and the mother of John S. H. Frink, Esq., both of whom stand high in professional and political relations in New Hampshire—worthy descendants of a worthy ancestry, noted for great native abilities, honesty, industry and perseverance.

The boyhood of Col. George, as contemporaries say, was unmarked by any special indication of that decided description which sometimes heralds a boy's preference for a life pursuit. He was slow neither at learning or at play. If he had a prevailing passion it was for the possession and care of domestic animals, on which he lavished great wealth of kindness, a quality which has grown with his growth and strengthened with his strength. His farm manager is authority for the opinion that "he would kill his animals with kindness were they so unfortunate as to have his constant personal attendance." His love for rural pursuits was a hereditament, and also clings to him with increasing vigor unto this day.

He was educated at the public schools in Concord, and was fitted for college at the Old Academy in that city. He entered as a student at

Dartmouth college in 1840, without having any special profession in future view, and deported himself with credit while there. When his father died, some three years afterward, he had to resign his college course, but his graduating degree, and that of Master of Arts, was subsequently conferred on him by the Faculty of Dartmouth.

It was fortunate for him, and largely also due to the promising character of young George, at this most important period of his life, that his family enjoyed the friendship of Ex-President Franklin Pierce. All who were privileged with the personal acquaintance of that eminent man knew the peculiar skill he had in the discovery of latent merit among the youth whom he honored with his friendship, and the more than kindly interest he took in many, who, only for his encouragement, would have lacked the spirit to aspire. Without previous consultation concerning his inclination towards the study of law, Gen. Pierce invited young George to enter his office and prepare for admission to the bar. That the youth had what is called "a legal mind" had been a quiet discovery made by his friend and patron, who was then at the head of the law-firm, in Concord, of Pierce & Fowler. Here, for three years, Col. George applied himself diligently to his studies, passed a reputable examination, and was admitted to the bar in 1846, and at once entered into partnership with Gen. Peaslee, and on the practice of law under the firm-name of Peaslee and George, which united interest continued until 1851, when he formed a copartnership with Sidney Webster, Esq.

Prior to his majority Col. George had been hovering round the verge of politics, and, at every circuit of the whirlpool he was drawn nearer to its vortex. For many years, and with but few interruptions, the Democracy had guided the politics of New Hampshire up to 1847, when the Colonel held his first public office as clerk of the State Senate. This office he filled in 1848, and again in 1850. In 1849 he was appointed Solicitor for the county of Merrimack, re-appointed in 1854, and removed by address, solely for political reasons, in 1856.

The same year in which he was made Solicitor for Merrimack county he was married to Miss Susan Ann Brigham, daughter of Levi Brigham, Esq., of Boston. Mrs. George died in 1863, leaving five children—three sons and two daughters. In 1865 he was again married to Miss Salvadora Meade Graham, daughter of Col. James D. Graham, of the United States Engineers. He has had one daughter by this marriage. His eldest son, John Paul, graduated last year at Dartmouth college, and is now studying at Harvard Law School. His eldest daughter, Jane Pierce, is married to Mr. H. E. Bacon, of Portland, Maine, and his second son, Charles Peaslee, is at the United States Naval School at Annapolis, Md. A son and daughter—Benjamin Pierce and Ann Brigham—are at home.

Famous as the bar of New Hampshire has been for its eminent men, few of their number gained, so early in their legal career as did Col. George, such reputation for skill and devotion to the interests of clients. His success was remarkable, and yet it was simply the meet reward of the most devoted study and perseverance in professional duty. Gifted with a powerful physical organization he accomplished miracles of labor in the legal and political fields. He was fortunate in the sympathy and aid he received in both relations from his partners, Gen. Peaslee and Sidney Webster, Esq., and until the latter gentleman, in 1852, became the private Secretary of President Franklin Pierce, when the brief copartnery was dissolved. In 1853 he formed another partnership with Judge William L. Foster, with which Hon. Charles P. Sanborn, ex-Speaker of the New Hampshire House of Representatives, subsequently became associate. The firms thus severally constituted held high reputation in the locality and state, and managed, with admirable skill, and great success, many of the prominent civil and criminal cases in Merrimack,

Grafton, and other counties in the state. Our gleanings are defective in their record of the leading cases—civil and criminal—in which Col. George had prominence as leading counsel, as public prosecutor, or otherwise. He was prosecutor in the case of State *v.* Haskell, a negro man, and wife, in 1855, when sentence of death passed on Haskell for murder, which doom was commuted to imprisonment for life. Being officially engaged on this trial the memory of the writer enables him to state that the conduct of this case by the prosecutor was managed with great skill, and without that redundancy of immaterial testimony, and surplusage of words in argument, which very often render trial proceedings, which ought to be of grave and dignified character, almost ludicrous. Other capital cases, defended by Col. George, and followed by acquittals, were those of State *v.* Scammel, tried in Grafton county; State *v.* Young, tried in Rockingham county, and State *v.* Sawyer, decided in Grafton county. Among Col. George's more memorable civil cases were those of Smith *v.* the Boston, Concord and Montreal railroad; Concord railroad *v.* Clough; Frost *v.* the city of Concord; Tufts' Brick Company *v.* Boston and Lowell railroad, and, recently, and still unfinished, the suit Commonwealth of Massachusetts and the pier accident case at Salem.

In 1851 and during the two succeeding years, and again in 1856, he was chairman of the Democratic state committee, during which he did much active service. He was especially prominent in organizing the Presidential campaign which resulted in the election of his intimate personal friend—Gen. Franklin Pierce. From 1852 until 1860 he was a member of the national Democratic committee; and, from 1853 until 1858, he was United States Attorney for New Hampshire. In 1853 he was elected a member of the state legislature, but he resigned his seat on accepting the appointment of U. S. Attorney.

It may properly be mentioned here that Col. George had a narrow escape from becoming Secretary for the territory of Minnesota. That appointment was offered him and accepted, and all arrangements were made to enable him to go to the north-west. On going to Washington he was informed by President Pierce that he need not hasten his departure for a couple of weeks, nor until the President and he should have an opportunity to talk over old home matters; but some business having been left undone in New Hampshire by the colonel, he sought permission to return and complete it, for which he had leave. On arriving at home such was the pressure brought to bear on him by his old clients, and such the importance and value of new encouragements presented him, as to induce him to give up the Minnesota appointment and resume his profession in Concord, greatly to the satisfaction of his friends in social, political and business relations.

Although primarily, in his military career, he was a member of that numerous body which hold colonelcies by a merely ornamental tenure, it cannot be said of him that he "never set a squadron in the field;" for, besides being aid-de-camp and chief of staff of Gov. Dinsmore during three years, up to 1850, for several years from the organization he commanded company A. of the "Governor's Horse Guards," one of the finest, best equipped and most thoroughly drilled cavalry corps in New England, and one in which the people of the state had just pride.

From 1847 until 1866, Col. George was clerk and counsel for the Concord railroad. In 1867 he moved his office to Boston, he having accepted the position of Solicitor for the Boston and Lowell and associate railroads—a position he now holds. He has a peculiar fitness for this office, through his being thoroughly conversant with railroads, their laws and modes of their management. In February, 1870, at the special request of the leading citizens of Concord, he delivered a public address on "Railroads and their Management," which was exhaustive of the subject and created great local as well as wide national interest. It was reported by a shorthand expert, published and extensively circulated, and is held as reliable authority regarding the theory of railroad management. His connection with railroads has been intimate and extended. He is director of the Mount Washington, the Profile and Franconia, and also of the Peterborough railways. He was one of the originators and earliest advocates of the Concord and Claremont and Contoocook Valley roads, and has aided largely in the construction of the various lines which have conserved to Concord its centrality. There are ways and means whereby men receive much popular reputation and credit for services as hollow and objectless as those of Col. George were substantial and valuable; yet it is but just to say in behalf of the wise and discriminating among our people that they put the genuine patriotic value on his efforts and esteem the man accordingly as a people's friend.

Last year Col. George was appointed a Trustee for the N. H. Asylum for the Insane. He has largely and influentially participated in local affairs in Concord. For many years he labored earnestly in the improvement of the public schools, and took deep interest in the elevation of the standard of education taught therein. He invariably upheld that the perfection of the school buildings was essential, as a precursor of the required improvement in the educational course. Because of this sentiment, he was employed on building committees chosen to manage the erection of several of our school buildings, which, for completeness and adaptability to their uses, Concord is so justly noted. In 1877 he was chosen a member of the Board of Education of the Union District. In course of his very active service in these relations, he has never made pecuniary charge on his fellow citizens for his labors, whether rendered as a lawyer or as a citizen. If the city records bear any evidence of such charge having been recognized, whatever it may be, the amount was never received by the colonel, but went back to the city schools in some shape or another, useful and necessary. When the effort to remove the State Capitol was made, he exerted every energy in his power to prevent the success of this design, and labored with great diligence and self sacrifice in that direction.

As previously stated, Col. George entered the arena of politics almost at the outset of his active life. Nature and mental acquirements combined to give him prominence in politics while yet almost a youth. His recognized energy and executive skill gave him the chairmanship of the committee appointed to receive President Franklin Pierce on his visit to his native State and home in 1854, and many will recollect the success attending that great event. In 1859 he was the Democratic nominee as candidate to represent the Second District in the House of Representatives of the United States, but failed of an election. In 1863 he was again nominated for that office, and made a vigorous canvass of the district—making twelve addresses per week during a month or more—but was again defeated after a very close vote. In 1866 he was the nominee of the Democratic members of the legislature of that year as candidate for the United States Senate. His fellow Democrats gave him the full strength of their vote, but the Republicans were largely in the majority against him.

A man may be mistaken in his notions, and be very earnest and persistent in their assertion, but he will be always respected when his views are believed to be honestly entertained and pronounced. The people only hold in contempt a man who has convictions, and who is afraid to express them when circumstances demand their explanation. Col. George is no such man. He is credited with thinking profoundly of what he says, and saying firmly what he has thought. He may offend men's opinions or prejudices by what he says, but he seldom or ever loses their respect, because of their conviction of his rigid honesty of argument or purpose. Socially speaking, and notwithstanding his variance in political opinion with the majority of his fellow citizens of

Concord, no public man can count more devoted personal friends and admirers amid his political opponents than he. His experiences have proved the falsity of the poet's contrary assertion, and that honesty is not a ragged virtue, but a covering which no good and patriotic man, and worthy citizen, can reputably refuse or decline to wear. In all respects, aside from politics or matters of public dispute, Col. George's social character stands high among his fellow citizens.

The "brethren of the mystic tie" have in him an exalted member of their most worthy fraternity. He exists among their number as a "Sovereign Grand Inspector" of the 33d and final degree in Masonry, and as an active member of the "Supreme Council of the Ancient and Accepted Scottish Rite of the Northern Jurisdiction of the United States," and has taken all the lower degrees. He is a member of the Blazing Star Lodge, and of the Mount Horeb Commandery of Concord, and was, for several years, Commander of the latter organization. Of most of our local charities, he is a quiet but liberal supporter; and the incidental demands of benevolence find him always a ready friend.

Notwithstanding the great pressure of professional and other duties, much attention is given by Col. George to agriculture, and those improvements connected therewith, sanctioned alike by modern science and experience. He owns a fine farm just over the western boundary of Concord, in the town of Hopkinton, where the improvement and enrichment of the soil, and the breeding and raising of horses and Jersey cattle form part of his summer pursuits. It is not certain that he will add largely to his fortune by his efforts as a "gentleman farmer;" but the external aspects of his management are such as to make those efforts valuable, at least, as examples. His rules providing for cleanliness, comfort and kindness towards his farm animals are seen in their fine condition, and reported to be profitably justified by their superior produce. No better proof of a man's nobility in the ranks of humanity can be found than in his kindness towards his dumb animals.

And now, in conclusion, a few words as to Col. George's status as a politician and a lawyer. As has already been shown he is a Democrat. Keeping always in view the foundation principles on which that policy rests, he is what may be properly called a progressionist. He recognizes—what many cannot do—the fact that the science of politics advances, as does every other, and that, while fundamental principles never vary, circumstances occur to change the rigid rule of their application, though not to materially vitiate its force or shut it out of due consideration. The political influences of today may not be fit to govern in what those of tomorrow may demand; and he can only be a narrow-minded man who can think otherwise and act accordingly. He certainly can have no pure element of statesmanship within him. But associated with this progressiveness there is no feature of vaccillation or radical change and departure from the organic principles of his party in Col. George. He is as true as steel to both, and no man among the Democracy of New Hampshire has a larger share of the confidence and respect of his compatriots. His public addresses are held by his admirers as models of honest, terse, pertinent and well-judged and founded argument; and he certainly carries an audience along with him, not by the use of clap-trap and sensationalism, but by the bold, acutely analytical, and forcible representation of sound logical facts. He is held to be one of the most solid, as well as most influential, stump speakers in New Hampshire, and his political opponents do not deny this. His memory acts as an encyclopedia of political history, state and national, and this always gives him wonderful advantage as an impromptu orator—a duty he has invariably to attend to when many or few are met together for political deliberation.

When his reputation and character as a lawyer comes up the writer confesses that the task of describing the latter puzzles him somewhat. There is no room for hesitation in saying that, in eminence of ability, determination in arranging the means of success, preparation to meet and confute opposing arguments, and unwavering general devotion to what he deems the just interests of his clients, no professional man in New England is more than his peer. To gainsay this fact would be to controvert the opinions of the best men on the bench and at the bar, and to attribute solely to friendly admiration what is assuredly a well recognized truth. So much for reputation; but what can, or should, be said as to Col. George's manner as a lawyer? It is confident, aggressive, bold and independent of every consideration but directness; it shows no aspect of favor for aught but the purpose in issue. Something has been here recorded of the qualities of his political addresses. The same bold fearlessness of men, and of opposing opinions, the same integrity of sentiment and expression, the same disregard of what offence the truth, as he views it, may give to the opposition, are characteristic of him as a pleader at law. Here, also, what may, and does seem to sound harshly from his lips is materially reconciled to the listener's favorable judgment by the pleader's manifest earnestness, honesty and unadulterated devotion to the truth, and the interest of his client, founded on his views thereof. There is no surplusage of words in Col. George's legal prelections. He is a very Gradgrind for facts, and uses them always with direct and sledge-hammer force, cultivating catapult pith rather than the pelting of his opposition with roses. Every energy is directed towards power and conquering effect. To use the expression of one who thoroughly knows the subject of this imperfect sketch: "the man in trouble who has Col. George for his friend and advocate is lucky indeed: he who is in legal difficulty, and has him to oppose him is assuredly to be pitied."

Col. George is of robust build, about five feet ten inches in height, approximates two hundred pounds weight, is of strong constitution, enjoys excellent health, has immense working power of mind and body; and, if all reports are true, it is not likely that he will live a long and active life and go "over the hill to the poor-house" at its close.

IN RUINS.

BY ABBA GOOLD WOOLSON.

All through the summer's rosy hours
  I built my castle fine;
And not a soul should dwell therein,
  Save only mine and thine,
    My Love,
  In loneliness divine.

No cost of make, or wealth of hue
  I spared from base to dome;
Where lordly monarchs choose to bide
  They rear a kingly home;
    And so
  This rose like silver foam.

Stand here upon the sunlit plain
  And see how fair it shines;
Untaught I planned its airy towers
  And shaped its perfect lines;
    For love
  All excellence divines.

But while I gaze, a dusky film
  Across its splendor falls;
My purples and my gold are dim—
  What ails the reeling walls?
    What doom
  Sends terror through its halls?

The keen air sweeps adown the hill:
  Give me a hand to hold;
I shiver in these breezes chill
  That grow so fierce and bold,
    Yet hearts
  May laugh at Winter's cold.

That hand of thine, so fair and strong,
  I thought could clasp me warm;
It melts within my burning grasp
  Like touch of ghostly form;
    I hear
  No heart-beat through the storm.

Great winds from out the heavens leap;
  No castle-dome appears;
Rain dashes on mine upturned face,
  To quench the hope of years:
    Pour, floods;
  Yet faster flow my tears.

MARCH.

BY ALICE ESTELLE FRIESE.

It was a fierce, wild March night. One can fancy such scenes quite comfortably in cheerful, well-lighted, close-curtained rooms; but to breast the driving storm of sleet and rain outside, is quite another matter. So thought Mr. Thorpe, a respectable tradesman in the thriving, bustling town of L——, as he hurried on through the darkness, and the ever increasing violence of the gale. Visions of the cosy parlor, with its tempting tea-table so daintily arranged, and the pretty, charming wife who presides so gracefully, flit across his brain; but even their alluring promises cannot blind him as to the discomforts of the present; and with a gasp of despair he tucks the wreck of an umbrella under his arm, buttons his heavy coat closer around him, and strides on through the gloom. No one is astir tonight; no sign of life meets him in the usually well-filled streets. "Everyone is safely housed, but myself," he mutters to the unpitying darkness. But even as he is speaking, a form, tall and slight, starts out from the shadows a few paces ahead, and pauses for a flash of time under the uncertain light of the solitary street-lamp, which lamps in our aspiring villages are placed at undeterminable distances from each other, wherever one long straggling street happens to meet another, seeming to say to the night pedestrian, "you have safely traversed the impenetrable darkness thus far, behold I invite you to a continuation of the same."

As the figure, evidently a woman's, stands thus for a moment clearly defined against the dark background, Mr. Thorpe is half inclined to fancy that it turns to meet his advancing steps with a gesture of entreaty; then suddenly and swiftly glides on, and is lost from sight.

I say he is inclined to fancy that she appealed to him for aid; but being an extremely practical man, he never allows himself such vagaries; so he banishes the fancy, and hurries on. At last he has reached his own home. The cheery, welcoming light streaming out from the windows, sends a cheerful, happy feeling through his entire being; and with a laugh of defiance at the mad fury of the storm, he springs up the steps to the sheltering porch, when suddenly at his very door his foot touches something soft and yielding, while at the same time, a little troubled cry is heard, mingled with the weird, uncanny voices of the wind. Half in wonder, half in fear he seizes a mysterious bundle at his feet, and presently appears before the astonished gaze of his wife, half drenched with the storm, a hopeless expression of bewilderment and perplexity upon his countenance, while in his arms he holds out the same mysterious bundle, from which various small cries issue, from time to time, at irregular intervals. The contents of the aforesaid bundle being duly examined, they prove none other than a round-faced, charmingly beautiful, black eyed baby girl. There is nothing in the "make-up" of the child or its wardrobe that even the most fastidious might criticise; every article of clothing is of the finest texture, and delicately wrought. Evidently this is a waif from the very lap of luxury, and refinement; and yet an outcast and homeless.

Tenderly, lovingly, pretty Mrs. Thorpe touches and caresses the little stranger, saying half hesitatingly, "we will care for her tonight, Charles, and tomorrow we must make an effort to find her parents; or if they cannot be found, perhaps the matron of the orphans' home would take her; she seems so unusually interesting, that I should like to be sure she is well cared for, if no one is to claim her."

"Claim her!" impatiently interrupts Mr. Thorpe; "You talk like a woman! As if any one ever claimed what they were glad to be rid of." "But,"—his voice softening a little as he spoke, for in spite of himself the remembrance of the unknown woman under the street-lamp, and her mute appeal to him for sympathy and help, clings to him; and for once, without arriving at his conclusion by a careful method of reasoning, very unlike his usual self, he in some strange, undefined way, closely associates in his mind the memory of this woman, and the presence of the little stranger in his home—

"But, Mary, you might as well keep the child; she seems as well disposed as such afflictions usually are, and although I don't approve of babies, and therefore wash my hands of the whole affair, still it might be a good thing for you; the vacant place in the household, you know, will at last be filled."

Still later, after Mrs. Thorpe had succeeded in coaxing the smiles to chase away the tears, and to play hide and seek among the convenient dimples in the baby's cheeks and chin, she ventures the question, "What shall we call her?" for of course every baby must have a name.

"Call her March; it would be quite apropos," suggests her husband quickly. "Yes, but," said Mrs. Thorpe, "it seems almost like an evil omen to give her such a dreary, cheerless name." "Nonsense, my love," returns Mr. Thorpe, "What's in a name?" And so it is settled, and baby March henceforth becomes an important member of the Thorpe household.

If I were giving a sermon, instead of attempting to write a story, I should here remark that Mrs. Thorpe was of the type of women that many men most desire for a wife—pretty, gentle, submissive, yielding, and for the good of the human race in general. I would urge the fair sex to fashion themselves in an entirely different mould; and, whether matron or maid, to stand firm and self-reliant in their own true womanhood; for, although these shy, helpless, clinging ways may seem to the masterful lover the very embodiment of womanly grace, yet they only tend to make the one selfish and arrogant, and the other abject and unwomanly. But as such is not my purpose, I shall leave all this unsaid, and proceed at once with the story.

Time drags wearily with the heavyhearted, and all too quickly speeds with the gay. To Mr. Thorpe's quiet home it has brought no sudden transformation. The head of the house has gone on in his matter-of-fact way, adding, year by year, to his well-filled coffers, until he has come to be acknowledged in business parlance, "one of the heaviest men of the town," which is quite as true literally. Mrs. Thorpe, the matron, is as charming and pretty as the Mrs. Thorpe of earlier years; while March has grown from babyhood past childhood into dawning womanhood, the pet and idol of the home. No clue has ever been given as to her mysterious advent among them; no trace of the unknown woman who, solitary and alone, traversed the deserted streets on that wild March night. Incredulous people have long since ceased to regard this phase of the night's experience. For how could any strange person, and a woman, go in and out among them, without the fact being noted and commented upon by some of the news-mongers. An utterly impracticable story! Thus the matter has been satisfactorily settled to their minds. And even Mr. Thorpe, from puzzling over the perplexing question so long, has been inclined to doubt its reality, and has even allowed himself to think that possibly it might have been a sort of optical illusion; or, more improbable still, an unreal presence from the shadowy land, supposed to be inhabited by the guardian attendants of finite creatures, and conditions. But be that as it may, he has somehow during these years fallen a victim to the strange lovableness and fascinating wiles of his adopted daughter; and has grown fonder of her than he would be willing to acknowledge.

A rare, beautiful creature she certainly has become, with a dusky, richly colored style of beauty quite unknown among the passionless, phlegmatic people of our sturdy north. A form, slight, childlike, with a peculiar undulating grace of movement, a complexion brown as the nuts of our own forests, yet crimson as the reddest rose; wavy masses of ebon hair, catching odd gleams in the sunlight, blue-black and purplish like a raven's wing, eyes capable of wonderful transitions, now full of joy, laughter, and sunshine, now flashing scorn and defiance, or heavy with midnight gloom. A strange child, full of wild vagaries and incontrolable impulses. Mrs. Thorpe could no more understand her nature or check her fierce impetuosity, than she could with her weak hands stay the torrent of the mountain stream, or control the headlong speed of the wind, as it eddies and whirls in its mad dance. And so, unchecked and unrestrained, March has entered upon her regal, imperious womanhood.

Naturally, of course, there are many manly hearts eager to pay homage at so fair a shrine; but Mr. Thorpe with paternal pride, has set his heart on securing an eligible partner for his darling. And so it begins to be rumored around town, that Hon. Elwyn Reeves has out-distanced all competitors, and is in fact, the betrothed husband of the beautiful March. To be sure, he is her senior by many years, but he comes from a long line of aristocratic ancestors, and has added to his proud name a princely fortune, as his solid, elegant home, away upon the hill, frowning in its imposing stateliness upon its humbler, less aspiring neighbors, attests.

"A very good match indeed, considering her mysterious and somewhat doubtful parentage, a remarkable *chef-d'œuvre* of fortune for her ;" say anxious mammas and disappointed maidens, Mr. Thorpe is pre-eminently satisfied, and if March herself shows no gratification in regard to her good fortune, it is to be attributed to her peculiar disposition, at times so reticent and reserved. Thus Mr. Thorpe quiets any scruples he may have entertained as he remembers how listlessly and wearily March replied, when he had mentioned Mr. Reeves' proposal, and dwelt warmly upon the happiness in store for her as his wife. "It shall be as you wish, papa, you may, if you desire it, give Mr. Reeves a favorable answer when he calls." But of course she was happy ; any sensible person would be with such a future in anticipation.

All are therefore quite unprepared for the announcement that Mrs. Thorpe with ashen face, and broken, quivering voice, first communicates to her husband, that the servants quickly catch up and carry into the streets ; that in an incredibly short time is upon every tongue—March has left them, as mysteriously and silently as she came among them.

"Where had she gone, and why?" These were questions with which speculative minds were for sometime busy, and anxious. Questions which were never answered to them. She had gone, leaving no trace behind. In a little note addressed to her foster-parents, she left them her dear love and a farewell. She should never, never forget their goodness and tenderness to her ; she had been happy with them, but she had chosen for herself another life, and a happier, and she must needs live it. That was all. After a while other faces came, and crowded the memory of her's away. The house on the hill soon found a mistress, who brought to her husband as a dower in the place of March's queenly beauty, a fortune equal in magnificence to that of its owner, and so he was content. It is one of the laws of compensation that gives one good in the place of another taken. Only Mr. and Mrs. Thorpe long remembered, loved, and waited for the lost one.

Every story must have its sequel, so has mine. I think it was five years before it came.

In a tiny cottage, embowered and hidden by luxuriant vines and thick, swaying foliage, in a quaint little town, in a clime where the warmth and glory and brightness of the midday sun is never paled and dimmed by snow-hung clouds, where the air is heavy with the perfume of a thousand flowers, and balmy with the luscious breath of tropical fruits ; where over the senses, and into the soul, steal a dreamy, blissful languor, and a strange, beautiful peace, a woman in all her glorious womanhood lay dying. And yet, death does not seem very near to that young creature who reclines on a low couch by the open window, watching and dreaming with a far away look in the shadowy eyes, and a beautiful smile upon the radiant face. A man with blue eyes, full of woman's tenderness, and hair and beard of silvery whiteness, is standing at her side. And now the woman, turning her large, dark eyes full upon him, speaks in a low, musical voice that thrills the listener with a subtile sense of pleasure and of pain. "Dearest and best of friends, I am come very near to the place where the finite and the infinite meet, and blend together, and are lost in one. The past is vanishing like a glad dream, so brief, and yet so full of joy and completeness. All the unrest, and wild, passionate longing seem very far away from me now, such a strange, restful life has come to me. I have been thinking, perhaps it may be that some lives gather their full measure of sunshine and beauty in a very little time, while others are longer upon the way.

And so, I have taken my happiness in one delicious draught, and now hold life's empty goblet in my hands. I have been waiting for this; my fate was sealed when, a twelve-month ago, they told me that my voice was irrecoverably gone; for with it I had lost my art, and that to me was simply life. Well, it is best so. It may be in that unknown beyond, whither I am hastening, I shall find mine own again, and my soul shall be satisfied. Today I have been living again my old life, a stranger and an alien, and yet tenderly cared for by warm, loving hearts. I suppose they mourned when they discovered that their wild, willful March had flown. The remembrance of the pain I caused them has been my only regret in this new life of mine—this wonderful, grand life—and I owe it all to you, my mother's friend and mine. After I am gone, you will send to my dear foster-parents my good-bye message. I have told them all. Of my vain struggles to find my place among the eager, restless throng in the great, busy world, with only a wild, untrained voice and an unconquerable will to aid me. Of my finding a friend, the dearest friend of my angel mother, who patiently, lovingly bore with my capricious, impetuous nature, and with lavish prodigality helped me on toward the wished for golden goal. And then how destiny pressed close upon me, with his black pinions o'ershadowing me, and the fiat was—"Thus far shalt thou go, and no farther." Possibly they may not understand it all. They will think sadly that my life has been a failure, and it may have been; still I am glad to have lived it. It has been grand, glorious, and yet I am a little weary, and am impatient for the end.

And very soon it came, and March went from the storm, and the tempest, the longing and the pain, into light ineffable, and peace eternal.

PURE AS THE LILIES.

BY HENRIETTA E. PAGE.

She held out her hands for the lilies.
Her blue eyes so eager and bright,
And holding them close to her bosom,
She murmured her soft toned "Dood night."

"Ah! baby, my own little darling,
Though the lilies be never so fair,
The gold at their hearts is no brighter
Than the glinting strands of your hair."

As you in my arms slumber lightly,
Your bright lashes kiss your fair cheek,
I pray the kind God to keep safely
My own little blossom so meek.

Then laying her safe in her cradle,
The lilies clasped close to her breast,
And kissing her dewy lips softly,
I leave her alone to her rest.

The breath of the flowers is no sweeter
Than the breath of my babe I ween,
The petals no whiter or purer
Than the soul of my wee heart's queen.

South Boston, Mass.

MEN OF OLD NOTTINGHAM AT THE BATTLE OF BUNKER HILL.

BY JOHN SCALES, DOVER, N. H.

That old Roman, Sallust, says: "Surely fortune rules all things. She makes everything famous or obscure rather from caprice than in conformity with truth. The exploits of the Athenians, as far as I can judge, were very great and glorious, something inferior, however, to what fame has represented them. But because writers of great talent flourished there, the actions of the Athenians are celebrated over the world as the most splendid achievements. Thus the merit of those who have acted is estimated at the highest point to which illustrious intellects could exalt it in their writings."

Also, that latest of classical authors, Josh Billings, says: "Young man, blow your own horn!" These quotations express exactly the way in which the illustrious intellects of authors in Modern Athens (of America) have exalted the deeds of Massachusetts' heroes to such a degree that most people, outside of New Hampshire, do not suppose our state had much to do at the battle of Bunker Hill, whereas New Hampshire men constituted nearly four fifths of all the men and officers in that battle. Therefore I think I have just cause to "blow my horn" for my native town, and my ancestors who fought in that battle.

Old Nottingham comprised a tract of land supposed to be ten miles square, and which is now Nottingham, Deerfield and Northwood. It was incorporated in 1722, and settlements commenced in it soon after, at the "Square," a beautiful ridge of land about 450 feet above the sea level. At the beginning of the Revolution, Nottingham had 999 inhabitants, Deerfield 929, and Northwood 313. The records show that the people were making preparations for the coming conflict, and had sent generous assistance to the "Industrious Poor sufferers of the town of Boston" during the seige. During the winter of 1774-5, Dr. Henry Dearborn had a company of men which met at the Square to drill from time to time. In November, 1774, a town-meeting was held and a committee appointed to "Inspect into any Person," suspected of being a Tory.

On the 20th of April, 1775, news reached the Square that a battle had been fought the day before, and in the evening a large number of citizens assembled at the store of Thomas Bartlett. On the 21st, at 4 o'clock, a company of nearly one hundred men commenced their march for Boston, being armed and equipped as best they could at such short notice.

Some say that Joseph Cilley was the leader of this band of heroes, but others say Dr. Henry Dearborn was captain, and probably he was, as he had been drillmaster all winter, and was captain of the company after they arrived in Cambridge. They marched on foot all night, and arrived in Medford at eight o'clock on the morning of the 22d, some of the company having traveled, on foot, more than eighty miles since the previous noon, and over roads which were far from being in the best condition for rapid traveling.

I have searched records a great deal and inquired of the "oldest inhabitant," whenever I could find him, that I might secure a complete list of the men who constituted this company, but of the hundred I can only give the following names with certainty. If any reader of this article can add a name he will do me a great favor by forwarding it to me:

Dr. Henry Dearborn, Joseph Cilley, Jr., Thomas Bartlett, Henry Butler, Zephaniah Butler, John Simpson, Nathaniel Batchelder, Daniel Moore, Peter Thurston, Maj. Andrew McClary, Benjamin Johnson, Cutting Cilley, Joseph Jackson, Andrew Neally, Samuel Johnson, Robert Morrison, William Woolis, Eliphlet Taylor, William Blake, Nathaniel Twombly, Simon Batchelder, Abraham Batchelder, Simon Marston, Moses Gilman, William Simpson, John Nealey, and Samuel Sias. Let us briefly glance at the record of some of these men in the years that came after.

Henry Dearborn was born in Hampton, Feb. 23, 1751. He studied medicine and settled at Nottingham Square as a physician, in 1772. He married Mary D. Bartlett, daughter of Israel, and sister of Thomas Bartlett of Nottingham. He was always fond of military affairs, and is said to have been a skillful drill-master and well posted in the tactics in use previous to the Revolution. He fought with his company at the battle of Bunker Hill. In the September following, he joined Arnold's expedition to Quebec, accompanied by these Nottingham men,—James Beverly, John P. Hilton, Samuel Sias and Moses Gilman. They marched up the Kenebec river, through the wilds of Maine and Canada. In the assault upon that city, Captain Dearborn was taken prisoner. Peter Livias, the Tory councilor at Quebec, influenced the authorities to parole and send him home, on condition that Dearborn should forward his wife and children to him from Portsmouth to Quebec, which was done as agreed. In April, 1777, Capt. Dearborn was appointed Major in Scammel's regiment. He was in the battles of Stillwater and Saratoga and fought with such bravery, having command of a distinct corps, as to win the special commendation of Gen. Gates. In 1778, he was in the battle of Monmouth, with Col. Cilley acting as Lieut. Col., and helped retrieve Lee's disgraceful retreat. He was with Gen. Sullivan in his expedition against the Indians, in 1779, and was at Yorktown at the surrender of Cornwallis in 1781. Upon the death of Scammel, the gallant Colonel of the Third N. H. Reg., at the hands of a barbarous foe, Dearborn was made Colonel and held that position to the end of the war. After the war, he settled in Maine, where he was Marshal by appointment of Washington. He was two terms a member of Congress; Sec'y of War under Jefferson from 1801 to 1809; collector of the port of Boston between 1809-12; senior Maj. General in U. S. Army, 1812-13, and captured York in Canada, and Fort George, at the mouth of Niagara. He was recalled by the President, July 6, 1813, and put in command of the military district of N. Y. City, which recall was, no doubt, a great mistake. In 1822 he was appointed Minister Plenipotentiary to Portugal; recalled in 1824, at his own request; died at Roxbury, Mass. June 6, 1829. General Dearborn was a man of large size, gentlemanly deportment, and one of the bravest and most gallant men of his time.

Joseph Cilley, son of Capt. Joseph Cilley of Nottingham, was born in 1734; died 1799. He was engaged in the attack upon Fort William and Mary, in 1774; appointed Major in Col. Poor's regiment by the Assembly of N. H. in 1775; he was not present in the battle of Bunker Hill, as his regiment was engaged in home defence. He was made Lieut. Col. in 1776, and April 2, 1777, was appointed Colonel of the 1st. N. H. Reg. of three years' men, in place of Col. Stark, resigned. He fought his regiment bravely at Bemis's Heights, near Saratoga; and two weeks later was among the bravest of the brave, when Burgoyne made his final attack before surrendering his entire army of six thousand men. So fierce was the battle, that a single cannon was taken and retaken five times; finally, Col. Cilley leaped upon it, waved his sword, and "dedicating the gun to the American cause," opened it upon the enemy with their own ammunition. He was with Washington's army at Valley Forge, 1777-8; was at the storming of Stony Point; at Monmouth he was one of the heroes in retrieving Gen. Lee's retreat; was at the surrender of Cornwallis at Yorktown, and in other hard-fought battles of the Revolution. After the war he was Major-General of the 1st Div. N. H. militia, and as such headed the troops which quelled the insurrection at Exeter in

1786, with his own hand arresting the leader in the midst of his armed followers. Gen. Cilley was a man of great energy and industry, of strong passion, yet generous and humane. He was repeatedly elected representative, senator and councillor.

Thomas Bartlett was born Oct. 22, 1745; married Sarah, daughter of Gen. Joseph Cilley; was town-clerk twenty-six years; selectman thirty years; was the first representative from Nottingham to the General Court in 1784; was one of the Committee of Safety which managed the colonial affairs of New Hampshire during part of the Revolution; was captain of the 5th company of "six weeks" men at Winter Hill in 1775; was Lieut. Col. in Col. Gilman's regiment, in 1776; Lieut. Col. in Col. Whipple's regiment at Rhode Island, in 1778; also was Lieut. Colonel under Stark at the capture of Burgoyne. In 1780 he was Colonel of a regiment at West Point, when Arnold betrayed that fort. In 1790 he was appointed Justice of the Court of Common Pleas, and retained that office till his death in 1805. He was Major-General of first division of New Hampshire militia from 1799 to 1805, in which office he was preceded by Gen. Joseph Cilley, and followed by Gen. Henry Butler.

Henry Butler was a son of Rev. Benjamin Butler, the first settled minister in Nottingham, and was born April 27, 1754. He was captain of a company in Col. Thomas Bartlett's regiment at West Point, in 1780. He held many town and state offices; was the first postmaster in Nottingham, when Gideon Granger was Postmaster-General; and was Major-General of the first division of New Hampshire militia from 1805, for several years.

Zephaniah Butler, brother to Rev. Benjamin, was a school teacher in Nottingham for many years preceding the Revolution, and was one of Col. Cilley's staff officers during several campaigns. He married a sister of Col. Cilley; Gen B. F. Butler, whom everybody knows, is his grandson, he being son of Capt. John Butler of Deerfield, who was son of Zephaniah.

Cutting Cilley, brother of Col. Joseph Cilley, was born in 1738, and died in 1825; he held many town offices, and was captain of a company in one of the New Hampshire regiments during the Revolution.

John Simpson, born in 1748, and dying in 1810, is said to have been the man who fired the first gun at the battle of Bunker Hill. In 1778, he was lieutenant in Capt. Simon Marston's company, Col. Peabody's regiment; and was subsequently promoted to major. His brother, Robert, who also served in the Revolutionary army, is the great grandfather of General Ulysses Simpson Grant.

Nathaniel Batchelder, who was a brother-in-law of Col. Cilley, fought in the battle of Bunker Hill, under Capt. Dearborn, and was adjutant in Col. Drake's regiment, which did brave service in the battle of Stillwater, Saratoga, and the surrender of Burgoyne. He died of fever at Valley Forge, March 28, 1778.

Daniel Moore kept the first tavern at Deerfield Parade; fought at Bunker Hill and in subsequent battles; was captain in Col. Stark's regiment, and did valiant service during the war.

Andrew McClary was from Epsom and belonged to a family distinguished for its military men. He was plowing in his field on the 20th of April, 1775, when he *heard a horn blow*, which, on the instant, he knew was the tocsin of war; he left his plow in the furrow, and after the speediest preparation, hastened to Deerfield Parade and thence to Nottingham Square, where he joined Capt. Dearborn's company. After they arrived in Cambridge he was active in helping organize the New Hampshire men into companies and was himself appointed major in Col. Stark's regiment. He fought with his regiment at Bunker Hill, and was killed after the battle, in attempting to have "another shot at the enemy."

Robert Morrison was born and lived on the Square; he was a member of Dr. Dearborn's company, which drilled during the winter of 1774-5, and a private in Capt. Dearborn's company in the battle of Bunker Hill. In the September following he was bearer of dispatches from Washington to the Committee of Safety in New Hampshire, by whom he was treated with distinguished honors. In 1777 he was a private in Col. Stark's regiment, and fought bravely in all the battles till the surrender of Burgoyne. His son, Robert Morrison, Esq., resides in Northwood at the present time.

Joseph Jackson was sergeant in Capt. Dearborn's company at Bunker Hill, afterwards served in several campaigns and was captain of a company.

Samuel Johnson was not in the Bunker Hill fight, but was in the campaign of 1777, at Bennington, Stillwater and Saratoga, and took an active part under a commission which gave him the rank of colonel. He was one of the first settlers of Northwood at the Narrows, and was one of the selectmen of the town for fifteen years.

Simon Marston was from Deerfield, having settled on the Longfellow farm in 1763; he lived in the garrison house, erected by Jonathan Longfellow. He was sowing wheat when the courier, shouting the news of the battle of Lexington, rode past the field where he was at work. Marston left the measure, from which he was sowing, rushed to the house, filled his knapsack with pork and other necessaries, seized his gun, and hurried down to the Square. He acted in the capacity of an officer in Col. Reed's regiment at Bunker Hill; was an officer under Lieut. Col. Senter; was captain of 1st Co. Col. Peabody's regiment; was afterwards commissioned major and fought at Bennington, Stillwater and Saratoga. He was a brave man in war and energetic in peace. The others named, although they held no office of rank, were no less brave and faithful in performing perilous duties, and deserve to have their names recorded where they will never be forgotten.

After the Nottingham men arrived in Cambridge, and saw there was no danger of another attack immediatly by the troops in Boston, several returned home and commenced more thorough preparation for the coming conflict, but Dr. Dearborn and most of the men remained and were organized into a company, and Dearborn was elected captain the company became a part of Col. Stark's regiment and was stationed at Medford, whence they marched on the 17th of June and participated in the glories of "Breed's Hill." Captain Dearborn's company was No. 8, but he marched from Medford to the "Rail-fence," by the side of Col. Stark.

The following list of men comprising this company is no doubt correct, as it was furnished by Judge Nesmith for Cogswell's "History of Nottingham, Deerfield and Northwood," and the Judge is one of the best authorities in the State in such matters. The men were nearly all from old Nottingham:

Captain, Henry Dearborn, Nottingham.
1st Lieut., Amos Morrill, Epsom.
2d " Michael McClary, Epsom.
1st Sergt., Jona. Clarke, Nottingham.
2d " And. McGaffey, Epsom.
3d " Jos. Jackson, Nottingham.
1st Corp., Jonah Moody, "
2d " Andrew Field, "
3d " Jona. Gilman, Deerfield.
4th " And. Bickford, "

Privates.—Simon Dearborn, Gideon Glidden, James Garland, John Harvey, David Mudgett (of Gilmanton), Simon Sanborn, Robt. Morrison, John Runnels, John Neally, Joseph Place, Abram Pettengale, Andrew Nealley, Peter Severance, John Wallace, Theop. Cass (of Epsom), Israel Clifford, Nathaniel Batchelder (of Deerfield), Jacob Morrill, John Simpson, John Wallace, Jr., Neal McGaffey (of Epsom), Jonah Libbey, Moses Locke, Francis Locke, Zebulon Marsh, Solomon Moody, Chas. Whitcher, Marsh Whitten, Noah Sinclair (drummer), James Randell (fifer), Nich. Brown, Benj. Berry (of Epsom), John Casey, Jona. Cram (of Deerfield), Jeremiah Conner, Elisha Hutchinson, Dudley Hutchinson, Benj. Judkins, Josh. Wells, Jere. Dowe, Jona. Dowe, John Dwyer, David Page, Jr., Beniah Libbey, William Rowell, Weymouth Wallace (of Epsom), Thomas Walsh and William McCrellis (of Epsom).

THE N. H. SEVENTH AT FT. WAGNER.

[From sketch of Lieut. HENRY W. BAKER, in Coffin's History of Boscawen.]

The command had been entrusted to Gen. Trueman H. Seymour, who determined to make an assault. He knew nothing of the construction of Ft. Wagner. No information of the impediments to be overcome had reached him. Col. Putnam of the 7th, commanding the second brigade, opposed the contemplated movement.

"I do not think that we can take the fort," he said; and when Gen. Seymour reiterated his determination to make the attempt, Col. Putnam said, "We shall go like a flock of sheep."

The sun had set, and the twilight faded. The soldiers were ordered to remove the caps from the nipples of their rifles, and were told that they must depend upon the bayonet alone. In the 100th N. Y., which formed behind the 7th, this order was neglected.

In the darkness the assaulting column moved forward. The iron-clads, and the Union batteries opened a heavy fire, which was continued till the column was so near that further firing would endanger it, when, at a signal, all the Union batteries became silent. In an instant Ft. Wagner was aflame. Its heavy siege guns, howitzers, and forty-two pounder carronades burst forth, pouring a stream of shot and shell into the advancing troops. And now, in addition, the parapet of the fort swarmed with men, who, through the terrible cannonade of the day had been lying securely beneath the bomb proofs. Mingled with the roar of cannon were their volleys of musketry.

The first brigade had the advance. Its ranks went down like grass before the mower. Some of the soldiers fled, panic stricken. The second brigade, led by the 7th N. H., pressed on and filled the decimated ranks. Suddenly they found themselves confronted by a ditch fifty feet wide and ten feet deep, with four feet of water flowing into it. Only at the south-eastern angle was it dry. It was enfiladed by howitzers. Into the ditch leaped the soldiers. Grape and canister mowed them down, but others crowded on. The 7th N. H., led by Lt. Col. Joseph C. Abbott, made its way unfalteringly into the ditch, through it, and up the slope of the parapet. Cannon and musketry blazed in their faces; and now there was a flash behind them—the 100th N. Y., not having removed their caps, were firing into the dark mass, not knowing who was friend, who foe. All was confusion. All order disappeared. In the darkness no one could be recognized. Amid the groans of the wounded, the shouting of officers, the rattle of rifles, the roar of cannon, the bursting of shells, it was impossible to maintain discipline. Col. Putnam, a few of his subordinates, and one or two hundred men entered the fort. The enemy charged, but were driven back. Col. Putnam was killed; one officer after another went down. The reserve, which should have rushed up, did not come. The assault had lost its force. Like sheep the Union soldiers fled as best they could through the devastating fire, leaving a ghastly heap of dead and wounded in the ditch, and on the parapet of the fort. Among the killed was Henry W. Baker. By his side were Dexter Pritchard, Liberty G. Raymond, and Alexander F. Stevens, from Boscawen, and of his company, also killed.

Among the wounded was Samuel McEvely, and among the prisoners was John Clancy, who died in prison at Richmond.

In his first battle, Lieut. Baker gave his life to his country. Those who served under him speak of him with affection. He was cool and brave, and ever mindful of his duty. He was buried where he fell, with his commander, Col. Putnam, and his subordinates, Pritchard, Raymond, and Stevens.

UPWARD.

BY MARY HELEN BOODEY.

On the wings of my faith I aspire
O God ! to rise higher and higher,
    And to quaff of the scinctillant springs
That flow all exhaustless from Thee,
Who art fountain, and haven, and sea,
    And canst satisfy all who aspire.

I mount and I mount through the air,
Borne up by the breath of my prayer,
    Through waves of the sunshine of love ;
Thy presence, O God ! is the light,
Thou givest my spirit its flight,
    Thou rulest below and above.

I live in the glories of God,
I know that His merciful rod
    Extends o'er a sorrowful world ;
I see how His Providence glows
With sweet hues of azure and rose,
    His banner, the heavens unfurled.

The universe sings to my soul,
And I join with my voice in the whole,
    And God is the spirit of Law ;
The Power of blessing and blight,
The Giver of morning and night,
    Whose judgments are all without flaw.

Behold ! I am given to see
That the darkness and sorrow that be,
    Lie low and cling closely to earth ;
But the light of God's glory descends,
And the might of His justice attends
    The souls that are weeping in dearth.

A Hand that is brilliant with truth,
And gentle indeed in its ruth,
    Shall point out the way and defend,
And the gloom of each fearful abyss,
The serpents that threaten and hiss,
    Shall be conquered and slain to amend.

IN BATTLE AND IN PRISON.

A REMINISCENCE OF THE WAR OF THE REBELLION.

BY WILLIAM E. STEVENS.

The events I am about to describe took place at a critical period of "the war to keep the Union whole," and cover that date in the career of the army of the Potomac beginning with Hooker's flank movement against Lee, entrenched on the heights of Fredericksburg, and ending with the disastrous repulse which attended that finely planned, yet poorly executed, and ill-starred campaign. Of course, I am not writing history, except in a small way; nor do I essay to describe in detail or with accuracy the events in question. My purpose is to give my own observations and experiences, mainly from memory, reinforced by a few scraps and half-illegible memoranda saved from the accidents by flood and field.

I was a participant in many of the earlier battles fought by the army of the Potomac; but my opportunities for acquiring accurate information touching the general aspects of the field were necessarily limited to that part of it within my own immediate range of vision, and even here—so rigidly did our commanders aim to reduce us to mere automatons—we were often in the dark as to the meaning of this or that movement. I strove hard to master the situation, but not until the war closed and the reports of commanders were given to the public, did I have other than a very indefinite conception of much that transpired about me. Why we made this or that change of front; why we were kept for hours in line of battle beneath a broiling sun with no enemy in sight; why we were rushed from one point to another in an apparently hap-hazard manner, enduring fatigue and hunger and subsisting upon wormy "hardtack;" why we were pushed against impregnable positions, when a flank movement seemed to our inexperienced eyes the proper thing to do—now fighting, now building corduroy roads, digging rifle-pits or supporting batteries in our rear, which did more execution upon us, by reason of defective ammunition, than upon the enemy—concerning all these points, and many more we were anxious to be informed, but not one atom of information could we get.

"Ours not to inquire why,
Ours but to do and die."

Was this reticence in pursuance of the mistaken theory that machine soldiers are best? Or was it because "some one had blundered," and ignorance or incapacity, or something still worse, could be the more easily concealed? Whatever the reason, the fact remains that to the rank and file much of the campaigning done up to 1863-64 seemed to them worse than needless;—and looking back over that period with the light of history thrown upon it, I am not prepared to say the rank and file were mistaken in their estimate. I was impressed then, and the impression has never been effaced, that the reticence observed toward the men in the ranks touching what was going on about them, was a grievous error on the part of our commanders. It is a question, certainly, whether it would not have been better to have kept the "boys" informed of the real military situation and of what they were expected to achieve. The belief that much of the hardship endured was the result of blundering generals, or, worse, of criminal indifference, did much to unman our soldiers and cause them to lose faith and hope. Our volunteers were not machine soldiers, as some of the West Pointers seemed to presume, but patriotic, thinking and observing men who could fight best when they fought understandingly. I am told that the rebel commanders pursued a different policy, and although their soldiers were mentally inferior to ours, kept them apprized of the general situation and of what they must do to accomplish the end sought. Who shall say how many of the confederate victories may be accredited to this fact, if it is a fact? But our commanders, instead of trusting their men, either kept them in utter ignorance of movements or foolishly deceived them. How well I remember at the battle of Gaines's Hill, where Jackson thrashed Porter so soundly, and Sykes's regulars failed to stand their ground, that the story was industriously circulated along the thinned but unbroken ranks of Bartlett's Brigade, "McClellan's in Richmond, boys. One more effort and the day is ours!" And Meagher's Irish Brigade, hastening to our relief on the run, took up the cry and put on so determined a front that Jackson's veterans halted and reformed, giving our officers time to re-establish their broken lines and hold their ground until night came down and afforded them an opportunity to withdraw to the left bank of the Chickahominy,—not to enter Richmond, but to begin that celebrated "flank movement" which ended at Harrison's Landing. Again, at second Bull Run, when, after dawdling along all day on the road from Alexandria to Centreville, with the sounds of conflict in our front (making a long two hours' rest at Annandale, and then marching at full speed in a hot sun), we reached Centreville, we were told that Pope had whipped Jackson, and that Lee with his whole army was in full retreat. But when we reached Bull Run, "Linden saw another sight." Heavens, what a stampede! McDowell's and Sigel's corps in disastrous retreat,—cavalry, artillery, infantry, ammunition and baggage wagons in one confused, struggling mass, intent upon reaching the heights of Centreville.. Our corps (Franklin's, 6th) had just halted to rest, as the stragglers came into view. Deploying, we stopped the rout, and ended the retreat. Seizing the infantry stragglers, we placed them in our own ranks until our brigade swelled to twice its usual size. Night closed in, and we were marched to the front across Cub Run, and ordered to hold our position at all hazards. In that march every straggler deserted! Poor fellows, who could blame them? Had they been killed then and there who could have accounted for them? Most of them returned to their own regiments and thereafter did good service no doubt. Panics are liable to seize upon the best of troops. I cite these instances as partial corroboration of my point. What wonder if our troops came to distrust all reports and to depend only upon established facts. But perhaps our commanders were right in concealing information from the army in general, and Moore may have hit the nail on the head when he wrote:

"A captain has been known to think.
Even colonels have been heard to reason;
And reasoners whether clad in pink,
Or red or blue, are on the brink,
Nine cases out of ten—of treason."

At any rate they conducted the war in harmony with such a belief.

One battle only did I witness from the vantage ground of a non-combatant, the first Fredericksburg fight, and I found it vastly more interesting and conducive to personal ease and safety, if less glorious. But this is not what I started out to tell the readers of this Magazine. I am to relate my experience during that memorable episode referred to in my opening paragraph. I must say at the outset that it was an exceedingly checkered episode, so far as my memory serves me, for within the time outlined I ran the gamut of a soldier's emotions—anxiety, uncertainty, fear, hope, the thrill of victory succeeded all too quickly by the blackest despair; for success was followed by repulse, and from an elated victor I became almost in a twinkling, a captive in the hands of as ragged and as dirty a lot of Johnny Rebs as ever fought with a courage worthy of a better cause,—a part of Wilcox's Alabama brigade, McLaw's division. But I must not anticipate.

During the winter of 1862-63, our brigade lay encamped near White Oak church, a locality about equi-distant, if my memory serves me, between Falmouth on the Rhappahannock and Belle Plain on the Potomac. It had had ample time to recuperate from the fatigue of the "mud march," as Burnside's second futile attempt to dislodge Lee from his intrenchments about Fredericksburg, was facetiously termed, and as spring opened the routine of life in cantonment was relieved by parades, reviews, inspections, drills, and, occasionally, target practice. Meantime Hooker had superceded Burnside in chief command, and a new and more vigorous life had been infused into all branches of the service. This was particularly true of the cavalry, which had fallen into general disfavor. Under Hooker's discipline it became very effective. The high-sounding grand divisions had been broken up, and the over-cautious, phlegmatic Franklin, relieved. With other changes, came Sedgwick to the command of our corps—a great improvement in some respects on Franklin. The cool and sagacious Slocum, so long at the head of the red-cross division, had been promoted to the command of a corps, and Gen. Brooks, as brave, perhaps, but a far less skilful soldier, had succeeded him, having been promoted from the Vermont brigade. Gen. Joe Bartlett of New York, commanded our brigade—a fine officer, and a lion in battle. A brave man, too, was our Colonel, but deficient in tactical skill. He might not "set a squadron in the field," but he could face the enemy's line of battle without flinching. In action he was the embodiment of pluck, and at such times he looked as if he might be the very

"——Colonel
Who galloped through the white infernal powder
cloud."

in continental days. But he did not appear to advantage on parade, being undersized and awkward gaited, with a shrill, piercing voice, not unlike that of the late Isaac O. Barnes, or the irrepressible Mel. Weston. and totally indifferent to all the niceties of drill so pleasing to the holiday soldier. On one occasion he forgot his place at a Brigade dress parade, and was then and there rebuked sharply by the general. Meeting the latter at headquarters the same evening, where a "reception" to the officers of the brigade was in full career and good fellowship, aided by copious draughts of "commissary," abounded, the Colonel extended his hand and piped out in a high key which attracted the attention of all present: "Gineral. I'm not much at drill I confess, but I've got a hell-fired stomach for a fight!"

On the morning of the 28th of April, 1863, our regiment was ordered on picket duty, but scarcely had we relieved the old picket guard when orders came to return to camp, strike tents, and prepare to move at once in heavy marching order. This meant work. but was an agreeable change. I had only joined my regiment the day previous, after a brief leave of absence, and was resplendent in a new uniform, sword, etc. Of course I packed the uniform away, and left it in care of the sutler, while I donned a knit blouse, and with a due regard for sharpshooters of which the Confederacy had, as it always seemed to me when on the skirmish line, more than its share, put myself in condition for serious work, having nothing in the way of wearing apparel save my side-arms to indicate military rank. Meantime a great change had been effected in our winter quarters. The tents had been removed from the log huts to which they had served as roofs and windows, and now the bare interiors, with the debris strewn about, and broken chimneys and blackened walls alone remained. A more dismal or melancholy sight than a deserted cantonment cannot be conceived. "Warm work ahead, boys," gaily and cheerily remarked our jovial, stout-hearted adjutant, as he rode up to the head of the regiment. It proved to be particularly hot for him, for he received a wound in his head, in the charge on Marye's Heights, that he will carry to his grave, and which ended his military career, but not his usefulness; for he is now a popular clergyman, a true soldier of the cross, settled in Philadelphia, I believe. Our progress was slow, and darkness intervened just as we reached a ravine leading down to the narrow valley which skirts the river on that side. We bivouacked in our tracks, not being allowed to kindle fires. Back over the route we had come could be heard the rumble of artillery wagons and the tramp, tramp, of marching columns. In front, silence reigned. Orders are issued in a low tone; and that stern composure which soldiers assume when about to encounter the enemy was apparent in the bearing of all. The officers gather around their adjutant, who is a favorite at brigade and division headquarters, to learn his views touching the movement. He thinks we are in for a fight, and gives his opinion, as to Hooker's intentions. He is sanguine of success.—We have hardly closed our eyes in sleep, when some one calls out in a voice seemingly loud enough for the rebel pickets to hear, "Where is Colonel Blank?" "Here, sir," responds that officer, rubbing his eyes. "What's wanted?" "Gen. B. directs me to say that you are to march your regiment to the bank of the river, form in line of battle, and await further orders. You are to move expeditiously, with as little noise as possible, following the pontoons." The order is obeyed; the regiment marching away in almost spectral silence. Debouching from the ravine, the darkness deepens, for a dense fog hangs over the valley of the Rhappahannock like a pall. We file past the pontoon train, from which the engineer corps are detaching the boats, silently and with all the celerity possible—and stand upon the river's brink. In our rear come other regiments, until our whole brigade is closed in line five regiments deep.—It was a critical time. I recall it well. The silence was almost oppressive; orders were given in low tones, and nothing but the rattle of accoutrements broke the silence. The fog resembled a mirage. Objects a little way off took on gigantic proportions. I remember that a pontoon boat, borne on stout shoulders to the river's brink, resembled the immense hulk of a ship as it loomed into view, while at the distance of a few feet men took on colossal dimensions. Meantime we are tolled off in detachments to occupy the pontoons, along with the engineers who are to do the navigation, and our orders are to form instantly on reaching the other shore, dash forward and capture the enemy's picket line, or whatever force may be there to oppose us. At length there are sounds of commotion on the other side. The Johnnies suspect something. Splash! goes a pontoon into the water, followed by a deep curse from the officer in charge, brave old Gen. Benham, who cannot restrain his rage over the carelessness of his men. Meanwhile the fog has been gradually rising, and the gray of dawn appears. More stir on the other side, a rattling of equipments, hurried commands—then a sharp challenge, (some of our scouts are nearly over), followed by a single musket discharge, then a volley, and the whistle of bullets. Instinctively we do them low obeisance; the lines waver for an instant, then firmness and silence. So heavy a fire was not anticipated. It told of a large reserve which must have been brought up in expectation of an attack. All hope of a surprise was over. "Will the pontoons never be launched?" Yes, Benham has done his duty, and into them we scramble and push off, each boat for itself. The stream is narrow at this point, but we are not swift enough to check another volley, which being better directed than the first, killed and wounded a number of our boys in the boats. Almost at the same instant our pontoon touches the shore. There is a rush, a charge, a brief struggle, and that picket guard is *hors du combat*. Quickly deploying on the bank we advance, but the enemy retires more quickly; —and we have established a firm foothold, the pontoon bridge is laid, and the whole corps is streaming across as the morning sun rises above the horizon. The fog still clings, however, to the rising ground on which Franklin fought at the first battle of Fredericksburg, and we move with due caution, skirmishers well out, not knowing what sort of a reception Stonewall Jackson, whose corps is known to occupy the wooded heights beyond, may have in store for us. But no serious opposition is offered after the affair of the pickets, and gradually we occupy most of the ground previously held by the centre of Franklin's grand division. The fog lifts at last, and the sight revealed is a picturesque one. Before us, a level plain, extending on the right to the suburbs of Fredericksburg, and on the left, cut with ravines and hillocks somewhat, for a long distance. Back of us, the river; fronting, on either hand, the plain ending in a range of wooded hills, semicircular in shape, and dotted with fortifications. The enemy's picket line is well out upon the plain but touching the river above us near the city. Extending our left it soon came in contact with Reynolds' corps, which had effected a crossing a mile or two lower down, after a sharp artillery fight in which the enemy showed superior metal, but was obliged to retire after the infantry got over. Midway from the river to the range of hills, and parallel with the former, is a deep ravine where partial shelter from the concentric fire from the artillery posted on Marye's Heights on the right and on the hills in front, was afforded Franklin's troops in the previous battle. A few artillery shots are fired, soon after establishing our lines, and then all becomes quiet. What does this inaction portend? Evidently, Lee is acting on the defensive, and waiting for the development of Hooker's strategy. He does not have long to wait. Before us is the whole rebel army. Will it swoop down upon us before Hooker can develop his left and crush us? This is the conundrum with which we wrestle, as the hours wear away, varying it with a conjecture as to whether we shall be ordered to assault the enemy, in his chosen position, against which Burnside had thrown the flower of his army only to be hurled back discomfited. Another artillery duel between Reynolds and Jackson later in the day closes the fighting, and a night of repose follows. The succeeding day proved to be one of quiet, also, but there was a constant movement of troops in our rear on the heights of Falmouth, the line of march being directly up river.

"You see them on their winding way,
About their ranks the sunbeams play."

That night our regiment went on picket. Never shall I forget it. Strict orders had been received, prohibiting fires, or conversation above a whisper, and requiring the most vigilant watchfulness to prevent surprise, as the enemy in heavy force was directly in our front. Our eyes were kept constantly on the rebel sentinels moving ghost-like upon their beats: A dense fog settled down, cold and damp. The hours seemed leaden. The suspense became intense, unbearable. Suddenly a tremor sweeps along the line. Our boys are doubly alert. What does it mean? A message comes down the front line—"The enemy are advancing. Hold your ground until the reserves are formed, then rally upon them!" With muskets firmly grasped the Union pickets await the onset. A night attack is always dreaded by soldiers, and nothing is more trying to the nerves of veterans than the expectation of a conflict with an unseen foe. But our boys do not flinch; they feel the responsibility imposed upon them and resolve to do their duty. Minutes go by, and still no advance, although the weird line of sentinels has been succeeded by a line of battle. Momentarily we expect to see a sheet of flame burst from that compact mass, the components of which are indistinguishable in the fog and darkness, although hardly six rods distant. But it comes not. The mass recedes and fades out, leaving the sentinels pacing their posts, and we now know that the movement was only a reconnoisance. Morning dawns at length, and we are relieved without firing a shot. As we gain the shelter of the ravine near the bank of the river, we notice that Reynolds has recrossed with his whole corps and is marching in the direction taken by the main army. Looking toward the rebel position on our left, dark masses of men are seen moving over the hills, as if in retreat. Here again we have food for speculation. Has Hooker, whose guns are now heard on the right, outflanked the enemy? Later on we learned that these troops were Stonewall Jackson's rear guard, that intrepid commander being then in the process of executing that famous flank movement which put the 11th corps to rout and turned a Union success into a Confederate victory, the most signal ever achieved by its armies. About noon our troops made a demonstration, driving back the enemy's pickets, and later in the day rifle pits were dug under cover of army blankets hung up as if to dry—a device so simple as to deceive the Confederates, for otherwise, being commanded by their guns, it could not have been effected without serious loss.

The next day (Saturday, May 2), was comparatively quiet, although far to the right could be heard the deep, yet muffled sound of artillery firing, telling that Hooker was engaged. We made demonstrations all along our front, but did no real fighting. During the night, the firing on the right became very heavy,—and I was called into line at about 2 a. m., to go through ere another chance to sleep was afforded me, the most exciting experiences of my life. We were marched to the front, and posted in a ravine. With the first streaks of dawn came sounds of musketry firing on our right. It was the Light Division in the streets of Fredericksburg. Marching by the left flank we emerge from the ravine and take a position on the left, the second, and third and light divisions of our corps extending to the right. As we leave the ravine the enemy opens a heavy fire upon our devoted regiment, the hills on our front and right being aflame with the flashes of the "red artillery." We advance rapidly, our general leading; our batteries gallop to the rising ground, and open on the enemy's guns posted near the railroad embankment and which are doing the most execution. Our guns are splendidly served, and soon the rebel battery in front and its infantry supports are seen making quick time for the fortifications in the woods at the base of the hill. Now the guns on the hills redouble their fire, and the din is terrible. Men are falling at every step, and so fierce is the concentric artillery fire of the Confederates that our batteries have to be withdrawn. Not so the infantry. It is our part to keep the rebel force in front employed while the divisions on our right storm Marye's Heights. So we keep steadily on until a ravine is reached running at right angles with the one we have left, and leading nearly up to the rebel entrenchments. The air is full of screaming shot and whistling shell, and as we near the entrance to the ravine, which is filled with a thick undergrowth of trees and bushes, our boys are ready to insist that at least five hundred rebel cannon have the range and are peppering us accordingly. Through the hell of fire we go, marching by the left flank and closing up our ranks with each breach, and into the ravine from which the enemy's sharpshooters are seen to scamper like so many rats, as much to escape the range of their own cannon as that of our musketry, for we had not as yet fired a shot.—Here, by hugging the steep sides, we were partially sheltered and within half rifle practice of the foe posted behind their breastworks at the base of the hill. A brisk fusilade was kept up, and although we were unsupported and "in the air" we kept the Johnnies so busy that they did not attempt a sortie. By this time, also, the batteries on Marye's Heights, which had enfiladed us, had as much as they could do nearer home, for Howe and Newton had begun their advance. It being deemed useless to attempt to do more than keep the enemy in our front employed, our regiment was withdrawn from the ravine and the Parrotts were again opened on the position, which we had supposed was to be stormed.— "The war which for a space did fail," now opens furiously on our right, and we watch the advance of the light division with interest, although our regiment is still exposed to a galling fire from riflemen behind the railroad embankment. — The spectacle was a thrilling one. The 6th corps batteries were playing upon the heights, with might and main, and up the steep ascent our brave boys were climbing with all speed. Out hearts were in our throats as we watched. Could the heights be stormed? Could Sedgwick with 10,000 men do what Burnside failed to do with ten times that number? Our Colonel, who has been watching the conflict through his field-glass, electrifies us at last by exclaiming, "The heights are ours, boys!" "Our flag is there!" Such a cheer as went up must have astonished our friends just opposite. A rebel brigade, which had left the entrenchments near our front and was making all speed to succor its friends, suddenly halted, then taking in the situation turned about and ran back again, its pace being accelerated by shots from cannon just taken. The victory was ours thus far, but at what a cost! It was a brief triumph, alas! for disaster had overtaken Hooker, and he was a beaten general at that moment. We knew it not, however. Contrariwise it was announced that Hooker had been even more successful, and that Lee's routed army was in rapid retreat on Richmond. Joy filled our hearts, even though we mourned the death of many brave comrades whose last roll call on earth had been answered that morning. Hence, when orders came for our brigade to fall in and take the lead in the pursuit on our side, they were obeyed with alacrity, and up and over the battle-stained heights we marched, munching our hardtack as we went, and out upon the Chancellorsville pike, driving the enemy before us like chaff before the wind. Two miles out, a battery opened upon us, but we took little notice, pushing our skirmish line rapidly forward. It was a fatal discharge, however, to an officer on Brooks' staff, who fell from his horse, nearly decapitated by a shell.—One of our batteries is hurried to the front and a single discharge causes the enemy to retire on the double quick. We reach Salem church, nearly exhausted by our rapid marching, hoping for rest. But the worst is yet to come. Our skirmish line is held at bay. It cannot advance, and our brigade is formed for a charge —my own regiment, through the negligence of some one, going into the fight in heavy marching order, with knapsacks strung, and blankets strapped. Meeting a heavy fire of musketry at the edge of a piece of woods, the brigade halts. But Gen. Brooks, who has orders to effect a junction with Hooker, and deeming the enemy in front to be, the same we have been driving, orders another advance. Into the woods we go to be met by a terrific fire. We charge and drive the foe from his breastworks, but can go no further. Heavily reinforced he advances with yells. There is a continuous roll of musketry. The Pennsylvania regiments on our right and left give ground. We are outflanked and enfiladed. Then comes the order to fall back. It must be done quickly if we would not be entirely cut off from the second line. Burdened as many of our men are by their knapsacks, and fatigued by the march, they can not run. Such is my condition. Although with only a blanket to carry, I am quite used up physically. The double-quick is beyond my powers, and with every disposition in the world to run I cannot to save my life. Suddenly, one leg refuses to move, and I fall. A call to my men is unheard, or if heard, unheeded. I try to regain my feet, but cannot. My leg seems paralyzed. Am I hit? wounded? A brother officer sees me; hears my call for assistance; and proffers aid; helps me to my feet, and I stagger along for a few paces. Meantime, we have been left far in the rear and are between two fires. The air is laden with missiles. It is madness to proceed, and so we both hug the ground. Doubtless our lives are saved by this device, but, although we had not the faintest idea then that such was the case, it involved our capture and imprisonment. "The combat deepens." The din is awful. Line after line of Lee's veterans surges forward; they intermingle; halt, yell, fire; then rush on like a mob. It is not until they have fairly run over us that we realize our position—that capture is inevitable. Two lines pass us unnoticed, when a squad of skirmishers who have hung on our flank come up and demand our surrender. There is no alternative, and that brand-new blade goes into the hands of a rebel sergeant whose straight, black hair runs up through a rent in his hat like a plume. We are taken to the rear amid a rain of shot from our batteries, three men helping me along and two keeping close guard over my companion. They seemed in a hurry to get out of range, and glad of the opportunity our capture afforded them of retiring with eclat from the strife. Soon we came upon Gen. Wilcox and staff nicely ensconced in a position not accessible to Yankee bullets. He questioned us, but not getting satisfactory replies, sent us still further to the rear (after his Adjutant-General had purchased my sword of the hatless sergeant), where we were placed under guard near a field hospital. Here I found, upon examination, that I was not injured, but that my inability to walk without help was due to fatigue and a slight abrasion on the hip, occasioned probably by a spent ball. We were courteously treated by our guards but could get no food, Stoneman's raid having sadly interfered with the rebel commissariat. Next day we were taken to Spottsylvania court-house where we met nearly half of the 11th corps and learned for the first time the disaster that had befallen "Fighting Joe" Hooker. Of the kindness of one of my captors, Billy Peyton of Memphis, Tenn., but a member of the 9th Alabama, and his peculiarities, I should like to speak, but this sketch has grown on my hands, and I am compelled to omit an account of my first visit to Richmond, introduction to Major Turner, and incarceration in Libby. Should this sketch please the readers of this Magazine, I may essay another describing my prison life, and how near I came to being annihilated by a fierce Virginia home guard officer who commanded the escort which conducted the detatchment of prisoners, of which I made one, to the flag of truce boat on the James, going by the way of Petersburgh.

MANNERS AND CUSTOMS IN HOPKINTON—No. 2.

BY C. C. LORD.

RELIGIOUS.

At first, worship, both private and public, was conducted in the primative homes of the settlers of the township. On the erection of military posts, or forts, such edifices became natural, social centres, and worship was conducted in one or more of them. Rev. James Scales, first minister of the town, was ordained in Putney's Fort, in 1757. During the ministry of Mr. Scales, public worship was sometimes conducted at the Parsonage. The erection of a church determined a permanent place of public religious services.

The first meeting-house in Hopkinton represented a much larger territorial expanse of population than any church now extant. Denominational controversies had not divided the ranks of the worshipers, nor had local patrons of the one church demanded special privileges of their own. The distance to church was long in many cases, and the conveyances often only the locomotary means of nature.

In olden times in this vicinity, though people had the instinct of personal adornment the same as now, they often lacked the means of gratifying it. Extra articles of dress were so rare that people frequently walked to church in their daily accustomed garb, or trod the Sunday path with a most scrupulous care for their extra wardrobe. Women sometimes carried the skirts of their Sunday dresses on their arms till they arrived near or at the church door, when they let them fall. The Sunday shoes were often carried in the hand till the journey to meeting was nearly ended, when they were put on for entrance to the sanctuary. Present readers can comprehend the necessity of such care, when they reflect that in the olden time the price of a week's work of a woman was only equivalent to a yard of cloth, or a pair of shoes.

Church services in the former days were long, and savored of dogmatic theology. The principal prayer was much longer than the present average sermon, and the discourse proportionally extended. Such prolonged services were conducted in winter, at first, without the favor of any artificial warmth. In contemplating the situation of the worshipers in those old wintry days, the bleakness of the characteristic meeting-house of the times is to be taken into account. In the old Baptist church was an open aperture in an upper wall, where the crows have been known to perch while worship was in progress. The advent of foot-stoves gave much relief to the chilly congregations of earlier times, and the introduction of extremer experiences of the wintry the general heater put an end to the Sunday.

The representative minister of the olden time was a person of eminent scholarly culture and gentlemanly bearing. A thorough scholar and rhetorician, his discourses were framed with strict regard to the logical sequences of his subject. The numerical divisions of his theme often carried him among units of the second order; firstly, secondly, and thirdly were only preliminary to thirteenthly, fourteenthly, and fifteenthly; the grand category of predications was terminated by a "conclusion." In his loftier intellectual schemes, he sometimes elaborated whole volumes of disquisitional matter. Rev. Ethan Smith, third minister in the town, was the author of several profound theological treatises. There was a dignity and austerity of manner pertaining to the characteristic primative clergyman that made him a pattern of personified seriousness. His grave demeanor on his parochial rounds, when he spoke directly upon the obligations of personal religion, made his presence in the household a suggestion of profound respect and awe. He impressed his personality upon the receptive social element of his parish. The deacons became only minor pastors, and the whole congregation of believers expressed in subdued form the character of the shepherd of the flock.*

The support of a "learned and orthodox minister" was implied in the original grant of this township. In the strict construction of the text of the original compact, "orthodoxy" meant Calvinistic Congregationalism. The disturbed condition of the early settlement prevented the establishment of a permanent local pastorate till 1757. On the 8th of September of that year, it was voted to settle the Rev. James Scales, and that he should be ordained on the 23d of the following November. His salary was to be sixty Spanish milled dollars, or their equivalent in paper bills, a year. When the town became incorporated in 1765, the formal acknowledgment of Mr. Scales as legal pastor was renewed, it being the 4th of March, and his salary was named at £13, 10s.

---

*The austere influence of religion upon society in the olden time was attested by the legal strictures upon traveling, idling, etc., on Sunday, of which conduct the tything-men were to take cognizance. Tything-men were chosen in this town as late as 1843, when Charles Barton, Samuel Frazier and Daniel Chase were selected. The law requiring such choice had even then become virtually a dead letter.

In progress of time different religious societies became established in this town, but the Congregational alone drew support from any portion of the populace by a direct tax. People were taxed for the support of the Congregational ministry in this town as late as 1810. The warrant for a town meeting called for the 12th of March, 1811, contained this article:

"To see what method the town will take to raise money for the support of the Congregational minister in town the ensuing year, how levied, and how divided between the two meeting-houses."

At this time a meeting-house had been, for about ten years, in existence at Campbell's Corner, in the westerly part of the town, and since its erection the funds for the support of Congregational preaching derived from taxes had been divided between the east and west meeting-houses, as they were called. However, at the town meeting called for the above date, it was voted to "pass over the article" relating to the proposed support of Congregational religious services by the town, and we think the subject was never taken up again.

The minister's tax was never collected of any person who acknowledged a belief in the religious principles of any legalized society, other than the Congregational. The following vote, passed on the 25th of March, 1799, illustrated the method of raising the minister's tax:

"Voted to lay a ministerial tax on the Congregational inhabitants at twenty cents each on the poll, and upon all ratable estate in the same proportion, Congregational inhabitants to be ascertained by consent, individually, to either of the selectmen at the time of taking the inventory."

People liable to pay a minister's tax sometimes publicly, in town meeting, declared their adhesion to the principles of some one or other of the societies exempted from the payment of that tax.

The lease of the parsonage lands in 1798, incurred an annual revenue which was proportionately divided among the existing societies till the year 1853. In the year 1842, when the town for the first time published a printed report of its pecuniary transactions, the last division of parsonage money was declared to be as follows:

1st Congregational society,		$27.88
2d " "		4.39
Calvinist Baptist, "		13.88
Union " "		16.12
Episcopalian "		9.64
1st Universalist "		4.21
2d " "		10.31
Methodist "		1.43

The round total was set down at $88.00

The 2d Congregational society dropped out of the list in 1851. The last allowance to this society was fifty-six cents. The town report of the year 1853, contained the following and last list of apportionments of parsonage money:

Congregational society,		$30.09
Union Baptist "		19.04
Calvinist " "		15.72
Episcopalian "		4.40
1st Universalist "		7.57
2d " "		7.10
Methodist "		4.18

The total of this list was also set down in round numbers as $88.

The above figures are suggestive in presenting a view of the relative strength of the different societies at the specific times stated. It is interesting to note that certain of the societies soon lost all traces of even a nominal existence, after the suspension of the parsonage revenues. For some time they had kept up a show of vitality by making their portion of the parsonage fund a nucleus of an outlay for a few days' preaching in the year.

In the march of the years, the old peculiarities of local religious life have given place to new features and forms. It is needless to say that some of the old formalities died hard. Innovations were distrusted. The experience in view of proposed changes was substantially uniform in all the churches. Even the staid Episcopalians were ruffled by unaccustomed ceremonies. When, for the first time, the choir of the Episcopal church chanted the *Gloria Patri*, which before had been read only, an indignant lady abruptly shut her prayer book in unfeigned disgust. The greater jealousy formerly existing between different denominations is well known. It is said this inharmonious feeling was once sought to serve an innovating use. A person prominent in musical circles sought to influence the leading minds of the Congregational church in favor of the purchase of a bass viol. As an extreme argumentative resort he suggested, "The poor, miserable Baptists have got one." Tradition, however, doesn't relate the effect of this suggestion.

COMMERCIAL.

The country store of the earliest times was a more emphatic collection of multitudinous varieties of articles, if possible, than the later place of local public traffic. Then, as now, the local store was the principal resort of the great commonalty. Men of special vocations sometimes took a stock of products to the lower country and bartered for goods to bring back and distribute among their neighbors, and the itinerant merchant, or pedlar, reaped a much better harvest than now; but the country store was a popular necessity and well patronized. At first there was less trading in domestic luxuries; the goods in store represented the common necessities. Since the popular idea of necessity does not fully exclude the illusory principle, we have to admit rum, gin, brandy, etc., into the former list of domestic staples. Cash and barter were entertained by every tradesman, to whom the populace largely looked for advantageous exchanges of substance. The progress of the settlement was attended by the extension, and to some extent by the classification, of trade till the time when Hopkinton assumed the commercial importance described in a previous article.

The currency employed in the transaction of business was at first nominally English, though Spanish milled dollars were in circulation. One of the inconveniences of the early settlers of New England was a scarcity of money. The different provincial governments sought to relieve the public financial burdens by the issue of Bills of Credit, a currency mentioned in the records of this town as "old tenor." Such a circulating medium in such a time could only depreciate in value, but, following a custom obtaining in the old country, the purchasing value of these bills could from time to time be fixed by the local legislatures. About the year 1750, it was established throughout the provinces that £1 in the currency of the Bills of Credit should be equivalent to two shillings and eight pence lawful money, and that six shillings should be equal to one dollar.

The preliminary events of the Revolution involved the establishment of a system of Continental currency. At the time of the first issue of a paper circulating medium, in 1775, the Continental notes were nearly at par with gold, but they soon fell to comparative nothingness in value. The effect of this collapse in monetary matters was amply illustrated in the public transactions of the town of Hopkinton. At a town meeting held in 1781, it was voted that the price of a day's work on the highway, by a man, should be $30; the price of a day's work by a yoke of oxen, $10; the price of a plow and cart, $10 each. The salary of the Rev. Elijah Fletcher, second minister of the town, was also voted to be $4000 for the year, but the reverend pastor prefered to accept £70 in gold equivalents, and declined the larger nominal sum. The success of the American cause, and the permanent establishment of the public credit, gave a correspondingly improved aspect to local affairs, and in later times this town has experienced fluctuations in prices in common with the general country.

During the period of Hopkinton's greater importance as a commercial station, a bank was maintained here for a few years. The institution was known as the Franklin Bank, and was incorporated in 1833. The grantees were Horace Chase, Nathaniel Gilman, Isaac Long,

Jr., William Little, Joseph Stanwood, Matthew Harvey, Andrew Leach, Moses Gould, Ebenezer Dustin, Timothy Chandler, Stephen Darling, and James Huse. The operations of this bank seem to have been exceedingly bungling during the short term of its existence, and it finally settled with its creditors at ninety cents on a dollar. The Franklin Bank occupied the building now used by the Hopkinton Public Library.

The standard of quantities to be recognized in commercial transactions has, from remote times, been a subject of legal regulation. The weights and measures first used in this town were the standards of older communities. In a record made in the year 1804, the town of Hopkinton declared the local standard to be as follows:

WEIGHTS OF IRON.

1	.	.	56 lbs.
1	.	.	28 lbs.
1	.	.	24 lbs.
1	.	.	7 lbs.

WEIGHTS OF BRASS.

1	.	.	4 lbs.
1	.	.	2 lbs.
1	.	.	1 lb.
1	.	.	½ lb.
1	.	.	2 oz.
1	.	.	1 oz.
1	.	.	½ oz.
1	.	.	¼ oz.

For the use of the above weights the town recognized "two small scale beams with brass dishes," and also "one large scale beam with boards, and strung with iron wires." The *wooden dry measures* were specific as 1 half-bushel, 1 peck, 1 half-peck, 1 two-quart, and 1 quart; while the *copper liquid measures* were started to be 1 gallon, 1 two-quart, 1 quart, 1 pint, 1 half-pint, and 1 gill.

By legal requirement, the standard of weights and measures is regulated by a town sealer to this day, such officer being chosen annually at the town-meeting in March, but the modern improvements and facilities for determining quantities have made a practically dead letter of the present law requiring his selection.

For many years a public hay-scales occupied a site in the rear of the Congregational meeting house. It was simply an immense scale beam and platform, the whole apparatus being covered with a roof. It long ago passed away to give place to the modern hay-scales.

POLITICAL.

In the earlier history of this town, politics and religion were closely related. For many years the affairs of the legally established, or Congregational, church were arranged by vote of the town. The intimate relation existing between the church and the town made the meeting-house and town-house at first identical. The earliest town-meeting held in the first meeting-house was on the 2d of March, 1767. Previously, town-meetings had been held at private houses. Town-meetings continued to be held in the church till 1799, when use was first made of the old Hillsborough county Court House, the annual meeting of that year being held in the upper room of the county edifice. Town-meeting has since been held annually on the same spot.

At the time of the incorporation of the town, in 1765, annual town-meetings were legally held only on the first Monday in March. In the year 1803, the State legislature fixed the date of annual town-meetings at the second Tuesday of the same month. Till the year 1813, when the State established a law requiring the use of an alphabetical list of voters at town-meetings, public legal gatherings in town had been conducted with less formality than has been maintained since, but the regard for parliamentary proprieties had been sufficient to prevent any disorder or unskillfulness of a serious nature.

The instincts of the people of this town have always largely partaken of a Democratic character. There has been a prominent jealousy of individual rights. This feature of local political life was exhibited in the very earliest times, when individuals frequently appeared at the moderator's desk to record their names in opposition to some measure or other passed by the majority.

Even to this day the doctrine of individual rights is strongly asserted by the mass of persons of whatever party name. In the days of the prolonged supremacy of the Democratic party, the lines of party distinction were drawn so clearly that scarcly a Whig was ever permitted to represent the town at the General Court. Once, in 1844, there was a kind of general compromise between parties, and Moses Colby, a Whig, and Samuel Colby, a Democrat, were sent to the legislature together. For quite a number of years there was a compromise on the subject of selectmen, and a general consent gave the Whigs annually one member in a board of three; but this arrangement was broken up by a fancied or real attempt of the Whigs to take more than their customarily allotted portion of the chosen.

Till the year 1855, when the Democrats lost the general control of political affairs in town for the first time, the constantly prevailing superiority had prevented the practice or necessity of much caucusing. A few leading ones put their heads together and gave a definite impulse to the party movement. The process worked very well, except when an accident would happen, as, for instance, when a refractory candidate insisted in pushing his private claims at all hazzards. Caucusing, however, had been practiced more or less previously to 1855, but since this date the closeness of the popular vote has often led to a degree of figuring and planning that can be easily comprehended by all accustomed to watch the movements of political leadership in New Hampshire during the last quarter of a century.

We have shown, in a previous article, that the Democrats of this town held a majority on the Governor's vote till 1865. However, in 1855, the American party elected two representatives—Paul R. George and Timothy Colby—and three selectmen.

MALAGA.

BY VIANNA A. CONNOR.

[This article from Miss Connor, written from Malaga last summer, having been mislaid, after its reception, is published at this time as not without interest, notwithstanding the delay.—ED.]

The streets of Malaga always present an animated appearance. One never sees here that dead calm which pervades many of our northern cities in midsummer. At all hours of the day the air resounds with the sonorous voices of men and boys calling out whatever they may have to sell. Fish of all kinds, fruits, live turkeys and many other things may be obtained in this way, with the additional entertainment of listening to a loud and heated discussion between the servant and vender regarding the price. If the latter chances to be a boy, he summons a flood of tears to his assistance, having acquired, as a part of his occupation, the faculty of crying when occasion demands. The servant, accustomed to mechanical weeping, is immovable and the youthful imposter is finally compelled to receive a fair price for his wares.

Every afternoon at five o'clock, an old man with a bright, cheerful face passes our window calling out "barquillos" in a clear, musical voice which makes itself heard at a long distance.

The children crowd around him while he takes from a green box strapped over his shoulder, a tube made of light paste, on one end of which he puts a white foamy substance, composed of the whites of eggs and sugar. At this juncture, the little ones become frantic and jostle each other in a most unceremonoïus manner, in their eagerness to possess the delicate morsel. Each one is served and the poor old man goes on his way rejoicing ever the few quartas which will buy his daily bread. Barquillos are also obtained at restaurants as an accompaniment for ices, and seem to be relished by children of a larger growth, as well as others.

The business of the ware houses commences at an early hour and continues through the day; carts drawn by mules are constantly passing while the industrious little donkeys may be seen marching in a line, following their leader, who has a bell to announce his coming. During the vintage, long lines of donkeys laden with boxes of raisins come from the vineyards, horses never being used except in cabs and private carriages. The cab horses are poor, old animals which seem to have lived as long as nature intended, but are kept alive by some mysterious agency, and by dint of much urging and whipping manage to move at a slow pace. One day, when we were taking a drive, the horse suddenly stopped and the driver dismounted. To our inquiry, as to the cause of delay he replied, "*no es nada*" (it is nothing), resumed his seat and we started again, but had not proceeded far when the animal absolutely refused to go; this time we insisted upon alighting and were coolly informed that the horse was only a little *cansado* (tired). Many more instances might be cited illustrating the manner in which dumb animals are abused in a country where there are no laws prohibiting it, or if such laws exist they are not enforced.

The animation prevailing through the day by no means diminishes as night approaches, although of a very different character. At twilight, the higher classes sally forth to the Alameda or Muelle (mole), to enjoy the refreshing breeze from the sea, while those of lower estate seek some place of rendezvous and indulge in their idle gossip. An occasional troubadour steals to some obscure corner and sends forth plaintive sounds from his faithful guitar, not unfrequently some youthful swain is inspired to add the charms of his voice, and the "Malaguenas" bursts forth in all its primitive sweetness. The enthusiasm of the Spaniards on hearing their national airs is something remarkable, they become quite wild with excitement and applaud in the most vociferous manner. Foreigners, also, who have spent some time in the country, share this enthusiasm, which seems to be caused more by a certain rhthymical peculiarity, than by any extraordinary merit of the music itself.

The romantic days of Spain are past, when the lover stood beneath the balcony of his sweetheart, wooing her with the gentle strains of his guitar. To us it seems a matter of regret that this ancient custom no longer exists, but it undoubtedly relieves many anxious parents as it particularly favored clandestine courtships. A Spanish gentleman of our acquaintance who is blessed with seven daughters, and occupies a house containing twenty balconies, congratulates himself upon the change in love-making as it would be impossible to keep watch over all, even by constantly rushing from one balcony to another. At the present day the suitor is admitted to the salon, where he may converse with the object of his affections, but always in the presence of her parents. Spanish mammas would be shocked at the freedom allowed American girls in receiving visits from the opposite sex and accepting their escort to places of entertainment.

The feast of Corpus Christi was celebrated in Malaga with much *eclat*. For two weeks previous preparations were going on for the fair, which takes place at this time, booths being arranged on one side of the Alameda and filled with a variety of articles, useful and ornamental, calculated to please the eye and lighten the pockets of passers-by, while others were provided with these substantial things needful to satisfy the wants of the inner man. At night the Alameda was most brilliantly illuminated by long lines of lights extending the whole length on either side, also across the centre at intervals, with occasional circles and clusters, producing a most dazzling effect. At each end, in front of the fountains were erected two pavillions, one under the direction of a club styled the "Circulo Mercantil," the other by the members of the "Lycio" both of which were handsomely decorated with flags and flowers and provided with comfortable seats. We availed ourselves of the opportunity to attend the balls given in these pavillions, and found them exceedingly diverting. In the centre, a space was reserved for the dancers, who tripped the "light fantastic" with apparent enjoyment, notwithstanding the disadvantages of little room and much heat. The *toilettes* of the ladies were varied and elegant, displaying a taste which would do credit to Worth himself, while the national costume, worn by a few young ladies, far exceeded the most charming conceptions of that famous artist. This costume, called the "*Maja*," is extremely picturesque, especially when combined with the piquant faces and nonchalant airs of the Spanish girls. It consists of a skirt of bright red or blue satin, edged with a broad trimming of black *chenille*; with this is worn a black velvet bodice, the hair is arranged in finger puffs, with a high comb placed jauntily on one side, and a few flowers gracefully twined among the dark tresses; a Spanish mantilla, and laced slippers, just disclosed beneath the short skirt, complete this beautiful costume, rich in fabric, but simple in design, and above all allowing a graceful freedom which our present straight laced fashions render impossible. Weary of the brilliancy and animation of the ballroom, we passed to the garden where tables were arranged for refreshments, and amid the sound of inspiring music and the gentle murmur of the fountain, partook of delicate viands served by attentive waiters. The arrangement of these pavillions was perfect in every respect, contributing in the highest degree to the comfort of the guests, and long shall we bear in remembrance the pleasant evenings they afforded us.

On Corpus Christi day a long and imposing procession marched through the principal streets, carrying an image of the "Virgin" robed in black velvet elaborately embroidered in gold, and a large "*Custodia*" of solid silver containing the "*host*." The clergy, in their clerical gowns, with their faces plump and glossy, walked along in a self-satisfied manner, confident of good cheer in this world, whatever may await them in another. The civil and military authorities added their dignified presence, followed by a large concourse of people with wax candles. The streets and balconies were filled with men, women, and children of all ages and classes, every available space being occupied. In the afternoon a bull fight took place, and a ball in the evening ended the programme of the day.

In the midst of the festivities of the week, the Queen's illness was announced, causing a suspension of all gayety, and her subsequent death was followed by a season of mourning. The Alameda was stripped of its superfluous adornings, and the sound of music no longer filled the air with its sweet harmonies. Funeral services were solemnized in the Cathedral, and many a fervent prayer ascended to Heaven for the repose of the dead, and the resignation of the bereaved young King.

THE GRANITE MONTHLY.

A MAGAZINE OF LITERATURE, HISTORY, AND STATE PROGRESS.

VOL. II. MAY, 1879. NO. 8.

HON. LEVI W. BARTON.

Croydon, in Sullivan County, is situated on the highlands between Connecticut and Merrimac rivers. The north branch of Sugar River crosses it, dividing it into two nearly equal parts. The soil is diversified, and much of its scenery is wild and picturesque. "Croydon Mountain," extending across the western part of the town, is the highest elevation in the county and commands an extensive and beautiful prospect.

The charter of Croydon, signed by Benning Wentworth, was dated May 31, 1763. The township was divided into seventy-one shares, of which two were reserved as a farm for Gov. Wentworth; one, for the propagation of the gospel in foreign parts; one, as a glebe for the Church of England; one, for the first minister who should settle in town; one, for the education of youth, and the remaining sixty-five to as many different individuals.

The first meeting of the grantees was held at Grafton, Mass., June 17, 1763; and the first meeting in Croydon, Jan. 17, 1768. From Grafton, in the spring of 1766, came the first settlers of Croydon, and commenced the erection of cabins in the unbroken forest. They were hardy, brave men and grappled manfully and resolutely with the hardships of pioneer life.

Among those who came to Croydon, in the spring of 1766, was Ezekiel Powers, son of Lemuel and Thankful (Leland) Powers, born in Grafton, Mass., March 21, 1745. He 'was admirably fitted to endure the hardships and privations incident to a new settlement, being a man of rare physical power, but of an active, energetic and versatile mind. His children were Ezekiel, Jun., Abijah James and several daughters. Among his decendants are numbered some in each of the learned professions, and in the various walks of business life.

Bezaleel Barton, Benjamin Barton, and Peter Barton, brothers, came to Croydon, during the Revolution, from Sutton, Mass.

Levi W. Barton, grandson of Peter Barton and Ezekiel Powers, and son of Bezaleel Barton, 2d, and Hannah (Powers) Barton, the eldest of five brothers, was born in Croydon, on the first day of March, 1818. His father's business calling him from home much of the time, the care and management of the children fell to the lot of their mother, a woman well fitted to take the responsibility. After the death of her husband she, by untiring industry and the most rigid economy managed to keep her family together and in comfortable circumstances. But few mothers, if placed in her circumstances could "keep the wolf from the door." Levi W. early learned to share with his mother the cares and responsibility of maintaining the family, the pecuniary condition of which was such as to demand his time and labor even in early boyhood. He early learned the lesson of self-reliance and the necessity of economy and a proper use of time, a lesson which has contributed much to the success he has attained in life.

From the age of ten years till he left the district school at eighteen, his attendance was restricted to a short term in winter and this with frequent interruptions, he being engaged in manual labor all other parts of the year.

The condition of the family having somewhat improved, he left home when he was eighteen years old for the purpose of taking care of himself. But the way before him was beset with difficulties. He now wished to improve his condition and receive the advantages afforded to others; but he had not the means. He must labor. So he compromised the matter by taking his books with him as he went to his daily labor, and, as an opportunity presented itself, changed from labor to study. The writer well remembers the times, on rainy days, when Levi W. would call upon him, book in hand, for instruction in grammar or other common school branches. In this way, and by attending one term at the Unity Academy, then under the instruction of Alonzo A. Miner, now Dr. Miner, of Boston, he fitted himself for teaching. He now regarded his school days closed and cheerfully chose the occupation of a farmer.

In 1839, when twenty-one years of age, he married Miss Mary A. Pike, of Newport, a young lady of great worth, who died of scarlet fever in 1840, leaving an infant son five days old, afterwards the late Col. Ira McL. Barton. He placed his motherless boy in the care and keeping of a sister, Mrs. Amos Kidder, who tenderly cared for and reared the child.

By the death of his young wife, all his plans for life had perished. He could no longer endure a home so desolate. He spent a part of the following year with friends who extended to him every kindness in their power. The year following he collected together about one hundred dollars, all the worldly effects which he posessed, and commenced a classical course of study at Kimball Union Academy, then under the direction of Dr. Cyrus Richards, a distinguished teacher and educator. There he pursued his studies with a zeal which would listen to no discouragement. During his stay of three years, he taught school each winter and spent his vacations in manual labor to eke out his scanty means.

It being often a matter of doubt how he should meet even the most prudent expenditures, separated, as he was, from his son, and still laboring under the load of domestic affliction, few believed that he could complete a labor commenced and continued under such circumstances. Although laboring at first under disadvantages arising from lack of early school training, he rose by dint of application to stand abreast with his fellows in their usual studies, and to outrank them as a speaker and debater.

He entered Dartmouth College in July, 1844, being then twenty-six years of age. Few who had witnessed his course thus far, dared predict that he would hold on his course four long years. Especially was this true of those who knew that he must rely upon his own exertions to raise the means for his support. Still, nothing daunted, he entered upon his course and graduated in the class of 1848, with Hon. James W. Patterson, Hon. H. P. Rolfe, Hon. Anson S. Marshall, Dr. A. B. Crosby, and others who have done honor to their Alma Mater. Mr. Barton's standing in college was honorable, and his oration on the day of graduation was highly commended through the public journals of the day.

While in college, he also spent the winters in teaching and the vacations in manual labor. His custom, as he informed the writer, was, as soon as the last recitation of a term had been heard, to start on foot for his mother's house, a distance of twenty-one miles; and at the commencement of the next term he would return by the same conveyance.

Being anxious to enter upon the practice of his chosen profession at the earliest possible day, he commenced the study of the law with Hon. Daniel Blaisdell of Hanover, during his senior year.

Immediately after graduating, Mr. Barton commenced teaching the Canaan Academy, and at the same time entered as a student the office of Judge Kittredge, where he remained until January, 1851. While there he taught the Academy five terms, the Academy being then in a flourishing condition. He was also appointed postmaster of Canaan, which office he held until January, 1851, when he went to Newport, and completed his course of legal study with Messrs. Metcalf and Corbin, and where he was admitted to practice in July of the same year. In 1854 he became the law partner of Hon. Ralph Metcalf, and continued one year in business with him, when the latter was elected Governor of the State, and retired from practice. Mr. Barton then formed a partnership with Shepherd L. Bowers, Esq., then just commencing the practice of the law, and continued the partnership until 1859.

While his professional duties have claimed the greater share of his attention, he has found time to engage in house-building, having erected and completed four entire sets of buildings; in practical farming, for which he has a strong liking; in stock raising and in fruit growing, in both of which he has had much practical experience.

In 1855, 1856 and 1857 he was Register of Deeds for Sullivan county; was County Solicitor from 1859 to 1864; was representative to the State Legislature in 1863, 1864, 1875, 1876 and 1877, and State Senator in 1867 and 1868. During his entire term of service in both branches, he was a member of the Judiciary Committee, and for five years its chairman. In 1866 he was chairman of the board of Commissioners appointed by Gov. Smith to audit and report the war indebtedness of the state. In 1876 he was a member of the convention to revise the constitution of the state, and the same year, one of the Republican Electors of President and Vice-President of the United States. He was appointed Bank Commissioner by Gov. Harriman, but declined the office. In 1877 he was appointed by Gov. Prescott one of the Commissioners to revise and codify the laws of New Hampshire.

He has been twice a prominent candidate for Congress, but has failed of a nomination through local divisions, though his qualifications for the position no one questioned, nor could any one say that the nomination was not due to him if long continued, faithful, public service could confer such right on any one.

As a teacher, Mr. Barton had few superiors. He taught in all seventeen terms, the last three in Newport, after his admission to the bar. For four years following he had charge of the district schools of the town.

When he opened an office in Newport, he found there the Hon. Edmund Burke, Messrs. Metcalf and Corbin, Amasa Edes, Esq., David Allen, Esq., and William F. Newton, Esq., all in the practice of their profession. The field seemed to be fully and ably occupied. No wonder that some predicted that Mr. Barton would be starved out. But a man who had supported himself for sixty cents a week at the Academy, and for less than two dollars a week at College, was not the man to starve easily. He knew what economy meant, and how to practice accordingly. His early training had made him muscular and self-reliant. It soon became apparent that he had come to stay; for from the outset his success was assured. It immediately became apparent that he would bring to the discharge of the duties of his new position the same energy and devotion to principles, which had heretofore characterized his actions. From that time to the present he has enjoyed the confidence of the public.

As a counselor he is cautious and careful, dissuading his clients from engaging in litigation, rather than encouraging them to embark on that sea without a shore; as an advocate, he is eloquent, zealous, bold and persistent. In the preparation and trial of causes, he has few equals and no superiors at the Sullivan county bar. His faithfulness and devotion to the interests of his clients, appear in an unusual degree. Hon. Edmund Burke who has been opposed to him in many hard contested cases, has been heard to say to the jury that his "brother Barton's clients, in his own estimation, were always right and his witnesses always truthful, in fact, his geese were always swans."

Mr. Barton's first election to the House was in 1863, during the war of the Rebellion. Political feeling ran high. The Democracy were represented by their ablest men and best parliamentarians, skilled in all the rules and modes of procedure, which make minorities formidable. Never was a minority abler led by adroit leaders. Although Mr. Barton was a new member, unused to the rules of the House, still, he almost at once became the acknowledged leader of the majority. No other man was so much relied upon to meet the attacks of the opposition, and none did it with greater effect. Returned to the House in 1864, his position was the same as that in the former year. He urged the passage of the law allowing soldiers in the field the right to vote, and openly denounced the action of Gov. Gilmore in relation to the bill, though he well knew that it would cost him, as it did, his re-appointment to the office of solicitor.

In 1875 and 1876 he was chairman of the Republican legislative caucus, the labors of which were both extremely difficult and important. As to the manner of treating the Senatorial question then before the legislature, the Republicans were divided. Mr. Barton at once took his position and could not be turned aside. While he believed that Messrs. Head and Todd were entitled by right to their seats in the Senate, he did not believe it advisable under the circumstances, and looking to the final results, to insist upon these rights. Looking at the results which followed, who can now doubt the wisdom of the course pursued? Commenting upon the case at the close of the session, the Free Press remarks: "The cool course pursued is due in a great measure to Mr. Barton, sustained by the Governor. We think it will stand the test of time and recommend itself to all fair thinking men as the wisest course that could have been pursued under the circumstances." The Independent Statesman, in commenting on the Free Press article, says: "It is no doubt true that the course of Mr. Barton, sustained by the Governor, was what decided the matter. It turned the scale before hanging in the balance. In this they followed their convictions of right, and all the glory as well as the responsibility is theirs."

In the sessions of 1876 and 1877 his attention to business was such as to give him a commanding influence in the House. Always in his place, he was ready to lend a helping hand for any needed work. His large experience had made the various steps of legislation familiar to him. And the writer may be pardoned if he here adds the following as expressive of the views of those competent to form an opinion from actual observation. At the close of the session of 1877, the correspondent of the Manchester American, an able and sagacious observer of men and things, says:

"Barton of Newport is a man who brought with him an established reputation, and who has been one of the most prominent members of the House. He is a ready debater, quick to see a point and take it, popular with his acquaintances, and has had a large legislative experience, which gives him the full measure of his ability. He was the most prominent champion of the prison bill, which he managed with great tact and carried to victory, against odds which threatened at one time to defeat it. He has also been an active advocate of the various farmers' bills. If Sullivan county is permitted to name the successor of Col. Blair, an honor which her reliable Republican majority seems to entitle her, he will doubtless be the man."

Not less complimentary to Mr. Barton is the following truthful notice of his labors at that time, which appeared in the Statesman:

"One of the best men in the House was Barton of Newport. Suave and considerate at all times, and willing to take a hand in any discussion affecting the public weal, his cheerful, hearty voice striking in upon a dull or an acrimonious debate, had a pleasing and mollifying effect. Although careful and cautious, he has positive ideas, and while he respects the saying that "harsh words butter no parsnips," it cannot be assumed that he is not sufficiently aggressive in the maintenance of his convictions when they are assailed. Sometimes sharp in his personal sallies, they were singularly free from bitterness or malice, and no one, however much aggrieved at first, could hold resentment against him. Few members had more influence in the House, and his advocacy of any measure gave it strength. He made no long or labored speeches, nor did he attempt any learned expositions. Knowing the caliber of the average legislator in an unwieldy body of nearly four hundred men, his remarks were couched in off hand phrase more effective with the bucolic element than the most polished rhetoric or the severest logic. Perhaps, also, the secret of his influence with the House, was due in part to the fact that he seldom got on the wrong side of a question. On all moral questions, also, he was sound, foremost with voice and influence and vote."

In the legislative caucus, which nominated Hon. E. H. Rollins, for U. S. Senator, Mr. Barton received a handsome complimentary vote.

Thus it will be seen that Mr. Barton is a man of large experience in the duties of a legislator; and it may be added that through all of these years of political life he presents a record without a blemish.

In private as well as public life he has ever been upright and honorable. He is a self-made man, and we venture to say that few men have, unaided, surmounted greater difficulties. He does not claim to belong to the class of reformed men, as he never lapsed into bad habits, never having indulged in the use of intoxicating liquor, or of tobacco in any form. It was said of him, in 1877, that he was the "best preserved man in the House." We know not how this may have been, but it is true, that judging from his looks and appearance, one would say that he was at least ten years the junior of men of his age.

In 1852, he was married to Miss Lizzie F. Jewett, of Hollis, a young lady of culture, learning, and good sense. They have three sons and one daughter now living. The eldest, Herbert J. Barton, is a young man of great promise. He graduated at Dartmouth in the Class of 1876, among the first in a class of 69 students. He has since had charge of the Union School in Newport for two years, and now has charge of a school in Waukegan, Ill. His labors as a teacher have been attended with marked success.

Mr. Barton is highly esteemed as a citizen; he is kind as a neighbor, is strongly attached to his friends, generous to his opponents, and social with all.

In religious belief he is a Methodist, though reared in the Universalist faith. He is no bigot. He has always taken a strong interest in whatever affects the moral, social, or material prosperity of of those around him, and is always ready to lend a helping hand to every good work.

In conclusion, it may be stated that Croydon, though little in wealth and population, is great in the number and character of the men whom she has produced and sent abroad. The limits of this sketch forbid the mention of but few of them. The late William Powers and Gershom Powers, brothers, of Auburn, N. Y., were both self-educated and self-made men; William was Deputy Agent of the Auburn Penitentiary and Superintendent in the erection of a prison at Kingston, in Canada, and, for some years after, Warden of the same; and Gershom was a teacher, lawyer, judge, agent of the Auburn prison, and Member of Congress; the late Dr. Horace Powers, of Morristown, Vt., a man of extensive practice in his profession, sheriff of Lamoille County, Member of the Constitutional Convention, State Senator and bank director,— he was the father of Hon. H. H. Powers, now Judge of the Supreme Court of Vt.; the late Judge Cutting, of Bangor, was one of the Justices of the Supreme Court of Maine; the late Dr. Stow, of Boston, was, for many years, a leading clergyman of the Baptist denomination; the late Griswold .W. Wheeler, M. D., of St. Louis, Mo., was a scientist and member of a Philosophical and Scientific Society in St. Louis; the late William P. Wheeler, of Keene, N. H., was a leading lawyer in Cheshire Co.; the late Hon. Cyrus Barton was an influential editor at Concord, N. H.; Timothy C. Eastman, of New York city, is probably the heaviest exporter of fresh beef in the United States; George F. Putnam, of Haverhill, is a leading lawyer in Northern New Hampshire. But none among the sons of Croydon have done more to reflect honor upon the place of his nativity than the subject of this sketch.*

*It might properly be added, that Dr. William Barton, of Croydon, a brother of the subject of this sketch, is a physician of high repute, and was many years prominent in educational affairs, while a half-sister, Augusta Cooper Bristol, now of Vineland, New Jersey, is well and favorably known in literary circles.

ALL THROUGH THE NIGHT.

BY ABBA GOOLD WOOLSON.

All through the night,
Dear Father, when our trembling eyes explore
 In vain Thy heavens, bereft of warmth and light,
When birds are mute, and roses glow no more,
 And this fair world sinks rayless from our sight,
  O, Father, keep us then!

All through the night,
When no lips smile, nor dear eyes answer ours,
 Nor well-known voices through the shadows come;
When love and friends seem dreams of vanished hours,
 And darkness holds us, pitiless and dumb,
  O, Father, keep us then!

All through the night,
When lone despairs beset our happy hearts,
 And drear forebodings will not let us sleep;
When every smothered sorrow freshly starts,
 And pleads for pity till we fain would weep,
  O, Father, keep us then!

All through the night,
When slumbers deep our weary senses fold,
 Protect us in the hollow of Thy hand;
And when the morn, with glances bright and bold,
 Thrills the glad heavens and wakes the smiling land,
  O, Father, keep us then!

CONGRESSIONAL PAPERS, No. 5.—FORTY-FIFTH CONGRESS.

BY G. H. JENNESS.

The Forty-fifth Congress of the United States assembled at Washington in extra session, on Monday, October 15, 1877, in pursuance of the President's proclamation of the fifth of May preceding. The immediate reason for thus assembling Congress in extra session was the failure of the Forty-fourth Congress to make the usual annual appropriation for the support of the army for the fiscal year ending June 30, 1878. Nearly all the important legislation of the closing session of the Forty-fourth Congress had been delayed by the prolonged struggle over the electoral count, and when that memorable contest was ended, and Mr. Hayes declared the successor of President Grant, less than sixty hours remained in which to pass nearly all the great appropriation bills necessary for the support of the Government. On the Army bill there was a "dead lock" between the two houses, and as neither would yield, the bill failed. This necessitated a called session of the Forty-fifth Congress to remedy the omission of its immediate predecessor to provide for the maintenance of the army, and to transact such other business as the public needs might require. Its membership consisted of 76 Senators and 292 members of the House of Representatives. Of the former, Senator Hamlin, of Maine, was the oldest in years and term of service, and Senator Dorsey, of Arkansas, the youngest; 3 were less than 40 years of age; 17 were between the ages of 40 and 50; 39 between 50 and 60; 15 between 60 and 70; 1 (Hamlin) 71, and 1 (McCreary, of Kentucky) whose age was not given, but who was probably 70 or upwards.

The Senate was composed of 54 lawyers, 5 merchants, 3 doctors, 3 editors, 3 bankers, 1 planter, 1 farmer, 1 machinist, 1 manufacturer, 1 teacher, 2 miners, and 1 officer; 11 have performed service in the U. S. Army, and 10 in the Confederate Army; 13 have been governors' of their respective States, and 2 have served as territorial governors. 35 were educated in colleges, universities, or military schools, and 41 received only a common school or academic education; 10 were born in New York, 7 in Ohio, 6 in Pennsylvania, 6 in Virginia, 5 in Maryland, 4 in Massachusetts, 4 in Vermont, 4 in Tennessee, 4 in Kentucky, 3 in Georgia, 3 in Maine, 2 in Indiana, 2 in Delaware, 2 in New Hampshire, 2 in New Jersey, 2 in North Carolina, 1 in Connecticut, 1 in Louisiana, 1 in Michigan, 1 in Missouri, 1 in Rhode Island, 1 in South Carolina, 1 in Ireland (Jones of Florida), 1 in Scotland (Beck of Kentucky), 1 in England (Jones of Nevada), and 1 in Nova Scotia (Armstrong of Missouri); 11 states were represented in full by Senators who were born in the States they represented; 10 claimed 1 Senator as a native; 17 were wholly represented by Senators born in other states, or countries; and 16 states were denied the honor of being the birthplace of any member of the U. S. Senate in the Forty-fifth Congress.

Of their terms of service at the close of the Congress, 1 had served one year; 22 two years; 3 three years; 19 four years; 1 five years; 13 six years; 2 seven years; 3 eight years; 3 nine years; 2 ten years; 1 eleven years; 2 twelve years; 1 thirteen years; 1 eighteen years (Howe of Wisconsin); 1 twenty years (Anthony of Rhode Island); and 1 twenty-six years (Hamlin of Maine).

The House of Representatives was composed of 213 lawyers, 15 bankers, 11 merchants, 9 farmers, 7 manufacturers, 7 doctors, 4 editors 2 builders,

2 brewers, 1 barber, 1 clergyman, 1 mail contractor, 1 surveyor, 1 shipper, 1 real estate operator, 1 ticket agent, 1 railroad president, 1 leather dealer, 1 educator, 1 printer, 1 teacher, 1 planter, 1 pilot, 1 civil engineer, 5 whose occupation is not given, and 1 engaged in inland transportation.

Six have served as governors of their states. 150 were educated at colleges and universities, and 142 were educated in the common schools and academies, or were self-educated. 45 were born in New York, 38 in Pennsylvania, 32 in Ohio, 20 in Tennessee, 18 in Kentucky, 14 in Virginia, 12 in Massachusetts, 12 n North Carolina, 11 in Georgia, 10 in Indiana, 8 in Maine, 7 in Connecticut, 6 in South Carolina, 6 in Vermont, 6 in Maryland, 6 in New Hampshire, 5 in New Jersey, 4 in Illinois, 3 in Alabama, 3 in Missouri, 2 in Mississippi, 2 in Michigan, 1 in Arkansas, 1 in Florida, 1 in Iowa, 1 in Louisiana, 1 in Rhode Island, 4 in Germany (Schleicher of Texas, Muller of New York, Eickhoff of New York, and Morse of Massachusetts), 3 in England (Briggs of New Hampshire, Joyce of Vermont, and Dean of Massachusetts), 2 in Ireland (Walsh of Maryland, and Patterson of Colorado), 2 in Scotland (Phillips of Kansas, and Peddie of New Jersey), 1 in Canada, (Williams of New York), and 5 whose birthplace is not given.

Only 4 states were represented by members born in the states they represented, viz : Maine, North Carolina, Tennessee, and Georgia—though perhaps West Virginia ought to be reckoned in the list, inasmuch as her members were all born on the soil of the "Old Dominion" from which the state was set off ; 33 states were represented wholly or in part by members born in other states or countries (14 states wholly so) ; and 11 states claimed no member of the House of Representatives as a "favorite son."

1 member was less than 30 years of age (Acklem of Louisiana) ; 22 were between the ages of 30 and 40 ; 107 between 40 and 50 ; 108 between 50 and 60 ; 28 between 60 and 70 ; 3 between 70 and 80 ; and 1 above 80, (Patterson of New York, a native of New Hampshire), and 22 whose ages are not given.

At the close of the session, 1 member had served one year ; 124 two years ; 1 three years ; 94 four years ; 36 six years ; 15 eight years ; 9 ten years ; 1 fourteen years ; 3 sixteen years ; 3 eighteen years ; and 1 twenty-two years. Mr. Kelley of Pennsylvania was the "Father of the House" in point of consecutive service, having been in that body continuously for 18 years. Banks, of Massachusetts, and Cox, of New York, have each served 18 years, and Alexander H. Stephens of Georgia, 22, but neither of them consecutively. The terms of service of the remaining four members are not given ; 48 performed military service in the Union Army, and 58 in the Confederate Army.

The amount of business that the Forty-fifth Congress was obliged to pass its judgment upon, exceeded that of any preceding Congress since the organization of the government. In the House there were introduced 6525 bills, and 248 joint resolutions, of which number 478 bills and 44 joint resolutions became laws. In the Senate there were introduced 1865 bills, and 72 joint resolutions, of which number —— bills, and —— joint resolutions became laws (I have not the Senate Statistics at hand).

Col. J. H. Francis, the efficient Resolution and Petition Clerk of the House, informs me that 10,467 petitions were received, indexed, and referred to the appropriate Committee, which he has analyzed as follows :

Claims,	1,597
Commerce,	668
Currency,	196
Liquor Traffic,	264
Naval Affairs,	79
Patents,	192
Taxation,	254
Military Affairs,	376
Pensions,	878
Miscellaneous,	2,551
Polygamy,	431
Postal Matters,	541
Tariff,	2,440

A committee to which a petition may be referred, obtains jurisdiction of the subject matter thereof, and may report a bill thereon upon the call of committees. A large number of bills are reported from committees of Invalid, and Revolutionary Pensions, Post Office and Post Roads, Commerce, Military Affairs, Claims, and War Claims. Petitions are introduced in the House by members who endorse their names on the back of the documents and place them in a box in front of the Speaker's desk, from which they are taken to the Petition clerk, and thence distributed to the proper committees. Some of the petitions are huge rolls of manuscript, one of them in the second session of the Forty-fifth Congress containing the names of over 50,000 petitioners.

The New England temperance societies petition for the suppression of the liquor traffic in the District of Columbia, in the firm belief that sound legislation cannot be had while Congressmen obtain the morning "eye-opener" and evening "night cap." All the old maids append their authographs to formidable rolls of paper, insisting upon the abolition of polygamy in Utah, upon the ground, presumably, that a woman is entitled to a whole man, if she can get him, or none. The woolgrowers of Vermont petition for an increase of the duties on foreign wool, and others in Michigan pray, just as earnestly, for its removal. Pennsylvania and New England petition that existing tariff laws shall not be tampered with; while the South and West are equally clamorous for their modification or repeal. Among the "miscellaneous" are petitions from all classes of people for every conceivable object. One asks for an appropiation to test the efficacy of the theory that yellow fever and other similar diseases can be cured by the firing of cannon. Another believing, or assuming to believe that the light of the sun is soon to be extinguished proposes to light the world after Old Sol has departed. Still another is willing to accept a pension from the government for having succeeded, with the aid of his wife probably, in raising "one boy a year among the sand-hills of Florida," for several years past." The Common Council of Louisville ask the government "that the Howgate exploring expedition be directed to take the vessel making the exploration, after the colony leaves the same, out into the open Polar Sea and test the truth of the Symmes theory, and that Americus Symmes, a son of the author of said theory, be permitted to go on said vessel—."

A gentleman from New York with an eye upon posterity insists "that in the next census such necessary vital statistics be taken as will definitely settle all controversy upon the question of the effects upon the off-spring, of consanguineous marriage."

Forty-nine teachers in Illinois, who are evidently willing that country shall be spelled with a "k," ask "for the appointment of a commission to inquire into the propriety of a simplification of English orthography."

Another gentleman thinks he can secure an intelligent ballot "by the publication by the Government of a paper which shall be sent each week free to each family in the United States; in which paper shall be printed in the course of the year the Constitution of the United States and of the several States, the proceedings of Congress, the duties of the officers of the Government and their salaries, the reports of all Government expenditures, the amount of money received by the Government, the purposes to which applied, a monthly statement of the public debt."

The Lowell Operatives Reform Society want a territory set apart where "monogamic law shall not prevail."

A Maryland patriot wants pay for "two hogsheads of molasses destroyed by the British in 1814."

A Pennsylvania spinster, distressed by her lonely condition, and realizing the improbability of securing a man in any other way, asks Congress to enact a law, "compelling men to marry."

An evangelist whose penmanship and orthography needs reorganizing, wants the "religgun of Krist" made universal by Congressional enactments.

The petition box is alike the receptacle for business documents and the productions of disordered minds and visionary theorists. It also indicates the vast extent of our country, and the conflicting interests involved in its commercial and manufacturing industries.

It is not often that anything so prosaic as a House or Senate bill is made the vehicle of humor, but sometimes the scintillations of wit are found in the dryest places. For instance, while the discussion on financial legislation was in progress, some wag induced Senator Patterson of S. C., to introduce a bill (Senate bill 1383), providing "That the Congress of the United States of America will vote an appropriation, the same as a reward, to be paid the American citizen who shall produce a new foot-measure which shall divulge, in it, the truth of the meeting of parallel lines in exceeding great length."

The House also had its fun over the bill (House bill 4007); "For the relief of Private William Hines, Company F. Eighteenth United States Infantry, who lost his trousers and blanket by fire at Aiken, South Carolina." The amount of credit claimed was $8.50. The accompanying documents to the bill was a letter from the Secretary of War, the usual papers indorsed by all the military officers through whose hands it passed in the usual "red tape" style with as much formality, and through precisely the same channels as if it had been a claim for a million dollars. To those readers of the GRANITE MONTHLY who have been surfeited with partisan harangues, and have patiently waded through all the dreary twaddle of congressional debate, the following report of the House Committee upon Private Hines' trousers, is recommended as an antidote, with the writer's assurance that they will search the annals of Congress in vain for a parallel :

The Committee on Military Affairs, to whom was referred the bill (H. R. No. 4007), for the relief of Private William Hines, Company F. Eighteenth United States Infantry, having had the same under consideration, submit the following report:

The evidence is conclusive that Hines was a member of the company and regiment referred to, and that he lost his trousers and blanket by fire on or about the 11th day of October, A. D. 1876, while serving with his command at Aiken, South Carolina.

The time, place, and circumstances under which this loss occurred deserve much more than a mere passing notice. It was the year of the presidential election, and but one brief month prior to the time when the freemen of the Republic were called upon to cast their ballots for the men, or rather the electors of their choice. The air was filled with the eloquence of orators, both North and South, who spoke and labored for the success of their candidates. The propriety, not to say the constitutionality, of the presence of Federal troops in the southern section of our beloved country was a question that entered largely into the discussion of the day. Upon this subject there was then, as now, great difference of opinion; and without committing themselves upon this disputed point your committee find unanimously that Hines was there by order of the legally-constituted authorities; that he wore the usual and ordinary uniform of the private soldier; that he lost his trousers and blanket as set forth in the bill for his relief; that the loss occurred by fire; that a board of survey was called upon them, and that, in the language of that tribunal, "they were damaged to their full value," amounting to $8.65.

Your committee also find that this same board expressed the opinion that the fire was accidental; "that it originated at the top of the tent," and "that no one was to blame." There is no direct testimony upon this point, but it is fair to assume that Hines was lying down in his tent enjoying needed repose after a day's labor in asserting and maintaining the sovereignty of the General Government. It is true that those who seek to hold him responsible refer to the general and careless use of the pipe by our weary warriors; and others have attempted to account for the catastrophe by calling attention to the dangerous habit of soldiers carrying matches in their trousers' pockets. Both of these theories, although plausible, are rejected by your committee; and after patient investigation they are of the opinion that the fire originated in some unaccountable manner. If, as is altogether probable, Hines was recumbent in his tent, the conclusion is almost irresistible that he had disrobed and placed his blouse and trousers on the convenient and useful cracker-box; the progress of the flames from the top of the tent, where they originated, to his soldierly couch, doubtless aroused him from his reverie or sleep; and while the evidence is not entirely satisfactory on this point, your committee are of the opinion that Hines in his zeal to fight the fire and save Government property lost both trousers and blanket.

With this view of the case your committee accept the finding of the board of survey and discharge him from responsibility. No specific recommendations appear in their report, but through some misapprehension a gratuitous issue of trousers and blanket was made to him. As events proved, this was a fatal mistake. His commanding officer, misconstruing a mere suggestion, and perhaps unwilling that Hines should appear before the people of Aiken, trouserless, or, concluding that the honor and dignity of the United States would be put in jeopardy by his appearing on duty in a pair "damaged to their full value," made proper haste to rehabilitate him.

From this time Hines vanishes from the scene. How he disported himself in his new trousers nowhere appears. Unconsciously he had performed a great service to the Army and the country by causing an authoritative decision on a matter that had been involved in doubt. The question of a gratuitous issue of clothing is now settled, and while Hines may be indifferent to the trouble he has given captains, colonels, major-generals, a Secretary of War, and a congressional committee, he can content himself with the reflection that he has neither worn nor lost his trousers in vain.

In conclusion, your committee desire to call attention to the fact that they have devoted much time and thought to this case. The papers are voluminous, containing no less than seven distinct indorsements, commencing with a captain and concluding with the Secretary of War, who, in a communication to the Speaker of the House of Representatives, asks for the relief of Hines; or, to use his own well-chosen words, "requests the sanction of Congress for the issuing of said clothing to said Hines."

This communication is marked "A" and made a part of this report.

It is in no vainglorious spirit that your committee state that whatever delay there has been in this matter the blame does not attach to them.

The trouble with Hines began nearly eighteen months since, and the papers only reached the hands of your committee a few days ago; and in placing the final determination of the question with the Representatives of the people, they feel that they are discharged from further responsibility. They cannot, however, dismiss the subject without calling attention to the almost perfect system of checks and guards thrown around the issuing of Government property. The thoughtless may call it "red-tape," or circumlocution, but without it, Hines today would be in undisputed possession of a pair of trousers and a blanket to which he would have no legal title. As it is, the system has been vindicated, the right of the United States to Hines' trousers fully established, and his personal and pecuniary responsibility determined.

Under all the circumstances, your committee recommend the passage of the bill.

After all, the bill failed, with numerous others to reach the President, and the great question still remains unsettled.

In order to convey some idea of the amount of money required to carry on the Government, the following table of statistics compiled from official documents are given, showing the sums appropriated in each of the eleven regular annual appropriation bills.

FORTY-FIFTH CONGRESS.

First and Second Sessions.		Third Session.
Military Academy bill	$282,805.30	$319,547.33
Fortification	" 275,000.00	275,000.00
Consular	" 1,070,135.00	1,087,835.00
Navy	" 14,152,603.70	14,029,968.95
Post-Office	" 33,256,373.00	36,121,400.00
Pensions	" 29,371,574.00	29,366,000.00
Indian	" 4,721,275.79	4,713,478.58
Army	" 35,583,186.01	*
River and Harbor	" 8,307,000.00	7,842,100.00
Deficiency	" 14,534,672.52	2,961,478.42
Legislative	" 15,430,781.30	*............
Sundry Civil	" 24,750,100.06	18,414,171.51
Miscellaneous	" 1,572,659.50	
Arrearages of Pensions		26,807,200.00
Total	$173,308,165.79	$141,998,179.79

*Failed. †Not yet published.

In comparison of the above totals it should be remembered that the Army, and Legislative bills, had they become laws, would have added about $45,000,000 more to column of the "Third Session"; and the Arrearages of Pensions bill was an extraordinary appropriation, unlike any in the preceding Congresses. The Sundry Civil bill of the Second Session, also, was increased $5,500,000 by the Halifax fishery award, and the large Deficiency bill of over fourteen millions was ten or eleven millions above its normal amount, in consequence of deficiences extending over a period of several years previous.

Among the prominent measures,

aside from the appropriation bills that came before the Forty-fifth Congress for consideration, was a bill granting relief to the soldiers and sailors of the war of 1812; a bill to reimburse the trustees of the College of William and Mary for property destroyed during the late war; a bill for the relief of soldiers and sailors who served in the war with Mexico; a bill "to authorize the free coinage of the standard silver dollar, and to restore its legal tender character," known as "the silver bill;" a bill reorganizing the government of the District of Columbia; a bill providing for the reorganization of the army; a bill in relation to Pacific railroads; a bill to revise the patent laws; a bill to prevent the introduction of contagious and epidemic diseases into the United States; the Geneva Award bill; a bill to restrict Chinese immigration, and many others of greater or less importance. Of the few alluded to above, the bills relating to Mexican war pensions, the army reorganization, the Geneva Award, the revision of the patent laws, William and Mary College, epidemic diseases, and Chinese immigration, all failed to become laws—the latter being vetoed by the President. All the rest were approved except the "silver bill," which was passed over the President's veto, and thus became a law. Of measures political the "Potter resolutions" in the House, and the appointment of the "Teller Committee" in the Senate, were the most important. In the House the Potter resolutions were debated for several days, and "filibustering" resorted to to defeat their passage, which was finally secured by just a quorum, the Republicans refusing to vote. The history of these political committees being so well known, and their appointment of such recent origin, it is not deemed advisable to further allude to them here.

The third and final session of the Forty-Fifth Congress closed amid scenes of considerable excitement, at noon on the fourth of March, 1879, leaving two appropriation bills that failed to pass. These were the army, and the legislative, executive and judicial bills, upon which the conference committees could not agree, and so reported at the last hour. The amount involved in the two bills aggregated about $45,000,000; and the Forty-Sixth Congress, like the one of which a brief mention herewith closes, commences with an extra session to remedy the failure.

A BIT OF NEWSPAPER HISTORY.

The recent retirement of Messrs. Carleton & Harvey from the proprietorship of the *Argus* and *Spectator* newspaper at Newport, is a matter suggestive of far greater interest than usually attaches to changes in the control of county papers in our state. These gentlemen—Henry G. Carleton, and Matthew Harvey—had been editors and publishers of this paper for a period of nearly forty years, assuming the proprietorship January 1, 1840, and retiring therefrom April 1, 1879. It may be safely asserted that the entire history of the state furnishes no other example of equally long-continued, uninterrupted newspaper proprietorship and editorial management combined. And not alone from its long duration and unchanging character may the journalistic career of these men be regarded as remarkable and unique. Entering

A BIT OF NEWSPAPER HISTORY.

the office of the same paper, as apprentices together in boyhood, they learned the printer's trade, side by side, and worked together, harmoniously in the same way from first to last. By an arrangement entered into in the outset, when the establishment came into their hands, the editorial work was done by the two alternately, one editing the paper one week and the other the next, which arrangement was followed out without interruption to the close, Mr. Harvey acting as editor the first week of their proprietorship, and, in regular order, the last week also.

The early history of this paper was almost as remarkable for changes in proprietorship and management, as its after history for the reverse. The "*Spectator*" was established at Claremont, in August, 1823, by Cyrus Barton, who subsequently became well known as an able writer and a prominent Democratic politician. In January 1825, the paper was removed to Newport, and was there published by Mr. Barton, as sole proprietor, until September of the following year, when Dunbar Aldrich, a practical printer and a brother-in-law of the late venerable John Prentiss of the Keene Sentinel, became a partner in the concern. This partnership continued until April, 1829, when Mr. Aldrich withdrew, and Messrs. B. B. French and Cyrus Metcalf, the former a lawyer who came to Newport from the town of Chester, and the latter a printer, became Mr. Barton's partners in the business. Not long after Mr. Barton himself withdrew to assume an editorial connection with the *New Hampshire Patriot* at Concord, and the paper was conducted by French and Metcalf. This partnership was also of short duration, Mr. Metcalf going out, and Mr. Simon Brown a printer, and a brother-in-law of French, also from Chester, coming into the concern, which was then managed under the firm name of French and Brown. A few years later Mr. French disposed of his interest to his partner, removing to Washington, D. C., and Mr. Brown became sole editor and proprietor. About this time the "Argus" another Democratic paper, was established at Claremont, by a company of gentlemen, and Edmund Burke, then a young lawyer, who had been in practice two or three years at Whitefield, became its editor. Mr. Brown not giving satisfaction to many of the Democrats of Newport, they soon secured the removal of the *Argus* to Newport. This was in 1835. The two papers were run independently for a few months, when Mr. Brown sold out the "*Spectator*," the same being united with the *Argus* under the name of the *Argus and Spectator*, (by which it has ever since been known), the proprietorship being in a company of several gentlemen, mostly residents of Newport, and one of whom was Mr. Burke its editor, by whom it was conducted until his election to Congress a few years later, when the paper passed into the hands of Henry C. Baldwin and William English, two practical printers. Mr. English soon left to assume a position in the Boston Custom House, and Samuel C. Baldwin, a brother of Henry E., became a partner in the concern, which was, however, soon after sold to Messrs. Carleton and Harvey, who had learned and followed the printer's trade in the office, as has been suggested, entering in 1831, when French and Brown were proprietors.

In the seventeen years from the commencement of the paper in Claremont, till it passed into the hands of Messrs. Carleton and Harvey, nine different men had been actively engaged in its management—all men of more than ordinary ability, and several of whom acquired distinguished reputation in public life. Mr. Barton, the founder of the paper, was a State Senator and Councillor, State Printer, U. S. Marshal, and a member of the Constitutional Convention of 1850. He fell dead while making a political speech in the town of Loudon in the campaign of 1855. B. B. French became clerk of the National House of Representatives, and held various other offices at Washington, where he died in 1870. Simon Brown, who was subsequently editor of the *New England Farmer*, at

Boston, served in both branches of the Massachusetts Legislature and was elected Lieutenant Governor of that State. Edmund Burke, whose trenchant pen, won for the paper and himself an extended reputation in a very short time, was six years a member of Congress and subsequently Commissioner of Patents, under the administration of President Polk. Afterwards he was for a time editor of the Washington *Union*. As a ready and vigorous political writer he has had few if any equals—certainly no superiors in the country. Of all those engaged in the management of the paper, previous to the late proprietors, Mr. Burke alone survives.

Messrs. Carleton and Harvey went from the town of Sutton to Newport, when they became apprentices in the *Spectator* office. Mr. Carleton was a native of Bucksport, Me., born in Nov. 1813, but had removed to Sutton, when about ten years of age, where Mr. Harvey was born in Jan., 1815. The two are cousins, their mothers being sisters, whose maiden name was Greeley—half cousins of the illustrious journalist, Horace Greeley. The late Hon. Matthew Harvey of Concord, prominent in the history and politics of the State, and Jonathan Harvey of Sutton, also a member of Congress, were uncles of Mr. Harvey. Hon. George A. Pillsbury, formerly Mayor of Concord, now of Minneapolis, Minn., is a brother-in-law of Mr. Carleton, having married his sister.

Under their protracted management, the *Argus and Spectator* well maintained its reputation as a reliable exponent and advocate of the principles of the Democratic party, while, individually, each has held prominent and influential positions in the community of which they are now respected members. Mr. Carleton was Register of Deeds for the county of Sullivan in 1844 and 1845, and was appointed Register of Probate in 1854, being removed the following year upon the accession of the opposite party to power. He was also a member of the Legislature from Newport in 1853. Mr. Harvey held the office of Register of Deeds for five years, from 1846 to 1851.

The period covered by their newspaper proprietorship has been, indeed, a long and eventful one, witnessing great changes in national and state history. At its commencement there was not a railroad line in the state, and the telegraph was unknown. Of the more than fifty weekly newspapers now published in New Hampshire, not more than eight or ten have a history covering this period, and of these not a single one remains in the hands which then controled it.

AFTER MANY YEARS.

BY HELEN M. RUSSELL.

CHAPTER I.

Barbara Clay lived all alone in a little cottage toward the lower end of the small village of R——. Just opposite her humble home, stood the church wherein she worshipped, and every Sabbath, rain or shine, summer or winter, found her in her accustomed seat, listening intently to the good words which fell from Parson Downs' lips. She was apparently somewhere in the vicinity of forty years of age, and although she bore her years lightly, and the rippling brown hair was guiltless of a silver thread, her dark blue eyes were filled with a tender, mournful expression, and the sensitive mouth wore a look of subdued sorrow. She had come a perfect stranger nineteen years before, into this secluded village, and purchased the cottage which had ever since been her home. She mingled but little with her neighbors, and with the exception of attending church, was seldom seen away from home, unless it was to care for the sick and dying. The simple old-fashioned villagers respected and loved her. People said she had a story, but what it was they did not undertake to tell.

One dark, rainy afternoon in April, the lumbering yellow stage-coach drew up in front of the tavern, and the driver alighting from his elevated seat, approached his only passenger and said, with a low bow, "Where did you wish to stop, Miss; I believe you didn't state any partikler place, so I brought you to the tavern." A sweet, girlish voice replied, "I wish to know if a lady by the name of Barbara Clay resides in this village." "Yes, ma'am, she does," replied the driver. "Then, if you please, I will go directly to her home." The driver hastened back to his place, and gathering up his reins, drove on, leaving the knot of villagers in front of the tavern gazing in surprise after the departing vehicle. The coming of a young lady into their midst, and to see Barbara Clay of all persons, was an *event*, and it was something to wonder over and talk about, so when the stage-coach came slowly back again the driver found quite a crowd awaiting him, eager for a description of the stranger. "Don't know nothin 'bout her; I didn't see her face for she wore a vail over it. She got aboard the stage at Day's tavern, that's all I know about her." This explanation, as may be supposed, did not go far toward allaying their curiosity. In the meantime the young girl who had alighted from the coach in front of Miss Clay's cottage, stood patiently awaiting an answer to her repeated knocks upon the door. She was short and slight, with brown hair and dark blue eyes. Her dress was a rusty black alpaca; a coarse heavy black shawl and black straw hat trimmed with black ribbon, completed her attire. She had removed her well-worn vail, which she held in one slender ungloved hand; in the other she carried a small travelling bag. At length the door opened and Miss Barbara stood before her. "Are you Miss Barbara Clay?" questioned the girl, raising her eyes to the lady's face. "I am—will you please walk in," replied the lady, not without some surprise, as she turned and led the way into her small, neat sitting-room, where she placed a chair for her guest, and seated herself near by. As she did so her eyes fell upon a ring which the girl wore upon the third finger of her left hand. It was an old-fashioned ring, with two hearts linked together, and the initials B and C engraved beneath. She had in her possession a ring precisely like it, although for nearly twenty years she had not worn it.

Her face turned very pale and her voice trembled as she said, "Young lady, will you tell me your name?"

"My name is Etta Arnold, and if I mistake not you are my aunt Barbara," replied the girl with some hesitation.

For a moment the lady's face flushed crimson, and then the color receded, leaving her deathly pale as she sprang to her feet exclaiming, "Why are you here girl. Do you not know that your very presence is an insult to me?"

The girl half rose to her feet and then sunk back again, saying in a husky voice, "Oh, aunt Barbara, how can it be? I have never harmed you."

"You do not know the wrong your parents did me then," said the lady bitterly.

"I only know that in dying, my mother bade me go to you and ask your protection, and also to tell you of her continued love for you. I do not think she ever knowingly harmed you. Had you said my father had wronged you I should not have felt the least surprise, for he was capable of everything that was bad," said the girl bitterly. "Since my presence is not desired here, I will go at once," she continued, arising and turning toward the door.

"No, sit down; I wish to ask you a few questions; Is your father living?"

"No, he died three years ago," replied the girl.

"And you have no money, no home," said the lady, looking at the well-worn clothes of her niece.

"I have nothing, and no one in the world to care for me, except you and my father's brother," replied the girl, with a burst of tears.

"You would be much better off without *his* assistance than with it, I am thinking," returned the lady.

"He promised to provide a place for me as soon as possible, but I preferred coming to you as my mother requested me to do."

"How did your mother learn where I resided?" inquired the lady.

"She did not know, she told me to go to L——, her native place, supposing if you were yet living, I should find you there. I mentioned her request to my uncle, and he told me that my grandparents and uncle Oscar were dead, and no one knew anything concerning you whatever," answered the girl.

"How then did you discover my whereabouts?"

"Do you recollect a lady, Mrs. Eaton by name, who was ill here at the hotel some three years since? She came here to dispose of some land belonging to her, and was taken sick."

"Certainly I do," replied Barbara, quickly.

"You cared for her and doubtless saved her life. After my uncle's departure I mentioned your name to her, and she told me that a lady of that name lived in the village of R——, situated in New Hampshire. That you resided alone, and so far as she knew were without relations. By her advice I started immediately for your home, and here I am. I had no thought but that I should be welcome," concluded the girl in a husky voice.

"I do not mean to be unkind, but you do not know girl the wound your coming has reopened. I was learning to forget and I am sorry you came; however, since you are here I will try and make you comfortable. How strange that Mrs. Eaton should know you. Did you live near her?"

"She owned the house where my mother died and where we had lived for two years—that is we occupied two rooms in it. She was our only friend and the kindest lady I ever knew. Had it not been for her we must have starved, for I could not get work to take home with me, and I could not leave mother alone," answered Etta.

Barbara's eyes filled with tears as she arose and approaching the girl began to remove her outer garments, saying at the same time, "I have been too harsh with you my poor child. Will you forgive me?"

"Oh, aunt Barbara, I have nothing to forgive, but I will love you all my life, if you will let me stay with you," replied the girl, bursting into tears.

"There, there, my child do not weep, I shall not send you away. Draw your chair near the fire, and while you are warming, I will prepare you some supper," said Barbara, as she left the room. Not immediately did she begin her preparations for tea for her guest, however, for she sank down beside the window in her kitchen, and burying her face in her hands, burst into tears. It had all come back to her—the shame and agony of the day when she had found the sister she loved so dearly, the man she had reverenced above all others, alike false and unworthy of a single thought from her. She could see it all. The bright June day so fair and sweet, the air heavy with the perfume of flowers, the songs of thousands of birds, making the world seem so lively. She remembered how she had stood in the window of her room and listened to their songs, and wondered if anywhere in the world there was another creature so blest, so happy as herself, upon this her wedding morn. She had wondered as the moments passed on, that her sister Clarice did not come to her, and inquiring of her mother the cause, was told that she had retired the night before with a severe headache, and had not yet arisen. Then she had let them prepare her for her bridal, her pure heart full of happiness. The ceremony was to be performed at eleven, and when at length she stood ready, she glanced at her watch and saw that it was not quite half past ten. "I am going to surprise Clarice," she said to her bridesmaids, and with a gay, happy smile on her lips, she had stolen softly along the wide hall to her sister's room. She opened the door quickly, expecting to find her sister putting the finishing touches to her own toilet. To her surprise the room was in great disorder. Articles of wearing apparel were strewn about, lying upon the bed and upon chairs. Boxes stood open; in a word everything betokened that some unusual event had taken place, but her sister was not there. Approaching the dressing case she stood looking in surprise at the empty jewelry case which stood thereon, when her eye fell upon a letter directed to herself. Fearing, she knew not what, she opened it and read as follows:

"Dear Sister. Forgive me for causing you one moment's pain. All these weeks while you have been so happy, my heart has been full of deepest sorrow, but it is to end tonight. My Leonard and I are going away together, and before twenty-four hours have passed, I shall be his wife. I have deliberately chosen my path in life, and come weal or woe, shall abide by it. We knew that father and mother would never consent to our marriage, and have kept our love a secret from everyone. If we can be forgiven, an advertisement inserted in the *Herald* will bring us back, otherwise you will never again see your erring sister Clarice."

They had found Barbara lying senseless upon the floor with the cruel letter crushed in her hand, and every hope crushed out of her life. She remembered but dimly the events of the next three months, for a portion of the time she was ill with brain fever. Then, as she at length gradually came back to a knowledge of life, and realized the shame that her once idolized sister had brought upon them all, she secluded herself, keeping aloof from her acquaintances. Then came the terrible fever that swept down so many victims, her parents and only brother Oscar, among the first, and she was left alone. Rallying from the stupor of despair that at first overwhelmed her, she threw herself into the very midst of the pestilence, and her watchful care brought life and health to more than one poor victim. When at length the worst was over and she was at liberty to remain at home, she found the old house too full of sorrowful reminders of her happy past to be endured, so she had sold the place with all its furniture to a young couple recently married, and then she had left her once happy home, leaving no trace behind her. She had taken with her an elderly lady—Mrs. Lane by name, who like herself had been bereft of friends by the epidemic, and together they had lived in the village of R—— until Mrs. Lane's death.

For five years Barbara had dwelt there alone, and now this young girl, claiming to be her niece, the offspring of that guilty couple—her sister and Leonard Arnold—had come to her claiming her protection. Could she ever love her? "Forgive us our trespasses as we forgive those who trespass against us," she murmured softly. After all the girl was not to blame, and she would try and love her at least, and so, arising, she bathed her face—which, however, bore traces of her grief when she re-entered the sitting-room, bearing tea and toast for her unwelcome guest.

CHAPTER II.

Two months have come and gone, and the bright June days have come once more. The villagers have ascertained that the young lady who had come into their midst on that rainy April day is named Etta Arnold, and that she is Barbara Clay's niece. She goes and comes in and out among them with a kind word for everyone who addresses her, but her face is very sad, and she seldom smiles. It has been decided that she shall remain with her aunt, and Barbara is beginning to love the girl who is always so eager to please her and so gentle and fair. It is a lovely evening. The full moon is shining brightly, and the simple little village looks very peaceful, nestled in between high hills that rise on either side. It has become very dear to her —this home of her adoption, and Barbara thinks she shall never leave it while her saddened life lasts, and at its close she will be lain away in yonder cemetery whose simple headstones she can see shining in the moonlight. Etta has taken a walk over to the post-office, and her aunt sits by the window watching for her return. At length she sees her coming, walking rapidly up the path from the road. As she enters the house she says, in a glad voice, "At last, dear auntie, I have received my long looked for letter, and by its size I think I shall be repaid for waiting."

"I am very glad my dear. You can light the lamp at once."

Etta hastens to the kitchen and soon returns bearing a lighted lamp, and with an eagerness unusual to her, seats herself to read her letter. Barbara watches her and smiles to herself as she sees the girl's face light up with sudden joy as she reads. "She has a lover, and I shall lose her, when I prize her most," she thinks to herself, the smile dying away as she thinks how hard it will be to part with her. Etta rapidly scans page after page and her aunt notices that one sheet is carefully lain aside unread, and wonders at it. At length, Etta arises and extinguishing the light, says, "Aunt Barbara this moonlight is too lovely not to be enjoyed," and drawing a hassock to her aunt's feet she seats herself thereon.

"You are happier tonight than I have ever seen you before my dear. I hope you will always be so in the future. I have often thought you must be very unhappy with me, you always seem so sad," said Barbara, stroking the girl's hair tenderly.

"I am happy here with you aunt Barbara, and I do not think I am very sad. I was always different from other girls, for my life has been full of trouble," she replied sadly.

"You are so different from your mother, my dear. She was all joy and brightness, you are just the reverse," continued the lady.

"I can not remember the time that my mother was otherwise than sad. You have no idea of the unhappy life she led," returned Etta, in a choking voice.

For several moments the silence remained unbroken, then Barbara said gently, "Etta, I have refrained from asking you any questions concerning your parents, for your sake as well as my own, but tonight I feel that I would like to know something more concerning them. I hope Leonard Arnold was not unkind to the young girl he tempted away from her happy home," she concluded bitterly.

For several moments Etta made no reply, then she said in a voice slightly tremulous, "Aunt Barbara I have a story to tell you—which, however, I have not really understood myself until I received my long expected letter tonight. Dear aunt Barbara," she continued, caressing the little hand she held in her own, "you have been laboring under a cruel mistake ever since that morning, so long ago, that was to have seen you Leonard Clayton Arnold's bride."

"Etta, what can you mean," asked the lady in a tone of surprise.

"Did you ever have a thought that your sister cared for Clayton Leonard Arnold, twin brother to your lover?"

"No, Etta, most assuredly I never did. How could she? for although he was Leonard's exact counterpart in looks, he was just the reverse in everything else. In a word he was a spendthrift, a gambler, and all that was bad. I cannot understand your meaning Etta."

The moonbeams rested upon Etta's face, showing it deadly pale, and her voice was full of pain as she replied, "Aunt Barbara what you say of Clayton Arnold is true, but it is nevertheless true that he was my mother's husband and my father. They were married the day after she left her home. I have their marriage certificate and can prove what I am saying," said the girl in a low, firm voice.

"Then in Heaven's name why did she call him Leonard in her letter to me, and where, oh where was Leonard?"

"I do not positively know why she called him Leonard in writing you, but knowing as I do that she thoroughly disliked the name of Clayton, she had formed the habit of calling him Leonard, during their stolen visits, and therefore in the excitement of going away used the name unthinkingly. If I have been rightly informed—and I think I have—Leonard had been absent on business for two weeks, but was to return to L—— the night before the wedding. He did so and as he stepped from the train, he saw his brother and your sister just entering the forward car. With only one thought, and that to save her from such a mad act, he followed them. It was in vain, however, that he expostulated and even threatened, they were married as I told you the next day. He only went with them, however, as far as the city of A——, for being assured that Clayton really intended to marry her, and not having any authority to prevent it, he started to return to L——. When but a few miles from A—— a serious railroad accident occurred, and uncle Leonard was terribly injured. For three months, while you was thinking him false to you, he lay utterly unconscious, in a poor laborer's hut not fifty miles from L——. Then when he came slowly back to life again and discovered that three months had elapsed since the day which was to have been his wedding day, he fretted himself into a fever which again brought him nearly to the grave. When he at length began once more to recover he wrote to you, but at that time the fever was raging at L——, and you never received the letter. When he was able to travel he hastened to your old home at once, only to find you gone no one knew where. He searched for you, advertised for you in vain. Aunt Barbara my uncle Leonard is still living. He has never married. The letter I received tonight was from him in answer to one I wrote him soon after I came here. I have never seen him but once, and then only for a few moments soon after my mother's death. He gave me fifty dollars and desired me to remain with Mrs. Eaton until he could make arrangements for having me sent to school. The night before my mother died she told me how she had left her home and how bitterly she had always regretted it. She knew you had not married Leonard, and supposed her own marriage to have been the cause of a quarrel between you. Father had kept our whereabouts a secret from his brother, as he had forged his name soon after his marriage, thereby securing a thousand dollars. Mother desired me to write to him and tell him of my destitute condition, thinking that as he is very wealthy he would assist me to go to you. He came to me at once, and I had only to see him to love him dearly. In the box of old letters you gave me to overlook the week after I came here, I found the letter my mother wrote you ere she left her home. Not wishing to ask you anything in regard to the subject as I saw you avoided it, I wrote to uncle Leonard and enclosed a copy of the letter. And now I will leave you with his reply, and a letter for you which was enclosed in mine. Good night, dear aunt Barbara."

As Etta concluded she arose and throwing her arms around her aunt's neck, she pressed a kiss upon her brow, and stole softly from the room. Hour after hour passed and still Barbara sat there in the moonlight. Could it be true, this strange story her niece had told her. It seemed too much like a romance—such mistakes often happened in them, but in real life—never. And yet there were many circumstances that went to prove the strange story to be true. She remembered many incidents that had occurred at the time of Clayton Arnold's stay in L——, which should have told her the truth at the time. Yes, it must have been a mistake. How she had wronged her sister and Leonard all these years. The dawn of another day found her still sitting with his letter in her hand unread. It had been joy enough just at first for her to know that he had never been untrue to her. When, an hour after dawn, Etta came quietly into the room, her aunt arose and came forward to greet her with a face so full of joy that all the impress of grief her long suffering had placed there was effaced and Etta hardly recognized the voice that spoke to her, so full of happiness was it as she said, "He will be with us soon my dear, perhaps today, as he intended starting immediately after writing this letter. I can hardly realize the truth yet, it seems like a dream."

She said no more, and during the next few days she never once alluded to the subject, but kept quietly on in the same old routine of household duties. At length upon the fourth day after receiving the letter announcing Leonard Arnold's intended visit, as Barbara sat by her favorite window, a tall, gentlemanly form came slowly up the flower-bordered pathway to the door, and a moment later there came a low knock. Trembling like a frightened schoolgirl, Barbara arose to answer the summons. She opened the door, and stood face to face with her old lover. There was an eager, searching look into the tearful blue eyes raised to his face, and then the little hands were caught in a strong, firm clasp, and the words, "Barbara at last, thank God," and then he entered the little cottage and the door was closed. It chanced that Etta was away when he arrived, but when she returned two hours later she found a very happy couple awaiting her. "My dear," said her uncle, drawing her to his side, "we owe all our present happiness to you, for if it had not been for you I would never have found your aunt. I was away from home when your letter reached the city, therefore did not receive it until I returned home six weeks after its arrival. I was delayed three days by the sudden death of my partner, but I am here at last. And now Etta you must help me to prevail upon your aunt for a speedy wedding. I have waited nearly twenty years—it will be just twenty next Sabbath—and I think I should have my reward. Your aunt thinks she cannot possibly be ready in four days, but I insist that she can and you must help her."

"That I will dear uncle. We shall have ample time for what little preparation is really necessary," replied Etta, her face beaming with joy.

And so it came about that upon the next Sabbath a small bridal party consisting of Leonard Arnold and Barbara Clay, accompanied by Etta Arnold and the aged clergyman's sweet-faced granddaughter, entered the little church where the simple service was performed that made Barbara Clay the wife of Leonard Arnold, and the happiest woman the sun ever shone upon. The day following, Mrs. Arnold presented the good clergyman with a deed of the little cottage and its furniture, and bidding adieu to the village which had so long been her home, she and her husband, accompanied by Etta, set out for the elegant home awaiting them in a distant city. In the sunlight of her uncle's home Etta soon became light-hearted and joyous, in a measure forgetting the troubles of her early life, while Barbara resting content in the love of her noble husband, finds perfect happiness at last—AFTER MANY YEARS.

AN OLD SKETCH OF LANCASTER.

BY JOHN W. WEEKS.*

[From the Farmers' Monthly Visitor, conducted by Isaac Hill, October, 1839.]

Connecticut River, meaning in the Indian language, "the stream of many waters," passes the forty-fourth degree and thirty minutes of North Latitude and fifth degree and twenty-eight minutes East Longitude in a south westerly direction, being the north westerly boundary of the town of Lancaster, ten miles, exclusive of its windings, which are so remarkable that the country adjacent obtained from the Aborrigines the name of Coos, which in this language signified crooked, and known to the early hunters as the Upper Coos, to distinguish it from Haverhill and Newbury, which was also for a like reason called Coos by the natives, and by the hunters the Lower Coos. Colebrook has recently received, on the authority of friend Carrigain, the appelation of "Coos above the upper Coos."

Lancaster derived its name from a town of Massachusetts; it is delightfully located, the hills receding somewhat like an amphitheatre. Most of its lands are of excellent quality—its alluvials stretching nearly its whole length, and averaging about one mile in width. Israel's river rushes tumultuously westward, furnishing power for mills and machinery, to a great extent, near the centre of the town, where its waters become comparatively tranquil and gently meander for a long distance, through a most fertile soil, until they mingle with the more turbid Connecticut.

Lancaster was incorporated on the 5th of July, 1763, and owes its early settlement, like many other events in the world, to passion. David Page Esq., grand uncle of our present Governor, disatissfied with the division of the rights in Haverhill, and having been advised of the extent and fertility of our "meadows" by some of the survivors of that party of Rogers' Rangers, who, after the destruction of the village

*Hon. John W. Weeks, the writer of this sketch, and a prominent citizen of Lancaster, was a native of the town of Greenland, but removed in childhood with his father to Lancaster. His occupation was that of a house carpenter, but he took much interest in public and military affairs. In the war of 1812, he raised a company for the 11th Regiment, U. S. Infantry, which he commanded with credit. He was brevetted for gallant service at Chippewa, and commissioned Major at the close of the war. He lived thereafter upon a farm in Lancaster until his death in 1853. He was a State Senator in 1827 and 1828, served with Ichabod Bartlett and others on the New Hampshire and Maine Boundary Commission in 1828, and was a member of Congress one term, from 1829 to 1831. He also occupied the offices of Sheriff and Treasurer of the County of Coos. He left no children. He was an uncle to William D. Weeks of Lancaster, present Judge of Probate for the County of Coos, who now occupies the farm which he formerly owned, and also to Hon. James W. Weeks, a prominent citizen of Lancaster. In politics he was an ardent Democrat, or rather Republican as the party was then called (as will readily be seen from certain expressions in this sketch) and was the political associate of such men as Jared W. Williams, John S. Wells and John H. White.

of St. Francois, reached and passed down the waters of the Connecticut, being a man of great resolution, resolved to penetrate at once to the Upper Coos. With this view in the autumn of 1763, he sent his son David Page Jun., and Emmons Stockwell, to build a camp, and winter in Lancaster. They unfortunately erected their habitation on the meadow, from which they were driven the next March by the overflowing of the Connecticut river. In the year 1764, David Page, Esq. (called by the settlers Gov. Page) with his large family "moved" to Lancaster, followed by several young men, eager to improve, or rather make their fortune. The best tracts of land were immediately occupied, and were so productive that, for many years, manure was considered unnecessary, and was actually thrown over banks and into hollows, where it would be most out of the way. At this period there was no settlement between Haverhill and Lancaster, and but very few north of No. 4, (now Charlestown). There being no roads, the settlers suffered inconceivable hardships in transporting their necessaries, few as they were, being obliged to navigate their log canoes up and down the "fifteen mile falls," now known to be twenty miles in length, with a descent of more than three hundred feet; and in winter to pass the same dangerous rapids in sleighs and with ox-teams, frequently falling through the ice, and sometimes never rising above it. High water to decend, and low water to ascend, were thought the most favorable times, the canoes being drawn up by ropes; but when decending, one man stood in the bow with a pole to guard from rock to rock, while another sat in in the stern to steer with his paddle. In this manner the wife of Governor Page, when corpulent and infirm, was carried in safety to her friends "below." Her boatmen were her son David, and Emmons Stockwell who had married one of her daughters, men of great muscular power and of Roman resolution, equally persevering and collected, whether carrying packs of ninety pounds, or swimming in the foaming surge.

They afterwards commanded companies of militia, acquired large estates, and left many descendants, who, we hope, will emulate their example and transcend their usefulness. Edwards Bucknam, a young follower of Gov. Page, soon married one of his daughters, and settled at the mouth of Beaver brook; his daughter Eunice was the first white child born in Lancaster in 1767. He was a man of unbounded hospitality and usefulness, was a dead shot with his "smooth bore," could draw teeth, "let blood," perform the duties of priest in marrying, was one of the most skilful and accurate surveyors in the State, was proprietors' and town clerk, (his house and records were destroyed by fire in the year 1792;) afterward was General of the Militia; became regardless of property, and died poor.

The first town-meeting was held on the 11th of March 1769.

The first mill was operated by horse power, but so illy constructed, that it was little better than the large mortar and pestle attached to a pole, which was used by many. A "water mill" was erected, and soon after burnt; another, and another met the same fate. These disasters, with the revolutionary war, reduced the settlers to extreme distress. Newcomb Blodgett (who is now living) and some others being captured by the Indians and carried to Canada, led to the determination of abandoning the country; and for this purpose the settlers collected at the house of Emmons Stockwell, whose resolution never forsook him, even for a moment. "My family," said he, "and I shan't go." This remark changed the opinion of several families who remained, yet with but very few accessions to the end of the great and glorious struggle.

On the 7th of January, 1776, Joseph Whipple was chosen to represent the towns of Lancaster, Northumberland, Dartmouth (now Jefferson) Apthorp, (merged in other towns) and Stratford. Voted to give their representatives "instructions from time to time." At a subsequent meeting, Joseph Whipple was again elected to the same office; —a vote of thanks passed for his past services, and a committee of five was chosen to give him instructions for the future. Thus was the right of instruction established to govern the first representative ; may God grant that that right may never be subverted. Near and soon after the close of the war, several families, who had lost much of their property during the conflict, migrated to Lancaster. Maj. Jonas Wilder, with a large and highly respectable family, was of the number. He built a "grist and saw mill." In May, 1787, Capt. John Weeks, for a like reason, came to this town, bringing his eldest daughter and son, (the writer of this article, then six years of age) with him ; they rode on two horses, with bed and other furniture appended. The best of mothers and the other children followed the next October ; and the pleasure of meeting, in a neat log house, surrounded within a few rods by the dense and sturdy forest, will be among the last of our recollections. The town had now acquired the very respectable number of twenty-four families, exclusive of several young men. Our forests abounded with moose ; our rivers with trout, salmon, and various other kinds of fish—articles essential to even the existence of the settlers.

Nothing can exceed the symmetry and beauty of the limbs and horns of the moose ; the round part, or that near the head, is about fourteen inches in length, where it becomes palmated, and is, in some instances twelve inches broad, surmounted in one instance (seen by Edward Spaulding now living) by seventeen spikes on each horn. One, now before me, is one inch and a half in diameter at the base, and eight inches in length, terminating in a point.

The largest class of horns spread five feet, and weigh about one hundred pounds. Yet this enormous proportion of horn is of unusual growth, being moulted every February. Even at this early period, cars were used for the transportation of baggage ; not constructed however, precisely like those now employed on our railroads, as they were composed of two poles, one end of each resting on the ground, the other ends passing through the stirrups of a saddle, with two transverse sticks behind the horse, on which rested the load, and to one of which the whipple-tree was attached. Capt. John Weeks, as delegate from the upper Coos, on the 21st of June, 1788, attended the Convention for ratifying the Federal constitution, and was one of fifty-seven, who voted in the affirmative against forty-six negative voters. He was in favor of giving even more power to the Federal compact, and being an honest man (though deceived in this instance) he through life acted with the Federal party. He lived to his seventieth year, and probably never saw a moment when he would not divide the last dollar of his property with him who was in greatest need. Of course he early became poor, and cheerfully maintained that condition through life.

New Hampshire was the ninth state adopting ; consequently, every consideration within the reach of man was put in requisition during the deliberation of the Convention. And now, in the year 1839, we have more fear of consolidation than all other evils that can assail our unparalleled happiness and prosperity. At the March meeting in 1789, twenty votes were cast for State officers ; and even this small number were divided by important political considerations ; twelve friends to popular rights however prevailed. And we have reason to believe, that, at the remote period, when the other sections of our country shall have sunk below the standard of civil and religious right, the bracing atmosphere of the White Mountains will keep our inhabitants true to themselves, their country, and their God. In 1791, the town voted "to build a Meeting House," and chose a committee of five to fix the site and superintend the building. It was large, and many years elapsed before it was finished. A congregational church of twenty-four persons was gathered on the 17th of July, 1794 ; and on the 18th of the following September, the Rev. Joseph Willard was installed. He being the first settled minister, was entitled to the right of land (over 300 acres) voted by the original proprietors. The town agreed to give him fifty pounds per annum, and that his salary should rise, in the ratio of the inventory, to eighty pounds annually. He continued with the people of his charge, until the 16th of October, 1822. Some few persons, being inclined to what would now be called Burchardism, desired more fire in their worship; on learning that fact, the venerable Parson requested a dismission, which was granted on the above mentioned day. He afterwards preached in other towns, and was hired by his old congregation two years. He died July 22d, 1826, aged sixty-six. Mr. Willard served in the revolutionary army, and retained through life an elegant military figure and step. His sermons were written in a plain, easy, chaste style, sound in doctrine, yet liberal, as was his whole life and conversation. The church and congregation soon became much divided, which unhappily continues to be their state; and probably nothing short of a power like "a rushing mighty wind" will heal their dissentions and concentrate their efforts and affections.

Richard C. Everett, the first lawyer, settled in town in the year 1793. He enlisted into the army at the age of fourteen, served through the war, obtained by his own efforts a collegiate education, studied law, became a district judge; possessed a strong mind, was a man of honor, and much respected, and died on the 22d of March, in the year 1815, aged fifty-one years.

A slow yet regular and healthy progress has been made in the settlement and improvement of the town, from 1787 to the present time; nothing extraordinary occuring except the envenomed violence of party strife, during the embargo, non-intercourse and war. The parties being nearly equal in numbers, and so near the northern frontiers, that smuggling became the business of many of one party, and a few deluded unfortunates of the other, and was carried on to such a degree, that patriotism was put to the most severe test.

In the year 1813, the most malignant form of scarletina swept from the town most of our aged people, the infirm in younger life, and some whose hardy constitutions almost bid defiance to disease and death. Pulmonary diseases here, as in other parts of New England, have ever been active and relentless, alike destroying beauty, laying the mighty low, and sending piety on high. Fevers are comparatively rare. Dyspepsia, with its languid and downcast look, is beginning to make its appearance among us; but as farming and gymnastic exercises are becoming again fashionable, it is hoped that disorder will soon be as little known as it was among our fathers. The altitude of Lancaster, being about eight hundred feet above tide water, its proximity to the White Mountains, and high latitude, render some of its seasons too cold for maize; the mean temperature of the atmosphere through the year 1838, as indicated by Montandon's thermometer, which nearly agrees with Fahrenheit was 36 1-2 degrees above zero, yet out of fifty-two years past, that crop has wholly failed only three times. Wheat is very sure when sown late on ground well prepared, producing in very few instances forty bushels to the acre, and potatoes in one case over six hundred; and of a quality superior to those grown in most portions of our country. Rye does well on newly cleared land, but is subject to blight on old ground. The Hackmetack (Indian name of spruce, among the former tribes on the sea board, and those in the interior) abounds here. The Tamarack (Indian name for Larch) is frequent in low ground. The Moose Missie (Mountain Ash) in high hills and swampy low lands, is not unfrequent. Its Indian name was acquired by the fondness of the Moose for the bark and leaves of that tree. The most elegant and lofty white pines abounded on our highest alluvials. One shaft measured four feet in diameter at the base, was perfectly straight and without limbs ninety-eight feet, where it was twenty-two inches in diameter. The inhabitants are yet supplied with large quantities of sugar from the maple, which is abundant on the slopes of our hills. The beautiful elm with its sixty feet trunk, was found almost everywhere on our low meadows, before the axe had closed a war of extermination. The other forest trees common to New England are found here, except the Chestnut, Hickory, Pitch and Norway Pines, and White Oak. Granite of the most beautiful texture is found, not in large masses, but in detached blocks sprinkled over most of our high land; and if the distinguished industry and economy of our fathers shall be continued through the next generation, their houses, bridges and fences will be composed of that material. But few rocks of a secondary formation are found; consequently our soil partakes largely of the primitive character; covered by a deep rich loam, of decomposed vegetable matter. Lime is rare; but, as the various grasses flourish luxuriantly, animal manure is abundant for wheat and other crops.

About two miles southwest of the town's centre, there is a large tract of alluvial land, called Martin's Meadow, from an early hunter whose name was Martin. He caught immense numbers of beavers, from Beaver-brook, which meanders through the meadow. Beaver dams on and near this brook can yet be traced, in one instance, about fifty rods; another is near five feet high, and others of less extent and height; yet all exhibited extraordinary skill and ingenuity, superior to some bipeds, who attempt the erection of dams. The banks of this brook are perforated in hundreds of places, which show the former residence of bank bever; a kind smaller than those wonderful architects, who build dams, and erect houses several feet in diameter, with a layer of poles through the middle, which divides them into two stories, in one of which their food for winter, consisting of small poles, cut about two feet in length, is deposited; while the others covered with leaves, is their resting place during the inclement season. The entrance to both kinds of habitation is always below low water mark, from which they ascend through a subterranean passage, often several rods long to their dark, yet comfortable abode.

Immediately south of this meadow three conical hills, called Martin Meadow-Hills, gradually and beautifully rise several hundred feet, extending from the Connecticut river in an easterly direction two miles. On the sides of these hills reside ten aged farmers, who settled in the same neighborhood when young, and with little other property than their axes, having worked by the month, to pay for their respective lots of one hundred acres each. Most of them have become rich, and all enjoy a green old age, being able to labor on the same soil they occupied about fifty years ago. Phinehas Hodgdon is more than eighty years of age; Jonathan Twombly over seventy-eight; Walter Philbrook near seventy-five; William Moore in his seventy-sixth year; John McIntire in his seventy-fifth; Edward Spaulding (a decendant of the famous Mrs. Dustin) in his seventy-fourth; John Wilder in his seventy-eighth; Isaac Darby in his seventy-third; Menassah Wilder in his seventy-first; and Coffin Moore seventy-one. The same blast of a horn, well tuned, would now call them all to dinner; and although differing in politics and religion, they are all attached to the benign institutions of their beloved country.

On the south side of Martin Meadow-Hills, and washing their base, is Martin Meadow-Pond, a fine sheet of water, covering about four hundred acres. Here the first settlers repaired, whenever their stock of meat was exhausted, and their appetites satiated with fish, to watch and kill the noble animal, known by no other than its Indian name of Moose, which, during the hot season, spend its evenings in the pond to rid itself of myriads of flies, and to feed on its favorite food, the roots of lilies. An early settler, by the name of Dinnis Stanley, a man of strong mind and perfect veracity, informed the writer of this article, that being "out of meat" and wanting a moose skin, to buy a certain luxury, then much used, and too often at the present day, went alone to Cherry Pond for a supply, carrying his old gun, so much used that by turning powder into the barrel it would prime itself.

He had scarcely struck fire in his camp, when he heard several moose wading from the shallow side of the pond toward deep water. He then uncorked his powder horn, put several bullets into his mouth, and waited until the moose in front was nearly immersed in water. He waded in where the water was about one foot in depth, and took his position, not in rear of the moose, lest they should swim over the pond, but at a right angle with their track, and an easy musket shot from it. On his appearance, the four moose, as he had anticipated, chose rather to wade back than swim over, and commenced their retreat in the same order they had entered the pond; that was, one behind the other at some distance. In a moment the moose which had been in the rear, was now in front in the retreat; and, coming within reach, he was shot at. The powder horn was then applied to the muzzle of the gun, a bullet followed from his mouth, with the celerity which hunters only know. The second moose was fired at, the third, and fourth in rapid succession, when Lt. Stanley found time to give a fifth discharge to the moose then in the rear. Three fell at the water's edge, the other staggered to the top of the bank where he fell dead. But the greatest destruction of the moose occured in March, when the snow was deep and stiffened after a thaw. They were then destroyed without mercy by professional hunters who used only the skin, tallow, and nose; which last, and a beaver's tail, is probably more acceptable to the epicure than all the refinements of Roman luxury. One hunter, by name Nathan Caswell, killed in one season ninety-nine moose, most of them wantonly, not saving even the tallow or all of the skins. This brought him into disrepute among the settlers, who sometimes refused him their houses. The settlers however were more provident, always observing the injunction to Peter, with a slight modification, "Arise, slay," only "to eat." A moose of the largest class is about eight feet high and will weigh over nine hundred pounds. Deer and wolves were unknown till long after the first settlement, as were also eels, till the otter were exterminated.

From the village in Lancaster the roads diverge in four directions toward the sea board; in one toward Canada, and in another westward. This central location gives the town most of the business, mercantile and professional, in the counties of Essex and Coos, performed by five store keepers, seven lawyers, four physicians, one bank with a capital of fifty thousand dollars, and one Fire Insurance Company, to which may be added a flour mill with three sets of stones, four saw mills, three clapboard and three shingle machines, one extensive clothier's mill, a tannery, machinery for carriage making, blacksmith work, coopering and many other mechanical operations. Our religious establishments are very respectable, consisting of a Congregational Church, Methodist, Episcopal Society, three meeting houses, many Baptists, Unitarians, Freewill Baptists, some quakers, christians, restorationists, and no mormons. We have also an Academy in successful operation, and a very convenient brick Court House, and Jail often without tenants. There is also a Printing Press in town, from which issues a weekly newspaper entitled the Coos County Democrat. Its politics is indicated by its title. The town contains three hundred voters, and probably about fifteen hundred inhabitants.

One of the most magnificent spectacles I have ever witnessed, common in early times, now rare, was tracts of twenty, thirty, and sometimes fifty acres of heavily timbered land, a large proportion of which was evergreen, mixed with deciduous trees, cut down one or two years, and in a dry season, with fire attached to the windward side of the lot, the flame ascending with fearful velocity, far above the tallest of the trees (for it was a rule in those days, if the trees were felled by the job, to leave four of the largest on each acre standing) and the vast columns of dense and rapid smoke, obscuring the sun's brilliant light, nearly and perhaps quite equalling Napoleon's description of the burning of Moscow.

Our inhabitants begin to be aware, that one hundred years since, a smattering of Greek and Latin was a passport to honor and wealth, the learned profession then being scantily filled, which has led many parents and more young persons, at a time, when our professorships were over-flowing, to identify a collegiate education with ease, honor and wealth, and agricultural pursuits, with a life of meanness, of toil, and of no profit. Hence the rush of young men to colleges, academies, the yard stick, speculations, and even idleness, to avoid the low groveling pursuit of farming, as if agriculture did not require learning, and will not produce wealth and happiness preeminently over every other profession. The recent importation of bread stuff from Europe has, with its disgrace and pecuniary loss, produced one good effect. It has excited the attention of legislatures and scientific men to the "Art of all Arts:" It has convinced many that with a moderate share of industry, and the present enormous prices of the products of our northern region, they can become independent and happy, far, very far, beyond the care-worn speculator, the blasted hopes of those who depend on their diplomas, or even him who is a slave to his millions.

The character of our inhabitants is, in some respects, dissimilar to that of many other country towns, uniting the warm sensibilities of the heart, with the more profound researches of the understanding; enterprising, perhaps in the extreme; depending, however, more on individual effort, than on combined exertion; hospitable yet economical; aspiring, yet restrained within the bounds of propriety; independent in principle, even to a fault, if fault it can be; patriotic, only in accordance with their own perceptions of right; equally regardless of all dictums, unless clearly announced to their comprehension; patient and persevering, when cheered on by hope, yet possibly restless, when that "anchor to the soul" is "deferred." Lancaster, "with all thy faults, I love thee still."

August 4th, 1839.

MANNERS AND CUSTOMS IN HOPKINTON—No. 3.

BY C. C. LORD.

FUNEREAL.

Few customs in this town have changed more since the original settlement than those relating to the disposal of the dead. As soon as civilized society was established here, a spot was selected for a burial place. The first graveyard was on the top of Putney's Hill, being the lot now celebrated both on account of its antiquity and the elevated prospect afforded in the vicinity. This lot appears to have been at first selected by common consent, but, on the incorporation of the town, the subject of its legal ownership came up for public consideration. In 1766, the year after the incorporation, the subject of the ownership of the burial lot was set at rest by the following declaration inscribed in the record of the legal proceedings of the annual town meeting of that year: "The half acre of Land, which is voted to be procured for a Burying Plac on the top of the Hill, I give and Be Stow on the Town. John Putney."*

In the earliest days of this township, if a person died, the body was enclosed in a winding sheet, which enwrapped the form in such a manner as to favor the lapping of certain edges over the face of the deceased after the obsequies were performed and before the coffin was closed. The coffin was made by the local carpenter, who does not appear to have ever kept one on hand in case of an emergency, and was fitted with a pane of glass over the place alloted to the head of the corpse, through which glass the features were to be viewed by the mourners and friends. The funeral exercises being finished, the detached lid of the coffin was screwed over the pane, and the remains were ready for burial.

The preparations for burial being finished, the coffin was placed upon a bier, or barrow, and covered with a pall. The pall was a large piece of black cloth, about the size of a bedsheet, and served as a symbol of general solemnity and mourning. The pall was the property of the town. A pall was purchased in this town in 1768. The bier was at first borne on the shoulders of a number of men selected for the purpose; in later times, it was carried by the hands, as it is now, for short distances, on the way to the grave. The coffin was buried without any box, or other investing receptacle.

At first, there were sometimes attempts at preserving the memories of the dead by rude headstones of unhewn rock, in which were cut the initials of the deceased. A number of these headstones can be seen in the old cemetery on Putney's Hill. Only one of these bears a date. It is in memory of a child. The whole inscription is "1758, J. C.," the initials being cut below the date. As soon as the prosperity of the local settlement would allow, wrought gravestones began to be used. These were at first "with shapeless sculpture decked," being exceedingly rude. In the old graveyard on Putney's Hill are the two oldest artificial headstones in town. One is a memento of Lieut. Aaron Kimball, who died July 30, 1760, aged 50; the other, of Jeremiah Kimball, who died May 18, 1764, aged 56. These headstones are supplemented by corresponding footstones.

The gravestones of the older time sometimes exhibited a prolixity of inscription that was quite noticeable. The most remarkable case in kind is seen in the lower village cemetery.* On a large, slate headstone, finely sculptured on its face, is the following elaborate inscription:

In testimony of sincere
affection,
This humble monument was erected by
E. DARLING,
to inform the passing stranger that beneath rests the head of his beloved
ELIZA W. PARKER,
youngest daughter of Lt. E. P., who died of consumption, May 11, 1820,
Æt. 18.
Invidious Death! How dost thou rend
asunder
The bonds of nature and the ties of
love.
In Coelo optimus convenire.
We know that her Redeemer liveth.

*In 1766, the following act, doubtless relating to the original cemetery at the village, was passed by the town:

"Voted that half a nacor of Land Be Procurd for a Buring yard on the High way Leding to Concord Be tween the Land of Mr. Mark Jewet and Mr. John Blaisdel, a quarter out of Each of these Lands." Subsequently to a blank space immediately following this vote, this gratuity is expressed:

"a quarter of a nacor of Land for a Buring Plas which was Voted to Be Procurd on my Land I give and Be Stow on the Town. John Blaisdel."

The blank space in the record was doubtless intended for the accommodation of Mr. Jewett, who for some reason never used it.

---

*The public act of the town in advance of this gratuity is as follows:

"Voted that Half a Nacre of Land Be Procurd for a Buring Place where they have Be gun to Bury on the top of the Hill."

On the left of this inscription, according to the reader's observation, is the perpendicularly chiseled sentiment, "Her Eulogy is written on the hearts of her friends;" on the right, another, "Her friends were—ALL, who knew her."

The first artificial headstones in the town were of slatestone, rudely sculptured, with a death's head and wings. Afterwards came the improved slab of slate, on which the monument and weeping willow—one or both—were representative graven symbols of affliction. The marble slab followed, to be in its turn largely superseded by the more imposing stone or stately monument, the latter being usually of marble, though sometimes of granite.

The first tomb constructed in this town was built by Roger E. Perkins, and is located in the lower village graveyard. It received the bodies of numerous members and descendants of the Perkins family, but will receive no more. A few years ago it was closed and sealed for all time. In front of this tomb, on a slab of soft stone, is this inscription:

<blockquote>
ROGER E. PERKINS'
Tomb,
Erected July 11, 1821.
</blockquote>

It is an interesting fact that this inscription was cut by the late Rev. Edward Ballard, son of the late John Osgood Ballard, the renowned select school teacher, and that the sculptor used only his pocket knife in the operation.

The mention of the lower village cemetery suggests an interesting fact of local history. This yard, as originally laid out, extended two or three rods into the present main street. When the growth of the village demanded an increased width of street, the graveyard fence was set back the necessary distance at this point, and many bodies were disinterred and reburied in other places; but many others were left in their original positions, the mounds being smoothed off, and the thoughtless travelers to day tread above them while passing and repassing. The above change of outline occurred not far from the year 1820.

MATRIMONIAL.

There is less that need be said of matrimonial customs than of some others. There are some legal features of this part of the present subject that are worth noticing. The colonial statute of marriage required that an intention of matrimony should be attended by a certificate from the clerk of the town, or a license from the governor of the province, and be published on three several meeting days. Subsequently to Independence, in 1791, a law was enacted in New Hampshire, making it compulsory upon parties desiring to consummate marriage to have their "desire or intention published at three several public meeting days, or three Sabbath days," in town, or, if there was no clerk to publish, in the next adjoining town. The first publications of matrimonial intents were by open "crying" of the same by the town clerk at some interval in the religious services of Sunday. Afterwards notice was given by posting the legal evidence of the intent of parties in the entry, or porch, of the meeting-house.

The posting of marriages was kept up till a late period. In the rooms of the New Hampshire Antiquarian Society, at Contoocook, can be seen the last marriage notice posted in this town. It reads as follows:

Mr. Erastus Danforth, and Miss Mary S. Nichols, both of Hopkinton, intend marriage.

<blockquote>
F. P. KNOWLTON,
Town Clerk.
</blockquote>

Were married Aug. 23, 1854.

In later times, as is well known, the certificate of a town-clerk is a sufficient guaranty of the privilege of legal marriage.

BENEVOLENT.

Charity is an attribute of human nature in all times and places. Its formulated services are modified to suit the times and circumstances. In the earlier days of this town, the poor were assisted by the public, as now. Such of the poor as were homeless were at first boarded at the expense of the town. The board of paupers was sold at the annual town-meeting to the lowest bidder. This was a custom that was liable to abuses, like any other practice. At best, complaints would naturally arise from such a form of management. It is said that on one occasion, when it was proposed in town-meeting to sell the board of a certain pauper, the unfortunate man asked the privilege to speak. He said he did not wish to be sent to the place at which he had recently lived, for he "did not want to go to a place where they were poorer than he was." The practice of boarding the homeless poor around from place to place was, at best, objectionable, being excusable only on the ground of the poverty of the incipient township. The conduct of pauper affairs changed in 1833, when, on the 13th of March, it was voted in town-meeting to buy a pauper farm, Stephen Sibley, John Silver, and Daniel Chase being chosen a committee to effect the public purpose. The farm selected was one owned by Daniel Chase, and located on Dimond Hill, about two miles below the village, on the main road to Concord. This farm continued to be the home of the town's poor till the year 1872, when the property was sold in fulfillment of the vote of the town. The farm and its appendencies were sold in lots. Moses F. Hoyt purchased the main location and occupies it to this day. Since the sale of the town farm, the town's poor have been boarded, but by a management exempt from the objectional features of the first practice. The poor are no longer sold like worthless trumpery to the lowest bidder.

FINANCIAL.

As a public corporation, this town has enjoyed nearly or quite all the immunities and privileges implied in the right to buy and sell, borrow and lend, sue and be sued. It has collected its claims and paid its debts. We are not aware that any official of this town has ever been prosecuted for mal-administration or embezzlement. There has been a laxity of financial conduct that is apt to obtain in country towns. Men of no professional financial training are apt to transact business with regard only to present contingencies. As a consequence, the financial records of such managers are seldom what they should be. A citizen of this town, who has often been personally concerned in public affairs, tells us he once knew a time when there was not a scrap of an account to certify the amount of the indebtedness of the town in the possession of one of its officers. Its notes were out here and there, but nobody knew the amount in the aggregate. If the town chose to give its note, it was done; if it wished to cancel any indebtedness, it was accomplished.

In consequence of the indifferent local management, and the attendant popular inadvertence, the disposal of the town's revenues derived from the sale of public lands is a problem to many of our citizens to this day. We have been to some pains to uncover the facts, but as yet with incomplete success. From the sale of the parsonage lands, a fund of about $1000 was derived; from the sale of the school right, about as much more; from the sale of the training field, a considerable sum, be it more or less. The interest of these funds was devoted to special, distinctive uses. The parsonage fund was devoted to religion, the school fund to education, the training field fund to military affairs. We will give detailed information briefly.

With the above funds, bound in fulfillment of the original purposes to be invested, the officers of the town often experienced difficulties. Investments were not always easy. Reliable men were not always ready to take them. At length the parsonage fund was disposed of by a vote to appropriate the principle of the same to the discharge of any public indebtedness, and to raise the equivalent of the interest, annually, for distribution *pro rata* among the several religious societies. The plan worked only for a short time. It was soon objected that the nature of our civil compact forbade public assessments for the benefit of religious societies. The point was considered and sustained, and the collecting and disbursing of parsonage incomes ceased in 1853. The school fund was annihilated by the annual appropriation of the interest, with a certain part of the principle, for the support of common schools. The interest of the training field fund was annually devoted to military expenses till 1851, when the New Hampshire militia system was abolished, and we presume it was then absorbed into the general treasury.

The "surplus money" was for a time a thorn in the side of the financial body corporate. This product of the surcharged governmental treasury at Washington was received by Stephen Sibley, formally authorized receiving agent of the town.* Mr. Sibley rendered a report of his official services as receiver in 1838, and his report was accepted. On the 27th of April, 1839, the subject of the disposal of the surplus money came up for consideration. In the warrant for a town-meeting held on that date, an article was inserted to see if the town would divide the yearly interest accruing from this revenue equally among the ratable polls, and if, when so divided, the amount should be considered as a discharge of an equal sum of the annual poll tax. The town voted to pass over the article. At the annual town-meeting in March, in 1843, a vote was passed to divide annually one year's interest of the surplus fund, at the rate of six per cent., equally among all resident persons liable to taxation, until further ordered by the town. The matter rested till the 29th of November, 1845, when it was voted to reconsider the foregoing vote from and after the 1st of the following April. In March of the next year, an attempt was made to reconsider the vote of the 29th of November, but the article was indefinitely postponed. The contest over the surplus money arose from the protest against the anti-American idea of taxing the people to support individuals. The fund was absorbed into the town treasury.

INTER-COMMUNICATIVE.

We now touch briefly the subject of messages, the facilities for the conveyance of which having increased greatly since the earlier days of the town. At first, the ability to transmit messages depended upon the gratuitous accommodations of public travel. A person wishing to send a letter to a relative or friend, prepared it and forwarded by any person who happened to be journeying that way. By this popular method of transmitting messages, the taverns became general distributing post-offices. Sometimes a strip of tape tacked above the fireplace of the public house became a support for letters. The transient traveler looked over the list, and, selecting any bound in the direction he was going, took them along. By this method, the time required for conveyance from one point to another was governed much by uncertainties. Months were sometimes required for messages to reach their destination, at distances now accomplished regularly in less time than a day. The introduction of a public mail service removed a great inconvenience. The earlier mails were carried through this region by horsemen, and afterwards by drivers of vehicles. Subsequently, the public stage became the means of conveyance; the railroad crowned the accommodations in this direction till the telegraph* afforded the transportation of the most momentous matters.

The first post-office in Hopkinton was established April 1, 1811. John Harris was the first postmaster. The post-office at Contoocook was established March 5, 1831. Thomas Burn-

---

*In 1837, the town paid Mr. Sibley $2.17 for services as receiver, and for like services 1838, $4.31. The amount of surplus money received in two installments was not far from $6000, but it is a singular fact that neither in the records of this town, nor in those of the State Treasurer's office, at Concord, appear any figures to certify the sum.

*A telegraph office was opened in Contoocook in 1866. Levi W. Dimond was the first operator.

ham was the postmaster. The post-office at West Hopkinton was established May 29, 1857. Joseph P. Dow was postmaster.

MUTUAL AND PROTECTIVE.

In the earlier half of the present century, there were enterprises instituted in Hopkinton that, though in part maintained till now, would have advanced to schemes of greater public importance, if the public position once occupied by this town had never been changed. One of these enterprises was the Hopkinton Village Aqueduct Association. Water is a domestic necessity, and wells for water are contemporaneous with history. The first wells in Hopkinton village were in many instances impracticable for two reasons. The earth in this vicinity is sandy and porous to a great depth, and drawing water long distances is not a desirable employment.* Again, the quality of the soil is so slightly concreted that wells are in constant danger of falling in. A number of wells have disappeared in consequence of the lightness of the soil in this village. People have been disturbed by a rumble and tremor of the earth, and have investigated the phenomenon to find that their well had disappeared. Once an attempt was made to purify the old Wiggin well, better known as the "town well," since it occupied a position in the public street. Preparations were made for descent into it, and a man started down to begin the work of purification. He accomplished only a part of the descent, returning to state with much concern that there was a large chasm in the side, caused by the caving of the earth. The project of improvement was abandoned. This well has been closed a number of years.

A general need prompted the formation of the Aqueduct Association,

---

*An old well on the premises of Horace Edmunds is reputed to be seventy feet in depth.

which was incorporated in 1840. The grantees were Horace Chase, Nathaniel Curtis, Joseph Stanwood, Isaac Long, Moses Kimball, Ariel P. Knowlton, William Little and Reuben E. French. Water was drawn by means of logs from springs on the eastern slope of Putney's Hill, about half a mile from the centre of the village, the site of the supply being on the land of Abram Burnham. The water of these springs is very pure and sweet.

An important protective enterprise was implied in the formation of the Hopkinton Engine Company, which was incorporated in the year 1814. The grantees were Benjamin Wiggin, Joseph Town, Thomas Williams, Ebenezer Lerned, John O. Ballard, Stephen Sibley, Thomas W. Bailey and their associates. This company was in active existence till about 1852. During the warmer season of the year, it was its custom to meet monthly for a trial exercise. The company was marshaled by the strokes of the meeting-house bell, the engine taken to some reservoir, the tank filled by buckets, and the propelling power of the machine tested. The transaction was done with all the exactness of military drill.

About the time of the last practical usefulness of the Hopkinton Engine Company, an attempt was made to elevate the village into a precinct. A legal controversy thwarted the plan, which has never since been revived. For many years two tanks with pumps, supplied from the aqueduct, have been in existence in anticipation of dangers by fire. A chemical fire-engine was purchased by subscription in 1872 for use in Hopkinton lower village.

The Contoocook Village Engine Company was incorporated in 1831. Isaac Bailey, 3d, John Whipple, Rollin White, Joseph B. Town, and associates, were grantees. This organization is still in effective existence. Contoocook was elevated to a precinct in 1865.

THE GRANITE MONTHLY.

A MAGAZINE OF LITERATURE, HISTORY, AND STATE PROGRESS.

VOL. II.   JUNE, 1879.   NO. 9.

HON. ONSLOW STEARNS.

A large proportion of the men who have been elected to the chief magistracy of our state, have been to a greater or less extent engaged in political life during a considerable period of their existence. The men of essentially business tastes and occupation, who have been called to the gubernatorial chair, have been exceptions to the general rule. Nor is our state different from others in this regard. Everywhere, as a rule, the public offices which the people have at their disposal, are conferred upon men who have devoted their time and attention to politics and partisan management. Among the more conspicuous exceptions to this rule in this state, is the case of the late ex-Gov. Stearns, who, although a man of decided political convictions, was in no sense of the word a politician, and was never in any degree concerned in party management. Mr. Stearns was a business man in the full sense of the term, and, thoroughly identified as he was with the railroad interest of the state from its inception till the day of his death, he was unquestionably, from first to last, the most conspicuous representative of that interest in New Hampshire. A brief sketch of his career cannot fail to prove interesting to the readers of this magazine.

ONSLOW STEARNS was born in Billerica, Mass., August 30, 1810. The farm upon which he was reared, and which still remains in the family, being now owned by an older brother, Franklin Stearns, was the property and homestead of his grandfather, Hon. Isaac Stearns, a prominent and influential citizen of Middlesex County, and a soldier in the old French War, who was at one time a member of the Executive Council of the state and held other honorable and responsible offices. His father, John Stearns, who was also a farmer and succeeded in possession of the homestead, was killed in the prime of life by a railroad accident at Woburn. William Stearns, a brother of John and uncle of Onslow, was a soldier in the Revolution and fought at the battle Lexington. Onslow Stearns remained at home, laboring upon the farm and availing himself of such educational privileges as the public schools afforded, until seventeen years of age, when he went to Boston and engaged as a clerk in the house of Howe & Holbrook, afterward J. C. Howe & Co., where he remained about three years, and then left to join his brother, John O. Stearns, since famous as a railroad contractor and builder, who, then in Virginia, was engaged in the construction of the Chesapeake and Ohio canal. Subsequently he became interested with his brother in contracts for the construction of various railroads in Pennsylvania, New York and New Jersey, upon which he was engaged until the summer of 1837, when he returned to Massachusetts and engaged in contracts upon the Charlestown Branch and Wilmington & Haverhill Railroads, now respectively portions of the Fitchburg and Boston & Maine roads. Soon after he engaged in the work of completing the Nashua & Lowell Railroad, then in process of construction from Lowell to Nashua. This road was completed in the fall of 1838, when Mr. Stearns was made its superintendent, holding the position until July, 1845, when he resigned to become agent of the Northern Railroad Company of New Hampshire for the purpose of constructing its road from Concord to White River Junction. His first efforts in the interest of this road were directed toward obtaining the necessary legislation for securing a right of way for the road over the land where it was to pass, the law of 1840 having rendered it impossible. This legislation was secured in 1844, by which the state was empowered to take the land of the owners, making them compensation for damages, and leasing the same to railroad corporations, they repaying to the state the amount paid for damages.

Under the personal supervision of Mr. Stearns, the road was located, and the work of construction vigorously carried forward and completed, the Bristol branch included. After its completion he became manager of the road, which position he held till May, 1852, when he was chosen President of the Northern Railroad Company, continuing in that office until the time of his death. He was also general superintendent of the Vermont Central Railroad from 1852 till 1855, a director in the Ogdensburgh Railroad for some time, and for nearly twenty years up to 1875, a director in the Nashua & Lowell Railroad Corporation.

While president of the Northern oad Company, Mr. Stearns was president of the Sullivan, the Contoocook Valley, and the Concord & Claremont Railroad Companies, which were connected in interest with the Northern Railroad, and under his direction the Concord & Claremont Railroad was extended from Bradford to Claremont, being completed in 1872. The success of Mr. Stearns in the management of these various railroad enterprises caused his services to be sought by those interested in other railroads, and he was frequently solicited to take charge of railroad interests in Massachusetts and other states. These offers he uniformly declined till July, 1866, when he was induced to take the presidency of the Old Colony & Newport Railway Company, in Massachusetts, which position he held till November, 1877, when he resigned on account of failing health. During this time the Old Colony & Newport Railway Company and the Cape Cod Railroad Company were consolidated under the name of the Old Colony Railroad Company, and the South Shore and Duxbury & Cohasset Railroads, with others, were added to it. The Old Colony Steamboat Company was also formed, and purchased the boats of the Narragansett Steamship Company, thus forming, with the Old Colony Railroad, the present Fall River Line between Boston and New York. In 1874, Mr. Stearns was elected president of the Concord Railroad, and continued to manage the affairs of this corporation till his death.

The eleven years during which Mr. Stearns was president of the Old Colony Railroad were years of the most intense and constant labor on his part. For two years of the time he was governor of New Hampshire. He was president of the Northern Railroad and the other roads connected with it during all that time, and for three years he was also president of the Concord Railroad and of the Old Colony Steamboat Company, besides being a director and interested in the management of various other corporations. Mr. Stearns gave an active, personal supervision to all the corporate interests under his charge, embracing not only their general relations with other corporations and interests, but extending to the most minute details of their management. He was never idle. No man was ever more painstaking and faithful in the discharge of his duties. His papers and figures were carried with him, and studied as he journeyed between his home in Concord and the railroad offices in Boston; and when in Boston his labors almost always extended far into the hours of night. He lived in labor, and thought no plan complete till, by execution, it had passed beyond his power to labor upon it. His knowledge of the practical management of railroads was complete and perfect to the smallest details; and this, together with his unwearied industry, sound business judgment and foresight, and his knowledge and control of men, contributed to a success such as few railroad managers have attained. At his death he was the oldest railroad president in continuous service in New England, having been president of the Northern Railroad for twenty-seven years.

Although in no sense a politician, as has been stated, Mr. Stearns was a man of fixed political convictions, acting heartily with the Whig party from early life until the dissolution of the party, when he became a Republican. In 1862 he accepted the nomination of his party as candidate for State Senator in the Concord District and was elected, serving upon the committees upon railroads, elections and military affairs. He was re-elected the following year and was chosen President of the Senate, faithfully and acceptably discharging the duties of his responsible position. In legislation as in business life he was eminently a practical man. During his term of legislative service the war of the rebellion was in progress, and his efforts as a legislator, as well as a citizen, were freely and fully exerted in behalf of the Union cause. He was one of the prime movers in the formation of the New Hampshire Soldiers' Aid Society, an organization which contributed largely to the encouragement of enlistments and the assistance of the needy families of soldiers in the field.

In 1864 Mr. Stearns was a delegate-at-large from New Hampshire in the Republican National Convention, and was one of the vice-presidents of that body. Many prominent Republicans and personal friends had for some time urged his candidacy for the Republican nomination for governor of the state, and in 1867 he received a large vote in the convention which nominated Gen. Harriman for that office. Soon after the convention he was besought by a number of his friends and political associates, who were dissatisfied with the action of the convention, to allow the use of his name as an independent candidate, but declined to accede to their wishes.

In the Republican State Convention of 1867 no name but that of Mr. Stearns was presented for the gubernatorial nomination, which was conferred upon him by acclamation, a circumstance of rare occurrence in the case of a first nomination. He was elected by a decided majority—over Gen. John Bedel, the Democratic candidate, and was renominated the following year. He sent a letter to the convention, declining the re-nomination, on account of the state of his health and the pressure of business cares, but the convention refused to accept the declination, and a committee was appointed to wait upon him and urge its withdrawal, which was finally successful in its efforts. His re-election followed, and for another year he devoted no small share of his attention to the interests of the state, notwithstanding the varied demands of the extensive corporate interests under his management. To the financial affairs of the state his care was especially directed, and during his administration the state debt was reduced nearly one-third, while the state tax was also reduced in still greater proportion. He also took a lively interest in the management of the State Prison, and was instrumental in effecting great changes therein, securing more thorough discipline and putting the institution upon a paying basis, whereas it had long been run at a pecuniary loss to the state.

In the discharge of all his public duties, Mr. Stearns always sought to treat the matter in hand in a thoroughly practical and businesslike manner, exercising the same judgment and discrimination as in the management of his private and business affairs. Although firmly attached to his party, he was less a partisan in the exercise of his official functions than many of his predecessors had been, and was the first Republican governor of New Hampshire to nominate a Democrat to a position upon the Supreme Bench, which he did in 1870, when Hon. Wm. S. Ladd of Lancaster was made an associate Justice of the Supreme Judicial Court to fill the vacancy caused by the retirement of Judge Nesmith. This action, although denounced by many of his Republican friends, is now regarded by all as having been wise and judicious, inasmuch as the ultimate outcome has been a thoroughly non-partisan judiciary in our state, and a universal desire and determination to maintain the same.

The cause of education found in Mr. Stearns a warm friend, and in the welfare of Dartmouth College, which institution in 1857, conferred upon him the honorary degree of Master of Arts, he took special interest. His first public address after assuming the gubernatorial office, was upon the occasion of the college centennial, wherein he took decided ground in favor of such liberal aid from the state as might be necessary to make the institution permanently effective for the public good.

In religious sympathies and convictions Mr. Stearns was a Unitarian, and was an active and influential member of the Unitarian Society of Concord, during his long residence in the city, contributing liberally for the support of public worship, upon which he was a constant attendant, and for all its auxiliary purposes and objects. Thoroughly public-spirited, he never failed to give material support to all measures which seemed to him calculated to advance the interests of his adopted city as well as the state at large, nor were his social duties in the least neglected, notwithstanding the pressing cares of public and business life.

The long and arduous labor of his life was not without its substantial reward, and he became the possessor of an ample fortune, enabling him to dispense a liberal hospitality. Among the many distinguished persons entertained in his elegant mansion, were two incumbents of the chief magistracy of the United States—General Grant and Mr. Hayes, each of whom became his guest when visiting our State Capital. The estate which he left at his decease, amounted to upwards of three hundred thousand dollars in value, and exceeds any ever left by any other individual in the county of Merrimack, as the result of his own labors.

Mr. Stearns was united in marriage June 26, 1845, with Miss Mary A. Holbrook, daughter of Hon. Adin Holbrook of Lowell, Mass., and with her, established a home in Concord the following year, in the location where he continued to reside, making numerous improvements from time to time, throughout his life. Five children, a son and four daughters are the fruit of this union. The son, Charles O. Stearns is engaged in the office of Old Colony Railroad in Boston. The eldest daughter, Mary, is the wife of Brevet Brigadier General John R. Brooke of the United States Army now engaged in the frontier service; the second daughter, Margaret, is now Mrs. Ingalls of North Adams, Mass.; the other daughters, Sarah and Grace, remain with their mother at the family residence in Concord, where the husband and father, after a brief illness of a few days, quietly departed this life, December 29, 1878.

HISTORY OF THE FIRST CONGREGATIONAL CHURCH, CONCORD, N. H.

BY REV. F. D. AYER.

The First Congregational Church in Concord was organized November 18, 1730. The proprietors of the town, at a meeting in Andover, Mass., February 8, 1726, voted to build a blockhouse, which should serve the double purpose of a fort and a meeting-house. Early in 1727, the first family moved into the town, and Rev. Bezaleel Toppan was employed to preach one year from the 15th of May. Mr. Toppan and Rev. Enoch Coffin, both proprietors of the town, were employed by the settlers to preach till October 14, 1730, when it was resolved to establish a permanent ministry. Rev. Timothy Walker was at once called to be the minister of the town.

A Council met November 18, 1730, and organized, "in this remote part of the wilderness," a church of eight members, and Rev. Timothy Walker was installed its pastor. The Sermon by Rev. John Barnard, of Andover, Mass., was from Prov. 9 : 1–3. The Charge to the Pastor was by Rev. Samuel Phillips, of Andover, and the Right-hand of Fellowship by Rev. John Brown, of Haverhill, Mass. The church was orthodox and stable in its faith, and during the long ministry of Mr. Walker—fifty-two years—it was united and prosperous. Strong in the confidence and affection of the people, Mr. Walker always and actively opposed any thing which threatened division in the church or the town.

It is impossible to measure accurately the growth of the church during this period, owing to incompleteness of the records. No regular record is found after 1736, and the names of those who owned the covenant are gathered only in part, and these from entries made in his diary. While the names of only ninety-five who united with the church are known, many more than this must have become members, for, at the installation of his successor, though but few of those whose names were recorded were alive, there were one hundred and twenty members. The growth of the church must, therefore, have been rapid for those days, and its prosperity, stability and influence in the town and throughout the state are proof of a faithful ministry.

Rev. Timothy Walker, A. M., was a native of Woburn, Mass., and a graduate of Harvard College, in the class of 1725. His salary, at settlement, was £100, to increase forty shillings per annum till it reached £120; also use of parsonage. He died suddenly, on Sabbath morning, September 1, 1782, aged 77 years, deeply mourned by the people he had so faithfully served and led, and between whom and himself the mutual attachment had remained strong to the last.

The deep impress of this early ministry has never been effaced, and the influence of Mr. Walker, to a large degree, decided the moral tone and habits of the town. For more than half a century he directed the thought, and was the religious teacher of the early settlers ; and his clear convictions, his bold utterances, and his firm adherence to practical principles, made him a wise leader. He served the town as well as the church. His wise council and prompt and judicious action in relation to every matter of public interest, were of great benefit to the people, and gave him a wide and acknowledged influence. Three times he visited England, as agent for the town, to confirm its endangered rights, and was enabled by his personal influence and wisdom to make secure forever the claims and privileges of the settlers. His influence will be acknowledged, and his name remembered with gratitude by future generations.

Nearly seven years now passed without a stated ministry. In one case a call to settle was extended, but declined. September 1, 1788, Rev. Israel Evans was called by both the church and the town to settle as minister, and was installed pastor July 1, 1789. Installation sermon by Rev. Joseph Eckley, of Boston, Mass. His ministry continued eight years. No records of the church during this period can be found, and probably but few were added, as the number of members at his dismission was one hundred and twenty-four. Mr. Evans was a native of Pennsylvania, and a graduate of Princeton College, N. J., in 1772. He was ordained chaplain in the United States army, at Philadelphia, in 1776, and from 1777 till the close of the war, was chaplain in a New Hampshire brigade. He resigned his pastorate July 1, 1797, but resided in town till his death, at the age of 60 years, March 9, 1807.

The church, without delay, chose as successor to Mr. Evans, Rev. Asa McFarland, and the town concurring in the choice, he was installed March 7, 1798. The sermon was preached by Rev. John Smith, of Dartmouth College. The growth of the church under the ministry of Dr. McFarland was rapid and steady. Seasons of quiet, and also of deep religious interest, blessed it, and 429 were added to the membership, and 734 adults and infants received the rite of baptism. His ministry continued twenty-seven years, and closed March 23, 1825. Dr. McFarland was the last minister provided for by the town, his successor being supported by the society.

Rev. Asa McFarland, D. D., was born in Worcester, Mass., April 19, 1769. He graduated at Dartmouth College in 1793, and was for two years tutor in the college. He possessed a vigorous and active mind, was discriminating and sound in judgment; wise and diligent in action. His personal character and position secured to him a wide and lasting influence in the town and throughout the State. Eighteen discourses delivered on public occasions were published. In consequence of ill health he resigned his office as pastor. He, too, died among his people. By shock of paralysis Sabbath morning, February 18, 1827, he ceased from his labors, in the 58th year of his age.

The council which dismissed Dr. McFarland, March 23, 1825, installed as pastor, his successor, Rev. Nathaniel Bouton. Sermon was by Rev. Justin Edwards, D. D., of Andover, Mass.; Installing Prayer, by Rev. Walter Harris, of Dunbarton; Charge to the Pastor, by Rev. Asa McFarland, D. D.; Fellowship of the Churches, by Rev. Abraham Burnham, of Pembroke; Charge to the People, by Rev. Daniel Dana, D. D., of Londonderry.. The spirit of the Most High early rested on this ministry, and many seasons of revival blessed it. Bible classes and Sabbath-schools were organized in different parts of the town, and the faithful labors of the pastor in these, and in the large assembly of the people gathered in a single place of worship, were attended with great success. In connection with the meeting of the General Association of New Hampshire, held with this church in 1831, a deep work of grace began, and more than an hundred were added to to the church as the result. Large accessions were received in the years 1834, 1836, 1842, and 1843. During the forty-two years of this ministry, 772 members were added to the church, and 629 adults and infants were baptised. Three colonies were dismissed and organized into other churches, and the real increase of the church in strength and influence was very great. Churches of other denominations were also organized in town, yet this continued harmonious in action and steadfast in faith. This ministry was characterized by unity, stability and growth. Dr. Bouton resigned his pastorate, of marked and continued success, at the forty-second anniversary of his settlement, March 23, 1867, and was dismissed by council September 12, 1867.

Rev. Nathaniel Bouton, D. D., was a native of Norwalk, Conn., and graduated at Yale College in 1821, and at Andover Theological Seminary in 1824. He was not only a faithful minister of of Christ, but a citizen of valued and acknowledged influence, during a period of the great growth and prosperity of Concord, and bore for a generation an active part in questions of reform and public weal, both at home and abroad. A friend of learning and its institutions, he was a Trustee of Dartmouth College from 1840-1877. In the ecclesiastical bodies of this State, and in the benevolent organizations of the land, he was active and respected, and was a corporate member of the American Board of Commissioners for Foreign Missions, and of other charitable societies. In 1856 he published the History of Concord, and also published, during his ministry, many sermons, historical and biographical, and of public interest. Dr. Bouton was State Historian of New Hampshire from 1867-1877, and compiled the ten Volumes of Provincial and State Papers, which have been published.

On Sunday, March 23d 1878, the 53d anniversary of his settlement, he attended public worship for the last time, and died June 6th, at nearly 79 years of age.

His form was laid, as have been those of all his predecessors in this ministry, among the people he had so faithfully served for nearly half a century.

Rev. Franklin D. Ayer, a graduate of Dartmouth College in 1856, and of Andover Theological Seminary in 1859, was installed by the council which dismissed Dr. Bouton, September 12, 1867. The Sermon was by Rev. Eden B. Foster, D. D., of Lowell, Mass.; Installing Prayer, by Rev. J. M. R. Eaton, of Henniker; Charge to the Pastor, by Rev. P. B. Day, D. D., of Hollis; Fellowship of the Churches, by Rev. W. R. Jewett, of Fisherville; Address to the People, by Rev. W. T. Savage, D. D,. of Franklin. He is still the Pastor.

Thus this church has not been without a settled ministry since March 7th, 1798, and reaches nearly its one hundred and fiftith anniversary with its fifth pastor.

In the present pastorate 139 have been added to the church, making the total additions, 1,566.

OTHER CHURCHES FORMED.

For many years this was the only church in the town. The steady growth of the population at length called for other churches, and this church sent out three colonies of the Congregatonial order.

The West Parish Church. After mature deliberation, the families resident in the west part of the town decided to organize a new church. Eighty-eight members were dismissed, by unanimous consent, from this church, and April 22, 1833, organized into the West Parish Congregational Church, and the next day Rev. Asa P. Tenney was installed its pastor.

The South Church. Soon the interests of religion, and the increase of population in the southerly part of the village, required the establishment of a Congregational Church in that vicinity. February 1, 1837, the sixty-seven members dismissed by a vote, unanimous, and sealed with prayers and friendly wishes. were organized into the South Congregational Church. May 3d, Rev. Daniel J. Noyes was installed its pastor.

The East Church. In 1842 a new house of worship was built, on the east side of the Merrimack river, and a church formed of the forty-four members, dismissed from this church for that purpose.

HOUSES OF WORSHIP.

The first meeting-house of Concord was built of logs, in 1727, and served as a fort and a place of worship. It stood near West's brook, and was occupied by this church twenty-three years. The second house was that so long known as the "Old North." The main body of the house was built in 1751. In 1783 it was completed with porches and a spire, and in 1802 enlarged so as to furnish sittings for twelve hundred people, and a bell was placed in the tower. Central in its location, it was for a long time the only place of public worship in the town, and was used by this church for ninety years. It served the state also. In this house the Convention of 1778 met "to form a permanent plan of government for the state." Here, with religious services, in 1784, the new State Constitution was first introduced, and here, too, in June, 1788, the Federal Constitution was adopted, by which New Hampshire became one of the states of the Union. This was the ninth state to adopt that Constitution, the number required to render it operative; so that, by this vote, it became binding upon the United States. After another church edifice was built, this was used by the "Methodist Biblical Institute" till 1866. When it was destroyed by fire, on the night of November 28, 1870, there passed from sight the church building which had associated with it more of marked and precious history than with any other in the state.

The third house of worship, situated on the corner of Main and Washington streets, was dedicated to the worship of God November 23, 1842. In 1848 it was enlarged by an addition, giving twenty new pews. In 1869 the gallery was lowered, to make room for a new organ which was placed in the church; the inside of the house was repainted and the walls frescoed.

It was burned Sunday morning, June 29th, 1873.

At the rear of this building, a chapel was erected, in 1858, and enlarged in 1868.

The present beautiful and commodious house of worship is on the same site, built of brick with stone trimmings, and is cruciform in shape. It cost about $45,000, and was dedicated free of debt, March 1st, 1876.

CHURCH UNION.

As the church was about leaving the "Old North" as a house of worship, it was voted to invite all the churches formed from this to unite in a special religious service in that house. Says the record of it: "Religious services were attended at the Old North Church, on Thursday and Friday, October 27 and 28, 1842. On Friday the pastor delivered a discourse on the history of this church, and in the afternoon about 550 communicants of the four sister churches sat down at the table of the Lord. It was a season of tender and affectionate interest. Many wept at the thought of separation from the place where they and their fathers had worshipped." So happy was the effect of this meeting, that the next year one of like character was held in the New North Church, but on November 18, in commemoration of the organization of this church. Since that time, an annual union meeting of the Congregational churches in Concord, including that in Fisherville, has been held with the several churches in succession, and the meetings have always been precious seasons of Christian union and fellowship. At the twenty-fifth annual meeting, held with the First Church, 1867, it was voted that the union bear as its name, "The Concord Congregational Church Union."

THE SABBATH-SCHOOL.

Miss Sarah Kimball, in her annual report to the Female Charitable Society, in January, 1817, suggested that something more be done to get the children to meeting and to school, and that Sabbath-schools be commenced the coming spring or summer. It is probable that a small school was gathered the comming summer, by Miss Sarah Russell, a school teacher in the village. About the same time, also, Mr. Charles Herbert, a devoted christian, used to gather the small children of the neighborhood into the kitchen of his father's house, after the service on Sabbath afternoon, and teach them the catechism and scripture. In the spring of 1818, by advice of Dr. McFarland, Sabbath-schools were organized in four different parts of the town, viz., one in the Town House, superintended by Capt. Joshua Abbott; one in District No. 9, superintended by Hon. Thomas Thompson, and numbering 44 scholars; in the West Parish, one numbering 47 scholars; and in the school-house on the East Side, No. 13, one of 40 scholars. The two last named had no superintendents, but were taught by two young men—I. W. Dow and Ira Rowell. The school on the East Side was continued but a few years, but that in the West Parish was united with the church there organized in 1833, and still continues. The schools in the Town House and in No. 9 were united. At the settlement of Dr. Bouton, in 1825, the Sabbath-school was held in the Town House, assembling at the ringing of the first bell on Sabbath morning, and after the exercises, the scholars, attended by their teachers, walked in the order of classes to the church at the opening of morning service.

The returns made October 25, 1825, from seven schools held in as many different districts, from May to October, show 50 teachers, 334 scholars, and 88,122 verses of scripture recited. In 1826 there were twelve schools, with 70 teachers, 480 scholars, who recited 161,446 verses of scripture—five times the number in the whole Bible. This year a library was purchased and used. As most of those in the schools were young, not more than fifteen years of age, Dr. Bouton, soon after his settlement, organized five Bible classes in different sections of the town, for the youth and the older ones, and these continued, full of interest and profit, till the revival of 1831, and from January, 1826, to January, 1832, 81 were received from these classes to the church.

At the organization of each of the other churches, the schools near them were united and soon held during the interval of worship. Those of this congregation were united, and the sessions held after the morning service, and through the year. Adult classes were formed in 1838, and in 1842 the Sabbath-school Association, composed of all the teachers and scholars belonging to the school, was organized, and is still continued. Its anniversary is held on the last Sabbath of December, when reports are read and addresses made by the pastor and others. The Sabbath-school Concert was first held in 1851, and is observed on the second Sabbath of each month. There have been added to the church, by profession, since 1825, from the Bible class, 82; from the Sabbath-school, 346. Total, 428.

HUNGER.

BY LAURA GARLAND CARR.

'Tis not for bread alone
    That famished mortals cry;
What nourishment our bodies crave,
    We find in large supply.
O'er field and plain,
In rolling main,
    The waiting treasures lie.

But O, the hungry heart,
    With longings all untold,
Seeking such love and sympathy,
    As human hearts may hold;
Meeting the gloss
Of useless dross,
    Where should be purest gold.

And O, the hungry brain,
Eager for wisdom's lore,
Finding the way it seeks to tread,
Guarded by bolted door;
Looking afar
To many a star,
Which it may ne'er explore.

And O, the hungry soul,
Waiting what yet may come,
Striving with dim, short-sighted eyes,
To pierce the future's gloom;
Longing for life,
Immortal life,
While seeing but the tomb.

NEW HAMPSHIRE MEN AT BUNKER HILL.

BY HON. GEORGE W. NESMITH.

When the news of the Lexington engagement reached New Hampshire, a large number of her citizens soon assembled at Cambridge. They were without organization. Many were destitute of either arms or provisions. The New Hampshire civil authorities had not yet moved. The Massachusetts government felt the necessity of providing the means of defence, and employing men for that purpose. Her rulers organized forthwith her own regiments and companies, and issued commissions to her officers.

It appears they extended their patronage beyond their own limits, as proved by the following record. "The committee of safety for Massachusetts, on the 26th of April, 1775, issued the commission of colonel to John Stark, with beating orders. Under this commission he enlisted 800 men from the tap of his drum. Captain James Reed* of Fitzwilliam, Cheshire county, also, Paul Dudley Sargent of Amherst, Hillsborough county, received commissions as colonels, which were accepted upon the condition that they should continue until New Hampshire should act."

Stark soon enlisted 14 companies. Reed and Sargent only 4 each. After-

---

*Gen. Reed was granted half pay. We copy his petition and accompanying papers, as follows:

To the Hon. Senate and House of Representatives convened at Portsmouth, 1785:

Humbly shews James Reed. Esq., late Brigadier General in the Continental army, that in consideration of his unfortunate loss of sight in the service of his country, Congress granted the continuance of his pay and rations, calculated the amount due, and requested this state to pay the same, and charge it to the account of the United States; but notwithstanding repeated applications have been made, he has not been able to obtain either that or the half pay due to him by the resolves of Congress made in favor of the unfortunate sufferers in the service of the United States.

Your petitioner now reduced to the severest distress, with a large family dependent on him for support, robbed of the means of subsistence, incapable of performing any kind of business, which might contribute to his, and their relief, and having nothing to console him but an expectation that the representatives of a free and generous people will not suffer a person, who, to obtain their freedom, endured sufferings which have forever deprived him of the pleasure of

wards, New Hampshire gave commissions to Stark and Reed. Stark's regiment to be No. 1. The other commission was assigned to Col. Enoch Poor, as belonging to that part of the state where he resided. Early in May, the New Hampshire assembly voted to raise and equip 2000 men to be divided into three regiments of 10 companies each, Poor's regiment to be second in rank, Reed's third. Col. Sargent retired to Massachusetts, and during the siege of Boston had command of a small regiment of Massachusetts troops. Stark had some collision with Gen. Folsom, Hobart and others about his rank and supplies, &c. Yet he had early in June a large regiment of men ready for active service.

Two of his companies were ordered to be detached, and to be joined to Col. Reed's regiment to make up his quota of 10 companies. Still leaving to Stark 10 companies, exceeding Reed's regiment in numbers, as will appear by the following statement. Prior to the 17th of June, 1775, Stark's regiment was stationed at Medford. Reed's regiment was located near Charlestown Neck. On the 14th day of June, the effective men fit for duty, belonging to Reed's regiment, according to Adjutant Stephen Peabody's return, amounted to 488 men. Several of the men who had enlisted had not then joined. Others were furloughed, some were sick, some were on guard. The regiment of Stark as returned, amounted to 632 men, including rank and file.

Col. Reed returned his highest number of killed and wounded in the battle of the 17th, as 5 killed and 27 wounded. We have been able to ascertain the names of these men, with much certainty, at the expense of some labor.

Rockingham county furnished one company of 44 men to James Reed's regiment. It was commanded by Captain Hezekiah Hutchins of Hampstead; 1st Lieut., Amos Emerson, Chester; 2d Lieut., John Marsh. This company was enlisted from Hampstead, Chester, Raymond, Atkinson, Sandown and Candia. Candia suffered the greatest loss. Parker Hills of Candia, was mortally wounded and not heard from after the battle. John Varnum and Samuel Morrill, both of Candia, were severely wounded, and received afterwards invalid pensions from the United States government, as did Nathaniel Leavitt of Hampstead, who was also then and there wounded.

Second company, 44 men. Captain, Josiah Crosby of Amherst; Lieut., Daniel Wilkins, Amherst; Ensign, Thompson Maxwell. This company was from Amherst, which then embraced Milford and Mont Vernon. John Cole and James Hutchinson were both mortally wounded. Hutchinson died June 24, 1775.

Third company, 46 men. Capt., Philip Thomas of Rindge; Lieut., John Hooper; Ensign, Ezekiel Rand, Rindge. This company was from Rindge, Jaffrey, &c. There were returned 3 killed, viz: George Carlton,

---

viewing that country, which he helped to make free, he takes the liberty of entreating your Honors to take his melancholy situation into view and grant him such relief as your wisdom shall direct.

As in duty bound will ever pray.
BENJAMIN SUMNER,
In behalf of the petitioner.
June 10, 1785.

Nov. 30, 1786.
Cheshire, ss. Gen. James Reed came before the subscriber and made oath, that he is an inhabitant of the town of Keene in the county aforesaid.
Attest, DANIEL NEWCOMB,
Justice of the peace.

To the Hon. Com. of the Sick and Invalids:
Agreeably to your notice, I have con-
formed to the oath therein directed. I have had an opportunity of speaking with his Excellency the President of the State, and he informed me that as I had already transmitted certificates from the Director General of the hospital and Regimental Doctor, and other evidences of my entire disability while in the service of my country, both to Congress and the General Court of this state, that I had no further occasion of furnishing any further certificates at the time, than the one indorsed.
Attest, LOCKHART WILLARD,
JAMES REED.
Keene, Dec. 4, 1786.

Half pay, &c., allowed to Gen. Reed. He received 1162 pounds, 10 shillings.

S. Adams and Jonathan Lovejoy of Rindge; 3 wounded, John Thompson of Rindge, (rec'd half pay from the State) B. Parker of Swanzey, mortally wounded, Edward Waldo of Alstead, severely.

Fourth company, 44 men. Capt., Levi Spalding, who represented Lyndeborough in 1781-82; Lieut., Joseph Bradford; Ensign, Thomas Buffee. This company was chiefly from Lyndeborough, Temple, Hudson, &c. David Carlton and Jesse Lund were both mortally wounded, Carlton dying June 18. Lund was from Dunstable. Jacob Wellman of Lyndeborough, was wounded in the shoulder while employed in fixing a flint into his gun. He afterwards was an invalid pensioner.

Fifth company, 59 men. Capt., Jonathan Whitcomb, Swanzey; Lieut., Elijah Cloyes,* Fitzwilliam; Ensign, Stephen Carter. This company was from Keene, Swanzey, Fitzwilliam, &c. Joshua Ellis of Keene, was wounded; Josiah Barton, wounded in the side, his cartridge box being shot into pieces.

Sixth company, 54 men. Capt., Jacob Hinds, Hinsdale; Lieut., Isaac Stone; Ensign, Geo. Aldrich, Westmoreland. This company was from Hinsdale, Chesterfield and Westmoreland. John Davis of Chesterfield, killed, Lem. Wentworth, wounded.

Seventh company, 52 men. Capt., Ezra Towns of New Ipswich; Lieut., Josiah Brown, New Ipswich; Ensign, John Harkness, Richmond. This company was made up from recruits from New Ipswich. Also, Capt. Wm. Scott of Peterborough, furnished about half of his men and served as a volunteer himself. Josiah Walton of Chesterfield, was wounded, as was, also, Capt. William Scott, who fought bravely and was severely wounded, made prisoner and conveyed to Boston, from thence to Halifax. He escaped after a confinement of some months, and returned home. He in 1776, commanded a company in Col. Jackson's regiment of Massachusetts. David Scott of Peterborough was wounded.

Eighth company, 46 men. Capt., Wm. Walker, Dunstable; 1st Lieut., James Brown, Dunstable; 2d Lieut., Wm. Roby. Enlisted from Dunstable, Merrimack, Hudson, Amherst, &c. Joseph Greeley, son of Doctor Greeley, wounded; Paul Clogstone of Dunstable, wounded; died July 15, '75; Jonathan Gray, died of his wounds; Asa Cram, wounded.

Ninth company, 49 men. Capt., Benjamin Mann of Mason; 1st Lieut., James Brewer of Marlborough; 2d Lieut., Samuel Pettengill. This company composed largely from men of Mason, Wilton, Marlborough, Temple, &c. Joseph Blood of Mason, killed; Ebenezer Blood, Jun., was mortally wounded, not afterwards heard from. Their father drew their back pay. Both sons marked killed on company rolls.

Tenth company, 48 men. Capt., John Marcey of Walpole; 1st Lieut., Isaac Farewell of Charlestown; 2d Lieut., James Taggart of Peterborough. This company was enlisted from Walpole, Charlestown, Acworth, Cornish, &c. Joseph Farewell of Charlestown, was killed, and J. Patten and John Melvin were mortally wounded and not afterwards heard from. Marked both killed on rolls, in Adjutant Generals office.

The biographer of the town of Charlestown, says that N. Parker of Charlestown was killed at Bunker Hill, but we have not been able to find his name on the company rolls of Marcey. Probably to be found elsewhere. The aforesaid list of the killed and wounded is believed to be nearly authentic and generally fortified by record testimony. The 7th volume of Dr. Bouton's State Records embraces a statement of the property lost by the men of both Reed's and Stark's regiments, as inventoried, appraised and paid for by the state. Reed's regiment suffered most severely. The statement is, as the two regiments marched on to the hill, Reed's men deposited their packs and extra clothing, &c., in a building located near Charlestown Neck, and the building and contents

---

*Captain Cloyes was killed one hundred years ago, in Sullivan's expedition among the Indians.

were burned by a shot from the enemy's shipping, while our troops were engaged in the battle on the hill.

We here furnish the names of the several company officers attached to Col. John Stark's regiment, together with many of the killed and wounded in each company, in the battle of Bunker Hill. The list is not perfect, but as accurate as we can make it from the materials at our command. We also furnish the number of enlisted men according to the rolls or returns in June, 1775. The whole number of enlisted men was 632; The number of killed as returned by Col. Stark, 15 men; also, of the wounded, by Col. Stark, 45 men. Maj. Andrew McClary of Epsom, was of the staff killed. We give the companies in order of the numbers in each:

First company, 77 men. Capt., George Reid of Londonderry; 1st Lieut., Abraham Reid of Londonderry; 2d Lieut., James Anderson, Londonderry. This company was enlisted from Londonderry. We have the authority of Matthew Dickey to sustain the statement that a part of Capt. Wm. Scott's company joined the Derry company, and that Randall McAllister of Peterborough, was severely wounded in the shoulder while rashly standing upon the stone breastwork, located in front of the men. Also, Geo. McLeod and John Graham of Peterborough, and Martin Montgomery of Londonderry, were all slightly wounded. Thomas Green, afterwards of Swanzey, was also severely wounded. The Peterborough men were enrolled by Capt. W. Scott. The other part of his company were in Capt. Town's company.

Second company, 69 men. Capt., Daniel Moor, then of Deerfield, afterwards of Pembroke; 1st Lieut., Ebenezer Frye of Pembroke; 2d Lieut., John Moor. This company composed largely from Pembroke, Deerfield, Allenstown, Bow, &c. Nathan Holt and J. Robinson, both of Pembroke, were wounded, as were Josiah Allen of Allenstown, and J. Broderick.

Third company, 67 men. Capt., Elisha Woodbury of Salem; 1st Lieut., Thomas Hardy of Pelham; 2d Lieut., Jonathan Corliss of Salem. This company was from Salem, Pelham, Windham and vicinity. Moses Poor and Thomas Collins were both killed; Abner Gage of Pelham, afterward of Acworth, was severely wounded in the foot, and made lame permanently; John Simpson of Windham, lost a portion of one of his hands by a cannon ball, so certified by his captain and Isaac Thom his surgeon. Both Gage and Simpson received invalid pensions. Eph. Kelley of Salem, and Seth Cutter of Pelham, were also slightly wounded.

Fourth company, 66 men. On the day of the battle this company was commanded by Capt. John Moor of Derryfield; 1st Lieut., Thomas McLaughlin of Bedford; 2d Lieut., Nathaniel Boyd of Derryfield; 1st Serg., Wm. Hutchins of Weare. This company was enlisted from Derryfield, Bedford, Brookline, &c. Henry Glover was killed; Wm. Spalding of Raby, now Brookline, severely wounded; John Cypher and Saml. Milliken, also wounded. Capt. Moor was promoted to the rank of major of the regiment, upon the death of Maj. Andrew McClary.

Fifth company, 60 men. Capt., Gordon Hutchins of Concord; 1st Lieut., Joseph Soper; 2d Lieut., Daniel Livermore of Concord. This company was composed largely from Concord, Henniker and vicinity. Dr. Bouton gives 15 from Concord; Col. Cogswell gives 20 from Henniker. Geo. Shannon was killed, also James Reed of Henniker; Alexander Patterson of Henniker, wounded.

Sixth company, 59 men. Capt., Henry Dearborn of Nottingham; 1st Lieut., Amos Morrill of Epsom; 2d Lieut., Michael McClary of Epsom. This company was from Nottingham, Deerfield, Epsom, Chichester, Exeter, Barrington, &c. Wm. McCrillis of Epsom, was killed; Serg. Andrew McGaffey of Sandwich, Serg. Jonathan Gilman of Deerfield, and private Weymouth Wallace of Epsom, were wounded and received invalid pensions.

Seventh company, 55 men. Capt. Isaac Baldwin of Hillsborough, killed; 1st Lieut., John Hale, Hopkinton; 2d Lieut., Stephen Hoit, Hopkinton. Composed largely from the men of Hopkinton, Hillsborough, Warner, Bradford, &c. Capt. Baldwin was a valuable man, was a native of Sudbury, Mass. Had been with Stark in the French war; was one of the first settlers in Hillsborough; was mortally wounded in the battle of the 17th, by a shot through the body; was carried from the field by John McNeil and Serg. Andrews, his neighbors. Died about sunset of that day, aged 39 years.

Moses Trussell of Hopkinton lost his left arm by a cannon ball in that engagement. He says he came off the hill safely. Hearing that his brave commander was left behind, and that he was wounded, with others I returned back to help bring him off. While crossing the Charlestown Neck, I received the shot which disabled me. His narrative is embraced in a petition for half pay from the state, which he received.* He also was an invalid pensioner. He resided many years in New London in this state.

Eighth company, 53 men. Capt., Samuel Aaron Kinsman of Concord;

1st Lieut., Ebenezer Eastman of Concord; 2d Lieut., Samuel Dearborn. This company was made up from recruits from all parts of the state. John Manual of Boscawen, formerly of Bow, was killed; Abraham Kimball of Hopkinton, alias Henniker, was wounded.

Ninth company, 52 men. Capt., Samuel Richards of Goffstown; 1st Lieut., Moses Little; 2d Lieut., Jesse Carr of Goffstown. This company was enlisted from Goffstown, New Boston and Weare. Caleb Dalton was killed; Reuben Kemp of Goffstown was wounded and made prisoner, dying in Boston; Andrew McMillan of New Boston was wounded in his right hand, he losing the use of it; Peter Robinson of Amherst, was also wounded, losing his right hand by a cannon ball. Both received invalid pensions and half pay. We give Col. Stark's certificate:

March 17, 1777.

This may certify that A. McMillan of New Boston, and Peter Robinson of Amherst, were both of my regiment, and were with me at Bunker Hill, and were both wounded, and I knew them to behave very courageously in that action. I beg the Hon. Court would consider of their loss, and make them some consideration.

JOHN STARK, Col.

---

*We here give the petition of Moses Trussel, with the certificates:

To the Hon. Council and House of Representatives of the State of New Hampshire, at Exeter, convened:

Gentlemen: The petition of Moses Trussell, humbly sheweth that your petitioner early engaged in the service of his country by enlisting into the company of Capt. Baldwin, Col. Stark's regiment, in the year 1775. On the 17th of June, being invited to join the reinforcement going on to Bunker Hill, I cheerfully went on, and after standing the severe fire of the enemy until ordered to retreat. Then making the best of my way out, escaped over the neck safely. When hearing that Capt. Baldwin was left behind, and hearing that he was wounded, and that he would fall into the hands of a cruel and barbarous enemy, a motion was made for returning back to find him if possible. Your petitioner with several others returned, being zealously affected toward such a gallant and brave officer (notwithstanding the severity of the enemy's fire across the Charlestown Neck), and in my search, had the misfortune by a shot from the enemy to lose my left hand, it being shot so far off that it had only a little skin and a few tendons left. In this situation I returned to Plowed Hill, where a surgeon cut the tendons and remaining skin entirely off. We then had the misfortune not only of losing one member of my body, but also of having our worthy Capt. Baldwin mortally wounded. Being then conducted to Medford, I was put under the care of Dr. Williams, whose certificate will show. Being fatherless, my honored mother came to visit me and attended upon me about three weeks, and after about seven weeks I was committed to the care of Dr. Kittredge. I tarried there about two weeks, and from there went home to my brother. From which time I have had no allowance from the state, neither for attendance or other things. Finding myself incapable of performing the business of a farmer to which I had been brought up, as soon as I was able, I attended a school a while at Hampstead, then again

Tenth company, 65 men. Capt., Joshua Abbott, Concord; Lieut., Samuel Atkinson, Boscawen; 2d Lieut., Abial Chandler, Concord. This company had 23 men in it from Concord. The balance were from Boscawen, Salisbury and vicinity. William Mitchell of East Concord, was killed; Elias Rano of Salisbury, was wounded in his leg; James Robinson and Reuben Kemp were both prisoners in Boston, and were reported dead; Daniel McGrath was reported dead in Boston. In the returns, Charles Rice of Surry and James Winn of Richmond, were reported as wounded, and attached to Stark's regiment. The same may be said of Jacob Elliott, Andrew Aiken, and Wm. Smart; they all were reported to have been wounded at Bunker Hill; we are not able to assign them to any particular company. We thus have been able to give more than three fourths of the whole number of all the killed and wounded in that engagement with considerable accuracy. Stark's regiment was unquestionably the largest in numbers that was engaged on the American side. Captain Dearborn said in his report of 1818, that our two New Hampshire regiments marched on to the hill with full numbers. We make the full number of Stark's regiment, including rank and file, 632. Doubtless there were some sick and others left on guard at Medford, and smoe on furlough, for which a deduction may be made. We allow a deduction of 50 men. The numbers engaged in that battle on the British side must have exceeded 3000 men. The number of the Americans must have been nearly 2500, according to Frothingham. Mrs. Hannah Brown lost her husband in Bunker Hill battle, we cannot give the husband's name. There were eight Browns in Stark's regiment.

We claim in behalf of New Hampshire that she furnished nearly half of the men that fought on the American side. Though it may be admitted that those who fought in the entrenchment suffered most.

Poor's regiment was not sent for until after the battle of the 17th. It arrived at Cambridge, June 25. In addition to the numbers already stated, the men of the town of Hollis were found in Col. Prescott's regiment. They numbered 59, and were commanded by Captain Reuben Dow, who was wounded in his leg or ankle, and permanently lamed. Judge Worcester of Nashua has furnished a good, reliable record of his revolutionary fathers and their achievements. We are glad to know he is about to give to the public a history of his native town. Judge Worcester gives the loss in Capt. Dow's

---

returned to Hopkinton, the town for which I enlisted. There having the benefit of the pastor and the people I acquired so much instruction, so that in 1777 I was enabled to teach a small school, by means of which and the help of my kind mother I continued along, until at length the great arbiter of life and death called her to the world of spirits. And now being destitute of father and mother, and one hand, I should take it as a favor to have a claim with many others upon the public rewards. As in duty bound your petitioner will ever pray.
    MOSES TRUSSELL.
Hopkinton, Feb. 10, 1781.

STATE OF NEW HAMPSHIRE.
This certifies that Moses Trussell served as a private in Col. Stark's regiment in the year 1775, and that he has produced sufficient evidence that while in the service of the United States he lost his left arm by a wound received in it, and that we judge him to be entitled to a pension of twenty shillings per month, commencing on the 31st of July, 1786.
 JOSEPH GILMAN, } Committee.
 SAMUEL TENNEY, }
Exeter, Oct. 31, 1786.

      March 21, 1786.
This certifies that there appears to be due to Moses Trussell, an invalid, the sum of one hundred and fifteen pounds in full, for half pay from January 1st, 1776, to July 31st, 1785.
$115.00 JOSEPH PEARSON,
add 24.00 Register of Invalid Pensions.

$139.00 in the whole — 139 pounds half pay.

Reuben Trussell was wounded at Bennington, Col. Stickney's regiment, Stark's Brigade. Received as half pay 30 pounds, on account of his wound. He was from Hopkinton. We suppose him a brother of Moses Trussell.

company as follows, viz: 6 killed—Nathan Blood, Thomas Wheat, Isaac Hobart, Peter Poor, Jacob Boynton, Phineas Nevins; 5 wounded—Capt. Reuben Dow, Francis Powers, Wm. Wood, Eph. Blood, Thomas Pratt.

In Capt. Joseph Mann's company, private R. Ebenezer Youngman, killed; Thomas Colburn, killed; 4 in this company from Hollis. In Capt. Sawyer's company, of Haverhill, Col. Frye's regiment, 4 men from Plaistow, N. H. Of these, Simeon Pike was killed; his brother, James Pike, was wounded.

In this battle, Stark's regiment was opposed to the British 23d regiment, well known as the Royal Welsh Fusileers Recently, on the 12th of July, A. D. 1849, the late Prince Albert presented to this regiment a new stand of colors, and made an interesting speech on that occasion. We present a short extract from it:

"In the American war, the Fusileers were engaged in the first unhappy collision, which took place at Lexington. It also fought at Bunker Hill and at Brandywine. At Bunker Hill, its loss was so great, that it was said only one officer remained to tell the story. In 1781, they fought at Guilford Court House. Prince Albert added, this was one of the hardest and best contested fields in the American war."

American historians support the above facts. The British troops landed on the Charlestown beach, and marched up the hill in three separate columns. The Fusileers formed on the British right, in front of Stark's regiment, which was stationed on the extreme left of the American forces. The late Capt. David Flanders, who was a private in Capt. Joshua Abbott's company, stated to the writer, that his company was located down on the Mystic beach, wholly unprotected by any defence in their front. That the column of the Fusileers did not deploy until they passed Abbott's company, therefore, they were outflanked by us, hence we had a good chance to pick off their officers. This chance we improved, as we could distinguish the officers by observing the swords in their hands, and that they had occasion to use them in urging their own men into the fight.

We recapitulate the whole number of the New Hampshire men engaged in Bunker Hill battle, and their loss, as follows, viz:

Col. John Stark's regiment, rank and file, 632 men; deduct for the sick and those on guard, &c., 50 men; balance of men engaged, 582. Col. James Reed's regiment, deducting sick, &c., as returned June 14, 488 men; Capt. Reuben Dow's company of Hollis, men in Col. Prescott's Mass. regiment, 59; Capt. Mann's Hollis men, Prescott's regiment, 4; in Capt. Sawyer's company, Frye's regiment, Plaistow men, 4; whole number in battle, 1137; whole number killed as returned by Stark, 45; wounded, 15; whole number killed as returned by Reed, 5; wounded, 27; whole number killed as returned by Capt. Dow, 8; wounded, 5; whole number killed as returned by Plaistow men, 1; wounded, 1. Whole number of killed and wounded, 107.

THE HOME OF LADY WENTWORTH.

BY FRED MYRON COLBY.

I was at Portsmouth, that lovely old city by the sea, which has quite as much of the antique and the romantic about it as any spot in America, St. Augustine and Quebec not excepted. Several days had been spent in looking about the streets and wharves, visiting the grand mansions of the ancient aristocracy, the quaint churches, and the graveyards, where under escutchioned monuments the great men and beautiful women of colonial days lie quietly sleeping.

One beautiful June morning, when the sun flashed brilliantly on street and highway and river wave, and the air was fragrant with the breath of lilacs and apple blossoms, I took my way on foot along the Little Harbor road, my objective point being the old homestead of Gov. Wentworth, celebrated in prose as the home of New Hampshire's vice royalty for twenty years, and quite as much more in poetry as the home of the beautiful Lady Wentworth, whose romantic marriage our Longfellow has celebrated in his exquisite verse. The distance is only about two miles from the centre of Portsmouth, and the road is one of the most picturesque in New England, leading along delightful parks, elegant farm-houses, and well-cultivated fields, through romantic glens and vales, and over beautifully rounded hills, from which charming views are obtained of the adjacent city, the silvery Piscatasqua, and the broad open sea beyond.

It was with a singular emotion that I approached the mansion. Certain poetical emotions there are which have entered into our imagination in our youth, so as to take firm possession of us and affect us like reality; and when these phantoms suddenly evoked by the localities where we have seen them in our dreams start up from the depths of memory, a distinct echo, so to speak, of our youth and its ideal loves thrills through all our being. For a time we move in an atmosphere of enchantment, of romance, in which vague and shadowy figures of "ye ancient day" throng about one. More than once that morning I saw the glittering coach drawn by six spanking bays, flashing along the very highway I was traversing, on its panels shining the lion statant, the armorial device of the Wentworths since Sir Reginald buckled on his armor and went forth with the conqueror to win estates in England, and within the carriage the portly figure of the old governor, who has been dead under the sod for over a hundred years. I cannot tell of all I saw.

I was greeted at last by a huge rambling building of nondescript architecture, brown, decayed in some places, yet a noble pile withal.

"Baronial and colonial in its style;
Gables and dormer windows everywhere,
And stacks of chimneys rising high in air."

The site of the grand mansion is a picturesque one, sequestered in a lovely little nook, overlooking the broad bay of the Piscatasqua, with the sea waves rippling at your feet, and the hazy Isles of Shoals, the home of one of our sweetest singers, a faint line on the horizon. It is built close upon the water, and the luxuriant lawn in the rear needs a strong sea wall to protect it from tidal encroachments. Vast hedges of lilacs all in bloom, bordered the grounds and even swept up around one end of the old mansion with which they seemed to hold sweet communion. The broad open court was covered with green grass that rippled luxuriantly in the breeze and shook the golden chalices of the buttercups that opened in the sunshine. The shingled roof was shadowed by noble trees, some of which must have looked in their infancy upon the pomps and pageants of the vice regal proprietor.

Despite its air of grandeur the house is an architectural freak. It is seldom that one will find so large a house that is as irregular and straggling as this one is. The rambling old pile looks as if it had been put together at different periods, and each portion the unhappy afterthought of the architect who designed it. It is simply an extension of wing upon wing, and this whimsical arrangement is followed up in the interior. The chambers are curiously connected by unlooked-for steps and capricious little passages that remind one of those mysterious ones in the old castles, celebrated by the writers of the Anne Radcliffe school. Before we enter the building, however, let us glance for a moment at its founder, Gov. Benning Wentworth.

Few names hold more exalted rank in the annals of the old thirteen colonies than that of Wentworth. The progenitor of our colonial family was William, a cousin of the ill-fated Chancellor of Charles the First, who arrived in New Hampshire as early as 1650. Benning Wentworth was a great grandson of William. His father was John Wentworth, who was Lieutenant-Governor of New Hampshire from 1717 till 1730. The son graduated at Harvard, and afterwards was associated with his father and uncle in the mercantile business at Portsmouth. He several times represented the town in the Provincial Assembly, was appointed a king's councillor in 1734, and finally, in 1741, became the royal governor of the province. His life was long, active, and distinguished, and during his career New Hampshire advanced rapidly in wealth and prosperity, though not so fast as the governor did. He laid heavy tribute on the province, and exacted heavy fees for grants of land. He had the right perhaps. That he was a right brave and distinguised looking cavalier, and well fitted to lead society at a provincial court, his portrait at Wentworth Hall abundantly shows. It represents him dressed in the heighth of fashion, with a long flaxen peruke flowing in profuse curls to his shoulders. He has a handsome, dignified face, the lips wearing an engaging smile, and the air generally of face and figure of one who is "lord of the manor." Indeed there was everything in the career of the worthy governor to give him what in Europe used to be called the "bel air." Fortune had taken him by the hand from the very cradle, and some beneficent fairy, throughout all his life, seemed to have smoothed away all thorns in his path and scattered flowers before him. He died at the age of seventy-four, having lived as fortunate and splendid a life as any gentleman of his time in the new world.

It was in 1749 that he commenced to build this mansion, and it was completed the next year. He had been fascinated by the beauty of the place, and the magnificent structure which rose at his command was worthy of its situation. Where he obtained his plan no one knows, but perhaps the irregularity of the structure was compensated by the grandeur and sumptuousness of its adornments. Everything about the mansion was on a grand scale. The stables held thirty horses in time of peace. The lofty gateways were like the entrance to a castle. The offices and outhouses might have done credit to a Kenilworth or a Middleham. As it now stands, girt by its ancestral trees, looking out upon the sea, the house seems a patrician of the old regime, withdrawing itself instinctively from contact with its upstart neighbors. Having an existence of four generations and more, a stately, dignified, hospitable home before Washington had reached manhood, the Wentworth house may claim the respect due to a hale, hearty old age as well as that due to greatness.

The interior of the house is as worthy of inspection as the outside premises. The broad generous hall with its staircase railed in with the curiously wrought balusters, which the taste of the time required to be different in form and design, is suggestive of an old baronial castle. As I passed through it I was for a moment overcome with a halo of distinguished associations. The same floor had been pressed by the feet of brave soldiers, scholars, and grave dignitaries of state. Few houses in America have had as many illustrious visitors. Rooms under its roof have been occupied by Governor Shirley of New York, Lord London, commander in chief of the British forces in America, Sir Charles Knolles, Admiral Boscawen, George Whitefield, and other worthies of that period. Stately merrymakings have been celebrated in its old halls. The wide doors of the grandly carved vestibule have been flung open more than once upon festival times. Over this spacious staircase many a time half a dozen noble dames walked abreast, with their embroidered trains. Gay belles with stiff brocades, and hair three-stories high, and young gallants, with powdered wigs and the brave court costume of the Second and Third George's reign—the beauty, the wealth, the aristocracy of Portsmouth, have danced stately figures on the oaken floors. All this was long ago, but as you gaze on the high, dadoed walls, the solid floors, the carving, the staircase, it is easy to imagine it all. You can almost hear the rustle of the sweeping trains, and the patter of high heeled shoes, with a flutter of your imagination.

The first door on the right hand of the hall opens into the grand parlor of the old governor, which still retains all of its former magnificence. The paper on the walls is the same that was put on at the time the mansion was erected, and the carpet on the floor was put there by Lady Wentworth more than eighty years ago. The four windows draped by those blue woolen damask curtains with silken fringes, command a long stretch of out of door beauties in striking contrast to the antiquarian fireplace with tiled jams, brass andirons and fender, and the ancient stone hearth. Several portraits, those of Hancock and Washington, and Judge William Cushing, whom Washington wanted to be Chief Justice of the United States, among the number, adorn the walls, and there are several interesting relics of later families about the apartment.

In this room, surrounded by the wondering invited guests of the governor, was consummated the marriage ceremony which Longfellow has celebrated in his "Tales of a Wayside Inn," between Wentworth and his chambermaid. It was something of a change for Martha Hilton. She was a girl of matchless beauty, but very poor. When young she had scandalized her neighbors by glimpses of bare ankles and white shoulders as she promenaded the streets in scant costume. A puritanic dame one time remonstrated with the maiden in rather severe terms for exhibiting so much of her beauty to every passer in the street. But the sleek-limbed Martha answered not abashed, "never mind how I look; I yet shall ride in my own chariot, ma'am." It was a true prophecy. After a lapse of years, attracted by her grace, her beauty, her wit and good sense, Benning Wentworth offered her his hand. Of course she accepted it—what woman would have not? and they were married on the governor's sixtieth birthday, by Rev. Arthur Brown.

From the parlor the visitor passes into a large, roomy apartment, known as the Council Chamber. It was formerly the state apartment, and was truly magnificent, enough so, even for a vice regal Wentworth. The ceilings are high, and the wainscots, panels, and mouldings are enriched with carvings. The closely-jointed, smooth, white floor, despite a century's wear, looks as if laid but yesterday. The original fireplace is there, before which the royal governor and his friends discussed the tangled questions pertaining to the sway of his growing province. The room is finished in the best style of the last century. The ornamentation of the huge mantel was carved with knife and chisel, at which the artist worked constantly for a whole long year.

Around the Council Room are some grand old portraits, thirteen in all. They are all in handsome gilt frames, and some of them have rare histories if they could be told. A copy of one of

Vandyke's, representing Lord Strafford dictating to his secretary on the night before his execution, is quite prominent, as is also a portrait of Queen Christina of Sweden. The others are portraits of the governor's ancestors and relatives, among which is that of the beautiful Dorothy Quincey. This last is by Copley, and represents the colonial belle when she was about twenty years old. She wears, I think, a blue silk dress, cut in the Maria Stuart fashion, and fitting closely the queenly figure. The face is fair, with a pair of laughing blue eyes and a lovely mouth, framed in a mass of hair as golden as any of the Venetian beauties whom Titian has celebrated, and resting upon a neck as white and graceful as a swan's. Dorothy was the daughter of Judge Edward Quincey of Braintree, and was a niece of Gov. Wentworth. After having many suitors, Aaron Burr being one of them, the pretty and vivacious coquette married the princely merchant and distinguished patriot, John Hancock.

At the entrance of the Council Chamber are seen the racks for the twelve guns, carried when occasion required by the governor's guards. In the Billiard Room, which adjoins this apartment, still remains the ancient spinet, now time-worn and voiceless, but whose keys have many a time been touched by the jeweled white fingers of aristocratic belles. Washington listened to its music once when he visited here in 1790, the guest of the hospitable Colonel Wentworth. Here, too, is seen in one corner, the old buffet which in the olden time has held many a full and empty punch bowl. Opening out of the larger apartment are little side rooms where illustrious guests, General London, Admiral Boscawen, Lord Pepperell and many others, have played at cards and other games until the "wee sma' hours." About the whole hall there is a choice venerableness which the antiquarian can fully appreciate.

On the left hand of the great hall, stretches away, room after room which are in daily use by the household. Through the courtesy of the proprietor, I was permitted to visit the kitchen, dining, and sitting-room, and view the ancient commissariat of the governor, which was made on an extensive scale. The view from the west windows of the dining-room is as fine as any from the house, combining both land and ocean scenery. The old governor, good liver as he was, never was troubled with dyspepsia. The reason is evident, viz: good digestion, superinduced by the delightful prospect visible from his table.

In the second story a stranger would be very liable to get lost. The winding passages and numerous rooms are perplexing. The old house contained fifty-two rooms, formerly, every one of them wainscoted, but some of them have been given over entirely to rats. The State Chamber is immediately above the parlor, and is an elegant and luxurious apartment. On one side, the windows look down into the garden with its old box-bordered walks and its blossoming beauties of leaf and flower. Fruit trees were blushing scarlet and purple with flowers, the Pyrus Japonica shamed the sunlight with its gorgeous crimson bloom, and the odors rose from the white starred Spiraea and Deutzia gracilis. It was very natural that the lines should suggest themselves.

"A brave old house, a garden full of bees,
Large drooping poppies and green hollyhocks,
With butterflies for crowns, trapeonies,
And pinks and goldilocks."

Many and many a time this bed chamber wooed the slumbers of the sybarite Benning Wentworth, and here on a dull Sunday, Oct. 14th, 1770, the great man breathed his last in the arms of his faithful wife. The governor rewarded her care and faithfulness by bequeathing her his entire estate. The great house was not long without a master, however. Lady Wentworth after living single about a year, fell into the matrimonial traces again, but without changing her name. She outlived her second husband several years, and at her death, in 1804, left the old mansion to her daughter Martha, whom she had by Colonel Michael Wentworth. She was buried beside her first husband in the churchyard of St. John's, in Portsmouth.

The mansion at Little Harbor continued to be occupied by the second Martha Wentworth, who was also a Lady, her husband being Sir John Wentworth, until 1816, when they went to England, from whence they never returned. Charles Cushing, Esq., not distantly related to Hon. Caleb Cushing, purchased the place in 1817, and his widow, the daughter of Senator Jacob Sheafe, long resided there. The mansion and surrounding estate is now the property of Mr. Mathew B. Israel, whose wife has Sheafe, Cushing, and Wentworth blood flowing in one rich stream in her aristocratic veins.

THE COMING OF JUNE.

BY HOPE HUNTINGTON.

When the gladsome earth discloses
  All her fragrant, queenly roses,
And the thrush and swallow warble all in tune,
  And the wood and meadow smiling,
  Call their subjects all beguiling,
Then from up the shining orient comes the June.

  Lovelier than the springtime maiden,
  And with richer treasures laden ;
Come ! with deeper beauty on thy glowing mien !
  We would hear thy low, sweet singing,
  Over hill and valley ringing.
Come ! with sky-blue eyes, and breath of eglantine !

  Foam and wave, oh em'rald grasses,
  Make a pathway when she passes ;
Sing, oh lark, a merry welcome loud and clear !
  And with joy we'll end the measure,
  With a glad sweet cry of pleasure,
Shouting, "June, of months the fairest, June is here !"

  "Perfect bloom of rare completeness,
  Rich in fresh, unconscious sweetness,
Gladly would we yield her Earth's most precious boon !
  Yet the best that we could render,
  Would be lost amid the splendor,
And the ever-radiant glory of the June !"

MANNERS AND CUSTOMS IN HOPKINTON—No. 4.

BY C. C. LORD.

MILITARY.

In a previous article, we have given a sketch of military affairs in this town, viewing the subject in its more abstract relations. It is now our purpose to mention the local military element as an integral part of our earlier social system. In the colonial days of New Hampshire, the militia was in almost constant demand in anticipation of possible conflicts with the Indians. The first garrisons were manned by soldiers who were the natural protectors of the local settlement. The attendance of the military at public gatherings was often required. Arms bristled in the air, when, in 1757, the first ordination of a minister took place in Hopkinton. It is said that the present prevailing custom of seating the male members of religious congregations in the heads of pews arose from the primitive habit of locating the soldiery in a similar manner. It must be remembered, however, that, in the earlier times in this vicinity, every able-bodied man was considered in a general sense a person of military precautions, if not one of actual martial occupation.

The existence of an organized soldiery implies the practice of military evolution, or drill. A "training-field," for the accommodation of military practice, was selected very early in this town. The spot was on the top of Putney's Hill, a few rods distant from Putney's Fort. The determination of American Independence incurred a re-establishment of a military system. Under the new political regime, the law of 1792, with some modifications, provided for all the accidental, local military facts, it is necessary, in this connection, to mention, till the year 1851. This ancient law provided for practice at arms at least three times each year, by all persons liable to military duties. In compliance with legal provisions, for many years, the soldiery of Hopkinton were accustomed to practice tactics once in May and once in September, the days selected being known respectively as spring and fall training days, upon which company drill alone was practiced. A regimental muster occurred annually in the month of September, the date of the occasion being determined by the official authority of the regiment; the place of assembling was in some one of the towns represented in the command, the practice of alternating locations being in vogue.*

A soldier of the regular infantry was required to appear at training or muster, armed with a gun and bayonet of his own purchase, as well as equipped with a knapsack, canteen, cartridge-box and belt, priming-wire and brush, and two extra flints. In later years of the old military service, a member of an "independent" or uniformed company was furnished a gun by the state. Commissioned officers were required to procure their own arms. At company trainings, the three commissioned officers —captain, lieutenant and ensign, or 2d lieutenant—were charged with the duty of inspecting arms and equipments, imposing corresponding fines if any were found deficient in number or quality; at musters a similar duty devolved upon the regimental inspecting officer. The inspection finished, the company or regiment was duly exercised in military evolutions and in the manual of arms.

Public military parade was usually conducted with a decorum appropriate

---

*The plains land south of Contoocook village, the interval below Tyler's bridge, on the south side of the river, and the spot occupied by the new graveyard, east of the lower village, have been used as muster fields in this town.

to the imperative character of soldierly discipline. In some instances, the excellence in tactics was eminently superior. The best skill depended upon the executive character of the commanders. The system of general military practice sometimes developed officers that could direct a company through a variety of evolutions without speaking a word, the motion of the sword designating the order of movement. Col. William Colby, of this town, was one thus skilled. The use of gunpowder was not legally exacted upon the instance of parade, though powder was sometimes used by popular agreement, or custom. The sham-fight, a favorite exercise of muster day, was an occasion of much blank firing, when the whole regiment—cavalry, artillery, infantry and riflemen—divided in the semblance of two hostile bands, struggled in a grand melee for the honors of a *quasi* victory.

The legitimate programme of a sham fight implied the attempt of a contending force to surround and capture another, or to display its own ranks so skillfully as to prevent a surprisal, while all the time a great deploy of tumultuous gunnery was indulged. Such contests were always exciting and liable at any time to end in a riotous demonstration of local pride and jealousy. Local feuds engendered in sham fights were often perennial in duration, developing at times into such a fever of animosity that the officers of the regiment were impelled to make prudence the better part of valor and dispense with the fight altogether, lest it should become too dangerously real in character.*

---

*The dangerous heat of military enthusiasm was once emphatically illustrated by the boys of this town. Two rival companies of amateur militia—respectively from the upper and lower villages—met on the highway, in what is now the Gage district, and contended so desperately that the populace became alarmed and caused the arrest of the combat. The commanders of these companies were Benjamin Jewell, of the upper, and Hamilton E. Perkins, of the lower village. There was also about this time a third company of boys in the Blackwater district; it was commanded by Samuel B. Straw.

The time appropriated to a company training was generally half of a day. A general muster of the regiment occupied a whole day. No legal provision was made for the conveyance of soldiers to the place of rendevouz, and individuals often straggled along on the way to the training or muster field, their gay uniforms making them the observed of all observers. Since the place of the regimental muster alternated among the different towns represented in the command, the distance required to reach it often demanded a start of many hours in advance. The spot reached, both the tents of the regiment, and private or tavern accommodations were often required to lodge the troops. Experiences akin to the actual life of war were often realized in this military housing. Muster service was at best a hard one, and many a youth who looked forward with fond anticipation to the time when he, too, should be a happy soldier, lived to count the years that must pass away so slowly before he should be exempt from a duty that had become as irksome as it had once seemed fascinating. The duties of a common soldier of militia were performed without pay,* though he received his dinner, or its equivalent, on muster days. At first, the town provided a dinner of bread and beef for the regiment at muster; later, an equivalent of thirty-one cents was allowed; last, fifty cents were appropriated as a means of a soldier's refreshment. In later times, also, the members of uniformed companies received each a compensation of $1.50 a year, paid them at muster, and immediately after satisfactory inspection, by the selectmen. The sum paid was reckoned as the equivalent of fifty cents for each of two attendances at company training and one at muster.

Music is always regarded as an aid to the metrical execution of military drill. For the support of martial music,

---

*Commissioned officers of militia received no salary, but received such other compensation as was given to privates of the same command. They could be exempted from military duty, however, after an official service of a term of years.

the state provided each company with a fife, a snare drum and a base. drum.* If companies desired other instruments of music, they were allowed to provide, at their own expense, as many as they wished. The old military practices developed a good use in stimulating the musical talents of the young. Instrumental music was cultivated everywhere, and military bands frequently established. There was in Hopkinton, at the close of the old military system, a band of no mean ability, being composed of players upon clarionets, bugles, trombones, and other instruments. Subsequently to 1851, the interest in martial music rapidly declined to complete extinction. It revived again, however, in 1859, when the Hopkinton Cornet Band was organized, under the leadership of Melvin Colby. This organization expired in 1873, but in 1877 a new one was formed under the old name, and under the leadership of John F. Gage. The Cootoocook Cornet Band was organized in 1861, under the leadership of W. H. Hardy; re-organized in 1875, under the leadership of C. T. Webber. Amos H. Currier is the present leader.

A noted martial musician of this town was Mr. Jonah Campbell, a famous drummer, who died on the 6th of May of the present year, at the advanced age of 83 years. Mr. George Choat, a celebrated fifer, is still living at an advanced age.

MEDICAL.

Although this department of our present subject hardly comes within the domain of popular themes, yet the practice of the curative art has been modified so much since the beginning of civilized history in this town that some particulars cannot fail to interest the reader. It must be understood, too, that the curative art was very largely popular in the first years of this local community. A pioneer society in New England, a century ago, was forced to maintain existence in spite of many professional privations. In such a condition, people are accustomed to draw constantly upon such special resources as their domestic circumstances afford. A society so situated could not fail to produce local characters famed for their skill in emergencies. Among such characters, females would enjoy a generally allotted prominence in the department of remedial knowledge. However, experienced men and matrons in primitive circles would convey abundant traditions of the medical value of sundry herbs, roots, barks, and other domestic resources, in the instance of the various ills that afflict the human body. Confidence inspired from such a source annually replenished the earlier homes of this vicinity with a profusion of herbal packages and bundles, provided against the dreaded prospective wants of the sickened individual or household. Rummaging through this domestic *materia medica*, one could find specific reliefs for fevers, chills, aches, eruptions, etc., the efficacy of which was as firmly reputed as any specific in the officinal list of the professional corps today. The curative products of the concocting skill of some local or itinerant* domestic practitioner of extraordinary repute were often regarded as indispensable household equipments. Most likely some famous plaster or salve, or some renowned liniment, was included in the list of special reliances.

The professional physician of the earlier times was practically beholden, in a large degree, to his knowledge of the reputation of purely domestic remedies. The first physicians in this vicinity were often educated solely under the tutorship of reputable practitioners in their respective localities, and their practice was somewhat of an eclectic character. Yet they were relatively skillful, as a

---

*The first base drum used was proportionately longer in form than the present one, was slung horizontally from the neck, and played with two drum-sticks, one in each hand.

*An itinerant doctor of repute in this town was Dr. ——— Flagg, who carried a stock of medicines and travelled on foot. He seems to have been esteemed by many adults, but greatly feared by the children, who regarded him as a monster having mysterious and dreadful uses for children, especially if they had red hair.

body, in their day and generation, while one of them enjoyed extra repute. Laboring in an incipient community, much often depended on the personal self-possession of the primative physician. When a person is often called upon to represent the only individual reliance of a dependent circle, he naturally becomes an object of a confidence that rises to the degree of superstition. A resolute and prudent physician, the object of such intense regard, can use his position in promoting effects lying on the border land of mystery.*

Dr. Ebenezer Lerned, who became a resident of this town as early as 1793, was the first thoroughly educated physician practicing in Hopkinton. It will be interesting to note some of the leading points in the practice of the regular faculty at this period of our history. Practically speaking, the intelligent representatives of all schools of healing, hold one principle in an emphatic degree of prominence. The alternations of vital force between opposite extremes is, in the minds of the best practitioners, favorably related to conditions of bodily health. In general, too, disease is a result of a restriction of vital expression to one pole of the natural circuit. The terms tonic and atonic, action and reaction, elevation and subsidence, express the sum and substance of successful medical theorists from allopathists to pure hygienists. The choice of remedial agencies lies between stimulants and narcotics, tonics and relaxants, nutritives and depletories, action and rest.

The first school of practice known here was the allopathic. Its dominant methods of treatment were much more heroic than those of the same school of the present day. The processes of toning up and letting down were accomplished with a promptness and effectiveness that would at present fail of professional countenance. If a patient were seized with a violent fever or an apolexy, the physician pricked his lance into a vein in the arm and drew therefrom a quantity of blood sufficient in his estimation to produce sanguinary depletion and relaxation, and arrest the progress of the disease. In cases of local inflammations, leeches, to bite and suck out the superfluous blood, were applied to the affected part. If bloodletting were foreborne in any general case, the tonic state was counteracted by the great deobstruent, mercury, or some antimonial or opiate preparation. If an emetic were demanded, ipecac was the principal disgorging reliance. Blistering was also a potent means of diverting internal congestions and inflammations to the surface of the body.

In contemplating the ancient practice of medicine, one is struck with the comparatively exclusive prominence given to depressing agencies.* In fact, bloodletting, mercury, antimony and opium, seem to have been about the only great specifics in the whole list of remedies. Doubtless stimulating effects were more or less sought by alcoholic means, but in the list of tonics were admitted many of the simple substances and preparations familiar to every domestic household. Yet scientific reflection easily apprehends a reason for this state of things. A community of pioneers is of necessity vigorous and elastic in physical constitution. Full of blood and vital positiveness, its principal symptoms of illness would be of an acute character. The medical re-agents applicable to this class of ills being promptly em-

---

*Not to make this fact too historically exclusive, we may mention a comparatively recent case in illustration. A physician of repute in this town was called to a patient suffering a violent, intense pain. The doctor gave the sick man a roll of brimstone in each hand and bade him hold on hard when the paroxysm occurred. The man did as directed and was soon relieved. Two sticks of wood had doubtless been just as efficacious, except that brimstone appealed better to the imagination, a potent agency in the healing art. We have heard of another physician of this town who said he had often administered bread pills with satisfactory results.

*It is an interesting fact that blood-letting was even employed in paralysis, which would seem to demand a tonic rather than a depletory, unless the practitioners were indulging the theory of *similia similibus curatur*, or the disease were the result of an engorged brain.

ployed, the native elasticity of constitution readily restored the system to its normal condition. Consequently, tonics were of less importance in the remedial curriculum. The more composite state of older society, and the attendant mixture of constitutions, was, scientifically speaking, a prominent cause of the ultimate abandonment of the old practice.*

About the year 1820, a violent epidemic, known as the "throat distemper," sadly afflicted the people of this town. Mostly, or wholly, it attacked the children and youth of the locality, seventy-two of whom are said to have died by its stroke. This distemper, contrary to a conception sometimes indulged, was pathologically distinct from diphtheria, though it might have been somewhat similar in its manifestations. The physician treating this malady with the best success was Dr. Michael Tubbs, of Deering, who had nineteen patients in this town and saved them all, but one, whom he pronounced beyond help when called to the bedside. The principal remedy used by Dr. Tubbs was balsam of fir, employing at the same time a cervical bandage made of black sheep's wool saturated with vinegar.

SUPERSTITIOUS.

Superstition is the legitimate offspring of ignorance, which both creates fantastic ideals and magnifies mole-hills into mountains. In all societies where genuine intellectual culture holds but an insignificant sway, the imagination of the marvelously susceptible carries them to the extreme of absurdity in their conceptions of the mysterious. The part that superstition bore in the general history of New England, in the earlier times, is too well known to the reading public to need description here. It was only a natural consequence that the people of this town were, in a measure at least, involved in the general apprehension and mystified conception of occult and distressing influences.

In New England, in the days when Hopkinton was reclaimed from the wilderness, the popular definition of all that was socially occult and dangerous was embraced in the term witchcraft. Subject of Satan, indeed, the witch might be, but the accessory was more feared than the principal. Witchcraft was recognized in this vicinity in at least four forms. There were the occult influence exercised over the beasts of the field, the hidden danger that lurked about the path of the unwary traveller, the specter that haunted the sleeper by night, and the ghost that hung around its favorite stamping ground. Some details of the several forms and methods employed in these several departments of dreaded mystery will be interesting.

The live-stock of the husbandman was beset by witchcraft that either affected the disposition of the animal or the product of its economy. A beast would become ill-tempered or stubborn through the obsession of the witch. Cows, particularly, failed at times to yield their milk, or the lacteal product soured in an incredibly short space of time, or the cream in the churn refused, after prolonged agitation, to come into butter. Instances of this class occured quite frequently, and were of quite recent experience. Only a few years ago, a respectable lady, now living, related to us a case under personal observation, in which the milk of a cow, fresh from the pasture, turned to bonny clapper before it could be conveyed from the animal to the pantry.

The mysterious annoyance of the traveller by day was more likely to directly affect the beast than the driver. Persons in going abroad were sometimes troubled by a sudden refusal of a beast to continue tranquilly on its accustomed way. Balking and witchcraft became to an extent closely related phenomena. A mysterious case in kind occurred within the memory of the pre-

---

*We once conversed with an aged physician of the heroic school, who, speaking of the change in modern practice, said in substance: "During my earlier practice, we had remedies for various diseases, and they were successful; but in later times the old applications failed. There must have been some modification of the constitutions of people."

sent generation. A respectable lady, who died only a few years ago, related that, being on a solitary journey, she was accosted by an old woman who begged for the favor of conveyance. For some reason satisfactory to herself, the person accosted declined to grant the favor, but only to receive the vituperations of the stranger wayfarer, who avowed the refusing party would one day suffer for her stolidness. A while after the berated woman was journeying the same way again, when, being near the spot where she encountered the offended stranger, her horse balked and could not be induced to proceed further, and her journey in that direction was ended. The suggestion of witchcraft naturally came in as an aid to the solution of the problem.

The witchcraft of the midnight hour oppressed the innocent sleeper and made his couch a bed of horrors, wherein hags, specters and hob-goblins subjected him to a variety of tortures, if, by the exertion of mysterious powers, they did not even for the time being transmute him into the form of some beast of burden, drive him abroad under the expanse of heaven, and train him to severe discipline. Persons capable of this kind of obsession were to all appearences more fond of turning the objects of their torture into horses, riding them abroad with presumable gusto. Witches of this class were supposed to have at ordinary times, in some special repository, a bridle reserved for such abominable excursions. This bridle was supposed to be of blue, green, or some other fantastic color. Not far from the residence of the writer there once lived a woman who was reputed to possess a bridle of this kind.

Ghosts and witches are naturally contemporaneous, though, if anything, the former are more inclined to favorite places of resort, from which they seldom stray. Many towns in New England can show the once special haunts of ghostly inhabitants. Hopkinton has its former ghostly stalking place. Upon the northern brow of Putney's Hill, sometimes known as Gould's Hill, is a patch of forest long recognized as the "Lookout." From the reputed presence of ghosts, it received this appellation. Spectral appearances in different forms, manifested both by day and by night, were apprehended in this locality. The writer remembers a respectable man who believed to his dying day that he there saw an apparition in broad daylight. There is living in this town today an old and respectable gentleman who once averred that, passing the Lookout in the evening, returning from his day's work, he saw several balls of spectral fire appear and stand before him, keeping in his advance as he maintained his distressful march home.

There appear to have been but two great witches in this town. They were "Witch Burbank," whose home was in the vicinity of Contoocook village, and "Witch Webber," who lived on the southern part of Beech Hill. Witch Webber seems to have been willing to be recognized as a person of occult gifts, and her exploits also appear to have been more remarkable in reputed character. We judge so since Witch Webber is traditionally claimed to have acknowledged a journey to Lynn, Mass., where the famous Moll Pitcher resided, to attend a mutual convention of weird sisters. Witch Webber's statement of a journey to Lynn was confirmed, in the mind of one man at least, in a singular manner. In sailing through the air on the way to her destination, the witch averred that, in passing a barn on Dimond Hill,* she stubbed her toe on the roof and detached a few shingles by the suddenness of the contact. The owner of the premises, hearing the report of the exploit, mounted a ladder and examined the roof of his barn, finding, in the palpable evidence of a few lost shingles, a fact to himself satisfactory and indubitable that the witche's words were true.

We have discovered but little evidence that incantations for the defeat of witchcraft or the destruction of witches were practiced to any great ex-

---

*Witch Webber was not a geographer, or she would not have taken an air-line route to Lynn by the way of Dimond Hill.

tent in this town. We have heard a story of a man assaulting, axe in hand, an old woman whom he conceived might have obsessed his child, and threatening to destroy her if the annoyance did not cease. The child was relieved by the operation. There is also a story that incantation was once tried on a reputed witch, in consequence of an afflicted person, and the result affected the suspected witch with great and prolonged agony, if it did not destroy her. A successful trick was once played on Witch Burbank. Two young men, apprentices of David Young, cabinet maker, joiner, etc., were disbelievers in witchcraft. Seeing Witch Burbank passing the shop one day, one of the young men, remembering that silence must be maintained during incantation, motioned his companion to hand him a brad-awl, which he took and stuck in the track of the witch. She had passed but a few rods and sat down when the awl was applied to the earth. Pretty soon Mrs. Young, a person well remembered for her eccentricities, entered the shop in great concern, asking the young men what they had done to Witch Burbank to make her stop; for she feared the witch would obsess them all. The apprentices denied any action on their part, but, on Mrs. Young's return to the house, the awl was withdrawn from the earth, and Witch Burbank continued on her way. We presume the attitude of the young men towards witchcraft was afterwards somewhat modified.

We said at the beginning that superstition is the offspring of ignorance. We may add that the child is capable of great filial attachment. With the progress of popular intelligence many follies disappear. That there are occult phenomena constantly attendant upon human life cannot be denied. True knowledge, however, allows no absurd superstition, though it may entertain a rational mystery, which, though it transcends the intelligence, does not contradict it. Some of the affirmed facts of ancient marvel are too puerile for explanation. Others are subjects of frequent present elucidation by teachers of different branches of science.* There are still others that imply problems not yet solved in any uniform conception of the public mind, and which are open to such investigation as inquiring minds are able to bring to bear upon them.

---

*It is well known to the scientific world that stagnate water, when drunk by cows, will convey microscopic spores of infusorial life into the general circulation of the animal and, in the milk, cause a viscous and frothy condition, of mysterious origin to the uninformed. It is another scientifically apparent fact that dyspepsia, or indigestion, will induce a great variety of spectral illusions in the minds of sleeping persons, especially if they happen to be of active cerebral, and nervous temperaments. Alcoholic fermentation in cream, also, thwarts the manufacture of butter.

TOWN HISTORIES.

No state in the Union is richer than our own in the materials for history; yet the history of New Hampshire remains to be written. Belknap and Barstow blazed the pathway along the course of the early years; Bouton collected and arranged a great mass of information; Sanborn has contributed valuable suggestions; but the man who is to write a comprehensive history of New Hampshire, which shall tell the story of her growth and achievements, and her full contribution to the national life and honor, from the landing of the fishermen at Dover Point down through the first completed century of American Independence, has yet to make himself known. Let us hope that he may come forward ere many years have gone, and apply himself to the work with that patient devotion, loyal zeal, tireless energy and discriminating judgment which shall ensure its thorough and satisfactory completion.

In the meantime it is all-important that the materials themselves, as far as possible, be gathered and preserved, as the years go by. To this end, the compilation of town histories is beyond question the most effectual instrumentality; and yet to gather, arrange and embellish the materials requisite to a respectable history of one of our New Hampshire towns, or rather to properly select and arrange, from the mass of attainable facts, those of greatest interest and worth, is a task of no small magnitude, and one, which, it appears, few men have as yet assumed. Although several town histories have recently been produced in the state, and others are now in course of preparation, the entire number published thus far is quite small in proportion to the whole number of towns. In fact, not more than one in ten of all our New Hampshire towns have anything like a complete and substantial written history which has been given to the public in printed form.

A brief investigation, as thoroughly made as circumstances permit, shows that histories of the following towns have been published—mostly in well bound octavo volumes—the name of the author or compiler, date of publication, and number of pages, being also given:

Acworth—J. L. Merrill, 1869; 306 pp.

Barnstead—Jeremiah P. Jewett and R. B. Caverly, 1875; 463 pp.

Bedford—Compiled by Committee, 1851; 364 pp.

Boscawen and Webster—Chas. Carleton Coffin, 1878; 666 pp.

Charlestown—Henry H. Sanderson, 1876, 726 pp.

Chester—Benjamin Chase, 1869, 702 pp.

Concord—Nathaniel Bouton, 1856; 786 pp.

Croydon—Edmund Wheeler, 1867; 173 pp.

Dublin—Levi W. Leonard, 1853; 433 pp.

Dunbarton—Caleb Stark, 1860; 272 pp.

Gilmanton—Daniel Lancaster, 1845; 304 pp. 12 mo.

Londonderry—Edward L. Parker, 1851; 359 pp. 12 mo.

Manchester—Chandler E. Potter, 1856; 760 pp. John B. Clarke, 1875; 463 pp.

Mason—John B. Hill, 1858; 324 pp.

New Boston—Elliott C. Cogswell, 1864; 469 pp.

New Ipswich—Compiled by Committee, 1852; 488 pp.

Peterborough—Albert Smith, 1876; 735 pp.

Raymond—Joseph Fullonton, 1875; 408 pp.

Rindge—Ezra S. Stearns, 1875; 788 pp.

Temple—Henry Ames Blood, 1860; 352 pp.

Troy—A. M. Caverly, 1850; 299 pp. 12 mo.

Warren—William Little, 1870; 592 pp.

Earlier histories of some of these towns had been published, but the same were substantially embraced in, and superceded by, the later publications. Aside from these, there have also been publications embodying local history in the state, worthy of mention in this connection. "The Annals of Portsmouth," by Nathaniel Adams, 1825, 400 pp., embraces much of the early history of that old town; while the "Rambles About Portsmouth," by Charles W. Brewster, published in two series, in 1859 and 1869, have a considerable proportion of matter of much historical value. A history of "Old Dunstable," by Charles J. Fox, published in 1846, 278 pp., may also be classed with the New Hampshire town histories, as the larger portion of Dunstable lay within the limits of this state, including what is now Litchfield, Hudson, Nashua and Hollis, and portions of Amherst, Merrimack, Milford, Brookline, Pelham and Londonderry.

Besides these, quite a number of historical sketches of towns have been published, some of them of considerable extent. One of Candia, by F. B. Eaton, published in 1852 contains 152 pages. One of Antrim the same year, by John M. Whiton, has 95 pages. There are two old sketches of Amherst, by John Farmer, the last published in 1837 and containing 52 pages; a sketch of Hillsborough by Charles J. Smith, 1841, 72 pages; "Annals of Keene," by Salma Hale, 1826, 69 pages; a brief sketch of Epsom, by Rev. Jonathan Curtis, published in 1823, and one of Andover, by Jacob B. Moore in 1822.

There have also been published, several pamplets, embracing the proceedings at Centennial celebrations in different towns, including historical addresses and other matter of real historical value. Among these towns are Orford, Lebanon, Lancaster, Jaffrey, Wilton, Hampton, and perhaps others. Another work, worthy of mention in this connection is a 12mo volume of 240 pages, by Rev. Grant Powers, published at Haverhill, in 1841, entitled "Historical Sketches of the Discovery, Settlement and Progress of Events in the Coos Country and Vicinitry."

As will be noticed, several of the town histories mentioned are quite volumninous, involving much labor and research in their preparation, notably those of Concord, Chester, Charlestown, Rindge, Peterboro, Boscawen and Webster and Chandler's history of Manchester. A considerable proportion of the number, also, are illustrated with portraits, and engravings of buildings scenery, &c., that of New Ipswich being the first illustrated town history published.

As was suggested, there are now several town histories in course of preparation, or about to be issued. One of Newport, by Edmund Wheeler, author of the history of Croydon, is already in the hands of the binder. It is a work of five or six hundred pages, and will be illustrated by about thirty fine steel engravings, mostly portraits of prominent citizens or natives of the town. Gen. Walter Harriman, a native of Warner, has prepared an elaborate history of that town, which will make a volume of six hundred pages, and will also be finely illustrated, which is now in the printer's hands. Rev. M. T. Runnalls, of Sanbornton, is engaged upon a history of that town; Col. L. W. Cogswell is preparing a history of Henniker, Rev. Silvanus Hayward one of Gilsum, and D. F. Secomb, Esq., Assistant Assistant Librarian of the State Historical Society, is collecting the material for a history of Amherst. There are other towns in which steps have been taken by the people looking to the publication of their histories, among which are Walpole, Littleton, and Andover. C. C. Lord, of Hopkinton, has also collected material for a history of Hopkinton, much of which has been published in his series of interesting sketches in the GRANITE MONTHLY.

There remain to be mentioned two town histories, recently published, each of which forms a valuable contribution to the historical literature of the State—one, the history of old Nottingham, comprising Nottingham, Northwood, and Deerfield, by Rev. E. C. Cogswell, the historian of New Boston, who has been many years principal of Northwood Academy, and the other of Hollis, by Hon. Samuel T. Worchester, of Nashua, a native of that town. In a notice of the former, Prof. Sanborn, of Hanover, says:

"Town histories, like nouns, are both common, proper, and collective. They are common, because most of the larger towns in the state have made provision for the publication of their local histories. They are proper, because they snatch from

'Decay's effacing fingers,'

valuable records which would, otherwise, be lost. Acts of incorporation, town records, the origin of churches, schools and academies, and the civil and military history of many of our honored fathers, are today so 'tattered and torn,' as to be almost illegible. When the biographies of the first settlers are written, then the town history resembles a noun of multitude or a collective noun. Mr. Cogswell has rescued from oblivion the early history of three towns. The oldest Nottingham was the parent of Deerfield and Northwood. Nottingham was originally ten miles square. It was almost large enough to make three towns of the usual size, six miles square. In early times, the ecclesiastical history of new settlements was often more important than the civil history. The minister was settled by the town. The parsonage, the church, the call, the salary, and the ordination often filled the larger part of the town records. If there was a quarrel, the whole population were involved in it. Sometimes ministers sued their towns for arrears of salary; then the hearers became indifferent or hostile. It was a good day for the churches, when the towns ceased to call and settle ministers. Mr. Cogswell has given a faithful narrative of all the settlements that have occurred in these three towns; and thus has sketched the life and labors of many excellent men. The embellishments of his history are not the least valuable portion of it. He has, at large expense procured pictures of scenery, mountains, lakes, churches, and homes, which give great interest to the narrative. He has, also, given us the faces of many of the men and women who have enacted the history of these three towns. The work deserves the patronage of all the citizens who dwell in them. The labor of preparing it has been long, wearisome and comparatively profitless. It is a valuable contribution to the history of the state and has a special interest for the descendants of those who felled the trees, opened the roads, built the houses, and fought the battles of 'those times that tried men's souls.'"

The History of Hollis, by Judge Worcester, which has just been published by A. Williams & Co., of Boston, is embraced in a handsome octavo volume of 393 pages, embellished by twenty-five engravings, sixteen of which are portraits.

The town of Hollis, which was embraced in the territory of old Dunstable, and was first incorporated as the West Parish of Dunstable, has a history dating back a hundred and fifty years, the first charter of incorporation having been granted in 1739, but a settlement having been made within its limits nearly ten years previous, Capt. Peter Powers being the first settler. Upon the adjustment of the boundary between Massachusetts and New Hampshire, the line was so established as to leave the territory which is now Hollis, in the latter province, and the Massachusetts charter became worthless. A district organization was maintained until 1746, when a charter was obtained of the New Hampshire government, under the name of Hollis, or *Holles*, as it was originally spelled.

From its early settlement and generally continued prosperity, the town had come to be, at the time of the Revolution, among the more important in the state, having a population of 1255 souls, according to a census taken in 1775. It contributed quite a number of soldiers to the service, during the French and Indian wars, and in Col. Joseph Blanchard's regiment, raised in 1755, for the expedition against Crown Point, there were no less than thirty-four men from this town, among whom were Rev. Daniel Emerson (first pastor of Hollis), chaplain of the regiment, Dr. John Hale, Surgeon's Mate, and Jonathan Hobart, Adjutant. Hollis responded nobly to the country's call at the outbreak of the Revolution, sending a full company to Bunker Hill, which performed valiant service in that battle, and throughout the entire war the men of Hollis were largely engaged in fighting for our national independence. It appears in fact that over three hundred different men of Hollis, or one in four out of the entire population of the town, were enlisted, for longer or shorter periods, in the course of the war—a record of patriotism, not surpassed, if even equalled, by that of any other town in the state.

Rich in the material for historical narrative, the town of Hollis is equally fortunate in being favored with the services of one so eminently qualified as Judge Worcester, to collect, arrange, and present the same in the attractive form in which it now appears. Judge Worcester is a native of Hollis, and a descendant of one of its early and prominent families. His grandfather, Capt. Noah Worcester, was commander of the Hollis militia in 1775. His father, Jesse Worcester, was four times enlisted in the service during the Revolution. He reared a family of fifteen children, of whom fourteen became teachers in the public schools. Of the nine sons, five were college graduates, one being the distinguished lexicographer, Joseph E. Worcester. Samuel T. Worcester, graduated at Harvard in 1830, read law with Hon. B. M. Farley of Hollis and at the Cambridge Law School, and settled in the practice of his profession at Norwalk, Ohio, in 1835, where he remained for over thirty years in successful practice, in the meantime, serving as State Senator, District Judge, and Member of Congress. He returned to New Hampshire a few years since, and settled in Nashua, where he has since resided. He has devoted his leisure time for four or five years past to the preparation of this history of his native town, and it is but just to say that the work has been done in a manner which does full credit to his industry and ability, displaying alike extensive research and great facility of expression.

The material, political, military, educational, and ecclesiastical history of the town are all fully and appropriately considered, that covering the Revolutionary period being treated with great care and systematic detail. A prominent feature of the work is that of its biograpical sketches of citizens and natives of the town, who have attained distinction in the various walks of life, or have been prominent in the administration of public affairs. The substitution of these sketches in place of the dry genealogical data occupying so large a portion of many town histories, may justly be regarded as a decided improvement.

It is certainly not too much to say that this history of Hollis, takes rank among the best town histories yet produced. The author, the publishers, and the town whose honorable record it embodies, are all to be congratulated upon its appearance.

GRANITE MONTHLY.

A MAGAZINE OF LITERATURE, HISTORY, AND STATE PROGRESS.

VOL. II.   JULY, 1879.   NO. 10.

THE STATE SENATE OF 1879–80.

There appeared last summer in the GRANITE MONTHLY an article entitled "The Senate and its Presidents," supplemented with a sketch of Hon. David H. Buffum, President of the Senate for that year. It is proper at this time to allude briefly to the Senate of 1879–1880, the first to meet under the amended constitution of the state, providing for biennial sessions, whose regular session has just been brought to a close.

By the provisions of the amended constitution the number of Senators was increased from twelve to twenty-four, thus bringing in, to a greater degree, the popular element and, perhaps, modifying to some extent the conservative character and tendency of the body. It is safe to say, at all events, that, under the new arrangement, our State Senate proves to be more thoroughly a representative body than heretofore, and that, while perhaps yielding nothing of its traditional prerogative as a practical council of review in considering the action of the lower house, it appears far less inclined to confine itself to merely revisory work than was formerly the case. Indeed, during the late legislative session, the Senate manifested a capacity and a disposition to originate legislation almost if not fully equal to that of the House; while in the matter of debate it altogether surpassed the latter body. This fact may be attributed, however, in no small degree, to the presence of one or two active and aggressive members who would have found a more appropriate and congenial field of action in the other branch of the legislature.

It is but fair to add, without reference to the general character of the action taken during its late session, that the Senate of 1879–80 contains several members of marked ability, whose presence and action during the session has contributed largely to attract public attention, and increase the popular interest in the deliberations of the Senatorial body, and from whom the people may reasonably expect to hear again, and in other and even more important capacities in time to come.

The following short sketch of Hon. J. H. Gallinger, President of the Senate, whose portrait appears as a frontispiece in this number of the GRANITE MONTHLY, with brief notices of the individual Senators, will not be without interest. More extended sketches of several of the number, it is hoped, may be given upon future occasions.

PRESIDENT GALLINGER.

HON. JACOB H. GALLINGER, President of the Senate, is one of the rising young men in the Republican party of New Hampshire. Starting out in life a poor boy, he has fought his way up to his present position unaided and alone, overcoming obstacles before which a less ambitious and resolute spirit would have quailed and fallen back. He is emphatically a self-made man, and his success is due to a tireless energy and an ability of a high order. Commencing life as a farmer's boy, he has successively risen to the position of a printer, an editor, a physician, and a successful politician. In the *Independent Statesman* of February 28, 1878, appeared a lengthy sketch of Dr. Gallinger's eventful life, from which the following facts are gleaned :

"Dr. Gallinger is of German descent, and was born in the town of Cornwall, Province of Ontario, March 28, 1837, being the fourth son of a farmer, and one of a family of twelve children. At the age of thirteen, he entered that poor boy's college, a printing office, and served an apprenticeship of nearly four years. At the expiration of his term as an apprentice, he went to Ogdensburg, N. Y., where he labored one year as a journeyman printer. Returning to Cornwall, he took charge of the paper on which he served his apprenticeship, and during the next year he labored as a printer and editor, and was also under private instruction from a competent teacher. In 1855, he went to Cincinnati, Ohio, and began the study of medicine, graduating in May, 1858, having the honors of valedictorian. Between lecture terms he either worked in the office of the Cincinnati *Gazette* (as reporter, proofreader or compositor), or was engaged in literary labor. After a year's practice in Cincinnati, the doctor travelled and studied for a year, and then in July, 1860, came to New Hampshire, and in the fall of 1861, he became associated in practice with Dr. W. B. Chamberlain of Keene, now of Worcester, Mass., at which time he became a convert to the doctrines of the Homœopathic school. In the spring of 1862, Dr. Gallinger removed to Concord, opened an office, and became a permanent resident. During his citizenship here he has built up an extensive medical practice, and taken a front rank as a physician and an enterprising, public spirited citizen. He has contributed frequently to medical journals, has lectured extensively before lyceums, besides writing more or less for the daily press. For seven years he held the office of President of the New Hampshire Homœopathic Medical Society, and in 1868 he received an honorary degree from the New York Homœopathic Medical College and has been elected an honorary member of several medical societies."

Dr. Gallinger's first political office was that of Moderator of Ward 4, Concord, which he held for two years. In 1872 he was elected to the Legislature, and served as chairman of the Committee on Insurance, and was re-elected in 1873, and served as chairman of the Committee on Banks. He was a prominent member of the Constitutional Convention of 1876, and his plan for the reorganization of the House of Representatives, on the basis of representation by population, was adopted by a very large majority, although it was opposed by some of the ablest men in the convention. In March, 1878, he was elected to the State Senate, where he served as chairman of the Committee on Education, and took a front rank as a skilful parliamentarian and successful debater. In November, 1879, notwithstanding a strong effort was made to defeat him, there being three tickets in the field, he was handsomely re-elected, and when the Senate organized he was chosen President, a position that he has filled to the entire acceptance of Democrats and Republicans alike.

In addition to filling the offices named, the doctor has done a vast amount of work for the party, having served for several years as a member of the Republican State Central Committee, and chairman of the Merrimack County Committee, and, during the last political campaign he did effective service on the stump. He has been a frequent delegate to political conventions usually serving on the Committee on Resolutions, where his ready pen has been of great service to his party. That his political career is not yet ended is evident from the fact that he was never so popular as to-day, and although it is understood that his personal preference would be to devote himself exclusively to his professional pursuits, it is hardly to be presumed that he will be permitted to do so.

In August, 1860, Dr. Gallinger married Mary Anna Bailey, ot Salisbury, New Hampshire, daughter of Major Isaac Bailey, formerly of Hopkinton, and a well known business man. They have had six children, four of whom are living, viz., Alice M., aged 17 years; Kate C., aged 13; William H., aged 9; and Ralph E., aged 6.

Dr. Gallinger was reared in the Episcopal Church, but for many years past has been connected with the Baptist denomination, although it is well known that his religious views are exceedingly liberal, and that his mind is free from all denominational and sectarian prejudices. He is a firm believer in fraternal organizations, and in addition to being a member of several temperance societies he is connected with the Odd Fellows, and is a very prominent member of the order of Knights of Honor, having represented New Hampshire for three years in the Supreme Lodge, at one time holding the second highest office in the order.

Few men have the ability to accomplish the amount of work that Dr. Gallinger constantly performs. In addition to a healthy body he has a remarkably quick conception, executive ability of a high order, and an indomitable will, and these enable him to accomplish tasks that few others could possibly endure. He is a man of great industry, of profound convictions and positive ideas, and while he has a host of devoted friends, these very qualities make him some enemies, who are naturally ready to impugn his motives and misrepresent his acts.

The doctor has been foremost in the advocacy of all progressive reforms, but never in a fanatical way. He has been a life-long total abstainer from the use of intoxicants, and also of tobacco in all its forms. He is a staunch Republican, broad and catholic in his views, warm in his friendships, faithful to his convictions, accurate in his judgments, graceful and eloquent as a speaker, ready in debate, courageous and sagacious, and, in short, is admirably qualified for the work of legislation, and his friends will be greatly disappointed if his success as President of the New Hampshire Senate does not bring him so prominently before the people of the State as to secure for him future recognition in a sphere of still greater honor and usefulness.

Dr. Gallinger has lately been honored by an unsolicited appointment on the staff of Gov. Head as Surgeon-General, with the rank of Brigadier-General. At the close of the recent session of the Senate he was the recipient of the most flattering acknowledgements from his associates. The chair being occupied by Senator Burns, Senator Mann offered a resolution of thanks, and Senator Blodgett advocated the adoption of the resolution in eloquent words, from which the following is an extract:

It is with great pleasure that I rise to cordially indorse the resolution which has just been offered, and which I am confident will receive the approbation of every member. It expresses nothing more than the united sentiment of the Senate will recognize to be eminently fit and proper, as a slight recognition of the ability, dignity and unfailing courtesy which have characterized its presiding officer in the discharge of his duties. If he has made mistakes I know not what they have been; if he has been actuated by any desire other than to give to every Senator equal rights, I have failed to observe it. I am certain that I but re-echo the united voice of the Senate when I say that he has been the right man in the right place.

* * * * *

And as a more substantial evidence than words of our esteem for the presiding officer of this body, permit me, sir, through you, to tender to our President, in behalf of the Senators, the accompanying volumes—Appleton's New American Cyclopedia—which I trust may be to him a grateful gift.

The resolution was adopted by a unanimous vote, and President Gallinger made a very happy extemporaneous response, concluding as follows:

Senators, we are about to separate, and resume the duties that await us in our several spheres in life, and as we do so it is with peculiar satisfaction and pride that I recall the fact that nothing has occurred during the entire session to permanently mar the harmony that prevailed at the beginning. We met, most of us, as strangers; we part, all of us, as friends, and if in the future it be my privilege to meet any of you, be assured of a hearty welcome; and with renewed thanks for your bountiful kindness, and earnest wishes for the prosperity and happiness of you all, let me conclude in the words of Tiny Tim and say. "God bless us every one."

SHERBURNE R. MERRILL, Senator from the Coos District, No. One, which is territorially the largest in the state, embracing the entire county of Coos, is sixty-nine years of age, and the oldest member of the Senatorial body, having been born in the town of Fishersfield, now Newbury, Jan. 2, 1810. His father, Samuel Merrill, a farmer of that town, died when he was about sixteen years of age, leaving a family of seven children, of whom he was the eldest. Having his own way to make in the world, and being of an enterprising turn of mind, he soon left home and went to Boston, where he was variously engaged for several years. When about twenty-five years of age he located in the town of Woodstock, Grafton county, where he engaged in the manufacture of starch, operated a grist and saw-mill and engaged in land speculation to a considerable extent. From Woodstock he removed to Colebrook, where he has resided for the past twenty-six years, or more, and has been extensively engaged in starch making there, being a pioneer in that business in Coos county. His youngest brother, Seneca S. Merrill, who was in his employ at Woodstock, is a partner with him in business at Colebrook. They have several starch mills, and are also proprietors of a large general store with an extensive patronage, and operating very heavily in grain. Mr. Merrill has also dealt largely in real estate since his residence in Colebrook. He has done much to develop the resources of Northern New Hampshire, and has his substantial reward in an ample fortune. While in Woodstock he was several years one of the board of selectmen, and represented the town in the legislature in 1850 and 1851. He was also a member of the House from Colebrook in 1870 and 1871. He has been a working member of the Senate, acting upon the Railroad Committee, and upon the Committees on Towns and Elections.

Mr. Merrill married in March, 1836, Sarah B. Merrill of Nolesboro, Me., by whom he had six children, four of whom are now living, all married daughters. Of these, one is the wife of Wm. H. Shurtleff, Esq., of Colebrook, and another the wife of Maj. Irving W. Drew of Lancaster. His first wife died in 1877, and on the first of January last he married Sarah Butler of Plymouth.

EDWARD F. MANN, of Benton, Senator from the Grafton District, or No. Two, is the youngest member of the body, having been born in the town of his present residence, Sept. 7, 1845. He is a son of George W. Mann, an extensive farmer, contractor and builder of Benton, who has long been known in Grafton County politics, and has represented his town in the Legislature several years. He spent his early life upon the farm, enjoying such educational advantages as the common school afforded, supplemented by a short attendance at Tilton Seminary, and at twenty years of age went into the service of the Boston, Concord & Montreal Railroad Company, being first employed at the station at Tilton, subsequently for several years as brakeman, and afterwards as conductor, in which position he is now engaged, running the morning express train between Concord and Plymouth. In this capacity he has gained, in the highest degree, the confidence of the corporation, and of the public as a faithful and courteous official. He is an earnest Democrat, and a member of the present Democratic State Committee, has been actively engaged in political affairs in his county, and represented his town in the House in 1871 and 1872. He has been a working rather than a talking member of the Senate, and has served upon the Committees on Education, Claims, and Roads, Bridges and Canals. Mr.

Mann is unmarried. He is a member of Burns Lodge, F. & A. M., at Littleton, and Franklin Chapter, at Lisbon.

ALFRED M. SHAW, of the Third, or Lebanon District, is a native of Maine, having been born in the town of Poland, in that state, May 3, 1819, and is therefore just sixty years of age. His father was Francis Shaw, a merchant of Poland. He received a common school and academic education, learned civil engineering, and subsequently became largely interested as a railway contractor. He has been engaged to a greater or less extent in the construction of numerous railway lines in different parts of New England and New York, including, among others, the Boston & Providence, Old Colony, Kennebec & Portland, Air Line (from Rochester to Syracuse), Sugar River, and Peterborough roads. He has been for twenty years the regular civil engineer of the Northern Railroad. He has also been engaged in extensive building contracts outside of railroad work. He is pre-eminently a man of enterprise and action, and retains his youthful vigor in a marked degree. He has been for many years a resident of Lebanon, but previously had his residence in Cambridge, Mass., and in the town of Andover, in this state, where, in Dec. 1848, he married Caroline D. Emery, a daughter of William Emery, of that town. He is a Republican, but not an intense partizan, and has been considerably in public life. He served in the Legislature in 1862 and 1863, and was one of the Presidential electors for this state in 1868, a member of the Constitutional Convention of 1876, was a member of the Senate last year, and was also appointed a member of the commission to build the new State Prison, in the duties of which position he is still engaged. He is a man of action rather than words, and his judgment in practical matters is regarded as reliable. He has served this year upon the Committees on Railroads, Incorporations, and Military Affairs, being chairman of the former, a position usually of much importance and labor, and more than ordinarily so this year.

Senator Shaw is at present a Director of the Northern Railroad, and also of the Nashua & Lowell. He is a Royal Arch Mason, and a member of the Independent Order of Odd Fellows. His religious associations are with the Methodist denomination. He has two children, both sons, the eldest of whom is engaged in flour manufacturing at Lebanon.

HIRAM HODGDON, of Ashland, Senator from Plymouth District, No. Four, was born in the town of Northfield, Oct. 21, 1832, his father being John L. Hodgdon, a farmer of that town. He secured a first-class academical education, graduating at the N. H. Conference Seminary, and was engaged in teaching and farming until 1857, when he engaged in mercantile business at Holderness village, now Ashland, where he has since resided and continued in trade, with the exception of two years in the real estate business in Chicago, Ill.—1870 and 1871. He has recently, in company with a brother, engaged extensively in stock raising in Nebraska, and left home before the close of the late legislative session, to look after his interests there. He has not been engaged in public life, heretofore, with the exception of town offices, but was a member of Gov. Cheney's staff during his gubernatorial incumbency. In the Senate he served upon the committees on Military Affairs, Agriculture, and Roads, Bridges and Canals, being chairman of the latter.

Col. Hodgdon married in June, 1858, Miss Martha S. Webster, daughter of Nathaniel Webster, of Danville, but has no children. He is a member of Mt. Prospect Lodge, F. & A. M., at Ashland, and a liberal contributor to the support of the Free Baptist church at that place, and an active member of the society.

ISAAC N. BLODGETT, of Franklin, who represents the Fifth, or Laconia District, has been prominent at the bar and in public life for several years past. He was born in the town of Canaan, Nov. 6, 1838. His father was the late Hon. Caleb Blodgett, a prominent citizen of Grafton county, who served many years in the legislature, and was also a member of the Senate and of the Executive Council. Hon. Jeremiah Blodgett, of Wentworth, is his uncle. He received a thorough education at the Canaan Academy, read law with Hon. Wm. P. Weeks and Anson S. Marshall, and commenced the practice of his profession at Canaan in Dec., 1862. In 1867 he removed to Franklin, where he has since been engaged in legal practice, having been in partnership with Hon. Austin F. Pike until March last. Mr. Blodgett has been four years a member of the House of Representatives from Franklin, taking a leading position upon the Democratic side, and was an active member of the Constitutional Convention of 1876. He has taken strong interest in political affairs, and was chairman of the Democratic State Committee in 1876 and 1877.

Mr. Blodgett received the compliment of a nomination for President of the Senate by the Democratic members, served upon the Judiciary, Incorporations, and Finance Committees, and took a prominent part in the debates as well as the ordinary legislative work of the session.

In June, 1860, he was united in marriage with Sarah A., daughter of Rev. M. Gerould. They have one child, a daughter, now a member of Wellesley Female College.

DUDLEY C. COLMAN, of the Winnipesaukee District, or No. Six, is a native and resident of Brookfield, fifty-one years of age in September next. His father was Charles Colman, a farmer and school teacher of Brookfield. He received a good education in the common schools and at Wakefield Academy; taught school and was engaged in farming until thirty years of age, since which time he has been engaged in trade in the flour and grain business and country store, at Wakefield and Brookfield. He has been prominent in town affairs; has been selectman and town treasurer ten years; represented Brookfield in the Legislature in 1863 and 1864, and was a member of the Constitutional Convention in 1876.

He is a man of sound judgement but few words, and served efficiently upon the Judiciary Committee, and also upon the committees on Towns and Claims. Mr. Colman, although a decided Republican, represented a district ordinarily strongly Democractic, owing his position to a failure to elect on the part of the people, through the diversion of a considerable portion of the Democratic vote to the "Greenback" candidate, and a consequent choice by the Legislature in joint convention. In the absence of political measures of a partisan character, from the deliberations of the Legislature this year, however, the people of the Sixth District generally cannot fail to be satisfied with the action of their Senator, whose conduct has been creditable, both to himself and his district.

ALBERT PITTS, of the Sullivan District, No. Seven, is by occupation a commercial traveller, and has been for several years past a selling agent for the extensive dry goods firm of Brown, Durell & Co., Boston, travelling in the counties of Cheshire, Sullivan and Grafton. He resided for a time in Lebanon and afterward in Walpole, but has been for the past eight years a citizen of Charlestown. He married, in 1869, Alice S. Saunders, of Fall River, Mass., but has no children. He is a member of Franklin Lodge, F. & A. M., at Lebanon. He has been somewhat active in local politics, but held no public office previous to his election to the Senate, in which body he developed much aptness for legislative work, and served as chairman of the Committee on Military Affairs, and a member of the Committee on State Institutions.

CORNELIUS COOLEDGE, of Hillsborough, Senator from the Eighth, or Hillsborough District, is a native of that town, a son of Lemuel Cooledge, born Oct. 16, 1828. He received a common school education, and at fifteen years of age started out to make his way in life. He first went to Boston where he was for some time a clerk in a grocery store, was afterwards for two years in the service of the

Lancaster Mills Manufacturing Company, at Lancaster, Mass., and in 1849 went to California, where he remained six years, engaged in mining and in trade. In 1855 he returned to the old homestead in Hillsborough, where he has since resided. He has been a member of the board of selectmen of his town for twelve years, was in the Legislature in 1864 and 1865, and a member of the last Constitutional Convention. He has taken a lively interest in agricultural as well as political and public affairs, and was one of the leading spirits in the organization of the Contoocook Agricultural Society. His good judgment is largely and safely relied upon by his fellow citizens in all business matters. He is an earnest Democrat, but has always received more than a straight party support, when a candidate for office. Few members of the Senate have exerted greater influence during the session than Mr. Cooledge, and the judgment of none was more highly respected. He frequently occupied the chair, to the satisfaction of all, and served upon the Committees on State Institutions, Banks and Manufactures. He married, in July, 1855, Sarah N., daughter of Simeon W. Jones, a prominent citizen of the town of Washington, by whom he has three children. He has been a member of the Masonic organization for twenty years past.

NEHEMIAH G. ORDWAY, of Warner, Senator from the Ninth or Merrimack District, has been extensively known in public life for the past twenty years. He was born in Warner, Nov. 10, 1828, and passed his youth in that town, laboring upon his grandfather's farm, and as a clerk in different stores in the village. At the age of nineteen he purchased a stock of goods, and commenced business for himself as a country merchant. He served as doorkeeper of the House of Representatives at Concord, in 1855, and again in 1856. During the latter year he was appointed Sheriff of Merrimack County and removed to Concord, where he also held the office of City Marshal the following year. An active and zealous Republican, he was made chairman of the State Committee of his party in 1860, and in 1861 received an appointment as special agent of the Post-Office Department for New England. In 1863 he was elected Sergeant-at-Arms of the National House of Representatives, at Washington, which position he held for twelve years, until the Democracy regained ascendancy in that body. Returning to New Hampshire, and taking up his residence in his native town, where he had ever retained a citizen's interest, Mr. Ordway was elected a representative to the State Legislature in 1855, although the town had long been strongly Democratic, and re-elected in 1876 and 1877, taking an active part in the deliberations of that body each year. He served in 1875 and 1876 as chairman of the Railroad Committe, and in 1877 was chairman of the Committee on Finance. He served in the Constitutional Convention of 1876, and was prominent in the debates in that body. In November, 1877 he was appointed a member of the Tax Commission, established by act of the Legislature at the previous session, and devoted much time and labor to the work in which the commission engaged, the fruits of which were seen in a large number of bills reported to the next session of the Legislature, bearing upon the subject of taxation, and which engrossed the attention of that body to a very considerable extent, some of which, in modified form, found their way upon the statute book. Although not a member of the legislature in 1878, Mr. Ordway was in attendance during most of the session, engaged before various committees, urging the adoption of the several measures reported by the tax commission.

During the late session of the Senate he served as chairman of two committees, those on Banks and Elections, and was also a member of the committee on Towns; but devoted his attention and labor in the main to railroad affairs, making a single-handed contest against the railroad corporations, in an effort to secure legislation looking to the reduction and equalization of fares and freights, in the advocacy of which he was extensively engaged in debate. Mr. Ordway married in 1848, Nancy, daughter of Daniel Bean of Warner, by whom he has three children living, a son and two daughters. The eldest daughter is the wife of Col. E. L. Whitford, U. S. Pension Agent at Concord. The son, Col. Geo. L. Ordway, a member of Gov. Prescott's staff, is now located in the practice of law at Denver, Col.

CHARLES F. CATE, of Northwood, Senator from the Pittsfield District, No. Eleven, like Senator Colman of the Sixth District, is a Republican, representing a strong Democratic District, and owes his position to the same cause. Two other Senators, Mr. Hodgdon of No. Four, and Mr. Philbrick of No. Twenty-two, were also chosen by the legislature, but their Districts are ordinarily closely divided between the two parties. Mr. Cate is a son of Jonathan Cate, a prominent farmer of Northwood, who married Mary Johnson, daughter of John Johnson, a revolutionary soldier, and a representative of one of the first families of Northwood. He was born Sept. 19, 1841, received a common school education, and has devoted himself mainly to agriculture, remaining upon the old homestead, and still unmarried. An older brother, Hon. Geo. W. Cate, a lawyer of Amesbury, is now a member of the Massachusetts Senate. In addition to his farm work Mr. Cate operates a lumber-mill and grist-mill. He represented Northwood in the House in 1876, and was re-elected the following year. In the Senate he is a member of the Committees on Agriculture, Banks, and Towns, and chairman of the latter. He is a member of the Congregational church at Northwood, and of Equity Lodge, No. 33, I. O. O. F.

LUTHER HAYES, of Milton, who represents the Somersworth District, No. Twelve, was born in Lebanon, Me., Jan. 12, 1820. His father, George Hayes, was a farmer, who removed with his family from Lebanon to Roch ester, in this State, shortly after the birth of Luther. He received a common school education, and was engaged mainly in farm labor, until he attained his majority, shortly after which, Feb. 4, 1841, he married Louisa A. Bragdon, a daughter of Samuel Bragdon, of Milton, and removed to that town, where he has since resided, being extensively engaged in farming, and in lumber business. He has held a prominent position in connection with public affairs in his town and county, represented Milton in the Legislature in 1857 and 1858, and again in 1876 and 1877. He was elected a member of the Board of Commissioners for Strafford County in 1864, holding the office three years, and in 1866, was appointed Sheriff of the county, which position he occupied until 1871. In 1876 he was appointed by Governor Cheney a member of the State Fish Commission for the term of five years, which office he now holds, and to which he has devoted considerable time and attention. He served in the Senate as chairman of the Committee on Agriculture, a position to which he is well adapted, and was also a member of the Railroad Committee, and that on Roads, Bridges and Canals.

Mr. Hayes has been a long time a leading member, and President, of the Strafford County Agricultural Society, also a Vice-President of the State Agricultural Society. He is an Odd Fellow and a Royal Arch Mason. His first wife died in December, 1859, leaving five children, two sons and three daughters, another son having previously died, and one daughter since. In June, 1861, he married Sarah D., daughter of John Cofran of Pembroke, who died ten years later, leaving two sons and two daughters, the eldest son, Lyman S., having served as messenger of the Senate the past session. In Nov., 1872, he married his present wife, Nellie R., daughter of Asa Morrill of Pembroke, by whom he has one son.

[CONTINUED IN AUGUST NUMBER.]

NEW HAMPSHIRE HILLS.

BY GEORGE BANCROFT GRIFFITH.

'Twas well immortal Milton thanked the Lord,
For mountains, everlasting peaks, round which
Delight to anchor islands of the sky !
Famed Washington and proud Kearsarge I view,
Grand Monadnock, Chocorua's line of blue !
Sandwich and Sunapee, Moosehillock fair ;
A sea of summits rising everywhere !

Those tall and pathless crags whose shadows sleep
All day in linked embrace, far, far below,
Where verdant vales are bathed in welton light,
And lonely streams o'er beds of granite flow.

Go forth with me when kiss of rosy dawn
First warms the naked crest of yonder mount,
Or when the ling'ring sunsets, haloed wreath
O'er hoary brow dissolves in rainbow tints,
And ye, my thoughts divining, would exclaim :
" Were stony eyes of that huge Mountain Man
But blessed with sight how he amazed would scan,
And with a voice of thunder e'er extol,
The matchless charms that Nature's hand unrolls,"

Though 'gainst these lofty pinnacles are hurled
The lightning's fiery bolt, like arrows thrown
At each proud, flinty heart, they're set
To music evermore ! for tinkling rills
Gush swiftly from each breast of rock, and, lo !
The cataract's glitt'ring line, from melted snow,
Leaves glowing, moss and lichens richly spread
Where foot of man has never dared to tread !
And when a stream doth sound in joyful leap
God's praise forever on the flower-hung steep !
The wild cry of the plover echoes there,
There, too, the idle raven answers back
The taunt of eagles shrieked from eyre high,
And all the deep ravines are filled with sound,
When storm-king's chariot rolls along the sky.

Ascending billowy slopes, I seaward look,
When purple haze that rims old ocean melts
As Day-God rolleth up, and blue expanse
Lies boundless, sparkling, gladdening the eye.
White with their winged ships, the waters gleam.
And Portsmouth bar and Isles of Shoals appear,
And the tall beacons shining white and clear ;
White sea-gulls sail with pinions widely spread,
Or fearless dip, or sweep in throngs afar.

But greater still when mighty storm prevails,
And stray winds blow the gray fog off in clouds,
The "league long roller," that with easy grace
Moved shoreward in the calm, now white with foam.
Increased to giant size is madly hurled
With thund'rous shock upon the shud'dring coast !
Great fleets now rock within that havened bay ;
The endless reach of forest bows in fear,
From wilderness goes up despairing sigh,
Wide heaths seem paralyzed, and uplands fair
A lower bed would seek in sheer dismay ;
But still defiant, looming, firm, each head
Of solid granite fronts the scene of dread.

Still more impressive here to silent stand
When o'er the portals of magestic Night
Each star its brilliant torch resets and glows ;
The full orbed moon between the towering crags
To flood the hamlets with their tender light ;
The slumbering village nestled at their base !
When plumes of pine are stirred by lightest breeze
And blooms of white bedeck the orchard trees.
  * * * * *

For ages have the caves of mounts abroad
Gave shelter to the homeless. Noble saints
There refuge found when Bigotry pursued
With deadly fangs, in vain. From rock to rock
Have men of God like hunted chamois leaped ;
"In palace halls of ice undaunted stood,
Where Solitude sits throned forever more,"
And saw no light save smile of pitying stars !
The scent of sacrifice has rose for aye
In many a mountain defile ! Natives
Yet believe that ghosts of valiant heroes
Linger where they fell and deities decide
The fate of mortals in their highest mounts !

And so with reverence look we forth today
On our own "Crystal Hills," as yet unsung ;
This simple verse may wake some poet's lay,
Whose garland long may please the rising young.

East Lempster, N. H.

MAJOR GENERAL AMOS SHEPARD.

BY REV. SILAS KETCHUM, WINDSOR, CONN.

JONATHAN SHEPARD, of Coventry, Connecticut, a farmer of English descent, married Love Palmer, of Stonington, and to them were born seven sons and three daughters. He subsequently married Polly Underwood, probably in Connecticut, by whom he had one daughter.

His sons were Jonathan, Oliver, Nathaniel, Amos, Simeon, Joshua and Roswell. In this order are they given by Rev. Seth S. Arnold, in his *Historical Sketches of Alstead*, and in a memorandum, in the hand of Gen. Amos Shepard, 1777, and this is probably the order of their birth. His daughters, by Love Palmer, were Prudence, who married John Ladd, of Coventry; Anne, who married Silas King, of the same town, neither of whom resided in New Hampshire; and Love, who married (after April 24, 1788) Daniel Morley, of Alstead, and had daughters, Love, Percis-Scott and Anne; and sons, Daniel and Nathaniel.

JONATHAN (Jr.) married Hannah Benjamin, of Hartford, Conn., was a shoemaker by trade, and had six sons; among them Elisha, Ralph, Amos and Levi; and one daughter.

OLIVER married, in November, 1775, Zerviah Hatch, theirs being the first marriage in Alstead between parties both belonging in town. They had two sons; one of whom was William; and two daughters. He was a captain, probably in the Revolutionary war; certainly not in the militia reorganized in 1791; represented Alstead in the Provincial Congress at Exeter, 1775; and nine years in the legislature; and died August, 1830, Æ. 87.

NATHANIEL married Lois Marvin; no issue.

AMOS is the subject of this sketch.

SIMEON married Rachel Brooks, and had four sons; among them Gardner, Luke and Roswell; and four daughters.

JOSHUA married Lucy Farnsworth, and had three sons, Cadwell, Chauncey, and Joshua; and four daughters.

ROSWELL is said (by Arnold) to have died in minority. He died in 1776. He left an estate which was divided among his brothers and sisters. This estate was the proceeds of the lot of land, deeded 15 January, 1777, to his brother Amos (vid. *infra*), which was conveyed to him by deed from his father, 24 June, 1774, for £5, as per record in Cheshire County, *Lib.* B, *Fol.* 460.

Alstead is thought to have been first granted under the name of Newton, but that, the conditions of the grant not being fulfilled, the charter was forfeited. It was chartered under its present name in August, 1763, by Gov. Benning Wentworth, and settlements commenced soon after. It is well known that the peculiarly exposed and unprotected condition of these towns, in the western part of the state, prevented or retarded for some years their settlement and growth. But in 1771, Alstead had twenty-five families of actual residents, and ten other men improving their land with the intention of becoming such. Nevertheless, the terms of the charter not having been fully complied with, the inhabitants petitioned Gov. John Wentworth and His Majesty's Council, "13 Jeneuary, 1772," for an extension of time.

Jonathan Shepard, Senior, came from Coventry, Connecticut, to Alstead in 1768, and soon after, probably the next year, removed a portion of his family thither. Of his seven sons, Jonathan and Amos married in Connecticut; Roswell died unmarried; all the rest married in Alstead, where *all* became residents. Of the daughter by Polly Underwood I have not been able to ascertain the name. When the older sons came to Alstead is not certain, but it is probable that all save Jonathan and Amos came in 1771. To the above-mentioned petition only Oliver and his father were signers, indicating that the others were not then freeholders.

AMOS SHEPARD, the fourth son of Jonathan, became a noted man in New Hampshire. I have never met with any account of him in print or otherwise. But he was, for about thirty-five years, the most conspicuous man in Alstead, holding as to wealth, influence, and public service, much the same relation to that town that Col. Benjamin Bellows did to Walpole.

In 1878, Elijah Bingham, Esq., who was born in Lempster (24 February, 1800) but lived in Alstead, as a student-at-law and business-man, mostly from 1820 to 1835, presented to the New Hampshire Antiquarian Society all that are extant of Gen. Shepard's private papers. Mr. Bingham was a student of Dartmouth College at one time, but did not complete his course; studied law with his brother, James H. Bingham, Esq., (D. C. 1801); removed to Cleveland in 1835, and has been for many years an honored and respected citizen of his adopted city. He married Thankful-Cadwell, a daughter of Major Samuel Hutchinson, of Alstead, in 1827, who is still living. At the time of Gen. Shepard's decease, Maj. Hutchinson was his partner in business, to the whole of which he succeeded. He was also a legatee by, and sole executor of, Gen. Shepard's last will and testament; guardian of the widow's interest during her life-time; becoming also executor of her will, and residuary legatee of her estate.*

Among these papers appear to be all Gen. Shepard's commissions, both civil and military, signed by Gov. Jonathan Trumbull, of Connecticut, Presidents Meshec Weare, Josiah Bartlett and John Langdon, and Gov. John Taylor Gilman, of New Hampshire. Also, most of the deeds of conveyance to him of real estate in Alstead and vicinity, of which at least sixty-five are on record in Cheshire County, besides some in Vermont; several military orders, and papers relating to his service in the army and militia; many indentures of the partnerships he formed for the carrying on of the various branches of his extensive affairs, in his own and other towns; his own and his wife's wills; and his memorandum and account books from 1777 to 1784. All these (save the account books) have been copied and indexed in Volume VII, of the Society's *Manuscript Historical Collections*, and from them the present sketch has been mostly made up. By them much light has been thrown upon the employments and condition of the first settlers of Alstead, the location of farms and dwellings, and many other things not touched upon in this paper.

Gen. Amos Shepard was born in Coventry, Connecticut, in 1746, and died in Alstead, 1 January, 1812. Of his early life nothing appears in these sources of information. It is plain that his education was not extensive, although, like so many of the shrewd settlers of his day, he had learned the art of surveying land. But his syntax was scarcely according to Lindley Murray, and his orthography was decidedly phonetic. He married Thankful Cadwell, of Hartford, and settled in New Haven, where he was a freeholder as early as 1772 (see *New Haven Records*, "Ledger Book" 35. p. 350). In this deed he is described as a "joiner," which trade is found, after his removal to New Hampshire, to include the manufacture of coffins, cooperage, and household furniture.

He was commissioned a second lieutenant by Gov. Trumbull, 1 May, 1775, and accompanied the expedition which invaded Canada, under Gen. Richard Montgomery, in the summer

---

*Major Hutchinson's mother, the wife of Rev. Elisha Hutchinson (D. C., 1775), of Pomfret, Vermont, was a sister to Gen. Amos Shepard's wife; and Major Hutchinson's daughter, who married Elijah Bingham, Esq., above named, was a grand-niece of Mrs. Shepard, and was named for her.

and autumn of that year, and was present at the reduction of St. Johns, and the occupation of Montreal. Whether he accompanied Montgomery to Quebec is uncertain; but he did not return home till the spring of 1776, when he immediately raised a company and joined the American army above New York, returning before winter.

In January, 1777, he removed to Alstead, whither his father and brothers had preceeded him, and lived in the house of his brother Oliver, till the 9th of June, when he moved into Andrew Beckwith's house, probably while a log house, or other temporary residence was being constructed for himself. He purchased his first land, a lot of ninety-two acres, of the heirs of his late brother, Roswell, [see *Cheshire County Register*, Lib. 5, Fol. 131], 15 January, 1777, for £80; which became the nucleus of a prodigious territorial estate. In this deed, which was executed at Alstead, he is described by the grantors as "our brother, Amos Shepard of New Haven, state of Connecticut (joiner)." His accounts show that he commenced at once to work at his trade, manufacturing the various articles of household use most necessary in families situated as the earliest settlers then were.

But, before the 14th of September following, he had opened the first store in town, in which business he continued, constantly enlarging it, until it became very extensive, comprising not only branch stores in Croydon, Marlow and Newport, but also various manufactures, such as lumber, cooperage, leather, hats, and perhaps others.

He was commissioned captain by President Weare, 4 May, 1777, and on the alarm that Ticonderoga was in danger, marched to its defense, as adjutant of the regiment commanded by Col. Benjamin Bellows. He had scarcely returned home when he was again called into service, by order of Gen. Folsom, and marched, as captain of Co. 4 of the same regiment, to check the progress of Burgoyne.

After this he does not appear to have been in any active service in the field; but was rapidly advanced in the militia, being commissioned first major of the 16th Regiment, by President Weare, 16 March, 1782; lieut. colonel, 25 December, 1784, and colonel, 1 March, 1786, by President Langdon; brigadier general, 29 September, 1791, and major general of the newly organized militia, 27 March, 1793, by Governor Bartlett; which office he held until his resignation, 6 June, 1806.

He was commissioned a justice of the peace in 1785, and of the quorum in 1790; represented Alstead in the legislature several years; was councillor in 1785; and was president of the Senate from 1797 to 1804.

In 1786 he built for himself a mansion, corresponding to his improved circumstances, in which he lived in a style becoming his position. He possessed vast energy, great sagacity in business and an unusual capacity for public affairs. He had no children. By his will, after providing for his widow, he bequeathed the bulk of his property to his partner, Major Samuel Hutchinson, before mentioned, and to his three nephews, Levi, Roswell and Joshua Shepard. His widow died 7 June, 1817, aged 71. By her will she left $1,000 to the Congregational church in Alstead, and $1,000 to the New Hampshire Bible Society. Doubtless an examination of the town records, and of the sepulchral inscriptions of Alstead, would supply many additional facts in relation to Gen. Shepard, his father and brothers, but such examination I have not been able to make. In a future number I will give some account of Major Samuel Hutchinson and his connections.

HYMNOLOGY OF THE CHURCHES.

BY ASA MCFARLAND.

The circumstances under which some hymns, destined to hold a permanent place in "the tunes of the church" were written, are such as to show that their endurance is attributable rather to the fervor with which their authors were inspired, than the labor bestowed upon them. Perhaps no favorite production was ever so expeditiously written as the "Missionary Hymn," by Rev. Reginald Heber:

> "From Greenland's icy mountains,
> From India's coral strand,
> Where Afric's sunny fountains
> Roll down their golden sand," &c.

The author, then 35 years of age, was visiting his father-in-law, Rev. Dr. Shipley, in Wrexham, England. On a Saturday evening a few friends were assembled in the parlor of the rectory, when Dr. Shipley, aware of the ease with which his son-in-law composed verses, asked him if he could not write a hymn to be sung the next forenoon, as he was to preach upon missions. With this brief notice Heber retired to an adjacent room, and wrote three of the four stanzas of which this celebrated production consists, and, not long after the request was made, came back and read them. "There, there," said Dr. Shipley, "that will do." But Heber, thinking the idea had not been carried to completion, returned and wrote the fourth stanza, which is the bugle blast, or trumpet call of the Missionary Hymn, as follows:

> "Waft, waft, ye winds his story,
> And you, ye waters, roll;
> Till, like a sea of glory,
> It spreads from pole to pole;
> Till o'er our ransomed nature
> The Lamb for sinners slain,
> Redeemer, King, Creator,
> In bliss returns to reign."

The words were printed the same evening, and sung the next forenoon in Wrexham church. Such were the circumstances under which a hymn was written that bids fair to hold its place in the hymnology of the churches so long as the English language is spoken. Reginald Heber became Lord Bishop of Calcutta, and died in Trinchinopoly, India, April 3, 1826, aged 43.

HENRY FRANCIS LYTE, an Episcopal clergyman, was the author of a hymn the world will never let die, commencing:

> "Abide with me, fast falls the eventide,
> The darkness deepens—Lord, abide with me,
> When other helpers fail, and comforts flee,
> Help of the helpless, Lord, abide with me."

This hymn was a few years since printed in illustrated form, for Christmas and New Year presentation to friends. The author was pastor, from choice, of a poor people, many of them of sea-going occupation living on the coast of Devonshire, England, whose surroundings were bleak and desolate. In the autumn of 1847, the gloom of winter then settling upon the coast, his health having become impaired, Francis Lyte resolved to pass the winter in a more salubrious climate. On his last Sunday in England he dragged his weakened body into his desk, and delivered the discourse which proved to be his last, and drew tears from his weather-worn congregation. He ended the day by composing the memorable production here alluded to. The author soon sailed for Nice, on the shore of the Mediterranean, where he soon after died.

The hymn known as "Rock of Ages," found in books in use by people of Trinitarian belief, had its origin in one who writes as follows of himself:

"At the age of sixteen I went into a barn, in an obscure portion of Ireland, and heard an earnest but illiterate layman preach from the text: 'Ye who some time were far off are brought nigh by the blood of Christ.' Strange that I, who had so long been under the means of grace in England, should be brought nigh to God in an obscure part of Ireland, amidst a handful of God's people, met in a barn, and under the preaching of a man who could scarcely write his name." This was Augustus Montague Toplady, whose father fell in the battle of Carthagena, Spain, and the son was reared by a pious mother. He became a clergyman and died in 1778, aged 38. The hymn known as "Rock of Ages" was repeated on his dying bed by Prince Albert, husband of Queen Victoria, and a Latin version was written by Hon. W. E. Gladstone. It is one of those productions to the duration of which it is not possible to fix a limit.

"Blest be the tie that binds,"

is the first line of a hymn that is often sung, but the circumstances under which it was written are perhaps not generally known. Its author was Rev. John Fawcett, of Bradford, England. After a pastorate of seven years at Wainsgate, he was invited to become the successor of Rev. Dr. Gill, in London. The offer was in the highest degree flattering, and he made preparations to move to the great city—his church at Wainsgate being scattered over a large surface, and were not wealthy. His parishioners assembled to witness his departure, but so sad was the meeting—the poor people sorrowing with many tears—that Mr. Fawcett gave way with the remark, "Unpack my goods, and we will live lovingly together." This circumstance caused Mr. Fawcett to write the hymn:

"Blest be the tie that binds
Our hearts in Christian love;
The fellowship of kindred minds
Is like to that above."

A woman, in very humble condition, wrote a hymn, many years ago, which soon obtained a place in church hymnology which it bids fair to hold into the indefinite future. This position it obtained and will keep, not because of its merit as a metrical composition, but for its devout, humble spirit. This is the first stanza:

"I love to steal awhile away,
From every cumbering care,
And spend the hours of setting day
In humble, grateful prayer."

The author was Mrs. Phebe H. Brown, of Canaan, N. Y. She was a devout, christian mother, and was in the habit of resorting to a solitary grove, near evening, for secret prayer. For this she was severely censured by a wealthy neighbor, and her feelings deeply wounded. Mrs. Brown, like many others, "builded better than she knew," for a hymn written with no expectation that it would ever appear in print, is found in a multitude of collections of hymnology, and bids fair to remain there forever.

"I love thy kingdom, Lord,
The house of thine abode,
The church our blest Redeemer saved,
With his own precious blood."

The hymn of which the above is the first stanza is often sung at the Anniversary of the American Board, and other public assemblies for the promotion of missions. Its author was Rev. Timothy Dwight, D.D., President of Yale College in the early part of the present century. It has become a companion piece of the Missionary Hymn, by Heber, and holds a permanent place in the collections of people of Trinitarian belief:

"Jesus my all to Heaven has gone."

In the year 1730 there lived in Reading, England, a youth fond of cards and stage plays; not of decidedly vicious tendencies, but inclined to ways of folly. One day while walking in London, a mental reaction came upon him. To use his own language, "While walking hastily in Cheapside the hand of the Lord touched me, and I at once felt uncommon fear and dejection. I looked upon the past with regret, and the future afforded me no cheering prospect." In this condition I remained two years. He finally became a clergyman of the Moravian church, and died in 1775. This was John Cennick, author of several choice hymns, and among them:

"Jesus my all to heaven is gone,
He whom I fix my hopes upon;
His track I see, and I'll pursue
The narrow way till Him I view."

THE MESSAGE.

B. A. GOODRIDGE.

The wind blows loud; the sky is gray;
   The billows leap along the strand,
   And roar around me where I stand
Unmindful of their drenching spray.

I cannot pray, I cannot weep,
   My heart is cold, my brain is wild
   "O wind, blow soft! O sea, be mild!
And bring him safe across the deep."

The wind goes down, the sun gleams bright,
   O'er crested sea and dripping rocks,
   While sea-birds sport in screaming flocks,
And toss the foam from pinions white.

Day wanes, and sinks into the west,
   The long swell dies upon the shore,
   The seamew's cry is heard no more;
Still lies the ocean's placid breast.

I whisper to the dying breeze,
   "The hours drag on with drooping wings,
   I heed not though glad summer sings,
Oh, send him quick across the seas!"

The last faint gleam of light has fled,
   The tide creeps sobbing to my feet.
   I know on earth we shall not meet
Until the sea gives up its dead!

ITEMS AND INCIDENTS IN HOPKINTON.

BY C. C. LORD.

INTRODUCTORY.

The summary of social history is not complete without a notice of numerous facts that are outside of the prosaic experiences of every-day life. In the social career of any people, items and incidents are frequently developed to be often recounted in indulgence of the relishing tidbits they afford for the feast of local memories. Among such historical fragments are many interesting, romantic and amusing bits of experience that enliven social converse whenever they are told. The list of such relations afforded by the history of this town is too long for complete publication. We have therefore selected a few of the best, offering them as means of the lighter entertainment of our readers.

INCOGNITO.

In perusing the reminisences already recited to the public, the reader has noticed occasional mentions of Dolloff's brook. This rivulet courses its way from its source near the center of the town to a point near the north-eastern corner, where it empties into the Contoocook river. This tributary of the Contoocook receives its name from one Joseph Dolloff, or Dolph—the people pronounce it both ways. Quite early in the history of Hopkinton, Abraham Kimball, first male child born in town, built a mill on Dolloff's brook, at a point of the present highway running eastward to Buswell's Corner, where the remains of the ancient structure can be seen to this day. For the accommodation of the mill-hands, a dug-out was constructed close by the mill's location. Being intended for a temporary convenience, the dug-out was not always occupied. One day there came into the neighborhood two strangers—a man and a woman—with a few personal effects, which they brought along on foot, while they drove before them a cow in which they seemed to maintain exclusive proprietorship. They came from—nobody knows where—and, in want of shelter, took quarters in the aforesaid dug-out, otherwise unused at the time, and where the indulgence of the mill-owner allowed them to remain for a considerable period, subsequently to which a small framed house, standing to this day, sheltered them.

Dolloff and his companion lived in Hopkinton the balance of their lives, or at least till death severed their domestic bond. Dolloff was always poor, being more or less an object of charity, and when, at the age of at least one hundred years, he left this world, he took the secret of his personal history with him, excepting to claim that he was a soldier under Wolfe, in 1759, and was the first man to mount the ramparts of the enemy at the battle of Quebec. Whether this claim was true or not, Dolloff was not a person of much individual energy or intelligence.*

A BY-WORD.

A local proverb, or by-word, is often a product of the merest accident. Some time ago in the history of this town an instance in kind occured, developing a pass-phrase that was quite common twenty-five years ago or more, if it is not even now sometimes heard. The story is as follows :

Lois Eastman was a *non compos mentis*. Being a pauper, and living before the purchase of a town farm, she was annually boarded out in fulfilment of the prevalent custom of disposing of the homeless poor. For many years, Lois lived on Putney's Hill. At the time of which we speak, the present main road from the center of the neighborhood to the lower village had not been constructed, and the existing highways being rather indirect, stranger travellers were liable to the necessity of inquiring the way. One day a stranger, doubtful of his road, knocked at the door of the house where Lois lived, to ask the way to the center of the town. Lois responded to his knock, and in answer to his question said :

"You go right down by Joe Putney's turnip yard, and by the sweet apple tree, and so on down to John Gage's."

This was indeed a part of the way to the lower village, though the direction was altogether unintelligible to the

---

*It is an interesting fact in this connection that the name of Joseph Dolloff appears in the company of Capt. Nathaniel Folsom, of Exeter, in the regiment of Col. Joseph Blanchard, of Dunstable, in the expedition against forts DuQuesne, Niagara, and Crown Point, in 1755. The same name also appears in Capt. John Titcomb's company, in the regiment of Col. Nathaniel Meserve, of Portsmouth, in the expedition against Crown Point, in 1756.

entire stranger in the place, who ventured in reply:

"I don't know anything about Joe Putney's turnip yard, the sweet apple tree, or John Gage's, either."

The simple minded Lois lost her patience in view of what appeared to her as most intolerable ignorance.

"Well, then," said she, "you air one pesky, divilish fool, if you don't know the way to John Gage's!"

Out of this incident a by-word was born. For years afterwards, a person of less than average intelligence was liable to be designated as one "who didn't know the way to John Gage's."

LOVE'S LABOR LOST.

In the earlier days, the lower village Baptists used to immerse candidates in the waters of the brook that runs from Smith's pond northerly, through the village, on its way to become a tributary of Dolloff's brook. The spot selected for public baptisms was in a glen just north of the village, on land now owned by Mr. I. W. Fellows. The location, at the time of which we speak, was very romantic and beautiful. The glen was shaded by grand old forest trees. The brook was reached only by a foot-path winding down a precipitous cliff. In the bosom of the brook was a pool prepared for baptismal purposes, its bottom being paved with white pebbles. On a baptismal occasion, the people of the congregation were accustomed to file down the zigzag path, singing appropriate hymns; the bottom of the glen reached, the ceremony of baptism was performed with the usual solemnities. The place, the occasion and the formalities conspired to impress the imagination in a forcible manner.

On a certain occasion of baptism at this romantic spot, the rite was administered to a number of young ladies, who, for the occasion, were arrayed in robes of symbolic white. One of these persons was popularly recognized as the fairest of the fair, and her beauty was not diminished by her snowy dress and luxuriant, loose flowing hair. That day a young officer of the United States army arrived in town, and finding the tide of local population turned toward the scene of public baptism, wended his way thither, taking a position of observation on the summit of the cliff overlooking the glen. Sitting there, he saw the lovely maid, the fairest of the fair, plunged beneath the sparkling wave of the pellucid stream. The sight of so much beauty quickened an emotion coetaneous with human nature and made him feel a vacancy in his being that longed for occupancy by the adorable being before him. Imperative circumstances, however, prevent the immediate consummation of desired plans, and, discharging his personal errands, the young son of Mars returned from whence he came.

The fires of love, once kindled into a vigorous flame, are not readily subdued. The young military officer, feeling the yearnings of his heart constant toward the new-found attraction, embraced an opportunity of visiting these local scenes again. Years, however, had passed away since his first visit, but time and absence had not obliterated the traces of personal regard that were once wrought in his bosom. As he came and saw once, he determined to come and see again, possibly to conquer. He sought and found these streets again, and asked for the domicile of the fair one that had made his spirit glow with an intenser fire. He was pointed to a village house. He approached and knocked at the door. A plain, buxom woman responded. She was clad in a country house-wife dress, and her sleeves were rolled upon her arms. A peculiar odor filled the hall, and, if one had gone there, he would have heard a peculiar sizzling in the kitchen. The truth must be told. The fair maid of days ago stood before the martial visitor. She had become plain and stout; she was the wife of the village butcher; her husband had just killed a number of hogs, and a grand trial of lard was in progress; the good-wife was mistress of the performance. *Sic transit gloria amoris!*

A YARN.

A yarn is a distinctively qualified relation. While it assumes the appearance of veracity on its inception, the boldness of its progressive or final incidents must startle the incredulity of the most obtuse. Without this characteristic audacity of relation, no concatenated order of narrated particulars can legitimately claim to be a yarn. The implied characteristic of mental ingenuity being very prominent, few persons are capable of inventing a good yarn. The scarcity of the species makes a good narrator of yarns a person of local celebrity. Such a person lived years ago in this town, and, though he has gone, the memory of his yarns has not departed. We give one.

The tale includes assumed circumstances attendant upon a flood of the Contoocook river. The banks of this stream being low, a sudden rise of water often floods the adjacent meadows and intervales, sometimes also submerging the lower floors of dwellings in the vicinity. A considerable portion of Contoocook village has been thus sometimes flowed. On the occasion of one of the heaviest freshets on the Contoocook, a farm-house on one of its banks was suddenly partially engulfed. The occupants—husband and wife—were in a situation both unhappy and precarious. Their neighbors promptly determined to rescue them. Here the yarn begins.

The original narrator, who claimed to have been one of the rescuing party, stated that a boat was procured, into which a number of persons entered and pulled for the imperiled home. Having reached the house, they rowed into the front door and made their way into a room where the unfortunate inmates were found upon a bed, which supported them above the water. The boat being brought to the bedside, the relieved persons stepped gladly into it, and preparations were made to return to shore. Just then, however, one of the rescuing party suggested that a little cider would be an appropriate acknowledgement of a favor. The host was complacent. He immediately leaped from the boat, procured a light, went down cellar, drew some cider, returned and regaled the company, and then the whole party stood out for dry land. The reader will remember we have already made our comments at the beginning of this matter.

A DEED OF DARING.

Speaking of the floods of the Contoocook, we are reminded of an event which took place about seventy years ago, and which gave abundant attestation of the courage of a woman. The time was spring. The day was Sunday. The woman was Mrs. John O. Emerson.

Spring thaws often suddenly break up the ice in rivers and send it in fragments on a hasty march southward. The day we have in mind was one of the warmer days of the early season. In the morning, a party of perhaps a dozen persons, Mrs. Emerson among the rest, crossed the frozen river from the north side, to attend meeting at the old west meeting-house. As the day marched on to its meridian, the warmth increased, the snows melted, the waters swelled, the ice broke, and the surface of the river became strewn with the floating debris of the natural bridge of the morning.

Returning from church, the aforesaid party approached the river to find a most forbidding barrier to their direct progress homeward. They halted for reflection. The nearest bridge was three miles down the river. To reach home that way required at least six miles of travel. The party was on foot, yet the dominant opinion—the natural one—admitted no alternative. Mrs. Emerson, however, demurred in view of the popular decision. She could not think of wasting so much energy in a needless tramp. She would recross the river on the floating ice. Not to be deterred from her resolution, she sprang upon an icy float. Alert, she bounded to a second. A third was gained by a dexterious leap. In this manner she reached the opposite shore. Her friends stood still and

AN HYPERBOLE.

The use of figurative speech often implies expressions not subject to the narrow restrictions of simple prosaic interpretation. The intensity of emotion involved in the conception of a subject may sometimes engender an assertion which, while avoiding the ascription of a false attribute, presents the substance of the theme in only a too strong natural light, thus speaking hyperbolically. In all times and places the hyperbole has been recognized as a legitimate element of human language. Classical judgment has never been so inflexible as to deny the fervent soul the privilege of projecting its affirmations a little beyond the boundaries of abstract reality. How could it?

Many years ago there lived in this town a diligent knight of the lap-stone, the products of whose skill were of sufficient reputation to ensure him a decent activity in business. That a plain shoemaker should be able to indulge in a figure of speech that should impress itself upon the memory of future generations only proves how much talent is sometimes resident in humble situations. However, one day a citizen of recognized local prominence and influence called upon our friend, the shoemaker, and discussed the subject of a pair of new boots.

"Can you make a pair of boots that won't soak water?" asked the local patrician.

"Yes, sir," replied the humble disciple of St. Crispin.

"Very well. Make me a pair of boots that won't soak water."

The measure was taken, the boots made, and the customer served. In a short time, bearing an expression of displeasure on his countenance, the citizen returned.

"Mr. Leathers, these boots are not satisfactory."

"Why not?"

"They soak water badly. You agreed to furnish me a pair of tight boots."

"I think those you have must be tight ones."

"No, they are not."

The two began to argue with much earnestness. At length the customer insisted:

"They are the worst boots to soak water I ever had. You never saw such a pair of boots to soak water."

"I have seen a pair that soaked water worse than that," stoutly affirmed the shoemaker.

"I would like to know if there was ever a pair of boots that would soak water worse than this," warmly replied the customer.

"Why," said the shoemaker, "I have seen a pair that soaked so badly that it would draw the water right up out of a well."

The point taken by the shoemaker was irresistible. The boots were conveyed home again, and no further complaint was made or question asked.

LOVE'S OBJECT GAINED.

In a sparsely populated district, special gatherings are always of great general moment. In such a society, all legitimate causes of meeting enlist the popular attention. Be it politics, reform, or religion, the great commonalty is prepared to attest its interest. This fact of widely distributed popular life is always intensified in pioneer locations. In such, events which in other places are only local become territorial. The social ball once set rolling, it perambulates the extremest confines of adjacent domestic society.

On the 23d day of November, 1757, an ordination of a minister occurred in Hopkinton for the first time. In anticipation of the event, the hearts of the pioneer populace for many miles around were set agog. In expectation of a great gathering, the town made ample provisional arrangements. Entertainment was voted to be prepared at no less than six different places—the homes of Aaron Kimball, Matthew Stanley, Stephen Hoyt, Peter How,

---

watched her progress. Seeing her safely over, they made a practical adoption of the sentiment that the farther way around is the nearer way home and recrossed the stream by the bridge below.

Samuel Putney and Joseph Putney. The sum of £450* was appropriated for the expenses of the grand occasion.

The day and the company came duly as appointed and expected. Clergy and people, a numerous band, assembled. The solemn rights of ecclesiastical ordination were performed at Putney's Fort, near the top of Putney's Hill, and where also the military was gathered for greater security against possible Indian attacks. The ceremony was prolonged till late in the day, and the rays of the setting sun shed a calm, subdued radiance over the closing scene. As the company began to disperse after the dismissal of service, a young Salisbury man, whose eyes had been amorously wandering during the day, boldly approached a stranger lass and said:

"Ah! miss, you are the one for me."

The damsel replied with a manifest dignity peculiar to woman:

"What do you mean, sir?"

"I mean," respectfully explained the rustic swain, "that I am a young man in need of a wife and that you are the person I want."

Introduction followed; the lady was complacent; marriage occurred that night; and the next morning the bride began the journey to her new home in Salisbury.

AN EVEN SWAP.

A horse jockey is a representative of a distinct species of the genus *Homo*. His distinctiveness is asserted in the manifest particularities of his executive genius, whereby he performs marketing exploits of which men of usual commercial talents are wholly incapable. The exclusive capabilities of the characteristic horse jockey are suggestive of creative instincts, since they at times attest the faculty of producing as it were something out of nothing. We have a local instance in illustration. It is said there once lived in the Stumpfield district a jockey of most distinctive characteristic stripe. Taking into the tow of his executive genius a suitable representative of the equine species, he journeyed down to the vicinity of the mouth of the Merrimack, remained a few weeks, trading in the meanwhile an indefinite number of times, and then returned to Hopkinton, with the same beast he took away and $75 additional in cash.

Success and greatness, however, are often only stations in the highway to defeat and littleness, and our champion horse jockey was in time called upon to illustrate the fact at least in one instance. The event was on this wise. Taking along a semi-vitalized skeleton of a horse, the hero of this section of narrative wended his way to a favorite location in the lower county of Massachusetts, housed his skeleton, took position in the bar-room of a hotel, and awaited opportunities of business. It being a dull time for trade, and wishing to stimulate topics, our visitor from the north ventured to offer an even swap with the first man who accepted the proposition.

A customer was found, who asked for an exposure of property. The afore-mentioned bones were brought out and duly exhibited.

Proceeding to an adjoining shed, the customer returned with a saw horse.

"A trade's a trade," said the jockey. "How much will you take for your horse?"

"Five dollars," was the answer. The price was promptly paid and matters resumed their original status.

LEGENDARY.

In searching for knowledge of the past, unless assisted by honest and competent records, one encounters much that is visionary and uncertain. In intellectual as in physical observation, objects seen in the distance are tinged with illusive halos, and the dimly outlined forms and facts assume phantastic qualities proportional to the imagination. For this reason, the recollection of the "oldest inhabitant" of a local district is exceedingly unreliable when positive data are the special objects of historical research. We pre-

---

* This sum, payable in depreciated bills of credit, was equivalent to only $200.

mise thus in order that an approaching narrative may receive a qualified attention.

Among the tales of local Indian perils and distresses, afflicting this township in its earliest days, is one told us years ago by an aged woman, whose story fell upon our ears with that pleasure always enjoyed by youth, when listening to exciting tales of by-gone times. Once, in the primative days, she said, two stalwart young men of this town wandered, gun in hand, from the vicinity of Putney's Fort westerly to the plains on the bank of the Contoocook river. While wandering there, they discovered that their footsteps were closely tracked by Indians, who perhaps were more intent on capture than on destruction. Not knowing the number of their pursuers, and necessarily bent on personal safety, the young men beat a hasty retreat in the direction of Putney's Fort. They soon observed evidences of rapid pursuit. A number of Indians were scenting their track. Fortunately both the young men were skilful in the use of the gun, though not uniformly so. One of them could load a gun while running; the other was equally skilful in whirling suddenly and firing, hitting close to the mark. By a conjunction of separate personal skills, the two were enabled to keep up a successful running fight. They both escaped safely, but not till three Indians had been made, by their well-directed fire, to bite the dust. Having secured companions, the escaped men returned and picked up the bodies of the slain, which were buried just westerly of the present Contoocook road, in a lot now sometimes known as the tan-house piece, owned by Mr. Ira A. Putney.

Substantial record confirms a number of Indian encounters in this vicinity, but our present narration is not one of them. We give the old lady's narrative—which may be true—for the biased contemplation of our readers.

THE BEST OF FARE.

Several different times Hopkinton was the seat of the legal government of New Hampshire. Since the permanent location of a capital, she has been close to the center of functional state authority. In consequence of Hopkinton's peculiar privileges and situation, she was in former times a scene of frequent assemblies with their attendant features of social activity and recreation. In those days, the present railway thoroughfares not being in existence, the tide of travel towards the capital from the western part of the state either stopped at, or passed through, Hopkinton. In later times, too, a governor elect, if he happened to live in a westerly section, would likely enough be met at Hopkinton by a large delegation of officials and citizens, prepared to conduct or witness his escort to the state capitol. On such occasions, Perkin's tavern was the principal resort of the *elite*, as well as of as many others as could find room for accommodation at its hospitable board. We think it was on an historically later occasion of events anticipative of an inauguration of a supreme state official that, among all the assembled ones seeking hospitality at Captain Perkins', there was a country swain of self-possessed aspect and manner, having in escort his favorite rural lass. The pair having taken seats at a dinner table, surrounded by a large company of strangers of different social style and position, the confident swain was approached by a waiter who asked what dish would suit his special palate.

"The best you've got," promptly replied the rustic Lothario.

The patient waiter mentioned a number of palatable preparations devised in anticipation of the occasion. Would he name his choice?

Nothing seemed to excite his particular appetite. He ruminated. At length he inquired:

"Have you any salt mackerel?"

The waiter informed him there were mackerel in the brine, but they must necessarily be freshened before cooking, and the operation would unavoidably consume a considerable amount of time.

"Never mind the freshening," he suggested. "Bring me some cooked right out of the brine."

The dish was duly prepared and served according to direction. The suggestion of salt mackerel, cooked directly from the brine, being the best fare afforded at a first-class tavern, created a ripple of mirth that ran all round the table.

NEW LONDON CENTENNIAL.

ADDRESS OF HON. J. EVERETT SARGENT.

The town of New London was incorporated, June 25, 1779. Deeming the occurrence of the centennial anniversary an event of sufficient importance to warrant a formal observance, the citizens of the town, at the last March election, voted an appropriation of three hundred dollars for that purpose, and appointed Gen. Luther McCutchins, N. T. Greenwood, and James E. Shepard a committee of arrangements. The announcement of the celebration, with an invitation to be present, having been sent in due time to all likely to be interested, it soon became evident, from the responses received that there would be a large representation of the absent sons and daughters of the town in attendance upon the occasion ; and for several days previous to June 25, there were numbers, from all parts of the country, engaged in renewing youthful associations and revisiting the scenes of their childhood in that good old town amid the hills of western Merrimack. On the night previous to the celebration the capacity of the town for the accommodation of the guests was tried to the utmost ; and on the following morning, which broke clear and beautiful and was ushered in by the ringing of bells at five o'clock, the people began to come in from the surrounding towns in great numbers, and by every means of conveyance, until there was a larger gathering than ever before seen in New London.

At half past nine a procession was formed near the academy building, under the direction of Gen. J. M. Clough, Commander of the New Hampshire National Guard, as Chief Marshal, in the following order :

Chief Marshal, with John Seamans and Harry Greenwood, as aids ; Franklin Cornet Band ; Messer Rifles, Capt. W. A. Messer, as Escort.

First Division, Major A. C. Burpee, Marshal, with Robert Greenwood and Wilfred Burpee, as Aids ; Sabbath-Schools, with officers of the day, invited guests in carriages.

Second division, Col. J. H. Burpee, Marshal, Commanding Prescott Jones Post No. 32, G. A. R. ; citizens and former residents of town, and delegations from neighboring towns.

After marching and counter-marching, the procession reached the Baptist church at half-past ten, which large edifice was immediately filled to its utmost capacity, while large numbers, unable to gain entrance, lingered around the building. The church was beautifully decorated for the occasion, while flags and streamers displayed from the outside of other buildings gave the town a gala day appearance. The exercises in the church began with the effective rendering by the choir of the anthem, "Oh, Praise the Mighty God," followed by prayer by Rev. D. P. Morgan, of Beverly, Mass. An original hymn was then sung by the choir, written for the occasion by Mrs.

James B. Colgate, of New York, a daughter of the late ex-Gov. Colby, of New London, and set to music composed by Mrs. Nahum T. Greenwood. Gen. McCutchins, president of the day, then made a few remarks, welcoming the visitors to the town and its hospitalities, and closed by introducing Hon. J. Everett Sargent, of Concord, ex-Chief Justice of the Supreme Court, and a member of one of the largest of the old families of New London, as speaker of the day, who occupied about two hours in the delivery of his address, stopping twice to allow musical exercises, one being the rendering of a song written by Mrs. Geo. Rogers, of Charlestown, Mass. Music by the Franklin Band followed the address, and then came the poem, a fine production, by Mrs. Dr. R. A. Blood, of Charlestown, Mass., a daughter of Gen. McCutchins. The exercises in the church closed at twenty minutes past one, with the anthem "Strike the Cymbals." Dinner was served in a large tent, with tables set for five hundred people, where in the course of two hours about two thousand were fed, while the militia company, Grand Army post and band dined at Town Hall, where ample preparations were made. At half past three the church was again filled, and toasts, responses, &c., were in order, N. T. Greenwood, Esq., officiating as toast-master. Among the toasts offered were the following:

"The Bar"—responded to by Judge Sargent and by a letter from Hon. Walter P. Flanders, of Milwaukee, Wisconsin. "Our Ministers"—responses by Rev. D. P. Morgan, of Beverly, Mass., and letter from Rev. Francis A. Gates, of Iowa. The Press—response by James E. G. Shepard, Esq., of Attica, N. Y., formerly of the Nashville (Tenn.) *Union*. Our Home Interests—response by Gen. Luther McCutchins. Colby Academy and the Baptist Church—response by present pastor, Rev S. C. Fletcher. Interesting short speeches were made by several present and former residents of the town. These closed the public exercises of the day, which were naturally followed, by social reunions, the renewal of old acquaintanceships, &c. The arrangements were excellent and admirably carried out, and the occasion an enjoyable one throughout. A display of fireworks in the evening closed the festivities.

ADDRESS OF JUDGE SARGENT.

Mr. President, Ladies and Gentlemen:

We have met today to commemorate the one hundredth anniversary or birthday of the good old town of New London, as a municipal corporation. One hundred years ago today, June 25, 1779, the Great and General Court of the state of New Hampshire passed an act incorporating the town of New London out of a tract of land that had previously been known as "Alexandria Addition." The lines of the township were described in the act of incorporation, but we shall find that the town as at first incorporated contained much territory that does not now belong to it, and, also, that it did not contain considerable territory which now constitutes a part of it.

But although the town was not incorporated until 1779, it had been inhabited several years previous to that, and in giving a historical sketch of the town, it will be not only interesting but proper and necessary to go back as far as we can trace any step of the white man; and it would be interesting also, had we the means of doing so, to go even back of that, and to describe what savage tribes, what sons of the forest, what race of the red men formerly frequented these hills and mountains and tracked their devious ways through the dense forests that then covered these hills and valleys; who hunted their game in these regions while the woods were yet unbroken; and sailed upon our grassy lakes and ponds in their bark canoes, when as yet their waters had never mirrored forth the forms or the features of any of the race of pale faces, the descendants of the English. But all the facts in relation to these times have perished from human memory, and all the traditions in regard to former races of men who may have once in the ages of the past, inhabited these regions, are forgotten and have passed away forever, and we can only draw upon our imaginations to picture the races of men, the modes of living, the habits, pursuits and characteristics of the people who may at some distant day in the far past, have lived and labored, loved and hated, enjoyed and suffered, in these places which we now occupy.

What has been going on within the limits embraced in this single township during the long ages of the past, extending far back to the times of Greece and Rome, of Persia and of Egypt, to the times of Babylon and Nineveh; to the times of Abraham and of Noah, to say nothing of the centuries preceeding the flood? No man can tell us. Upon these points, while we know absolutely nothing, yet we are sure that we are as wise as the wisest. Oblivion has drawn her impenetrable veil over all of the events that have taken place in these regions for almost the whole of the nearly six thousand years since the creation. All that is left to us is to go back one hundred, and a little over, of the nearly six thousand years of the past and see what we can gather up of the history of that comparatively short period. For although a century seems a long time for one person to live, a long time to look forward to, and a long time to look back upon, when we consider all that has been accomplished in it, yet as compared with all of time that has passed, it is only as a drop in the bucket, a single grain of sand in the hour-glass of time.

Indian settlements in this town were far back before any white man had knowledge of these localities. The Indian wars were over and the few scattering remnants of the race that remained had retired from the unequal contest, had ceased their depredations and left the state (except perhaps in the extreme northerly portion) before this town was settled; and we look almost in vain for any trace of them in this region. The only name that I find anywhere in the neighborhood, that indicates that the Indians ever dwelt here, is the name of *Sunapee* Lake. That name is unmistakably Indian. But why did the Indians call it *Sunapee?* From the best information I have been able to obtain, I think the name means in plain English, "Goose" and Sunapee Pond meant simply Goose Pond. Our theory is that at sometime in the past this lake was found to be a favorite resting place for the Canadian wild geese, as they migrated from the regions of Hudson Bay southward at the approach of winter, flying as they always do at a great height, and like a well trained military company, following their leader in such a way as to describe the sides of a triangle with the angle in front, or as our farmers would familiarly express it in the shape of a harrow.

The size of the lake would cause it to be seen from a great distance on either side, and thus it would be sure to be sought as a place of rest and refreshment for a time by the wild geese, as they went southward in the autumn and northward in the spring, and we infer that the Indians were familiar with this fact and hence the name *Sunapee*,—Goose Pond.

We cannot doubt that the Indians also were familiar with the Little Sunapee Pond in the north-westerly part of the town and Messer's and Clark's or Harvey's Ponds in the southerly part, and crossed the height of land and descended to Pleasant Pond, in the north-easterly part of the town. But, however that may be, one fact remains, which is that New London is the highest land, or furnishes the dividing line between the Connecticut and the Merrimack rivers. There are upon the old farm on which I was born brooks on one side that ran into Little Sunapee and through to Sunapee Lake, and thence by Sugar River to the Connecticut; and brooks on the other side that descended to Pleasant Pond, thence into the Blackwater and so to the Merrimack; and it is said there are buildings in town from the roof of which the water descends from one side to the Merrimack and from the other side to the Connecticut River.

4

I find this account of traces of the Indians in Sutton, near Kezar's Pond, in the northerly part of the town and not far from the line of New London. Sutton was then known as Perrystown and was settled first in 1767, some eight years before this town was settled, and it was stated of the early settlers there, that though no Indian was seen by them, yet it seemed as though he had just put out his fire and gone away, as the white man came. His track was still plain and visible. On the west bank of Kezar's Pond were several acres of land which appeared to have been cleared by them of their original forests. Here were found several Indian hearths built with stone, with much skill and ingenuity. Here was found an Indian burying place. Gun barrels and arrows have also been found here, and near the pond were found stone mortar pestles and tomahawks.

It is certain that these regions were once, and that not long before the advent of the pale-faces, inhabited by the red man; he hunted his game over these hills and encamped and lived on the banks of our Great Lake, Sunapee, and of our smaller ponds, nestling as they do in beauty among our hills. Upon investigation I find that large numbers of Indian utensils and arms have been found by Mr. James M. Pike and Mr. Amos Currier in the west part of the town near Sunapee Lake, so that I am satisfied the Indians had a settlement on the border of the lake in that neighborhood, and that they had a track or path from such settlement down by Harvey's Pond to North Sutton, to Kezar's Pond, which we have just noticed. They also visited Little Sunapee Pond and had a settlement in the summer season on its easterly shore, and had a track or path from thence easterly over the height of land to the upper end of Pleasant Pond, where they also had another settlement, and where they had cleared up the forests, on the intervale; and this clearing was the first place occupied by the white man in that part of the town. They were in the habit of hunting in summer all over our hills, and their arrow-heads of stone have been found by Gen. McCutchins, by Mr. Nathan Pingree, Mr. Ransom Sargent and others; and a few years since Mr. Asa Ray plowed up an Indian gouge in the path leading from Little Sunapee to Pleasant Pond, which is now in possession of Mr. S. D. Messer.

New London was first settled in 1775, some four years before it was incorporated. James Lamb and Nathaniel Merrill were the first settlers, and they were soon followed, in the same season, by Eliphalet Lyon and Ebenezer Hunting. The next year, 1776, the first child was born within the limits of the town, a son of James Lamb, and they called his name John. James Lamb is said to have made the first settlement on the farm known as the Ezekiel Knowlton farm. It is also related that Moses Trussell came up from Hopkinton, in 1774, and camped in the wilderness and felled several acres of trees on the Morgan farm, so called, adjoining the Knowlton farm; that he burned off the land and planted it with corn; that in the autumn he returned again to harvest his crop, but finding that he had been anticipated by the hedge hogs and other wild animals, he returned to Hopkinton, and the next spring instead of coming to New London, he went to Bunker Hill, where he lost an arm and did not get back to New London until 1804, just thirty years after his first visit. Soon after 1775 came also Mr. Samuel Messer, Benjamin Eastman, Nathaniel Everett, Nathaniel Goodwin, Ephraim Guile, and John Austin, with Jedediah Jewett and Thomas Whittier and others; and in March, 1779, these citizens petitioned "the Honorable General Court of the State of New Hampshire then sitting at Exeter," that they might be incorporated into a town, which petition was afterward granted.

The act of incorporation was as follows:

" In the year of our Lord one thousand seven hundred and seventy-nine.

State of New Hampshire.

An act to incorporate a place called

Addition of Alexandria, in the county of Hillsborough.

Whereas, a petition has been prefered to the General Court in behalf of the inhabitants of a tract of land called Addition of Alexandria, in the county of Hillsborough, setting forth that they labor under great inconveniences for want of incorporation, and praying that they may be incorporated, of which public notice has been given and no objection has been made.

Be it therefore enacted by the Council and House of Representatives in general court assembled, and by authority of the same, that there be and hereby is a township erected and incorporated by the name of New London within the following bounds, viz.: Beginning at the south-westerly corner of Alexandria, aforesaid, on the patent line, and running on said patent line to Fishersfield Corner in great Sunapee Pond ; from thence east on the northerly side line of Fishersfield four hundred and seventy-two rods, to Perrystown Corner ; then north, eighty-five degrees east, about four miles to a beech tree marked on Perrystown line ; from thence north, thirty-nine degrees east, about sixteen hundred and seventy-two rods to a beech tree marked in Alexandria Corner ; from thence north, twelve degrees west, to the patent line aforementioned on the westerly side of Alexandria.

And the inhabitants of said township are hereby erected into a body politic and corporate, to have continuance and succession forever, and invested with all power, and enfranchised with all the rights, privileges and immunities, which any town in the state holds and enjoys, to hold to the said inhabitants and their successors forever.

Mr. Samuel Messer is hereby authorized to call a meeting of said inhabitants, to choose all necessary and customary town officers, giving fourteen days notice of the time and place and design of such meeting ; and the officers then chosen shall hereby be invested with all the power of such officers in any other town in the state, and every other meeting which shall be annually held in said town for that purpose shall be on the second Tuesday of March forever."

"State of New Hampshire. In the House of Representatives, June 24th, 1779. The foregoing bill having been read a third time, *voted* that it pass to be enacted.

Sent up for concurrence.

(Signed)
JOHN LANGDON, *Speaker*.

"In Council June 25th, 1779. This bill was read a third time, and *voted* that the same be enacted.

(Signed)
M. WARE, *President*.

Copy examined by E. Thompson, Secretary."

Mr. Samuel Messer called a meeting of the freeholders, and other inhabitants qualified by law, to vote in town affairs, on Tuesday the third day of August, 1779. of which he gave due notice, for the following purposes, viz :

Firstly—To choose a Town-Clerk.

Secondly—To choose Selectmen.

Thirdly—To choose a Constable and such other officers as shall be thought proper in town.

Fourthly—To see what method the town will take to have roads.

Fifthly—To know what sums of money shall be granted to pay the town charges for the present year.

Sixthly—To see if the town will vote to hire preaching.

Seventhly—To see if the town will hire any school for children.

In compliance with said warrant the inhabitants of New London met at the dwelling-house of Mr. Samuel Messer, at which time was read the copy of the act of incorporation of this town, Mr. Messer's power. given him by said honorable court, to call said meeting, after which was read the notification for said meeting, of which Mr. Messer was considered as moderator, and then proceeded to act on the business of the day.

Town officers chosen by written votes : Ebenezer Hunting, Town-Clerk ;

Mr. Samuel Messer, Mr. Benjamin Eastman, and Mr. Nathaniel Everett, for Selectmen ; and Mr. Nathaniel Goodwin, for a Constable ; Mr. Nathaniel Everett, for Town Treasurer ; and Mr. Benjamin Guile, and Mr. John Austin, for Surveyors. (All of whom were duly sworn.)

Voted, To choose a committee to lay out roads where, at present, necessary.

Voted, That Mr. Samuel Messer, Mr. Benjamin Eastman, and Mr. Nathaniel Everett, serve as a committee to lay out roads this year.

Voted, That roads be laid out three rods wide.

Voted, To purchase the land for said roads.

Voted, That four hundred and fifty pounds be raised for clearing roads, and that labor shall be three pounds per day.

Voted, That one hundred and eighty pounds be raised to pay town charges.

Voted, Not to hire any preaching this year.

Voted, To hire three months' schooling this year.

The meeting dissolved.

I have thus given you a full account of the act of incorporation, and the action of the town at its first meeting. The town is now fully organized, with its town officers, its three months schooling in a year, and its committee to lay out roads where necessary, and money raised to clear them out with. Having thus got our young craft fully rigged and fairly launched, we may leave her for awhile to prosecute her way upon the tide of successful experiment while we pause and examine some things that have been disclosed in our course thus far, which it may be profitable to consider.

1. It will be observed that the act of incorporation of this town was passed about midway during the time of the Revolutionary War. The first settlements were made in the year 1775. the same year that witnessed the commencement of the war at Lexington. Concord, and Bunker Hill. The first child was born here in 1776. the year in which, upon the 4th of July, the ever memorable Declaration of American Independence was adopted by the Continental Congress. This year was also noted for another event which no son of New Hampshire should forget, that is that on the fifth day of January of that year a temporary constitution was adopted by this State, which was the first written constitution adopted by any of the states now constituting the American Union. Under this constitution the State was prosperously governed for eight years. and until the new constitution of 1784, went into effect. The form of government was not much changed by the constitution of 1776.

Before that the Government of the State consisted of a Royal Governor, appointed and commissioned by the King of England, with a council, also appointed by the King, and an assembly elected by the people of the several towns in the province. After the separation from the mother country the State elected their Council and also their Assembly or House of Representatives ; and the Council elected their presiding officer, who acted for the time being as Governor ; hence the act of incorporation was passed by the House of Representatives, then by the Council, and was signed M. Ware, President. This was the form of government until the new constitution of 1784, when we had a President, and an advisory Council. with a Senate and House of Representatives, all elected by the people. Meshech Ware was President of the Council for the eight years that the temporary constitution continued, and one year under the new constitution. It will also be observed that our town was incorporated some two years, nearly, after the articles of confederation had been adopted by the American Congress, that having been done Nov. 15, 1777.

2. By examining the boundaries of the town as incorporated. we shall see that it was of very ample proportions as compared with its present size. It began at the southwesterly corner of Alexandria. on the patent line, &c. Alexandria was formerly much larger than

it now is, for besides several other pieces that have been taken off from it, the whole township of Danbury was incorporated June 18th, 1795, out of territory that before was the southwesterly portion of Alexandria, so that when New London, in 1779, began at the southwest corner of Alexandria it would be the same now as beginning at the southwest corner of Danbury on the patent line.

But what was this *patent line?* New Hampshire as it seems was granted by the Council of Plymouth, England, to one John Mason, in 1629. This patent included the land "from the middle of Pascataqua River and up the same to the farthest head thereof, and from thence northwestward, until sixty miles from the mouth of the harbor were finished; also, through Merrimack river to the farthest head thereof, and so forward up into the land westward until sixty miles were finished; and from thence to cross overland to the end of the sixty miles accounted from Pascataqua River; together with all Islands within five leagues of the coast." This tract of land was called New Hampshire. In 1768 the Masonian proprietors procured one Robert Fletcher, as a surveyor to run out their territory, claiming that their line should be a curve line drawn from the point on the south line of the State, 60 miles west from the sea-coast, to a point on the east line of the State sixty miles north of the sea-coast, in such a way that it should at every point be 60 miles from the coast. This claim of Mason, and after him of the Masonian proprietors, to this curve line had never been disputed by the government of England, and so Fletcher run the line as requested, starting on the south, on the west of the town of Fitzwilliam, and so running northerly and northeasterly through Marlow, Sullivan, Goshen, and so on what was afterwards the northwest line of New London and Wilmot, and thence through Hebron, Plymouth, Campton, and Sandwich, to the town of Conway. This was known as the westerly line of the Mason patent, and is hence called the patent line.

So New London after starting at the corner of Alexandria (now Danbury) on this patent line was to run on this patent line to Fishersfield Corner. Fishersfield had been incorporated the year before New London (1778, Nov. 27), and is bounded on the northwest by the same patent line. Its name was changed to Newbury in 1837. Then the line of the town runs easterly on the north line of Fishersfield, to the corner of Perrystown, now Sutton, thence on Perrystown north line a given number of rods to a marked tree, and there, turning off and running north, 39° east, to Alexandria Corner (now Danbury South Corner) and thence on Alexandria (now Danbury) to the place of beginning.

Perhaps I may here be allowed to state that this patent line remained unchanged, though undecided, marking the claim of the Masonian proprietors, until after the termination of the Revolutionary War in 1783, when various disputes arising, relating to the titles to the land, several parties petitioned the Legislature to locate and establish this line. Whereupon, by an act of 1787, the bound on the south line of the State was fixed near the southwest corner of Rindge, and thence running a straight line instead of a curved line to the bound on the easterly line of the State. This line run through Peterborough, Francestown, Hopkinton, Concord, Gilmanton, and so across the lake through Ossipee, making a difference, here in the centre of the line, of some 30 miles between the two lines.

Having thus ascertained what was meant by the patent line, the next question that arises is, how came the territory now known as New London to have been called "Alexandria Addition?" or the addition of Alexandria? It is so called in the petition of the inhabitants for their act of incorporation and is so designated in said act of incorporation. But *why* was it so called? I have looked in vain for an answer to that question among all the books of charters and acts of incorporation and other records in the office of the Secretary of State at Concord, where such records should be found. Upon going to the records of the town of Alexandria, I find that the town had been granted by the Masonian proprietors to Joseph Butterfield, Jr., and others, March 13, 1767, including much of what is now Alexandria, and all of Danbury. But the conditions upon which this grant was made were not performed by the grantees ; and so the grantors, the Masonian proprietors, re-entered upon the land, and thus became legally seized and possessed again of the lands.

On the 7th day of July, 1773, the Masonian proprietors at a meeting held at Portsmouth, issued a new grant of Alexandria, including the same land which had been included in the former grant, to Jonas Minot, Matthew Thornton and others. This grant was described as bounded on the northwest by Mason's patent line. The said Masonian proprietors at the same time, July 7, 1773, voted that there be and there hereby is granted unto the before named Jonas Minot, and others, upon the terms, conditions, limitations, and reservations hereinafter mentioned, "A certain tract of land situated in the county of Hillsborough and Province of New Hampshire, bounded as follows, viz. : beginning at the southwesterly corner of Alexandria, aforesaid, on the patent line, and running on said patent line to Fishersfield Corner in Great Sunapee Pond ; from thence east on the northerly side line of Fishersfield, 472 rods, to Perrystown Corner; thence north,eighty-five degrees east, about four miles to a beech tree marked on the Perrystown line ; from thence north, thirty-nine degrees east, about 1672 rods, to a beech tree marked in Alexandria Corner ; from thence north, 12 degrees west, to the patent line aforementioned on the westerly side of said Alexandria." One of the terms and conditions of the grant was, that "within ninety days from this date, the lots of said grantees shall be drawn or divided and a schedule of the numbers returned to the said grantors within that time, with a list of the settling lots and the lots thereto belonging, and that said grantees, within said ninety days, shall vote an acceptance of both said grants and make a record of such acceptance."

There was a meeting of the grantees of these lands, holden at Londonderry, September 7, 1773. at which it was voted "that the proprietors accept of the grant agreeably to the condition of the charter, granted to them by the proprietors of Mason's Patent, bearing date July 7th, 1773, which grant includes the township called Alexandria, in the county of Grafton, and the land called the "Addition of Alexandria," lying in the county of Hillsborough, both in the Province of New Hampshire."

Here we have the origin of the term *Addition of Alexandria*, which addition, as you see, was bounded precisely as the town of New London was when first incorporated. We also find that all the lands in the town of New London, and much of Wilmot. were lotted and drawn to the proprietors, while it was thus known as the Addition of Alexandria, and probably within the ninety days after the date of the grant, for the records of Alexandria show the drawing of these lots, and among the different lots drawn by one Robert McMurphy was lot No. 108, and at the end of his drawing it says, "and all the common land adjoining the lot 108 by Little Sunapee Pond." The records of the proprietors of Alexandria, to whom this addition was also granted, have been destroyed by fire. from 1779. the year New London was chartered, down to 1793. After this latter date I find that the Addition is often spoken of as the Alexandria Addition, *alias* New London, and a number of the meetings of these proprietors were held in New London after 1793, at the house of Joseph Colby, Esq.

Thus we see that the lands in New London were originally and are still held under this grant of the Masonian proprietors to Jonas Minot and others of this territory as an addition to the town of Alexandria; and all the plans of the town are based upon that grant and upon the allotments and drawings or purchase of lots under that title. But these grants of the territory gave only the title to the lands, and did not give any political or municipal rights, and hence when the inhabitants desired to act as a body politic, to lay out highways and build the same, to elect town officers, to impose taxes for town purposes, for schools or for preaching, they needed an act of incorporation by the state government, which was obtained in 1779, as has been seen, and the town organized and making progress under the same.

I find a difference of opinion in regard to the original name of New London. Some say its first name was Dantzick, others that it was first called Heidleburg. Which are right? The earliest writer I have been able to find on that subject is Dr. Belknap, the author of the early history of New Hampshire. In the third volume of his history of this state, he gives us a table of statistics, in which, on page 235, he mentions Fishersfield (now Newbury) and says of it "First called Dantzick," and on page 236, he mentions New London, and says of it, "First called Heidleburg." He mentions these both as facts that were to his mind well authenticated, and concerning which there was no dispute or doubt.

The N. H. Gazetteer of 1823 (Farmer & Moore's), says that Fishersfield was first called Dantzick, according to Dr. Belknap, and that New London's "first name was Dantzick, Dr. Belknap says Hiedleburg." But they give us no reasons why they differ in opinion with Dr. Belknap in this regard. Dr. Bouton follows Farmer & Moore and says that New London was first called Dantzick, but says nothing of Fishersfield. Fogg in in his Gazetteer says that Newbury (formerly Fishersfield) was originally called Dantzick, and says the same of New London. No one of them, subsequent to Dr. Belknap, has given any reason for differing from him, nor do they refer us to any books, maps or records, to substantiate their claim. I have been able to find nothing in the office of the Secretary of State, bearing upon the question. In the State Library are many maps and charts, which I have consulted. Carrigain's Map of New Hampshire, published in 1816, shows nothing on this point, but it shows the curve line which was for many years claimed as the western and northwestern boundary of the Masonian Grant. Neither does Dr. Belknap's map, in the first volume of his History, show any thing upon the point in controversy, while it does show the straight line, that was established in 1787, by the legislature as the northwestern boundary of said Masonian Grant. Holland's Map of New Hampshire, published in London, Eng., in 1784, from a survey made about 1775, gives us no aid in this matter.

But I find a large Atlas of Maps in the State Library, published in London, Eng., in 1768, in which is a map of New Hampshire, which is said to have been made from surveys of the State, made by Mitchell and Hazzen, in 1750. Upon this map we find put down Protectworth (now Springfield), Alexandria, Heidleburg, Dantzick, and Perrystown (now Sutton), and judging from that map, and comparing it with our modern maps, it would seem to leave no doubt that Dr. Belknap is right. Dantzick, on the map, covers nearly all the territory now covered by Newbury, and extends easterly so as to cover a considerable part of what is now Sutton; but it does not extend farther north than the north line of Newbury and Sutton, and Heidleburg lies north of Dantzick, and covers very nearly the ground afterwards covered by New London.

I also find another map of New Hampshire in the same atlas, prepared by Col. Joseph Blanchard and Rev. Samuel Langdon, at Portsmouth, N. H., in 1761. and engraved and published in London with the rest, in which the curve indicating the claim of Mason on the west and northwest, is well marked, and showing all the towns in the vicinity within that curve line, and scarcely anything outside of it, showing New Chester, Alexandria, Heidleburg, Dantzick, Perrystown, and other towns around it on the east and south; from all which I am led to the same conclusion, as to the location of Heidleburg, as before.

There is one other circumstance which has great weight with me. My father was born in Hopkinton, in 1768, and removed thence to New London, in 1781, when thirteen years old, and he was eleven years old when the town was incorporated as New London. He used to tell me often about his moving to New London with his father, that his father had been talking of moving there for several years before he did go, and that this tract of land was known in Hopkinton as Heidleburg until the time of its incorporation, and that in 1781, when he moved there, the name of Heidleburg was quite as frequently applied to it as New London, though both were used indiscriminately in common conversation. That Dantzick was the name applied to the region round the south end of Sunapee Lake, while Heidleburg was to the northeast of it.

The only trouble with these old maps is that Sunapee Lake being put down without regard to any actual survey, is often represented on them as extending much farther south than it should be as compared with the surrounding territory. All the authorities agree that Newbury (formerly Fishersfield) was originally called Dantzick; and I think upon investigation it is equally well settled that the original name of New London was Heidleburg. I have no partiality for one name more than the other, and have only endeavored to get at the truth in this matter. I am inclined to think that the first settlers were wise in selecting the plain English name of New London in preference to either of them.

Let us now return to the records of the town and see what progress our new municipal corporation has been making. They held their meetings annually for the choice of town officers, and many special meetings were also holden; one notified and held February 12, 1781, to see what method the town will take to procure a man for the Continental Army, and it was *voted* "That some man be procured for the Continental Army," also that "the selectmen be a committee to hire a man for this town to serve in the Continental Army for three years."

Also, at a meeting held September 24, 1781, "*Voted*, to raise silver money to pay for beef purchased for this year, and to pay the soldier hired for this year."

At the annual town meeting held in March, 1782, after choosing town officers, &c., they *voted* "twenty hard dollars to be raised for town charges."

Voted, To grant money for school.—twelve hard dollars granted.

Voted, Seventy-five dollars for highways; work to be three shillings per day.

Voted, To do something towards the support of Mr. Ambrose, preacher. Chose a committee to inquire into his wants, and supply according to our proportion, and that an average of the same be made. The committee was Nathaniel Everett and Mr. Samuel Messer.

Voted, To join Perrystown and Fishersfield, and petition the General Court that these towns may be joined in representation.

We find nothing to show that New London was ever classed with Perrystown and Fishersfield to send a representative, but it was soon classed with Perrystown, which was incorporated as Sutton in the year 1784, April 13.

The Town Records do not show who was procured as the soldier in the Continental Army. But I find in the Adjutant General's office, among a mass of old papers and records, one with the following heading:

"Return of Soldiers mustered in the years 1781 and 1782 to fill up the Continental Army with the towns and places they engage for, and time when mustered in, for each of which a bounty of twenty pounds was promised by the acts and resolves of the General Court."

[CONTINUED IN AUGUST NUMBER.]

ND
GRANITE MONTHLY.

A MAGAZINE OF LITERATURE, HISTORY, AND STATE PROGRESS.

VOL. II.   AUGUST, 1879.   NO. 11.

HON. JAMES A. WESTON.

There is but one member of the Democratic party in the state, now living, who ever held the office of Governor of New Hampshire, and he is the only Democrat, also, who has been elected to that position since the Republican party first gained ascendancy in the state, twenty five years ago. Considering the comparatively short periods of service filled by our chief magistrates the number of surviving ex-Governors of New Hampshire is remarkably small, being but eight, altogether, and yet the idea that there is any fatality consequent upon the occupation of the office is not so far prevalent as to be productive of difficulty on the part of either party in finding men willing to accept its nomination therefor. It is a somewhat remarkable fact, after all, that no Governor of our state has ever died in office, while the average age at decease of those who have occupied the position has been considerably in excess of the allotted three score and ten years.

For seventy-five years the name of Weston has been prominent in the history of Manchester. In 1803 Amos Weston removed with his family from Reading, Mass., and settled in the town of Derryfield, now Manchester. He was a descendant, of the fifth generation, from that John Weston, who came from Buckinghamshire, England, and aided in founding a colony at Weymouth, then Wiscassett, Mass., where he established himself as a merchant, being one of the first to engage in colonial trade, but returning to England after a few years, died suddenly in that country. In 1644 John Weston, a young son of the former, made his way to America, joining several of his kindred who had emigrated previously, and finally settled in Reading, and became the progenitor of the Weston family in question. This Amos Weston was a farmer and settled upon the now well known farm in the southeastern part of Manchester to which the name is still applied. That he was a man of substantial character and held in due esteem by his fellow citizens is attested by the fact that he was several times chosen one of the selectmen of the town, as appears from the records, and was a member of the committee chosen March, 1810, to petition the legislature to change the name of Derryfield to Manchester, which petition was granted by the legislature in June following. Amos Weston, Jr., son of the above, was born in Reading, Mass., in 1791, and removed with his parents to Derryfield. He succeeded to the family homestead and became an enterprising and prosperous farmer. He married, in 1814, Betsy Wilson of Londonderry, a daughter of Col. Robert Wilson, a prominent citizen of that town, and grandaughter of James Wilson, who came from Londonderry,

Ireland, one hundred and fifty years ago, and settled at the place now known as Wilson's Crossing, in Londonderry. A man of sound judgment and superior business capacity, his services were called into requisition by his townsmen in the direction of public affairs. Between 1820 and 1841 he served five years as town-clerk, fifteen years as selectman, being eleven years chairman of the board, and three years as the representative of the town (then entitled to but one member) in the General Court. Of his union with Betsy Wilson (an estimable woman, endowed with the most amiable and exemplary traits of character) five children were born, but only one survives.

JAMES ADAMS WESTON, the youngest and only surviving child of Amos and Betsy (Wilson) Weston, was born in Manchester, August 27, 1827, being now just fifty-two years of age. He passed his time in early life at home upon the farm, in attendance upon the district school, and the academies at Piscataquog and Manchester, developing a strong taste for mathematics, to which branch of study he applied himself with much earnestness, and at an early age determined upon civil engineering as his avocation in life. Persistently continuing his studies in that direction, and in the meantime teaching school successfully two winters, in Londonderry and Manchester, he was appointed, in 1846, at nineteen years of age, assistant civil engineer of the Concord Railroad, and immediately commenced his labors in that position in attending to the work of laying the second track of the road. Three years after he was promoted to the office of chief engineer of the road, which position he has holden to the present time. At the time of his promotion, in 1849, he established his residence in Concord, where he retained his abode until 1856, having married in the meantime (1854) Miss Anna S., daughter of Mitchel Gilmore, Esq., of Concord. In connection with his duties as chief engineer, he for several years discharged the duties of road master, and master of transportation of the Concord and Manchester and Lawrence Railroad. He superintended the construction of the Concord & Portsmouth Railroad, between Manchester and Candia, and of the Suncook Valley Railroad, from Hooksett to Pittsfield. In 1856 he removed to Manchester, where he has ever since resided, devoting himself assiduously to the duties of his position in connection with the railroad, and the general pursuit of his profession as a civil engineer, together with the responsible public duties to which he has been called.

Never a politician in the ordinary sense of the term, taking no part or interest in the manipulation of partisan machinery, cherishing no ambition for the distinction of public position, Mr. Weston has always entertained decided political convictions, and has, from youth, been a consistent and persistent supporter of the principles and policy of the Democratic party. Guided in his political action by the conservative influence of reason, allied with the spirit of just liberality instead of the blind partisan zeal and intolerance which too often directs and distinguishes the conduct of public men and political leaders of either party, Mr. Weston has won and retained the personal respect of his political opponents even, so that whenever yielding to the solicitation of his party friends, and accepting their nomination for official position, he has never failed to receive more or less support from members of the opposite party, within the circle of his acquaintance. His first nomination for public office was in 1861, when he was persuaded by the Democracy of Manchester to allow the use of his name as their candidate for mayor. Manchester had always been known as a strong Republican or Whig city, and with the exception of two years, when the late Hon. Edward W. Harrington, a man of great personal popularity was the Democratic candidate and secured the election by a narrow majority, had never failed to elect an anti-Democratic mayor and city government, and at the election next previous to Mr. Weston's candidacy the Republican nominee had received a majority of nearly four hundred and fifty. Mr. Weston was defeated by a majority of some two hundred and fifty. At the election the following year he was again the Democratic candidate and was only defeated by a majority of eighteen votes by Theodore T. Abbott, the Republican candidate, an ex-Mayor of exceptional strength, who had previously polled a larger vote than had ever been cast for any other man for mayor in Manchester.

In 1867 Mr. Weston was again prevailed upon to accept the Democratic nomination for Mayor, and the election resulted in his choice, over Joseph B. Clark, then mayor and Republican candidate for re-election, by a majority of two hundred and seventy-two, his vote being larger than ever before cast for the candidate of any party, in the city, with the single exception of that cast for Mayor Abbott in 1855, the time of the great "know-nothing" excitement. A very spirited contest at the next election resulted in Mayor Weston's defeat for re-election by Isaac W. Smith the Republican candidate, upon a heavy vote, by a majority of just twenty-three. In 1869 he was again the Democratic candidate, and defeated Mayor Smith's re-election, receiving a majority of one hundred and thirty-eight. Renominated in 1870, he was again elected, receiving a majority over both the Republican and Prohibition candidates.

Mayor Weston's efficient and successful administration of the municipal affairs of the city of Manchester, and the great popular strength which he had developed in that important manufacturing metropolis of the state, directed the attention of the Democracy of the state generally to his fitness and availability for the gubernatorial nomination of the party, and at their nominating convention in January, 1871, his name was placed at the head of the state ticket. The election resulted in the first defeat which the Republican party had experienced in the state since it came into ascendancy in 1855, there being no choice of governor by the people, though Mr. Weston received a decided plurality over Hon. James Pike, the Republican candidate, and lacked but a few votes of a clear majority. Elected governor by the legislature in joint convention, he entered upon the duties of the office and devoted thereto his best efforts and most earnest labors in behalf of all the material and popular interests of the state dependent in any degree upon executive action or influence.

In 1872 the Republican leaders determined upon the restoration of their party to power, and fully appreciating the importance of the vote of the city of Manchester, as affecting the result, secured the nomination as the Republican candidate, of Hon. Ezekiel A. Straw, the able and popular agent of the Amoskeag Manufacturing Company, the largest and most powerful manufacturing corporation in that city, and in the state—a man of great popularity and influence not only in Manchester, but in all manufacturing communities throughout the state. The election resulted as was readily to be apprehended in a Republican triumph, followed by the re-election of Gov. Straw in 1873; but in the campaign of 1874, Gov. Weston, who had continued as the standard-bearer of his party upon earnest solicitation, again defeated the Republican nominee, Gen. Luther McCutchins, by a handsome plurality, although failing of an election by the people as before, and was chosen governor by the legislature. At the municipal election in Manchester, in December previous, he had been for the fourth time elected mayor of the city, a distinction which no other citizen, except ex-Gov. Smyth, has ever enjoyed. As before, he discharged the duties of both his important executive positions with eminent ability and fidelity, and retired therefrom with the full confidence and respect of the people of his native state and city.

No man has taken a deeper interest in the welfare of the city of Manchester or labored more devotedly to promote its prosperity, than has Gov. Weston. The important enterprise known as the City Water Works, by which the city is furnished with an abundant supply of the purest water from Lake Massabesic,—a supply equal to the necessities of a city of four times the present population of Manchester, and consequently ample for all demands of the future,—owes its inception and its successful organization largely to his individual efforts. There had been for some time previous much agitation of the question of a new and increased water supply for the city, and various surveys and estimates had been made —Gov. Weston himself having been engaged therein, and during the year 1871, while he was at the head of the municipal government, the matter culminated and took shape in definite action. Actively instrumental in securing the legislation necessary to allow the prosecution of the work by the city government, he became chairman of the board of commissioners established to have charge of the work, by virtue of his office as Mayor, and through this position, and his sound judgment, practical knowledge as an engineer, and deep interest in the enterprise, he gave careful direction as well as strong impetus to the preliminary work, which insured at an early day the establishment and successful operation of the noble system of water supply with which the city of Manchester is so happily favored.

Gov. Weston has been intimately connected with various other public enterprises in his native city, and was chairman of the building committee of the soldiers' monument, now just completed, and about to be dedicated with imposing ceremonies. In 1871, while Governor, he was appointed a member of the New Hampshire Centennial Commission, of which body he was chairman, and in the following year was appointed by Congress a member of the Centennial Board of Finance. His efforts were second to those of no other man in the state in promoting the excellence of the New Hampshire exhibit, and the general success of the exposition.

In his profession as a civil engineer Gov. Weston occupies the highest rank, and his services have been largely in demand in making important surveys. He surveyed proposed routes for the Manchester and Keene, Monadnock, Concord and Pittsfield, and Lowell and Windham railroads, and has made surveys and estimates for water works for various towns and cities. When the city of Concord decided upon the establishment of water works and the introduction of water from Lake Penacook he was selected as chief engineer, and carried out the work with eminent success

Notwithstanding the extent of his professional and public official labors he has been and is now actively and prominently connected with important business interests. He is one of the trustees of the Amoskeag Savings Bank, and has recently been chosen president of the City National Bank. He is the treasurer of the Suncook Valley Railroad, and a director and clerk of the Manchester Horse Railway, of which enterprise he was an active projector. He is also, and has been from its organization, vice-president and managing director of the N. H. Fire Insurance Company, and to his practical judgment the remarkable prosperity of that corporation is largely due.

Faithful and zealous in the discharge of all official duties, governed by the strictest integrity in all his business connections, his relations in social and private life correspond harmoniously therewith, and justify and increase the general esteem in which he is held. His residence, at the corner of Maple and Myrtle streets, combines the elements of modesty, comfort and taste, and is indeed the abode of a happy home circle, as well as the scene of much social enjoyment. Five interesting children grace this pleasant home : Grace Helen, born July 1, 1866 ; James Henry, July 17, 1868 ; Edwin Bell, March 15, 1871 ; Annie Mabel, September 26, 1876 ; Charles Albert, Nov. 1, 1878.

THE STATE SENATE OF 1879-80.

EDWARD GUSTINE, Senator from the Keene district, No. thirteen, was born in the town of Winchester, September 2, 1819, being now sixty years of age, the past twenty years of his life having been spent in Keene, where he now resides. His father, Edward Gustine, was a merchant. He received a common school education, learned the business of a machinist and has been mainly engaged, since entering active life, as a gas and water engineer. He has had contracts for extensive works, both gas and water, at different places in this state, Massachusetts, Vermont and New York, all of which have been carried out in a thorough and satisfactory manner.

A decided Republican, though never an active politician, Mr. Gustine has not been largely in public life, but served as a member of the House in 1865 and again in 1875 and 1876, acting as chairman of the Committee on State Prison the latter year, and was also a member of the last Constitutional Convention. He enjoys the full confidence of his fellow citizens regardless of party, and whenever a candidate for office receives many votes of those opposed to him upon political questions. In the Senate he served upon the Committee on Incorporations, Banks, and Manufactures, being chairman of the latter. He frequently participated in debates, and, although making no pretentions to oratory, his suggestions, practical in their character, were not without influence.

Mr. Gustine married Miss Sarah H. Worcester, of Lebanon, Maine, by whom he has two children, a son and daughter. The son, Edward W. Gustine, is engaged in mercantile business in Keene. In religion he is a Unitarian and an active member of the society in Keene. He has long been prominent in the Masonic organizations, local and state, having been Master of both lodges and High Priest of the Chapter at Keene, and was Grand High Priest for New Hampshire in 1870 and 1871, and has held various other honorable positions in masonic bodies. Thoroughly public spirited and a friend of all progressive enterprises, he has contributed in no small degree to the prosperity of the flourishing city in which he resides.

CHARLES J. AMIDON, of the Cheshire District, No. fourteen, is a native of the town of Chesterfield, a son of Otis Amidon, a merchant of that town, born April 23, 1827. He received his early education in the common school and at Chesterfield Academy, then a well known literary institution. He became interested in politics in youth, uniting with the Whig party and casting his first vote for Gen. Taylor for President. In 1849, at twenty-two years of age, he was appointed postmaster at Chesterfield, and held the office until his removal to Hinsdale in 1851, in which town he has since resided, and is engaged in manufacturing, doing an extensive business, giving employment to about eighty hands, in the production of cassimere and other woolen goods.

Mr. Amidon was appointed a Bank Commissioner by Gov. Ralph Metcalf, holding the office for the term of three years. He has served several years as a member of the board of selectmen of the town of Hinsdale and represented the town in the Legislature in 1861-2-3-4, serving as chairman of the committee on Claims the first three years, and of the Committee on Towns and Parishes in 1864. He was elected a representative again in 1876 and re-elected the following year, when he served as chairman of the Railroad Committee. He held the office of postmaster at Hinsdale for twelve successive years, from 1861. He was also a delegate to the Constitutional Convention in 1876, and took a prominent part in the deliberations of that body. In March, 1878, he was chosen Senator from the old ninth district, and during the legislative session of the following summer he was recognized as a leading member of the senate on the side of the majority and occupied the responsible position of chairman of the Judiciary Committee, there being no lawyer among the Republican senators that year. He also served upon the Finance Committee and the Committee on Towns.

Entering the present senate with a legislative experience more extended than that of any other member of the body he naturally exercised a strong influence in shaping its action, if not so conspicuous in debate as some of the new members. He served as chairman of the Committee on Education, and was also a member of the Judiciary Committee and of the Committee on Manufactures.

Mr. Amidon's name has been frequently mentioned in connection with the congressional nomination of his party in the third district, and it is not improbable that, whenever the nomination shall be accorded to his section of the district, he will find a strong support, should he choose to be regarded as a candidate.

Mr. Amidon was married in May, 1851, to Miss Mary J. Harvey, daughter of Loring Harvey, Esq., by whom he has three children living, two sons and a daughter.

CHARLES H. BURNS, senator from the fifteenth or Peterborough district, was born in the town of Milford, January 19, 1835, being a son of Charles A. Burns, a farmer of that town, now deceased. He completed his education at the New Ipswich Academy, under the instruction of Prof. Quimby, and having determined to enter the legal profession he entered the law office of the late Col. O. W. Lull, in his native town, where he diligently pursued his studies, and finally attended the Law School of Harvard University, where he graduated in the class of 1858. In May of that year he was admitted to the Suffolk bar in Boston, the late Chief Justice Shaw presiding, and in October following he was admitted to the New Hampshire bar, and in January, 1859, he located at Wilmot, where he has since remained in the practice of his chosen profession, to which he has been thoroughly devoted, and in which he has achieved enviable distinction and success.

A decided Republican in his political convictions, although never neglecting his professional business, he has frequently rendered his party efficient service upon the stump, where he has gained the reputation of being one of the ablest campaign speakers in the state. He was a delegate at large to the Republican National Convention at Cincinnati in 1876, and represented the New Hampshire delegation in the Committee on Resolutions. He was selected to preside at the last Republican State Convention, holden in Concord September 10, 1878, and upon assuming the chair, made a forcible and earnest speech, in which he enunciated decided hard money doctrines, notwithstanding the apparently discouraging result of the election in Maine on the preceeding day. Referring to this address in its report of the convention the *Boston Journal* said: "Although Mr. Burns' ability and scholarship have for years been known to the public, yet it is only justice to him to say that his address today was the grandest effort of his life and places him in the very front rank of the earnest, eloquent and impassioned speakers of our state."

Mr. Burns was elected to and discharged the duties of the office of Treasurer of Hillsborough County in 1864 and 1865. In 1876 he received an appointment as County Solicitor from Gov. Cheney, which office he still holds, having been elected thereto by the people at the late election under the amended constitution. In 1873 he was a member of the senate, from the old seventh district, in which body he was at once accorded a leading position and served as chairman of the Judiciary Committee, to which position he was promptly assigned by President Gallinger in making up the committees of the present senate, and was also appointed upon the Claims and Finance committees. To the consideration of the many important matters coming before the Judiciary Committee at the late session of the Legislature he devoted the most careful attention, giving all questions effecting the public interest in the committee as well as in the senate, as full an investigation as circumstances would permit, and fair treatment in all respects. A ready debater, combining clearness of statement with vigor of speech, yet speaking only when impelled by judgment of the merits or the necessities of the case, he exercised an influence in the deliberations of the senate second to that of no other senator. It cannot be regarded improper to remark that no man in the state stands higher in the confidence of his party today, than Mr. Burns, and should he be inclined to pursue a public career, there is no position in the gift of his party to which he may not reasonably aspire.

Mr. Burns was united in marriage with Sarah N. Mills, of Milford, upon the twenty-first anniversary of his birth, Jan. 19, 1856, by whom he has four children, two sons and two daughters. He has a fine estate in Wilton, and is known as one of the most public spirited citizens of the town. His religious faith is of the liberal order. He has taken thirty-two degrees in masonry and is a prominent member of the organization. In 1874 he received the honorary degree of Master of Arts from Dartmouth College, and in the recent organization of his military staff he was designated by Gov. Head, Judge Advocate General with the rank of Brigadier General.

GEORGE W. TODD, senator from the Amherst district, No. sixteen, was born in Ridge, November 19, 1828, being the son of a farmer of that town. He received his education in the common schools, at the academies in Jaffrey and Marlow in this state, and Brattleborough. Vt., and under private tutors. He studied medicine two years, but relinquished the same for the study of law, which he pursued in the office of Pierce & Tyler at Winchendon, Mass., and that of Hon. Edmund L. Cushing, late Chief Justice of this state, at Charlestown, and graduated at the end of a four years' course, at the State and National Law School, at Poughkeepsie, N. Y., and was admitted to practice in the courts of New York and this state, and subsequently those of Vermont ; but after a few years' practice of his profession has devoted his life mainly to teaching, in which occupation he has met with marked success. He became principal of the Orleans Liberal Institute at Glover, Vt., in 1858, where he was engaged for seven years, was subsequently three years principal of Marlow Academy ; one year principal of the High School at Edgartown, Mass. ; three years at Lenox, and three years at Great Barrington in the same state ; also as principal of their High Schools, and had been for six years previous to election to the senate principal of McCollom Institute, the well known academy at Mont Vernon, which institution under his management attained a high and extended reputation among the educational institutions of the state. Mr. Todd has served for fourteen years altogether upon school-boards in the various places in which he has resided, but held no political office previous to his election to the present senate, with the exception of that of representative in the legislature, to which he was chosen by the citizens of his native town in 1857 and again in 1858, only two votes being cast against him the latter year. He served each year upon the Committee on Education, and in 1858 was the Cheshire County member of the select committee appointed to draft resolutions upon that portion of the governor's message relating to national affairs, the adoption of which resolutions by the house he advocated in a strong speech. In the senate he has been known as an active working member, serving upon the Committees on Claims, Education, and Roads, Bridges and Canals, being chairman of the first named committee.

Mr. Todd was married, Aug. 16, 1857, to Mary A. H. Blodgett, of Jaffrey, who deceased Dec. 31, 1864. He subsequently married Sarah J., daughter of Dea. Harvey Chapin, of Holyoke, Mass., his present wife. He has no children living.

ORREN C. MOORE, Senator from the seventeenth district, which embraces the city of Nashua, has been well known in political life in New Hampshire for several years past, holding a prominent position among the leaders of the Republican party in the state. There may be others who have attained more exalted official position at as early an age in life at the hands of one or the other of the great political parties in our state, but no man in New Hampshire, of equal years, within the last quarter of a century at least, has engrossed public attention in larger measure, exerted a stronger influence in shaping the action of his party or directing the legislation of the state than has Mr. Moore during the last six or eight years. Born in the town of New Hampton, Aug. 10, 1839, he is now just forty years of age. His father, J. H. Moore, was a country merchant in limited circumstances, who was engaged in trade for a time in Holderness, and subsequently removed to Manchester, where he died. Young Moore was early thrown upon his own resources for his support. He labored for a time in the employ of one of the corporations at Manchester and obtained such education as he was enabled to secure in the time at his command in the public schools of that city. In 1855, at sixteen years of age, he went to LaCrosse, Wisconsin, where he learned the printer's trade in the office of an older brother, F. A. Moore, remaining in his service three years. Returning to New Hampshire, he worked at his trade in different offices in Manchester, and was for several years foreman of the news room of the *Daily American* of that city, until its consolidation with the *Mirror*.

In 1866 Mr. Moore became editor and part proprietor of the weekly *Telegraph*, at Nashua, and removed to that city, where he has since resided, engaged in the management of the same paper, which has come to be regarded as one of the ablest exponents of Republicanism in New England. In 1869 he established a daily in connection with the weekly paper, there being previously no daily paper published in the city. Last year Mr. Langley, who had been his partner in the business, withdrew, and he is now sole proprietor of the newspaper and printing establishment, in connection with which there is also an extensive bindery.

For five years previous to his election to the present senate, Mr. Moore was a member of the House of Representatives from Nashua, and during the entire period of his service in that body it may be safely said that no member labored more diligently in the interest of all measures which he regarded as essential to the welfare of the state, none watched more closely the general course of legislation or participated more earnestly or effectively in debate upon all important questions than did Mr. Moore. In 1878 he was particularly conspicuous as the champion of several important measures recommended by the Tax Commission appointed by Gov. Prescott in accordance with the act of the previous legislature, of which commission he was a member and of whose report he was the author. Whatever was accomplished by the legislature last year in the direction of the equalization of taxation is due in the main to Mr. Moore's efforts. In the senate the present year he has maintained his high rank as a debater, as well as a laborious and earnest legislator, persistently supporting all measures which, to his mind, the best interest of the state demanded. As chairman of the Committee on State Institutions he favored the most liberal policy with reference to the State Normal School, of which institution he has ever been a strong friend, and was mainly instrumental in securing the appropriation for the instruction of the inmates of the Reform School in industrial trades and callings. He was also an active member of the Committee on Education and Railroads.

What is rarely the case with a ready and incisive writer, Mr. Moore is equally ready and forcible in debate, and is a vigorous and effective speaker upon the stump, where his services are frequently called in requisition by his party in this and other states. In 1873 he served as chairman of the Republican State Committee, has been often called into service in framing the party platform, and once as president of the Republican State Convention. He was also a member of the New Hampshire delegation to the last Republican National Convention. In the recent Senatorial caucus which nominated Col. Blair, he received a handsome vote, and is likely to be warmly supported by his friends for the next Republican Congressional nomination in his district. Yet after all, journalism is his real forte, and in the opinion of those who know him best the highest success is attainable for him in that field.

Mr. Moore married, Nov. 29, 1860, Miss N. W. Thompson, a daughter of J. H. Thompson, Esq., of Holderness, and a sister of Maj. A. B. Thompson, present Secretary of State, by whom he has one child, a daughter.

ELBRIDGE G. HAYNES, senator from the Manchester or eighteenth district, was born in Allenstown, Jan. 29, 1815, his father being James Haynes, a farmer by occupation, and his mother's maiden name was Sally Clarke.

His parents resided in Epsom until 1827, when they removed to New London, and two years later to Fishersfield, now Newbury.

His early educational advantages were limited, comprising but little beyond eight or nine weeks each winter in the district schools, between the ages of eight and sixteen years.

In the spring of 1831 he "bought his time" of his father, paying one hundred and fifty dollars therefor, and started on foot for Boston to seek his fortune. From Sutton he accompanied a team loaded with cider as far as Lexington, where the apple-juice was sold, and he continued on to Boston, making his appearance on Haymarket Square with his trunk on his shoulder, and fourpense-ha'penny in his pocket, as the remains of the two dollars with which he had started. He speedily found employment, and remained in Boston, in the wholesale provision business, until 1840. He witnessed the burning of the Ursiline Convent, the execution of the pirates of the brig Mexican, and the "Broad street riots." The sight of the mob marching Garrison through the streets of Boston had a powerful influence in shaping his political convictions, and he became and ever remained a zealous advocate of the anti-slavery movement.

In 1840 he returned to Newbury, and was married, Nov. 1, to Caroline R. Knowlton, daughter of Capt. Nathaniel W. Knowlton, of Sutton. Four children have resulted from this union: Col. Martin A., now editor of the *Lake Village Times*, and clerk of the court for the county of Belknap; Addie M., wife of Dr. C. W. Clement, of Manchester; Charles F., recently deceased, and Cora M.

The year of his marriage he bought a farm in Springfield, and lived there and in Sutton until 1846, the fall of which year he removed to Manchester, and learned the mason's trade, which he has ever since followed.

He has been for a long period almost continuously in public office in Manchester as Alderman, Selectman, Moderator and Councilman, two years in each position; as Assessor four years, and as Supervisor and Inspector of Elections three years, besides other minor offices.

His first legislative service was in the senate this year, but his extended experience in the practical affairs of life has given him ample qualification therefor. In committee work he served efficiently upon the committee on State Institutions, Incorporations and Military Affairs.

In religious preferences Mr. Haynes is Universalist, having attended that church for the past thirty years.

WILLIAM G. PERRY, who represents the Amoskeag District, No. Nineteen, in the senate was very appropriately selected as the first senator from the new district, which embraces the manufacturing centre of the state, whose leading corporation has given its name to the district, and to the successful service of which corporation Mr. Perry has devoted the best energies of his life. A native of the state of Rhode Island, the son of Geo. C. Perry, a farmer of South Kingston in that state, born Aug. 5, 1818, he spent his early life in his native state, his educational advantages being such as the common school afforded. In early youth he entered the service of a manufacturing establishment, and has been for over forty-eight years engaged in cotton manufacturing and in the building of machinery, residing at Providence until twenty-three years ago, when, in November, 1856, he came to Manchester and engaged in the service of the Amoskeag corporation as superintendent of the manufacturing department, which position he has holden to to the present time, contributing in a large degree, through his sound judgment and superior executive ability, to the prosperity of that great corporation.

Mr. Perry, although devoting himself without reserve to the onerous duties of his position as superintendent of the Amoskeag Manufacturing Company's Mills, has not been unmindful of his duties as a citizen, has taken a strong interest in public affairs in the city of his adoption, and has been called into service under the city government as a member of the school committee and of the Board of Aldermen. He also efficiently represented his ward in the legislature in 1875 and again in 1876, and there as in the senate this year, proved himself a safe and practical conservator of the public interests. He served upon the Senate Committee on Finance, Elections and Manufactures.

Mr. Perry was married in 1837 to Miss Nancy A. Shrieve, who died in December, 1874. By her he had eight children, five of whom died in infancy. The surviving children are Hon. Geo. T. Perry, M. D., of Natick, R. I., surgeon of the Rhode Island State Prison and State Farm; Mrs. William A. Champlain, of Providence, and William A. Perry, clerk in the office of the Amoskeag Co., at Manchester. Mr. Perry worships with the Second Congregational church at Manchester, and is a member of Lafayette Lodge I. O. O. F., and Trinity Commandery of that city.

WILLIAM H. SHEPARD, of the Londonderry Senatorial District, No. twenty, was born in the town of Holderness, in this state, May 16, 1819, his father being William B. Shepard, a farmer. He spent his early life upon the farm, and obtained a good English education in the common schools and at Plymouth Academy. Not content with such opportunities for advancement as his native place afforded he went, in youth, to Massachusetts, where he succeeded in making his way in life prosperously, as many a New Hampshire youth has done. He engaged in woolen manufacturing and was for a long time superintendent and purchasing agent for a Lawrence manufacturing company. In 1869, after thirty-three years of successful labor in the Bay State, he returned to New Hampshire, and established his residence in the town of Derry, where he purchased a large farm, and has since devoted himself to rural pursuits, making a specialty of fruit and vegetables, of which he produces a larger and finer variety than is often found in this or any other New England state. Since his residence in Derry Mr. Shepard has served the town upon the board of selectmen, and in the legislature for the years 1875 and 1876, giving eminent satisfaction in each position, as has also been the case in his senatorial service this year. He served upon the committees on Towns, Education, and Roads, Bridges and Canals. Mr. Shepard was married in Dec., 1841, to Miss Anna E. Johnson, daughter of D. A. R. Johnson, of Springfield, N. H., by whom he had three children, one dying in infancy. One son, Edgar H. Shepard, was a member of the 18th Reg. N. H. V., and died in Concord in 1865. The remaining son is now a farmer at Derry.

GREENLEAF CLARKE, Senator from the Rockingham District, No twenty-one, is a member of the well known Clarke family of Atkinson, children of Greenleaf and Julia (Cogswell) Clarke. The eldest brother, William C. Clarke, attained a high position at the bar of this state, and in addition to other important offices, held the position of Attorney-General of the state from 1863 till his death in 1872. Another brother is John B. Clarke, state printer, and the well known proprietor of the *Manchester Mirror*. Greenleaf Clarke, the senator in question, is a farmer and occupies the old homestead in Atkinson, upon which he was born, May 7, 1816, and which ranks among the best farms in the county of Rockingham. He received a good practical education in the common schools and at the old Atkinson Academy, formerly one of the best educational institutions in the state, and at an early period of life was somewhat prominent in politics as an active Democrat, serving in various town offices, as representative in the legislature, and as a member of the Executive Council during the last two years of the administration of the late Governor Dinsmore. Latterly he has not been prominently engaged in politics or public life, though retaining a strong interest in national questions, and changing his connection from the Democratic to the Republican party during the war period, until within the last few years. In 1876 he was chosen a delegate from his town to the state Constitutional Convention and was elected representative the following year. He served in the Senate as chairman of the Committee on Incorporations and as a member of the Railroad and Agricultural Committees. He may well be designated as a "plain, blunt man," never speaking except when occasion requires and then clearly and without circumlocution.

Mr. Clarke has been largely engaged in other business aside from farming, such as lumbering, contracting, surveying, etc. He is a director, and was one of the grantees and surveyors of the Manchester and Lawrence Railroad. In religious preference he is a Congregationalist, and is also a Royal Arch Mason.

He married, in 1855, Miss Sarah J. Noyes, daughter of Cyrus Noyes of Atkinson, by whom he has three children, two daughters and a son, Greenleaf Clarke, Jr.

EMMONS B. PHILBRICK, of Rye, represents one of the "close" political districts in the present senate—the Newmarket District, No. 22,—in which the people failed to elect : Mr. Philbrick, the Republican candidate, who had received a plurality vote, being chosen Senator by the Legislature in joint convention. Mr. Philbrick is a son of Josiah W. Philbrick a Rye farmer, and was born in that town November 14, 1833. He took a scientific course of study at Hampton Academy, with a view to pursuing the profession of a civil engineer ; but upon the death of an only brother, at the earnest solicitation of his parents he surrendered his plans in that direction, and after teaching school successfully for some fifteen terms in this state and Massachusetts, settled in his old home and took charge of the farm, where he has since resided, devoting himself in the main to agriculture, but taking an active part in developing the summer boarding interest, now an important factor in the prosperity of his town and section. He is also engaged to some extent in surveying and does a large business as a justice of the peace, an important item in a town like Rye where there is no lawyer located. He has been prominently connected with town affairs, although a member of the minority party in the town, holding the offices of selectman and superintending school committee, his large experience in teaching and deep interest in educational affairs giving him especial qualifications for the latter position. He was a member of the last senate from the old First District, and served as chairman of the Finance Committee in that body, which position he has also acceptably filled the present year, serving also upon the Judiciary and Election Committees.

Mr. Philbrick has been twice married, first in April 1859 to Vianna M. Dalton, daughter of Michael Dalton of North Hampton, who died in 1869, and again to Mary C. Seavey of Rye, in October, 1875. He has had two children by each marriage, three of whom survive—two sons and a daughter. His religious associations are with the Christian church at Rye. He is a member of the Odd Fellows organization.

CHARLES E. SMITH of the Dover District, No. Twenty-three, which embraces the city of Dover and the town of Rollinsford, has been a resident of Dover for some ten years past, where he is landlord of the Kimball House, a hotel near the Boston & Maine railway station, and favorably known to the traveling public under his management. Mr. Smith is a native of Newmarket, born January 5, 1831, his father, Daniel R. Smith, being a farmer and carpenter, resident in that town. His educational advantages were limited to the common schools, and most of his early life was passed in farm labor. Subsequently he engaged for a time in trade, and afterwards went into the hotel business at South Newmarket, where he remained until his removal to Dover. Wide awake, public spirited, and active in political life while in South Newmarket, he held nearly every position in the gift of the town, being selectman, collector of taxes and representative in the legislature, and was for nine years chief of police of the village. During his residence in Dover he has given a hearty support to all progressive enterprises, and taken special interest in the welfare of the Strafford County Agricultural society. He is an active member of the order of Knights of Pythias. In his religious views he is liberal, but attends the services of the M. E. Church. In the senate he has been one of the working rather than talking members, serving upon the Committees, on Claims, Elections and as the senate member of the joint Standing Committee on State House and Yard, and to his sensible efforts is due largely the adoption of the resolution authorizing the removal of the fountain from the centre of the walk approaching the front of the State House, which has long been regarded a public nuisance. Mr. Smith was united in marriage in Dec., 1865, with Miss A. Augusta Burley, an accomplished young lady of Newmarket, daughter of Jonathan Burley of that town.

JOHN H. BROUGHTON, Senator from the Portsmouth District, No. Twenty-four, is a native of that city, born July 11, 1830, and has always resided there. He is a lumber dealer by occupation, and a member of the well-known firm of Samuel Adams & Co. Mr. Broughton is emphatically a self-made man. Favored with but slight opportunities to procure an education in youth, his strong native sense and indomitable energy and industry has won for him an honorable and enviable position among his fellow-citizens. A man of sound sense and correct business principles, honorable and just in all his dealings, he has not only worked his way to an ample fortune, but also to the esteem and confidence of the community in which he resides. He represented his ward in the legislature in 1872 and 1873, discharging his duties most creditably to himself and his constituents. In 1876 he was elected Mayor of Portsmouth and was re-elected the following year. In his election to the present senate the people of Portsmouth gave another strong testimonial of their appreciation of his ability and faithfulness in the public service, which his course during the session has unquestionably justified. He served upon the Committees on Banks, Manufactures and State Institutions, being chairman of the former committee, which position in the sketch of Senator Ordway last month was erroneously accorded to him.*

Mr. Broughton was married Nov. 29, 1854, to Miss Mary E. Patch, of Portsmouth, a sister of the gallant Lieutenant Charles W. Patch, of the Second N. H. Regiment, who was mortally wounded at the battle of Gettysburg.

* Another error in the Senatorial Sketches last month occurred in the misprinting of the Christian name of Senator Shaw, which was printed *Alfred*, instead of Albert as it should have been.

LINES ON THE DEATH OF THACKERAY.

BY MARY HELEN BOODEY.

'Twas night in the great city, and the sound
  Of passing thousands echoed forth less loud
Through the dim streets. The noisy bound
  Of human footsteps, gay, and soft, and proud,
All, all had passed as passed the fleeting crowd,
  Some heavy with a weight of untold woe,
Some gay and light as though no sorrow cloud
  Had bowed them to the earth beneath its blow ;
All these had fled and only now and then
Broke on the ear the voice and tread of men.

Yet there was one of all that mighty throng,
  One glorious by intellect and fame,
One now the theme of many a mournful song,
  Whose glowing, burning words engrave his name
In characters of pure, undying fame
  Upon the hearts of men. Yet in the gloom of night
Alone he struggled and alone he died.
  Died ! Passed away ! Fled to a world of light,
Where, casting off the robings of his soul,
Beauty and glory crowned his kingly brow,
Before whose splendor angels, e'en, might bow.

O Death ! relentless, stern and unsubdued,
  Thou "lovest a shining mark ;" well didst thou choose
This one from others ;—many hearts have sued
  In vain for that one fearful power, to lose
Their own existence ;—to precipitate
  Themselves into Eternity ; to test
That strange hereafter, life in which men date
  These longings for the beautiful, this eager quest
For happiness and rest. But Thackeray's death
Was like some glorious noon shaded by Tempest's breath.

KEARSARGE MOUNTAIN.

FROM HARRIMAN'S HISTORY OF WARNER.*

The late Dr. Bouton called Kearsarge "the peerless mountain" of Merrimack county. It is closely identified with Warner. It lifts its head 2943 feet above the sea level. It has no immediate competitor. To the traveller on the Northern railroad it presents a bold and striking outline. It is a prominent landmark within a circle whose diameter is one hundred miles.

A controversy in relation to the origin of the *name* of this mountain sprang up a few years ago. Somebody set afloat the absurd story that an English hunter, by the name of Hezekiah Sargent, came, some time previous to 1750, and made his home somewhere on this mountain, and hence its name; that, furthermore, the said Hezekiah died about the year 1800, and was buried—but, as in the case of Moses, "no man knoweth of his sepulchre unto this day."

It is a sufficient answer to this, to say that no such man ever lived on Kearsarge mountain, on the top or on either side of it. The story is a fabrication. The best authority for it, so far as the writer knows, is a visionary, crazed man (now dead), who, in his last will and testament, bequeathed to his daughter *four hedgehogs*, when she should catch them on his mountain ledge!

Two hundred years before the ridiculous tale is told of this Hezekiah Currier Sargent, the mountain bore the name of Kearsarge, in some of its variations; and a hundred and seventy-five years before this remarkable character is placed on the mountain at all, or is ever heard of anywhere, even in tradition, Kearsarge was known by its present name. This hero of the wild hunting-grounds puts in an appearance too late.

The name unquestionably comes from the Indians, who sojourned at its base, who roamed over its steep declivities, or who saw it from afar. It is not easy to convey, by the use of English letters, the precise sounds of the unlettered wild men of the forest. The thing is impossible, and, in attempting it, we have the orthography of the name in almost an unlimited number of forms. The still further difficulty may be noticed, that, even among the Indians themselves, the pronunciation of the word varied as much as the orthography of it has varied among white men.

In 1652, Gov. Endicott's exploration of the Merrimack river to Lake Winnipesaukee was executed. The Endicott rock, at the outlet of the lake, was then marked. A plan was made of this survey, and the proof is at hand that this plan must have been made *before* 1670. It is thus endorsed: "Plat of Meremack river from ye See up to Wenepeseoce Pond, also the Corses from Dunstable to Penny—cook.

Jn⁰ Gardner."

Kearsarge mountain is on this plan, and the name is spelled *Carsaga*.

Capt. Samuel Willard, of Lancaster, Mass., the prince of Indian rangers, saw this mountain from the top of Monadnock, July 31, 1725, and called it *Cusagee* mountain.

On the margin of the ancient plan of Boscawen, which was granted by Massa-

---

*This work, recently issued, is embraced in a handsome octavo volume of 581 pages, finely printed, substantially bound, and embellished by a map of the town and twenty-three portraits of distinguished citizens or natives of the town, several of which are steel engravings. To the production of this work General Walter Harriman, a distinguished son of the old town of which he writes, has devoted much care and labor, and has given the public one of the most systematic, comprehensive and thoroughly interesting town histories yet produced.

chusetts, as a township, in 1733, appears a rude representation of an irregular hill along the northern boundary line, with this appended inscription: "Supposed to be one of ye *Kiasaga* Hills."

A plan of Kearsarge Gore, drawn by Col. Henry Gerrish subsequent to 1751, bears the following title: "A plan of *Kaysarge* Gore, near *Kyasarge.*"

An English map, published according to act of Parliament, in 1755, by Thomas Jeffreys, geographer to His Royal Highness the Prince of Wales, near Charing Cross, and taken from actual surveys made in 1750 by Mitchell and Hazzen, puts our mountain in its true place, and spells it *Kyasage*.

The proprietor's records of Sutton state that a township of land "was granted to Capt. Obadiah Perry and others, in 1743, lying on the west side of *Kiasarge* Hill."

In June, 1750, a meeting of the proprietors of that town was called by Thomas Hale, who represented that the land laid "on the westerly side of *Ciasarge* Hill." Again, the proprietors of that town spell the name, *Ciasargey;* again, *Chia Sarge;* and again, *Keyasargy*. But words need not be multiplied. The position here taken required, perhaps, no substantiation at all. The story of Hezekiah Sargent is a myth. The mountain has been known, continuously, as *Kearsarge* more than two hundred years!

But another controversy concerning this mountain has arisen still more recently. The birth of this latter controversy, so far as the public are informed, was in 1875. The Union corvette, or sloop of war, *Kearsarge*, became famous by sinking the Confederate Alabama, June 19, 1864. Eleven years afterwards the question is raised, whether this gallant vessel took its name from the Kearsarge of two hundred years standing, or from a mountain in Carroll county.

The Kearsarge was built at Portsmouth, N. H., in 1861. Major Henry McFarland, of Concord, a paymaster in the army, wrote a letter to the assistant secretary of the navy (G. V. Fox), on the first day of June, 1861, suggesting that one of the sloops of war, which were then being built at Portsmouth, be called *Kearsarge*. Gideon Wells, of Connecticut, was secretary of the navy. He accepted this name. He thought, at first, that *Kearsarge*, with the final "r" left out, was the true orthography, but the secretary of the treasury, Salmon P. Chase, corrected him. Concerning this matter, Secretary Wells wrote as follows: "I first directed that the corvette should be called Kearsage; but Mr. Chase, a New Hampshire man, corrected my pronunciation and orthography. We had, I recollect, a little dispute, and that I quoted Governor Hill, but Mr. Chase convinced me that he was correct."

Major McFarland says, with much force and beauty, "The corvette appears to me to have been named when she received the precise designation which she defiantly carried through storm and battle." It will be well to remember here that Salmon P. Chase was a native of Cornish, a New Hampshire town, which has the Kearsarge of Merrimack county in plain view.

Mr. Wells "quoted Governor Hill." This is further proof that it was the mountain in Merrimack county for which he named the corvette, Governor Hill having been a citizen of Concord, a large land-owner on that mountain, and an enthusiast in setting forth its lofty grandeur.

About 1865, a large hotel was built on the Wilmot side of this mountain, and named in honor of the ship's captain, the "Winslow House." That hotel was destroyed by fire in 1867, and was rebuilt on a larger scale. A reception was given to Admiral Winslow, in the first house, and he was present at the opening of the second, in 1868, when he gave the proprietor a stand of colors and a picture of the battle.

Men of high station, both in the state and country, as well as others, were present on these occasions, participating in the festivities and congratulations of the hour. Nobody whispered that we were on the wrong mountain. Probably, into no one's mind, *at that time*, had the idea entered that a rival mountain was entitled to these honors.

In due time Admiral Winslow died, and a boulder was taken from the original Kearsarge to serve as a monument at his grave. And now the controversy as to the origin of the ship's name began; but the family of the Admiral stood by *our* Kearsarge, and the boulder is found in Forest Hill Cemetery, Boston Highlands, supporting a bronze tablet with the following inscription:

> Rear Admiral
> JOHN ANCRUM WINSLOW,
> U. S. Navy,
> Born in Wilmington, N. C.,
> Nov. 19, 1811,
> Died in Boston, Mass.,
> Sept, 29, 1873.
> He conducted the memorable
> Sea-fight in command of
> U. S. S. Kearsarge,
> When she sank the Alabama in the
> English Channel, June 19, 1864.
> This boulder from
> Kearsarge Mountain, Merrimack County, N. H.,
> Is the gift
> Of the citizens of Warner, N. H., and is erected
> to his memory by his wife and
> surviving children.

A correspondent of the Boston *Journal*, writing from Petersburg, Virginia, July 16, 1864, says,—"The sinking of the Alabama by the Kearsarge gives great joy to the soldiers. They are as much gratified as if *they* had won a victory. The men of the Kearsarge were mainly from New Hampshire. Their ship was built there, and it bears the name of the grand old mountain, beneath the shadow of which Daniel Webster passed his childhood. The name was selected for the ship by one of the publishers of the *New Hampshire Statesman*. The tourist, passing through the Granite State, will look with increased pleasure upon the mountain whose name, bestowed upon a national vessel, will be prominent in the history of the republic."

Warner, Wilmot, Andover, Sutton, and Salisbury all claim ownership in this mountain. Warner and Wilmot meet on the very summit; Andover comes near the top; Salisbury and Sutton not quite as near.

The summit of Kearsarge is a bald rock. It was once mostly covered with wood; but about seventy-five years ago the fire ran over the top of the mountain, increasing in intensity for several days, and consuming not only the dead and living trees, but burning up the greater portion of the soil itself.

Standing on the majestic height, one feels that he is, indeed, on the king mountain of all this region. It stands there without a rival. It has no neighbor on the east—nothing to intercept a view of the ocean. At the south, fifty miles away, rises the grand Monadnock, its equal, and its solitary neighbor in that direction. At the west lies old Ascutney, triple-pointed, and grand beyond description in the evening twilight, but this mountain is "over the border," for, by the decree of King George the Third, in 1764, the west bank of the Connecticut river is our boundary. Then, to the northward and in fair view, though from thirty to sixty miles away, the nearest equal neighbors are Cardigan, White Face, and Chocorua, the summit of the two latter being seldom trodden by human feet. Each of these mountains is sublime in its way, but *Kearsarge* stands alone in solitary grandeur—the Mont Blanc of central New Hampshire.

HYMNOLOGY OF THE CHURCHES.

BY ASA McFARLAND.

The purpose of this and the preceding article (Monthly for July), is only to make mention of a few of the hymns which hold a permanent place in the books in use by most churches, accompanied by a statement of the circumstances under which some of them were written. With this brief statement we proceed to speak of Isaac Watts, D. D., whose metrical productions occupy large space in books devoted to sacred song. Watts died in 1748, in the seventy-fifth year of his age. He was one of the dissenting clergymen of England, and several years pastor of a church in London. He was a better versifier than poet: but his productions are full of scripture, abound with individual life and reality; were written in pure English, and are adapted to the experience of all Christian people; are correct in rhyme, and came from a devout heart. He was an earnest and eloquent preacher, and the congregation greatly increased under his ministration. But his health failed, and he was compelled to cease preaching. He was then invited by Sir Thomas Abney, one of the aldermen of London, to visit him at his residence in the country. This visit, intended to be of only a few weeks, was extended to more than thirty years. The country abode of the London alderman was upon the shore of that arm of the sea known as "Southampton Water." Living upon the margin of that body of water, and looking across it, how natural that hymn of Watts:

" Sweet fields beyond the swelling flood,
 Stand dressed in living green;
So to the Jews old Canaan stood,
 While Jordan rolled between."

Mrs. Sarah Flower Adams, wife of an English civil engineer, was the author of a hymn that is in as general use as any metrical production in our language, for it is sung in the churches of all denominations. This is the well known production of which the following is the first stanza:

" Nearer, my God, to thee,
  Nearer to thee!
 E'en though it be a cross
  That raiseth me!
 Still all my song shall be,
 Nearer, my God, to thee,
  Nearer to thee."

Mrs. Adams was a Unitarian, and her celebrated hymn was written for an English magazine, with no expectation that it would find a place in the hymnology of the churches. Another instance of an author "building better than she knew."

Rev. Philip Doddridge. D. D., wrote much that holds a permanent place in the books of the present day. He was a native of London; was author of the "Family Expositor," and "Rise and Progress of Religion in the Soul." He died in Lisbon, whither he went for the benefit of his health. Oct. 13, 1751. He was a laborious and successful preacher of the gospel, and was in the habit, occasionally, of writing and appending a hymn to his discourse, suggested by its topic. Preaching on one occasion from the text, " There remaineth, therefore, a rest for the people of God," he appended a hymn which has come down to us, and is found in a multitude of books, of which the following is the first stanza:

"Thine earthly Sabbaths, Lord, we love,
 But there's a nobler rest above;
To that our longing souls aspire,
 With cheerful hope and strong desire."

Church hymnology is not wanting in productions of heroic or triumphant cast. Of such is the hymn by Martin Luther, commencing:

"A mighty fortress is our God,
A bulwark never failing;
Our helper he, amid the flood
Of mortal ills prevailing:
For still our ancient foe
Doth seek to work our woe;
His craft and power are great,
And, armed with cruel hate,
On earth is not his equal."

Hymns of that cast or tone might properly be expected of the great German Reformer, but of Henry Kirke White, who died at only a little over twenty-one, we would not look for productions of heroic character. He was a native of Nottingham, England, and a young man of such rare promise, that a memoir of him was written by the poet Southey. He died in 1806. Here are three verses of a hymn by this young man that are of the heroic cast:

"The Lord, our God, is clothed with might,
The winds obey his will;
He speaks, and in his heavenly height,
The rolling sun stands still.

Rebel, ye waves, and o'er the land
With threatening aspect roar;
The Lord uplifts his awful hand,
And chains you to the shore.

Howl, winds of night, your force combine—
Without God's high behest,
Ye shall not, in the mountain pine,
Disturb the sparrow's nest."

And a third example is by William Shrubsole, Esq., of Sheerness, England, one of the founders of the London Missionary Society, commencing—

"Arm of the Lord, awake, awake;
Put on thy strength, the nations shake;
Now let the world, adoring, see
Triumphs of mercy wrought by thee."

No writer of hymns, not himself a clergyman, is held in greater favor by devout people, than William Cowper, and no poet ever wrote productions so entirely dissimilar. It is one of the curiosities of English Literature, that the author of the "Diverting History of John Gilpin," and the hymn commencing:

"Oh, for a closer walk with God;
A calm and heavenly frame;
A light to shine upon the road
That leads me to the Lamb,"

were one and the same man. Such productions of Cowper as are brought into the service of sacred song are known in his works as "Olney Hymns," because written when the author dwelt in that town with the Unwin family. These hymns are sixty-eight in number, and found in most collections. Perhaps the following is as much a favorite as any of the Olney Hymns:

"God moves in a mysterious way,
His wonders to perform;
He plants his footsteps in the sea,
And rides upon the storm.

Deep in unfathomable mines
Of never failing skill,
He treasures up his bright designs
And works his sovereign will.

Ye fearful saints, fresh courage take!
The clouds ye so much dread,
Are big with mercy, and will break
In blessings on your head.

Judge not the Lord by feeble sense,
But trust him for his grace;
Behind a frowning Providence
He hides a smiling face.

His purposes will ripen fast,
Unfolding every hour;
The bud may have a bitter taste
But sweet will be the flower.

Blind unbelief is sure to err,
And scan his work in vain;
God is his own interpreter,
And he will make it plain."

Although the greater portion of hymns in use for church service were written by clergymen, yet laymen have written much and well. Wordsworth, Bryant, Montgomery, H. K. White, Thomas Moore (the Irish melodist), Geo. P. Morris, Browning, Addison, Dryden, Oliver W. Holmes, and W. B. Tappan are of this number, and many might be added. Addison was one of the most eminent literary men of the age in which he lived. The Spectator (for which Addison was chief writer), dated

Sept. 20, 1712, contained a hymn that has lived 167 years. The author had encountered a storm at sea, and narrowly escaped death. The hymn is founded upon the 107th Psalm, which commences, "Oh, give thanks unto the Lord, for he is good; for his mercy endureth forever." The following is the first stanza:

"How are thy servants blest, O Lord;
How sure is their defense!
Eternal wisdom is their guide,
Their help, Omnipotence."

The third and fourth stanzas are supposed to have been suggested by the terrific storm the vessel encountered:

"When by the dreadful tempest borne,
High on the broken wave,
They know thou art not slow to hear,
Nor impotent to save.

The storm is laid, the winds retire,
Obedient to thy will;
The sea, that roars at thy command,
At thy command is still."

That Cowper, subject to mental depression much of his life, should have been the author of "John Gilpin," is no more surprising than that the rollicking song writer, Thomas Moore, should have been the author of the following hymn, which has a place in the singing-books of sedate christians of most denominations:

"The bird let loose in eastern skies,
Returning fondly home,
Ne'er stoops to earth her wing, nor flies
Where idle warblers roam.

But high she shoots, through air and light,
Above all low delay,
Where nothing earthly bounds her flight,
Nor shadow dims her way.

So grant me, Lord, from every snare
Of sinful passion free,
Aloft, through Faith's serener air
To hold my course to thee.

No sin to cloud, no lure to stay
My soul, as home it springs;
Thy sunshine on her joyful way,
Thy freedom in her wings."

Many years ago there appeared with much frequency in public journals the productions in rhyme of William B. Tappan, a bookseller of Philadelphia. Under the title of "Heaven" is one from his pen, which became a universal favorite, and is found in books in use by many congregations. The following is the first stanza:

"There is an hour of perfect rest
To mourning wanderers given;
There is a joy for souls distressed,
A balm for every wounded breast—
'Tis found alone in Heaven."

Further extracts might be made from the works of laymen who furnished much of the hymnology of the churches, such as Wordsworth, Bryant, James Montgomery, Bowring, and others; but we bring this article to its close by adding a production from the pen of a native of Exeter, this state—Rev. W. B. O. Peabody:

"Behold the western evening light,
It melts in deepening gloom;
So calmly Christians sink away,
Descending to the tomb.

The winds breathe low, the withering leaf
Scarce whispers from the trees;
So gently flows the parting breath,
When good men cease to be.

How beautiful on all the hills
The crimson light is shed!
'Tis like the peace the Christian gives,
To mourners round his bed.

How mildly on the wandering cloud
The sunset beam is cast!
'Tis like the memory left behind
When loved ones breathe their last.

And now, above the dews of night,
The rising star appears;
So faith springs in the heart of those
Whose eyes are bathed in tears.

But soon the morning's happier light
Its glory shall restore,
And eyelids that are sealed in death
Shall wake to close no more.

A SUMMER'S DAY.

BY ABBA GOOLD WOOLSON.

Black bees on the clover-heads drowsily clinging,
 Where tall, feathered grasses and buttercups sway,
And all through the fields a white sprinkle of daisies,
 Open-eyed at the setting of day.

O, the heaps of sweet roses, sweet cinnamon roses,
 In great crimson thickets that cover the wall!
And flocks of bright butterflies giddy to see them,
 And a sunny blue sky over all.

Trailing boughs of the elms drooping over the hedges,
 Where spiders their glimmering laces have spun;
And breezes that bend the light tops of the willows
 And down through the meadow-grass run.

Silver-brown little birds sitting close in the branches,
 And yellow wings flashing from hillock to tree,
And wide-wheeling swallows that dip to the marshes,
 And bobolinks crazy with glee;—

So crazy, they soar through the glow of the sunset
 And warble their merriest notes as they fly,
Nor heed how the moths hover low in the hollows
 And the dew gathers soft in the sky.

Then a round beaming moon o'er the blossomed hill coming,
 Making paler the fields and the shadows more deep;
And through the wide meadows a murmurous chirping
 Of insects too happy to sleep.

Enchanted I sit on the bank by the willow
 And hum the last snatch of a rollicking tune;
And since all this loveliness cannot be heaven,
 I know in my heart it is June.

NEW LONDON CENTENNIAL.

ADDRESS OF HON. J. EVERETT SARGENT.

Upon this paper I find the names of the different towns entered, with the names of the soldiers and the date of their mustering in. Under the heading "New London" is the name "Francis Coums, 1781, April 23." The town is also credited in another place on this paper with one man for the year 1781, £60.00; one man for the year 1782, £60.00; one man for the year 1783, £54.12. We find that the army was disbanded November 3, 1783; our independence having been secured by treaty before that time.

At the annual town meeting in March, 1783, held at the house of Lieut. Levi Harvey at the mills in said town, said Harvey was chosen moderator, Ebenezer Hunting, town-clerk; Samuel Brocklebank, Levi Harvey and Ebenezer Hunting, selectmen; Peter Sargent, constable; John Morgan and others, surveyors of highways.

Voted, To concur with the Council and House of Representatives for this state that the present government be continued in full force until the 10th day of June, 1784, according to their resolve passed the 27th of February, 1783.

Our constitution was adopted only to continue during the war with England. The war had virtually ceased in January, 1783, but our state recommended that the government be continued until the meeting of the Legislature in 1784, when the new constitution took effect.

Voted, To Mr. Nathaniel Everett one pound, five shillings and six pence, it being for expense in removing Mr. Ambrose from New Plymouth to Perrystown; also, voted that the selectmen give security to Levi Harvey for the purchase of land and defending of privileges for a mill, according to former bond; and also, that "grinding days this year be Tuesdays and Fridays of each week."

Thus we see that at first the only currency was the depreciated continental money, a pound of which was only equal to a shilling in silver, and three of either were equal to a bushel of corn or a day's work.

• Peter Sargent, my grandfather, who was first elected constable in 1783, was born in Amesbury, Mass., married Ruth Nichols of Amesbury or Newbury, and removed to Hopkinton, N. H., before 1760, where he had a large family, and then removed to New London with his family in 1781. Most of his children settled in New London.

We find that the Rev. Samuel Ambrose, who had been living at Plymouth (then called New Plymouth), had visited Perrystown in 1781, and preached to them a while, and that he finally removed there in February, 1782, and that he preached to the people in New London a portion of the time, in connection with the people of Sutton, for several years, the town contributing something annually towards his support, until they were able to settle a minister for themselves. It appears, also, that Levi Harvey had built a grist-mill at the outlet of Harvey's pond, being the only grist-mill in town, and that two days in each week were assigned as *grinding days*.

In 1784, the town *voted* to raise twenty-five dollars for Mr. Ambrose for his services the year past; also, to open a road from Kearsarge Gore to Protectworth, upon the request of the latter place; also, *voted* to lay out one hundred days' work in opening said road this season, and also to "raise ten gallons of rum, on the town's cost, for the opening of the road before mentioned." This was the main road from Sutton to

Springfield, as it used to come up by Esquire Jonathan Harvey's in Sutton to the Daniel Woodbury place, thence over the hill where the meeting-house now is, and by Little Sunapee pond, and thence over Addison hill, as it was termed, to Springfield.

This year the town first voted for president of the state, as the governor was called, under the new constitution of 1784, and they all voted for Col. Josiah Bartlett, of Kingston, for president, he having 24 votes; in 1785, John Langdon, of Portsmouth, had 25 votes for president.

In March, 1786, the town *voted* to build a meeting-house fifty feet long, and height and width in proportion. *Voted*, to set the meeting-house not more than 40 rods distant from the mouth of the Hutchins' road, so called. *Voted*, Samuel Messer, Nath'l Goodwin and Samuel Brocklebank a committee to pitch the place to set the meeting-house, sell the pews, and go forward with the same as far as the money that the pews are sold for will forward the building of said meeting-house. *Voted*, to have a burying-yard near where said meeting-house is to stand. This meeting was adjourned several times, and the committee appointed had located the house and sold the pews and provided that those who bought them might pay for the same in corn at four shillings and rye at five shillings per bushel. *Voted*, to raise twenty dollars for preaching this year, and that Levi Harvey see the same expended, and that the selectmen should settle with Mr. Ambrose and pay any balance due him for preaching out of the town's stock.

In these votes of 1786 originated the old meeting-house (which was located on the ground which now constitutes the southerly part of the cemetery) and also the burying-ground which adjoined it, and which has since been enlarged and improved. The Hutchins road, referred to in the location of the meeting-house, was the road that led across from the four corners to the other road on which the cemetery is now located.

I find that this year, also, 1786, a census was ordered by the legislature of the state by a resolution passed March 3d. We find New London responded to this call, which is the first census of the inhabitants of the town that I have been able to find. The return is as follows:

The number of inhabitants of New London in 1786 are as follows:

Males 21 years of age and upwards, 46
Males under 21 years of age, 66
Females 18 years of age and upwards, 46
Females under 18 years of age, 61

Total, 219

The above is a true account, as witness our hands.

LEVI HARVEY. } Selectmen
JOHN ADAMS. } for
JOHN MORGAN. } New London.

New London, June 5, 1786.

In 1787, at the request of many of the people who had come here from Attleborough, Mass., and had there known Elder Seamans, he visited New London and preached here June 24, 1787. That autumn the town,

Voted, To give Elder Seamans a call to settle in this town as a minister of the gospel.

Voted, To give him forty pounds yearly as a salary, three pounds in cash and thirty-seven pounds in labor and grain and other produce that he may want, all to be paid at the common price, and all ministerial privileges in town except one half the parsonage lot.

In February, 1788, Elder Seamans visited New London again and spent some two months there in preaching from house to house and in visiting the people, and it seems that he concluded to accept the call, for in March of that year the town instructed a committee to engage Mr. Seamans' salary to him; that in paying the part to be paid in corn and grain, corn should be reckoned at three shillings and rye at four, and

Voted, To remove Mr Seamans' family from Attleborough to New London on the cost of the town, and that his salary begin on the 24th day of February last and that the selectmen do forward the moving of Mr. Seamans' family.

On the 20th day of June of that year the arrangements for moving had been completed and he started with his family for New London, where he arrived July 1, and as he says in his diary, "went into a very poor house of Mr. James Brocklebank."

He commenced his labors at once, working on his farm through the week and preaching on Sunday; he studied his sermons while engaged in manual labor.

A church of eleven members was formed October 23d, 1788, over which he acted as pastor, and on the 25th day of November of the same year, at a town-meeting called for the first time at the meeting-house, the town voted to unite with the church, in the call they had given Mr. Seamans, and arrangements were made for his reinstallment as pastor of the church and minister of the town. At this town-meeting, the town also elected singers to sing at their public religious meetings, as follows:

Voted, For singers, Ebenezer Hunting, Lieut. Samuel Messer, Nathaniel Fales, Asa Burpee, Moses Hill, Jonathan Adams and Capt. Samuel Brocklebank. The time for the reinstallment was fixed for the 21st of January, 1789.

On the 13th of December, 1788, Elder Seamans gave his final answer to the town, approving of their arrangements and consenting to the reinstallment as proposed, and the same came off, with all proper ceremonies, on the day appointed. Mr. Ebenezer Hunting had been elected by the church as deacon, January 8, 1789.

At the reinstallment of Mr. Seamans, on January 21st, the exercises were held in the meeting-house, on which occasion Rev. Amos Wood, of Weare, preached the sermon; Rev. Thomas Baldwin, of Canaan, gave the charge to the candidate; and Rev. Samuel Ambrose, of Sutton, announced the fellowship of the churches. On the next Sunday, Jan. 25th, the church and their new pastor had their first communion season together.

The meeting-house in which these exercises were held was only partly finished, being without pews or seats (except such as were extemporized for the occasion) and mostly without floors, but there was a large gathering of the people, and everything passed off in a satisfactory manner.

In 1790, the census taken in the state shows that New London had 311 inhabitants, a gain of ninety-two in four years. I find the first mention made of Joseph Colby, as a citizen of New London, in March, 1788, when he was elected as a surveyor of highways. In 1792 the town voted against adopting the amendments to the constitution, proposed by the convention of that year, seventeen votes being recorded in the negative and none in the affirmative.

The church, which commenced with eleven members, Oct. 23, 1788, had gained but seven members up to 1792, consisting then of eighteen members, and there were then about fifty families in town. An extensive revival broke out that year under the preaching of Elder Seamans, and in that year there were about fifty conversions, and the work continued through the years 1793 and 1794, so that in the last year the members of the church had increased to 115, the additions having been made from all classes and of all ages, from seventy down to eight or ten, and what was quite remarkable, there were thirty-seven men who, with their wives, were members of the church,—the united heads of thirty-seven out of the fifty families in town.

In 1795 they had got their meeting-house so far completed, that the town voted to hold their meetings in it for the future. They had but recently built the pulpit, and got the floors laid in the porches above and below, but it was only partially glazed, and not painted at all, and the singing pew, as they called it, was not completed, nor was the house finished without or within. During this year, also, the town appointed a committee to confer with Elder Seamans, and see upon what terms he would give up the bond he held from the town, to ensure his annual salary. The town had already got in arrears, and were largely indebted to him, and they evidently desired to close up their contract with him as a town, and leave it for the church, and for voluntary contributions to supply his salary. The committee waited upon the Elder, and he, after due consideration, made the town a proposition in writing, giving them a choice of three alternatives, as follows :

1st. That he receive a dismission from his pastoral and ministerial office in church and town, together with such a recommendation as he brought to them from Attleborough ; that his salary should cease from the date of such dismission, and he to give up said bond when his salary should be paid up to such dismission.

2d. The church and town should wholly surrender, give up and relinquish his ministerial services in church and town, and he would surrender, give up, and relinquish his salary, so that it shall be a matter of judgment and conscience between them, he to serve them as much in the work of the ministry as his judgment and conscience should dictate, and they on their part to communicate of their temporal good things toward the support of himself and his family, as much as their judgment and conscience should dictate to them, and that, too, in such a way as they might choose.

3d. But if neither of these offers should prove satisfactory, then he requested the town to unite with him in calling a mutual council to look into any matters of dissatisfaction between them on either side, and decide upon the whole whether it was not best for him to ask, and for them to give him such a dismission and recommendation as above mentioned ; and if such council should be in favor of such dismission, then that they should also settle the conditions, after being informed what the town had done for him, and of his services in return, whether the town should pay him his salary in part or in full or give him something more, or whether he should relinquish his salary, which shall be then due either in part or in whole, or shall give the town something more, for reasons which to the council may appear.

It was very evident that it was of no use to seek a controversy with a man who was so willing to settle in any way, and the town, by vote, accepted of his second offer, by which the town gave up all claim to his ministerial services and he gave up all legal claim to his salary, and after that his support was derived mainly from the church and from voluntary contributions. The town at the same time voted not to unite with him in calling a council.

In 1797 they also voted that those inhabitants of the town that do not belong to the Baptist society, so called, have a right to invite preachers of the gospel into the meeting-house to preach such part of the time as shall be in proportion to the interest they own in the meeting-house, and this was so voted for several years. Almost every year there was an article in the warrant to see about finishing the singing pew or to see about finishing off the meeting-house, but there seemed a great reluctance to complete the house, and the town refused to act.

Thus we come down to the year 1800, the close of the eighteenth century. By the census of that year it appears that New London then had 617 inhabitants, having gone from 311 to 617, in ten years. But while they had been thus prosperous in that particular, their meeting-house was still unfinished. It was only partially glazed, the gallery was not completed, the singing pew was not built, nor was it plastered or painted at all. A controversy between Levi Harvey and the town had arisen, about his mills, which was still undisposed of, and many were the articles in the warrants for town-meetings, and many were the special town-meetings called to consider and act upon these two subjects, but the town never seemed ready to finish either the meeting-house or this controversy

Perhaps at this point it may occur to some of you to inquire a little more particularly in relation to the Masonian proprietors, who they were, and who were the original grantees of the land granted as the Addition of Alexandria, afterwards New London, and how was the land divided among them?

Capt. John Mason, of London, to

whom the grant of New Hampshire was made in 1629, as we have seen, died in 1635, and his heirs held and tried to enforce his claims to the land till about 1692, when they sold and conveyed the same to one Samuel Allen, of the same London, who came to this country to enforce his claims. But Allen died in 1705, and the lands descended to his heirs, who prosecuted his claims vigorously for a time, until the heirs of Mason found some defect, either real or pretended, in Allen's title to the lands, and set up a claim to them for themselves.

One John Tufton Mason, a descendant of Capt. John, the first grantee, came to this country, claiming to own the Masonian Patent, and sold his rights to certain parties in Massachusetts and New Hampshire, and conveyed to them by deed in 1746. The names of these purchasers were as follows: Theodore Atkinson, Mark H. Wentworth, Richard Wibird, John Wentworth (son of the governor), George Jaffrey, Nathaniel Meserve, Thomas Packer, Thomas Wallingford, Jotham Odiorne, Joshua Pierce, Samuel Moore, and John Moffat. Atkinson had three-fifteenths. M. H. Wentworth had two-fifteenths, and all the rest one-fifteenth each. These men were afterwards known as the Masonian proprietors.

The persons to whom they granted the town of Alexandria and also the Addition were as follows: Jonas Minot, of Concord, in the county of Middlesex, gentleman; Jonathan Bagley, Esq., and William Bailey. gentleman, both of Amesbury, in the county of Essex, and all in the Province of Massachusetts Bay; Matthew Thornton, Esq., and Robert McMurphy, gentleman, both of Londonderry; John Talford, Esq., and William Talford, gentleman, both of Chester; and Daniel Rindge, of Portsmouth, all in the county of Rockingham and Province of New Hampshire; and Joshua Talford, of New Chester, in the county of Grafton, and Province last mentioned, husbandman.

In the deed of the Addition of Alexandria the original grantors, the Masonian proprietors, reserved one third part of said land to themselves, their heirs, and assigns forever; one half of the balance, or one third of the whole, was conveyed to said Minot; and the other half of the balance, or third of the whole, was conveyed to the remaining grantees in the following proportions, viz.: to Matthew Thornton, twelve forty-ninths; to said J. Bagley, five forty-ninths; to the said W. Bailey, five forty-ninths; to the said John Talford, seven forty-ninths and one third; to the said William Talford, eight forty-ninths and one third; to said Robert McMurphy, eight forty-ninths and one third; to the said Daniel Rindge, two forty-ninths, and to the said Joshua Talford, one forty-ninth. The grant to said William Bailey was conditional upon his accepting the rights granted him in the new charter of the town of Alexandria in full for his claims under the old charter, which he refused to accept, and therefore he drew no lots in the Addition, which was afterwards New London.

The Addition was surveyed and laid out in 137 lots of 150 acres each. Certain lots were reserved for schools, for the first settled minister, etc. There were reserved for the Masonian proprietors 45 lots and two fractions; and drawn to Capt. Jonas Minot 44 lots and two fractions: to Col. Matthew Thornton, ten lots and a fraction; to Robert McMurphy, seven lots and two fractions; to Deacon William Talford, seven lots and a fraction: to Maj. John Talford, six lots and a fraction; to Jonathan Bagley, Esq., five lots and a fraction; to Hon. Daniel Rindge two lots; and to Joshua Talford, Esq., one lot.

These lots were drawn Sept. 7, 1773. I have a plan of the drawing, with the numbers of the lots drawn to each owner.

Having gone along in the order of time for the first twenty-one years of the town's history up to the year 1800, let us now go forward for a similar period of twenty-one years to the year 1821, and there make a stand, and from that stand-point look back over that space of time, that second period of twenty-one years of the town's history. Let us select our time now with some particularity—well, suppose we call it the ninth day of September, 1821. It is one of the earliest days that I can remember, and yet, though I was then only five years of age, I shall never forget it. The day was Sunday. The morning was bright and sunny. The air was soft and balmy. The day was hot, and especially in the afternoon was still and sultry. About five o'clock there were signs of a thunder shower, dark clouds gathered in the west, and soon overcast the sky. The stillness that precedes the storm was soon interrupted by the mutterings of the distant thunder, the clouds grew darker and blacker, until presently a strange commotion was seen among them in the west; vivid lightnings light up the dark and angry masses, the roaring of the distant tornado is heard as it approaches, and anon the most terrible whirlwind ever known in the state burst upon the terror-stricken inhabitants of New London.

I gather the following facts from a description of the great whirlwind of 1821, as found in the collections of the N. H. Historical Society, vol. 1, page 241. The whirlwind entered the state in Cornish, and moving easterly through Croydon, demolished the house and barn of Deacon Cooper, thence through Wendell (now Sunapee) to near Sunapee Lake, where it blew to pieces the house, barn and out-buildings of Harvey Huntoon, destroying and blowing away all the furniture and other property in his house, and the contents of his barns and other buildings, and blowing an infant nearly a year old, that was lying on a bed in the house, away into the lake, where the mangled body was found the next Wednesday, on the opposite side of the lake, and the feather bed on which the child was sleeping was found in Andover by a Mr. Durgin and restored to Mr. Huntoon. A horse was blown up hill a distance of forty rods, and was so injured that it was necessary to kill him. No human lives were lost in that town except the child, though the other seven members of Mr. Huntoon's household were injured, and some of them very severely. From Wendell the hurricane passed across Lake Sunapee in a most terrific manner, assuming the form of an inverted pyramid in motion, and drawing up into its bosom vast quantities of water. Its appearance on the lake was in the highest degree sublime and terrible, apparently about twenty rods in diameter at the surface of the water, it expanded on each side towards the heavens, its vast body as dark as midnight, but occasionally illuminated by the most vivid flashes of lightning.

From the lake it passed into New London and through the southerly part of the town, destroying property to the estimated value of $9,000 or $10,000. But fortunately no person in the town was killed. The house and other buildings of John Davis, standing directly in the path of the tornado, were entirely demolished. Not a timber nor a board was left upon the ground where the house had stood, and not a brick in the chimney remained unmoved. A huge hearth stone weighing some seven or eight hundred pounds was removed from its bed and turned up on one edge; all the furniture of the house, beds, bedding and clothing was swept away, and not the value of five dollars of it was ever found. The family chanced to be absent from the house. Three barns belonging to Josiah Davis, with their contents, were blown entirely away, and his house much shattered and damaged. A house belonging to Jonathan Herrick was unroofed, the windows broken out, and much furniture and clothing blown away, but fortunately none of the family were injured. A new two-story house frame, nearly covered, belonging to Nathan Herrick, and two barns, were blown down. A house and barn of Asa Gage were unroofed, and two sheds carried away. Anthony Sargent had one barn demolished, another unroofed, and two sheds blown away. Deacon Peter Sargent had a barn blown down, another unroofed, and a shed blown away. A barn of J. P. Sabin was torn to pieces; another barn of Levi Harvey was blown to pieces, his saw-mill demolished, and some twelve thousand feet of boards in the mill-yard carried away; his grist-mill was moved some distance whole, and was left standing on dry land, and a hog house, containing a hog weighing from three to four hundred pounds, was carried away whole several rods and dropped on the top of a stone wall, where it fell into fragments, and the hog released from his prison walked away unhurt. A pair of cart wheels strongly bound with iron and nearly new, with the spire and axle, were carried ten rods, the spire broken off in the middle, all the spokes but two broken out of one wheel and more than half out of the other. All the trees in an orchard of one hundred, without a single exception, were prostrated, and one half of them were wrenched up by the roots, and carried entirely away, root and branch. The trunk of one of these trees, divested of its principal roots and branches, was found half a mile distant and at the top of a long hill ; near the top of this hill was an excurvation some forty feet long, and in places two to three feet deep, partly filled with mangled boards and broken timbers, apparently made by the perpendicular fall of the side of a barn, which must have been blown whole at least eighty rods.

The track or path of the whirlwind in New London, was some four miles long, and varied in width from one fourth to one half a mile as the column rose and fell, and passed off upon the north side of Kearsarge Mountain. In passing, it seemed to hug to the mountain, so that its course was changed more to the south, and it passed down the mountain on the easterly side into the Gore, touching a corner of Salisbury and into Warner, and finally terminated in the woods of Boscawen. A great amount of property, many buildings, and several lives were destroyed in the Gore and in Warner.

The track of the whirlwind is thus described : " It appeared as if a rushing torrent had been pouring down for many days ; the dwellings, buildings, fences and trees were all swept off in its course. The earth was torn up in places, the grass withered, and nothing fresh or living was to be seen in the path of the desolation." It is difficult for us to conceive the horrors of that instant—for it was but an instant—when horses, barns, trees, fences, fowls, and other moveable objects were all lifted from the earth into the bosom of the whirlwind and anon dashed into a thousand pieces. Probably no event has occurred in this town during the hundred years of its existence, that was so well calculated to teach man his utter impotence, and to impress upon his mind the awful sublimity, the terrible grandeur of the scene, where the hand of omnipotence, even for a moment, displays its resistless power, as the great whirlwind of September 9, 1821.

Let us now look back and briefly review the events that have occurred since the year 1800. June 9, 1801, the Social Library was incorporated, which had about one hundred volumes of very valuable books. The library was kept at the house of Josiah Brown, Esq. I recollect that from about the year 1825 to 1833 I obtained most of my reading matter from this library and found it very profitable and interesting. Whether this institution yet remains I do not know. In 1803 the town first had the necessary number of ratable polls to entitle it to send a representative alone, and Joseph Colby, Esq., was elected as the first representative of the town, and he was re-elected every year until 1816.

In 1817 there was a political revolution in the town, and everything was changed. Daniel Woodbury, Esq., was the moderator, first selectman, and representative for that and several succeeding years ; and the dominant party held a celebration over their victory, in the spring of 1817, at which, as I am informed, the liberty pole was erected, which used to stand in front of the old meeting-house, around which the people in the olden time used to congregate, and spend their intermissions between the forenoon and afternoon services on Sunday. My first recollections of attending church are associated with hearing Elder Seamans preach, and Elder Ambrose pray ; of riding to church in the wagon with father and mother,— standing up behind and holding on to the back of the seat in order to preserve my perpendicular equilibrium. This I did until growing older I preferred to walk rather than to ride in that way. It was the fashion in those days for the whole family to go to church as soon as the children were large enough to be carried. But to return from this degression.

In 1804 a committee was appointed to cause an accurate survey of the town to be made. This was in pursuance of a law requiring each town in the state to make a plan of the same and return it to the secretary of state, with a view to the making of a state map, which was afterward published by Philip Carrigain. This committee consisted of Green French, Levi Harvey, Jr., and Anthony Sargent.

The meeting-house was still a subject of contention. Articles were frequently inserted in the warrants for town-meeting to see if the town would vote to finish glazing the house, or to plaster the house, or to paint the house, or to finish off the house, but the town uniformily voted in the negative upon them all. Probably some of this work was done by voluntary subscription or contributions, and the house was occupied for all purposes. Finally, in 1818, at a special meeting holden for that purpose, June 1, it was voted to raise $300 for the purpose of repairing and finishing the outside of the meeting-house in this town, and Joseph Colby, Esq., was appointed as agent of the town to see to repairing and finishing the outside of the meeting-house, and I find no further articles in the warrants for their town-meetings relating to finishing the meeting-house. Thus, the house which was commenced in 1786, was finished in 1818, having been thirty-two years in building.

The controversy concerning Levi Harvey's mill privilege and flowage rights arose in this way. Away back in 1780, an article was inserted in the warrant to see if the town would adopt any method to build mills in said town, but the vote was that as a town they could not do anything as to building mills. But it seems that some individuals gave said Harvey a bond that they would purchase the land on which he was to set the mill, and would defend him against claims for flowage by the owners of land around and above his mill-pond, if he would erect a saw and grist-mill upon a certain lot of land owned by some absent proprietor; and in 1783 the town, at their annual meeting, voted to clear those men that were bound in a bond to Levi Harvey to purchase land and for defending of privileges as mentioned in said bond; also, that the present selectmen be empowered to give security to said Harvey for the purchase of land and the defending of privileges as mentioned in former bond. The selectmen for that year were Samuel Brocklebank, Levi Harvey, and Ebenezer Hunting. In compliance with this vote of March, 1783, said Brocklebank and Hunting gave to said Harvey a bond conditioned like the previous one, and the former bond was cancelled. The mill and the dam was built, and everything went along smoothly for several years.

But after a time a controversy arose about the land where the mill was located, and the owners of lots above the mill began to claim damages for flowage by the dam, and Harvey appealed to the town, and Brocklebank and Hunting also claimed to have the town act in the premises, but the town declined, and upon one excuse and another refused to act. In 1802 the town appointed a committee to act in the premises and to make a final settlement between said Harvey and the town; but in 1804 they again voted to let the matter take its due course in law. An article was inserted in the annual warrants for town-meetings on this subject, and special meetings were called to act upon it, but the town would not act.

Finally suits were brought by the parties agrieved against Harvey, as of course they must be, and damages recovered against him for flowage by the owners of lands above his mill and by the claimant of the land where his mill was located. These damages were collected of Harvey, and then he called on his bondsmen, Hunting and Brocklebank, to respond. They called on the town, but the town was still deaf to the call ; so after various town-meetings, Harvey sued Hunting and Brocklebank on their bond. The town still refusing to come to their rescue, they defended themselves as best they could in the suit, but were finally beaten and a judgment recovered against them for the whole amount that Harvey had been obliged to pay. Then there were more town-meetings,.but the town was still persistent in doing nothing.

I infer that in the mean time Brocklebank had become irresponsible, and as Hunting was good, Harvey at length arrested Deacon Hunting and lodged him safely in jail for the non-payment of the debt. Hunting was stubborn, and Harvey was resolute, so Hunting laid in jail over a year ; but finding that Harvey would not yield, he finally paid the money and went home to his family. Then he called on the town, and the town refusing to act, he brought his suit against the town, and then more town-meetings followed ; but the suit went along, and the town in the end was beaten, as it deserved to be, and a judgment was recovered against the town.

On the 24th day of May, 1808, a special meeting was called on that matter, and the town voted, that there be assessed upon the polls and estate in this town, and that part of Wilmot which was taken from this town in June last, a sum of money sufficient to satisfy the judgment rendered against the town in favor of Deacon Ebenezer Hunting, at the last term of the supreme court in this county. They do not state how large the sum thus raised was ; but it is reported that the amount of this claim had by this time, with all the costs of the various suits, reached the sum of nearly $1500, which for those times was a large amount.

In 1809 there was an article in the warrant to see if the town will pay Deacon Ebenezer Hunting the amount of interest which he has been obliged to pay on the execution which Levi Harvey, Esq., obtained against him. But the town passed over the article. Again, on the 13th January, 1812, a special meeting was called to see if the town will pay to Deacon Ebenezer Hunting a sum of money equal to the amount of interest which he paid on the Harvey execution, and also to see what compensation the town will make Deacon Ebenezer Hunting for damages he sustained by being imprisoned on said execution. But the town made quick work of it by voting at once not to do anything about it. This ended the controversy which had been in agitation more than twenty years in town.

Let us now look for a moment at the boundaries of the town at different periods of its history. When the town was incorporated it was, as you have seen, in very regular shape, extending from Alexandria to Fishersfield and Sutton in length, and of about equal width between the patent line and Kearsarge Gore. June 19, 1793, the Legislature disannexed lots No. 19, 20, 21, 22, 23, 24 and 25 from the northwesterly part of Kearsarge Gore, and annexed the same to New London. By this change the southerly line of New London was extended east to the northeast corner of Sutton. The piece thus annexed was a triangle, with its base resting on Sutton north line. December 11, 1804, the Legislature disannexed a large number of lots from Wendell and annexed the same to New London ; and on the 19th of June, 1817, another tract was taken from Wendell and annexed to New London, so that the line between these towns was described as follows : Beginning at a point in Sunapee Lake, which is described, "thence running north 16° east, 108 rods to Otter Pond and thence on the same course across said pond to Springfield south line." By these two additions to New London, it was intended to make the line between Sunapee and New London one continuous straight line from Fishersfield (now Newbury) northwest corner through Otter Pond to Springfield line. I find by your town records that the old patent line run over the top of Burpee Hill, a little above the house where Nathaniel Messer and his son lived and died.

The old school-house that used to sit there on the top of the hill on a ledge of rock, was on the patent line which originally divided this town from Wendell. By these additions another triangle was added to the town on that side, with its base resting on the old patent line, and bounded west by Wendell and north by Springfield.

On the 18th of June, 1807, the town of Wilmot was incorporated out of the north-easterly part of New London, a part of New Chester, and all that part of Kearsarge Gore that laid northerly of the summit of Kearsarge Mountain.

The part taken off from New London was described as follows : " Beginning at the south-easterly corner of lot No. 22, and the south-westerly corner of lot No. 21, on the south-easterly line of said New London, thence running westwardly across said New London on the northerly sides of lots numbered 22, 35, 54, 70, 78, 90, 112 and 130, over to Springfield line," so taking all the land that lay north-easterly of that line in New London. This part of the town thus set off to Wilmot contained about 9000 acres of land.

From 1812 to 1815 the country was engaged in its second war with England, which was substantially closed by Gen. Andrew Jackson, at New Orleans, on the 8th of Junuary, 1815.

In 1819 the toleration act, as it was called, was passed by the legislature and became a law, which separated the civil and religious elements in our organization, so to speak. It took from the towns, in their corporate capacity, the power to raise money for the support of preaching of any kind, or to build meeting-houses, or for other religious purposes, leaving it to religious societies to do this work, each to suit its own views of propriety and duty. But this act did not affect religious matters in New London at all. The town had, in fact, anticipated the law many years. They had raised no money as a town, for preaching, since 1795, as I can find, and they had voted to let each denomination in town occupy the meeting-house according to their interest therein, each sect being thus left free to advance their own views, in their own way, and at their own expense. This has been the policy of the law ever since, and was the policy of the town long before the law was passed.

From this time forth we shall find the history of the town and the history of the church entirely separate and distinct. Yet every one knows, whether he believes in the doctrines of a church or not, that wherever a church has been long established, and has been made up of any considerable portion of the people, it has and will have its influence upon the community to such an extent that no history of the town would be complete without a history of its church, or its churches, where there are more than one. Particularly is that true of a country town like New London, where there has been, from the earliest times, a leading and influential church, which has taken the lead in all great moral questions and reforms.

The church had, in this period of twenty-one years, seen two seasons of revival under the preaching of Elder Seamans. In 1809 some forty were added to the church, and in 1818 and 1819 occurred what was long known as the great reformation, in which between eighty and ninety were added to the church.

But during all these years there was much hard and disagreeable work to be done ; many labors with the brethren were instituted, and many were the letters of admonition and expulsion that were issued and recorded on the church records.

In the year 1801 the first Baptist society was formed in town, which was kept up and had its annual meetings down as late as 1846, when its records cease, and the church has gone along so far, as appears, without the aid of the society.

Within this period, too, the institution of Free Masonry had arisen and flourished in this town quite extensively. King Solomon's Lodge of Free and Accepted Masons, No. 14, was chartered and located at New London, in the county of Hillsborough, on January 27, 1802, by the Most Worshipful Grand Lodge of the State of New Hampshire. The Lodge flourished well here for many years, and had become quite numerous previous to the anti-masonic wave that swept over the eastern and middle states about 1826, when the excitement run so high and the opposition was so strong that the masons, thinking that discretion was the better part of valor, suspended their meetings for a time altogether, and the lodge in fact never did much more work in its old locality. But in June, 1851, it was removed to Wilmot, where it remained in good working order until 1878, when it was again removed and located at Scytheville, in New London, where it now remains, enjoying a fair share of prosperity.

The population had gone on increasing since 1800, though somewhat irregular. In 1810 the census showed 692, gaining only seventy-five in that decade ; but in 1820 there were 924, a gain of 232 in that decade, and the town had also made rapid progress in education, wealth and position, and was now enjoying a large share of the comforts and conveniences of life for that day.

The County of Merrimack was incorporatd July 23, 1823, and consisted of twenty-six towns, from Rockingham and Hillsborough counties. New London, which had been a part of Hillsborough County hitherto, now became a part of Merrimack, of which it still forms a part.

On July 4, 1826, the new meeting-house, the house in which we are to-day assembled, was raised. The corner-stone had been placed with appropriate ceremonies before that, at a public gathering, with a procession, music and religious ceremonies. The Fourth of July was a pleasant day, and at sunrise the work of raising was commenced, and it was substantially finished the same day, except what could be done with the force that was to be permanently employed upon it. From that time forward the work was prosecuted with vigor, so that before the winter closed in it was completed, with steeple and bell ; the slips were disposed of and the house ready for use, and all that I find in the records concerning it, anywhere, in either church or society, is the following vote by the society at their regular meeting on the third Monday of December, 1826, viz. :

Voted, "To accept of the new meeting-house, built by David Everett and Anthony Colby, and the common around the same. Chose Joseph Colby and Jonathan Greeley to take a conveyance of said meeting-house and common."

It seems that it had been arranged that the house should be appraised so as to cover expenses, and a sufficient number of the society had subscribed, or in some way became responsible to take the slips at the appraised value, so as to secure those who did the work in the first instance ; and then those two built the house and conveyed it to the society.

I can well remember the procession and proceedings when the corner-stone was laid, and the day of the raising of the house. After it was completed we used to alternate between the new house and the old, one Sunday at each in turn for many years. In the old meeting-house were the square pews, with the seats on all four sides of them, with the high pulpit and the great sounding-board over it, which would be sure to fall upon the minister's devoted head, should he depart but the breadth of a single hair from the truth. In the new meeting-house there was some improvement, the slips were all facing the same way and towards the pulpit, which originally was at the other end of the house, directly in front of the singing gallery, and but little lower than that.

On May 30, 1830, Rev. Samuel Ambrose died. He had for several years been a member of this church, the original church at Sutton having become at one time nearly or quite extinct ; and on October 4th, in the same year, Elder Seamans died. Thus these two men, who had labored side by side so long in the cause of the master, were called very nearly together to their reward.

In 1830 the population was only 913, a loss of 11 from 1820.

In 1831 and 1832 the church was visited by one of its most remarkable revivals, under the preaching of the Rev. Oren Tracy. The whole town seemed to be reached and affected by it. During the fall of 1831, and the next winter, evening meetings were kept up in the different parts of the town, in the school-houses and in private houses, on Sundays and on weekdays, to which large numbers were drawn, and the interest in religious matters was deep and wide spread. On the first Sunday of January, 1833, which was the first day of the week, and of the month, and of the year, an addition of forty-three was made to the church; on the first Sunday of March thirty-six more were added, and during the following summer several more, making between eighty and ninety in all.

In the fall of 1832 another event took place which was at the time of great interest to the people of New London. During that autumn the first stage coach took its regular trip through New London upon the route from Hanover to Lowell. This new road had been before the public for several years in one form and another, and was strongly favored by one party and opposed by another. But it had finally, through the efforts of Col. Anthony Colby more than of any other man, probably, been laid out and built and a stage company had been formed, horses and coaches purchased, and arrangements made for stageing.

This fall of 1832 J. Everett Farnum was teaching a private school for a term in the red school-house at the four corners, and it was announced that on a certain day in October, I think, the stage coach would make its appearance. It was to go through here in the afternoon to Hanover, and start the next morning early for Lowell. As the expected event drew nigh, study was out of the question, and our kind teacher gave us all permission to gaze for a time, to the extent of our capacity, for the long expected stage coach with its four horses in hand. It finally came and went, as all things come and go, and we resumed our studies again; but it took some time to fully comprehend and realize the importance of the fact that New London was henceforth to have a daily stage and a daily mail both ways.

In 1837 the New London Academy was incorporated and went into successful operation, and continued prosperous under different teachers for several years, up to about 1850, when its operations were suspended for a time. It commenced in 1837 as a ladies' school, with Miss Susan F. Colby as principal. In the autumn of that year Prof. Dyer H. Sanborn became principal and Miss Colby continued as principal of the Ladies' Department. After some years Mr. Sanborn resigned, and Truman K. Wright succeeded him as principal; after Mr. Wright, a Mr. Meserve, a Mr. Averhill, and a Mr. Comings followed. Then Mr. Alvah Hovey, now president of Newton Theological Institution, taught one year; then Mr. Joseph B. Clarke, now of Manchester, followed for a year; then a Mr. V. J. Walker followed, who was the last, or among the last who taught under this arrangement.

In 1840 the population of New London reached 1019, a gain of 106 in the last ten years, and this was the largest number that were ever in the town at the time of any census, and the town was in a condition of prosperity, wealth and influence, perhaps equal to that of any other period in its history.

[CONTINUED IN SEPTEMBER NUMBER.]

THE GRANITE MONTHLY.

A MAGAZINE OF LITERATURE, HISTORY, AND STATE PROGRESS.

VOL. II.   SEPTEMBER, 1879.   NO. 12.

COL. JOHN B. CLARKE.

BY HERBERT F. NORRIS.

The subject of this sketch, as editor and publisher of the most widely circulated newspaper in the state, probably exerts an influence upon public opinion second to that of no other man within its borders.

Commencing his journalistic career without training and without capital, he has by his energy, enterprise and sagacity built up an establishment yielding him a handsome income, and made the "*Mirror*" the most valuable newspaper property in the state.

John Badger Clarke was born in Atkinson, Jan. 30, 1820, the son of Greenleaf and Julia Cogswell Clarke.

His mother was the daughter of Dr. William Cogswell of Atkinson, and Judith Badger of Gilmanton, and was one of a family of nine, of whom still survive, Francis Cogswell of Andover, Mass., formerly president of the Boston and Maine Railroad, and George Cogswell, a physician of Bradford, Mass.

Mr. Clarke had one sister, the wife of Col. Samuel Carlton, of Haverhill, Mass., and four brothers; of the latter, three, Francis, a physician, settled in Andover, Mass., Moses, a physician of Cambridge, Mass., and William C. late Attorney-General of New Hampshire, have died. The remaining brother is the Hon. Greenleaf Clarke, the present senator from the Rockingham district, who lives on the paternal homestead at Atkinson.

Spending his boyhood upon the farm, where with pure air and healthy exercise he laid the foundation of the excellent physical man he now is, Mr. Clarke supplemented his common school advantages by attendance at the Atkinson Academy, entered Dartmouth College at the age of nineteen, graduating in the class of 1843 with high honors, having among his classmates the late Prof. J. N. Putnam (the only member of the class that outranked Mr. Clarke in scholarship), Hon. Harry Bingham, Col. A. O. Brewster of Massachusetts, Hon. L. D. Stevens, Col. James O. Adams, Prof. Jonathan Tenney, and others now well known in the literary world. Of Mr. Clarke, Prof. Tenney, in his memorial of the class, says: "As a writer he is terse, piquant, and positive. His paper is leading and popular, always on time with the latest news and free discussions of all sorts, sparing neither friends nor foes when he has a point to carry or readers to entertain."

Leaving college, he was for three years Principal of the Academy at Laconia, exhibiting an aptness for teaching rarely found, and binding himself to his students by ties that will long exist, and make his name a popular one in many a household. While thus engaged in teaching, Mr. Clarke found time to engage in the study of law and connected himself with the office of Stephen C. Lyford, Esq., and upon leaving the Academy removed to Manchester, continuing his studies with his brother, William C. Clarke, and was admitted to the bar of Hillsborough County in 1848. The next year he was seized by the California fever, being the first of a large number from Manchester who decided to go to the newly discovered gold fields.

Spending about two years on the Pacific Coast, at work in the mines, practicing law, and traveling in Central America and New Grenada, he returned home in February, 1851, and went to Salem, Mass., with a view of establishing himself, but soon removed to Manchester, where he opened a law office and applied himself to the practice of his profession until February, 1852, when at the request of the publisher, Joseph C. Emerson, he took charge of the editorial department of the *Daily Mirror*, agreeing to devote half of his time to the work.

This he continued till the September following, when financial embarrassments compelled the publisher to dispose of the *Mirror* property, and on the 20th of October it was sold at auction, Mr. Clarke being the purchaser of the daily and weekly *Mirror* and the job printing establishment connected therewith, of which he has ever since been the sole owner and manager. Subsequently he purchased the daily and weekly *American* (in which the weekly *Democrat* had been previously merged) and the New Hampshire *Journal of Agriculture*. These were combined with the *Mirror* and the name of the daily changed to *Mirror and American*, and the weekly from *Dollar Weekly Mirror* to *Weekly Mirror and Farmer*. Both papers have been twice enlarged since he became the publisher. At the time he took possession of the *Mirror*, the weekly had but a few hundred subscribers, and the daily not a quarter of its present circulation, but Mr. Clarke's indomitable will, great energy, persistence and executive ability, combined with a keen insight into men and measures, a ready perception of the drift of public sentiment, and the hearty enthusiasm which enters into everything he undertakes enabled him rapidly, to increase its circulation and influence until it was brought to the foremost place among the newspapers of the state. Previous to the war of the Rebellion, the *Mirror* had been non-partisan in politics, but at that time it came out boldly on the side of the administration and has ever since espoused the principles of the Republican party.

Of his editorial management a few extracts, gathered from the press, when Mr. Clarke was more actively at work, writing not only editorials but attending to all the details of the publishment of the paper, will show the esteem in which he was held by his contemporaries.

The *Oasis* (Nashua) says: "The *Mirror* is placed under the conduct of John B. Clarke, Esq., a gentleman of wit, wisdom, and worth; a gentleman and a scholar as well as a traveller."

"Mr. Clarke has long been in the newspaper business, is an enterprising man, an able writer and he is on the right side."—*Lowell Citizen*.

Compelled to increase the price of the *Mirror*, during the war of the Rebellion, the Boston *Commercial Bulletin* notices the advance as follows: "The Manchester (N. H.) *Mirror*, whose enterprise gives it a monopoly of all the local business and circulation in that city, has made a slight advance in its terms. The *Mirror* has displayed much tact and industry in advocating the interests of Manchester. Its editor is a gentleman and an able writer, and we doubt not that he will secure a continuance of the same liberal patronage that has thus far rewarded his efforts."

The *Portsmouth Chronicle*, in 1867, from the pen of Col. W. H. Hackett, says: "Among the prominent institutions in the city is the *Daily Mirror*, one of the smartest papers of its class in the United States. We called on its editor, Hon. John B. Clarke, and found him seated in his handsome sanctum (by the way, why can't other editors have a decent place to sit down in?) busy with piles of papers, but received a hearty welcome. His jolly face betokens great good nature; but there is a certain snap in his eye indicating no want of 'grit.' We judge him to be a good friend, but a hard enemy to encounter. He may not be 'fast;' but surely, the man who drives a fast horse, fights the railroads, edits the *Mirror*, and publishes the handsomest calendar in the world, is by no means '*slow*.' Success, say we, to the *Mirror*, and its stirring editor; 'long may they wave.' "

In general, Mr. Clarke, as he talks, writes with great positiveness and at the same time with a vein of humor that makes everything readable. He attacks his opponents boldly, exasperates them with sarcasm and ridicule, thoroughly demolishes the groundwork of their argument, and then, as if in pity, advises them to try again. With a supply of this kind of ammunition always at hand, he is a dangerous man to meet in a journalistic encounter.

In connection with his daily and weekly papers, Mr. Clarke has an extensive book and job printing business, and has published many valuable works, including, "The Londonderry Celebration," "Sanborn's History of New Hampshire," "Clarke's Manchester Almanac and Directory," "Clarke's History of Manchester," and many smaller works.

Both in college and later as teacher and editor, Mr. Clarke has been much interested in the study of elocution, and in 1874 offered Dartmouth College one hundred dollars yearly, for five years, to be awarded in prizes for excellence in public speaking. This generous offer awakened a lively interest in that branch, bringing out the best men of the college, among whom were his two sons, who each secured the first prize during their course of study. He also gave great stimulus to the interest in good reading and speaking in the Manchester public schools by his agitation of the subject in the *Mirror*, and by the bestowal of forty dollars in prizes to the High School for two successive years for the same object.

During his senior year in college, Mr. Clarke was president of the Social Friends' Society, and in 1863 was elected president of the Tri Kappa Society of Dartmouth College.

In 1866 he was appointed by Gov. Smyth one of the trustees of the New Hampshire College of Agriculture and Mechanic Arts, and has been one of the trustees of the Merrimack River Savings Bank since its organization in 1858. He was one of the first to welcome the order of Patrons of Husbandry to New England, and through his efforts Amoskeag Grange, No. 3, was instituted in 1873, Mr. Clarke being its master for three years.

He was for two years Lieut. Col. of the Amoskeag Veterans, and was twice elected commander, but declined to hold that position.

It was through his connection with the Veterans that he obtained the title of "Colonel" that is now so familiar as to become almost a part of his name.

Although always a wide awake politician he has not often held political office, refusing to be a candidate because it might interfere with his position and power as an independent journalist, and for similar reasons has declined offices of honor and trust in the various agricultural societies of New England; yet few men have had more influence in shaping the policy and action of his party in the state during the past fifteen years than he, while his political sagacity is so well known that in a doubtful contest his opinions are sought by both friend and foe. Having served for years on the state committee and in the conventions of his party, he is eagerly sought by the anxious candidate, and many a successful one owes his nomination to the championship of the energetic colonel.

He was a delegate to the Baltimore Convention, that nominated Abraham Lincoln for the second time to the presidency, and was elected one of the National Committee of seven (including ex-Gov. Clafflin of Mass., ex-Gov. Marcus L. Ward of New Jersey and Hon. Henry J. Raymond of the New York *Times*) that managed that campaign.

Six times he has been elected state printer, in 1867, '68, '69, and 1877, '78,

'79, being the present incumbent of that important office, and to say that he well sustains his past reputation for energy, promptness and skill is but to do justice to the work he has given the state.

Mr. Clarke is a very positive man; forms his opinions quickly, whether right or wrong, and acts upon them with the utmost directness. He will decide upon a project, map out a plan for its execution, select the men to carry out its details, and have the whole thing substantially disposed of while many men would be halting and trying to determine whether the matter was feasible.

He never does anything lukewarmly. Whatever cause he espouses he enters into heartily, bending all his efforts to bring about success and make certain the desired end.

If he would do his friend a favor he devotes himself to that purpose with as much zeal as if its attainment were the chief object of his life. He is not the ideal politician, "all things to all men," for he never wears two faces; whether your friend or foe, you will know his position from the start. Naturally a man so positive and determined as he makes many enemies, but it is seldom that the malice of rivals, or the bitterness of opponents deters him from pursuing his own course.

Doubtless much of his success is due to his knowledge of men, by which he selects the best suited to carry out his purposes, whether as assistants in the various departments of his business or to attend to details in any measures in which he takes an interest.

Not to speak of him as an ardent lover of the horse and dog would do Mr. Clarke injustice, for no man in the state has done more to bring before the people the value of a good horse, or the rare sport found in anight's hunt for that much hunted animal, "the coon."

An enthusiastic believer in the saying, "Blood will tell," he has brought into New Hampshire the best blood of the best stock-farms in the country and urged upon all, through the press and in private, the necessity of breeding well if they would improve their stock. Seen at his best one must meet the Colonel socially, and with him visit his farm in the suburbs of the city, ramble over his well cultivated fields, learn of him of his stock, view the excellent horses always in his stable, and at night with his dogs capture the wily coon: then one sees it all; the determined business man, the successful publisher, the thoroughly generous man, and the affable and agreeable gentleman.

He has learned by experience that there is a limit to the amount of care and business the strongest man can undertake, especially when everything is done with the intensity characteristic of his nature. Being obliged by advice of physicians to abstain from all business for several months, in 1872 he visited Great Britain, France and Germany to regain the health too close attention to business had temporarily destroyed. He now applies the wisdom thus dearly bought by limiting the time to be devoted to business, rarely allowing himself to overstep the bounds.

Generous to a fault, Mr. Clarke has contributed liberally to all measures calculated to advance the interests of his city, and hardly a public work in Manchester now exists that does not owe something to his influence or pecuniary aid.

Mr. Clarke's family were strong in the Orthodox Congregational faith, two of his uncles having been ministers of that denomination, viz., Rev. William Cogswell, D. D., for a time professor of History in Dartmouth College, afterwards president of the Theological Seminary at Gilmanton, and Rev. Nathaniel Cogswell; and he has always adhered to the faith in which he was reared, being a liberal supporter of the Franklin Street Congregational Church in Manchester, a constant attendant upon its worship, and has been elected to the various offices in the society.

He married, July 29, 1852, Susan Greeley Moulton, of Gilmanton, and they have two children, Arthur E., and William C., both of whom graduated at Dartmouth College and are now employed as reporters on the *Mirror*.

WILLIAM CULLEN BRYANT.—1794-1878.

BY REV. SILVANUS HAYWARD.

Poet, in whose loving heart
Nature fondly set apart
For herself a temple rare,
Shrine of all things pure and fair !
There she placed her royal seat,
And her chorus round her feet
Ever sang their sweetest strains,
Echoes from Elysian plains.

Thanatopsis calm and fair
Marched in stately beauty there.
There the maples on the hill,
"Warbling waters" of the rill ;
Sporting by its "oozy brink"
Thrasher sweet and bob-o-link ;
Flora's gems in emerald set,
Gentian blue and violet,
Windflower, lodged in sunny nook,
And the "sunflower by the brook ;"
When their brightness passed away,
Sweet he sang of their decay.

There he saw "the ages" press
Forward in their course to bless.
There the "unrelenting past"
Knotted "fetters, sure and fast ;"
But he broke their ruthless power,
Sang of Truth's triumphant hour,
When it "crushed to earth shall rise,"
Be re-knit Affection's ties ;—
Then with unabated breath
Raised the noble "Hymn to Death."

Calmly waiting by that gate,
Which his song did celebrate,
When the hinges slowly turned,
Flashing forth to glory burned,
And its "radiant beauty" shed
In an aureole round his head,
While a voice was heard to fall
Like a herald's trumpet call :—
"Victor, lay thine armor down,
And receive the laurel crown !"
With a look of "sweet surprise"
Stealing from his earnest eyes,
Like a weary child he seems,
"And lies down to pleasant dreams."

ITEMS AND INCIDENTS IN HOPKINTON.

BY C. C. LORD.

EXPLANATORY.

In reciting the items and incidents embraced in this and our immediately preceding article, an unusual carelessness of statement has been indulged. Only so far as any involved particulars have a direct historical character has attention been paid to exactness of narrative. In fact, many of these fragmentary reminiscences have been gathered from miscellaneous sources and are of such an unauthoritative character as to be entitled to only a qualified credence. Probably based upon a substratum of truth, frequent repetition has undoubtedly modified widely their original forms. The safest present rule, is to allow them to pass gratuitously at their face value with the distinct understanding that they are not to be redeemed at any price.

A CASE OF BODY SNATCHING.

To advance at first into the domain of undisputable narrative, we mention an event that in its time moved the heart of local society to the profoundest depths. The natural sentiment of mystery and awe that is associated with death and the grave is only intensified by acts of grave-yard desecration. This fact, if in any degree different, could only be more real in earlier times. The case under narration is, we believe, the only one of its kind ever happening within the limits of this township.

In the year 1831, Mr. Joseph Philbrick died and was buried in the then new grave-yard in the village of Contoocook. A few days after, his widow followed him in death, expressing tenderness of conjugal affection in her last hours, and wishing that, in the grave, her coffin might be allowed to rest in actual contact, side by side, with that of her husband. In the proposed fulfillment of this dying wish, the new grave was dug unusually close to the one enclosing Mr. Philbrick's body so recently. Such close proximity revealed the unexpected fact that a quantity of rubbish was contained in Mr. Philbrick's grave, and which could not have been there at the time of his burial. Suspicion was aroused, investigation instituted, and discovery made that the grave had been robbed. Mr. Philbrick's body was missing.

Great excitement, profound suspicion and diligent search followed upon this shocking discovery. All this heated activity, however, failed of any practical result. The body was not found through any public detective skill. Some time after the event of the discovery of the empty coffin, the lost body was discovered in a swampy place in the southern part of the town, by a party engaged in building fence, which fact only tends to support the proposition that the act of desecration was performed by persons living not far away. The body was reburied in its original spot.

PRESUMPTUOUS GUESTS.

Keepers of public houses, like people of other vocations, are not without their particular liabilities to annoyances incident upon their peculiar calling. In the great incongruous mass of individuals steadily seeking the advantages of a prominent public house are many whose freaks of fancy or deceit are a constant source of vexation to the landlord, though his customary aspect of outward complacency may seldom allow of an expression of the impatient fervor that dwells within. The executive authority of Perkins' Tavern, so prominently connected with the history of this town, was in no sense exempt from the common lot of all those offering their hospitalities to public patronage.

Among the guests seeking hospitality at Perkins' Tavern was the eccentric Mrs. Royal, well know for her assumed interest in the political conduct of our great and mighty nation. Mrs. Royal's sense of privilege implied the exercise of private judgment of the qualities of her acquaintances, who were respectively recorded in either her "red book" or her "black book," as, in her estimation, they were either good or bad. Being at one time a visitor at Perkins' Tavern, this model critic allowed her sense of privilege to extend to the voluntary appropriation of a portion of a fowl unremoved from the vessel for cooking, and which she abstracted with her naked fingers ; and when the landlady, who formerly figured more prominently than now in the domestic affairs of the public house, looked remonstratingly at her, she only replied, "Its Mrs. Royal to whom you have the pleasure of addressing yourself.", However, the presumption of Mrs. Royal was outstripped in an eminent degree by a plain, unassuming wayfarer who called at Captain Perkins' on a wintry day, and in a pathetically pleading voice, said, addressing the landlady :

"Good lady, will you be kind enough to give me a few potatoes to eat with my cold meat?"

It was a frequent custom in those days for travelers to carry a portion or all of their provision on their way, and this fact doubtless prevented any surprise at the implied dietary situation of the suppliant visitor, who, in the apprehension of the landlady, appeared as only a person of partial charitable needs. With a heart full of sympathy for want, she supplied the applicant for charity with a stock of potatoes sufficient for a generous meal. The needy individual received them, buried them in the hot embers of the ancient fireplace, watched them during the progress of roasting, removed them when done, and finally brushed and blew off the clinging ashes nicely. Then he resumed his former suppliant attitude again and said :

"Good lady, will you be so kind as to give me a little cold meat to eat with my roasted potatoes?"

Though a person of resolute mind, the landlady was more impressed by the ingenuity of the presumptive guest than by his perpetrated imposition, and she allowed him to partake of a repast of cold meat and roasted potatoes at the expense of the house.

A LEGAL TRAGEDY.

From a short time subsequently to the incorporation of Hillsborough county, in 1771, till the erection of Merrimack county, in 1823, Hopkinton was one of the shire towns of Hillsborough. Consequently, in this town occurred courts, trials, convictions and commitments, the county jail being located in the southerly outskirts of the village, the edifice, outwardly unchanged, being now the residence of Mr. B. O. Kimball. A series of legal events memorable in the history of this town embraces the detention, trial, conviction and execution of Abraham Prescott, who killed the wife of Chauncey Cochran of Pembroke, in the year 1833. The execution of Prescott was the only event of the kind occuring in Hopkinton during its career as a shire town, and was attended by peculiarly lamentable circumstances.

Prescott was a feeble minded youth, who, being a kind of *protege* of the Cochran family, conceived, as the story goes, that by getting rid of the responsible heads of the Cochran household he should surely inherit their property. In fulfillment of a stupid though tragical project, he succeeded in decoying Mrs. Cochran into a secluded place where he stealthily dealt her a fatal blow. For this crime, he was convicted of murder at the September term of the Superior Court, at Hopkinton, in the year 1834. An alleged irregularity secured a motion for a new trial, which took place at the September term of court of 1835, when the accused was again convicted, and sentenced to be hung on the 23d of the following December.

Very strenuous efforts were made for

a commutation of sentence, the miserable youth's mental condition being urged as a motive for legal consideration. A reprieve to the 6th of January was obtained, but no appeals affecting the executive attitude of the Governor and council, the doomed culprit went to his fate on the expiration of the reprieve.

The direct fatal result in the experience of the prisoner was not the only culminating tragical feature of this painful affair. The criminal executions of the day being public, immense crowds assembled to witness the morbidly fasinating scenes. On the day first appointed for the execution of Prescott, a large crowd gathered about the jail, not at first knowing of the judicial reprieve. When the news of this fact came to the ears of the company, it raised such a tumult that a lady under confinement in the jailor's family died from incurred excitement and dismay.

Prescott was executed as above stated in an open lot just north of the village, on land now owned by George W. Currier, Esq. The miserable culprit died almost or quite without a struggle. Imbecility, fear, and long suffering, either one or all, had made him comparatively impassive and lifeless when he ascended the scaffold.

A CRAZY PRISONER.

Not far from the year 1830, Benjamin Rowell shot William Holmes in cold blood. Rowell was a lunatic, and Holmes had angered him in some way. Rowell was apprehended and confined in jail, but, being well known as a lunatic, though formerly considered harmless, he was never punished as a responsible culprit, though he was kept under legal confinement or surveillance till the erection of the New Hampshire State Asylum for the Insane, in 1843, when he became an inmate of that institution, remaining till his death, a few years ago.

While in jail in this town, being considered worthy of so much trust, Rowell was sometimes allowed the "freedom of the yard." There being no adequate inclosure about the premises of the county prison, such freedom as was sometimes allowed to trusted prisoners implied the privilege of strolling up and down a certain distance of highway. While enjoying the described privilege, Rowell, on one occasion, ventured to abuse the confidence imposed in him so far as to relieve the irksomeness of constraint by a little amusement at the expense of legal authority. Indulging an emphatic pretense of running away, he suddenly disappeared from sight, to be followed in rapid pursuit by the jailor and a posse of citizens,—all eager to restore to confinement the absconding culprit. As the whole company was tearing along the highway in the direction Rowell had apparently taken for flight, the pursuers were suddenly halted and vexed by the appearance of the prisoner far in the rear, shouting, "Here he is! Why don't you catch him?" Turning upon his heel, Rowell ran in the reverse direction, and the excited posse rushed pell mell after him again, but only to be tricked the same as before.

"Ben," said the jailor, "if you don't stop, I'll shoot you."

"Guess you'll have to go home first and get your gun," quietly replied Ben.

A gun was brought and Ben walked quietly back to his old headquarters.

Benjamin Rowell represented a family of unusually keen intelligence. In his earlier years, he served an apprenticeship with a carpenter. Having completed his service, he was sent into the woods to select timber and construct a frame. Being ambitious, anxious and nervous, the burden of his responsibility weighed upon him and broke his reason. In justice to the unfortunate man, it is gratifying to be able to say that the frame, in the construction of which he lost his reason, proved to be a perfect one.

STEADY WORK AND READY PAY.

While almost all people clamor for success and prosperity in the conduct of this world's affairs, there is a lamentably large quota of individuals who are exceedingly slow to avail themselves of the most reliable means of temporal advantage that society has ever found. The exercise of a vigorous and persistent continuity is eminently repulsive to many unfortunate persons, who seem incompetent to consider, and even less to realize, that what often appears as a sudden, triumph of genius is only the result of a diligent and prolonged uniformity of application, pursued in chambers where the eye of popular observation seldom penetrates. The idea that working on and on, doing the same things over and over again, is the experimental lot of thousands that the world calls successful, and that permanently gratifying accomplishments can be obtained only by following in the same path of protracted samenesses, hardly enters the consciousness of multitudes who can only wonder that their success is small, and that their lines fall in unpleasant places.

A certain rich man in this town was sometimes solicited by needy individuals in search of work. The urgency of application indulged by supplient industrial callers was doubtless at times of such a character as to awaken the most dormant element of sympathy. The part of wisdom in such instances often implies a proper test of a man's disposition to help himself. This part was once illustrated by our late wealthy townsman in an emphatic manner. Receiving an application for work, he agreed to employ at the expense of one dollar a day. Taking the laborer into an out-building, he pointed to an accumulation of earthy *debris* and required that it be shoveled out through a window in the side of the edifice. The laborer consumed a whole day in the accomplishment of this task, and received the prompt payment of a dollar for the service.

"Do you want to work to-morrow?" asked the employer.

"I should like to," answered the employee.

"Very well; come to-morrow and work, and I will pay you another dollar."

"What do you wish me to do?"

"It matters not; only understand that I will provide you with work."

Next morning the employee appeared for work, and the employer pointed to the pile of *debris* removed from the building on the previous day, and gave his directions.

"I want you to shovel that pile all back into the building," said he.

The laborer patiently resumed work, and at the end of the day had removed the *debris* to its former inside position, and received his dollar in regular payment.

"Do you want to work to-morrow?" again inquired the master of hiring.

"I should like to," replied the servant of wages.

"Very well: come again and work to-morrow, and I will pay you another dollar."

The next morning saw the workman promptly on hand again, and his employer, pointing to the afore-mentioned accumulation said:

"I want you to go to work and shovel that all out-doors again."

The same alternations of labor were required and performed several times, and the employee duly received his daily dollar in payment. In time, however, the sense of irksomeness overcame the dispostion to industry. The workman refused to accept the task and received, with his discharge, a gratuitous expression reflecting uncomplimentarily upon the principle of laziness. It was a hard situation, but no worse than that of thousands of tradesmen and clerks who are all their lives reenacting the same uses.

AN IMPERILED SITUATION.

In contemplating the earliest history of a New England township, one cannot fail to notice the frequency with which certain personages appear in places of public trust. In fact, in the times under retrospection, there were few men out of the whole number in a local community who either considered themselves proper candidates for office or were considered such by their contemporaries. The consequence of prevailing social conditions made the earlier official status generally uniform throughout New England. In time, however, in accordance with the increase of general prosperity, circumstances changed, and the conception of general official possibilities was widely indulged, and the number of candidates was multiplied.

The town of Hopkinton was passed into the second stage of local political life and ambition, when a person of official aspirations began to prospect in anticipation of the desired prize. The amount of recognition and influence requisite to secure the object of ambition accumulated slowly. However, deserving patience has its frequent reward, and the aspirant for political honors at last found himself a hopeful candidate. However, time had advanced upon him till his personal vital career was past its meridian; he was verging towards the season of life when many individuals step into the back-ground of public notice.

Town-meeting day arrived, and the great company of voters gathered at the polls to fulfil the rights of American citizens. The extensive excitement and impetuosity too frequently incidental upon public elections, was abundantly illustrated. The party entering upon the life of full-fledged official candidacy was of dignified mien and counsel, and righteously deplored the too prevailing rudeness of the crowd at town-meeting. On this particular occasion, seeing a brusk voter elbowing his way impetuously towards the polls, he accosted the hasty individual, saying, in an admonitory tone of voice :

"Don't hurry so. There is plenty of time. What is your haste?"

"I want," said the impetuous individual, "to get to the polls to vote for you. I have been waiting a long time for a chance to vote for you, and if I don't get a chance to cast a ballot for you pretty soon, you will be too old to hold any office."

We presume the enquirer saw the peril of the situation and admitted the pleaded cause of increased motivity.

A DOUBTFUL COMPLIMENT.

Among all the forms of human utterance that excite our risibles, there are none more forcible than those that are the manifest offspring of a predisposition to absurd verbal blundering. The aspect of this class of *lapsus linguæ* is often eminently laughable. We admire a keen stroke of wit for its sublety. We smile at a dash of lively humor, for it lifts us out of the slough of abstract and oppressive seriousness, and sheds a cheering light upon our otherwise too prosy pathway. The sudden ingression of a bold ludicrosity upon our ordinary mental rectitude upsets the very foundations of our gravity, and the unrestrained torrent of emotive drollery sweeps us away. There is no such thing as anticipating, perfectly, when a demonstration of our incidental liability to any ludicrous *contretemps* may not occur ; and, when surprised, we are always, in some sense at least, ungovernable.

No one occupies a more critical social position than a new minister. Being not only the observed of all observers, and the special object of every conversational reflection, there is an illusive glare attendant upon his moral position that strains and inflames the eyes of the collective laity and often makes them see with distorted vision. Even in the absence of any unjust intent, the mystified vision of the observer will often incite attitudes and observations closely bordering upon the realm of undeserved severity. In such a situation and case, the gospel of a good word, even from a weaker representative of faith, affords a cheer that goes to the root of inner consciousness.

Many years ago a certain church and society in this town was favored with a new clergyman. Like all persons similarly situated, he was subjected to the ordeal of socially inductive criticism. Not long after his advent in the locality, certain of the sisters of his congregation were gathered at a quilting. Diligently plying their needles around the borders of the prospective bed-spread, their reflections and conversation naturally turned towards the new minister. It is needless to say that the merits of that individual were thoroughly canvassed. There were observations of approval and disaproval. There were reflections *pro* and *con*. At length a pious sister, full of interest in the theme in progress, in substance thus gave expression to her honest thought:

"I think brother Solomon is a real good man. I think he is just as good a minister as anybody needs to have. I don't mean to say that I think he is quite equal to Christ, but I think he is fully equal to Anti-Christ."

There is no doubt of the place of the good dame's heart, though her remark has given more than one person a side-splitting recreational exercise.

A BIG TREE.

When, in 1750, the proprietors of this township renewed their grant, procuring a title from the Lord Proprietors of John Tufton Mason, they became bound to a stipulation that all suitable pine trees should be reserved, for the use of His Majesty's navy. The local supply of pine trees of primitive gigantic size furnished one representative that has inspired an interesting chapter in the historic roll of the town. The particulars of the story, with a few later data necessarily added, are included in the following sketch. written by a former professional gentleman of Hopkinton, and originally published in the Worcester (Mass.) *Palladium:*

"Some time previous to the Revolution, a gentleman by the name of Chamberlain, purporting to be an agent for the King of Great Britain, came into this section of the country in pursuit of trees suitable for the masts for the Royal Navy. He found one in the westerly part of Concord, and another in Hopkinton, of enormous size. The one in Hopkinton was a white pine. It grew on the farm lately owned by Mr. Isaiah Webber, about one mile north of the east village. The King's agent employed Capt. Jonathan Chase, the grandfather of the late Bishop Chase, one of the first settlers in the place, with several other persons, to cut the tree and draw it to Sewell's Fall, in the Merrimack river, a distance of eight or ten miles. When the tree was fallen, it was cut off one hundred and ten feet in length, and then measured three feet in diameter at the top. The exact dimensions of the stump I cannot ascertain, but it is certain that Dr. John Webber, father of Samuel Webber, the President of Harvard College, who lived near by, drove a yoke of large oxen upon the stump and turned them about upon it with ease. Fifty-five yokes of oxen were employed to draw the mast to the river, and a road was cut the whole distance through the forest for that purpose; and it is said to have often happened, while passing over the rough country, that several yokes of oxen were suspended by their necks from the ground, by the force of the draught of those forward of them. In passing down a steep hill in the west parish of Concord, the team was divided, and a portion of it put in the rear; but the holdback chains broke, and the immense burden slid forward with fearful velocity, crushing off the horns of the oxen upon the tongue, and stopping finally against the trunk of a large tree. That place to this day goes by the name of 'tail-down hill.'

The mast was floated down the Merrimack at high water; but in passing over Amoskeag Falls, about twenty miles below the place where it was put into the river, it broke in the middle. The butt end floated out of the current into a small cove in Andover, in Massachusetts, where it remained until it decayed. It was often resorted to as a curiosity, and, tradition says, it was so large that no man could be found who could leap upon it from the ground.

When the mast broke, the king's agent, Chamberlain, was sitting upon his horse on the bank of the river; he exclaimed, 'I am ruined!' and putting spurs to his horse, he rode off, leaving his bills unpaid, and was never seen or heard of afterwards."

MAJOR SAMUEL HUTCHINSON.

BY REV. SILAS KETCHUM, WINDSOR, CONN.

On the 6th of September, 1770, Rev. Bezaleel Woodward, writing from Lebanon, Conn., to Rev. Eleazer Wheelock, then at Hanover, preparing a cradle for the infant college, says: "We have all of us been endeavoring to expedite the removal. . . . . But I fear madam will not be able to set out so soon [as the 18th inst]. She, with Miss Nabby, propose to ride in the Post-Chaise, as soon as they can possibly be ready. HUTCHINSON is to drive it for them."

The HUTCHINSON here named, to whom was committed the important trust of conveying through the wilderness, a distance of nearly or quite two hundred miles, the wife and daughter of the president of Dartmouth College, was ELISHA, a son of Samuel, born in Sharon, Conn., 22 Dec., 1749. He was then fitting for college under the instruction of Dr. Wheelock; was one of the company of seventy who shared with its founder the toils and privations of those first years of struggle which led to victory. He pursued his studies at the college, and graduated in 1775, in the same class with Nathaniel Adams, the Annalist of Portsmouth. He gave three years to the study of divinity, and was ordained pastor of the Congregational church in Ashford, Conn. (not *Westford*, as Chapman has it, in his *Alumni of Dart. Coll.*), in March, 1778. On the 16th of July following, he married Jerusha Cadwell, described by Chapman (*Alum. D. C.*, 18.) as being of Westford; but her sister, Thankful, who married Gen. Amos Shepard, is said by Arnold (*Hist. Sketches of Alstead, 28*) to be of Hartford. In Sept., 1783, Mr. Hutchinson was dismissed from his pastorate in Ashford, and was installed the first minister of Pomfret, Vt., 14 Dec., 1784; dismissed 8 Jan., 1795. After this he appears to have resided in Pomfret till 1800, when he went to Zoar, Ms., where he united with the Calvinist-Baptist denomination and removed to Susquehanna, Pa., from which place he was compelled to flee by the Indians, who at that time invaded our western frontier, under Butler and Brandt, and committed that massacre at Wyoming. He next settled in Marion, Wayne Co., N. Y.; and in 1814 became pastor of the Baptist church in Newport, N. H., where he continued in the active duties of the ministry till 1821, and where he resided till his death, 19 April 1833,—instead of April 9th, as Chapman has it. He married, for a second wife, Martha, daughter of Samuel Eddy, of Washington Co., N. Y.

SAMUEL HUTCHINSON was his son, and was born in Ashford, Conn., 9 July, 1779; and died in Alstead (N. H.), 14 May, 1819. As a boy he labored on his father's farm in Pomfret, and attended school, when there was any, till he was fifteen years old. But, possessed of an active mind, and displaying some capacity for business, an opportunity was improved of introducing him to a different sphere, and to far other scenes, than his Vermont home afforded.

In the July No. of this Magazine, I gave an account of Gen. Amos Shepard, who, as above stated, married a sister of Maj. Hutchinson's mother. In 1794, Gen. Shepard had been a merchant in Alstead seventeen years, held the highest military office under the governor, was one of the wealthiest and most conspicious men in the western part of the state. The following extract from a letter shows the manner of young Hutchinson's introduction to the care of his distinguished uncle:—

"*Pomfret. 17th July, 1794.*

"Sir!

"I understand you are in want of a lad to assist in tending your store, and that you had entertained a favorable idea of my son in this view. I think it proper to give you some information respecting this matter. * * * * I can assure you that Samuel is very fond of the idea of living with you—I shall therefor permit him to make trial, to see whether he will answer your purpose. He is something apt to learn—but has had little advantage for it as yet. He is rather of a slender constitution, not able to endure hard labor, and naturally inclined to learn, and to tend a store. With proper advantages to learn, and your instructions with respect to tending store. I apprehend he might in a short time be advantageous to you. He is naturally reserved, and so far as I know, faithful and just in business with which he is entrusted. He is at present not remarkably fond of company, nor inclined to drinking, or any hurtful vice, that I know of; and I can always depend on his word.

"If he should answer your purpose and be inclined to remain with you, we have determined that he shall be yours until of age. We hope you and Mrs. Shepard will consider him as being under your care and direction; and esteem it your duty to train him up in the way of virtue, as well as business.

After haying is over, we shall embrace the first opportunity to send him to you. But if he should not come till fall, you will yet understand, that we determine to send him then. * * * * If you have opportunity you might send for him after the middle of August next.

"We present our dutiful respects.

"I am, sir, with respect and
"esteem your humble servant,
"E. HUTCHINSON.
"Hon. Gen. Shepard,
"Alstead."

The intention of the above letter was carried out. The boy became a clerk in his uncle's store and a member of his family. He was quick to learn the details of business, attentive to the interests of his employer, prompt and courteous in his intercourse with customers, and soon gained the good will of the people and secured their confidence. The affection and care which they would have expended upon their own, had they been blessed with children, Gen. Shepard and his christian wife bestowed upon this sister's son, who in all his relations approved himself worthy of such distinction.

On reaching his majority, he was received as a co-partner in the business, which was, for the next eleven years carried on under the name of Shepard & Hutchinson. They supplied from distant markets every kind of merchandise required by their customers, and afforded them a market for all the products of the farm and shop. Their trade increased. They established a branch store at Newport, of which William Cheney and Joseph Farnsworth took charge. They had an interest in a store in Croydon, and in various manufactures.

On the first day of January, 1812, there was a heavy snow-storm in Alstead; so severe that, contrary to their custom, neither Gen. Shepard nor Maj. Hutchinson—each of whom lived near the store, though in opposite directions—did not go home to supper, but spent the evening with some neighbors who happened in, in social enjoyment at the store, separating about nine o'clock. Gen. Shepard was in good health and spirits, and had been entertaining his friends by his conversation. On reaching his house he fell to the floor, and expired in a moment. The doctors said of apoplexy. He was a man of full habit, a hearty eater, enjoyed his meals, and extended to his friends, and to all visitors to Alstead, a most bountiful hospitality. He had been an honored man among "the great ones" of the state. He was *the* man of the town. The sensation caused by his death was startling and profound.

By his will, dated 25 June, 1808, it was found that he had bequeathed to Thankful, his wife, all his household furniture, the farm stock and utensils, and $1000 in money, in her own right, and the use of all his estate, both real and personal, during her life. After her decease were to be paid legacies, amounting to $1890, besides $400, and a certain farm, which were left to Maj. Hutchinson. The balance was to be equally divided between three of his nephews and the said Hutchinson. Maj. Hutchinson was appointed executor, and Mrs. Shepard executrix of the will. The latter declined the trust, and Maj. H. administered alone. The estate was appraised at $46,231.54, of which $38,211.21 was "personal."

MAJOR SAMUEL HUTCHINSON.

How much was realized upon it does not appear.

Mrs. Shepard died in 1817. Her estate was appraised at $12,144.50. Of this amount, $5660, two farms and various articles of personal property were parcelled out by her will in legacies, and the residue she bequeathed to Maj. Hutchinson, whom she appointed her executor.

After Gen. Shepard's death, Maj. Hutchinson extended his business widely. He established a commercial house at Potsdam, N. Y., under the management of Samuel Partridge, who had been with him some years in the store at Alstead, whom he admitted to a partnership. On similar terms he opened another store at Canton, N. Y., which was in charge of Sartel Prentice, a native of Alstead. Of the home establishment he continued his personal supervision. His ventures were successful, the opportunities being chosen with much prudence and sagacity. All were in full operation up to the time of his death.

The title, by which he was best known in his day, he received by commission from Gov. John Taylor Gilman, who appointed him on the staff of Maj. Gen. Shepard, with the rank of major.

On the 6th of May, 1804, Mr. Hutchinson married Hannah Pratt, daughter of Levi Pratt, of Pomfret, Vt., who was born in Middleboro', Ms., 7 July, 1783. Their children, all born in Alstead, were:—

1. Thankful Cadwell, born 9 June, 1805; married, 1827, Elijah Bingham, a brother of Hon. James H. Bingham (Dart. Coll. 1801), with whom he studied law. In 1835 they removed to Cleveland, O., where both are still living (1879), in the enjoyment of honorable old age.

2. Hannah Emily, born 6 Jan., 1807; married Charles F. Brooks, of Westmoreland.

3. Amos Shepard, born 21 April, 1809; married (1) Harriet E. White, of Plattsburg, N. Y.; (2) Ann DeWitt, of Cleveland, where he died 26 April, 1875.

4. Samuel Richards, born 28 Oct., 1811; married Catherine M. White, of Plattsburg; removed to Cleveland, where she died 2 Jan., 1855, and he 1 Oct., 1869.

5. Susan Pratt, born 1 Aug., 1813; married Geo. W. Lynde, of Cleveland, and died 25 July, 1853.

6. James Bingham, born 31 May, 1815; married Sarah Cook, of Cleveland; removed to Madison, Ind., where both are still living.

7. Elisha Cheney, born 28 May, 1817; died in infancy.

8. George Cheney, born 6 April, 1819; died in Cleveland, 26 April, 1838.

To Elijah Bingham, Esq., above named, I am indebted for the principal facts relating to Major Hutchinson. Concerning Mrs. Hutchinson he says: "By the death of her husband, she was left with the care of these seven children, the oldest not fourteen years old. But she had an abiding sense of a parent's duty, and her good judgment never forsook her. She sent her children to the best schools, and had the satisfaction of seeing, in after years, that she had pursued the right course. * * * * She was a noble woman; noted for deeds of charity and benevolence; always ready to contribute of her means to every good work. She lived the life of a consistent christian."

After her husband's death her parents came from Pomfret and resided with her; she ministering to their comfort and supplying their wants. Her father died in 1846, aged ninety-seven; her mother in 1848, aged ninety-two. After this she disposed of her property in Alstead, followed her children to the west, and spent the remainder of her days with them, dying at the residence of her daughter, Mrs. Bingham, in Cleveland, 21 May, 1867, aged eighty-four.

Major Hutchinson was a life-member of the New Hampshire Bible Society, to which he left a legacy of $500, and also $1000 to the Congregational church in Alstead. Hon. James H. Bingham, his legal advisor, was named by him executor of his will, who assumed the management and settlement of his large property. To his ability and integrity Rev. Seth S. Arnold, minister of the church, in his *Historical Sketches of Alstead*, pays a high tribute. Concerning Major Hutchinson the same writer says: "By his honesty, diligence, amiable and correct deportment; and especially by his public spirit and generous benevolence, he merited and secured the good will of all with whom he was acquainted. He died * * * in the midst of his usefulness; and his death was generally felt and lamented."

A COTTAGE.

BY LAURA GARLAND CARR.

By a road-side, hot and dusty,
   Is a wide gate, old and gray.
Lift the latch, time-worn and rusty.
   Heavily 'twill backward sway,
While the iron hinges mutter
   In a dull complaining way.

Down a long hill slowly wending,
   Wheels and hoofs with muffled sound,
On the grass-grown path descending,
   Reach at last the level ground,
And an humble low-roofed cottage
   With rose bushes hedged around.

Cherry-trees, with ripe fruit teeming,
   Almost hide the house from sight—
Just a hint, through green leaves gleaming,
   Of the low walls, snowy white.
Does the fragrance from the roses
   Thrill you with a keen delight?

This small window, almost hidden
   By the climbing, twining sprays,
Out from Memory's stores has bidden
   Fair sweet scenes from childhood's days,
Framed and perfumed with the roses,
   Vaguely seen through Time's rich haze.

In a bed that trundled under
  One of wide and higher frame,
In the corner bed-room yonder,
  I have slept and waked again,
With a sense of dewy sweetness
  Flooding all my drowsy brain.

Sometimes morning dreams were shattered
  By a wet touch on my face—
Dew and blossoms o'er me scattered
  Roused me from my resting place,
While a laugh came through the window
  Where the branches interlace.

Did the roses bloom all summer
  In that lovely far off time?
Did the breezes ever murmur,
  Like low sentences that rhyme?
Ah! no thorn, no blight, no blemish
  Mar these memories of mine.

Many useful lessons taught me,
  In that cottage snug and small,
To the changing years have brought me,
  Help that I shall oft' recall;
But the memory of the roses
  Clings the closest of them all.

NEW LONDON CENTENNIAL.

ADDRESS OF HON. J. EVERETT SARGENT.

In 1843 Joseph Colby, Esq., died. He had passed most of his life in New London, and few men have had a wider or a better influence in the town than he had. He was born in Plaistow, N. H., March 24, 1762, moved to Hopkinton, N. H., about the time he became twenty-one years old, and lived there a few years; while there he was married to Miss Anna Heath, of Hampstead, N. H., Dec. 21, 1785. They moved to New London March 10, 1786, and at first lived in a log-house on the shore of Pleasant Pond, at the upper end, near where Stephen Sargent now lives, where the Indians had formerly cleared up a few acres of the intervale, to raise their corn and beans. He enlarged this clearing and made a valuable farm. He moved from there and lived at other places in town; built the house on the Elder Seamans' place, opposite where the buildings now stand, which has since been burnt down; then moved on to the road that leads from here directly to the low plains,—where Anthony and the youngest daughter, Mrs. Burpee, were born; and then moved to the farm on Main street, in the year 1800, where he ever after lived, and where he died April 19, 1843.

He was for many years the agent of Jonas Minot, one of the original and the largest of the proprietors of the grant, and in that way he had opportunities for learning more of the situation and value of the land in the different localities than most other men. He dealt largely in real estate in the town. He served the town well in various capacities; for many years as one of the selectmen, and was its first representative to the General Court, and was re-elected every successive year from 1803 to 1816 inclusive. He was early a member of the church, and I think the records will show that he acted on more committees in the church than any other man during the same period of time. He was also a leading magistrate in the town for many years.

In 1846, ANTHONY COLBY, of New London, was elected governor of the state. He was a native of this town, the son of Joseph and Anna Colby, born Nov. 13, 1792. He received his education mainly in the common schools of his native town. But he had a wonderful capacity for business, and was always active in matters of a public' character. He built the original stone dam at the outlet of Pleasant Pond, and built a grist-mill there, which was a great public benefit. He was largely instrumental in getting the new road laid out and built, and started the line of stages upon it, that for a long time run through from Hanover to Lowell in a day, a distance of 100 miles or more; and he readily lent a helping hand to the enterprise, started by another son of New London, of establishing the business of manufacturing scythes, where the same has been so successfully carried on ever since. He was one of the two men who built the new meeting-house; in fact few men have ever lived a more active life than he did.

He was a friend of education, and of the common school, and for a long time was one of the superintendents of the schools in town, and was among the earlier advocates of the temperance reform. He went through all the grades of military promotion, from captain to major-general, and had represented the town in the legislature in the years 1828, 1829, 1830, 1831, 1832, also in 1837, 1838, 1839; and in 1846

3

was the chief magistrate of the state. His administration of the affairs of the state government was characterized for integrity, true economy, and a spirit of progress and reform. In the position in which the political parties then stood, it was simply impossible that he could be re-elected.

He was again elected to the legislature in 1860, from New London, and was appointed by Gov. Berry, in 1861, as adjutant-general of the state, at a time when the best man in the state was needed for that responsible position, made so responsible by the great importance of the struggle in which the country was then engaged. He performed the duties of this office in a manner entirely satisfactory to the government and the people, and resigned in 1863. He was long an active and influential member of the church here, as well as a leading member in the denomination in the state. He died July 20, 1873. He always lived in this town, and always, except the first eight years of his life, in the house into which his father moved in 1800, and where both father and son have died. No man ever devoted himself more fully and constantly to the building up of what he believed to be the best interest of his native town than he did. He married for his first wife, Miss Mary Everett, of New London, and for his second, Mrs. Eliza Richardson, of Boston, who survives him, and continues to live in your midst.

In 1847, the union meeting-house, sometimes called the Free Church, was built at the Four Corners. This remained for several years, but was finally sold, and removed and converted to other uses, it being wisely concluded that one good strong church in a place is far better than two or three feeble ones, and that one meeting-house well filled is far better than several empty ones.

In 1850 the population was 945, being a loss of 74 from 1840. Benjamin R. Andrews was the delegate from New London to the Constitutional Convention of that year in this state.

In 1853 the new town-house was built, near the new meeting-house. There was quite a struggle upon the question of removal, the subject having been voted on at no less than three town-meetings, held in rapid succession, in the spring and summer of that year.

In 1853, when the academical and theological school, under the patronage of the Calvinist Baptist denomination, was removed from New Hampton to the state of Vermont, it left the denomination without a school in this state. They soon resolved that this state of things ought not to be, and they at once looked about for the best place to locate their seminary of learning. The friends at New London offered to give the denomination their academy, and put it in good repair, and build a ladies' boarding-house, and furnish various other accommodations. This proposition was favorably considered by the denomination, and the preference was given to New London. Accordingly a new act of incorporation was obtained in 1853, and "The New London Literary and Scientific Institute" was incorporated that year, and the school put in successful operation that fall, and in course of its first year enrolled upon its catalogue some 335 scholars. The property of the New London Academy was transferred to the Institute. In 1855 an alteration was made in its name, changing the word Institute to Institution, and modifying some of the provisions of its charter, and its name has remained unchanged from that time to the year 1878, when it was changed to that of "The Colby Academy" at New London, which name it now holds.

In 1854 the old town-meeting house was sold, by vote of the town, and removed to this neighborhood and converted into a boarding-house for the use of the academy.

Benjamin P. Burpee, of New London, was elected a county commissioner for Merrimack county for the years 1852, 1853 and 1854. He was also the representative of the town for the years 1853 and 1854.

In 1856, George W. Everett, of this town, was appointed solicitor of Merrimack county, which office he held for five years, until 1861. He was the representative of the town in the years 1852 and 1856.

RICHARD H. MESSER was elected a member of the Governor's Council for the years 1857 and 1858. He was a native of the town, the son of Isaac and Martha Messer, born October 20th, 1807. He received a common school education only, and when of age he went to Massachusetts and learned the trade of manufacturing scythes; he then came back to New London, and uniting himself with Mr. Phillips and Anthony Colby, introduced the business here, at the place where said Colby had early built the second* grist-mill in town, and where the enterprising village of Scytheville has since grown up. The town is greatly indebted to Mr. Messer as being the originator and the active agent in introducing and building up this great industry in your town, and the gentlemen who first were associated with him in the business were also benefactors of the place. He was elected to the legislature in the year 1858. He continued in his favorite occupation, devoting himself to business with all his energies until he died, May 15, 1872, aged sixty-five years.

In 1860 the population of the town was 952, a gain of only seven in ten years.

In 1860 Gov. Colby was again elected representative, and in 1861 he was appointed adjutant-general of the state, which place he held till 1863, when he resigned and his son, Daniel E. Colby, was appointed to the same place in August, and held the place till March, 1864, when he resigned the position. He had been representative of the town in the legislature in 1857, and was afterwards a member of the Constitutional Convention of 1876, and still resides upon the old homestead of his father and grandfather.

---

*I am told that some one had built a small grist-mill here on this site before that time, but it was of no account. Colby's mill was from the first and is today substantially *the* mill of the town.

The academy, as organized in 1853, had been doing a good work and doing it well, and had been prospered. At first a fund of $25,000 was raised, which for a time seemed to meet the demand of the institution, but presently the need was felt of more ample accommodations and a better location; and it was a grave question where the funds were to be obtained to meet this new want, this growing necessity. In 1866 Mrs. James B. Colgate, a daughter of Gov. Colby, offered $25,000 towards establishing the necessary fund, provided that the amount should be made up to $100,000 within a given time. This was accomplished by the aid of the Rev. W. H. Eaton, D. D., who had assisted in raising the previous fund of $25,000, and at the anniversary in 1867 the subscription was filled and the object secured.

The present site was then obtained and the present buildings were erected, and in 1870 they were completed and dedicated, upon which occasion Rev. Dr. Cummings, of Concord, the president of the institution, delivered an able and interesting historical address.

This school has been placed under great obligations to Mrs. Colgate, of New York; Ex-Governor Colby, of New London; John Conant, Esq., of Jaffrey; Messrs. H. H. & J. S. Brown, of Fisherville; Nahum T. Greenwood, Esq., of New London, and many others, by their liberal contributions to its fund.

In 1853 George W. Gardner was appointed principal, who continued in that place seven years, and was followed by Rev. George B. Gove for three years, who was succeeded by Rev. A. W. Sawyer, who remained about seven years, to 1870. He is now president of Acadia College, N. S. Then Horace M. Willard was appointed principal, who was followed in 1872 by Laban E. Warren, who was succeeded by A. L. Lane in 1875, who in turn gave place to J. F. Morton in 1876, who remained two years, to 1878, when the present principal, E. J. McEwan, was elected, who still holds and very acceptably fills that position today.

Several have held the place of lady principal. Miss Mary J. Prescott from 1853 to 1857, Miss Harriet E. Rice, Miss Julia A. Gould, Miss Adelaide L. Smiley, Miss Lucy Flagg, Miss Mary A. Davis, Miss Mary O. Carter (who became Mrs. Warren in 1872), Miss Hannah P. Dodge; and in 1877 Miss Smiley was again appointed, who continues to hold the position still.

Mr. Ephraim Knight was appointed associate principal and professor of mathematics, at the commencement in 1853, which place he held down to 1873, a period of twenty years, when, in consequence of declining health, he resigned the post, and died here March 4th, 1878.

In 1870 the population of the town was 959, a gain of 7 from 1860, and just the same made in the last previous decade. Since 1870 but few matters of general interest have occurred in New London.

In 1874 you came very near furnishing another governor for the state. Gen. LUTHER MCCUTCHINS was born in Pembroke, N. H., in 1809; first came to New London in 1837, and remained two years; then went to Connecticut for some four years, returning to New London in 1843, where he has since lived. He received the Republican nomination for governor in 1874, and received the full strength of his party, and a vote very complimentary to him, and only failed because, as the issues were then made up and the parties were then organized, the Republicans could not elect anybody that year. He has been your representative in the legislature in 1850, 1851, 1873, 1878, and also the present year, 1879. He is a practical farmer, who takes a deep interest in whatever is calculated to advance the agricultural interests of the state.

In 1875 George M. Knight, Esq., of this town, was elected county commissioner for the county of Merrimack, which office he held for the term of three years, 1875, 1876 and 1877.

In 1878 you commenced preparations for your centennial reunion in this hundredth year from the date of your charter as a town, and the success of your enterprise today shows how well and how faithfully you have made your preparations.

We have thus come down to the close of the first century of New London's history. I have endeavored to give you a fair and impartial statement of the facts of that century, without any attempt at embellishment. There are a few other facts that may properly be alluded to before we close, and first, the *patriotism* of the town. We have seen that the town voted at once, after it was incorporated, to furnish a soldier for the continental army; this they did furnish and paid him, as we have seen, through the war until its close. We have no evidence that the Mr. Coums, who went from the town, was an inhabitant of the town; our impression is that he probably was not, but was a substitute, or a man hired by the town to fill the place. But New London had its revolutionary heroes in abundance. In fact it seemed a favorite resort for those soldiers who had gone from other places and served through the war, and then looked about for the most desirable places for settlement in the new country. The fresh breezes of your hills, and the views of the noble mountains in your neighborhood, are all congenial to a love of freedom and independence. Hence we find that immediately after the war many who had been in the continental army came at once to New London and settled here; others came later. There was Thomas Currier (known as Capt. Kiah), Edmund Davis, Josiah Davis, John Dole, Jesse Dow, Levi Everett, Penuel Everett, Eliphalet Gay, Zebedee Hayes, Ezekiel Knowlton, Thomas Pike, David Smith, Moses Trussell and Eliphalet Woodward. Most of them came from Massachusetts,— from Attleborough, Dedham, New Rowley (now Georgetown), and Bradford; but Moses Trussell came from Hopkinton, N. H., in the year 1804.

Capt. Currier not only served through the revolutionary war, but no sooner was the war of 1812 declared than he entered the regular army. He went through the war, fought in several battles, and came safely home when the war was over. I remember him as he used to come to church on Sunday, and other days, for he was a man who loved his God as well as his country, and he knew no fear in the service of either. Levi Everett was another man whom I well remember. He lived near my father, and I never wearied of listening to him when he was telling his stories about the wars and the battles he had seen. Then there was Moses Trussell, with one arm gone from below the elbow. I knew him well. I understood that he lost his arm in the war, but did not know where, or when, or how; but a paper has recently been found that explains these matters, of which I have a copy that I will read you. (This paper is published at length in the second volume of the GRANITE MONTHLY, page 270.) Such were some of the men of those days. Mr. Trussell, you will remember, had been here in 1774 and cleared a piece of land; the next year he went to Bunker Hill, and in thirty years' from his first visit, he returned to live and spend the rest of his days here, and died in New London.

So in the war of 1812, New London did her full proportion. At the first alarm of war many left and joined the regular army and followed its fortunes through the war, like Capt. Currier, of whom I have spoken. But few, comparatively, were called into active service from this state in that war; but whenever the call came the men were ready. I find that among the companies that were called out and ordered to Portsmouth there were, in Capt. Jonathan Bean's company, one sergeant, Robert Knowlton from New London, and four privates, John Davis, David Marshall, Nathaniel Messer and David Gile; and that in Capt. Silas Call's company, Stephen Sargent was first lieutenant, and Capt. Call having died before his term was out, said Sargent was in command of the company for a time. There were in the same company, as privates, Samuel Messer, Zenas Herrick, and Nathan Smith, all from New London.

And in the late war of the rebellion New London did not falter, but promptly met the call of the country and sent her sons to the conflict without reserve, as they were needed, furnishing such officers as Capt. Andrew J. Sargent, Major George W. Everett of the ninth regiment, and Lieut. Col. J. M. Clough of the eighteenth regiment, who, since the war was over, is doing good service in our state militia, as a brigadier-general. The town also furnished men for the ranks in the various stations and places where they were needed, who were true as steel and faithful unto death to the trust reposed in them. The reputation of the town for patriotism is established beyond a peradventure.

That the town is a place of good morals would follow almost naturally from the fact that the people of the town are an agricultural people, who have always believed that a good education is of the highest consequence, and have had good schools, and for the last forty years a very good academy. These facts, in connection with the religious training of the people under such men as Elder Seamans and his successors, could hardly fail to make the population what it has been,—an industrious, an intelligent, a patriotic, a moral, and a happy people. Wherever the criminals come from that fill our jails and prisons, very few of them have ever come from New London, or ever will, until the town forgets the lessons of the first hundred years of its history.

There are a few more general facts and a few more individual notices that I desire to refer to.

The following persons have graduated from college, who were natives or residents of New London at the time, with the year of graduation:

John H. Slack, Dartmouth College, 1811.

Benjamin Woodbury, Dartmouth College, 1817.

J. Everett Farnum, Waterville College, now Colby University, 1833.

Daniel P. Woodbury, West Point, 1833.

Francis A Gates, Waterville College, 1836.

Daniel E. Colby, Dartmouth College, 1836.
J. Everett Sargent, Dartmouth College, 1840.
Robert Colby, Dartmouth College, 1845.
Edward B. Knight, Dartmouth College, 1861.
Dura P. Morgan, Brown University, 1869.
Carl Knight, Dartmouth College, 1873.
William Knight, Brown University, 1877.
Charles M. Sargent, Bates College, 1879.

PHYSICIANS IN NEW LONDON.

SAMUEL FLAGG was a travelling doctor, whose route extended from Pembroke and Dunbarton to Enfield, through Hopkinton and New London, usually coming this way two or three times a year, but irregularly. He always travelled on foot and carried his saddlebags of medicine over his shoulder. He had no fixed residence, but wandered from place to place; a man of considerable skill, but intemperate, and took great delight in making himself a terror to children. He was found dead in a mud hole, into which he was supposed to have fallen in a fit of intoxication.

JOHN CUSHING was a resident of New London for many years; came here before the year 1800; was a skillful physician, and for a time was quite popular here. He was engaged to be married to Phebe Messer, the daughter of Samuel Messer. The day was appointed for the wedding; the friends were invited; the guests came; the bride, in expectancy, was attired, and the waiting maids in attendance. The only absent one was the bridegroom that was to be, who did not put in an appearance; and as there could not be much of a wedding without a bridegroom, the result was that the wedding did not come off according to programme. This was in 1802 or 1803. But this disappointment proved a blessing in disguise to the intended bride, for Cushing, who was then somewhat given to drink, went on from bad to worse and became very intemperate, lost his practice and the confidence of the community, and finally moved to Fishersfield and died there in poverty. He always rode on horseback to visit his patients. He never married.

ROBERT LANE came to New London, from Newport, about the year 1808, after Cushing had lost his practice and moved from town. He lived here some two or three years, then moved to Sutton, where he was living and in practice in 1811, and remained there a few years. He then returned to New London, where I find that he was residing in 1814, and he remained in town through 1815 and 1816, for he was one of the selectmen of the town in these latter years. After this he went to Mobile, Ala., and was absent a year or two, when he returned and stopped a short time at New London, and then took up his permanent residence in Sutton, at the north village, where he ever afterwards lived. He had an extensive practice, became quite distinguished in his profession, was much respected, and died a few years ago at a good old age. You knew him well.

CHARLES PINNEY came to New London about 1810, when Dr. Lane first went to Sutton. I find that Pinney was here and in full practice in 1811, when Lane was also in full practice in Sutton. Pinney married a daughter of Mr. Edmund Davis. After Dr. Lane returned to New London they both remained awhile, and then Pinney moved away. He returned to live here again after several years, and remained here, I think, till his death; at least he is buried in your cemetery. I knew him well after his return, but he was not then in practice as a physician.

ISAAC COLBY followed Dr. Lane, coming soon after he left, in 1817 or 1818, and remained till about 1821, when he removed to Hopkinton.

HERBERT FOSTER was here in the year 1822, may have come in 1821, but did not remain but a year or two.

JONATHAN DEARBORN came soon after this, perhaps in 1823, or a little later; was a skilful physician, but left town suddenly in 1829. You that can remember back as far as that know well why he left.

SAMUEL LITTLE followed Dr. Dearborn, coming about 1830, and remained till 1838, or thereabouts; was town-clerk several years; then moved to Thetford, Vt., thence to Lebanon, and thence to Rumney, N. H., where I used to see him frequently when I lived at Wentworth. He afterwards moved West, where he died a few years ago.

ROBERT COPP was here for a few years, during the time that Dr. Little was here. 'I remember him well. He was here in 1836, but left soon after; may have been here some three or four years in all.

REUBEN HOSMER followed Dr. Little in 1839, and remained till 1848, some ten years.

HEZEKIAH BICKFORD came back in 1848, for he was a native of this town, and remained till 1851, some four years.

S. M. WHIPPLE came into town in 1849, and remains here still, having lived longer in town than any other physician,—near thirty years. He was a native of Croydon, N. H.; attended medical lectures at Dartmouth college, and commenced practice at New London in the year 1849. Since he came to New London several others have been here for short periods, as follows:

OTIS AYER, from 1855 to 1857, three years.

LEVI PIERCE (Homœopathic), from 1861 to 1864, four years.

N. T. CLARK, from 1870 to 1871, two years.

R. A. BLOOD, from 1871 to 1873, three years.

J. P. ELKINS (at Scytheville), from 1878 to 1879, two years.

There have also been several physicians raised up in town, from its native-born or adopted citizens, who have gone to other places.

JONATHAN E. HERRICK, son of Esquire Jonathan and Rhoda Herrick, who is now in practice in New York.

GEORGE H. W. HERRICK, son of Dea. Joseph C. Herrick, who was in practice at Charlestown, Mass., and who died abroad in 1877.

CHARLES PIKE, in practice in Peabody, Mass.

ASHLEY WHIPPLE, son of S. M. Whipple, of New London, now at Ashland, N. H.

MINISTERS OF NEW LONDON.

JOB SEAMANS was born in Reheboth, Mass., May 24, 1748; was the son of Deacon Charles Seamans, and Hannah his wife. His father was a farmer at Reheboth; moved to Swansea, Mass., when Job was about a year old, residing there about four years; then removed to Providence, R. I., where he lived about ten years. He then moved to Sackville, Cumberland county, Nova Scotia, where he lived about eight years, and where he died in the year 1771, aged 71 years. Job, the son, followed the farm until the father died. He was about fifteen years old when he moved from Providence to Sackville; and on August 10, 1769, he married, at Sackville, Miss Sarah Esterbrooks, a daughter of Valentine Esterbrooks, Esq., and who was born at Johnson, R. I., April 14, 1750.

He began to preach at Sackville, having united with the Baptist church there, when about twenty years of age, and about one year before his marriage. Soon after his father died, in 1771, he returned to New England, and in 1772 he was preaching to the church at North Attleborough, Mass., and on the fifteenth of December, 1772, he was ordained as its pastor. He continued a successful ministry there for about fifteen years. In 1787 he first came to New Hampshire. The entry in his diary is as follows: "Lord's day, June 17, 1787, I preached in Sutton, in the State of New Hampshire." The next entry is, "Lord's day, June 24, I preached in New London, in the same state." He came to New London again in February, 1788, arriving on the 22d, at Deacon Hunting's, and remained some two months, preaching from house to house. Many of the early settlers of New London were from Attleborough, Mass., and the towns in that neighborhood, who had long been acquainted with him there, and it is not strange that they should be anxious to obtain him for their minister here, and so we find him listening to their call, and willing in the end to cast in his lot with these old friends; and after considering the subject fully he started with his family for New London, June 20, 1788, and arrived there July 1st, and he says in his diary, "went into a very poor house of Mr. James Brocklebank. The same night our youngest child (Manning) was taken sick."

He was, as you see, twelve days in moving from Attleborough to New London, a distance of 130 or 140 miles perhaps; as long a time as would be necessary to go to San Francisco and back again. Time enough now to go to London or Paris.

His first work here was to found a church. This was done Oct. 23, 1788. The churches from Sutton and Wendell being present, by their ministers and delegates, to counsel and assist. The church consisted at first of eleven members, and Mr. Seamans was installed as pastor of the church and minister of the town, Jan. 21, 1789. Of the exercises at his installation, the gathering at the unfinished meetinghouse, and the salary paid him by the town, we have already spoken; also of the seasons of reformation in the church from time to time under his preaching.

The church records also show a vast amount of labor done in the church. Those were the days for laying foundations, and Elder Seamans laid his foundations for church order and discipline deep, broad, and permanent. Were members guilty of any immorality, they were dealt with? Did they absent themselves from the communion of the church, that was cause for labor? All members were required to do their share, according to their means, for the support of the gospel. Many was the labor, frequent the letters of admonition, and not unfrequent the final letters of expulsion sent to members of the church for the sole reason that they were unwilling to pay their due proportion, according to their ability, for ministerial support.

While all the poor were welcomed to the privileges of the gospel, without money and without price, yet it was held to be the duty of those church members who were known to be able, and could not deny the fact of their ability, to pay accordingly; and if they would not, no amount of profession, no quantity of apparent sanctity and long-facedness was sufficient to screen the delinquent miser from merited expulsion.

The christians of those days evidently believed that no amount of grace was sufficient to save a man, unless it was sufficient to sanctify his love of gain as well as his other affections; and that a man's conversion, in order to be genuine, must reach not only his head but also his heart, and not only his head and heart but also his pocket book. For the last years of his life he was not able to preach, except occasionally; he did not preach much after the year 1824, though, so far as I can find, his pastoral relation to the church continued up to 1828, some forty years. That year Mr. Tracy was ordained as his successor in that office. Elder Seamans died Oct. 4, 1830, aged eighty-two years, four months and ten days, among the people with whom and for whom he had labored. He married for his second wife, Nov. 30, 1819, Mrs. Mary Everett, widow of Jonathan Everett, deceased.

Elder Seamans was a man of medium stature, light complexion, marked features, and in advanced life had a commanding and venerable appearance. It is said that he never wrote a sermon in his life. Yet he always preached his two sermons on Sunday, and frequently a third, besides many on week days, and was always acceptable and interesting, and an earnest preacher of the gospel of the Son of God. His long ministry in this town was no insignificant element in advancing the temporal and spiritual welfare of the people and the church of New London.

JOSEPH DAVIS moved into town in

November, 1824, and commenced preaching at once. He remained in town about three years, as a stated supply. Then Oren Tracy was called; but having some engagements that detained him for a while, his brother, Leonard Tracy, preached here one season, and until his brother was prepared to come.

OREN TRACY was born at Tunbridge, Vt., June 18, 1798; was the son of Cyrus and Hannah Lillie Tracy. He was educated at Waterville college, Me., but did not graduate. He took what was then termed the short course in theology, and was ordained at East Stoughton, Mass., in October, 1825. He was married there during the first year of his ministry to Miss Marcia Billings of Royalton, Vt. After remaining there some two years or more, very pleasantly located, his physician recommended his removal from the seaboard, and he accepted the call from New London and moved there in the fall of 1827, and was ordained as the successor of Elder Seamans, January 30, 1828, and remained there till 1836, a period of about nine years. Under him the cause of education received a new impetus in town. Teachers were more thoroughly and systematically examined, and a higher standard in our common school education was at once attained; all our schools seemed to catch an inspiration from his spirit and efforts. He had great sympathy with, and great influence over young people. All the children loved Elder Tracy. I was twelve years old when he came here, and no man did so much as he to arouse in me a love of learning, and a determination to obtain a liberal education, at whatever cost. Mr. Tracy, I need not say, was my favorite minister; and Mrs. Tracy was a good, kind, pleasant, motherly woman, who seemed to take as much interest in the people and in the children as he did.

He was also a pioneer in the cause of temperance. When he came here it was the fashion to set on the decanter of liquor, with sugar and water, whenever the minister made a friendly call. It would have been considered almost disrespectful not to have done so. This fashion was soon changed under his administration, for he would not taste of distilled spirit at all, not even wine or cider, as a beverage. I remember that he delivered a course of lectures on temperance on Sundays, at the intermission between the forenoon and afternoon service; and besides he usually held his third meeting on Sunday, also. I have spoken of the revival of 1831 and 1832 under his preaching, when nearly a hundred were added to the church.

Many who are here today will never forget that first Sunday in January, 1832, and also the first Sunday in March of the same year, upon each of which occasions about forty, standing on both sides of the broad aisle in the old meeting-house, received the right hand of fellowship from Mr. Tracy, on being received as members of the church. On these occasions Mr. Tracy seemed to be inspired. I was absent at school for the last year or two of his residence here, and entered college in 1836, the year he moved away. I have never found and never expect to find another minister who, in all respects, would quite fill Mr. Tracy's place with me.

From New London he went to Newport, N. H., thence to Townsend, Mass., afterwards to Fitchburg, Athol and Greenfield in that state. From 1847 to 1849 he was agent of the A. B. Missionary Union in New England, residing at Springfield, Mass., and Hartford, Conn. From 1851 to 1862 he was agent of the A. B. Home Missionary Society, residing at Concord, N. H. From Concord he went to Greenfield, Mass., where he died September 6, 1863, aged 65. Mrs. Tracy still survives him, residing with her daughter, Mrs. Elliott, of Boston.

REUBEN SAWYER was born in Monkton, Vt., March 11, 1798; was married to Laura Wyman, at West Haven, Vt., in 1819. After this he was converted and baptized by his father, Rev. Isaac Sawyer, of Brandon, Vt. In 1822 he entered the Theological Seminary at Hamilton, N. Y., but owing to failing health he did not complete his course. He was ordained pastor of the Baptist church in West Haven, Vt., in 1824. He remained there as pastor until he came to New London early in 1836, where he became a member of the church, and was received as its pastor July 3, which place he held until April 8, 1844, when he resigned his pastoral charge, but remained with the church in the service of the New Hampshire Baptist convention until autumn, when he removed to Chester, Vt., where he was pastor of the church for some ten years. From there he removed to Leyden, N. Y., where he remained as pastor of the church for some ten years, when he returned to Vermont for a few years, at Hinesburg and in that vicinity, when he returned to Leyden, where, after a protracted illness, he died June 29, 1869, in the 72d year of his age.

He gave the prime of his life, the vigor of his manhood, to the church here. Large additions were made to it during his stay. The demands upon his time and strength were such as in these days would be deemed severe, with three preaching services on the Sabbath most of the time, and two or three other meetings during the week. In speaking of these arduous duties, his son, Rev. A. W. Sawyer, D. D., president of Acadia College, N. S., in his line to me, says: "But he was strengthened by the sympathy and affection of his people. The memory of the kindness he there experienced and the friendships he there formed were cherished by him to the last, and lightened the burdens of his declining years. His last year in New London was less pleasant to him because of his opposition to the anti-slavery agitation, but his views afterwards changed somewhat, so that he firmly held the conviction that the United States should be a land of freedom." He took an interest in whatever benefited the people with whom he lived. He was one of the founders of the original New London Academy, and always was deeply interested in the school. But first of all he felt that he was called to preach the gospel. This work he loved. He enjoyed most the presentation of those doctrines termed evangelical. Feeling the strength and comfort of these truths in his own soul, his presentation of them to his people was often with remarkable clearness and power.

The ministers that have followed Mr. Sawyer, are all, as I am informed, still living, and are known much better to you than they are to me, therefore any sketch of their lives will not be attempted by me. They are as follows:

Mark Carpenter, came in 1844, left in 1849—6.

Ebenezer Dodge, came in 1849, left in 1853—5.

Peter M. Hersey (Christian), came in 1849, left in 1853—5.

H. F. Lane (C. B.), came in 1854, left in 1857—4.

Lucien Hayden, came in 1857, left in 1869—12.

Asa Randlett (F. W. B.), came in 1859, left in 1861—3.

F. D. Blake (C. B.), came in 1870, left in 1873—4.

S. C. Fletcher, came in 1874, and remains in 1879—6.

The church frequently, and I think generally, depends as much upon the character and conduct of its deacons, for its standing and reputation with the world, as it does upon its ministers. so I have examined your church records to see who have been the deacons in New London, and so far as I know the church has been very fortunate in the selection of its deacons.

Ebenezer Hunting, elected January 8, 1789.

Matthew Harvey, Zebedee Hayes, elected July 5, 1793.

Jonas Shepard, Peter Sargent, Jr., elected April 3, 1812.

David Everett, Dexter Everett, elected June 16, 1825.

Joseph C. Herrick, Micajah Morgan, elected April 21, 1849.

Hunting was alone for about four and a half years, then Deacons Harvey and Hayes for nineteen years, then Deacons Shepard and Sargent for 13 years, then the two Deacons Everett for 24 years, and last Deacons Herrick and Morgan for 30 years.

NEW LONDON CENTENNIAL ADDRESS. 379

Ministers who have gone out from New London:

Enoch Hunting (C. B.), ordained March 15, 1814.
Benjamin Woodbury (Cong.), ordained about 1820.
Theophilus B. Adams (C. B.), ordained May 29, 1821.
Joshua Clement (C. B.), ordained about 1834.
Valentine E. Bunker(C. B.), licensed April 8, 1836.
Francis A. Gates (C. B.), licensed May, 1837.
Robert Stinson (Universalist), ordained about 1840.
Sylvan Hunting (Unitarian).
James Phillips (Methodist).
Lewis Phillips (Christian).
Dura P. Morgan (C. B.), ordained about 1872.

LAWYERS OF NEW LONDON.

STEPHEN C. BADGER, a native of Warner, N. H., graduated at Dartmouth College in 1823; studied law with Henry B. Chase, of Warner; commenced practice in New London in 1826, where he remained till 1833, a period of eight years, when he removed to Concord; was clerk of the courts for Merrimack county; police justice for Concord; a civil engineer; died at Concord, October 29, 1872. He married Miss Sophronia Evans, of Warner.

WALTER P. FLANDERS, also a native of Warner, N. H., graduated at Dartmouth, 1831; studied law with Hon. John D. Willard, of Troy, N. Y., and Hon. George W. Nesmith, of Franklin, N. H.; commenced practice in New London in 1834; was a member of the N. H. Legislature, from New London, in 1841 and 1842; and in 1849 he removed to Milwaukee, Wis., where he still resides. He married Miss Susan E. Greeley, of this town, youngest daughter of Jonathan Greeley, Esq.

GEORGE W. EVERETT, a native of New London, born Nov. 19, 1819; was educated at the public school and academy of this town; studied law with Walter P. Flanders of this place; was admitted to the bar in 1847, and soon began practice here. He was a member of the legislature, from this town, in the years 1852 and 1856; and was solicitor for Merrimack county for five years, from 1856 to 1861. In 1862 he received a commission as major of the ninth regiment of volunteer militia, which was ordered to the south-west; remained with the regiment one year, showing himself a brave and faithful officer. In August, 1863, as his regiment was coming up the Mississippi river from Vicksburg, Miss., he was taken dangerously ill, and stopping at Cincinatti, Ohio, he sank rapidly and died on 27th of August, 1863, just one year and a day from the date of his commission. His remains were brought to his native town and buried with masonic honors. He married Miss Ellen T. Lane, of Gloucester, Mass.

EDWARD B. KNIGHT, who was a brother of Professor Ephraim Knight of this town, graduated at Dartmouth in 1861; studied law with George W. Everett, of this place; was admitted to the bar in 1864, and commenced practice at Dover, N. H., but soon removed to Virginia, where he still resides in the practice of his profession.

I might perhaps, without impropriety, have mentioned my own name as one who went out from New London, and who has been engaged in the study, and the practice, and the administration of the law. That has thus far been my life work, and whatever of success I may have achieved it has been simply by patient toil and steady perseverance towards a single object, and by practicing upon the lessons of economy and industry, which I learned in my youth here in New London. When I heard that the good people of my good old native town were to have this centennial reunion, it met with my most unqualified approval, and when I received the summons, from your executive committee, to come here today and speak to you, I cheerfully obeyed without a single excuse, and I come today without a single apology, and only regret that I have been able to perform my allotted task no better. Yet I feel that I have done the best I could under all the circumstances of the case.

But I feel, my friends, that this is a day of jubilee. The town welcomes home her children; the mother calls home her sons and her daughters from afar, to mingle in the general joy. The citizens of the town have opened their houses and their hearts to bid us all welcome. As we return to the old places we see many of the old familiar faces that we left behind us. We find the same old pictures on the walls, the same curtains by the windows, as smooth and as white today as they were when we were children, and perchance some of the old crockery on the table. These things recall to our minds pleasant reminiscences of early days. They fill the memory with images of the past. They speak to us of childhood, and in fancy we will live over again for a few brief hours our childhood's happy days.

But while we thus go back in memory to recall the joys of youth, we are reminded that many others of the familiar faces of those days are with us no more forever here on earth; that in the beautiful cemetery yonder repose the ashes of the fathers and the mothers, while the green turfs of the new-made graves tell us of griefs more recent still, and of the inroads of death upon all classes and ages of our friends. Thus it is ever with us here on earth. Sadness and joy, sorrow and gladness, are strangely commingled in a day like this, and such is human life. Its little history is made up of joys and sorrows, following each other in such rapid succession that it is often impossible to distinguish the line that separates them.

But my friends, when this reunion is over, and we again leave these homes of our childhood and go out again into the battle of life, may it be with fresh strength and firmer wills and renewed courage for the performance of all life's duties, and as generation after generation shall come and go in the future centuries, as we have come and shall go in this, may the virtues of our fathers never be forgotten. May their principles of justice and truth and patriotism ever be maintained. May peace and prosperity forever dwell in the midst of this people, and may the God of the fathers of this goodly town be the children's God and portion forever.

ALOFT.

BY MARY HELEN BOODEY.

Oh! little do we know what shining heights
  Do wait for our ascending, nor can we
Measure, with mortal eyes, the heavenly flights
  The soul may take when light as air, and free,
Like the sweet lark it upward mounts and sings,
  The rainbow of life's morning on its wings.

WILLIAM LLOYD GARRISON.

BY PARKER PILLSBURY.

"The emphasis of death makes manifest
The eloquence of action in our flesh;
And men, who living were but dimly
  guessed,
When once free from their life's en-
  tangled mesh,
Show their full length in graves."

No truer words than these, by Mrs. Browning, were ever spoken; and to none did they ever apply better than to Mr. Garrison. Before his mortal remains were committed to the dust, the pulpit and the press were sounding his praises from ocean to ocean. And in the next hour the electric nerve under the Atlantic, had waked the sympathetic echoes of the Eastern Hemisphere.

And now the theme, the song, the joy are one with few discordant notes, to the farthest verge of Christian, or enlightened civilization.

And though the GRANITE MONTHLY be to some extent *local* in its contemplated themes, a tribute to Garrison cannot be out of place in its pages. He was born *for* New Hampshire if not in it. His newspaper, *The Liberator*, bore for its motto the words: "My Country is the World; my Countrymen are all Mankind." And his life-work to the very going down of its sun, was a rich, and finally a ripened fulfillment of so noble promise and prophecy.

Mr. Garrison belonged to Universal Humanity. To him were no high nor low, no great nor small, no male nor female. When he read, "All men are created equal," he understood *all* men. Not a part. And all men meant all *women* as well.

Garrison was born a truly natural, but in no sense a radical man, as the word is now understood. And yet rightly considered, the truest, or most natural man, is the most radical, or best rooted man; deepest rooted down among the laws and principles which underpin the material, moral and spiritual universe.

Newburyport, like most of Massachusetts, has been renowned more for conservative, calculating, conforming principle and policy, than for the spirit of innovation and advancement. There, have been builded the tombs of the Revolutionary prophets; there, the sepulchres of the sages and heroes of 1776, of Bunker Hill and Faneuil Hall, have been well kept and garnished. But when Garrison arose with his new Evangel, he was hated, hunted, imprisoned, haltered and barely escaped hanging by an infuriated mob of Boston's best men. "Gentlemen of property and standing," in beaver hats and broadcloth; and in broad day-light too!

Such was Boston, such Massachusetts. And such pre-eminently, was Newburyport, where, on the twelfth of December, 1804, William Lloyd Garrison first saw the light.

It had respectable slave traders and religious slave holders; one wizzard, a boy; and one witch, an old woman. Her, the church persecuted, the courts prosecuted and held and hunted two full years, and then sentenced, "to be hanged by the neck until you be dead." But subsequently, she was reprieved and died in her bed (the Reverend John Hale testifying), "praying to, and resting upon God in Christ for salvation."

Mr. Garrison first roused the wrath of the slave power by a newspaper article, charging a Newburyport sea captain, Francis Todd, with engaging in the coast-wise slave-trade between Baltimore and New Orleans. This cost him two suits at law, a fine of fifty dollars and forty-nine days' imprisonment in a Baltimore jail. It was, however, proved in court, that the number of slaves carried was much greater than the article specified. The fine was generously paid by Mr. Arthur Tappan, a wealthy anti-slavery man of New York, and Mr. Garrison was released.

On the first of January, following, (1831) Mr. Garrison issued the first number of the *Liberator*. In it, he demanded the "immediate and unconditional emancipation of every slave." He made that demand "in the name of justice and humanity, and according to the laws of the living God."

And the world now very well knows that he did not cease to press that claim, nor suspend the publication of the *Liberator* till the very last slave in the nation was set free by presidential proclamation. Thus wondrously did he fulfill his own prophetic announcement: "I am in earnest. I will not equivocate. I will not excuse. I will not retreat a single inch ; *and I will be heard!*"

In his youth, Garrison was a pronounced politician of the Newburyport whig, or conservative school. But the sound of the Greek revolution against the Moslem power reached his ear and fired his soul with the spirit of freedom. The powerful appeals of Henry Clay and Daniel Webster in the United States Congress fed the flame. Webster became to him the divinity of the forum, and he named him the "*God-like*." He even contemplated at one time entering the military school at West Point and hastily preparing himself to take the field in person in behalf of the Greeks. John Randolph had not then told him and Clay and Webster that the "*Greeks were at their own doors.*"

But when Garrison became a grown-up man and abolitionist, he firmly and religiously abjured all violence and the whole spirit of war among men.

When he espoused the cause of the American slave, and the American Anti-slavery Society was formed, the constitution contained this emphatic clause : "But this society will never, in any way, countenance the oppressed in vindicating their rights by resorting to physical force."

Mr. Garrison was at this time a Christian, as he understood the word, in all the word can be made rightly to mean. And most of all, he reverenced the doctrines of freedom and peace. "Peace on earth, good-will to men," were his proclamation and song. To "preach deliverance to the captives, and opening of the prisons to them who were bound," were his mission and work.

Human life he held as sacred above all other things. And so capital punishment and war, as well as slavery, were to him an abhorrence. And hence logically, he renounced allegiance to human governments founded in force and military power ; and to announce, defend and extend that high, and to him holy and divine philosophy, he with a few others organized the *New England Non-Resistance Society*, of which he was chosen first corresponding secretary and member of the executive committee.

And many, if not most of the official papers of the association bear unmistakable marks of Mr. Garrison's pen, brain and heart.

A portion of the Preamble to the Constitution reads thus :

Whereas, the penal code of the first covenant has been abrogated by Jesus Christ : and whereas our Savior has left us an example that we should follow his steps in forbearance, submission to injury, and non resistance, even when life itself is at stake ; and, whereas the weapons of a true christian are not carnal, but spiritual, and therefore mighty through God to the pulling down of strongholds :

And whereas, we profess to belong to a kingdom not of this world, which is without local or geographical boundaries, in which there is no division of caste nor inequality of sex ; therefore, we the undersigned, etc., etc.

A part of the second article of the Constitution is in these words :

"The members of this society agree in the opinion that no man nor body of men however constituted, or by whatever name called, have right to take the life of man as penalty for transgression: that no one who professes to have the spirit of Christ can consistently sue a man at law for redress of injuries, or thrust any evil doer into prison; or hold any office in which he would come under obligation to execute penal enactments; or take any part in the military service; or acknowledge allegiance to any human government."

At this time, it cannot be doubted that the faith of Mr. Garrison in the inspiration and authority of the Bible and the Trinity, and especially in the teachings and precepts of Christ, was substantially such as is *professed* by the whole evangelical church. And on that faith and philosophy alone were the New England Non-Resistance Society and all its auxiliaries founded.

Among Mr. Garrison's poetical effusions, this "Sonnet to the Bible," may be found:

O Book of books! though skepticism flout
  Thy sacred origin, thy worth decry :
Though transcendental folly give the lie
To what thou teachest; though the critic
  doubt
This fact; that miracle: and raise a
  shout
Of triumph o'er each incongruity
He in thy pages may perchance espy!
As in his strength the effulgent sun
  shines out,
Hiding innumerous stars, so dost thou
  shine,
With heavenly light all human works
  excelling.
Thy oracles are holy and divine;
  Of free salvation *through a Savior*,
  telling.
All Truth, all Excellence dost thou enshrine;
  The mists of sin and ignorance dispelling.
Boston, Nov. 1, 1841.

Such was Mr. Garrison as a Christian, as a follower of Christ. And sublimely consistent with his faith, were his spirit, his life, and his whole character.

At home, or abroad; in private, or in public; as writer, or as speaker; as husband, father, friend, or in whatever human position, or relation; after long and wide acquaintance with men, in pulpit, in church, in politics and in the world at large ; for the constant exercise of what are called the Christian virtues and graces, I surely have seen few the peer, none the superior of William Lloyd Garrison. Mr. Emerson says, " Swedenborg seemed, by the variety and amount of his powers, to be a composition of several persons." For *powers*, read moral goodness and excellence, and the remark applies well to him.

Revering the New Testament as divine authority, he kept its teachings. When he read, "swear not at all," he let his communication be, "yea and nay." And no more. Did he read, " Resist not evil;" he observed the sublime requirement; and preached it in his paper, *The Liberator*, and practiced it everywhere. Hence arose the Non-Resistance Society; I think the truest *Christian* Association ever formed under heaven, or known among men ; with Garrison, its very chiefest apostle.

When he read, " Love your enemies," it never meant to him, shoot them in war ; nor imprison, nor hate, nor hang them, in peace. And the *Liberator* was not only a proclamation of freedom, and of peace on earth, but of universal unfolding progress and reform, to all man and woman kind.

Mr. Garrison early lost his father, but became the hope and joy of an excellent mother, of English birth, and devout member of the Baptist church. He ever cherished fervently her memory ; and never spoke of her but in tones of tenderness and affection. He never united with any sect, but respected the true Christian faith and work, wherever found. The God he worshipped was " no respecter of persons." No more was he.

But chained down to no dogmatic ringbolt, he had an eye and ear ever open to discover new truth, in whatever book or religion it might be found. Ten years of violent opposition and persecution from almost the whole American church, on account of his profound adherence to the Christian doctrines of peace and liberty, as he had learned them from the Sermon on the Mount and the example of its great Author, might have clarified and quickened his vision, mentally and spiritually. At any rate, he subsequently re-examined the doctrines and dogmas of the evangelical sects, their avowed faith in the plenary inspiration of the scriptures, included. As one result of such further investigation, he attended a convention in Hartford, Connecticut, in 1853, called to consider the claims and character of the Jewish and Christian Scriptures. The meeting was very numerously attended, most of the Northern and Western states having representation, and continued four days, with three long sessions each day. In one of them Mr. Garrison offered, and defended very ably, a series of resolutions, the first of which was to this purport:

Resolved, That the doctrines of the American church and priesthood, that the Bible is the word of God; that whatever it contains was given by divine inspiration, and that it is the only rule of faith and practice, is self-evidently absurd; is exceedingly injurious both to the intellect and the soul; is highly pernicious in its application, and a stumbling-block in the way of human redemption."

And yet to the end of his life, no man more venerated, or made wiser, better or more frequent use of the Bible than did Mr. Garrison. In an article from his pen, now before me, he writes: "I have lost my traditional and educational notions of the holiness of the Bible, but have gained greatly, I think, in my estimation of it. * * I am fully aware how grievously the priesthood have perverted it and wielded it as an instrument of spiritual despotism, and in opposition to the sacred cause of humanity. Still, to no other volume do I turn with so much interest. No other do I consult so frequently; to no other am I so indebted for light and strength; no other is so identified with the growth of human freedom and progress; to no other have I so effectively appealed in aid of reformatory movements I have espoused; and it embodies an amount of excellence so great, as to make it in my estimation, THE BOOK OF BOOKS."

Garrison long ago learned to doubt nothing only because it was new; and to accept nothing unless it had more than the moss and mold of age to recommend it. He found the world, even the best of it, most enlightened of it, most Christian, "dead in the trespasses and sins of Intemperance, Slavery, War, Capital Punishment, and Woman's Enslavement." He lived to set on foot, or largely and liberally to cooperate in enterprises and instrumentalities for correcting all these fearful abuses, righting all these wrongs.

Then another stranger came to his door. With characteristic hospitality that door was again opened. The new guest was Spiritualism; another "sect everywhere spoken against," as anti-slavery had been, half a generation before. Even abolitionists, many of the most zealous of them, treated the new stranger with scorn.

Not so Garrison. And in giving the new idea recognition, he found, and ever after confidently believed, that he had been literally "entertaining angels;" though not "unawares!"

And spiritualism too, he yoked to his great "chariot of salvation;" perhaps in the full faith and hope of the eminent Lord Brougham, when he said: "*Even in the most cloudless skies of skepticism, I see a rain-cloud, if it be no bigger than a man's hand; and its name is Modern Spiritualism.*"

CONTENTS OF VOL. II.

Affections, The, 171
After Many Years, 239
All Through the Night, 230
Aloft, 380

Baker's River, 135
Baker, Capt. Thomas and Madame Christine, his wife, 17
Barton, Hon. Levi W., 225
Birth-place of Gen. Stark, 101
Boston Port Bill, The, 126
Bryant, William Cullen, 357

Churches in Hopkinton, 22
Coming of June, The, 277
Congressional Papers, No 2, 48
Congressional Papers, No. 3, 109
Congressional Papers, No. 4, 177
Congressional Papers, No. 5, 231
Contoocook River, 103
Cromwell, Oliver, 112
Currier, Hon. Moody, 129
Clarke, Col. John B., 353
Cottage, A, 367

Day at Old Kittery, A, 68
Deacon's Prayer, The, 145
Dead of 1878, The, 144
December 2, 1878, 100
Decisions of Chief Justice Smith, 172

Early History of the Concord Press, 164
Early History of the Methodists in New Hampshire, 12

Finitio, 37
First Congregational Church in Concord, 261
Forest Vegetation in New Hampshire, 76
Forgetfulness of Sorrow, 12
From the German of Heine, 160

Garrison, William Lloyd, 381
George, Col. John Hatch, 193
Good Luck, 176

Head, Gen. Natt, 97
Hutchinson, Major Samuel, 364
Hunger, 265
Hymn, A, 94
Hymnology of the Churches, 302, 335

Illegible Manuscript in Printing Offices, 61
In Battle and in Prison, 210
Industries in Hopkinton, 121
In Ruins, 108
Items and Incidents in Hopkinton, 304, 358

Kearsarge Mountain, 334

Lady Wentworth, The Home of, 273
Lancaster, An Old Sketch of, 245
Lawyers and Politicians, 132

Library Questions, 149
Love Wins Love, 38

Malaga, 11, 222
Manners and Customs in Hopkinton, 186, 217, 251, 278
March, 199
Mary and Martha, 20
Men and their Professions, 82
Men of Old Nottingham at the Battle of Bunker Hill, 204
Message, The, 304
Military Affairs in Hopkinton, 152
Miron, 75
Mt. Kearsarge, To, 10
My Friends and I—Memories, 7, 52

Nature's Creed, 6
New Hampshire Hills, 131, 207
New Hampshire Men at Bunker Hill, 266
New Hampshire Seventh at Ft. Wagner, 208
New London Centennial Address, 311, 341, 369
Newspaper History, A Bit of, 236
Norris, Herbert F., 161

Old Time Trip in New Hampshire, An, 28

Poem by Rev. Silvanus Hayward, 47
Politics in Hopkinton, 43
Potter, Richard, 56
Proceedings of the New Hampshire Antiquarian Society, 63
Pure as the Lillies, 293

Rhapsody on Old Clothes, A, 79
Reviewer Reviewed, A, 191

Sagamores of the Newichawannock, The two Last, 95
Sanborn, Dyer Hook, A. M., 91
Senate and Its Presidents, The—Hon. David H. Buffum, 1
Shepard, Maj.-Gen. Amos, 299
Sorrow, 120
State Senate of 1879-80, The, 289, 321
Stearns, Hon. Onslow, 256
Summers's Day, A, 340
Sunshine After Clouds, 180

Thackeray, Lines on the Death of, 333
Town Histories, 285
Traveling Accommodations in Hopkinton, 71

Upward, 209

Variations, 163

Way to Grandpa's, The, 81
Weeks, Hon. Joseph D., 33
Weston, Hon. James A., 321
Widow's Mistake, The, 165

www.ingramcontent.com/pod-product-compliance
Lightning Source LLC
Chambersburg PA
CBHW022121290426
44112CB00008B/764